D1222194

Eighteenth Century Emigrants

from the Northern Alsace

to America

by

Annette Kunselman Burgert,

FGSP, FASG

PICTON PRESS
CAMDEN, MAINE

The floral decorations on various pages of the text are from *Fraktur* documents made by Johann Adam Eyer, son of Johann Martin Eyer who emigrated in 1749 from Feldbach near Kutzenhausen.

All rights reserved
Copyright © 1992 Annette Kunselman Burgert
International Standard Book Number 1-882442-00-8
Library of Congress Catalog Card Number 92-74115

No part of this publication may be reproduced or transmitted in any form or by any means, electronic or mechanical, including photocopying, recording, or any information storage and retrevial system, without permission in writing from the author.

This volume was prepared for distribution to members of The Pennsylvania German Society during 1992, as Volume XXVI in its series of publications on Pennsylvania German history and culture.

Available from:

AKB Publications
691 Weavertown Road
Myerstown, Pennsylvania 17067-2642

Picton Press
P. O. Box 1111
Camden, Maine 04843-1111

Manufactured in the United States of America
Printed on 60# acid-free paper

I dedicate this volume to our grandchildren
Kyle Badertscher
Longmont, Colorado
and
Beth Baumgartner
Oak Harbor, Ohio
with the hope that they will always appreciate
and cherish their Pennsylvania German heritage.

Contents

Illustrations

Maps

Preface

This volume of European ancestral origins continues a series of publications attempting to locate and identify the village of origin of the many German-speaking settlers who came to the American colonies in the eighteenth century.

There have been many volumes published containing lists of emigrants and giving villages of origin; these publications have been compiled primarily from emigration materials located in European archives and the majority of the records pertain to those emigrants who were given permission to leave. But the clandestine emigration was large, and for many of the immigrants, there are no archival records available to document their departure. In a few cases pastors made notations in the German church records about individuals who had gone to the new world. However, for a large majority of the emigrant families, no such notations were located; they could be established in fact as immigrants only by the judicious use of supporting evidence. When a familiar name was located in a German church record, a series of research steps then produced the following additional information:

1. The family in question disappears from the German records at a certain date.

2. The name appears in Pennsylvania records or the existing ship passenger lists about the same time.

3. If located in the ship lists, arrival with other families from the same village or general area.

4. Supporting evidence from Pennsylvania records, showing association with other families from the same European area, a coinciding date of birth, a corresponding list of children, a wife with the same given name as that found in the German record.

Step four was no easy task. Children often died young and their deaths were not always recorded. Sometimes the wife and children died on the voyage, and the immigrant remarried after arrival. Single young men are the most difficult to conclusively identify since the available evidence is so sparse. Several families are presented in Appendix C, page 582-589, who could not be identified without question; possibly a descendant has the needed data to verify or disprove their emigration.

The decision to limit this volume to a relatively small geographical area was difficult, knowing that families who came from other, equally important areas would not be represented. But the amount of information found made that decision inevitable. Enough immigrant families were found in just the northern part of Alsace to produce a volume. A few places which may not be considered a part of Alsace today are included and occasionally records of adjoining villages not thoroughly studied in this book were examined for data about families who moved around.

Since the material was obtained by an examination of church records something should be said about the nature of the primary source used. Congregations of Lutherans, Reformed and some Roman Catholics existed in the area, depending upon the overlord of the village in question. Each of these religious denominations required their pastors to keep records of the pastoral acts they performed involving their parishioners or others who came to them for ministry. They preserved, therefore, registers of baptisms, marriages, burials, confirmations, and communicants. In some instances registers of the congregation arranged by family were also kept. In every village such records were probably begun shortly after the Reformation in the sixteenth century, but not all of the records still exist from that period. The Thirty Years' War (1618-1648) and subsequent conflicts contributed to the destruction of some records. The religious situation is further complicated by these factors: 1) some church buildings changed hands as the result of political changes of administration; sometimes new records were begun by the pastor of the new confession, sometimes the old was simply continued in use; 2) pastors then as ever since have sometimes simultaneously served two or more congregations which adjoined one another. The result is that parishioners sometimes had their ministerial acts performed in either of the congregations the pastor served; 3) people moved about far more than American researchers often realize. Fortunately some pastors noted former home villages in making entries in the records.

In only a few cases the original church books were used. The majority of the documentation from Alsace provided here was compiled from microfilms of the records made by the Genealogical Society of Utah. When a record is microfilmed some of the quality of the original is lost. Some records are thick books with the dates entered close to the inner margins of the pages. These are lost in microfilming, and if there is a questionable date in the text below, it might be more clearly legible in the original record. Faded entries might also be more legible in the original. Handwritings vary in legibility as well and styles of German script changed considerably as time went on. Sometimes there are periods of years when no records were entered.

All of which is a way of saying that researchers finding a family of interest in this book are urged to consult the original records (most of them now in the archives at Strasbourg). An intensive study of the family in the village cited here and in neighboring villages will undoubtedly be fruitful. The student should be aware that the data given here on a family is not intended to be complete. Only enough has been cited to identify the immigrant and his *Heimat* (hometown). Some of the records are so complete that if a family was native to the village, by no means always the case, several more generations can be added to the lineage. There are also civil records available for some of the Alsatian villages to which we did not have access, such as probate, land and tax records from which a fuller picture of the immigrant and his family might be gained. A few of these records are presented in Appendix A, concerning persons who emigrated from the Nassau-Saarwerden County; they were kindly supplied by Dr. Bernd Gölzer from a series of records that have been compiled by Dr. Gerhard Hein.

All dates are given as they appear in the old records, both German and Pennsylvanian, with no transposition for the change from the Julian to the present Gregorian calendar. That change seems to have taken place about 1697 in the German-speaking areas. English lands, including the colonies made the change in 1752, at which time 11 days were dropped from the calendar here. In some of the church records only one date is given for the children without any statement as to whether the date is for birth or baptism. When this is the case, since most of the books are baptismal records, the date is given here with bp. preceeding it, signifying that it is a baptismal record. In a few instances, however, it might actually be the date of birth (and in some, of course, of both, since it was customary to baptise at once). Some of the records contain both a date of birth and a date of baptism.

Throughout the text, the spelling of both village names and surnames are given as they appear in the records. Although the old spelling of place names is maintained, the modern version, complete with a five-digit zip code identification is given in each family entry. Each village in this area has a German version and a French version of the placename. Certain places mentioned in the text no longer exist, or the place names have changed. Examples are Feldbach, near Preuschdorf; Liniehausen, near Langensoultz-bach; Katzenthal, near Lembach; and Trautbronn, near Langensoultzbach.

It would not be accurate to claim that this volume names every emigrant from the northern part of Alsace to Pennsylvania. There are some persons in Pennsylvania with names and association so close to known emigrants from the area that one would guess their origin was there, but all efforts to locate them have failed. Undoubtedly some have simply been overlooked. One of the reasons that some emigrants from these villages may not be included here is simply because the name could not be found in the ship lists and Pennsylvania records. In some instances enough information could be found in both German and American records to narrow the probable time of immigration to within a year or two. When this was the case, a thorough search of the ship lists for those years was often rewarding. The second volume to Strassburger-Hinke, which contains the signature lists, was frequently consulted and proved to be invaluable. Several of the immigrants were located by using the signature lists rather than the printed translation. This does not intend any criticism of Hinke's monumental task of transcribing those lists. One reason the signatures were published was because of the problems in reading them. Hinke himself commented in the introduction to *Pennsylvania German Pioneers,* "in some cases no man living can decipher with certainty the awful scribbles of some of the writers." Any person working with this old handwriting is going to have a margin of error in interpreting certain letters. No translation of these records can be completely accurate, since the translator is limited by many factors: old faded ink, torn pages, ink that bled through the paper making both sides of the page illegible. Most of all the translator is limited by the writer's ability to make clear, distinct and consistent letters. This is not only true of the signatures on the ship lists, of course, but is is a valid comment on some of the German script church records in Germany, Alsace, Switzerland and Pennsylvania. Another reason that an emigrant from this region is not included in this volume is that records were simply not found. An example may be found in the family of an immigrant named Georg Rupp who is identified in Charles Roberts et al, *History of Lehigh County, Pennsylvania*, Vol. III: 1106. The article states that he was born in Wimmerau in Lower Alsace on 11 Aug. 1721, son of Ulrich Rupp and Margaret Holtz. This place appeared likely to be Wimmenau, and the records there were searched for the family. The church book at Wimmenau starts in 1724, too late to locate a birth that occured in 1721; however, it is likely that the immigrant was from this village since an Ulrich Rupp was located in the burial records at Wimmenau, died 29 Aug. 1727, aged 50 years. Other Rupps appear in the Wimmenau KB, but no mention of Georg Rupp could be found there. A second example may be found in the immigrant Georg Ruch who is identified in Charles Roberts et al, *History of Lehigh County, Pennsylvania*, Vol. III: 1098-1099. His tombstone at Jordan Lutheran Church was said to give the information that he was born in Zizendorf in Elsas 1664. The records at Zutzendorf were searched, and although the surname Ruch appears in the records there, this Georg Ruch does not appear. One Melchior Ruch had a son Hans Georg b. 29 Dec. 1682, bp. 2 Jan. 1683 in Zutzendorf. The Ruchs were shepherds and moved freely throughout the area. They may yet be located in a record in the vicinity of Zutzendorf. It was not possible to completely search every record in this area due to the large number of records available. Yet another reason for omitting a family may be because they do not appear in the existing records. It is known that there were colonies of both Mennonite and Amish in the Alsatian region, but they do not appear in the Lutheran, Reformed and Catholic records in this area.

In preparing the family entries, I have tried to locate some evidence of the precise year of arrival. For those who appear in the ship lists, the page reference in Strassburger and Hinke, *Pennsylvania German Pioneers*, Volume I, is given. The useful abbreviation S-H, I is used to indicate this source. The page number is cited, along with the ship's name and year of arrival, because in a few instances, ship's names are duplicated in the lists. Two *Sallys* arrived in 1767, so that the page numbers become important.

The Pennsylvania documentation involved the use of hundreds of records, both published and unpublished sources. Charles Glatfelter's *Pastors and*

People, Volume I, identifies 525 Lutheran and Reformed congregations that existed at some time or other between 1717 and 1793. Not all of these records were searched, but many of them, especially the earliest ones, were. To simplify the task of citing these sources, certain key words are used to identify the congregational records. *Hill Lutheran KB, Lebanon co.* is used to designate the Lutheran church book of the congregation located in North Annville township, Lebanon county, also known as Quitopahilla, Quittapahilla, and Hill. A separate record for the Reformed congregation here is listed as *Hill Reformed KB, Lebanon co.* KB is standard German genealogical abbreviation for *Kirchenbuch,* church record volume. There were other Hill churches, but only one in Lebanon county. Researchers who are not familiar with the exact location or history of the early congregations mentioned in the text should refer to the two volumes by Dr. Glatfelter already mentioned.

Where will and probate record citations are used, I have relied, of necessity, quite heavily on previously compiled abstracts and indices. Some contain errors and omissions and the original wills should be consulted. The decision to include this material was difficult, but the knowledge that a probate record exists outweighed the disadvantage of using secondary sources.

The Pennsylvania research has been compiled from previously translated or transcribed sources and is also subject to any errors of transcribing that might have been made. It would have been more satisfactory to work entirely from primary sources, but neither time nor the availability of the original records permitted such research. The Pennsylvania documentation on these families is not intended to be exhaustive. On some families the available information is far too extensive to publish here in its entirety. On other families only the arrival on the ship list was found and no other information could be located. A thorough search of all county estate records, deeds and assessment lists would probably yield much more information about some of these families. The few Pennsylvania records presented here are offered as a guide for others who might be interested in developing the family's history. The researcher should be aware that ages given in the ship lists and dates of birth given on tombstones or in church records in obituary notices are often incorrect.

For brevity, certain short citations are used for frequently cited records. For full title or citation see list on page xix. Under American records, where church books and court records are cited, if no state is given after the county designated, it is assumed to be PA. If the church or court record or other source is from a state other than PA, the standard state abbreviation is used: e.g. NC for North Carolina. A list of abbreviations appears on page xviii. Throughout the text, bold face type has been used to designate the sources of the data presented. The immigrants who actually appear in the passenger lists are presented in bold type, when presented within the family group. It is possible that others within the family group also emigrated, but do not appear in the ship lists, perhaps because they were under 16 years of age.

With all the limitations stated, we present the following list of 628 emigrant heads of households, being fully aware that there may be errors in identification. Exact identification requires extensive study of the families. The repetition of both given and surnames in some villages makes unquestionable identification impossible in some cases. As is true in all of the questionable areas, or in incomplete entries, additions or corrections to the material here will be welcomed.

This book would not have been possible without the assistance of some very special people.

Pastor Frederick S. Weiser, who served as editor of The Pennsylvania German Society for quarter of a century, provided guidance, suggestions and assistance to this project for fifteen years. No words can adequately express my gratitude for his efforts.

The microfilming program of the Family History Library in Salt Lake City has made the Alsatian church records available for the intensive study needed for a project of this scope. The cooperation and help of Noel R. Barton, Regional Manager, U.S. Acquisitions, Genealogical Society of Utah, is deeply appreciated.

Dr. Bernd Gölzer provided much archival material that would not have otherwise been available for this volume. His many contributions are cited throughout the text, and Appendix A was created as a result of his efforts.

Dr. Gerhard Hein has compiled a wealth of material concerning families from Nassau-Saarwerden County. His work is gratefully acknowledged, and his many volumes include data on these families that is not available on microfilm.

Klaus Wust and Peggy Joyner have always shared much material on the Shenandoah Valley Germans. Special thanks also to Peggy Joyner for providing some Maryland naturalizations and denizations from "Commission Book, 82", published in *Maryland Historical Magazine,* XXVI (1931) and XXVII (1932).

Most of the photographs illustrating this volume were made by the author; special thanks to Guy Slaughenhaupt for his assistance in preparing some of the illustrations for publication; Clifford Canfield for his photographs of

Wingen; Mary Lou Mariner and Jane Knous for sharing their photographs of Niederbronn; Betty Bunting, Ruth Renton and Annabelle Hoffman for sharing a wonderful day photographing Alsatian villages and their help in making notes for later photo identification.

Alice Spayd devoted many hours entering the manuscript into the computer. Her knowledge of the Pennsylvania German dialect, her interest in genealogical research and her computer skills, were of great help.

Cleta Smith has discovered the origins and completely researched several of the families presented in this volume. She generously shared the results of her efforts on the Bietinger, Ensminger, Franckhauser, Nonnemacher and Schnepp families, plus providing notes and clues on several other immigrant families. My heartfelt thanks for her research.

Others have submitted helpful data on one or more of the families in the text. They include Marolyn N. Adams, Richard Bassett, Raymond Bell, FASG, Jean Bonham, Betty Bunting, Jane Adams Clarke, George H. Custard, Jeannette Harper, Jack Heck, Raymond Hollenbach, Alice Morrison, Shirley Pahl, Kenneth Smith, Ernest Thode, Grace Thompson, and Frederick S. Weiser

Last, but certainly not least, my husband, Richard A. Burgert, has provided support, encouragement, advice and most of all, understanding throughout the fifteen years of this project.

Annette K. Burgert

Myerstown, PA
August, 1992

Abbreviations

A. or a.	acres
adj.	adjoining
Adm.	administration, administrator of estate
appt.	appointed
b.	born
bp.	baptized
ca.	circa (about)
CH-	Switzerland (Confederatio Helvetica). Used in connection with a four-digit number it designates a Swiss postal code.
co.	county
conf.	confirmed
d.	died
dec'd.	deceased
exr, exrs.	executor(s)
Joh.	Johann (the form of Johannes used preceding another name, as Johann Martin; an alternative is Hans. The full name alone is Johannes.)
KB	Kirchenbuch, church book or parish register. This term is used to designate any form of church record in Germany or America.
KY	Kentucky
Luth.	Lutheran
m.	married
MD	Maryland
mo.	month(s)
Mstr.	Meister = master tradesman
nat.	naturalized
NC	North Carolina
NJ	New Jersey
N.N.	no surname or given name entered into the cited record
O.C.	Orphan's Court
OH	Ohio
PA	Pennsylvania
Pat.	Patent for land
q.v.	which see (refers to another emigrant listed in the text)
Ref.	Reformed
Rev.	Reverend
S-H, I:	Strassburger and Hinke, *Pennsylvania German Pioneers.*
II:	The number designates the volume used for the citation.
III:	

sp.	sponsors at baptism
twp.	township
VA	Virginia
W-	When used preceding a four-digit number, this signifies a postal code for a village in Germany.
w.	weeks
wit.	witnesses, witnessed
y.	year(s)

Short Citations

Rev. Abraham Blumer's records:

Unpublished nineteenth century copy of records of marriages and burials by Abraham Blumer, Reformed clergyman. The original appears to be lost; copy in the Historical Society of the Evangelical and Reformed Church, Philip Schaff Library, Lancaster Theological Seminary, Lancaster.

Burgert, *The Northern Kraichgau*

Annette Kunselman Burgert, *Eighteenth Century Emigrants from German-Speaking Lands to North America, Volume I: The Northern Kraichgau.* The Pennsylvania German Society, Vol. 16. (Breinigsville, PA, 1983).

Burgert, *The Western Palatinate*

Annette Kunselman Burgert, *Eighteenth Century Emigrants from German-Speaking Lands to North America, Volume II: The Western Palatinate.* The Pennsylvania German Society, Vol. 19. (Birdsboro, PA, 1986).

Burgert, *Hochstadt Origins*

Annette K. Burgert, *The Hochstadt Origins of Some of the Early Settlers at Host Church, Berks County, PA.* (Worthington, OH, 1983).

Chalkley's Chronicles

Lyman Chalkley, *Chronicles of the Scotch-Irish Settlement in Virginia; Extracted from the Original Court Records of Augusta County,* 1745-1800. 3 vols. (1912; reprinted Baltimore, 1974).

Chambers, *Early Germans of New Jersey*

Theodore F. Chambers, *The Early Germans of New Jersey.* (Baltimore, 1969).

Glatfelter, *Pastors and People*

Charles H. Glatfelter, *Pastors and People: German Lutheran and Reformed Churches in the Pennsylvania Field,* 1717-1793. 2 vols. (Breinigsville, 1979, 1981).

Hocker, *German Settlers of Pennsylvania*

Edward W. Hocker, *Genealogical Data Relating to the German Settlers of Pennsylvania and Adjacent Territory.* (Baltimore, 1981).

Rev. Jacob Lischy's records:

Unpublished private records of Rev. Jacob Lischy, a Reformed minister who served congregations in York County, PA.

Muhlenberg's Journals

Theodore G. Tappert and John W. Doberstein, trans. and ed., *The Journals of Henry Melchior Muhlenberg.* 3 vols. (Philadelphia, 1942-1958; reprinted, 1982).

PA:

Pennsylvania Archives, together with the *Colonial Records,* a 135-volume set published between 1838 and 1935 in several series of many volumes each.

Rupp: I. Daniel Rupp, *A Collection of Thirty-Thousand Names of German, Swiss, Dutch, French, Portuguese and other immigrants in Pennsylvania, chronologically arranged* 1727 to 1776 (Harrisburg, 1856, reissued and revised Philadelphia, 1876, numerous reprints; also printed with a German text, most recently Leipzig, 1936).

S-H, I: Ralph Beaver Strassburger and
S-H, II: William John Hinke, *Pennsylvania*
S-H, III: *German Pioneers*. 3 vols. (Norristown, 1934).

Rev. Daniel Schumacher's records: Frederick S. Weiser, "Daniel Schumacher's Baptismal Register," in *Publications of the Pennsylvania German Society*, Vol. I, (Breinigsville 1967), 185-407.

Rev. John Casper Stoever's records: [F. J. F. Schantz, trans.] *Records of Rev. John Casper Stoever, Baptismal and Marriage,* 1730-1799. (Harrisburg, 1896; reprinted Baltimore 1982). This translation contains errors and omissions.

Swiss in Hanau-Lichtenberg   Walter Bodmer, *L'Immigration Suisse dans le Comté de Hanau-Lichtenberg au Dix-Septième Siècle.* (Strasbourg, 1930).

Rev. John Waldschmidt's records: "Baptismal and Marriage Records. Rev. John Waldschmidt, 1752-1786, in *Pennsylvania Archives*, Sixth Series, Vol. 6, pages 147-282. (Harrisburg, 1907).

1790 Census: Heads of Families at the First Census of the United States Taken in the Year 1790. Pennsylvania. (Baltimore, 1970).

Zweibrücken Manumissions Protocoll   1726-1749 published in:
Annette Kunselman Burgert, *Eighteenth Century Emigrants from German-Speaking Lands to North America, Volume II: The Western Palatinate.* The Pennsylvania German Society, Vol. 19. (Birdsboro, PA, 1986). 1750-1771 published in: *Yearbook of the Pennsylvania German Folklore Society,* Vol. 16. (Allentown, 1951). Reprinted in: Don Yoder, Ed., *Pennsylvania German Immigrants, 1709-1786.* (Baltimore, 1980, 1984, 1989).

Annotations

The German church records have been studied by the author on films made by the Genealogical Society of Utah, Salt Lake City, all of which are available to other students through the genealogical society's branch library system. Most of the originals are in the Strasbourg Archives.

The Pennsylvania Church records have been studied from existing translations and/or microfilms of the originals in various libraries and archives.

Naturalizations: 1) Pennsylvania: Acts of the colonial legislature in *Statutes at Large,* M. S. Giuseppi, *Naturalizations of Foreign Protestants in the American and West Indian Colonies* (London, 1921; reprinted Baltimore 1964, 1969, 1979). See also Pennsylvania Archives, Second Series, 2:347-486; 2) Maryland: Jeffrey A. Wyand and Florence L. Wyand, *Colonial Maryland Naturalizations* (Baltimore, 1975).

Newspaper citations: All of the newspapers cited in the text have been microfilmed. A handy guide to references to Germans in them: Edward W. Hocker, *Genealogical Data relating to the German Settlers of Pennsylvania and Adjacent Territory* (Baltimore, 1981).

As an accommodation to American readers, the entries have been arranged and indexed without reference to umlauts. These two marks above an a, o or u amount to adding an e behind them. In German alphabetizing these letters are treated as ae oe and ue.

Deeds	References to deeds are abstracted as follows: Deed book references; date of transaction; seller, his occupation, his residence, his wife, to purchaser, his occupation, his residence, acreage or lot number, location of land sold; how seller acquired it.
Wills	References to wills are abstracted as follows: Decedent's name, location, occupation if given, date of will-date of probate. Wife; children (or other heirs). Executors; Witnesses.
Zip code identification of European villages	Modern zip codes have been inserted throughout the text to assist with village location and identification. A five-digit zip code refers to villages located today in France. A four-digit number preceded by W- indicates villages today in Germany. A four-digit number preceded by CH- indicates villages in Switzerland.

Glossary

Certain words have been left untranslated in the text, and appear in italics. These words usually refer to an occupation or an official status, and often have no equivalent English translation. Other words appear in the eighteenth century records that are now obsolete. An approximate meaning is offered for some of these phrases. The spellings are given as they appear in the eighteenth century records and may differ slightly from the currently accepted spelling.

Ackermann	small farmer, farm hand
Amtmann	bailiff
Amtschreiber	official clerk
Baumeister	architect; building contractor
Bildweber	picture or tapestry weaver
Censor	church official
Erbestander	hereditary tenant
Ertzgräber	digger of ores

Fuhrknecht	carriage servant
Fuhrmann	driver
Gemeinsmann	member of the community
Gerichtseltesten	court warden
Gerichtsmann	?councilman; member of the court
Gerichtsschöffen	court lay assessor or lay member of the court
Handelsmann	tradesman; shopkeeper
Hausknecht	house servant
Herrsch. Hoffmann	administrator of a manorial farm or estate
Hoffbestander	tenant farmer
Hoffmann	farmer on a manorial farm
Kirchschaffner	church steward
Kohlenbrenner	charcoal burner
Lehnsmann	vassal; feudal tenant
Melcker	milker
Meyer	dairy farmer
Oberförster	head forester
Rathwirth	town innkeeper
Rebmann	vinedresser
Rosshirt	horse herdsman
Rothgerber	red tanner
Saltzpeterseider	saltpeter boiler
Schirmer or	a resident with protected
Schirmsverwandte(r)(n)	religious priviledges
Schlossmeyer	steward of the manorial estate or dairy farm
Schultheissen	town administrator
Stabhalter	administrative official
Stubenhitzer	room heater
Stundenruffer	town crier
Tabackspinner	tobacconist
Vorsinger	chior leader
Vorsteher	church warden, Elder
Ziegler	brick or tile maker

The Northern Alsace

Introduction

For the purposes of this study, the area covered is designated the Northern Alsace, and comprises only that northernmost part of Alsace that borders on Germany and the northwestern portion that is today known as Alsace Bossue, in German Krummes Elsass. During the sixteenth and seventeenth centuries, Alsace was a country divided into numerous small domains; the area covered by this study belonged to the Grafschaft of Nassau-Saarwerden, the Grafschaft of Hanau Lichtenberg, the Lützelstein jurisdiction and the Duchy of Zweibrücken. Today the region is located in the northern part of the Département of Bas-Rhin in France.

Outline map of Département Bas-Rhin showing the
approximate outline of the area studied for this volume.

In the eighteenth century, the northwestern section belonged to the Counts of Nassau and was known as the Grafschaft of Nassau-Saarwerden. Several of the families mentioned in the Reformed parish records at Diedendorf actually lived in the neighboring territories of Lixheim and Vinstingen, which are today located in the neighboring Département of Moselle. Members of these families emigrated to Pennsylvania in the eighteenth century and are included in this study, although the villages are not located in Bas-Rhin today. This area is approximately forty miles northwest of the city of Strasbourg.

The village of Sarrewerden remains today, perpetuating
the name of the former Grafschaft of Nassau-Saarwerden.

As early as 1559, the Count of Nassau granted refuge in Nassau-Saarwerden to Huguenots who were expelled from French territory for religious reasons.

The Grafschaft of Nassau-Saarwerden was occupied by France and Lorraine from 1649-1670 and during this period the Lutheran religion was forbidden and the Catholic church was the official church. After a brief interval, Louis XIV invaded in 1676. In 1698 the county was returned to the jurisdiction of the Counts of Nassau, and the Lutheran religion was once more the official religion.

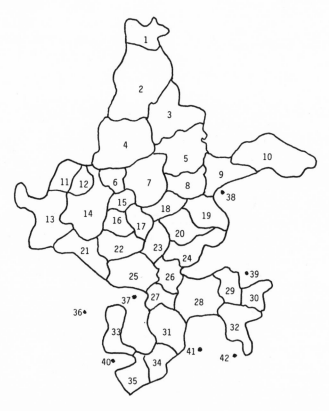

Territory of the Counts of Nassau-Saarwerden in the eighteenth century.
Key to the map:

1. Siltzheim	15. Neu-Sarrewerden	29. Drulingen
2. Herbitzheim	16. Zollingen	30. Ottwiller
3. Oermingen	17. Sarrewerden	31. Hirschland
4. Keskastel	18. Rimsdorf	32. Siewiller
5. Voellerdingen	19. Mackwiller	33. Kirrberg
6. Schopperten	20. Thal	34. Rauwiller
7. Bockenheim	21. Diedendorf	35. Goerlingen
8. Domfessel	22. Pisdorf	36. Fénétrange
9. Lorentzen	23. Burbech	37. Postorf
10. Butten	24. Berg-Rexingen	38. Diemeringen
11. Hinsingen	25. Wolfskirchen	39. Asswiller
12. Bissert	26. Eywiller	40. Helleringen
13. Altwiller	27. Eschwiller	41. Schalbach
14. Harskirchen	28. Weyer	42. Hangviller

Modern map of the area showing locations of villages in
the Nassau-Saarwerden and Lützelstein jurisdictions.

Several families came from Kirberg, and this village provides a good
example of the different jurisdictions as they existed in the seventeenth and
eighteenth centuries: in the 1600's Kirberg was in the Grafschaft of Nassau-
Saarwerden, the nearby village of Helleringen (today Hellering-lès-
Fénétrange) was in the Lordship of Lixheim, and Vinstingen (today
Fénétrange) was the county seat of the Lordship of Vinstingen. But families

from all three places appear in the Reformed church book at Diedendorf.

A Reformed parish centered at Diedendorf, where the records start in 1698, was established after the military defeat of Louis XIV in 1697, and the restoration of this area to the Counts of Nassau. This parish served all of Nassau-Saarwerden and also the remaining Huguenot families in the neighboring territories of Lixheim and Vinstingen. After the defeat of Louis XIV in 1697, many Reformed Swiss families came into the area to repopulate and they appear in large numbers in the Reformed parish records at Diedendorf. Diedendorf was one of seven villages that were founded by the Huguenots in 1559 with permission of the Counts of Nassau. Several of the families that appear in the Diedendorf records, Schneider, Wotring (Vautrin), Balliet, Marx and Hahn, also all appear in the Egypt Reformed church records in Lehigh co., PA.

This area was peaceful and prosperous until the time of the Thirty Years' War (1618-1648). In 1629 the Grafschaft of Nassau-Saarwerden was occupied by the Duchy of Lorraine. The Catholic Lorraine occupation resulted in the immediate expulsion of all Reformed pastors in Nassau-Saarwerden. From 1635 to 1648, the political jurisdictions (and official religions) changed several times. Many of the early Huguenot families fled from the area; others died from hunger, pestilence and the evils of warfare.

In 1649, the Lorraine troops returned to the area. Many of the Huguenot families fled to Bischweiler, fifty miles to the east, the closest settlement with a Reformed congregation. In 1670 the Lorraine occupation ended and Saarwerden County was returned to the Counts of Nassau. Peace did not last, and King Louis XIV of France again occupied the region in 1676. In 1685 he revoked the Edict of Nantes which led to a mass emigration of Huguenots from the French occupied territories. A new edict stated that the Reformed people should convert to Catholicism, and this edict was also applied by the local commanders to the Lutheran inhabitants of the Grafschaft of Nassau-Saarwerden. This edict also threatened the death penalty to those who attempted emigration. Louis XIV of France withdrew from the Nassau-Saarwerden territory in 1697, but parts of the area remained under Lorraine influence and Protestant services were still not permitted, although forced conversions to Catholicism ceased.

Just as the village names in this area have both a German and French spelling (vis: Vinstingen=Fénétrange) so, too, the surnames: Vautrin appears in some of the area records as Wodring; Brodt as DuPain, Dupin, and Pain; Join as Longjoin, Joing, and Schwing. These names provide just a few examples. Others appear in the individual family entries in the main text.

At the time of the emigration the county of Nassau-Saarwerden was German territory. This county was annexed to Alsace on 23 Nov. 1793.

The Northern Vosges region was divided into numerous small domains such as the Lützelstein jurisdiction. Many of the villages belonged to the Counts of Hanau-Lichtenberg, and as was the case in Nassau-Saarwerden, these villages also had a large influx of Swiss in the late seventeenth century and continuing on into the early eighteenth century.

Villages in the Lützelstein jurisdiction:

1. Waldhambach	14. Durstel
2. Volksberg	15. Petersbach
3. Rosteig	16. La Petite Pierre
4. Wingen-sur-Moder	17. Lohr
5. Weislingen	18. Schoenbourg
6. Frohmühl	19. Eschbourg/ Graufthal
7. Puberg	20. Hangviller
8. Adamswiller	21. Wintersbourg
9. Tieffenbach	22. Zilling
10. Struth	23. Vescheim
11. Hinsbourg	24. Berling
12. Gungwiller	25. Pfalzweyer
13. Bettwiller	26. Weinbourg

The religious complexity in this entire area presents its own set of problems when researching families. The majority of the church books are Lutheran, and there are a few Reformed parishes; there are also Catholic records. All must be studied to completely document the families. An example may be found in the records studied to compile just one immigrant family: Georg Dierenberger [Dürrenberger] who arrived on the *Phoenix* in 1750. He was born in Mertzweiler and married there in 1729. Five children were born in Mertzweiler, before the family moved westward to Volksberg. Four more children were born while the family resided in Volksberg, and these four children were found recorded in three different church books: Dehlingen Lutheran KB, Waldhambach Lutheran KB, and Tiefenbach Catholic KB.

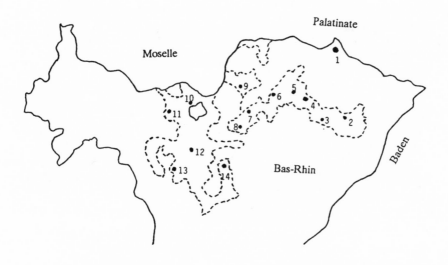

Partial territories of the Counts of Hanau-Lichtenberg within the studied region.

1. Wissembourg
2. Hatten
3. Betschdorf
4. Kutzenhausen
5. Preuschdorf
6. Woerth
7. Gundershoffen
8. Mietesheim
9. Niederbronn-les-Bains
10. Lichtenberg
11. Wimmenau
12. Bouxwiller
13. Hattmatt
14. Alteckendorf

Slightly southwest of Wissembourg were the territories of Cleebourg and Catharinenberg that belonged to the Duchy of Zweibrücken. Wissembourg is the northernmost city of Alsace, and is located on the border of the Palatinate. The town dates from the seventh century, with the founding of a Benedictine Abbey. To the south of Wissembourg, between the Rhine, the Lower Vosges and the Haguenau forest, stretches a vast plain. In this area are a number of small towns and villages where the architecture, dialects, costumes and religious practices have been preserved. Seebach, Hunspach, Soultz-sous-Forêts, Betschdorf, Hoffen, Hatten, and Kullendorf, all had eighteenth century emigration to America. Hunspach is a particularly charming village, with many half-timbered houses with canopies in the distinctive Alsatian style. Part of this area is today known as the Outre-Forêt region. In the eighteenth century, some of the villages south of Wissembourg belonged to the Duchy of Zweibrücken. The Zweibrücken District of Kleeburg embraced Schloss Kleeburg and Kleeburg village and the villages of Rott, Steinselz, Oberhofen, Ingolsheim, Hunspach, and Hoffen; the District of Katherinenburg included the villages of Birlenbach, Keffenach, half of the village of Schöneberg, the Wernershäuser Mill and the Welchen Mill near Memmelshofen.

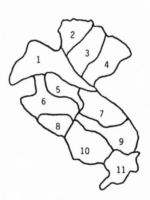

Villages belonging to the Duchy of Zweibrücken:

1. Cleebourg	5. Bremmelbach	9. Hunspach
2. Rott	6. Birlenbach	10. Schoenenbourg
3. Oberhoffen	7. Ingolsheim	11. Hoffen
4. Steinseltz	8. Keffenach	

Modern map of the villages, today in France, that belonged to the
Duchy of Zweibrücken in the eighteenth century

In all of the northern Alsace, only these villages that belonged to
Zweibrücken have had lists of emigrants published, and those published lists
are limited to the emigrants who applied for permission to leave. The
Zweibrücken Manumissions Protocoll, 1724-1749, has been published several
times, the most recent and complete version in:

Burgert, Annette Kunselman. *Eighteenth Century Emigrants from German-
Speaking Lands to North America, Vol. II: The Western Palatinate.* The
Pennsylvania German Society, Vol. 19. Birdsboro, 1985. Appendix B, pages
361-376: Zweibrücken Manumissions Protocoll 1724-1749, contains a list of
emigrants from Oberamt Cleeburg (villages today in Bas Rhin.)

Yoder, Don, ed. *Pennsylvania German Immigrants, 1709-1786.* Baltimore:
Genealogical Publishing Co., 1984. Contains two lists of emigrants from the
Zweibrücken territories, including Cleeburg and Catharinenberg juris-
dictions, located today in Bas-Rhin.

Other available titles to assist the researcher in this area are:

Hall, Charles M. *The Atlantic Bridge to Germany, Vol. IV. Saarland, Alsace Lorraine, Switzerland.* The Everton Publishers, Inc. 1976.

Macco, Herman F. *Swiss Immigrants to the Palatinate in Germany and to America 1650-1800 and Huguenots in the Palatinate and Germany.* 1954. Salt Lake City, Family History Library, typescript and microfilms # 823,861, and 823,862, with index.

Thode, Ernest. *Genealogical Gazetteer of Alsace-Lorraine.* Indianapolis: Heritage House, 1986.

The church books were the major source of information on the families documented in this volume. All church books cited in the text are available in this country on microfilm and may be consulted at the Family History Library in Salt Lake City, or at any of their branch libraries located throughout the country, through their microfilm rental program. Their locality catalog, available on microfiche, will help determine the records that are available for study. Another source that lists the church books of Alsace is:

Koch, Herbert. "Die Kirchenbücher von Elsass-Lothringen" in *Mitteilungen der Zentralstelle für Deutsche Personen=und Familiengeschichte*; Vol. 9: The Lutheran Church; Vol. 10: The Reformed Church. Leipzig, 1911, 1912.

The large number of Swiss families who moved into the area were Reformed, but they often settled in an area where there was no nearby Reformed parish, and entries on their families are found in the Lutheran records. As these territories changed hands after each of the many wars affecting the region, the religious denominations also changed. In a few of the records, there are notations entered by the pastor concerning these changes; an example is found in the Birlenbach Lutheran record: the earliest church book here starts in 1616, and until 1685 all entries are recorded in German script. Then in 1685, the Lutheran pastor Michael Steckh indicates a conversion to Catholicism; no entries are recorded until 1688 and the record resumes that year with all entries in Latin and continues until 1701. A new church book starts in 1702, with the title page again indicating a Lutheran record, and entries from that date are again recorded in German script. In another nearby village, Oberseebach, the entire church book is recorded in Latin, signifying a Catholic parish; but entries in the record indicate people of all denominations in the area are recorded in this single church book, and those parishioners who were Lutheran or Reformed are so designated. If no designation is given, Catholic may be assumed.

The amount of information given in each record varies from one village to another. In the Lutheran church book at Hirschland, there is a baptismal entry recorded for a son of Johann Adam Schneider and his wife Martha; the sponsors of the child are listed with the first sponsor being Johann Nickel Gerber, an innkeeper at Drulingen. Below the entry in the church book is the added notation "the first male sponsor is this child's great-grandfather". This type of entry is a genealogist's delight. But other records are not so detailed: in the Hunspach Reformed record the following burial entry is frustrating: died 25 Sept. 1728, the old Greth [Margretha], at Hunspach, and buried on the 26th, her age 108 years. You would think that anyone who had lived for 108 years should at least get their surname recorded! By contrast, consider the wealth of information in this burial record at Durstel:

Buried 22 March 1747, Maria Catharina Weiss, nee Bohn, daughter of the deceased J. Martin Bohn, farmer. She was born in 1689. She married 1 May 1714 Johannes Weiss, son of Philipps Weiss. They had __? sons and two daughters; one son married and went to America. She died aged 58 years.

Canton Bern provided the majority of Swiss into the Alsatian territories. In Nassau-Saarwerden a total of 441 families with identified origins arrived in the late seventeenth and early eighteenth centuries, over 400 of them from Canton Bern, and only 14 from Canton Zürich, plus a few from other Cantons. In Hanau-Lichtenberg there were more than 1100 Swiss with Cantons identified; 972 are identified from Canton Bern; about 70 came from Canton Zürich, and only a few from other Cantons. Several published works are available to help with the study of Swiss into this area:

Bodmer, Walter. *L'Immigration Suisse dans le Compté de Hanau-Lichtenberg au Dix-Septième Siècle.* Strasbourg: Imprimerie Heitz & Cie, 1930.

Grieb, Robert. *L'Immigration Suisse dans les paroisses du Comté de Nassau-Sarrewerden après la Guerre de Trente Ans.* Saverne: Société D'Histoire et D'Archéologie de Savern, 1971.

Joder, Karl. "Swiss Emigrants from 1694-1754 who Settled in the Palatinate, Alsace-Lorraine, Baden-Württemberg and Pennsylvania", in *Mennonite Family History,* Vol. 2, no. 4: Elverson, PA, Oct. 1983.

Stricker, Eberhardt. "Schweizer Einwanderung ins Elsass". Extract from *Jahrbuch der Elsass-Lothringischen Wissenschaftlichen Gesellschaft zu Strassburg,* 1937. Salt Lake City, Family History Library, microfilm # 1,071,428.

At least 75 of the families presented in this volume have identifiable Swiss origins given in the Alsatian records.

Several sources have been used to prove the emigration of the individuals or families mentioned in the text. The church books have already been mentioned as the primary source of information about the families. A few of the church books consulted also contained emigration notations. These may be located in the baptismal records, the marriage records, and even a few in the obituaries. There are emigration notations for 65 of the families in the village church records, and these are cited throughout the text.

Pastor Joh. Jacob Lucius served the Hirschland Lutheran parish for 56 years. He frequently made notations in the records about people from his parish who emigrated, many to America and some to Prussia. This pastor often crossed out the baptismal entry of a person who emigrated, and he also crossed out entries when people died. His handwriting is difficult to read, even without these slash marks through the entries, nor did it improve with age. His daughter Anna Regina Lucius married (1) Johannes Juncker, who died in 1733. She married (2) Simon Conrad Gryneus and they emigrated to America with others from the parish, and with her children from both marriages. Although the pastor placed an emigration notation by her birth entry, he did not cross out his own grandchildren's entries, as he did so many others, nor did he mention their emigration to America; however, they are found in Pennsylvania church records.

A thorough study of the records at Hirschland revealed that there were other emigrants from that parish who were not so noted in the pastoral notations. We will never know why the Pastor was inconsistent in making these emigration notations in this record.

In addition to the church books, there are various county records available at the Strasbourg Archives that offer information about emigrants who left for America or other destinations. These records include several groups, such as inheritance records, estate inventories, and notary public records. As an example of the type of information that can be found:

Catharina Schneider d. 5 Oct. 1764, leaving no children or siblings in Saarwerden Co. The enumeration of her heirs includes a genealogical chart of all descendants of her grandfather, the Swiss Joseph Schneider of Diedendorf, made by the county office on 18 Oct. 1764. In this record, eight families or individuals in Joseph's family are mentioned to be in the New Land, and one family moved to Lithuania. More than 100 of the following immigrant families were verified through the use of these county records.

This group of records is not available on microfilm, but many of these county records have been abstracted by a German genealogist, Dr. Gerhard Hein. He has compiled a series of privately mimeographed publications that are available in a few libraries in Germany and France. See Appendix A for additional information about these records.

One of the remarkable features of many of the Alsatian church books that have been studied for this publication, is the fact that often starting in the 1730s, the people involved in the KB entry sign the church record entry; if it is a baptismal entry, the father of the child signs, the mother sometimes signs but more often makes her mark, and the sponsors sign.

If it is a marriage entry, the groom signs, the bride often makes her mark, and the fathers of both bride and groom (if living) sign the entry. Occasionally, other witnesses to the event also sign. So there are a large number of signatures available for comparison purposes.

These signatures are of great value in verifying that you have located the right immigrant; it virtually proves the emigration in some cases. An example: Johann Nicolaus Schneider is an immigrant documented in this volume. In Europe, he served as the schoolmaster at Rauwiller. His signature is available from documents there. Three men named Johann Nicolaus Schneider appear in S-H, I. One arrived in 1738, another in 1749 and the third in 1764. All signed the passenger lists. A fourth immigrant with just the name Niclaus Schneyder (without the Johann) also arrived in 1749. A simple comparison of the signature from the Rauwiller records with the passenger's signature on the *Robert and Alice* in 1738 provides an almost perfect fit; the other signatures are not even close. Even without verifying data from the European records concerning this man's emigration, there is no doubt that we have the correct identification for the 1738 immigrant.

Another example of the value of these signatures can be found in the case of the immigrant Peter Bene. Sufficient information was found in the Alsatian records and Pennsylvania records on him and his family to verify his emigration, but no listing could be found in the ships lists as translated by either Rupp or Strassburger/Hinke. He last appeared in the European record in 1749, and had a child baptised in the Tulpehocken Lutheran Church, Berks co., PA in 1752, narrowing his emigration to the period between those dates. A comparision of his signature from the European record with the signature lists published in the second volume of S-H, *Pennsylvania German Pioneers* finally located him on the ship *Phoenix* arriving in 1750; his signature was translated in Rupp as Peter Bem and in S-H as Peter Ber! Im many cases it is only by using these signature lists that these immigrants can be identified; finally after many years, the signature volume has been reprinted with two new editions available to researchers.

The signature of another immigrant (Hans Peter *Voltz*) found in the Gundershoffen KB, enabled his precise identification in S-H, although his name was translated as Hans Peder *Goltz*. It was known from the Heidelberg Moravian KB in Berks county that Peter Foltz was born in Gundershoffen, and indeed Peter Voltz was located in the KB there; two children were born before the family emigrated, the second child being baptized in Gundershoffen on 1 Apr. 1749. This ruled out an immigrant named Johan Peter Voltz who arrived in 1748 [S-H, I: 383, 385.]. There was an immigrant named Peter Foltz who arrived on the ship *Patience*, in 1750 [S-H, I: 427], but his signature did not match the signature of the Peter Voltz who married and had two children in Gundershoffen. Signature comparison revealed that he was the immigrant translated as Hans Peder G̲oltz, who arrived on the *Dragon*, 17 Oct. 1749 [S-H, I: 423].

These signatures can also be used to verify an immigrant who does not appear in the ship lists for one reason or another. Perhaps an immigrant came through another port such as Baltimore, where no passenger lists were maintained. He may be mentioned in the Pennsylvania or Maryland or North Carolina records, but he does not appear in the passenger lists. If there exists a will or other document that he signed (road petitions, other petitions for the creation of new townships, etc), and if the signature of a person with the same name appears in an Alsatian record, the signatures can be compared and perhaps a match will be made. A careful search of both European and American records then narrows the emigration to a short period. This technique is also valid with certain immigrants who did not sign, provided they made a rather distinctive mark. The more common (X) does not work in this case, but many of those who made their mark used initials or some distinguishing feature when making their mark, and they usually did this in the same fashion throughout their lives.

Adam Kober, who emigrated from Oberbronn in 1751, made his mark in the church record by the baptismal entry of his son Philip Jacob Kober in 1737. His mark was (AKO) and it is the same mark found in the ship list that is reproduced in S-H, II: 542. There are numerous other examples of coinciding signatures and marks throughout the text. Sixty of the immigrants in this volume have been identified through the comparison of their signatures or marks in the Alsatian church books and the Pennsylvania oath lists in S-H, II.

Many of the emigrant's occupations are given in the Alsatian records. Many of the persons who emigrated were farmers. After the many wars that swept through this area, the noble families invited the Swiss into the area to repopulate and work the farms. The Swiss Reformed families who moved into these Lutheran territories were offered a religious tolerance and protection; they appear in the area records designated as *Schirmer* and *Schirmsverwandten.* The Huguenot families who fled into this area from the adjacent Catholic Lorraine territories were artisans and weavers. Various obsolete terms that reflected the village social order are found in the eighteenth century records and these terms are left untranslated in the text, since there is often no good English equivalent. This is also true of certain untranslated eighteenth century occupations. See the Glossary on page xxiii.

Included in the immigrant families were colonial clergymen, schoolmasters, a prominent physician, and other families who made their mark in American history. John Peter Saling of Virginia came from Alsace. David Schäffer, a Philadelphia sugar refiner, was the father-in-law of Frederich Augustus Conrad Muhlenberg, the first Speaker of the House of Representatives. Nicolaus Hauer was the father of the famous Barbara Fritschy. John Adam Eyer, the son of an immigrant, would make a lasting mark on *Fraktur.*

In the course of this study, only one archival list concerning the emigration was located in the Archives du Bas-Rhin at Strasbourg. This document, numbered E 4367, concerned the clandestine emigration of a group of families from Niederbronn in 1738. It is indeed fortunate that this document was preserved, since several of the emigrants died on the voyage and their names do not appear in the Pennsylvania lists. The Niederbronn group chose a disastrous year to emigrate. In 1738, due to increased solicitation by newlanders and shipping agents, large groups of emigrants gathered in Rotterdam for departure to the American colonies. The numbers that arrived exceeded all expectations and ships were not immediately available for their transport. The Palatines, Swiss, and other foreigners were sent to a holding area outside of Rotterdam city to await the arrival of the emigrant ships. A tent city was established and poor sanitation and immoderate weather conditions caused an epidemic of dysentery and malignant fevers. Nearly 80 small children died within a short time. After the ships arrived, they were overloaded, under provisioned, and to add to the misery, after sailing the vessels encountered heavy seas and a violent storm. Many of the passengers were sickly when they boarded the vessels, and on four of the 1738 transports, there were 425 deaths noted. The estimated number of deaths at sea in 1738 range from 1600 to over 2000. When the ships arrived at Philadelphia, they presented a health hazard to the inhabitants there. The *Charming Nancy* had loaded 312½ freights in Rotterdam; a surviving passenger on this ship, Johann Heinrich Keppele, recorded that 250 souls died at sea. The survivors of the Niederbronn group appear on the list of 65 surviving passengers who arrived on the *Charming Nancy* in 1738. How many other Alsatians perished on voyages that year may never be known.

An excellent article giving further detail of this terrible emigration year is found in *The Report, 40. A Journal of German-American History*, published by the Society for the History of the Germans in Maryland (Baltimore, 1986), titled "The Emigration Season of 1738- Year of the Destroying Angels" by Klaus Wust. Wust estimates that the mortality rate of this emigration year was close to 35% of those who set out for the New World. A detailed account of this disaster was sent back to Europe, and possibly discouraged emigration in some areas. But conditions in the German-speaking lands were such that many were still willing to risk everything to come to the New Land.

They came to America to improve their lot in life, and many of them found success; but others may have regretted their decision to leave their homeland. For those who survived the voyages, other perils awaited. Several of the Alsatian immigrant families were involved in the Indian massacres in the area that is today Lehigh county, PA. The following were killed by the Indians: the children of Adam Clauss; Jacob Wetterhold; Henry Frantz; Johannes Schneider, his wife, and three of their children. Two other

Schneider children were injured in the attack, and the homes of Nicholas Marx and Georg Graff were destroyed.

Although the emigration process was difficult and hazardous, the following pages attest that many of the immigrants survived both natural and man-made disasters, and the survivors and their descendants did find a better way of life.

The Bischtroff church has a square steeple.
Bischtroff-sur-Sarre appears in earlier records as Pisdorf.

The Emigrants

The Protestant church at Harskirchen, built in 1768,
designed by the architect Stengel. The records of this
church and more than one hundred other church books in
the northern Alsace have been the basis for the European
data in this volume about more than 600 families
who left the area to come to the American Colonies.

1. ABERT, PHILIP   67250 Soultz-sous-Forêts
Ship unknown
Not in S-H

EUROPEAN RECORDS

Soultz Lutheran KB:
Philipp Abert, son of Joh. Philip Abert, citizen at Hermersweiler
[Hermerswiller=67250 Soultz-sous-Forêts] m. 21 Nov. 1757 Catharina,
daughter of Jacob Scheib. Children:
1. Philipp b. 6 Aug. 1758
   Sp.: Martin Abert; Michael Bergmann; Christina Scheib
2. Johann Jacob b. 12 Jan. 1760
3. Johann Martin b. 4 Dec. 1761, bp. 6 Dec.1761
4. Georg Heinrich b. 5 Mar. 1764, bp. 7 Mar. 1764
5. Maria Magdalena b. 5 Feb. 1767, bp. 7 Feb. 1767
6. Joh. Georg b. 26 Jan. 1769, bp. 28 Jan. 1769
7. Anna Barbara b. 16 Feb. 1771, bp. 17 Feb. 1771

AMERICAN RECORDS

Frederick Lutheran KB, Frederick, MD:
Philip Abert and wife Catharina were sp. in 1785.
Martin Abert m. 10 Mar. 1789 Catharina Diederle. They had a son:
1. Martin b. 7 Jan.1790, bp. 10 Jan. 1790
   Sp.: Philipp Abert and wife Catharina

Jacob Abert and wife Anna had a son:
1. Jacob b. 9 Apr. 1792, bp. 8 Aug. 1792
   Sp.: Wilhelm Gutmann

Buried 14 Mar. 1792 - Wednesday, Jacob Abert, son of Philipp Abert and
his wife Catharina, b. 12 Jan. 1760 in "Sultz am Stade in Elsasischen."
Married 19 Feb. Henrich Meyer's surviving widow Anna, died of high fever,
aged 32 years, 2 months.

2. ACKER, CHRISTIAN   Lampertsloch
Neptune, 1755   & Preuschdorf=
S-H, I: 677, 678, 679   67250 Soultz-sous-Forêts

EUROPEAN RECORDS

Preuschdorf Lutheran KB:
Died 27 Sept. 1738 - Anna Maria nee Burckardt from *Wangen in*

Wirtenberger Land, [several Wangens] wife of Heinrich Acker, citizen here. Her age 67 y., 7 mo., and 7 days. The burial entry is signed by Heinrich Acker the widower (his mark) and Christjan Acker the son, Catharina Barbara the daughter (her mark), Christoff Burchardt her brother, Johannes Dräher, son-in-law & Hans Michel Acker a friend.
[Christian Acker's signature on this burial record matches his signature in S-H, II: 767, list 234C].
Hans Heinrich Acker d. 13 May 1741, age 82 y., 3 mo., 7 days.

Christian Acker married in 1728 [date faded-unreadable] Anna Margaretha Motz, daughter of the late Theobald Motz of Lampertsloch. She was b. __ Feb. 1708, daughter of Diebolt Motz and wife Anna Catharina. Children:
> 1. Joh. Georg b. 14 Sept. 1729, bp. 16 Sept. 1729 [q.v.]
> 2. Christian b. 20 Jan. 1735, died 1738
> 3. Joh. Christian b. 26 Oct. 1742, bp. 28 Oct. 1742
> 4. Joh. Heinrich b. 27 Jan. 1747, bp. 28 Jan. 1747
> 5. Anna Margretha b. 13 Dec. 1749, bp. 15 Dec. 1749

AMERICAN RECORDS

New Hanover Lutheran KB, Montgomery co.:
Died 21 May 1773, Christian Acker age 76 years, 9 months, 4 weeks.
Died 7 Apr. 1777, Margretha Acker, age 69 years.

Johann Christian Acker (b. 1742) m. 25 Apr. 1769 Elisabeth Fuchs. They had children:
> 1. Johann Adam b. 14 Mar. 1770
> 2. Christian b. 23 Sept. 1772
> 3. Eva Maria b. 28 Feb 1774
> 4. Heinrich b. 29 Aug. 1775
> 5. Elizabeth b. 5 Nov. 1778
> 6. Catharine b. 28 Feb. 1780
> 7. Barbara b. 25 Feb. 1783

3. ACKER, GEORG   Lampertsloch
Bennet Gally, 1750   & Preuschdorf=
S-H, I: 428   67250 Soultz-sous-Forêts
EUROPEAN RECORDS

Preuschdorf Lutheran KB:
Christian Acker [q.v.] and wife Anna Margretha nee Motz had:
> 1. Joh. Georg b. 14 Sept. 1729, bp. 16 Sept. 1729
> [See Christian Acker for further family records].

AMERICAN RECORDS

New Hanover Lutheran KB, Montgomery co. & St. Joseph's Lutheran KB, Oley Hills, Berks co.:
Georg Acker & wife *Ursula* had children:
1. Joh. George b. 13 Oct. 1758, bp. 26 Oct 1758 (New Hanover)
   Sp.: Joh. Leonhard Klotz and Hannah Gilmore
2. Joh. Martin b. 9 May 1760, bp. 1 June 1760 (Oley Hills)
   Sp.: Martin Glotz and Barbara Lober
3. Anna Margaretha b. 14 Nov. 1761, bp. 15 Nov. 1761 (Oley Hills)
4. Christian b. 9 Dec. 1762, bp. 27 Feb. 1763 (New Hanover)
   Sp.: Johann Christian Acker and Margareth
5. Christian b. 8 Apr. 1764, bp. 11 June 1764 (New Hanover)
   Sp.: Christian Acker and Elisabeth Fuchs

Trappe Lutheran KB, Montgomery co.:
Johann Jürg Acker m. 8 Aug. 1757 at New Hanover in Mr. Campbel's house, *Susanna* Klotz. [Perhaps her full name was Susanna Ursula Klotz - see Klotz sp. for Georg Acker's first and second children.]

St. Joseph's (Oley Hills) Church, Pike twp., Berks co.:
Georg Acker and wife Ursula had children:
6. Joh. Jacob b. 19 Sept. 1765, bp. 24 Nov. 1765
   Sp.: Joh. Jacob Klotz and wife Sophia
Susanna Acker, widow, had a son:
7. Leonhard b. 27 Aug. 1767, bp. 4 Oct. 1767.
Other later Ackers appear in this church book.

4. ACKER, JOH. HEINRICH Age 32   Preuschdorf=
Loyal Judith, 1732   67250 Soultz-sous-Forêts
S-H, I: 88, 90, 92

EUROPEAN RECORDS

Preuschdorf Lutheran KB:
Hans Heinrich Acker m. (between May & Nov. - faded) 1728, Anna Catharina Schäfer, daughter of Balthaser Schäfer of Preuschdorf. (Marginal note in KB: "Went to the new land.") They had children:
1. Anna Dorothea b. 13 Feb. 1730, bp. 15 Feb. 1730
2. Hans Jacob b. 14 Oct. 1731 at Lampertsloch bp. 17 Oct. 1731
   Sp.: Hans Jacob Martin; Dorothea, daughter of Georg Conrad Stepp of Preuschdorf; Hans Jacob, son of Hans Jacob Beck.

Anna Catharina Schäfer was b. 4 Mar. 1711, daughter of Hans Balthaser Schäfer and his wife Anna Catharina Stepp. For a complete record of this Schäfer family, see immigrant Friedrich Schäfer who also arrived on the *Loyal Judith*, 1732.

An old half-timber constructed building in Preuschdorf

AMERICAN RECORDS

Rev. John Casper Stoever's records:
Heinrich Acker (Hanover) had:
>   3. Georg Heinrich b. 3 Jan. 1734, bp. 7 Jan. 1734
>   Sp.: George Michael and wife

St. Michael's Lutheran KB, Germantown:
Heinrich Acker and wife Anna Catharina had:
>   Elisabetha b. 13 Mar. 1746, bp. 6 Apr. 1746
>   Sp.: Jacob Stiefell [q.v.] and Catharina Stiefelin.

Keller's Lutheran KB, Bucks co., Family register, 1751:
Henry Acker, age 51 years, b. 1700, son of Henry Acker and Anna Maria of Spachbach [Spechbach = 68720 Illfurth] in Hanau, Alsace. Married 1728 at *Prischdorf* Anna Catharina (b. 1710), daughter of Balthasar Schäfer and Anna Catharina; lived there until the year 1732 when they came to America. Children:

1. Anna Dorothea b. 1730, m. Michael Fischer
2. John Jacob, died
3. George Henry b. 1733
4. Anna Catharine, died
5. George Michael b. 1736, conf. 1751
6. Eva Catharina b. 18 July 1738, conf. 1752
7. Margaret b. 3 Mar. 1742 [note: Jordan Lutheran KB, Lehigh co., gives her birthdate as 3 Mar. 1741.]
8. Anna Maria, died
9. Christian, died
10. Elizabeth, died
11. Barbara, died
12. Magdalena b. 10 Oct. 1749
13. John b. 18 July 1751

Henry Acker d. 14 Oct. 1752

Philadelphia Will Book K: 20:
Henry Acker, 12 Oct. 1752 - 8 Nov. 1752.
Wife: Anna Catharina; children: only John and Mary Magdalena are named. Exrs: Philip ?Gary and Samuel Mummy. Wit: Abraham Beck, schoolmaster, and John Goodshires of Philadelphia who certify that said will was reduced to writing at the request of the testator on 12 Oct. 1752 and that he was unable to sign it.

New Hanover Lutheran KB:
Died 28 Mar. 1775 - Catharine Acker, age 66 years.

Henry Acker, Bucks co., nat. Sept. 1743

5. ACKER, PHILIP JACOB age 36   Preuschdorf=
Loyal Judith, 1732   67250 Soultz-sous-Forêts
S-H, I: 88, 90, 92

EUROPEAN RECORDS

Preuschdorf Lutheran KB:
Philip Jacob Acker, single son of Heinrich Acker, citizen at Preuschdorf, was

a sp. for Johann Philip Burckhardt, b. 22 Jan. 1724, son of Johan Georg Burckhardt [q.v.], also a passenger on the *Loyal Judith*. [see also his brother, Heinrich Acker.]

AMERICAN RECORDS

Jordan Lutheran KB, So. Whitehall twp., Lehigh co.:
Philip Jacob Acker was sp. in 1743 for Anna Maria, daughter of Henrich Acker and Anna Catharina.
Jacob Acker and wife Erhartina [Eberhardina in other records] had:
1. Christian b. 25 Dec. 1755
2. Philip Jacob b. 30 Aug. 1757
3. Lenhardt b. 22 Sept. 1759
4. Jerg Heinrich b. 10 Dec. 1761
5. Johann Michael b. 5 Dec. 1766
6. N.N. given b. 3 Aug. 1771
7. Mary Magdalena b. 11 Jan. 1775 [Jordan Reformed KB].

Philip Jacob Ackre, Bucks co., nat. Sept. 1743.

6. ALLIMANG, JACOB   Schalbach=
   ALLIMANG, JACOB   57370 Phalsbourg
[unnamed ship] 20 Oct. 1747
S-H, I: 369, 370

EUROPEAN RECORDS

Rauwiller Reformed KB:
Jacob Allemand [also Allemang in records] of Schallbach and wife Anna Maria nee Balliett had children:
1. Jacob b. 26 Apr. 1729
2. **Joh. Jacob** b. 26 Apr. 1730
3. Anna Elisabetha b. 14 Feb. 1732
4. Elisabetha b. 25 Mar. 1735
5. Christina b. 16 Jan. 1738
6. Christina b. 24 Feb. 1740
7. Heinrich b. 27 Sept. 1742
8. Joh. Nicklaus b. 8 Sept. 1745

AMERICAN RECORDS

Rev. Daniel Schumacher's records:
Jacob Allemang and wife Elisabetha Barbara had a son:
     Johann Friderich bp. 9 Nov. 1760 in Lehigh Church

Sp.: Daniel Hundsrücker; Friderich Kuntz;
Maria Catharina Sold(en); Salome Bähr(en)
Jacob Alleman and wife Elisabetha Barbara also had:
    Christian b. 6 Dec. 1766 [Egypt Reformed KB, Lehigh co.]
    Catharine Elisabetha b. 31 July 1768 [Schlosser's Reformed KB]

Westmoreland Co. Will Book l, p. 187:
Nicholas Allimang, yeoman, of Buffalo Twp., Armstrong co., 6 Sept. 1803-
21 Nov. 1803. Wife: Mary Magdalena. Children: Jacob, Margaret,
Barbara, daughter Magdalena's children, Susanna, Elizabeth.
Exrs: Jonathan Roerig and son Jacob Allemang.
Wit: Daniel Eshbach and Solomon Shoul.

Jacob Almand, Lehi twp., Northampton co., nat. Autumn 1765.
Nichs. Almand, Lehi twp., Northampton co., nat. Autumn 1765.

7. ALTMANN, GEORG   Herbitzheim=
   ALTMANN, ANTHON   67260 Sarre-Union
Phoenix, 1749
S-H, I: 405
EUROPEAN RECORDS

Keskastel Lutheran KB:
Hans Georg Altmann, son of Johannes Altmann, citizen at Ehrmingen, m.
19 Nov. 1715 at Ehrmingen, Johanna Sophia, daughter of Mathias Nehling
former *Graffischen Meyer* at Dehlingen. Children:
    1. Maria Catharina bp. 6 Sept. 1716 at Ehrmingen
    2. Philipps Peter bp. 14 Apr. 1718
    3. Hans Nickel bp. 14 Apr. 1720, conf. 1736 at Herbitzheim.

Herbitzheim Lutheran KB:
Georg Altmann from Ermingen and wife Sophia had:
    4. Maria Elisabetha bp. 5 June 1722
       Sp.: Joh. Nicol Werckle, Elisabetha Bentz, single and Maria
       Salome Weinland, single
    5. Eva Catharina b. 20 Aug. 1724, bp. 31 Aug. 1724
    6. Johannes b. 21 July 1727, bp. 23 July 1727
    7. Johann Anton b. 7 Aug. 1729, conf. 1743
       Sp.: Joh. Anton Jung; Hans Adam Reb; Maria Barbara Fuhrer;
       all Ermingen
    8. Catharina Magdalena b. 25 Apr. 1732, bp. 27 Apr. 1732
    9. Maria Salome b. 5 Nov. 1735, bp. 7 Apr. 1735

Maria Catharina Altmann, daughter of Georg Altmann, citizen and inhabitant at Ermingen, had an illegitimate child:

      Johann Georg b. 8 June 1741, bp. 11 June 1741

The father was named Caspar Hallauer, single butcher's apprentice from St. Johann by Saarbrücken.

AMERICAN RECORDS

Lehigh Lutheran KB, Lower Macungie twp., Lehigh co.:
Antoni Altmann (wife not named) had a son:

      1. Johann Wilhelm bp. 22nd p. Trin. 1755 (no sp. given).

Rev. Daniel Schumacher's records:
Anthony Altmann and wife Maria had a daughter:

      Anna Maria bp. 12 June 1766 at Ziegel Church.

Anna Maria Altman sp. a child of Jürg Wannemacher [q.v.] in 1760 at Lehigh.

One of the signers on a petition for protection from the Indians, dated 5 Oct. 1757, Forks of the Delaware:

      George Altman

Northampton co. estate records:
George Altman, Lehigh twp., adm. 20 Mar. 1761 to the widow Mary Elisabeth Altman and Jacob Altman, George Meyer and Jacob Roth. Inventory dated 21 Feb. 1761 by Michael Reed and Peter Andoni [Anthony, q.v.]. Vendue on 2 Apr. 1761 by *Anna Mary* Altman, widow. Mentions articles bought by Elizabeth Altman, Casper Altman and Peter Anthony.

Westmoreland co. Will Book 1: 235:
Anthony Altman, yeoman, Hempfield twp., 3 Feb. 1809- 25 Feb. 1809. Children: Mary, wife of Jacob Cribs, and their children Philip and Barbara, wife of John Herold; grandson John Noble; plantation adj. Hanspeter Altman and Valentine Scheafer. Exrs.: Joseph Weigley and John Shotz. Wit.: Valentine Shaeffer and Godfrey Zinber.

8. ALTMANN, JACOB   Herbitzheim=
   ALTMANN, WILHELM   67260 Sarre-Union
Phoenix, 1749
S-H, I: 405

EUROPEAN RECORDS

Herbitzheim Lutheran KB:
Jacob Altmann m. 22 Feb. 1724 Anna Maria Isenmann. They had:
1. Joh. Wilhelm b. 14 Nov. 1724 bp. ?1 Dec. 1724; conf. 1739
   Sp.: Stephan Bentz, Hans Martin Weyer, miller, and
   Anna Elisabetha Isenmann
2. Anna Margretha, b. 8 June 1727, bp. 11 June 1727; conf. 1741
   She m. George Ecker [q.v.]
3. Catharina Elisabetha b. 23 June 1729, d. 1 Apr. 1730
4. Sophia Elisabetha b. 20 Mar. 1731, bp. 22 Mar. 1731, conf. 1745
5. Johann Peter, b. 27 June 1735, bp. 30 June 1735
6. Anna Catharina b. 14 Aug. 1738, bp. 17 Aug. 1738
7. Johann Caspar b. 15 Apr. 1741, bp. 16 Apr. 1741
8. Johann Jacob b. 25 Apr. 1744, bp. in house
9. Catharina Margaretha b. 17 Apr. 1747, bp. 19 Apr. 1747

AMERICAN RECORDS

St. Paul's (Indianland) Lutheran KB; Lehigh co.:
Johann Peter Altmann and wife Christina had a son:
   Jürg Peter bp. 7 Nov. 1762
   Sp.: Jürg Eckert [q.v.] and wife Anna Margaretha;
   J. Peter Ruch and Catharine Margaretha Altmann

Rev. Daniel Schumacher's Records:
Peter Altman and Caspar Altman sp. a child of Jurg Ecker [q.v.] in 1760.
Johan Caspar Altmann and Christina Altmann sp. a child of Jacob Stroh in 1761.
Joh. Peter Altmann and wife Christine had:
   Jurg Jacob b. 5 May 1768, across the Lehigh
   Sp.: Jurg Eisemann [q.v.] and Catharina Ecker [q.v.]

Caspar Altmann and wife Susanna had:
   Maria Barbara bp. 5 May 1771

Emanuel Reformed KB, Moore twp., Northampton co.:
Caspar Altmann and wife Susanna had:
   Christine b. 29 Nov. 1767
   Sp.: John Peter Altmann and wife Christina.
Valentine Altmann and wife Catharina had:
   Maria Catharina b. 2 Mar. 1769.

One of the signers on a petition for protection from the Indians, dated 5 Oct. 1757, Forks of the Delaware:
   Jacob Altman

Westmoreland co. Will Book 1: 161:
John Peter Altman, yeoman, of Hempfield twp., 1 Dec. 1799-16 Mar. 1801.
Wife: Barbara. Children: Sallomon, George Peter, Andrew, Susanna wife of
Peter Eisenman, George Jacob, Catharine wife of Philip Miller, Michael,
Christina wife of Peter Miller, Barbara wife of Joseph Gongawere, and
William. Anna Maria was a daughter of the testator's first wife Christina;
Sallomon, Christina, Labina and Catharina are children of testator's present
wife Barbara. Exrs.: wife Barbara and Peter Wendling.
Wit.: James Guthrie, Adam Wendling, Daniel Williams.

9. ANGSTATT, HANS GEORG age 37   Gumbrechtshoffen=
Richard & Elizabeth, 1733   67110 Niederbronn-les-Bains
S-H, I: 127, 128, 129, 130
    with Eva Catharina _____, age 31; George Angsted, age 6; Johannes
Angsted, age 1; Eva Catharina _____, age 4.

EUROPEAN RECORDS

Zutzendorf Lutheran KB:
Georg Angstatt, citizen and widower here, m. 10 Oct. 1684 Anna Maria,
daughter of Jacob Schneider, citizen and *Gerichtsschöffen.* They had a son:
        Georgius bp. 23 Feb. 1696

Gumbrechtshoffen Lutheran KB:
Hans Georg Angstätt, son of the late Georg Angstätt, former citizen at
Zutzendorff, m. __ Feb. 1726 Eva Catharina, daughter of the late Hans
Adam Schäfer, citizen here. They had children:
        1. Hans Jacob b. 29 June 1724
        2. Hans Georg b. 29 Nov. 1726, bp. 2 Dec.
        [The father's signature by this entry in the KB matches his
        signature in the ship list, S-H, II: 120.]

AMERICAN RECORDS

Christ Lutheran KB (Mertz's), Bieber Creek, Berks co:
Eva Catharina Angstat sp. in 1747 a child of Joh. Heinrich Merz and wife
Anna Maria nee Rosmann.

Johann Angstaet [q.v.] and wife Margretha nee Dürrenberger had a son:
        Joh. Georg b. 29 Mar. 1751, bp. 12 May 1751
        Sp.: Georg Angstaet and wife Eva Catharina

Georg Angstaet and wife Sophia nee Nothart had:
1. Anna Rosina b. 14 Oct. 1749, bp. 15 Nov. 1749
   Sp.: Johannes Angstaet; Anna Rosina Voglin
2. Anna Maria b. 27 ?Sept. 1750, bp. 5 Oct. 1750
3. Esther b. 10 Feb. 1755, bp. 13 Apr. 1755
4. Joh. Georg b. 6 June 1756
5. Johannes b. 22 Dec. 1760
6. Magdalena b. 27 Jan. 1766

Jacob Zanger and wife Eva Catharina nee Angstaet had:
1. Anna Maria b. 7 Aug. 1756

Johannes Angstaet, master weaver, son of Georg Angstadt, m. 14 Dec. 1756
_____ (N.N. recorded).

10. ANSTETT, JOHANNES   67580 Mertzwiller
Speedwell, 1749
S-H, I: 410
EUROPEAN RECORDS

Mertzweiler Lutheran KB:
Hans Anstätt and wife Maria Margaretha had children:
1. Maria Magdalena b. 13 Sept. 1734, bp. 15 Sept. 1734
   [The father signed this entry in KB as Hans Anstett,
   and the ship list as Johannes Anstett; the Anstett
   part of his signature matches S-H, II: 460.]
2. Anna Margaretha b. ?10 May 1737, bp. 12 May 1737

AMERICAN RECORDS

Christ Lutheran KB (Mertz's), Bieber Creek, Berks co:
Johann Angstaet and wife Margretha nee Dürrenberger had a son:
Joh. Georg b. 29 Mar. 1751, bp. 12 May 1751
Sp.: Georg Angstaet and wife Eva Catharina

Hocker, *German Settlers of Pennsylvania:*
Pennsylvanische Geschichts-Schreiber, newspaper dated 1 June 1750:
Martin Schroeter, with Johannes Schneider, Lancaster, indentured his four
children last autumn, and wants to know what became of them. They are:
daughters, Christina and Elisabeth; stepsons, Hansz Georg Wambach and
Peter Wambach. He also seeks his brother-in-law, Johannes *Anstert.*

Jno. Angstet, Rockland twp., Berks co., nat. autumn, 1765.

11. ANTHONI, PAULUS   Langensoultzbach=
Brigantine *John,* 1736   67360 Woerth
S-H, I: 167,168
[Signed Paulus Andoni]
EUROPEAN RECORDS

Langensoultzbach Lutheran KB:
Joh. Paul Anthoni, son of Hans Adam Anthoni, *Schirmsverwandter,* m. 24
Nov. 1722 at Sultzbach Maria Ursula, daughter of Jonas Sadler,
Gerichtsschöffen. Children:
  1. Maria Catharina bp. 11 Oct. 1723
  2. Georg Friedrich bp. 6 Feb. 1725, died 1727
  3. Philipp Henrich bp. 12 Mar. 1727
  4. Joh. Philipp bp. 28 Feb. 1729
  5. Joh. Henrich bp. 20 May 1731, died 12 Aug. 1731
  6. Joh. Michael bp. __ Nov. 1733

AMERICAN RECORDS

Lynn twp., Lehigh co. tax list, 1762:
Philip Anthony

Chambers, *Early Germans of New Jersey,* pg 235:
Paul Anthony came from Germany in 1736. His name is on the Foxenberg
subscription list before 1749; probably came from Strasburg; had only one
son so far as is known:
     Philip m. Elisabeth Dewitt
     [article continues with their descendants.]

One Paul Anthony, Upper Hanover twp., Philadelphia co., nat. by
affirmation, 25 Sept. 1752. [There were 2 immigrants with this name].
One Philip Anthony, Linn twp., Northampton co., nat. Autumn 1765.

12. ASCH, NICHOLAS age 25   Hunspach=
Barclay, 1754   67250 Soultz-sous-Forêts
S-H, I: 595, 597, 599

EUROPEAN RECORDS

Hunspach Reformed KB:
Nicolaus Aesch, residing at the Neühoff, and wife Maria Eva had a son:
     Nicolaus b. 21 Dec. 1730, bp. 25 Dec. 1730, conf. 1745

Died 6 Apr. 1739:
Nicklaus Esch, residing at the Neuhoff, his age 47 y., 6 mo., and several days.

Died 5 May 1756:
Maria Eva, widow of Nicklaus Esch, age 59 y. 8 mo. 10 days.

Zweibrücken Manumissions Protocoll, Clee- and Catharinenburg, 1754:
Nicolaus Esch of Hunspach leaves for America.

A house in Hunspach, built in 1719 as the date
carved in the corner timber suggests.

A group of farm buildings located in the former Grafschaft of Nassau-Saarwerden.

Baerendorf dates from the eighth century when it was called Berunwillare;
a picturesque village located between Postorff and Rauwiller.

13. BACH, ANDREAS   Herbitzheim=
Betsy, 1768   67260 Sarre-Union
S-H, I: 725 [with Philipp Rippel, q.v.]

EUROPEAN RECORDS

Herbitzheim Lutheran KB:
Andreas Bach, born in Lorentzen [= 67430 Diemeringen], m. 9 Apr. 1765
Catharina Magaretha, widow of the late Peter Bauer.
   Peter Bauer from Dehlingen m. 11 Sept. 1758 Catharina Margaretha,
widow of Georg Philipp Rippel [see immigrant Philipp Rippel for additional
data.] They had children, surname Bauer, who likely emigrated with their
mother and stepfather.
      1. Johann Peter Bauer b. 21 Oct. 1759, bp. 20 Oct. 1759
      2. Catharina Eva Bauer b. 10 Apr. 1761
Peter Bauer, the smith, d. 27 Mar. 1763, age 34 y. 2 mo. 21 days. His widow,
Catharina Margaretha nee Jesel had another child after his death:
      3. Susanna Margaretha Bauer b. 27 Oct. 1763, bp. 30 Oct. 1763

Verification of this emigration supplied by Dr. Bernd Gölzer, from the
county records of Nassau-Saarwerden, compiled by Dr. Gerhard Hein:
Records of the Notary Public for Dehlingen:
25 Apr. 1782, inventory of Anna Margaretha Bauer, mentions that two
children of Peter Bauer are in America.

14. BACHMAN, JACOB   Altwiller=
   BACHMAN, JOH. JACOB   67260 Sarre-Union
   BACHMAN, LORENTZ   Hirschland=
Edinburg, 14 Sept. 1753   67320 Drulingen
S-H, I: 522, 524
EUROPEAN RECORDS

Diedendorf Reformed KB:
Jacob Bachmann was a grandson of Ulrich Bachmann from Laubersweiller,
BE [CH-3438 Lauperswil, BE].
Jacob Bachman from Hirschland, son of the late Niclaus Bachman from
there m. 15 Jan. 1704 Elisabeth Carl, daughter of the late Jacob Carl from
Reichenbach: They had a son:
      1. Hans Jacob bp. 24 Aug. 1704
      (Recorded with 1706 baptisms, pg. 24)

Jacob Bachman, son of Jacob Bachman of Hirschland, m. 5 Mar. 1726
Magdalena Zinck from Altweiller. Children:

1. Christina Margaretha bp. 16 Mar. 1727, Hirschland
2. Maria Elisabetha bp. 18 Sept. 1729
3. **Jacob** bp. 30 Nov. 1731
4. **Lorentz** bp. 23 May 1734
5. Susanna Catharina bp. 20 Jan. 1738
6. Anna Outilia bp. 27 Aug. 1741
7. Johann Nicklaus b. 19 May 1744
8. Paul b. 28 Jan. 1748

AMERICAN RECORDS

Jacob Bachman, Sr. brought a passport with him, dated 16 Mar. 1753 at Saarbrucken; it releases Jacob Bachman, Sr. and his wife and eight children from Hirschland from their hereditary obligation.

Lowhill Lutheran and Reformed KB, Lehigh co.:
Nicholas Bachman and wife Maria Magdalena had:
  1. Daniel b. 4 Dec. 1768, bp. 5 Jan.1769
  2. Maria Magdalena b. 20 Sept. 1770, bp. 13 Dec. 1770
  3. Jacob b. 22 Mar. 1772, bp. 17 May 1772
     Sp.: Jacob Bachman and Elisabeth
  4. Paulus b. 15 Sept. 1773, bp. 10 Oct. 1773
     Sp.: Paul Bachmann and Margaretha
  5. Anna Maria b. 8 Feb. 1776, bp. 17 Feb. 1776
  6. John Nicholas b. 18 Apr. 1778, bp. 28 May 1778
  7. Jonathan b. 1 Mar. 1780
  8. Rachel b. 30 Sept. 1781, bp. 13 Jan. 1782
  9. Andreas b. 29 Apr. 1784, bp. 30 May 1784
  10. John Peter b. 18 Apr. 1787, bp. 28 May 1787

Lorentz Bachmann and wife Susanna had:
  1. Jacob b. 9 Nov. 1773, bp. 7 Dec. 1773
     Sp.: Jacob Bachmann and Elisabeth
  2. Abraham b. 27 Sept. 1777, bp. 13 Mar. 1778

Paulus Bachmann and wife Margretha had:
  1. Johann Jacob b. 15 Apr. 1770 [Schumacher's records]
  2. Johannes b. 13 Feb. 1775, bp. 30 Apr. 1775
     Sp.: Jacob Bachmann and Elisabeth
  3. Maria Margaretha b. 22 July 1776, bp. 13 Oct. 1776
  4. Christian b. 30 Sept. 1777, bp. 25 Dec. 1777
  5. Maria Magdalena b. 2 July 1782, bp. 18 Aug. 1782
  6. Lorentz b. 17 Nov. 1783, bp. 10 Apr. 1784
  7. Daniel b. 12 Apr. 1787, bp. 13 May 1787

8. Andreas, bp. 13 May 1787
9. John Peter, bp. 13 May 1787
10. Esther b. 26 Aug. 1788

Cemetery Records, Lowhill Church, Lehigh co.:
Jacob Bachman
b. 25 July 1714? [stone worn; Lehigh county history says b. 1704]
d. 11 Nov. 1788
[This is the grave of Jacob Bachman Sr. who donated the first land for the church. It is the oldest burial with a legible stone.]

The grave of a Paul Bachman is in the next row. The inscription is only partly legible; no dates legible.

Jacob Bachman
b. 30 Dec. 1731
d. 28 Mar. 1796
[Served in Revolutionary War, private in 1st Class, 4th Co., 6th Battalion, Lowhill, Northampton co., militia].

Nicolaus Bachman
[broken stone, entirely illegible except name;
Lehigh County history says he d. 1802].

L. B. [Probably the grave of Lorentz Bachman]; 1830

Rev. Johannes Heinrich Helffrich's records: Burials at Lowhill:
Buried 14 Apr. 1791 - Paul Bachman's wife, aged 46 y. 7 mo. 1 day
Buried 20 Aug. 1794 - Nicholas Bachman's wife Elisabeth, age 54 y. 4 mo.

Northampton co. Wills:
Jacob Bachman, Sr., Weissenberg twp., yeoman. 30 Apr. 1787-27 Oct. 1789.
Names wife Catharina, who was the widow of the late William Schmetter of Albany twp., Berks co. Sons Paul, Jacob, Laurence, Nicholas. Daughters: Christina, Elizabeth, Susanne, Ottilia, Mary Elizabeth.
Wit: Jacob Horner and Nicholas Schwatz.

Lowhill Church Account Book, List of Contributors; 1769:
Jacob Bachman
Niclos Bachman
Lorentz Bachman
Jacob Bachman, *der alte.*
Paul Bachman

Weisenberg Lutheran and Reformed KB, Weisenberg twp., Lehigh co.:
Jacob Bachman, of Lowhill, and wife Elisabetha nee Reichel, had children:
1. Jacob b. 29 July 1761
2. Nicolaus b. 19 Aug. 1763
   Sp.: Nicolaus Bachman and Margaretha Heintz
3. Simon b. 8 Aug. 1765
   Sp.: Simon Georg and Maria Blos

Lowhill Lutheran and Reformed KB, Lowhill twp., Lehigh co.:
4. Johannes b. 21 Oct. 1768, bp. 14 Jan. 1769
   Sp.: Johannes Georg
5. Johan Adam b. 28 Jan. 1771, bp. 31 Mar. 1771
   Sp.: Johannes Reichel and Catharina
6. Lorentz b. 3 July 1773, bp. 18 July 1773
   Sp.: Lorentz Bachmann and Susanna
7. Paulus b. 26 Mar. 1776, bp. 14 Apr. 1776
   Sp.: Paulus Bachmann and Margaretha
8. Eva Elisabetha b. 14 July 1780

Jacob Bachman, Lowhill, Northampton co., nat. Fall, 1765.
Jacob Bachman, Weisenberg, Northampton co., nat. Fall, 1765.

See **Charles Roberts et al,** *History of Lehigh County, Pennsylvania,* **Vol. II:** 24,
for additional data on this Bachman family.

15. BALLIET, JOSEPH   Schalbach=
Lydia, 1749   57370 Phalsbourg
S-H, I: 421
EUROPEAN RECORDS

Diedendorf Reformed KB:
Abraham Baillet, son of Jacob Baillet of Schalbach, m. 22 Oct. 1708 Susanna
Catharina Hahn, daughter of Jacob Hahn of Fleissheim.

Rauwiller Reformed KB:
Abraham Balliett and Susanna nee Hahn had:
   Joseph b. 11 May 1729 in Schalbach.

AMERICAN RECORDS

Rev. Daniel Schumacher's records:
Joseph Balliet and wife Barbara had:
   Maria Barbara bp. 15 Mar. 1764, 13 days old, in Egypt.

Sp.: Paul Bohl; Maria Barbara Wodring; Dewald Kendell; Maria Salome Bär.

Northampton co. Will Abstracts:
Joseph Balliet was a witness to the 1777 will of Paul Baliet, Whitehall twp.

Joseph Baliet appears on the 1762 tax list, Whitehall twp, Lehigh co.

Charles Roberts et al, *History of Lehigh County, Pennsylvania*, Vol. II: 48:
Joseph Balliet was a relative of Paul Balliet, and lived in Whitehall as early as 1762. He and his wife Mary Barbara had sons Jacob, Leonhard and Daniel b. 13 Sept., d. 18 Oct. 1773. Jacob and Leonhard subsequently resided in Northampton co., east of the Lehigh.

[A later immigrant, Peter Balliet, also settled in Northampton co.:
Emmaus Moravian records, Northampton co.: Peter Balliet died 21 Aug. 1849, aged 52 y., 10 mo., and 8 days. He came to the U.S. in 1828, born near Rauweiler; he m. (1) Laetitia Everitt and had 3 children; m. (2) Esther Schaeffer and had 2 children, both dead.]

Entries for the Reformed families of Schalbach appear in the Diedendorf parish records and the Rauwiller Reformed church book.

16. BALLIET, PAULUS   Schalbach=
Robert and Alice, 1738   57370 Phalsbourg
S-H, I: 213, 215

EUROPEAN RECORDS

Diedendorf Reformed KB:
Stephan Paillet from Schalbach, son of Jacob Paillet, m. 26 Apr. 1707 at
Burbach, Maria Catharina, daughter of Niclaus Schweitzer of Schalbach.
They had a son:
> Paulus bp. 16 Aug. 1716
> Sp.: Paulus, son of Nicklaus Schweitzer of Schalbach; Jacob,
> son of Jacob Toussin of Weyer; Maria Margaretha Wibel, wife
> of Johann Schweitzer of Schalbach.

AMERICAN RECORDS

Egypt Reformed KB, Lehigh co.:
Paulus Pahjet (also Paljet) and wife Maria Magdalena had children:
> 1. Joh. Jacob b. 23 Dec. 1750
>   Sp.: Jacob Meckle and Lucae Flickinger
> 2. A daughter b. 28 July 1752
>   Sp.: Peter, son of Ulrich Burckhalter; Maria, daughter of
>   Joseph Kennel [q.v.], both single and from Egypt.
> 3. Eva bp. 26 Mar. 1760
>   Sp.: Johann Nicolaus Schneider [q.v.]; and Maria Catharina
>   wife of Johannes Solt.

Egypt Reformed KB, Lehigh co., footnotes in published record:
Adam Deshler was a son of Adam Deshler and was born 1 Oct. 1745, and
d. 24 Feb. 1790. He was a prosperous farmer of Whitehall township. He
married Maria Catharina Balliet and had nine children.

Stephen Balliet, son of Paul Balliet, was born in 1753. In Dec. 1776, he was
a Lieut. Col. in the Revolutionary army, and in 1781 a Colonel. In 1783 he
was elected a member of the Supreme Executive Council for a term of three
years, and in 1789 a member of the House of Representatives. In 1797, he
was appointed revenue collector for the Second District of Pennsylvania. He
married Magdalena Burkhalter and died August 4, 1821.

Unionville Cemetery, tombstone inscription:
Maria Magdalena Balliet (nee Wotring); b. 1727, d. 1802, aged 75 years.

Rev. Abraham Blumers records, Lehigh co.:
Buried 21 Mar. 1777 - Paul Balliet, age 60 years, 7 months.

Northampton co. Will Abstracts:
Paul Baliet, Whitehall twp.; 15 Mar. 1777-2 Aug. 1777.
Son Stephan given plantation in Towamensing twp. where Samuel Sommery
now lives. Mentions son John, and minor sons Paul and Nicholas. Wife
Mary Magdalena. Mentions plantation bought of Samuel Morris, and his
son-in-law Adam Deshler. Wit: David Hahn, Joseph Balliet, Nicholas Mark,
Samuel Somery.

The village of Ballietsville in Lehigh co. is named for the family.
see **Charles Roberts et al,** *History of Lehigh County, Pennsylvania,* **Vol. II:** 48
for additional family data. Nine children are listed in this article for Paul
Balliet and his wife Maria Magdalena, daughter of Abraham Wotring [q.v.].

Unionville Cemetery, No. Whitehall twp., Lehigh co.:
Paul Balliet   Col. Stephen Balliet
Died 19 Mar. 1777   1758-1821 age 68 years
Age 60 years

Paul Balliet, b. 24 May 1766, d. 17 Feb. 1845,
m. 20 years to Elisabeth Deschler

Paul Baillet nat. at Philadelphia, 10 Apr. 1759.

17. BANNWART, HENRICH   Vinstingen=
[unnamed ship] 20 Oct. 1747   57930 Fénétrange
S-H, I: 369, 370 [appears on list as Henry Bawngwar - did not sign.]

EUROPEAN RECORDS

Diedendorf Reformed KB:
Johann(es) Bannwarth, single tiler, son of Johann Banwarth, also tiler at
Herrschaffl. Ziegelscheuer in Vinstingen, born in the Landgericht Sefftigen,
[CH-3136 Seftigen, BE], Canton Bern, m. 6 Apr. 1717 Eva, daughter of
Nicklaus Koch, residing at the Vinstingerhoff, born in Landvogtey Nidau,
Canton Bern. [CH-2560 Nidau, BE]. They had a son:
    Johann Henrich bp. 15 Sept. 1720; conf. 1735 as *Hennrich Baumwart.*

Henrich Bannwart, son of Johannes Bannwart, tiler at *Ziegelscheuer* in
Vinstingen, m. 27 Aug. 1743 Elisabetha Bendel, daughter of the late Nickel
Bendel of Oberpib, Canton Bern. [CH-4538 Oberbipp, BE]. Children:
    1. Catharina Elisabetha bp. 7 July 1744
    2. Anna Barbara bp. 31 May 1746

Johannes Baunewart at the Vinstinger Ziegelhut, born in Switzerland, died 2 Sept. 1732, aged 68 years.

Johannes Baunwart, tiler at the Vinstinger Ziegelhutt, born in Sefftigen, Canton Bern, died 20 Jan. 1743, aged 46 years.

18. BARON, ANNA ELISABETHA   Postroff=
possibly with husband Georg Schleicher   57930 Fénétrange
Sally, 1770
S-H, I: 731

EUROPEAN RECORDS

Hirschland Lutheran KB:
Joh. Baron from Wintersburg [Wintersbourg=57119 Lixheim] m. 15 Jan. 1743 Anna Magdalena, daughter of Hans Nickel ?Schlimmer from Postroff. Johannes Baron and Anna Magdalena from Postorff had:

    1. Hans Nickel b. 19 Nov. 1748
       Sp.: Joh. Philipps Dettweiler, schoolteacher at Postorf;
       Hans Nickel Stephan, innkeeper at Wintersburg;
       Anna Margreta Gangloff
    2. Jacob b. 12 Feb. 1750 at Postorff
    3. Anna Elisabetha, bp. not located, b. ca. Sept. 1751

AMERICAN RECORDS

St. Michael's and Zion KB, Philadelphia:
Buried 31 Oct. 1791: Anna Elisabetha, daughter of Joh. Berrons and Maria Magdalena from Postroff, Nassau-Sarrewerden. Wife of Georg Schleicher. Age 40 y. 1 mo.

Notary Docket of John Morris, Esq., York co.:
Power of Attorney dated 1801: Peter Stephan and wife Magdalena of Franklin co; inheritance due from the estate of Nicholas Stephan, dec'd, and Anna Magdalena Beron, eldest daughter of John Beron, Jr. who was heir of John Beron, dec'd, late of the County of Litzelstein in Wintersberg, France.

19. BARON, NICKOLAS   Postroff=
Neptune, 1752   57930 Fénétrange
S-H, I: 492

EUROPEAN RECORDS

Hirschland Lutheran KB:
Hans Nickel Baron from Postorff and wife Anna Magdalena had a daughter:
Anna Magdalena b. 24 Nov. 1743

AMERICAN RECORDS

Moselem Lutheran KB, Richmond twp., Berks co.:
Nicholaus Baron and wife Catharina Christina had:
1. Johannes b. 27 Sept. 1765, bp. 27 Oct. 1765
   Sp.: Joh. Georg Mergel and Maria Magdalena
2. Joh. Philipp b. 9 Sept. 1767, bp. 11 Oct. 1767
   Sp.: Ludwig Otterman and Fransina

Nicolaus Baeron and Catharina Barbara Guth were sp. in 1765 for a child
of Heinrich Guth.

Salem Reformed KB, Hagerstown, MD:
Niclos Baron and wife Catharine were sp. in 1772 for a child of Johannes
Schneider.

Niclos Baron and Catharina had:
Johann Adam b. 16 Aug. 1774, bp. 26 Dec. 1774
Sp.: Georg Jung and wife Elisabeth

20. BASTIAN, JOHANN GEORG   67690 Hatten
BASTIAN, JOH. HEINRICH
Minerva, 1770
S-H, I: 730

EUROPEAN RECORDS

Hatten Lutheran KB:
Hans Georg Bastian and wife Anna Catharina nee Heyd had a son:
Johann Georg b. 9 Apr. 1721, bp. 11 Apr. 1721
Sp.: H. Adam _____?, weaver; Hans Georg Trion;
A. Christina, wife of Philips Faulstich.

Joh. Georg Bastian, locksmith, and wife Salome nee Drion had sons:
Joh. Georg b. 3 Nov. 1747
Joh. Heinrich b. 31 Jan. 1749

AMERICAN RECORDS

St. Michael's and Zion KB, Philadelphia:
Buried 18 Dec. 1783- Heinrich Bastian, born near Strasburg, son of Georg
Bastian; wife Catharine Salome; aged 34 y.

21. BAUER, CONRAD   Dehlingen=
    BAUER, LINHARD   67430 Diemeringen
Polly, 1764
S-H, I: 690

EUROPEAN RECORDS

Dehlingen Lutheran KB:
Hans Matheiss Bauer, tailor at Dehlingen, m. 18 July 1730 Maria Christina
Weinland. They had children:
    1. **Conrad Friedrich** b. 30 July 1731; conf. 1746.
      He m. 15 Apr. 1764 Catharina Margretha Dormeyer [q.v.]
    2. Anna Maria b. 9 Mar. 1735; conf. 1749.
      She m. 26 Mar. 1772 Paulus Nehlich
    3. **Johann Leonhard** b. 25 Sept. 1737 or 1738; conf. 1753.
      He m. 8 Nov. 1763 Carolina Christina Dormeyer [q.v.]
    4. Elisabetha Catharina b. 31 July 1740, d. 1784
    5. Maria Catharina b. 12 June 1743; conf. 1759
    6. Christina Margaretha b. 17 Jan. 1746, d. 1750
    7. Johann Ludwig b. 16 Nov. 1748; conf. 1762
    8. Philipp Clemenz b. 6 Mar. 1751; conf. 1765
    9. Johann Heinrich b. 28 Oct. 1755

Verification of this emigration supplied by Dr. Bernd Gölzer, from the
county records of Nassau-Saarwerden, compiled by Dr. Gerhard Hein:
Records of Saarwerden county office for Dehlingen:
1779 inventory listing Bauer children and their whereabouts: eldest son
Conrad moved away 16 years ago; son Leonhard is "in the New Land",
moved away with his brother Conrad, and nothing is known beyond that on
their whereabouts.

AMERICAN RECORDS

Hocker, *German Settlers of Pennsylvania:*
Philadelphische Correspondenz, newspaper dated June 3, 1783:
Leonhard Bauer seeks information about his wife's brother, Peter Dormeyer,
born in Diemringer Amt, Dorf Deringer, who in 1764 came to America, with
his sister, Carolina Christina, and her husband, and was indentured.
Dormeyer is believed to be in the dry lands near Bethlehem. Notify Jacob
Friesz, innkeeper, Salem County, N.J.

Emanuel Lutheran KB, Friesburg, Salem co., N.J.:
Conrad Bauer and wife Margareta had:
    1. Leonard b. 23 Sept. 1773, bp. 3 Oct. 1773
      Sp.: Leonard Bauer & wife Carolina
    2. Carolina Christina b. 27 Nov. 1775, bp. 1 Jan. 1776,
      d. 16 Feb. 1783. Sp.: Leonard Bauer & wife Carolina
    3. Jacob b. 9 July 1779, bp. 26 Sept. 1779
      Sp.: Jacob Miller & wife Catharina
    4. Johann Peter b. 4 Jan. (1782); bp. 16 June (1782)
      Sp.: Peter Mensch & Mrs. Elisabeth Schimpf.

Anna Margaretha, wife of Conrad Bauer, was born in Germany, died 10 Aug., buried 12 Aug. 1782.

Leonard Bauer and wife Carolina sp. a child of Conrad Schaefer in 1775.

Conrad Bauer, Greenwich twp., Berks co., nat. Autumn, 1765.

22. BAUER, HANS PETER   Schopperten=
Phoenix, 1750   67260 Sarre-Union
S-H, I: 442
              EUROPEAN RECORDS

Keskastel Lutheran KB:
Hans Peter Bauer, single linenweaver, son of Hans Georg Bauer, citizen and tailor at Altweiler, m. (1) 6 May 1732 at Schopperten, Justina, daughter of the late Niclaus Röhrer.

Hans Peter Bauer, citizen, linenweaver and widower, and inhabitant in Schopperten, m. (2) 9 June 1739 Magdalena, daughter of Hans Jacob Mog, the cowherder at Schopperten. Children:
    1. Anna Margaretha bp. 31 Mar. 1740;
      Record extracted 24 Apr. 1749
    2. Johann Georg bp. 27 Dec. 1741
    3. Maria Elisabetha bp. 8 Sept. 1743
    4. Hans Jacob bp. 12 May 1745, d. 5 Aug. 1745
    5. Anna Elisabeth bp. 3 Aug. 1746
    6. Maria Magdalena bp. 10 Nov. 1748

Verification of this emigrant provided by Dr. Bernd Gölzer from the compiled records of Dr. Gerhard Hein:
Records of Saarwerden county office for Schopperten:
1762, inventory of the property of the deceased Jacob Moog, cowherder of

Schopperten, mentions daughter Magdalena who went to the New Land with her husband Peter Bauer 12 years ago.

AMERICAN RECORDS

St. Paul's (Blue) Lutheran KB, Upper Saucon, Lehigh Co.:
One Johann Peter Bauer m. 19 Nov. 1751 Catharina (widow Indorth).

Kilian Indorht d. 7 Aug. 1751 age 33 y. 8 days.
He came to PA on the *Vernon,* 1747. Name on list, Indorff.

Peter Bauer, killed accidently 23 July 1757 by his horse kicking him; buried Upper Saucon cemetery.

Philadelphia Will Book L: 37:
Hans Peter Bauer, yeoman, Upper Saucon, Northampton co. 4 June 1754 - 15 Dec. 1757. Wife: Catharine, Exr. Wit: Joseph Powell, A. Bomper, James Burnside.

23. BAUER, MARIA CHARLOTTA   Oberbronn-Zinswiller=
_____, 1791   67110 Niederbronn-les-Bains
(not in S-H)
EUROPEAN RECORDS

Oberbronn Lutheran KB:
Georg Bauer and wife Charlotta nee Preysach had a daughter:
>   Maria Charlotta b. 1 Apr. 1774, bp. Festo Paschatus
>   Sp.: Matthias Haus, son of Joh. Jacob Haus; Eva Catharina, wife
>   of Joh. Valentin Helm; Anna Maria, daughter of Joh. Philipp
>   Preysach; Margaretha Ursula, daughter of Joh. Jacob Müller.

AMERICAN RECORDS

Easton Lutheran KB:
Maria Charlotta Bauer b. 1 Apr. 1774, d. 10 Aug. 1829, daughter of Georg and Charlotta Bauer, b. in Oberbronn in Alsace; came to this county in 1791; married Christian Jacob Hutter, Esq., 9 Dec. 1805. Had 2 sons and 2 daughters. Consumption.

BAUER see also BAUR

24. BAUMBERGER, HEINRICH
BAUMBERGER, HEINRICH
Robert and Alice, 1739
S-H, I: 264, 267, 271
[Bamberger on list - did not sign].

Vinstingen=
57930 Fénétrange
Wolfskirchen=
67260 Sarre-Union

EUROPEAN RECORDS

Diedendorf Reformed KB:
Heinrich Baumberger, residing on the *Ziegelscheuer* by Vinstingen, [today Fénétrange], and wife Anna Maria Schlabacher (Schlebach in some records) had children:
1. Johann Heinrich bp. 25 Dec. 1716; conf. 1732
   Sp.: Johann Jägi from Melchenau, Canton Bern; [CH-4917 Melchnau, BE]; Johann Banghart, son of Johann Banghart, tile maker at Vinstingen; Margaretha wife of Nicklaus Koch.
2. Johann Adam bp. 21 Mar. 1719
   Sp.: Johann Adam Hauer, citizen and smith at Vinstingen; Heinrich Stam, citizen and linen weaver, Vinstingen; Magdalena, wife of Heinrich Reiff, citizen and carpenter at Vinstingen.
3. Johannes bp. 17 Nov. 1721
4. Anna Catharina bp. 22 Oct. 1724
5. Lorentz bp. 11 May 1728, Wolfskirchen
   Sp.: Ulrich Roth and Lorentz Bamberger, Diedendorf; Barbara Iss and Elisabeth Fischer, Wolfskirchen.
6. Joh. Georg bp. 15 June 1731

Earlier entries in the KB indicate that the Baumberger family came into this area from Döss in Canton Zürich [today Töss, ZH= CH-8406 Winterthur].

AMERICAN RECORDS

Indian Creek Reformed KB, Montgomery co.:
Henry Bamberger and wife had a son:
   Georg Ludwig bp. 16 May 1756
   Sp.: Andrew Trumbauer and wife

Indianfield Lutheran KB, Montgomery co.:
Henry Bamberger (Reformed) and wife Elizabetha had:
   Maria Magdalena b. 5 June 1753, bp. 24 June 1753
   Sp.: Kilian Hager and Maria Magdalena Kuntzert, single

Confirmed 1753:
>   Andrew Bernhard, age 15, step-son of Henry Bamberger.
>   Elisabeth Bernhard, age 13½, step-daughter of Henry Bamberger.

New Goshenhoppen Reformed KB, Montgomery co.:
Undated marriages (between 1747 and 1758):
Lorentz Bamberger m. Scharlotta --- (n.n.)
J. Kugeler m. Catharina Bamberger

Buried 6 Apr. 1767: Henrich Bamberger of the Old Goshenhoppen congregation.

Georg Kugler had a daughter:
>   Maria Gretha bp. 6 July 1765. Sp.: Henrich Bamberger and wife

Old Goshenhoppen Lutheran KB, Montgomery co.: List of members:
Georg Kugler, b. 2 Feb. 1726 in Pennsylvania, son of Joh. Michael Kugler
of [W-7105] Grossgartach in Württemberg. On 29 Jan. 1747, he married
Anna Catharina, b. 1724, daughter of Henrich Bamberger and Anna Maria,
deceased, both Reformed. Four children listed in family record.

Lorentz Bamberger, Reformed, and wife Elisabetha, Lutheran, had:
>   Maria Elisabetha b. 16 Nov. 1756, bp. 30 Jan. 1757

Buried 24 Nov. 1753: Georg Henrich Bamberger, aged 1 y., 3 mo., b. 22 Aug.
1752, died 22 Nov. 1753. Father: Lorentz Bamberger, Reformed. Mother:
Elisabetha, Lutheran.
Buried 11 Mar. 1755: Johannes Bamberger, b. 15 Nov. 1748, d. 10 Mar. 1755.
Parents: Lorenz Bamberger, Reformed, and Maria Elisabetha, Lutheran.
Sponsors: Henrich Bamberger, Reformed, and Maria Elisabetha, Lutheran,
the grandparents of the deceased child. Aged 6 y., 3 mo., 25 days.

Philadelphia Will Book O: 107:
Henry Bamberg, Marlborough twp., Philadelphia co., 28 Apr. 1767.
Wife: Mary Elisabeth. Children: Henry, Lawrence, Catharina.
Exrs: Daniel Kister, Valentin Nungesser. Wit: Christian Sheid, Casper Kam,
Henry Schneider.

Henry Bumbarger (Bumberger) Rockhill twp., Bucks co., nat. 24 Sept. 1753.
Henry Bumbarger, Upper Salford, Philadelphia co., nat. 11 Apr. 1763.
Laurence Bumberger, Northern Liberties, Philadelphia, nat. Autumn 1765.

BAUR see also BAUER

25. BAUR, JACOB   Griesbach=
Edinburgh, 1751   67110 Niederbronn-les-Bains
S-H, I: 460

EUROPEAN RECORDS

Gundershoffen Lutheran KB:
Hans Adam Bauer, son of the late Andreas Bauer, former citizen at
Senfelden in Herzogth. Wurtemberg, m. 22 Nov. 1712 at Griesbach, Eva,
daughter of Michael Mallo. They had a son:
        Johann Jacob bp. 23 Feb. 1720

Johann Jacob Baur, single, from Griesbach, son of Joh. Adam Baur, m. 7
Feb. 1747 Anna Barbara, daughter of Joh. Georg Lindemann [q.v.].
[The signature of Jacob Baur by this marriage entry matches the signature
of the immigrant in S-H, II: 540.]
They had children:
        1. Eva Barbara b. 8 Apr. 1748
        2. Esther Elisabetha b. 27 Nov. 1749

Signature from KB: Signature from S-H, II: 540:

AMERICAN RECORDS

A Jacob Bower, Philadelphia, nat. autumn, 1765.

26. BECKER, PETER   Langensoultzbach=
Perhaps on *Anderson,* 1750   67360 Woerth
S-H, I: 436
[John Peter (H) Becker - others from Langensoultzbach on ship;
 several other Peter Beckers in S-H]

EUROPEAN RECORDS

Langensoultzbach Lutheran KB:
Hans Becker, citizen at Sultzbach, and wife Anna Barbara had a son:
        Johann Peter b. 31 May 1733

AMERICAN RECORDS

Trinity Lutheran KB, Lancaster:
Peter Becker from Langen Sulzbach in Alsace, m. 22 Apr. 1760 Susanna
Margaret Schweickart.

27. BECKH, BLASIUS   Oberbronn=
Edinburgh, 1751   67111 Niederbronn-les-Bains
S-H, I: 462
with Georg Walker [q.v.]

EUROPEAN RECORDS

Oberbronn Lutheran KB:
Blasius Beck, single butcher's apprentice, born in [W7470] Ebingen in
Wurtemberg, m. 2 Jan. 1741 Anna, widow of the late Matthis Walcker,
former citizen and nailsmith at Mühlhausen. [Mulhausen=67350
Pfaffenhoffen]

Blasius Beck, citizen and butcher here, and wife Anna nee Schmid, had
children:
1. Johannes b. __ July 1742, bp. 11 July 1742
   Sp.: Andreas Haas, master tailor here; Joh. Jacob Müller, master
   baker here & Barbara wife of Philip Kirsch, master butcher
2. A stillborn child July 1744
3. Johann Philipp bp. __ Oct. 1745
   Sp.: Joh. Philipp Kirsch, Joh. Jacob Lips, Maria Catharina,
   daughter of Diebold Schreiber.

[For children of her first marriage, surname Walcker, see immigrant Georg
Walker.]

AMERICAN RECORDS

St. Michael's and Zion Lutheran KB, Philadelphia:
Buried 25 Apr. 1768 - Philip Beck, stepbrother to Mr. Walker, born at
Oberbronn in Elsass. Came here 16 years ago. Age 22 y. 6 mo. 2 weeks.
Buried 19 July 1763 - Blasius Beck, a butcher, died after a long illness, aged
44 y., 7 mo., and several weeks.
Buried 23 Dec. 1764 - Anna, widow of Blasius Beck, Reformed religion, aged
56 years.

Muhlenberg's Journals, I: 610, 612, 646, 652:
23 Mar 1763 - "About two o'clock I went to visit Blasius Beck, a man who
has ruined his bodily and mental powers through excessive drinking. He

acted very wildly and strangely, since the *habitus mali* has become very strong."

Muhlenberg visited him again on 27 Mar. 1763. 1 July 1763 - "I visited sick Blasius Beck." 18 July 1763 - "Blasius Beck died today."

Philadelphia Will Book N: 11:
Blasius Beck, City of Philadelphia, butcher. 24 June 1763-12 Aug. 1763. Wife: Anna. Children: Philip, John. Stepsons: Jacob and George Walcker. Exr: wife Anna. Wit: Peter Miller, John Thomas (X) Bach.

28. BELLMANN, HANS GEORG age 40   Preuschdorf=
Loyal Judith, 1732   67250 Soultz-sous-Forêts
S-H, I: 88, 90, 91
   [John Jurgh Pelman on A list.]

EUROPEAN RECORDS

Preuschdorf Lutheran KB:
Johann Georg Belman, son of Joh. Heinrich Belman, citizen at ?Klein Fröschling [?6731 Kleinfischlingen?] m. (? Nov. or ? Dec) 1718 Maria Barbara, daughter of the late Hans Martin Pfeiffer, former citizen at Preuschdorf. [See Frederick Pfeiffer, 1730 immigrant for Pfeiffer]. They had children:
   1. Joh. Georg b. 16 May 1719, bp. 17 May 1719
      (father given as herdsman in Preuschdorf)
   2. Anna Catharina b. 23 Feb. 1721, died.
      (father given as herdsman in Mitschdorff)
   3. Hans Michel b. 1 Apr. 1727, bp. 3 Apr. 1727, d. 1729
      (father: herdsman at Preuschdorf)
      Sp.: Hans Michael, son of Hans Michael Dreher; Johannes, son of Hans Clauss; Maria Barbara, daughter of Hans Georg Ayermann, all of Preuschdorff.

AMERICAN RECORDS

Hans Georg Bellmann arrived with Acker, Burghart and Kuntz [all q.v. - from Preuschdorf].

Charles H. Glatfelter, *Pastors and People,* **Vol I**: 238-239, Belleman's Church. Congregations once in Bern twp., now Centre twp., Berks co., probably date from the later 1750s or the 1760s. Unfortunately, there is no old register. The land adjoining the church was warranted by Adolph Henry in 1740,

Philip Jacob Rhoad in 1746, and George Bellman (for whom the church was named) in 1750.

Philadelphia Orphan's Court Abstracts, 14 Apr. 1742:
George McCall owned 14,000 acres in Philadelphia co. called Douglas Manor. Allottments of this land and the names of landowners are listed in the OC records. Among those listed:
George Bellman

29. BENE, JACOB   Griesbach=
before 1743   67110 Niederbronn-les-Bains
Not in S-H
EUROPEAN RECORDS

Gundershoffen Lutheran KB:
Johan Reinhard Bene, citizen at Griesbach, and wife Agnes, had a son:
Johan Jacob b. 29 Nov. 1701, bp. 31 Nov. 1701
[See Reinhard Bene, 1738 immigrant for further data.]

Johann Jacob Bene, son of Reinhard Bene of Griesbach, m. 27 Jan. 1722 at Gundershofen, Anna Catharina, daughter of the late Hans Sieg, *Schirmsverwanten* at Guntershoffen. They had:
1. Johann Reinhardt b. 9 Oct. 1727, bp. 12 Oct. 1727
2. Joh. Stephan b. 4 July 1730, bp. 6 July 1730

AMERICAN RECORDS

Frederick Lutheran KB, Frederick, MD:
Jacob Bene and wife Catrina were sp. in 1743 for a child of Joh. Michel Teuffel.
Jacob Bene appears on the list of subscribers for the purchase of the church book in 1743.

Buried 23 Nov. 1774: Anna Juliana Benesin, born 1715 in Neuwieden [Neuwied], father was Gottfried Wittmann. In 1730 she married the preacher Philipp Streiter with whom she had 11 children of whom 3 sons and 3 daughters are still living, from whom she had 29 grandchildren, of whom 20 now live. She lived with him 26 years. After his death she married the widowed Jacob Bene with whom she lived 17 years. Her sickness was consumption from which she died Nov. 20, aged 59 years.

Buried 12 Sept. 1778: Jacob Bene, b. 31 Oct. 1701, at Mertzweiler in Alsace [67580 Mertzwiller]. His third and last wife was Preacher Streiter's widow.

Died of dysentery on Sept. 11, aged 76 years, 10 months, 10 days.

[Note: Although Jacob Bene's burial record names [67580] Mertzwiller as his birthplace, the records there were checked and his bp. does not appear there; only the Johan Jacob Bene b. 1701 in Griesbach appears in the records in that vicinity. Griesbach and Mertzwiller are located near each other.]

Colonial Maryland Naturalizations:
Jacob Baney, Lutheran, Fredericktown, nat. 10 Sept. 1761.

30. BENE, PETER   Griesbach & Gundershoffen=
Phoenix, 1750   67110 Niederbronn-les-Bains
S-H, I: 440
[translated in Rupp as Peter Bem;
translated in Hinke as Peter Ber]

EUROPEAN RECORDS

Gundershoffen Lutheran KB:
Melchior Bene, Jr., son of Melchior Bene, citizen at Griesbach, m. 26 Nov. 1711 Anna Barbara, daughter of Michael Mallo. They had a son:
    Joh. Peter b. 11 Apr. 1715

Peter Bene of Gundershoffen and wife Anna Barbara had children:
    1. Anna Barbara b. 14 Jan. 1740
        Sp.: Joh. Jac. Baur, single; Christina, daughter of Phil. Jac. Römer; Anna Barbara, daughter of Joh. Georg Löwenguth
    2. Johann Jacob b. 12 May 1741
        Sp.: Christman Diemer; Joh. Jacob Baur; Anna, wife of Ulrich Bielmann, weaver here.
    3. Anna Margaretha b. 8 Mar. 1743
    4. Hans Melchior b. 24 Sept. 1744
        Sp.: Johannes Wahl; Hans Jacob Bene of Griesbach; Anna, wife of Ulrich Bielman.
    5. Eva b. 6 Dec. 1746
        Sp.: Jacob Baur [q.v.]; Anna Margaretha, wife of Joh. Adam Bürry, citizen at Griesbach; Eva Mallo, wife of Joh. Georg Mallo.
    6. Maria Elisabetha b. 22 Mar. 1749

[the father signed the bp. entries in the KB in a clear script; his signature in the KB matches the immigrant's signature on S-H, II: 511.]

AMERICAN RECORDS

Christ Lutheran KB, Tulpehocken, Stouchsburg, Berks co.:
Peter Behne and wife Barbara had:
>Christina Elisabetha b. 3 Jan. 1752
>Sp.: Elisabeth Stamgast

Conf. 1774: Barbara Behne, daughter of Peter Behne, age 18.

Peter Behny, widower, m. 10 Mar. 1777 Christine Hartman, widow. They had children:
>Johannes b. 8 Feb. 1779
>Elisabet b. 8 Apr. 1781

Adam Bender, single son of the late Valentin Bender of Tulpehocken twp., m. 13 Apr. 1773 Christina Behny, single daughter of Peter Behny in Heidelberg twp., Lancaster co.

Johann Kempel, surviving son of Joh. Kempel, m. 6 Apr. 1779 Marie Magdalene Pehnich, daughter of Peter Pehny.

Peter Sattezahn m. 20 Mar. 1781 Barbara Behni.
Georg Peter Behny m. 22 June 1784 Anna Maria Deck.

Lancaster co. Will Book D-I: 420:
Peter Beany, Heidleberg twp., 2 Jan. 1784 - 6 Feb. 1784.
Wife: Christiana. Children: Jacob, George, Melchior, Eve, Elisabeth, Christiana, Barbara, Magdalena, and John.
Exrs: Christopher Leese, George Awinger.

31. BENE, REINHARD   Griesbach=
St. Andrew, 1738   67110 Niederbronn-les-Bains
S-H, I: 236, 238, 239
[did not sign; appears on A list: Hans Rinerd Bene; on B list: Reynard (H) Rene; on C list: Reinhart (H) Böning.]

EUROPEAN RECORDS

Gundershoffen Lutheran KB:
Johann Reinhard Bene, single journeyman, son of the late Jacob Bene, former citizen and *Gerichtsschöffen* at Griesbach, m. 18 Jan. 1695 Agnes, daughter of Magnus Mallo, also citizen and *Gerichtsschöffen* there. They had a son:

Joh. Reinhard b. 28 Mar. 1705, bp. 30 Mar. 1705

AMERICAN RECORDS

Northampton co. Wills:
Johan Reinhard Benne, Whitehall twp.; 22 Sept. 1751 - 2 Sept. 1758. Mentions wife Regina Louisa, brother Jacob Benny [q.v.-Jacob Bene], cousin Andreas Deemer. Exr: Andreas Deemer [q.v. Diemer]. Wit.: John Georg Smith, John Nicholas Schneider.

Inventory of the estate of John Rinerd Benny, dated 30 Sept. 1758, by Fridrich Neihardt and Anthony Able; improvement valued at £250.

Pennsylvania Patents, book AA-4: 179:
Under a warrant dated 25 Nov. 1737 there was surveyed to Daniel Rhode [q.v. Roth] 150 acres in Whitehall twp., then Bucks, now Northampton co. Rhode sold his right to Hans Reinard *Denny* alias *Benny*, and a new warrant was issued to Benny; also a second warrant 12 Jan. 1753 to a tract of 66 acres adj. Rhoad, Godfrey Knouse, and vacant land, and 12 Jan. 1753 for 47 acres. John Reinard Benny left the land to his wife Regina Louisa in a will 2 Sept. 1753. Another warrant was issued 5 Aug. 1757 to Daniel Rhode, son of the first named Daniel, for 18 acres adj. Gottfried Knouse, Jacob Yunt, and John Eigners. Regina Louisa Benny m. Gottfried Knouse and they sold the several tracts 21 Aug. 1761 to Daniel Roth the son, who by deed 25 June 1761 had conveyed to Knouse. Pat. to Knouse 12 Jan. 1763, recorded 18 Jan. 1763.

32. BERLIN, JOHANN JACOB age 22   67110 Niederbronn-les-Bains
    BERLIN, GEORG FRIEDRICH age 18
    BERLIN, ABRAHAM age 16
Charming Nancy, 1738
S-H, I; 246, 247, 248

EUROPEAN RECORDS

Niederbronn Lutheran KB:
Johann Georg Berlin and wife Anna Elisabetha had children:
1. Maria Barbara b. 16 Apr. 1714
2. **Johann Jacob** b. 17 Dec. 1716
3. **Georg Friedrich** b. 24 May 1720
4. **Joh. Abraham** b. 10 Dec. 1722
5. Maria Elisabetha b. 20 Apr. 1728
6. Georg Jacob b. 4 June 1732

7. Maria Elisabetha b. 23 Sep. 1736

Archives du Bas-Rhin, Document E 4367:
Hans Gerg Berlin is listed in this document, emigrating from Niederbronn in 1738. He evidently was one of the many who died on the voyage that year, since only his sons appear on the ship list.

AMERICAN RECORDS

Rev. John Casper Stoever's Records:
Jacob Baerling [Berlin], Codorus, had children:
    1. Jacob Cunradt b. 16 Nov. 1740, bp. 25 Nov. 1740
       Sp.: ___ Lau and his wife Anna Kunigunda
    2. John Frederick b. 3 Apr. 1742, bp. 6 Apr. 1742
       Sp.: John Frederick Geelwuchs and wife

PA, Second Series, Vol. IX, pg. 137:
Friedrich Berlin [Berling] m. 24 June 1744 Eva Hauck (Hauk). They had a son:
    Johann Michael b. 21 June 1752, bp. 5 July 1752
    (St. David's, Sherman's, Church, York co.)

York co. Will Book A: 200
Frederick Barling, 27 Mar. 1759 - Letters of Adm. to Eva Barling.

Barnard Houch [See Bernhard Hauch] names his grandchild Michael Bearlinguer, son of Eva, in his will dated 30 Aug. 1762.

Easton Reformed KB, Northampton co.:
Abraham Berlin and wife Anna Maria had:
    1. Abraham b. 14 May 1777, bp. 6 July 1777
       Sp.: Abraham Berlin and wife Catharina, the grandparents.
    2. Isaac b. 9 July 1779, bp. 20 Aug. 1779
    3. Johan Wilhelm b. 28 Jan. 1783, bp. 3 Aug. 1783
    4. David b. 9 Feb. 1790 [Easton Lutheran KB]

Abraham Berlin, Easton, Northampton co., nat. Apr. 1761.

33. BERSY, JOHANN JACOB   Neusaarwerden=
    BERSY, JOHANN LUDWIG   67260 Sarre-Union
Halifax, 1752   67320 Drulingen
S-H, I: 482   Waldhambach=
                        67430 Diemeringen

EUROPEAN RECORDS

Neusaarwerden Lutheran KB; Drulingen Lutheran KB; and Waldhambach Lutheran KB:
Johann Jacob Bersy (also Persie), shoemaker at Neusaarwerden, m. 15 May 1737 Anna Kunigunda Tittel, daughter of Nickel Tittel, schoolmaster at Neusaarwerden. They resided in Neusaarwerden 1731-1734, then moved to Drulingen, where Johann Jacob Bersy was schoolmaster from 1734-1738. By 1740, they were residing in Waldhambach, where he served as schoolmaster until emigrating in 1752. Children:

1. Maria Elisabetha b. 13 July 1732, Neusaarwerden; conf. 1745, Waldhambach Luth. KB
2. Johann Nicolaus b. 8 Dec. 1733, Neusaarwerden; d. - June 1738 in Drulingen, aged 5 years.
3. Ludwig b. 4 Feb. 1736, Drulingen; conf. 1749, Waldhambach.
4. Catharina Margaretha b. 3 Oct. 1738 at Drulingen; conf. 1752 at Waldhambach.
5. Johann Jacob b. 7 Nov. 1740, Waldhambach.
6. Carl Friedrich b. 20 Jan. 1743, d. 8 Apr. 1743, Waldhambach.
7. Christian b. 24 Jan. 1744, Waldhambach.
8. Child (N.N.) b. 26 Dec. 1745
9. Philippina b. 30 May 1748
10. Philipp Georg b. 9 Oct. 1750

Verification of emigration from Saarwerden County office records, provided by Dr. Bernd Gölzer: Dated 19 June 1765: Anna Kunigunda, daughter of Nickel Tittel, and her husband Jacob Bersy are in the New Land.

AMERICAN RECORDS

St. Michael's and Zion KB, Philadelphia:
Buried 17 June 1767 - Philippina Persie, daughter of Jacob and Cunigunda Persie, b. 18 May 1748 in Nassau Saarbrücken in *Teutschland.* Came here as a child and was indentured with the English. Aged 19 years, 1 month.

34. BERTSCHI, ISAAC   Goerlingen=
Boston, 1764   67320 Drulingen
S-H, I: 702

EUROPEAN RECORDS

Rauwiller Reformed KB:
Joseph Bertschi, carpenter at Görlingen, m. - Dec. 1732 at Rauweiler, Susanna Ernst of Görlingen. They had a son:

Isaac b. 20 Oct. 1737

Isaac Bertschi, citizen at Görlingen, and wife Elisabetha nee Isch, had:
1. Maria Eva bp. 16 Dec. 1758
   Sp.: Jacob Jiradon, citizen at Görling(en); Stephan, son of
   Louis Welshans; Maria Eva, wife of Isaac Ponain and Maria,
   daughter of Jacob Kreup.
2. Johann Michel bp. 23 Sept. 1761
   Sp.: Michel Isch, citizen at Görling(en); Jacob, son of
   Philip Witterhold, shepherd at Hirschland;   Margaretha,
   daughter of Joseph Bertschi.

AMERICAN RECORDS

1790 Census:
Isaac Bartgey, Lancaster (Borough), Lancaster co., 1 male over 16; 1 female.

35. BESINGER, PHILIP JACOB   Merkwiller-Pechelbronn=
Minerva, 1770   67250 Soultz-sous-Forêts
S-H, I: 730
EUROPEAN RECORDS

Kutzenhausen Lutheran KB:
Philip Jacob Besinger, son of Jacob Besinger, herdsman at Hermersweiller
[= 67250 Soultz-sous-Forêts], m. 27 Oct. 1767 Maria Dorothea, daughter of
the late Hans Peter Dreher, former herdsman at Fröschweiler [= 67360
Woerth]. The bridegroom's mark (B) by this marriage entry is the same
mark he used in the ship list. The bride's step-father, Hans Georg
Schopffer, also made his mark in this entry.
Philipp Jacob Besinger and Maria Dorothea had children:
1. Catharina Barbara b. 27 July 1768

AMERICAN RECORDS

Trinity Lutheran KB, Lancaster:
Jacob Besinger and wife Dorothea had:
2. Peter b. - Nov. 1772, bp. 10 Aug. 1773
3. Georg b. - July 1774, bp. 1 Aug. 1780
4. Michael b. - Nov. 1776, bp. 1 Aug. 1780
5. Anna Maria b. 17 Nov. 1779, bp. 1 Aug. 1780.

36. BEYERFALCK, MICHEL   Steinseltz=
_____, 1738   67160 Wissembourg
                      EUROPEAN RECORDS

Steinseltz Reformed KB:
Joh. Michael Beyerfalck, son of Hanns Michael Beyerfalck of Steinseltz,
m. 8 Feb. 1729 Dorothea, daughter of the late Jacob Schuler. Children:
  1. Anna Maria Elisabetha b. 17 May 1731, bp. 20 May. 1731
  2. Joh. Martin b. 29 Apr. 1732, bp. 4 May 1732
  3. Anna Catharina b. 3 Feb. 1734, bp. 7 Feb. 1734
  4. Maria Margretha b. 1 Apr. 1737, bp. 22 Apr. 1737

Zweibrücken Manumissions Protocoll, Cleeburg, 1738:
Michel Beyerfalck of Steinseltz moves to Pennsylvania.

                      AMERICAN RECORDS

Christ Lutheran KB, York co.,:
Moritz Müller m. 18 June 1739 Dorothy Beyerfall.

Andrew Fuhrman m. 9 Feb. 1743 Dorothy Beyerfalck.

Hocker, *German Settlers of Pennsylvania:*
Philadelphische Correspondenz, newspaper dated -- June, 1781:
Inquiry for Johann Michael Beyerfalck, who, with his wife and one daughter,
came to Pennsylvania about forty years ago from Zweibrücken and settled
near Georgetown, in the Holz Schwamm. The daughter married a European.

37. BIEBEL, HANS DANIEL   Goersdorf=
Edinburgh, 1750   67360 Woerth
S-H, I: 431 [name on list: Bübel]

                      EUROPEAN RECORDS

Preuschdorf Lutheran KB:
Hans Jacob Biebel, son of the late Anthoni Bibel, citizen and
Gerichtsschöffen at Preuschdorf, m. 28 Apr. 1722 Ottilia Reblaub, Reformed,
daughter of the late Johannes Reblaub of Gundershoffen [=67110
Niederbronn-les-Bains]. They had:
  1. Hans Jacob b. __ Mar. 1723, d. 1731
  2. Maria Elisabetha b. __ Mar. 1725
  3. **Johann Daniel** b. 30 Oct. 1727, bp. 4 Nov. 1727
     [faded notation in KB: "given taufschein 7 Apr. 1750?"]

Sp.: Johann Daniel Müller; Michael _____?; Anna Maria, daughter of Conrad Stepp

AMERICAN RECORDS

Trinity Lutheran KB, Lancaster, PA:
Johann Daniel Biebel from Gerssdorf in Alsace, single, m. 14 May 1754 Maria Margaret Grob from [W-6921] Ittlingen. [See Burgert, *Northern Kraichgau*, p. 140 for information on the Grob family of Ittlingen.] Daniel Biebel died 2 Sept. 1773, age 45 years, 10 mo. 3 days.

Salem Lutheran KB, Lebanon, PA:
Died 24 Apr. 1800 - Maria Margaretta Biebel, age 64 years, 2 days. Daughter of Johann Knob [Grob] and wife Christina, b. 9 May 1736 in the Pfalz, Germany. Was bp. in childhood. In her 7th year she came to this country with her parents and lived with them in Conestoga. In her 16th year she was conf. in the Lutheran Religion. In 1754 she m. Daniel Biebel and lived with him 19 years and 5 months, and had 9 children; 5 children are living [1800], 1 son and 4 daughters. She has a widow 27 years. She was confined to her bed 3 weeks; died yesterday at 10 o'clock.

Died 22 Feb. 1804 - Anna Maria Shammo, nee Bibel, age 42 years, 8 months, 10 days. Daughter of Daniel Bibel and wife Margreta. Born 11 June 1761. Bp. and conf. in the Lutheran Church. In 1785 she married Joseph Shammo; had 4 children and 4 sons survive. Sickness: Consumption.
[See Peggy Shomo Joyner, *Ancestors & Descendants of Joseph Shomo,* Baltimore, 1983; p. 66-68 for Shomo-Biebel descendants].

38. BIEBEL, JOH. ADAM   Goersdorf=
Sandwich, 1750   67360 Woerth
S-H, I: 449

EUROPEAN RECORDS

Preuschdorf Lutheran KB:
Georg Bibel, son of Mathis Bibel, citizen at Goersdorf, m. 11 May 1723 Maria Eva, daughter of Christoph Burckhardt, citizen and mastersmith and *Gerichtsschöffen* at Preuschdorf. Their son:
    Joh. Adam b. 2 Apr. 1728

Adam Biebel, single son of Hans Georg Biebel, m. 19 Nov. 1748 at Görschdorff [Goersdorf] Maria Eva Müller, eldest daughter of Otto Philipp Müller, the miller at the Görschdorffer Mill. They had:
    1. Johann Georg b. 22 Apr. 1749, d. 1749

[Hans Adam Biebel's signature in the marriage record and bp. record in this KB matches his signature on list 160 C, S-H, II: 524.]

Hans Adam Biebel was a brother-in-law of Nicklaus Schäfer [q.v.] who emigrated in 1767 with his family.

AMERICAN RECORDS

New Hanover Lutheran KB, Montgomery co:
Adam Biebel and wife Eva had children:
> 2. Johan Christian b. 7 Jan. 1752, bp. 9 Feb. 1752
> Sp.: Christian Kurtz and Elisabeth Borchart.
> 3. Eva Catharina b. 31 Oct. 1756, bp. 28 Nov. 1756
> Sp.: Jacob Mäyer and Eva Krebs

Died 13 Dec. 1750: John Adam Büebel, no age given.

39. BIEBER, HENRICH   Hirschland=
Brothers, 1751   67320 Drulingen
S-H, I: 463

EUROPEAN RECORDS

Hirschland Lutheran KB:
Joh. Georg Biber, tailor in Hirschland, and wife Anna Magdalena had a son:
> Joh. Henrich bp.9 Mar. 1757; conf. 1740

He appears to have emigrated in 1751, after the other members of this family emigrated in 1744. See father Jurg Bieber and brothers Johann and Dewald Bieber on *Friendship,* 1744 for more detail on family.

AMERICAN RECORDS

Rev. Daniel Schumacher's records:
Henrich Biber and Eva Catharina Driessen had a son:
> Johann Georg bp. 4 July 1773 in the new church in Allemangel,
> six weeks old; sp.: Jurg Kustler, Jr. and wife Christina.

40. BIEBER, JACOB   Asswiller=
Betsy, 1768   67320 Drulingen
S-H, I: 724
> [appears on list as Jacob Bever - did not sign]

EUROPEAN RECORDS

Assweiler Lutheran KB:
Joh. Michael Biber of Assweiler and wife Anna Barbara nee Hofmann had
a son:
>   Jacob b. 17 Mar. 1750, conf. 1762

Annotation in the Assweiler Lutheran KB:
"He traveled to Pennsylvania in May, 1768". Obituary of parents, 1773: "they
had 10 children, 8 sons and 2 daughters; of the four living sons, one has
traveled to PA, one is married, and two are still single."

AMERICAN RECORDS

One Jacob Bieber, Maxatawny, Berks co., nat. Autumn, 1765.

41. BIEBER [BIEWER], JERG   Hirschland=
BIEBER, JOHANN   67320 Drulingen
BIEBER, DEWALD
Friendship, 1744
S-H, I: 357

EUROPEAN RECORDS

Hirschland Lutheran KB:
Dietrich Bieber of Hirschland and wife Eva had a son:
>   Joh. Georg bp. 9 Mar. 1698
>   [Notation by baptism: to America]

Georg Biber m. 26 Nov. 1720 Anna Magdalena Schaffer.
Joh. Georg Biber, a tailor in Hirschland, and wife Anna Magdalena had
children:
>   1. **Johannes** bp. ?27 or ?29 Jan. 1722. [No emigration note]
>   2. Joh. Georg bp. 23 May 1723. One died 14 Mar. 1725;
>   however there is an emigration notation by his baptism.
>   3. Joh. Henrich bp. 9 Mar. 1727; conf. 1740 [q.v.]
>   4. **A son (n.n.)** bp. 22 Oct. 1729; Hans Theobald was conf. 1742;
>   also to America.
>   5. Anna Margreta bp. 10 Feb. 1732. To America.
>   6. Bernhard, twin, bp. 27 Feb. 1735
>   7. Dietrich, twin, bp. 27 Feb. 1735 "all went to America".
>   8. Anna Magdalena bp. 16 Oct. 1740. To America.

Verification of this emigrant also provided by Dr. Bernd Gölzer from the compiled records of Dr. Gerhard Hein:
Records of Saarwerden county office for Eyweiler: Dated 7 Apr. 1763:
Hans Georg Bieber lives in "Maxadamy", Pennsylvania, and writes a letter requesting his inheritance be fetched by David Hahn [q.v.]. Hans Georg Bieber has five children living; he is related to the mayor Peter Ludmann of Eyweiler and sends greetings to various relatives and friends.

AMERICAN RECORDS

Christ Lutheran KB (Mertz's), Bieber Creek, Rockland twp., Berks co., Cemetery, tombstone inscriptions:
Georg Bieber, 1698 - 1775

Jacob Biber, master shoemaker, son of Johannes Biber, m. 7 Nov. 1758 Christina Catharina Steinbrenner, daughter of Joh. Michel Steinbrenner.

Johannes Bieber and wife Marcretha Barbara had:
1. Maria Catharina b. 11 July 1746
2. Johannes b. 1 May 1748
3. Dewald b. 29 July 1756
4. Magdalena Sybilla b. 5 Sept. 1764, bp. 14 Oct. 1764

Georg Bieber and wife Catharina and Dewald Bieber were sp. for the first two children of Johannes Bieber.

Joh. Dieter Biber and wife Mar. Elisabeth nee Kiefer had:
Johan Georg b. 29 Apr. 1755, bp. 21 May 1755
Sp.: Johan Georg Biber and Anna Catharina
Abraham b. 11 Feb. 1761 or 1762? bp. 8 Mar. 1762.

Berks co. Wills:
Theobald Bieber, Maxatawny, Feb. 2, 1793 - Feb. 25, 1793. Provides for wife Elisabetha including use of real estate until son John is 21, when he is to have said real estate, to be appraised and the amount divided among children (not named). Brother Jacob Bieber and wife Elisabeth, exrs.
Wit.: Christian Seiwer and John Bieber.

Berks co. Adm.:
Dietrich Bieber of Maxatawny; Adm. granted 15 May 1787 to Elisabeth Bieber, the widow.

John Bieber, Maxatawny; Adm. granted 8 Mar. 1788 to George Bieber, eldest brother.

Kutztown Lutheran and Reformed Cemetery:
Dewald Bieber b. 16 Oct. 1729, d. 26 Jan. 1808

Johan Bieber, son of Johannes and Margaretha
b. 1 May 1748, d. 17 Apr. 1844

John Dewald Bieber, son of Theobald and Sibilla,
b. 21 Sept. 1758, d. 14 Sept. 1827.

Dewald Bebber, Maxatawny, Berks co., nat. 10/11 Apr. 1761.
George Beeber, Maxatawny, Berks co., nat. 10 Apr. 1760.
John Beeber nat. 10 Apr. 1760.
Dietrich Bieber, Maxatawny, Berks co., nat. Autumn, 1765.

42. BIEBER, JOHANNES   Hirschland=
Brothers, 1751   67320 Drulingen
S-H, I: 463
                        EUROPEAN RECORDS

Berg und Thal Lutheran KB:
Christoph Bieber, *seiler* at Hirschland, son of the late Hans Bieber, citizen
and farmer at Hirschland, m. 18 July 1719 Anna Elisabetha, daughter of
Lorentz Ludman, *censor* at Eyweiler.

Johannes Bieber, son of the late Christoph Bieber, inhabitant at Hirschland,
m. 23 Oct. 1742 Anna Magdalena Heckel, daughter of Nickel Heckel of
Eyweiler [Eywiller = 67320 Drulingen]. [For additional data, see immigrant
Bernhard Klein, who m. the widow of Christoph Bieber].

Hirschland Lutheran KB:
Johannes Biber of Hirschland and wife Anna Magdalena had children:
　　1. Maria Eva b. 10 Nov. 1743
　　　　Sp.: Maria Eva and Anna Elisabetha Heckel; Jacob Tussing;
　　　　Hans Michel Schmitt, Hirschland.
　　2. Hans Nickel b. 19 Dec. 1745
　　3. Catharina Elisabeta b. 16 Nov. 1747
　　4. Maria Magdalena b. 22 July 1749

He is possibly the Johannes Bieber who returned to Hirschland in 1753 and
appears in the KB as a baptismal sponsor.

                        AMERICAN RECORDS

Christ Lutheran KB (Mertz's), Bieber Creek, Berks co:
Johannes Biber and wife Magdalena nee Haegel [Heckel] had:
>   5. Bernhard b. 6 Nov. 1751, bp. 9 Nov. 1751
>   Sp.: Bernhard Klein [q.v.] and wife Elisabeth
>   6. Johannes b. 11 Aug. 1754, bp. 1 Sept. 1754
>   7. Christoph b. 19 Feb. 1756, bp. 23 Feb. 1756
>   Sp.: Paulus Charetin [Sharadin, q.v.] and Elisabetha Bader.

Philadelphia Adm. G: 337: estate # 14, 1762:
John Beiber, late of Gwynedd, Innholder; papers taken out by Magdalena
Beiber, the widow; David Shaffer [q.v.], shopkeeper of Philadelphia; and
Peter Miller of Philadelphia, dated 8 Dec. 1763. Inventory of the estate
made by Jacob Wentz and Melchior Waggoner, and the appraisement papers
mention that the deceased John Beiber "died on his voyage from
Philadelphia to England". [Although the name is recorded in the estate
records as Beiber, the adm. bond signed by the widow was signed Magdalin
Biberin in German script].
The account papers dated 18 Jan. 1769, distribution of estate:
£183.14.5 to Jacob Heister for his wife's third
£122.9.8 to the eldest son, two shares
£244.19.4 divided equally among four other children.

John Bebber, Richmond twp., Berks co., nat. 10/11 Apr. 1761.

43. BIEBER, LORENTZ   Hirschland=
Robert and Alice, 1739   67320 Drulingen
S-H, I: 264, 268, 271

EUROPEAN RECORDS

Hirschland Lutheran KB:
Theobald Biber [q.v.] from Hirschland m. 14 Jan. 1717 Sara Ludmann from
Eyweiler, [Eywiller = 67320 Drulingen]. Their first child was:
>   1. Laurentius bp. 28 Oct. 1717. A notation in the KB by his
>   baptism indicates that they all went to America.

There were eight children in this family, and there are emigration notations
in the KB by all baptismal entries. Lorentz arrived in 1739; other members
of the family arrived on the *Lydia* in 1741. See Theobald Bieber for more
detail.

AMERICAN RECORDS

Christ Lutheran KB (Mertz's), Bieber Creek, Rockland twp., Berks co:
Lorentz Bieber and wife Catharina sp. a child of Jacob Bieber in 1761.

Moselem Lutheran KB, Richmond twp., Berks co.:
Lorentz Biber and wife Catharina nee Adam had:
    1. Nicolaus, bp. not located; named in father's will.
    2. Anna Catharina b. 4 May 1745, bp. Trinity
       Sp.: Gottfried Kramer and Catharina Christina
    3. Christina b. 11 Aug. 1747, bp. 30 Aug. 1747
       Sp.: Conrad Maneschmit and Agnesia
    4. Debald b. 8 Apr. (?1749), bp. Sept. 1749
       Sp.: Jacob Laipe and Ottilia
    5. Anna Maria b. 15 July 1752, bp. 9 Aug. 1752
       Sp.: Friederich Kraemer and Anna Maria
    6. Maria Eva b. 20 June 1754, bp. 4 Aug. 1754
       Sp.: Gabriel Eisenberger
    7. A. Maria Margaret b. 21 May 1758, bp. 18 June 1758
       Sp.: Michael Haefele and Maria Margaret Spohn

Niclaus Bieber and Anna Elisabeth had:
    1. Christina b. 2 July 1765, bp. 14 July 1765
    2. Catharina b. 16 Aug. 1767, bp. 20 Sept. 1767
       Sp.: Catharina Bieber, Anna Kraemer
    3. Joh. Jacob b. 17 Jan. 1772, bp. 23 Feb. 1772
       Sp.: Jacob Bieber and Christina
    4. Anna Maria b. 25 Dec. 1773, bp. 20 Feb. 1774
Their marriage is recorded in the **Weisenberg Union KB, Lehigh co.:**
Johann Nickolaus Biber m. -- 1763 Anna Elisabetha Scheuer, old Johannes
Scheuer's single daughter.

Berks co. Wills:
Lorentz Bieber, Greenwich twp., Feb. 19, 1787 - June 14, 1787 (translation)
To son Nicholas 15 shillings beforehand, and thereafter Nicholas Bieber,
Theobald Bieber, Philip Miller, Adam Retriner, Jacob Zettelmoyer and
Peter Bieber shall stand in equal shares, and Christian Braucher and his
heirs are excluded, and my daughter Eva shall have one English shilling, and
Adam Keel and his heirs have nothing to demand because he has already £5,
my daughter Margaret one shilling and wife Eva articles named. Exr.: Jacob
Leiwig (Leiby); wit.: John Kohler and Henry Kohler.

One Nicholas Beeber of Rockland twp. died intestate, and adm. was granted
to his widow Susanna on 26 Mar. 1787.

Lawrence Beber, Greenwich twp., Berks co., nat. 24 Sept. 1762.

44. BIEBER, MATTHIAS   Eywiller=
Between 1762 and 1766   67320 Drulingen
                        EUROPEAN RECORDS

Verification of this emigrant provided by Dr. Bernd Gölzer from the
compiled records of Dr. Gerhard Hein:
Records of Saarwerden county office for Eyweiler:
Dated 11 Nov. 1761, inventory of Matthias Bieber: the son Matthias is 14
years old.
Dated 5 Dec. 1766, inventory of Magdalena nee Schäfer Bieber: the son
Matthias is 19 years old and has been taken "for several years" to PA by his
father's brother Peter Bieber. The grandfather is Michael Bieber of
Hirschland. [See Peter Bieber, 1741 immigrant, who must have made a
return trip ca. 1761 or 1762.]

45. BIEBER, MICHAEL   Hirschland=
Brothers, 1751   67320 Drulingen
S-H, I: 463
                        EUROPEAN RECORDS

Hirschland Lutheran KB:
Hans Michel Biber from Hirschland, son of Jacob Biber, m. 16 Jan. 1728
Maria Magdalena, daughter of Joh. Henrich Schäffer, church *Censor and
Gerichschöffner* at Hirschland. Children:
> 1. Hans Georg b. 16 Dec. 1732
> 2. A son bp. 1 Aug. 1735
> 3. Johannes b. 30 Mar. 1738
> 4. Hans Michel b. 15 Feb. 1740

Hans Michel Biber and wife Anna Elisabetha had:
> Theobald b. 4 Aug. 1746

                        AMERICAN RECORDS

Moselem Lutheran KB, Richmond twp., Berks co.:
Joh. Michael Biber and wife Elisabetha had a child:
> Joh. Theobald b. 12 Aug. 1769, bp. 15 Aug. 1769
> Sp.: Joh. Theobald Biber; Magdalena Sohm.
See 1741 immigrant Theobald Bieber, for records on a Michel Biber with
wife Maria Barbara who appears in Rev. Daniel Schumacher's records 1763-
1766.

One Michael Bieber, Weisenberg twp., Northampton co., nat. Autumn, 1765.

46. BIEBER, PETER   Hirschland=
Lydia, 1741   67320 Drulingen
S-H, I: 303
[He appears only on the C list as Peter (X) Beaver].

EUROPEAN RECORDS

Hirschland Lutheran KB:
Petrus Biber, son of Theobald Biber of Hirschland, m. 1 Mar. 1707
Margreta, daughter of Lorentz Ludmann, citizen at Eyweiler [Eywiller =
67320 Drulingen]. [Notation in KB: "sind in Americam gezogen". However,
this notation in the KB appears to be one of several such notations that are
in error; the Eyweiler KB indicates that he died there on 6 Nov. 1716,
leaving four children.]. The Peter Bieber who emigrated was:

Joh. Michael Bieber of Hirschland and wife Anna Margaretha nee Karcher
had a son:
          Peter bp. 20 Sept. 1711

Peter Bieber m. 24 Nov. 1735 Anna Margaretha Meyer of Merzig [67190
Mutzig]. They had one child bp. there:
          1. Hans Martin bp. 14 May 1740

Verification of this emigrant provided by Dr. Bernd Gölzer from the
compiled records of Dr. Gerhard Hein:
Records of Saarwerden county office for Hirschland:
Dated 30 Dec. 1762: Peter Bieber is in America, believed to be alive.
The family is not listed on the 1742 census of Hirschland.

AMERICAN RECORDS

Weisenberg Union KB, Lehigh co.:
Peter Biber was sp. in 1766 for a child of Jacob Rau. Peter Biber and wife
Christina, and Margaretha Stedler, were sp. in 1767 for a child of Henrich
Schäffer.

Peter Bieber and wife Christina had:
          1. Christoph b. 19 Sept. 1768, bp. 23 Sept. 1768
               Sp.: Stophel Drescher and Maria Margaretha.

Rev. Daniel Schumacher's records:
Peter Biber was a sp. in 1764 for a child of Michel Bieber in Weisenberg
twp., (Lehigh co.)

47. BIEBER, THEOBALD   age 43   Hirschland=
  BIEBER, HANS GEORG   age 21   67320 Drulingen
  BIEBER, THEOBALD, JR.   age 16
Lydia, 1741
S-H, I: 300, 301, 302, 303
[appear on list as: Dieble Beaver; Hans Geo. Beaver; Dieble Beaver, Jr.]

EUROPEAN RECORDS

Berg und Thal Lutheran KB:
Thiebold Biber from Hirschland, son of Hans Dieterich Biber, citizen and
farmer there, m. 21 Jan. 1717 Sara, daughter of Lorentz Ludman, citizen and
Herrschaffl. Schäffen at Eyweiler.

Hirschland Lutheran KB:
The same marriage is recorded at Hirschland, but with a date discrepancy:
Theobald Biber from Hirschland m. 14 Jan. 1717 Sara Ludmann from
Eyweiler. A notation by this marriage record indicates that they emigrated
to America. Children:
  1. Laurentius bp. 28 Oct. 1717 [q.v.]
  2. **Joh. Georg** bp. 12 Dec. 1717
  3. Joh. Theobald bp. 19 May 1722
  4. **Theobald** bp. 18 Sept. 1727, d. 31 Dec. 1730
  5. Hans Michel bp. 10 Jan. 1730
  6. Johann Jacob bp. 17 Dec. 1731
  7. Anna Magdalena bp. 26 Sept. 1734
  8. Anna Eva bp. 24 Mar. 1737
  There are emigration notations in the KB by the bp. records of all
of these children, except #7. [There appears to be some confusion on the
ship list between the names Brua and Bieber; both Theobald Brua [q.v.] and
Theobald Bieber emigrated from Hirschland with families and members of
both families appear to have arrived on this ship.]

AMERICAN RECORDS

Philadelphia Adm. Book D: 266:
Est. #10 - Letters of Adm. on est. of Dewald Bibber, yeoman, to Sarah
Bibber, widow, 12 Jan. 1742/3.

Berks co. Wills and Administrations:
George Beeber, Oley, no date, prob. May 14, 1753. To my mother Sara
Beeber all estate and after her death £3 to brother Lorentz Beeber and £3
to sister Otila, and all remainder to brother Jacob and sister Magdalena.
Letters of Adm. to Sarah Beeber. Wit.: Frederick Ullrich, Mathias Beeber,

Martin Boger. Translation.

Sarah Bieber, widow, Richmond, Sept. 22, 1764, adm. to Lawrence Bieber, eldest son.

Theobald Bieber, Greenwich, Aug. 31, 1769, adm. to Lawrence Bieber, eldest son.

Christ Lutheran KB (Mertz's), Bieber Creek, Rockland twp., Berks co:
Jacob Bieber and wife Christina had children:
  1. Dewald b. 19 July 1759
     Sp.: Dewald Bieber and wife Sybilla
  2. Jacob b. 13 Oct. 1761, bp. 1 Nov. 1761
     Sp.: Lorentz Bieber and wife Catharina

Michael Biber and Jacob Biber sp. a child of Michael Klein [q.v.] in 1751.

Mertz's Cemetery, tombstone inscriptions:
Jacob Bieber; b. 7 Feb. 1731, d. _ Aug. 1785

Rev. Daniel Schumacher's records, Zions Lutheran KB, Upper Macungie twp., and Stone Church, Kreidersville:
Michael Biber and Maria Barbara had:
  1. Jacob b. 8 Nov. 1761 [Zions, Upper Macungie]
  2. Anna Margaretha bp. 1 Apr. 1763 in Weisenberg
     Sp.: Henrich Schäffer; Margreth, wife of Eberhard Smidth;
     Maria Bibern. [Schumacher's]
  3. Peter b. 21 Sept. 1764, bp. 7 Oct. 1764 in Weisenberg
     Sp.: Peter Biber; Maria Margaretha, single daughter of
     Jacob Schneider, Lowhill. [Schumacher's]
  4. Christian bp. 2 Dec. 1766, 8 weeks old; died.
     Sp.: Christian Müller, Jr. and wife Maria. [Schumacher's]
  5. Elisabetha b. 23 July 1769 [Weissenberg KB, Lehigh co.]
  6. Henrich b. 8 May 1773 [Stone Church, Kreidersville]
  7. Johannes b. 26 June 1775
  8. Regina b. 8 Dec. 1779
  9. Joh. Friederich b. 28 Feb. 1783 [all Stone Church].

St. Paul's (Blue) Lutheran KB, Northampton co:
George Henrich Müller m. 28 Apr. 1757 Maria Magdalena, daughter of the late Theobald Biber, from the Blue Mountain.

Jacob Bieber, Maxatawny twp., Berks co., nat. Autumn, 1765

48. BIEBER, ULRICH   Hirschland=
Jeneffer, 1764   67320 Drulingen
S-H, I: 700

EUROPEAN RECORDS

Hirschland Lutheran KB:
Conf. 1724 - Joh. Ulrich Beber from Hirschland.

Ulrich Biber from Hirschland m. 25 June 1743 Elisabeta Biber.
Ulrich Biber from Hirschland and wife Anna Elisabeth had:
1. Utilia b. 21 July 1744
   Sp.: Catharina Lang, Wolffskirchen; Utilia Schneider, Hirschland;
   Hans Martin Petri, Wolffskirchen; Hans Michel Biber, Hirschland.
   Ulrich Biber's daughter died 1744, age 24 weeks.
2. Anna Elisabetha b. 26 Sept. 1745
   Sp.: Ann Elisabetha Biber; Catharina Biber; Hans Michel
   Schneider; Hans Michel Biber.
3. Christian b. 8 Sept. 1748
   Sp.: Christina Biber and Hans Gerg Lang from Wolffskirchen,
   Anna Elisabetha Schneider.
4. Johann Michael b. 20 Dec. 1753, died.
5. Anna Maria b. 19 July 1755
   Sp.: Joseph Siegel from Hirschland; Joh. Peter, son of Matthias
   Biber, Eyweiller; Ottilia, wife of Johannes Gangloff; Anna Maria,
   Schneider, daughter of the late Johannes Schneider of Hirschland.
   Notation in KB: "this Ulrich Bieber went to America".
6. Maria Katharina b. 8 June 1759, bp. 10 June 1759
   Sp.: Johannes Gangloff; Peter, son of Peter Schmidt; Maria
   Margaretha, daughter of Jacob Hartmann; Katharina Schall
   from Niedersteinsaal [Niederstinzel = 57930 Fénétrange].

AMERICAN RECORDS

Weisenberg Union KB, Lehigh co.:
Burials, 1765 (no other date given): Ulrich Biber was buried.

49. BIETINGER, HANS ADAM age 39   Durstel=
Samuel, 1737   67320 Drulingen
S-H, I: 169, 171, 172
   [Beidinger on A list, Biediger on B & C list]

EUROPEAN RECORDS

Ingenheim Lutheran KB:
Peter Bietinger from Gemmerswyl, [possibly ?CH-4918 Gondiswil, BE] Canton Bern, Switzerland, son of Hans Bietinger, citizen there, and *Schirmsverwandten* at Zutzendorff, [Zutzendorf=67330 Bouxwiller] m. 4 Feb. 1687 Maria Sabina, daughter of the late Hans Braun, former citizen in Würtenberger land. They moved to Ottweiler [Ottwiller=67320 Drulingen] and records of their children are found in the Drulingen Lutheran KB and Waldhambach Lutheran KB.

Drulingen Lutheran KB:
Peter Bietinger, inhabitant and daylaborer in Ottweiler, died 27 Apr. 1725, in his 64th year.
Maria Sabina, widow of the late Peter Bietinger of Ottweiler died 13 Jan. 1733, aged 66 years.

Drulingen Lutheran KB and Waldhambach Lutheran KB:
Peter Bietinger and wife Maria Sabina, nee Braun, had children:
  1. Christian conf. 1703/4 (Waldhambach KB)
  2. Johann Georg conf. 1703/4 (Waldhambach KB)
     He m. 4 June 1720 Apollonia Hert (Drulingen KB)
  3. Johann Adam b. ca. 1798, conf. 1715 in
     Schwindratzheim [=67270 Hochfelden] (Drulingen KB)
  4. Nicolaus b. 12 Aug. 1701, bp. 14 Aug. 1701 in
     Gottesheim [=67490 Dettwiller] (Printzheim KB)
  5. Hans Peter [q.v.] b. ca. 1703, conf. 1717 in
     Waldhambach [=67430 Diemeringen] (Drulingen KB)
  6. Hans Jacob, single in 1734.

Durstel Lutheran KB:
Joh. Ad(am) Büttiger, apprentice tailor at Ottweiler, son of Peter Büttiger, inhabitant at Ottweiler and Maria Sabina, m. 28 Nov. 1724 at Durstel, An. Margretha nee Schuh, widow of Joh. Georg Hausknecht. (Anna Margreth Schuh, daughter of Johann Adam Schuh and Anna Margreth nee Marx, m. (1) 5 Mar. 1715 Joh. Georg Haussknecht who d. 12 Apr. 1724.) Joh. Adam Büttiger and Anna Margreth had children:
  1. Johann Nicolas b. 26 June 1725, bp. 29 June 1725
  2. Johann Adam b. 31 July 1727, bp. 3 Aug. 1727, d. 15 Apr. 1728
  3. Johann Henrich b. 20 Mar. 1729, bp. 23 Mar. 1729
  4. Georg Michael b. 17 Dec. 1731, bp. 21 Dec. 1731
  5. Johann Peter b. 29 June 1734, bp. 2 July 1734

AMERICAN RECORDS

Lancaster Moravian KB, Lancaster co.:
Niclas Büdinger m. 14 June 1747 Christina Reinboldt.

Adam Bedinger [surname also appears in records as Beetinger, Bittinger, Beedinger] purchased land 3 miles Northwest of Hanover, York co. A warrant dated 3 Aug. 1750 to John Shauman for 100 A, called "Shauman Tract" was surveyed 4 Mar. 1760 for Adam Beetinger [Survey Book A-7; 26]. This land, including an additional 90 A, was patented to Adam Beetinger on 13 Sept. 1760 [Patent Book AA-2:30].
Adam Bittinger's first wife died ca. 1750 and he m. (2) Sabina. They had:
  6. Maria Elisabeth (called Marrillis in Orphan's Court records)
  7. Georg Adam b. 7 Dec. 1754, bp. 25 Dec. 1754, at St. Matthew's Lutheran KB, Hanover
  8. Christian/Christopher b. ca. 1758
  His Revolutionary War pension application says he m. 10 Aug. 1786/7 in Morris co., N.J. Mary Sanders. He d. 23 July 1824 in Hardy co., (W)VA.
  9. Frederick
  10. Eva

Adam Bittinger died before 1 Sept. 1768, when his oldest son Nicholas petitioned the York co. Orphans' Court, stating that his father had lately died leaving a widow Sabina and issue: Nicholas, Henry, Michael, Peter, Marrillis, George Adam, Christian, Frederick and Eva, and holding a 192 A tract in Berwick twp., [OC-B:202]. The tract was awarded to Nicholas [OC-C:19].

Johann Nicolas Bittinger m. ca. 1747 Maria Christina Reinholdt. He d. 2 May 1804 in Abbottstown, Adams co.
Johann Henrich Bittinger m. Mary Magdalena, daughter of Christopher Slagle. He d. 22 Jan. 1772 in Jefferson co., (W)VA.
Johann Peter Bittinger also went to Shepherdstown, Jefferson co., (W)VA, where he d. ca. 1801.

A special thank you to Cleta Smith, Silver Spring, MD for sharing her excellent research on these Bietinger families.

50. BIETINGER, PETER age 34 Ottwiller=
Samuel, 1737 67320 Drulingen
S-H, I: 169, 171 172
  [Beidinger on A & B list, Buidicer on C list]

EUROPEAN RECORDS

Drulingen Lutheran KB:
Peter Bietinger and wife Maria Sabina, nee Braun, had a son:
>Hans Peter b. ca. 1703, conf. 1717
>[See his brother, Hans Adam Bietinger, for additional family data].

Hans Peter Bietinger, weaver at Ottweiler, son of Peter Bietinger, m. 4 May 1728 Anna Maria Pfirsch. (Anna Maria Pfirsch was conf. 1719 in Neuwiller, [Neuwiller-les-Saverne = 67330 Bouxwiller] age 14, daughter of Christian Pfirsch and Anna Margareth nee Kruck.) Children:
>1. Anna Elisabetha b. 19 Dec. 1728 at Ottweiler, bp. 21 Dec. 1728. She d. 2 Jan. 1729.
>2. Anna Margretha b. 23 Nov. 1729, bp. 27 Nov. 1729
>3. Johann Adam b. 6 Dec. 1732, bp. 12 Dec. 1732. He d. 7 Aug. 1733 at Ottweiler.
>4. Johann Georg b. 13 Oct. 1734, bp. 16 Oct. 1734

AMERICAN RECORDS

Lancaster Moravian KB, Lancaster co.:
Peter Büdinger and wife Anna Maria had:
>Georg b. 22 Nov. 1744, bp. 27 Nov. 1744
>Susanna b. 9 Jan. 1745, bp. 13 Jan. 1745

York co. Adm. Book A: 50:
13 Jan. 1752, Adam Beedinger was appointed adm. of the estate of Peter Beedinger.

York co. Orphans' Court A: 100, dated 19 Aug. 1758:
George Bittinger, a son of Peter Bittinger, deceased, asked the court to name a guardian for his brother Adam, age 13 years and 10 months. Michael Charles was appointed. Young Adam Bittinger was bound to George Blenzenger, tailor, of Manheim twp., until he was age 21.

York co. Orphans' Court A: 131, dated 28 Nov. 1759:
Adam Bittinger, adm. of the estate of Peter Bittinger, reported a balance of over £57, to be distributed to the widow, Anna Margaretha, now the wife of Mathias Ehmich [Emig], and the children: George, Katrina wife of Leonhard Stephen, Peter, and Adam.

51. BIGLER, MARX age 28
Richard & Elizabeth, 1733
S-H, I: 127, 129, 130

Ingolsheim=
67250 Soultz-sous-Forêts

EUROPEAN RECORDS

Hunspach Reformed KB:
Hans Thomas Büchler, son of Henrich Büchler, former citizen at Leitersweyler [Leiterswiller = 67250 Soultz-sous-Forêts], m. 7 Jan. 1698 Maria, daughter of Jacob Vogler of Ingelsheim.
Hans Thomas Bögler of Ingelsheim and wife Anna Maria had:
1. Hans Georg b. 10 Feb. 1703, bp. 18 Feb. 1703
2. **Marx** b. 17 Apr. 1705, bp. 19 Apr. 1705
    Sp.: Hans Jacob Heckel, schoolteacher at Hunspach; Marx Weimer of Hofen; Magadalene (N.N.) of Leiterschweiler.
3. Hans Michel [q.v.] b. 3 Dec. 1707, bp. 4 Dec. 1707

AMERICAN RECORDS

Rev. John Casper Stoever's Records:
Marx Biegeler (Conewago) had a daughter:
    Anna Maria b. 30 Mar. 1741, bp. 21 Aug. 1741
    Sp.: Andreas Hill and Catarina Kuntz

Marx Biegler and wife were sp. in 1739 for a child of Joh. Michael Carl.

Colonial Maryland Naturalizations:
Mark Pickler nat. in MD, October Term, 1743.

52. BIGLER, MICHAEL   Ingolsheim=
Francis and Ann, 1741   67250 Soultz-sous-Forêts
S-H, I: 292, 293

EUROPEAN RECORDS

Hunspach Reformed KB:
Hans Thomas Büchler, son of Henrich Büchler, former citizen at Leitersweyler [Leiterswiller = 67250 Soultz-sous-Forêts], m. 7 Jan. 1698 Maria, daughter of Jacob Vogler of Ingelsheim. They had a son:
    Hans Michel b. 3 Dec. 1707, bp. 4 Dec. 1707
    [see his brother Marx Bigler for additional data.]

AMERICAN RECORDS

Rev. John Casper Stoever's Records:
John Michael Biegler m. 14 Dec. 1741 Susanna Reuscher, Conewago.

Frederick County Will Abstracts in *Western Maryland Genealogy*, Vol. 2, no. 3, 1986: Will Book A I: 227-8:
Michael Beigler of Frederick co., farmer. 21 Sept. 1763 - 20 Nov. 1764.
To Mark Beigler, son of my brother Mark: £5. To wife Bosenah [?Susanna]: all moveable and real estate; she also exr. /s/ Michael Beigler.
Wit: Daniel Leatherman, Matthias Hurnman?, John Arnold, Bartel Booker.

Colonial Maryland Naturalizations:
Michael Bigler of Frederick co., German, a member of Baptist congregation, nat. 21 Sept. 1763.

53. BILLMAN, H. DEWALT   Ingolsheim=
St. Andrew, 1752   67250 Soultz-sous-Forêts
S-H, I: 484
EUROPEAN RECORDS

Hunspach Reformed KB:
Diebolt Billmann, *Gemeinsmann* at Ingelsheim and wife Anna Appollonia had:
    1. Hans Michael b. 8 Mar.1708
    2. Hans Michel b. 12 Mar. 1710
    3. Maria Barbara b. 20 Aug. 1712
    4. Catharina Kunigunda b. 1 Apr. 1716
    5. Maria Magdalena b. 19 Mar. 1719. She m. 1739
       Martin Hauck [q.v.]
    6. Anna Maria b. 22 Feb. 1724
    7. **Hans Diebolt** b.15 July 1726, conf. 1741
    8. Martin b. ca. 1730, conf. 1744

Zweibruecken Manumissions Protocoll, Clee- and Catharinenburg,: 1752:
Theobald Billmann leaves for America.

AMERICAN RECORDS

Lynn twp., Lehigh co., tax list, 1762:
Dewald Billman

54. BIRCKER, ANDREAS   Uttenhoffen=
Dragon, 17 Oct. 1749   67110 Niederbronn-les-Bains
S-H, I: 423

EUROPEAN RECORDS

Gundershoffen Lutheran KB:
Andreas Bircker, weaver at Uttenhoffen, and wife Ottilia had a son:
Andreas bp. 6 Jan. 1717

Andreas Bürcker, son of the late Andreas Bürcker, former weaver and citizen at Uttenhoffen, m. 11 Apr. 1741 Christina, daughter of Abraham Huser, citizen here. Children:
1. Catharina ? bp. 22 Dec. 1743
2. Andreas bp. 3 Oct. 1745
3. Georg Friedrich b. 13 Oct. 1747
   [father's signature by this bp. matches signature on ship list S-H, II: 482]

AMERICAN RECORDS

Trinity Lutheran KB, New Holland, Lancaster co.:
Andreas Bürger and wife Christina nee Huserin had:
Georg b. 25 July 1751, bp. 29 Sept. 1751
Sp.: Matthaeus Hafner

55. BIRCKI, JACOB   Gundershoffen=
Betsey, 1765   67110 Niederbronn-les-Bains
S-H, I: 707

EUROPEAN RECORDS

Gundershoffen Lutheran KB:
Hans Jacob Bircke, *weberknapp* here, m. 29 Jan. 1722 Anna Catharina, daughter of the late Peter Hauser, former citizen and linenweaver here. They had a son:
Johann Jacob b. 10 Feb. 1723, bp. 12 Feb. 1723

Jacob Bircki, single linenweaver, son of Joh. Jacob Bircki, citizen and linenweaver, m. 22 Nov. 1746 Anna Barbara Uhlmann, daughter of Ulrich Uhlmann, citizen and linenweaver at Mietesheim [=67580 Mertzwiller]. Children:
1. Johann Jacob b. 19 May 1749
   [the father's signature by this baptism matches his signature in the ship lists].
2. Johann Peter b. __? Nov. 1750, bp. 10 ? Nov. 1750

Signature from KB: Signature from S-H, II: 809:

56. BIRSON, HANS PHILIPUS   Schalbach=
Phoenix, 1749   57370 Phalsbourg
S-H, I: 405

EUROPEAN RECORDS

Diedendorf Reformed KB:
Heinrich Pierson, son of Hans Philipp Peirson, linenweaver of [57119]
Lixheim, m. 23 Nov. 1713 Elisabetha, daughter of Nickel Schweitzer of
Schalbach. Children:
    1. Maria Catharina bp. 30 Mar. 1717
    2. Maria Magdalena bp. 11 Jan. 1722
        She m. 30 Apr. 1743 Johannes Huntzinger [q.v.]
    3. Elisabetha bp. 16 Mar. 1727

Rauwiller Reformed KB:
Heinrich Piercon, citizen and shoemaker at Schalbach and wife Elisabetha
nee Schweitzer had:
    4. **Joh. Philipp** bp. 20 Feb. 1729
    5. Anna Maria b. 19 Apr. 1731
    6. Catharina Margaretha b. 27 Mar. 1734
    7. Maria Elisabetha b. 10 Oct. 1738

AMERICAN RECORDS

Tohickon Reformed KB, Bucks co:
Philip Bierson [also appears as Berson, Person and Parson] and wife
Elisabetha had children:
    1. Henry b. 29 Oct. 1759, bp. 2 Dec. 1759
        Sp.: Henry Gut and Margaret Oberbeck
    2. Maria Catharina b. 14 Mar. 1770, bp. 15 Apr. 1770
        Sp.: Adam Graff and Catharina
    3. Margaret b. 2 June 1773, bp. 1 Aug. 1773
        Sp.: Jacob Guth and Elisabetha
    4. John Philip b. 25 Feb. 1777, bp. 6 Apr. 1777
        Sp.: Michael Schuck and Margaretha

Stone Church, Kreidersville, Northampton co.:
Cemetery, tombstone inscription:
    Philip Bierson, born in the year 1730 in Deutschland at Schallbach.
    His father was Heinrich and his mother Elisabeth Bierson.
    He died 7 Sept. 1802.

Philip Person, Hilltown, Bucks co., nat. Autumn, 1765.

57. BISCHOFF, HEINRICH age 20
Samuel, 1733
S-H, I: 106, 110, 111

Langensoultzbach=
67360 Woerth

EUROPEAN RECORDS

Langensoultzbach Lutheran KB:
Hans Bischoff, age 52, of Jägerthal [=67110 Niederbronn-les-Bains]
was buried in Sultzbach 7 Oct. 1729. His daughter Christina Margaretha m.
in 1732 Christian Krebs [q.v.].
It is probable that Henrich Bischoff was also a son of Hans Bischoff from
Schönechen Ampt. Hans Bischoff, herdsmann at Nähweiler [Nehwiller-pres-
Woerth=67110 Niederbronn-les-Bains], first appears in the bp. records here
in 1722. Hans Bischoff and wife Elisabetha nee Schwartz had children:
  1. Christina Margaretha
  2. probably Heinrich b. ca. 1713
  3. Anna Eva bp. 22 Oct. 1722
  4. Anna Maria bp. 8 Feb. 1725 at Liniehausen
  5. Hans Peter bp. 26 Dec. 1729

AMERICAN RECORDS

Trinity Lutheran KB, New Holland, Lancaster co.:
Heinrich Bishoff m. 4 June 1736 Elisabetha Ellrodt. They had children:
  1. Maria Magdalena b. 11 Feb. 1738, bp. 25 Feb. 1738
    Sp.: Christina Margaretha, wife of Christian Krebs.
  2. Johannes b. 14 Feb. 1740, bp. 2 May 1740
    Sp.: Wilhelm Ellrodt and wife Anna; Christoph and Jeremias
    Ellrodt.

St. Matthew's Lutheran KB, Hanover, York co.:
Henry Bishoff had a son:
    Jeremias b. 7 Mar. 1748, bp. 24 Apr. 1748
    Sp.: Augustus Scherer and wife Anna Magdalena.

58. BISH, THEOBALD
Minerva, 1770
S-H, I: 729

Preuschdorf=
67250 Soultz-sous-Forêts

EUROPEAN RECORDS

Preuschdorf Lutheran KB:
Hans Diebold Bisch, baker at Preuschdorf, and Anna Barbara had a son:
  Theobald b. 18 Dec. 1733, bp. 20 Dec. 1733

Theobald Bisch, baker and widower at Preuschdorf, m. (2) 24 July 1736 Anna Maria, widow of the late Joh. Georg Schindler, shepherd at Lampertsloch [=67250 Soultz-sous-Forêts].

AMERICAN RECORDS

Salem Lutheran KB, Lebanon, Lebanon co.:
Deobald Busch [also appears in record as Tiewald Pisth] and wife Elisabeth had children:
1. Joh. Heinrich bp. 20 June 1773
   Sp.: Joh. Heinrich Seyler [q.v.] and his wife Catarina
2. Catharine b. 17 July 1775, bp. 3 Aug. 1775
   Sp.: Henry Seiler and wife Eva Catherine

59. BLESCH, JOSEPH   67510 Lembach
Hamilton, 1767
S-H, I: 716

EUROPEAN RECORDS

Lembach Catholic KB:
Josephus Blesch from Geroltzheim [W-6711 Gerolsheim], son of the late Sebastian Blesch and his wife Margaretta, m. 15 June 1761 Dorothea Karst, daughter of the late Valentin Karst and his wife who was a daughter of Ludwig Meyer of Lembach. Witnesses to the marriage were: Theobald Schlosser, Johannes Rehm, Joseph Herdt and Michael Still. Joseph Blesch signed his marriage record in the KB, and the signature matches that in S-H, II: 824.

AMERICAN RECORDS

Michael Tepper, ed., *Emigrants to Pennsylvania,* Baltimore, 1975, p. 261:
[Excerpted from *Pennsylvania Magazine of History and Biography,* Vol. XXXIII, no. 4, p. 501, 1909]
The following list of German families arrived at Philadelphia, appears in an advertisement in Henry Miller's *Staats Bote* of Feb. 9, 1758. [Note by compiler: this date of the newspaper is obviously in error, and should be 1768. See corrected list in Appendix B of this volume].
"The following German families, and a couple of unmarried persons, are now in the city; all held for their passage from Holland, and desiring to bind themselves out for same ......" Among those named in this list are:
Joseph Bläs, tailor, from the Chur-Mannz jurisdiction, village of Burtzele; his wife Dorothea Kartz(in), born in Alsace, Dorfschaft Lembach.

60. BLEY, PHILIP Birlenbach=
ca. 1748 67160 Wissembourg
EUROPEAN RECORDS

Birlenbach Lutheran KB:
Philip Bley, citizen at Birlenbach, and wife Anna Maria had children:
1. Anna Barbara b. 7 Dec. 1716
2. Anna Maria b. 10 Dec.1717
3. Hans Martin bp. 19 July 1720
4. Maria Catharina bp. 18 Oct. 1722
5. Catharina Margaretha bp. 30 Nov. 1724
6. Hans Michel bp. 6 May 1726
7. Eva Barbara bp. 16 Jan. 1729

Philip Bley, citizen and widower at Birlenbach. m. 28 Nov. 1730 Feronica
Müller from Kutzenhausen. They had:
8. Maria Barbara b. 27 May 1735

Friedrich Krebs. "Annotations to Strassburger and Hinke's Pennsylvania German Pioneers," in *The Pennsylvania Genealogical Magazine,* Vol. 21 (1960):
Philipp Bley, son of the citizen and cooper Hanss Werner Bley of Hornbach and his wife Elisabeth Huber, "twenty-two years ago went into Alsace and married at Trachenbronn, from where he removed to America." Deposition made in 1770; (hence Philipp migrated about 1748).

61. BLOCH, JOHANNES Butten=
BLOCH, GEORG 67430 Diemeringen
BLOCH, MICHAEL Hirschland=
Patience, 1751 67320 Drulingen
S-H, I: 456
EUROPEAN RECORDS

Diedendorf Reformed KB:
Johannes Bloch, tile maker from Bitten, son of Moritz Bloch *"aus der vogtey finaleshoch Lobl. Berner gebiets",* m. 24 Jan. 1722 Maria Magdalena, daughter of Moyse Villerd from Görlingen [=67320 Drulingen]. They had:
1. **Georgius** bp. 8 Nov. 1722
Sp.: Georg Blais from Rauweiller; Jacob Bruard; Christina, daughter of Fritz Friederich; Frantzin(a), daughter of Joh. Peter Witersheim.
2. Anna Margaretha bp. 10 Mar. 1726
Sp.: Jacob Zins from Weyher; Jean Pierre Villard; Anna

Margaretha Mertz, wife of Abraham Wotring; Anna Elisabeth, daughter of Joh. Adam Dormeyer, Schalbach.

Rauwiller Reformed KB:
3. Joh. Michael bp. 26 Feb. 1728 at Hirschland
4. Joh. Friederich bp. 23 July 1730
5. Abraham bp. 4 Apr. 1734

Hans Görg Bloch from *Hirschlander Ziegelhut* m. (1) 21 July 1732 Anna Maria, daughter of Abraham Welschans, Kirberg.
Johan Görg Bloch from the *Hirschlander Zigelhud* m. 17 Nov. 1744 Anna Elisabetha Gelbach from Kirberg .

AMERICAN RECORDS

German Reformed KB, Germantown, Philadelphia co:
Magdalena Bloch, wife of Michael Bloch was a sp. in 1756 for a child of Jacob Kerty.

George Bloch and wife Anna Elisabeth had:
1. John bp. 25 Feb. 1753; Sp.: Martin Jost
2. Barbara bp. 31 Mar. 1755; Sp.: Barbara Walter
3. Anna Elisabeth b. 13 Dec. 1756, bp. 26 Dec. 1756
   Sp.: Henrich Bloecker and wife Louisa
4. Mary Magdalena b. 1 Sept. 1758, bp. 8 Oct. 1758
   Sp.: Michael Bloch and wife Mary Magdalena

Michael Bloch m. 3 Feb. 1756 Maria Magdalena Leebrock.

62. BOCK, LEONARD age 33   Goersdorf=
Britannia, 1731   67360 Woerth
S-H, I: 47, 49, 50, 51, 53
   With Elisabeth age 36, Maria Katharina age 10, Maria Sabina age 8,
Leonard age 5, Maria Elizabeth age 2 ½, Hans Michel age 1.

EUROPEAN RECORDS

Preuschdorf Lutheran KB:
Hans Heinrich Bock, son of Hans Bock of Goersdorf, m. 8 Jan. 1666 Anna
Barbara Trautmann, daughter of Michel Trautmann.   Their son, Hans
Niclaus Bock (b. 1668 - d. 1704) m. 12 Jan. 1693 Anna Margaretha, daughter
of the late Jacob Stocker, citizen at Görstdorff. They had a son:
      Joh. Leonhard b. 25 May 1698

Joh. Leonhard Bock, son of the late Hans Nicklaus Bock of Gerstorff, m. 19
Sept. 1719 Maria Elisabetha, daughter of Hans Conrad Kieffer of Gerstorff.
(Notation in KB: "Went to the new land.")   Children:
      1. Maria Catharina b. 6 July 1720, bp. 7 July 1720
      2. Maria Salome b. 6 July 1722, bp. 7 July 1722
      3. Joh. Leonhard b. 6 Dec. 1724, bp. 9 Dec 1724
      4. Maria Elisabetha b. 16 Nov. 1728, bp. 18 Nov. 1728
      5. Hans Michel b. 13 Feb. 1731, bp. 15 Feb 1731
         One of the Sp. at his bp. was Hans Michel Stocker [q.v.]

AMERICAN RECORDS

New Hanover Lutheran KB, Montgomery co:
Leonard Bok sp. a child of Georg and Francisca Burghart [see Burckhardt]
in 1748.

New Goshenhoppen Reformed KB, Montgomery co:
Georg Schütz and Anna Christina had a daughter:
      Maria Lisabeth bp. 11 Apr. 1737
      Sp.: Leonhardt Bock and wife Maria Lisabeth.

St. Paul's (Blue) Lutheran KB, Lehigh co:
Leonhard Bock and wife Christina had:
      Anna Maria b. 29 June 1757, bp. 17 July 1757
      Sp.: Johann Schmid and Anna Maria Koch

Leonhardt Bock and Christina were sp. in 1750 at Great Swamp Reformed
Church, Lehigh co., for a child of Theobald Breuchler and wife Anna Maria.

St. Michael's and Zion Lutheran KB:
Buried 8 Sept. 1780 - Leonhard Bock from Gersdorf, age 55 years.

Rev. Daniel Schumacher's records:
Michael Bock and wife (Maria) Salome had:
    1. Carl Jacob b. 9 May 1758 [Weissenberg Union KB, Lehigh co.]
    2. Johann Henrich b. 19 Apr. 1760.

Leonard Buck, Philadelphia co., nat. Apr. 1743

63. BOH (POH), HANS JACOB   Langensoultzbach=
Ship data not located.

67360 Woerth

EUROPEAN RECORDS

Langensoultzbach Lutheran KB:
Hans Jacob Boh (elsehwere Poh), son of Philips Boh, *Erbbeständer* in
Günstell [?Gunstett=67360 Woerth] m. 19 May 1733 Maria Elisabetha,
daughter of Hans Jacob ?Widdels, *Erbbestander* at Windstein [=67110
Niederbronn-les-Bains]. Children:
    1. Maria Margaretha bp. 14 Oct. 1733
    2. Maria Elisabetha bp. 9 Jan. 1735
    (no further record)

AMERICAN RECORDS

Rev. Daniel Schumacher's records:
Jacob Poh and wife Anna Maria had:
    Johannes bp. 24 July 1757 in Allemangle, 5 weeks old
    Sp.: Johannes Hein and Anna Maria
    Ferdinand b. 9 Oct. 1764, bp. 3 Dec. 1764 in Allemangel
    bp. at Strassers. Sp.: Ferdinand Ritter and Susanna

Conf. 1757? or 1761? in Allemangel: Jacob Poh.

Berks co. wills:
Jacob Poh, Albany twp., 5 May 1804 - 30 Nov. 1804 (trans.)
Provided for wife Elizabeth the land in Beaver township, Northumberland
co. To sons Sebastian and Michael and son Henry shall have 1 English
shilling, no more. Remaining children, George, John, Ferdinand and
Magdalena shall be no heirs to the property which I now have in possission
becuase they have already received their inheritance. Exrs: Adam Reyer, and
Bernd Eberhard. Wit.: Jacob Kummerer and Philip Bauscher.

64. BOLLINGER, CHRISTOPH   Altwiller=
Robert and Alice, 1739   67260 Sarre-Union
S-H, I: 263, 267, 270

EUROPEAN RECORDS

Diedendorf Reformed KB:
Christoff Bollinger, single smith from Stinsell, son of Bernhard Bollinger, m.
16 Sept. 1716 Anna Maria daughter of the late Johannes Zinck, *Ackermann*
at Altweiler.
Christoph Bolinger, farrier at Altweiler, and wife Anna Maria Zinck had:
1. Anna Margareta bp. 12 Feb. 1719
2. Johannes bp. 25 Jan. 1721
3. Anna Maria bp. 12 Apr. 1722
   Sp.: Joh. Georg ?Veich or ?Urich, Vingstingen; Joh. Nicolaus
   Bulinger, joiner at Niederstinsel; Johannetha, daughter of
   Johann Juin, Altweiller; Anna Maria Sarein, step-daughter of
   H. Modera, Altweiller.
4. Maria Catharina bp. 3 Oct. 1724
   Sp.: Joh. Peter Georg Burger; Ulrich Witmer, citizen at Altweiler
5. Christophel bp. 19 May 1727
   Sp.: Joh. Wendel Muller, Altweiller; Christian son of Johannes
   Schat, Altweiller; Eva Zinck, wife of Christian Stam, Altweiller;
   Anna Barbara, daughter of Ullrich Witmer, Altweiller.

AMERICAN RECORDS

Muddy Creek Reformed KB, Lancaster co.:
A Christopher Bollinger and wife Catharine were sp. in 1743 for a child of
Fritz Recher.
There were two immigrants of this name, the one arriving in 1737 from W-
6661 Winterbach [S-H, I: 175, 177, 178; see Burgert, *Western Palatinate* for
this other Bollinger family.]

Rev. John Casper Stoever's Records:
A Catarina Baulinger was sp. in 1741 for a child of Niclaus Layenberger
(Conewago).

65. BONN, NICOLAUS   Postroff=
    BONN, JOHANNES   57930 Fénétrange
Brotherhood, 1750
S-H, I: 448
EUROPEAN RECORDS

Hirschland Lutheran KB:
Joh. Sebastian Bon and wife Anna Margretha had:
    Johannes bp. 19 Sept. 1706

Johannes Bon of Postorff m. 7 July 1732 Anna Margreta Fus, daughter of
Hans Peter Fus. Children:
    1. **Hans Nickel** b. 13 Oct. 1734
    2. Johannes b. 24 June 1738
    3. Anna Catharina b. 2 July 1741
        Sp.: Anna Regina, wife of Conrad Grynius [q.v.]; Maria
        Barbara Klein, Niederstensel [Niederstinzel = 57930 Fénétrange];
        Philipps Dettweiler, schoolteacher at Postorff; Johannes Gangloff
    4. Joh. Theobald bp. 18 Nov. 1744
        [Emigration notation in KB: to America]

AMERICAN RECORDS

Frederick Lutheran KB, Frederick, MD:
Johann Nicolas Bohn and wife Anna Maria had a daughter:
    Catharina b. 10 July 1763, bp. 22 Mar. 1789
    [In the bp. record, she is named as the wife of John Scott].

Colonial Maryland Naturalizations:
One Nichole Boon nat. 11 Sept. 1765.

66. BRAUN, ANTON   Diedendorf=
Halifax, 1754   67260 Sarre-Union
S-H, I: 653, 654
EUROPEAN RECORDS

Diedendorf Reformed KB:
Anton Braun, son of Johannes Braun of Diedendorf, m. 11 Sept. 1753 Anna
Elisabetha Frantz, daughter of Jacob Frantz of Wolfskirchen. [See her
brother Debalt Frantz for additional Frantz data.]

Verification of this emigration supplied by Dr. Bernd Gölzer, from the
county records of Nassau-Saarwerden, compiled by Dr. Gerhard Hein:
Records of the Notary Public for Wolfskirchen:
Dated 1 Dec. 1756, inventory of Anna Maria Dintinger Frantz; the daughter
Anna Elisabetha, 35 years old, emigrated to America in 1753; the daughter
Catharina Barbara, 33 years old, emigrated to America in 1749; the son
Theobald Frantz [q.v.] has died in America, according to a letter written by
his sisters.

67. BRENDEL, JOHANN GEORG age 28   Langensoultzbach=
Snow *Two Sisters*, 1738   67360 Woerth
S-H, I: 209, 211
[his wife and children do not appear on list]

EUROPEAN RECORDS

Durstel Lutheran KB:
Johann Heinrich Brendel, schoolmaster at Durstel, and wife Barbara had:
1. Johann Georg bp. 20 July 1713

Langensoultzbach Lutheran KB:
Hans Georg Brendel, single son of Johann Henrich Brendel, schoolteacher at Sultzbach, m. 26 Spr. 1735 Eva Catharina, daughter of Henrich Frey [q.v.], *Hofmann auff Trautbronn.*
[See brothers Johann Philipp and Joh. Henrich Brendel for earlier family data].

Lembach Lutheran KB:
Johann Georg Brendel, linenweaver *aus dem Trautbronn*, and wife Eva Catharina nee Frey had children:
1. Eva Christina b. 9 Dec. 1736, bp. 11 Dec. 1736
2. Johann Martin b. 29 Dec. 1737, bp. 31 Dec. 1737
   Sp.: Johann Martin Dielmann, citizen and hunter;
   Maria Elisabetha, wife of Georg Diebold Anna, carpenter
   at Langensultzbach; & Martin Schlestein.
[His signature in the KB by these baptisms matches his signature on list 54 C, S-H, II: 218.]

AMERICAN RECORDS

Muddy Creek Moravian, Lancaster co:
Georg Brendel, b. 18 June 1713 in Lorraine. His wife Eva Catharina, nee Freyin, b. 11 Sept. 1717, bp. 12 Sept. 1717, m. 1735. Their children:
3. Anna Maria, b. 9 Aug. 1739, bp. 12 Aug. 1739
   Sp.: Henr. Schmidt
4. Susanna Catharina, b. 15 June 1741, bp. 12 July 1741
   Sp.: Martin Frey and wife
5. Georg, b. 12 Aug. 1743, bp. 14 Aug. 1743
   Sp.: Georg Hege
6. Eva Catharina, b. 25 Feb. 1745, bp. 24 Mar. 1745
   Sp.: Georg Hege and wife. Died 15 Oct. 1747, st.v.
7. Johannes, b. 23 June 1746, bp. 24 June 1746
8. Heinrich, b 8 Mar. 1748, bp. 21 Mar. 1748
9. Elisabeth, b. 30 Jan. st. v. 1750, bpt. 15 Feb. 1750

Heidelberg Moravian KB, Berks co:
   10. Maria Barbara, b. 19 Feb. old style 1752, bp. 11 Mar. 1752
   11. Christian, b. 25 Dec. 1753, bp. 27 Dec. 1753
   12. Philippus, b. 22 Oct. 1755, bp. the Saturday thereafter
       Died 23 May 1760
   13. Friedrich, b. 26 Apr. 1757, bp. 28 Apr. 1757
   14. Christina, b. 18 Apr. 1759, bp. the following day
   15. Jacob, b. 5 Sept. 1760, bp. 11 Sep. 1760; d. 23 Mar. 1762.

Berks co. wills:
George Brendle, Heidelberg twp. dated 10 June 1783; prob. 30 Aug. 1783.
Wife Eva Catharine. Children: Anna Maria, John George, Eve Catharine,
Johannes, Henry, Elisabeth, Maria Barbara, Frederick and Christina. Letters
to John George Brendel. Wit.: Philip Meyer and John Tobias Böckel.

Eva Catharina Brendel, Heidelberg twp., 3 Aug. 1784 adm. was granted to
Henry Brendel, son, and Mathias Sommer, son-in-law.

68. BRENDEL, JOHANN PHILLIP age 20   Langensoultzbach=
     BRENDEL, JOH. HENRICH age 11 [age incorrect]   67360 Woerth
Snow *Two Sisters,* 1738
S-H, I: 209, 210, 211

EUROPEAN RECORDS

Oberbronn Lutheran KB:
Johann Henrich Brändel, son of Joh. Henrich Brändel, citizen and tailor
here, m. 14 Oct. 1710 Anna Barbara Bältzer, daughter of Johannes Bältzer.

Langensoultzbach Lutheran KB:
Johann Henrich Brendel, schoolteacher at Sultzbach, and wife, Anna
Barbara nee Beltzel had children:
   1. Johann Georg [q.v.- also arrived on the *Two Sisters,* 1738]
   2. Johann Friedrich bp. 26 May 1715, d. 31 Dec. 1749
   3. **Johann Philipp** bp. 9 Apr. 1716
   4. **Johann Henrich** bp. 17 July 1718
   5. Johann Friedrich bp. 6 July 1721
   6. Johannes bp. 16 May 1723
   7. Maria Dorothea bp. 5 Oct. 1727

Died 30 Dec. 1737, Anna Barbara nee Boltzel, wife of Heinrich Brendel who
has been the teacher here for 23 years.
Johann Heinrich Brendel, the diligent schoolmaster and widower, m. 1 July

1738 at Langensultzbach Anna Maria Waltzinger, widow of Frederich Waltzinger, *Reeb u. Mallermeister* in Oberbronn [=67110 Niederbronn-les-Bains].

Half-timbered Alsatian houses in Langensoultzbach

AMERICAN RECORDS

Muddy Creek Moravian KB, Lancaster co:
Heinrich Brendel, fourth son of Heinr. Brendel, schoolmaster at Langen Sulzbach in Alsace, and Anna Barbara, nee Bölzelin. [Langensoultzbach, Alsace, France] He was born legitimately to these his parents in June 1720. He came to Pennsylvnia in 1740 and married Anna Barbara, Henr. Aurwasser's daughter in Muddy Creek, She was born around St. Michael's Day [29 Sept.] 1727. They were m. Dec. 1741. Children:
    1. Henrich, b. 26 Nov. 1741, bp. Dec. 1741
    2. Anna Barbara, b. on Wednesday before Pentecost 1744 and
       bp. four weeks later

3. Anna Maria, b. 27 Jan. 1747 st. v., bp. 18 Feb. 1747
Sp.: Barbara Beckin, Barbara Stöhrin, Mar. Magdalena
Schmiedin, Judith Hirschin and Christina Rihmin.
Died 20 Oct. 1747 st. v.

Berks co. wills:
Henry Brendel, Brecknock twp. 22 Dec. 1795 - 18 Apr. 1799.
Wife: Barbara. Children: Abraham; Henry; Mary, wife of Wendel Kremer;
Barbara, wife of Abraham Kern; Dorothy, wife of Mathias Deck; Susanna,
wife of John Huber. Son Henry and son-in-law Wendel Kremer, exrs.
Wit.: Christopher Schlebach and Samuel Addams.

69. BRION, ABRAHAM age 32   Kirrberg=
Lydia, 1741   67320 Drulingen
S-H, I: 300, 301, 302

EUROPEAN RECORDS

Diedendorf Reformed KB:
Jacob Brion, miller at Kirberg, son of Abraham Brion, m. 6 Feb. 1706,
Maria Jouin, daugher of Jean Jouin. [In one record, her maiden name is
given as Schwing]. They had:
1. Peter Paul bp. 14 Nov. 1706
2. Abraham bp. 31 Oct. 1708
3. **Abraham** bp. 8 Jan. 1710
   Sp.: Abraham Brion from Kirberg; Samuel Wenger from Kirberg;
   Maria Catharina Widersheim, nee Brion.
4. Joh. Jacob bp. 31 July 1712 [q.v.]
5. Anna Catharina bp. 24 Feb. 1715
6. Maria Magdalena bp. 1 Jan. 1718
7. Anna Margaretha bp. 9 Mar. 1721
8. Johann Franciscus bp. 6 Feb. 1727

AMERICAN RECORDS

First Reformed KB, Lancaster:
Abraham Welschhans [q.v.] and wife Margaret nee Bryon [Brion] had a
daughter bp. in 1742. 8 other children are recorded in Rev. Lischy's records
in York co. from 1745 to 1764. See Welschhans for a list of these children.

Moselem Lutheran KB, Richmond twp., Berks co.:
Johann Georg Olinger, weaver and widower, m. Dom. 13 Trinitatis 1745,
Anna Maria Brion, single daughter of Jacob Brion.

Johannes Kunz m. Dom. 13 p. Trinit. 1745?, Anna Catharina Brion, single daughter of Jacob Brion in *Deutschland*.

70. BRION, JACOB   Kirrberg=
Lydia, 1741   67320 Drulingen
S-H, I: 300, 301, 302

EUROPEAN RECORDS

Diedendorf Reformed KB:
Jacob Brion, miller at Kirberg, son of Abraham Brion, m. 6 Feb. 1706 Maria Jouin, daughter of Jean Jouin. Their son:
>   **Joh. Jacob** bp. 31 July 1712
>   [See his brother Abraham Brion for more family data.]

AMERICAN RECORDS

Moselem Lutheran KB, Berks co.:
Jacob Brion and wife Anna Maria nee Kaemp (Kamp) had:
>   1. Daniel b. 17 Mar. 1752, bp. 22 Mar. 1752
>   Sp.: Daniel Kaemp and Eva Kelchner
>   2. Catharina Eva b. 20 Sept. 1753, bp. 12 Oct. 1753
>   Sp.: Maria Catharina Kamp and Eva Hafner
>   3. Eva Margaret b. 26 Dec. 1754, bp. 26 Jan. 1755
>   Sp.: David Kamp and Eva Frey
>   4. Johan Georg b. 12 Apr. 1756, bp. 24 Apr. 1756
>   Sp.: Geo. Kamp and wife Anna Maria

Berks co. wills and adm:
Jacob Brion, Richmond twp. Adm. was granted on 23 May 1760 to Melchior Fritz and his wife Anna Maria, late the widow of said intestate.

71. BRODT, PAUL   57119 Lixheim
Christian, 1749
S-H, I: 399

EUROPEAN RECORDS

Diedendorf Reformed KB:
Paul Brodt, tanner at Lixheim, son of Simon Brodt, citizen and tradesman there, m. 22 Jan. 1715 Maria, daughter of Jacob Gassert, citizen and inhabitant at Heilringen [Hellering-lès-Fénétrange = 57930 Fénétrange]. They had:

1. Johannes Simon bp. 9 Feb. 1721

Paulus Brodt, citizen and tanner at Lixheim, widower, m. 23 Oct. 1722
Maria, daughter of the late Jacob Rieger. They had 9 children, including:
Johann Paul b. 19 Sept. 1733
[See Samuel Brodt, 1753 immigrant for a list of all of the children.]

AMERICAN RECORDS

Williams twp. KB, Northampton co.:
Paul Brodt and wife Maria Barbara had children:
1. Bernhard b. ca. 1768; conf. 1783
2. Margaretha b. 2 May 1772, bp. 7 June 1772
   She m. 13 May 1794 Jacob Rösly (Lower Saucon Reformed KB).
3. Johann Michael b. 20 Dec. 1773, bp. 27 Feb. 1774
4. Maria Catharina b. 30 June 1775, bp. 17 Mar. 1776
   Sp.: Bernhard Miller and Maria Catharina Tropp
5. Anna Rosina b. 1 June 1778, bp. 12 June 1778
   Sp.: Heinrich Müller and wife
6. Jacob b. 3 May 1780, bp. 3 p.trin. 1780
   Sp.: Valentin Müller and wife
7. Susanna b. 24 Apr. 1782, bp. 2 June 1782 (Lower Saucon Ref.)
   Sp.: Valentine Miller and Susanna

72. BRODT, SAMUEL   57119 Lixheim
Edinburg, 14 Sept. 1753
S-H, I: 522, 524

EUROPEAN RECORDS

Diedendorf Reformed KB:
See Paul Brodt for marriage records.
Paul Brodt of Lixheim and wife Maria nee Rüger had children:
1. Susanna bp. 1 Mar. 1725 [Diedendorf]
2. **Samuel** b. 24 Feb. 1726
3. David b. 27 Apr. 1727
4. Maria Elisabetha b. 6 Feb. 1729
5. Maria Susanna b. 22 Oct. 1730
6. Johanetha b. 27 Feb. 1732
7. Johann Paul b. 19 Sept. 1733 [q.v.]
8. Christophel b. 25 May 1735
9. Johannes Simon b. 30 May 1737

AMERICAN RECORDS

Indian Creek Reformed, Montgomery co. and Tohickon Reformed KB, Bucks co. and Springfield Lutheran KB, Bucks co.:
Samuel Brodt m. 16 Nov. 1756 Maria Salome Steckel. They had children:
> 1. Anna Christina b. 10 Nov. 1757, bp. 16 Dec. 1757
>   Sp.: Jacob Sterner and wife. Conf. 1772 at
>   Indianfield [Indian Creek].
> 2. Anna Elisabeth b. 1 Jan. 1759, bp. 14 Jan. 1759
>   (Springfield KB)
> 3. Johann Michael b. 6 Dec. 1759!, bp. 30 Dec. 1759
>   (Springfield KB) Sp.: Joh. Michael Melcher and Elisabeth Keil.
> 4. Susanna b. 21 Nov. 1761, bp. 25 Nov. 1761
>   Sp.: Parents [Tohickon]
> 5. Maria b. ca. 1764, conf. 1779 [Indian Creek]
> 6. Samuel b. 13 Mar. 1767, bp. 12 Apr. 1767 [Indian Creek]
> 7. Salome b. ca. 1769; conf. 1784, age 15, at Tohickon.
> 8. Charlotta b. 20 Jan. 1773, [Indian Creek]. Conf. 1790, age 17.

Indian Creek Ref. KB, Montgomery co:
Buried 28 Sept. 1793 - died 27 Sept. of dysentery, Samuel Brod, aged 67 y. 7 mo. 2 days.

73. BRUA, LORENTZ   Hirschland=
Robert and Alice, 1739   67320 Drulingen
S-H, I: 264, 268, 271

EUROPEAN RECORDS

Hirschland Lutheran KB:
Meister Joh. Adam Bruah and Anna Catharina *auf der Ischermühl* had a son:
> **Laurentius** bp. 21 Jan. 1714, conf. 1728
> Sp.: Joseph Tussing of Weyer; Joh. Adam, dairy farmer from
> Schallbach; Anna Maria Tussingern from Weyer.
> (Entry not crossed out - no emigration notation in book. See David
> Schäffer, on same ship; also no emigration notation in book.)

Verification of this emigration supplied by Dr. Bernd Gölzer, from the county records of Nassau-Saarwerden, compiled by Dr. Gerhard Hein:
Records of Saarwerden county office for Weyer: dated 16 Dec. 1757: Lorenz Brua, son of the deceased miller of Ischermühl Hans Adam Brua, has moved to America. The siblings want his share.
Dated 1 Nov. 1758: Lorentz Brua, who more than 20 years ago moved to America, with no ther news of him only that he died without having children.

74. BRUA, THEOBALD   Postroff=
Lydia, 1741   57930 Fénétrange
S-H, I: 301, 302, 303
[See also Theobald Bieber for comment
about surname confusion on ship list].

EUROPEAN RECORDS

Hirschland Lutheran KB:
Theobald Bruah m. 1 (?) Feb. 1719 Catharina nee ?Rhein from Postorff.
[Her name is clearly given in this marriage record as Catharina, but in all of
the baptismal records she is named Anna Margretha. There is an emigration
notation by the marriage record, and also emigration notes by each of the
baptisms.]

Theobald Brua(h) and wife Anna Margretha had children:
1. Anna Utilia bp. 4 Jan. 1720. She m. 1739 Carl Schmitt [q.v.].
   Notation by bp: went to America and died.
2. Anna Christina bp. 31 Jan. 1721. To America.
3. A son (n.n.) bp. 29 Nov. 1724
   [This child was possibly Hans Michael who died 25 May 1732.
   The record mentions that the father, occupation *Huffschmitt,*
   went to America.]
4. Catharina bp. 4 Jan. 1726. To America.
5. Joh. Theobald bp. 19 June 1727. To America.
6. A son (n.n.) [Peter] bp. 9 Feb. 1729. To America.
7. Hans Görg bp. 25 Aug. 1730
   Entry crossed out; no emigration note.
8. Hans Michel bp. 12 Jan. 1734. To America.
9. Gustavus b. ca. 1736 - bp. not located.
10. Hans Nickel bp. 20 Nov. 1739. *"Sind auch Dorthen."*

AMERICAN RECORDS

Christ Lutheran KB, Stouchsburg, Berks co:
Conf. 1754 - Gustavus Bruah, son of Theobaldus Bruah, age 18.

Gustof Bruah and wife Magdalena had:
1. Peter b. 31 Jan. 1757, bp. 13 Feb. 1757
   Sp.: Peter Bruah and Regina Koppenhoefer

Peter Bruah and wife Anna Maria had:
1. Henry bp. 3 July 1763
   Sp.: Joh. Nicholas Kurtz and wife

2. Jacob b. 23 Feb. 1765, bp. 3 Mar. 1765
   Sp.: Martin Stupp and wife
3. Catharina b. 20 Oct. 1768, bp. 3 Nov. 1768
   Sp.: John Kurtz and wife
4. John Peter b. 19 Feb. 1771, bp. 3 Mar. 1771
   Sp.: Mr. Peter Spicker and Maria Margaret

Henry Bruah m. 14 May 1787 Maria Stup.
Henry Brua, widower, m. 17 Nov. 1793 Catharina Schmidt.

Christ (Tulpehocken) Lutheran Cemetery Records, Stouchsburg, Berks co.:
Peter Brua b. 2 Feb. 1729; d. 1 Oct. 1808
Maria Brua, wife of Peter, b. 1731; d. 13 Feb. 1804

Peter Brua, Tulpehoccon, Berks co., nat. Autumn, 1765.

For additional Brua data, see *The Historical Review of Berks County*, Vol. XIV, No. 3, April, 1949: 80-82.

Cut-out heart in the door
of a very old building in Postroff.

75. BRÜCKER, JOH. PETER age 32   Langensoultzbach=
Snow *Two Sisters*, 1738   67360 Woerth
S-H, I: 209, 211
   with Barbara Pickering age 34

EUROPEAN RECORDS

Langensoultzbach Lutheran KB:
Hans Ulrich Brücker and wife Anna Margareth had children:
   1. Anna Margaretha b. 17 Feb. 1697
   2. Johann Georg b. 21 Sept. 1699
   3. Johann Jacob b. 15 Dec. 1701
   4. Joh. Peter b. 8 Apr. 1704
   5. Christian b. 25 Apr. 1707
   6. Anna Magdalena b. 9 Apr. 1709
   7. Maria Catharina b. 7 Aug. 1712
   8. Johann Peter b. 29 Mar. 1715

Joh. Peter Brücker, single, master tailor, son of Mr. Ulrich Brücker, citizen
and tailor, m. 9 July 1737 Maria Barbara, daughter of Heinrich Frey, [q.v.]
Hoffmann in Trautbronn.

[Note: the ages given on this ship list are almost all inaccurate; this couple
presents an excellent example. Joh. Peter Brücker was 23 (not 32). His wife
Maria Barbara Frey, was b. 13 June 1715 in Lembach, so her age was also
23, not 34].

AMERICAN RECORDS

Muddy Creek Lutheran KB, Lancaster co.:
Peter Brücker evidently died soon after arrival in America. His widow
Maria Barbara Brücker m. 23 Oct. 1739 at Muddy Creek Joh. Heinrich Stöhr
[q.v.]. Her date of birth is verified in the Muddy Creek Moravian KB,
Lancaster co., and also in the Heidelberg Moravian KB, Berks co.

76. BRUNGART, MARTIN   Mackwiller=
Halifax, 1752   67430 Diemeringen
S-H, I: 484
EUROPEAN RECORDS

Bütten Lutheran KB:
Martin Brunckhardt, Lutheran, stonemason of Mackweiler, son of Christian
Brunckhardt of Mackweiler, m. 14 Feb. 1744 Christina Krug, dau. of Simon

Krug and Maria Eva nee Hafner of Mackweiler. Children:
1. Johann Peter b. 27 Jan. 1745
2. Johann Adam b. 4 Oct. 1746
3. Johann Theobald b. 2 May 1750, d. 21 June 1751

Verification of this emigration supplied by Dr. Bernd Gölzer, from the county records of Nassau-Saarwerden, compiled by Dr. Gerhard Hein: Records of Saarwerden County office for Mackweiler:
Dated 10 Dec. 1767, inheritance of Simon Krug: the daughter Christina is married to Martin Brunckhardt of Mackweiler. They moved to America ca. 1751.

AMERICAN RECORDS

St. David's (Sherman's) Lutheran and Reformed KB, York co.:
Martin Brunkhard and wife Catharine had:
Maria Elizabeth b. 17 Aug. 1776, bp. 1 Sept. 1776
Sp.: Adam Brunkhard and wife

Martin Brungert and wife Catharine were sp. in 1792 for a child of Jacob Baer.

77. BÜHLER, ANTHONI   Diedendorf=
Robert and Alice, 1738   67260 Sarre-Union
S-H, I: 213, 214, 216
(Biehler on list)

EUROPEAN RECORDS

Diedendorf Reformed KB:
Anthonius Bühler, son of Ullerich *Biehler* from Sigeriswill, Canton Bern, [CH-3655 Sigriswil, BE], m. 10 June 1723, Anna Maria, daughter of Nicolaus Ebele from Saarwerden [Sarrewerden = 67260 Sarre-Union].
Anthoni Bühler *von die den Dorff* and Anna Maria nee Ebele (Eebel) had:
Marx Christian bp. 14 May 1724
Sp.: Marx Weiss, schoolteacher in Diedendorff; Christian Stutzman, born in Siegersweil, Bern; wife of the Pastor; Regina, daughter of Mathias Müller.

AMERICAN RECORDS

Muddy Creek Reformed KB, Lancaster co.:
One of the signers of the Reformed Church doctrine, dated 19 May 1743, was: Antoni Bühler

Muddy Creek Lutheran KB, Lancaster co.:
Antonius Buhler had a son:
>   Joh. Michael b. 9 Aug. 1740, bp. 29 Sept. 1740
>   Sp.: Joh. Michael Schumacher and Barbara Frey

78. BÜHLER, DAVID   Niederstinzel=
Robert & Alice, 1739   57930 Fénétrange
S-H, I: 263, 267, 270

EUROPEAN RECORDS

Diedendorf Reformed KB:
David Bühler, born in Schwanden, Canton Bern [there are 4 Schwandens in
Canton Bern, but this is likely CH-3657 Schwanden (Sigriswil), BE], m. 26
May 1724 Veronica Kern, widow of the later Peter Tritt of Niederstinsell.
[See Christian Tritte and Hans Peter Tritte for additional data.]
David Bühler, citizen at Niederstinsel, and wife Veronica Kern, had children:
>   1. Marx bp. 2 Mar. 1725
>   Sp.: Herr Marx Weiss, schoolteacher at Diedendorf;
>   Joh. Nicolaus Pollinger at Stinsel; Veronica, wife of Jacob
>   Stirnemann; Anna Maria, wife of Joh. Nicolaus Herman, hunter
>   at Niederstinsel.
>   2. Joh. Jacob bp. 28 Sept. 1727, d. 30 June 1728
>   Sp.: Jacob Schneider of Diedendorf; Jacob Allemang of
>   Diedendorf; Anna Catharina Stroh of Niederstinsel;
>   Christina Lung of Wibersweiler.
>   3. Johann Bernhardt bp. 6 May 1731
>   Sp.: Johannes Schlichter of Diedendorf; Bernhardt, son of
>   Sebastian Klein of Niederstinsel; Anna Catharina, wife of
>   Caspar Klein, of Niederstinsel; Anna Maria, daughter of
>   Joh. Jacob Schuster of Niederstinsel.

AMERICAN RECORDS

Muddy Creek Reformed KB, Lancaster co.:
A David Boller signed the Reformed church doctrine in 1743. Christian
Tritt and Peter Tritt, step-sons of David Bühler, also appear in the
Muddy Creek Reformed KB.

79. BURCKHARDT, FRIEDRICH age 30   Preuschdorf=
Loyal Judith, 1732   67250 Soultz-sous-Forêts
S-H, I: 88, 90, 92

EUROPEAN RECORDS

Preuschdorf Lutheran KB:
Friedrich Burckhardt, smith at Goersdorf, son of Joh. Christoph Burckhardt and wife Sophia Magdalena Dorothea nee Müller of Preuschdorf, m. 21 May 1726 Maria Dorothea Aniss, daughter of the late Peter Aniss, smith at Preuschdorf.
Marginal note by m. record: "went to the new land."
[Maria Dorothea Aniss was a granddaughter of Peter Anis from Sahnen, Bern [CH-3792 Saanen, BE].
Friedrich Burckhardt and Maria Dorothea had children:
    1. Joh. Christoph b. 25 Mar. 1727, d. 1729
    2. Maria Dorothea b. 14 Apr. 1729, d. 1729
    3. Maria Magdalena b. 27 Feb. 1730, bp. 2 Mar. 1730

AMERICAN RECORDS

New Hanover Lutheran KB, Montgomery co.:
Frederick Burckhart and wife Dorothea had:
    A child (n.n.) b. 27 Sept. 1747, bp. 8 Nov. 1747
    Sp.: Friderich Bender and wife

80. BURCKHARDT, HANS HEINRICH   Preuschdorf=
    _____, 1753   67250 Soultz-sous-Forêts
Not located in S-H
EUROPEAN RECORDS

Preuschdorf Lutheran KB:
Hans Heinrich Burckard, son of Christoph Burckard, citizen, *Gerichtsschöffen* and smith at Preuschdorf m. (1) 5 Feb. 1726 at Lampertsloch [=67250 Soultz-sous-Forêts] Maria Catharina Motz, daughter of Hans Georg Motz, citizen at Lampertsloch. They had:
    1. Catharina Elisabetha b. _ Mar. 1727, bp. 1 Apr. 1727; died.
A marginal note by this first m. in the KB: "she died, he went to the New Land."
Hans Heinrich Burckardt, widower, m. (2) 14 June 1729 Maria Barbara Rössel, daughter of Hans Georg Rössel. Note in KB: "went with all children to the New Land 1753". Children:
    2. Anna Catharina b. 21 July 1729, d. 1730
    3. Hans Stephan b. 18 July 1730, d. 1733
    4. Anna Catharina b. 21 Feb. 1732, bp. 23 Feb. 1732
    5. Eva Margaretha b. 4 July 1734, bp. 11 July 1734
    6. Hans Michel b. 27 Apr. 1736, bp. 28 Apr. 1736

7. Georg Heinrich b. 9 Sept. 1737, d. 1738. (Entry faded)
8. Georg Friedrich b. 26 May 1739, died
9. Joh. Heinrich b. 28 July 1740, d. 1749
10. Hans Georg b. 8 July 1743, bp. 10 July 1743
11. Anna Maria b. 23 June 1745, d. 1751

The Preuschdorf parish records include the
nearby villages of Goersdorf, Mitschdorf, and
Lampertsloch. The records date from 1659.

81. BURGHARDT, GEORG age 56   Preuschdorf=
Loyal Judith, 1732   67250 Soultz-sous-Forêts
S-H, I: 88, 90, 91

EUROPEAN RECORDS

Preuschdorf Lutheran KB:
Johann Georg Burckardt, herdsman at Preuschdorf, m. __ Feb. 1711
Catharina, daughter of the late Andreas Beurlin, former citizen at Ingweiler
[=67340 Ingwiller]. Children:
1. Catharina b. 28 Jan. 1712, d. aged 9 days
2. Joh. Wilhelm b. __ July 1713, d. 12 Aug. 1713
3. Maria Barbara b. 15 Apr. 1715
4. Johann Georg b. 8 Jan. 1718
5. Johann Heinrich b. 19 July 1720, d. y.
6. Anna Catharina b. 15 Sept. 1722, d. y.
7. Johann Philip b. 22 Jan. 1724
   One of his sp. was Philip Jacob Acker [q.v.],
   son of Heinrich Acker of Preuschdorf.
8. Elisabetha Margaretha b. 8 Dec. 1725
9. Maria Dorothea b. 19 Jan. 1727
10. Joh. Jacob, twin, b. 21 July 1729, d. 11 Mar. 1731
11. Maria Catharina, twin, b. 21 July 1729, d. 7 Dec. 1729
    One of her sp. was Maria Dorothea, wife of Friedrich
    Burckardt [q.v.]

AMERICAN RECORDS

New Hanover Lutheran KB, Montgomery co.:
Georg Burckhard d. 19 Apr. 1745, aged 69 y.

The mother of Georg Burghart d. 31 Jan. 1748, aged 69 y.

Anna Barbara, dau. of Georg Burckhard, d. 25 Dec. 1747.

Anna Maria Burckhard d. 3 Jan. 1748.

Catharine Burghart d. 30 Sept. 1748, aged 59 y.

Conf. 1754 - Elisabetha Catharina, daughter of Jürg Burckhard, age 14.
Conf. 1756 - David, son of Jürg Burchard, in his 14th year.
Conf. 1756 - Anna Maria, daughter of Jürg Burchardt, 15 years.
Conf. 1759 - Barbara, daughter of Jürg Burchardt, in her 14th year.

New Hanover Lutheran KB, Montgomery co.:
Several Georg Burckharts appear in the bp. records of this congregation:

Georg Burckhardt and wife Maria Margaretha have children in 1745 and 1747.

Georg Burckhart and wife Maria Frederica had a child in 1745.

Georg Burckard and wife Maria Fronica had 2 children 1759 and 1762.

Philadelphia Adm. F: 210: estate # 11, 1748:
Estate of Catharine Burkhard. Adm. Bond on 31 Oct. 1748 to George Burckhard, Mardin Bitting, David Jaag, all of the county of Philadelphia. Georg Burckhard was named adm. of the estate of his mother Cathrina Burchard, deceased. The inventory of her estate was dated 1 Nov. 1748 and signed by Martin Bitting and David (X) Jag.

Philadelphia Will Book M: 311: estate # 178, 1762:
Will of Philip Burkart (Burckhart), prob. 2 June 1762. Wife: Barbara. Children: Nicholas, Phillip, Daniel, William, Jacob, Michael, Anna, Margret, Dorothea, Mary Elizabeth, Marria Fredrica and "if my wife should be pregnant then it shall have an equal share." Wit.: Johannes Gamber, Rufinus Scherer, Wm. Clampffer.

Account of Barbara Burkart, ex. of Philip Burkart, deceased. filed 17 Dec. 1763. Inventory dated 16 Dec. 1763: (1) a frame house, 2 story (built this 17 years) situated in Quarry St. adj. house of Conrad Schweitzers; (2) another lot and frame house ajd. the house of John Kuhn on said street, but built by the widow; inventory also mentions other interesting items including one book of sermon and an old Bible; one old gun with a bayonet; one book called *Die Sterbens Kunst* in English *The Dying Art*; and a note that the inventory does not include four articles her son Jacob Miller had borrowed and are yet in his hands. (One of the appraisers was a Jacob Miller.)

A John Philip Burkhard and a Geo. Burkhard nat. 10 Apr. 1760, no residence given.

82. CARLE, ELIZABETH   Mattstall=
Samuel, 1733   67510 Lembach
S-H, I: 108
[appears on list as Elizabeth Kollren age 50]

EUROPEAN RECORDS

Matstall Lutheran KB:
Elisabeth, daughter of the late Christian Carle (originally from CH-3753
Diemtigen, BE) was a sp. in 1727 for Johann Daniel Haller, son of Hennrich
Haller and his wife Anna Catharina nee Carle [q.v.]. She arrived with the
Haller family on the *Samuel* in 1733. There is no marriage or death record
for her in Mattstall.

83. CARLE, JOHANN THEOBALD   Hirschland=
Robert and Alice, 1739   67320 Drulingen
S-H, I: 264, 271
[Appears on A list as Hans Leobald Karli, on C list as Dewald (D) Carel].

EUROPEAN RECORDS

Diedendorf Reformed KB:
Johann Carle, citizen and shoemaker at Burbach [=67260 Sarre-Union], m.
6 Sept. 1708 Maria, daughter of Melchior Weiss, linenweaver in Niderstensel
[Niderstinzel=57930 Fénétrange]. Children:
　1. Johann Heinrich bp. 24 May 1711
　2. Johann Theobald bp. 26 Feb. 1713
　3. Gertrud bp. 5 Mar. 1715
　4. Johann Theobald bp. 30 Mar. 1717 in Hirschland.
　　Sp.: Johann Jacob son of Johann Frölich, Hirschland; Frantz
　　Ludwig, son of Joh. Peter Ponsin, church *censor* in Burbach;
　　Elisabetha, daughter of Melchior Weiss, inhabitant at
　　Niderstinsel.
　5. Catharina Elisabetha b. ca. 1720

AMERICAN RECORDS

Old Goshenhoppen Lutheran KB, Family Register:
Valentin Nungässer m. 3 Mar. 1743 Catharina Elisabetha Carl, born about
Michaelmas, 1720. Her father: Joh. Carl; her mother: Anna Maria, of
Hirschland "in Nassauischen".

Longswamp Reformed KB, Longswamp twp., Berks co.:
Theobald Carl and wife Anna Maria nee Meer had children:
  1. Anna Maria b. 16 Jan. 1744
     Sp.: Leobolt Greber [q.v.] and wife Anna Maria
  2. Catharina b. 1 July 1746
  3. Peter b. 11 Apr. 1748
     one of the sp. was Adam Göry [see Geri].
  4. Johannes b. 5 Mar. 1750
  5. Elisabeth b. 20 Oct. 1752; Sp.: Elisabeth Göry
  6. Georg b. 10 Feb. 1754
  7. Michael b. 16 Mar. 1756
     Sp.: Michael Bieber [q.v.] and Maria Burger
  8. Theobald b. 1 July 1758
  9. Jacob b. 1 Dec. 1760
  10. Niclas b. 15 Mar. [1764]
     Sp. for last two children were Jacob Weimer [q.v.]
     and wife Maria Salome.

Berks co. wills:
Theobald Carl, Longswamp twp. 25 Feb. 1799-3 Feb. 1800.
All est. to wife Anna Maria; at her decease, est. divided among children in
equal parts. Children of deceased daughter Elisabeth to have her share. Son
George and Samuel Butz, exrs. Wit.: Michael Dress, Adam Helwig.

84. CHRIST, HEINRICH   67690 Hatten
Pennsylvania Merchant, 1732
S-H, I: 66, 67, 69, 70
[appears on list as Christen]
   with Anna Christen, Margaret, Magdalen, Jerich, Hendrick, Eva,
Catharine, Salme, Maria

                        EUROPEAN RECORDS

Hatten Lutheran KB:
Joh. Heinrich Christ, single cooper, born in Switzerland, Canton Bern, two
hours from Araw [CH-5000 Aarau, AG], son of the late Joh. Heinrich
Christ, former citizen at Niederseebach [= 67160 Wissembourg], in the
Baronie Fleckenstein, m. 8 Jan. 1715 Anna Götz, daughter of the late Joh.
Jacob Götz, here in Hatten. Children:
     1. Catharina Margaretha b. 5 Oct. 1715
     2. Maria Magdalena b. 23 Feb. 1717
     3. Joh. Georg b. 13 Aug. 1718
     4. Joh. Heinrich b. 26 Jan. 1721

5. Maria Eva b. 30 Nov. 1722
6. Maria Catharina b. 16 Mar. 1725
7. Maria Salome b. 21 Sept. 1726
8. Anna Maria b. 27 Nov. 1728
9. Andreas b. 16 Nov. 1730

AMERICAN RECORDS

Rev. John Casper Stoever's Records:
Heinrich Christ and Eva Kuhn sp. a child of Joh. Michael Henninger [q.v.] in 1736.

Moselem Lutheran KB, Berks co.:
Christian Jace (Jacki), single son of Christian Jace, m. 11 Nov. 1745 Maria Catharina Christ, daughter of Christian Heinrich Christ.

Johan Heinrich Christ, Jr., single son of Joh. Heinrich Christ, Sr., m. 25 Jan. 1748 Apollonia Richter, single daughter of the late Johannes Richter.

Maria Magdalena nee Christ, wife of Johannes Scheurer, is mentioned in the record in 1744.

Heinrich Christ and wife Apollonia had:
1. Anna Barbara b. 30 Dec. 1748, bp. 1 Jan. 1749

Anna Maria, nee Christ, mentioned as wife of George Wagner in 1749.

Trinity Lutheran KB, Reading, Berks co.:
Joh. Heinr. Christ and wife Apollonia had:
Johannes b. 25 Apr. 1766, bp. 7 June 1766

Died 13 Aug 1789: Heinrich Christ, Sr., Esq., age 68 y. 6 mo. 2 weeks 3 days.

Died 8 July 1805: Appollonia Christ, widow of Heinr. Christ, nee Richter; born in Hatten, bp. 30 Jan. 1721 [Note by compiler: it was her husband who was born in Hatten and bp. 30 Jan. 1721]. Her age about 84 years, 6 months.

Susanna Christ, daughter of Henerich Christ of Reading, m. 9 Mar. 1779 Friedrich Gossler, son of Hener. Gossler.

Jacob Christ, second son of Henr. Christ, Esq. of Reading, m. 27 Sept. 1785 Susanna Gross, daughter of the late Joh. Gross of Maxatawny.

Daniel Christ, youngest son of Henrich Christ of Reading, m. 25 Apr. 1790 Catharina Miller, oldest daughter of Philip Miller.

Henry Christ, Jr. and wife Catharina had children:
1. Johannes b. 27 Mar. 1776, bp. 28 Apr. 1776
2. Benjamin b. 11 Aug. 1782, bp. __ Nov. 1783
   Sp.: Heinrich Christ, Sr.
Died 24 Dec. 1784- Joh. Heinrich Christ, Jr. aged 29 y., 10 m., 3 weeks, 5 days; he leaves a widow Catharina nee Schumacher and 3 minor sons.

Berks co. Wills and Adm.:
Henry Christ, Reading : adm. granted on 5 Sept. 1789 to Appolonia, the widow, Jacob Christ a son, and Jacob Graul, son-in-law.

Appolonia Christ, widow, Reading: adm. granted on 21 Feb. 1806 to Samuel Grauel, a grandson.

85. CHRIST, JACOB age 54   Gosselming=
    CHRIST, MARCUS age 17   57930 Fénétrange
Richard and Elizabeth, 1733
S-H, I: 127, 129, 130
   other passenger on ship: Magdalena Christ age 44

EUROPEAN RECORDS

Diedendorf Reformed KB:
Jacob Christ, son of Niclaus Christ, from Rockwill [CH-4914 Roggwil, BE], now residing at Goselmingen [Gosselming= 57930 Fénétrange], m. 28 Jan. 1709 Magdalena, daughter of Durst Schwab residing at the *Bettlinger Weyer by Saarburg,* born in Eberweil, Graffschaft Buren [possibly CH-8925 Ebertswil, ZH]. Children:
1. possibly Maria Magdalena b. ca 1710, conf. 1724 [parents not given in confirmation record; bp. not located]
2. Johann Jacob bp. 15 Dec. 1711 in Diedendorf.
3. Margaretha Christina bp. 22 Jan. 1713, d. 1714
4. **Johann Marx** bp. 21 Dec. 1714
   Sp.: Johann Georg Urich, citizen and smith at Vinstingen [=57930 Fénétrange]; Herr Marx Weiss, schoolmaster and *Vorsinger* in Diedendorf; Magdalena Pons, wife of Jacob L'Amy, *Rebman* in the *Schloss* in Diedendorff.

AMERICAN RECORDS

Moselem Lutheran KB, Berks co.:
Marcus Christ and wife Maria Apolonia, nee Haas, had a daughter:
Anna Margaret b. 1 Dec. 1743, bp. Rogate 1744.

Johannes Scheurer [q.v.] and wife Maria Magdalena, nee Christ, had a daughter:
Anna Margaret b. 28 Feb. 1744, bp. Rogate 1744.

86. CLAUSS, ADAM　　　　　　　　　　　　　　　　Volksberg=
Ship data not located　　　　　　　　　　67290 Wingen-sur-Moder
After 1748- before 1757

EUROPEAN RECORDS

Waldhambach Lutheran KB:
Johann Matthias Clauss of Volksberg and wife Maria Elisabetha nee Fleckenstein had a son:
Hans Adam b. 1 Apr. 1725, conf. 1738
He last appears in the Waldhambach KB as a sponsor in 1748.

AMERICAN RECORDS

Charles Roberts et al, *History of Lehigh County, Pennsylvania,* **Vol. III:** 187:
"Adam Clauss of Lynn township, who appears to have been a relative of George, Sr., and John, Sr., of Bethlehem township, was probably attracted to Lynn by the settlement there of Moravian families. As early as 1757 he was a resident of Lynn township, as on July 9, of that year, one of his children was killed by Indians. This melancholy affair happened while three or four neighbors were cutting Adam Clauss' corn, and as they were eating their dinner they were fallen upon by a party of savages. Two men, two women, and one girl escaped; but two men, three women, and children were killed. This occurred four miles from Fort Everett and near what is now Lynnport and the Indians were pursued by Lieutenant Jacob Wetherhold and seven men for four miles, when they came upon nine Indians, who shot at them. The lieutenant shot one and wounded another. The rest escaped in the thick forest, but the soldiers secured a mare and two saddles, bridle and halter, a keg of liquor, and cloth and a brass kettle and four Indian cakes baked in the ashes of wheat meal."

"Adam Clauss was taxed in Lynn township in 1762, £9. He secured 136 acres by warrant in 1767. He was still living in 1781."

Rev. Daniel Schumacher's records:
Adam Clauss and wife Anna Maria were sp. for a child of Johann Jürg
Sprecher in Linn twp., 1760. They were sp. for a child of Johann Jacob
Hoffmann in Linn twp. in 1759.

Adam Klauss, Lynn twp., Northampton co., nat. Autumn, 1765.

87. CLAUS, CHRISTINA   Volksberg=
CLAUS, GEORG   67290 Wingen-sur-Moder
CLAUS, JOHANNES
Phoenix, 1750
S-H, I: 442
                          EUROPEAN RECORDS

Waldhambach Lutheran KB:
Johannes Clauss and Christina nee Seyfried [her name also given as Sybart
in some records] had children:
    1. Johannes b. 6 May 1717, d. 16 Apr. 1721
    2. Anna Maria b. 2 Oct. 1719, d. 16 Apr. 1721
    3. **Johann Georg** b. 26 Feb. 1722, conf. 1735
    4. Christina Sophia b. 24 Nov. 1724, conf. 1738
       She m. 1748 Johann Christian Giess [q.v.]
    5. Maria Eva b. 30 Oct. 1727
    6. **Johannes** b. 14 Feb. 1734, conf. 1749
    7. Jeremias b. 15 Sept. 1737

Johannes Clauss d. 27 Dec. 1748, age 59 years less 12 days.
[His widow Christina emigrated with the surviving children.]

Johann Georg Claus of Volksberg and wife Anna Christina nee Kühn had
children:
    1. Anna Christina b. 1 Jan. 1746, d. 18 Jan. 1746
    2. Johann Georg b. 17 Mar. 1747
    3. Johann Philipp b. 13 Feb. 1749

                          AMERICAN RECORDS

Emmaus Moravian KB, Northampton co.:
Georg Claus and wife Christina had children:
    4. Philipp b. 23 Dec. 1751, bp. 3 Jan. 1752
    5. Maria Christina b. 10 Feb. 1755, bp. 11 Feb. 1755
    6. Anna Catharina b. 18 June 1756, bp. 21 June 1756
    7. Anna Maria b. 18 Jan. 1759, bp. 19 Jan. 1759

Johann Claus and wife Catharina had:
>   1. Johann Georg b. 16 Nov. 1762, bp. 17 Nov. 1762
>   one of the sponsors was the widow Christina Claus.

Schoeneck Moravian Graveyard, Upper Nazareth twp., Northampton co.:
John George Clauss, born in Alsace 28 Feb. 1722, d. 12 Feb. 1763.

Old Moravian Cemetery, Bethlehem, PA:
Christina Claus, 1695-1775, born at Rosteig, Alsace. Her husband, John Claus, departed this life in 1748, whereupon she emigrated to America to find religious liberty. Her son, J. George, lived near Bethlehem.

Eva Lorenz, m. n. Clauss, 1727-1811, from the Alsace. She came to Pennsylvania in 1751 with her mother, in order to escape compulsory conversion to the Romish Church. She was married to Geo. N. Lorenz of Schoeneck, who bought a farm near Bethlehem.

Northampton Co. Wills:
John George Clowse, Bethlehem twp., farmer; 5 Feb. 1763 - 28 Feb. 1763.
Wife: Christina. Children: George, minor, and other children (not named).
Exrs: Wife Christina and William Edmonds of Bethlehem.
Wit: Ephriam Colvil, Andreas Folk.

John Clauss, Bethlehem twp., yeoman; 13 Dec. 1794 - 24 Feb. 1796.
Wife: Elizabeth. Children: George, Henry, Philip, John, Abraham, Daniel and Mary. Exrs: Son Henry and Thomas Hartman.
Wit: Thomas Hartman, Samuel Coleman, Michael Koehler.

Additional data on the Clauss family may be found in **Charles Roberts et al,** *History of Lehigh County, Pennsylvania,* **Vol. III,** pg. 186-187.

John Clowes, Allen twp., Northampton co., nat. Autumn, 1765.

88. CLOR, JACOB   Keffenach=
_____, 1749   67250 Soultz-sous-Forêts

EUROPEAN RECORDS

Hunspach Reformed KB:
Jacob Clor, a linenweaver, son of Peter Clor, citizen at Keffenach, m. 28 Feb. 1747 Elisabetha, dau. of Jacob Steinmann from Breidenacker Hoff.
>   [No children recorded in this KB]

Zweibrücken Manumissions Protocoll, Cleeburg, 1749:
Jacob Clor of Bremmelbach [= 67160 Wissembourg] moves with wife and one child to America.

89. CONRAD, GEORG   Mietesheim=
CONRAD, JACOB   67580 Mertzwiller
St. Andrew Galley, 1737
S-H, I: 179, 181, 184

EUROPEAN RECORDS

Mietesheim Lutheran KB:
Hans Cunrad, son of Hans Cunrad, m. 24 June 1703 Fronic(a), daughter of Jacob Staub. They had children:
1. Elisabeth b. 20 Apr. 1704
2. **Joh. Georg** b. 5 Jan. 1706, bp. 6 Jan. 1706
3. Maria Elisabetha b. 20 Nov. 1708
4. Anna b. 18 Oct. 1710
5. Johann b. 27 Dec. 1713
6. **Johann Jacob** b. 2 Feb. 1717, bp. 4 Feb. 171

The father's occupation is given as swineherder in several entries.

AMERICAN RECORDS

Heidelberg Moravian KB, Berks co., family register:
Jacob Conrad was born in Mietesheim in Lower Alsace on 3 Feb. 1717 and baptized at the same place the next day. The sponsors were Jacob Rebmann from Merzweiler and Anna Catharina Scheffer, Matthaus Scheffer's wife from Uhrweiler. His father was (name not recorded). He was married in January 1741 by Pastor Conrad Tempelman of the Reformed church in Warwick, to Miss Maria Catharina Reyer, daughter of Bastian Reyer, citizen of Behl near Landau [W-6737 Böhl-Iggelheim] in the Palatinate and his wife Agnes. Maria Catharina was born Sept. 23, 1725 in the Palatinate. [He d. 5 Sept. 1798; she d. 8 Mar. 1797]. They had children:
1. Jacob b. Jan. 1742 in Warwick, Lancaster co. Died beginning of Mar. 1742.
2. Christian b. Jan. 1743, died.
3. Christian, b. in Quittopehille, Lancaster co., 13 Dec. 1744
4. Johannes, b. in Heidelberg, Lancaster co., 15. Jan. 1747, bp. 25 Jan. 1747.
5. Maria, b. in Heidelberg, Lancaster co. 5 Mar. 1749, bp. 9 Apr. 1749. She d. 4 Aug. 1757.

6. Johann Jacob, b. 7 Sept. 1751, old style, in Heidelberg, Lancaster co., bp. 24 Sept. 1751.
7. Johann Heinrich, b. 25 May 1753 in Heidelberg, bp. 29 May 1753 He d. in Bern twp. 17 Aug. 1754.
8. Elisabeth, b. 8 Oct. 1755, bp. 12 Oct. 1755, died 19 Nov. 1755 and was buried on our God's acre in Heidelberg the following day.
9. Johann Heinrich Conrath, b. 9 Nov. 1756, bp. 12 Nov. 1756. He d. 7 July 1757.
10. Joseph b. 6 Jan. 1759, bp. 7 Jan. 1759
11. Friedrich, b. 31 Mar. 1761, bp. 9 Apr. 1761; Died 7 Nov. 1761.
12. Elisabeth b. 1 Jan. 1763, bp. 2 Jan. 1763, died.
13. Friedrich, b. 18 Aug. 1764 and on account of weakness was bp. soon after birth. The child died 18 hours old.
14. Gottfried, b. 24 Feb. 1744, died.

Berks co. Wills and Administrations:
Jacob Conrad, Bern twp.; 18 Mar. 1797 - 26 Sept. 1798.
Names sons Christian, Johannes, Jacob, and Joseph. Names granddaughter Elisabeth, daughter of son Joseph.
Exrs: Peter Kerschner and Christian Reyer.
Wit: Conrad Christ and John Bright.

Warwick Lutheran KB, Brickerville, Lancaster co.:
One Joh. Georg Conradt had a son:
> Johannes b. 5 Sept. 1757, bp. 18 Sept. 1757
> Sp.: Johannes Mor and wife Susanna

Another Görg Conrad with wife Catharina appears in Rev. Jacob Lischy's records in York Co., having children 1744-1750.

90. CULMANN, PHILIPP Hermerswiller=
Hamilton, 1767 67250 Soultz-sous-Forêts
S-H, I: 717
EUROPEAN RECORDS

Birlenbach Reformed KB:
Philipp Culmann, son of the late Caspar Culmann, former citizen at Hermersweiler, m. 2 Dec. 1754 Margaretha, daughter of Philipp Clauss, citizen at Hoffen [=67250 Soultz-sous-Forêts].

Rott Lutheran KB:
Philipp Culmann and wife Margaretha nee Claus had:

1. Johann Georg b. 10 Apr. 1755, bp. 12 Apr. 1755
2. Philipp Heinrich b. 4 Jan. 1757 bp. 7 Jan. 1757
3. Johann Georg b. 23 Aug. 1758, bp. 25 Aug. 1758

91. CUNTZ, HANS GEORG age 55   Preuschdorf=
CUNTZ, HANS GEORG age 19   67250 Soultz-sous-Forêts
Loyal Judith, 1732
S-H, I: 88, 90, 92

EUROPEAN RECORDS

Preuschdorf Lutheran KB:
Michell Cuntz, son of Peter Cuntz from Ober<u>bach</u>? *in der Obermarg-graffschafft Durlach,* m. 23 Jan. 1672 Margretha, daughter of Arbogast Schäffer, citizen here.
[There is a gap in the baptismal record from 1674-1683].

Hans Georg Cuntz, son of Michel Cuntz, citizen at Preuschdorf m. __ Nov. 1703 Margaretha, daughter of Hans Biebel, *Gerichtsschöffen* at Goerstdorf [Goersdorf]. They had children:
     1. Joh. Georg b. 17 Jan. 1706, died
     2. Maria Barbara b. __ Mar. 1708. She m. 1725 Hans Dreher
        [see emigrant Georg Dreher].
The first wife died in 1711.
Hans Georg Cuntz, widower at Preuschdorf, m. (2) __ Aug. 1712 Catharina, daughter of Georg Schwanger, citizen at __ Lusan, *Fleckensteinischen Herrschafft.* [Notation in KB by marriage record: "Went to the new land."]
They had children:
     3. Joh. Georg b. 5 May 1713, bp. 6 May 1713
     4. Joh. Jacob b. 5 July 1715, died 1717
     5. Hans Diebold b. 25 May 1720
     6. Joh. Michel b. 2 Oct. 1722, died 1723
     7. Elisabetha b. 2 May 1724
     8. Joh. Martin b. 8 Nov. 1726
     9. Anna Margretha b. 4 Nov. 1729
     10. Joh. Philip b. 2 Mar. 1732

AMERICAN RECORDS

Frederick Lutheran KB, Frederick co., MD:
Georg Kuntz had:
     Johann Martin b. 22 Jan. 1749, bp. 2 Apr. 1749
     Sp.: Martin Wetzel [q.v.] and wife

Philipp Kuntz had:
>Jacob b. 14 Sept. 1754, bp. 6 Sept [read Oct.] 1754
>Sp.: Andreas Berger and daughter
>Christina, widow of Henrici Faurtne.

92. CUNTZ, HANS MICHAEL
possibly: *Dragon,* 17 Oct. 1749
S-H, I: 423 or
Phoenix, 1750
S-H, I: 440 with Dewald Kuntz

Preuschdorf=
67250 Soultz-sous-Forêts

EUROPEAN RECORDS

Preuschdorf Lutheran KB:
Hans Diebold Cuntz of Preuschdorf, *Herrschafflichen Jäger,* m. (1) Anna Catharina ? Reinbold. She died in 1685. He m. (2) Anna Logel. She d. 20 Feb. 1729, age 61 years. A son of the second marriage was:
>Hans Michael Cuntz b. __ Dec. 1710

Hans Michael Cuntz, son of Theobald Cuntz, m. 9 May 1730 Anna Eva Bender, daughter of Hans Jacob Bender, forester at Langensoultzbach. Notation in KB, by marriage entry: "went to the new land." They had children:
>1. Anna Catharina b. 4 Nov. 1731, bp. 6 Nov. 1731
>2. Hans Theobald b. 10 Nov. 1733, died 1733
>3. Joh. Theobald b. 11 Dec. 1734, bp. 13 Dec. 1734
>4. Hans Georg b. 12 May 1736, bp. 14 May 1736

Langensoultzbach Lutheran KB:
Hans Michel Cuntz, citizen and farmer at Sultzbach, and wife Anna Eva nee Bender, had:
>5. Johann Jacob b. 27 Sept. 1738, bp. 24 Sept. 1738
>6. Johann Michael b. 15 Nov. 1740, died 1741
>7. Johann Bartholomäus b. 16 Apr. 1742
>8. Johann Daniel b. 1 Oct. 1747, bp. 3 Oct. 1747

AMERICAN RECORDS

St. Michael's and Zion KB, Philadelphia:
One Eva Kuntz sp. a child of Johan Jacob Raht in Feb. 1749
One Michael Kuntz was a witness to marriages in Philadelphia in 1749, 1751 and 1753.
One Michael Kuntz m. 7 Jan 1753 (name of bride not given).

Jordan Lutheran KB, Lehigh co:
Dewald Cuntz and wife Anna Maria had children:
1. Johannes b. 31 Mar. 1753
2. Philip Jacob b. 6 Dec. 1755
3. Georg Friedrich b. 22 Dec. 1759
4. Johann Philip b. 3 May 1762
5. Johann Henrich b. 22 Mar. 1766
   All bp. 27 Mar. 1766, Sp.: Georg Matz & wife Dorothea
   [see also Hans Diebold Cuntz b. 25 May 1720 son of 1732
   immigrant Hans Georg Cuntz].

Theobold Kuntz and wife Margaretha had:
1. Theobold b. 30 Sept. 1777, bp. 19 Oct. 1777
   Sp.: Georg Frederich Kuntz & Elisabeth Steininger
2. Elisabeth b. 15 Mar. 1782, bp. 29 Mar. 1782
   Sp.: Johan Philip Kunze & Elisabeth Steininger
3. Maria twin b. 13 Sept. 1787
4. Margaretha twin b. 13 Sept. 1787
(Many other Kuntz entries in record).

Hocker, *German Settlers of Pennsylvania:*
Newspaper dated 9 Nov. 1759: Dewald Kuntz, Macungie twp. (Lehigh co.)

Muhlenberg's Journals, I: 582:
13 Dec. 1762 - Visit from Michael Kuhntz.

Another Dewaldt Kuntz appears in **Rev. Daniel Schumacher's records:**
Dewaldt Kuntz and wife Catharina had children:
1. Elisabetha Barbara bp. 12 Sept. 1762, bp. 17 days old,
   in Allemangel.
2. Eva Maria b. 2 May 1764, bp. 8 July 1764 in Allemangel
3. Johann Frantz b. 29 Sept. 1766, bp. 2 Nov. 1766 in
   Allemangel. Sp.: Johannes Frantz, Barbara Stambach.
4. Maria Barbara bp. 21 May 1769, 9 days old.
   Sp.: Philip Probst and Maria Barbara.

93. CUNTZ, PETER age 47   Preuschdorf=
Samuel, 1733   67250 Soultz-sous-Forêts
S-H, I: 106, 110, 112 [Coonts on A list]
   with Maria Barbella age 45; Maria Barbella age 19; Michall age 13; Hans
Jerick age 9; Maria Crete age 7; Maria Catharina age 5.

EUROPEAN RECORDS

Preuschdorf Lutheran KB:
Michel Cuntz and wife Margretha nee Schäffer had a son:
 Peter b. __ July 1687

Peter Cuntz, son of the late Michael Cuntz of Preuschdorf m. 9 Feb. 1712
Maria Barbara Clauss, daughter of the late Phillips Clauss of Preuschdorf.
Notation in KB by marriage record: "went to the new land." They had
children [surname spelled Kuntz in some records]:
 1. Joh. Georg b. __ Dec. 1712, died
 2. Maria Barbara b. 25 Mar. 1714, bp. 26 Mar. 1714
 3. Joh. Stephan b. __ Feb. 1716, died 1717
 4. Maria Margaretha b. 6 Apr. 1718, died 1723
 5. Hans Michel b. 13 Dec. 1719, bp. 17 Dec. 1719
 6. Maria Dorothea b. 14 May 1722, died
 7. Hans Georg b. 11 Mar. 1724, bp. 13 Mar. 1724
 8. Anna Margretha b. __ Mar. 1726
 9. Maria Catharina b. 4 May 1728, bp. 6 May 1728

Maria Barbara Clauss was a daughter of Phillip Clauss of Preuschdorf, who
m. at Wörth in 1681 Anna Dorothea Jacobs, daughter of Hans Jacobs,
Gerichtsschöffen at Preuschdorf.

CUNTZ, see also KUNTZ

94. DAMRONG, HANS JACOB (sick)   Langensoultzbach=
Samuel, 1733   67360 Woerth
S-H, I: 106, 107, 109
 [apppears on list as Hans Jacob Tamooroon with
 Barbara and Hans Michael]

EUROPEAN RECORDS

Langensoultzbach Lutheran KB:
Hanns Christoph Damrong, citizen at Sultzbach, and wife Maria Gertruda
nee Weiss had a son:
 Johann Jacob b 11 Nov. 1697

AMERICAN RECORDS

St. Michael's and Zion KB, Philadelphia:
Buried 15 Mar. 1771: Jacob Tameron from Muestrom?, Grafschaft Hanau
in Elsass; b. 1700; came here 37 years ago; first settled between Philadelphia

and Germantown, later lived in Tewksbury twp. in Jersey. Had a son Michael in Phildadelphia.

95. DÄRENDINGER, JOHANNES   Ingolsheim=
DÄRENDINGER, JOHANNES, JR.   67250 Soultz-sous-Forêts
John and Elizabeth, 1754
S-H, I: 667, 669, 671

EUROPEAN RECORDS

Hunspach Reformed KB:
Hans Därendinger, son of Urs Dären(din)ger, inhabitant of ?Klingen, Herrschafft Gugenberg, Solothurn Geb. [? CH-4524 Günsberg, SO], m. 17 Feb. 1722 Catharina, daughter of Michel Hüller, citizen and inhabitant at Ingelsheim. Children:
1. Anna Catharina b. 22 Nov. 1722, bp. 29 Nov. 1722;
   she m. 1746 Henrich Heckmann [q.v.]
2. Maria Margaretha b. 1 June 1724; m. 1750 Jacob Ganther [q.v.]
3. Hans Michel b. 15 July 1728, bp. 18 July 1728, conf. 1743
4. Johannes b. 7 Sep. 1732, bp. 14 Sept. 1732, conf. 1748

Died 11 Mar. 1748- Anna Catharina, wife of Johannes Dörredinger, *des Gerichts* at Ingelsheim; age 51 y. 6 m. and several days.
Johannes Döredinger, widower, citizen and *des Gerichts* at Ingelsheim, m. (2) 1 Dec. 1750 Agatha, widow of the late Georg ?Keusch, former citizen at Ingelsheim.

Zweibrücken Manumissions Protocoll, 1754:
Johannes Daerendinger of Ingelsheim leaves with his family, one son and two daughters, for America.

AMERICAN RECORDS

First Reformed KB, Lancaster:
John Derendinger m. 26 Aug. 1766 Margaret Carl.
Christian Kautz m. 22 May 1785 Elizabeth Darretinger.
Michael Derretinger m. 23 Mar. 1792 Margaret Mayer.

96. DETTWEILER, CATHARINA   Bischtroff-sur-Sarre=
Ship data unknown   67260 Sarre-Union
before 1759   Bütten=
                                       67430 Diemeringen

EUROPEAN RECORDS

Pisdorf [Bischtroff] Lutheran KB:
Philipp Dettweiler and wife Dorothea had:
    Maria Cathrina b. 26 Dec. 1734 in Pistorff
    She was conf. 1750 in Bütten.

Joh. Philipp Dettweiler was the schoolteacher in Bütten and appears in the records there from 1750 to 1762.

AMERICAN RECORDS

Trinity Lutheran KB, Lancaster:
Georg Richter, carpenter, m. 2 Oct. 1759 at Lancaster Catharina Dettweyler of Bütten in Saarbrucken.

97. DIEFFENBACH, BALTHASER   Oberseebach=
Jeneffer, 1764   67160 Wissembourg
S-H, I: 700 [appears on list as B. Dieffenbach]

EUROPEAN RECORDS

Oberseebach KB: Catholic, Lutheran, and Reformed entries all combined in one KB, with the entries recorded in Latin:
Henrich Tieffenbach, Lutheran, and wife Barbara, Reformed, had:
    1. Johannes Henricus bp. 1 Oct. 1725; conf. 1740 at Hunspach
    2. Johannes Martinus bp. 7 June 1728; conf. 1743 at Rott
    3. Christophorus bp. 10 Apr. 1732; conf. 1746 at Rott
    4. Maria Margaretha bp. __ Nov. 1734
    5. Johannes Georgius bp. 19 Oct. 1737; conf. 1752 at Hunspach
    6. Johannes Wendelinus bp. 29 Nov. 1740; conf. 1755, Hunspach
    7. Johannes Balthasar bp. 5 Jan. 1743; conf. 1757 at Hunspach
        Sp.: Johannes Balthasar Vieth; Barbara Erismann
    8. Anna Maria bp. 7 May 1748

Hunspach Reformed KB and Rott Reformed KB:
Heinrich Tieffenbach of Seebach, had children conf. in these two KB as noted above.

AMERICAN RECORDS

Extracts from the *Memorandum Buch* of Rev. Henry Diefenbach, Hinke collection, Philip Schaff Library, Lancaster:
    "Johann Balthasar Diefenbach was my father. He was born in Deutschland, in Elsass, in the Dorf Obersebach. His parents were Henrich

Diefenbach and his second wife Cathrina. His grandfather was Jacob Diefenbach from the Pfaltz.

My grandfather Henrich had with his first wife 3 sons but no daughters. With his second wife he also had 3 sons of whom my father was the youngest. Also, my father had one sister, and this child died of the measles.

My father was born 8 Jan. 1743 and came to America when he was 21 years old, arriving in 1764. He already had a half-brother in America named Christoph Diefenbach [q.v.]. Also, his father's brother lived in Baltimore, a smith by occupation. [note by compiler: a Michael Dieffenbach, inhabitant in Baltimore town was nat. 9 Apr. 1760, colonial MD naturalizations.] He was wealthy, and without male heirs, and requested Baltasar Diefenbach to come to America.

My father's brothers and half-brothers were: Martin, Henrich, Christoph, Wendel, Georg and Joh. Baltasar, this was my father.

Johann Balthasar Diefenbach married Anna Maria Becker in 1768 or 1769. [See Burgert, *Hochstadt Origins* for Becker family data.] They lived two miles from Williamsport and ½ mile from the Batomeck [Potomac] River, eight miles from Hägerstown, Washington co., MD, until 8 Nov. 1784. They moved to VA near Stentaun [Staunton], Augusta co. They had 8 children, 2 died young, a son named David and a daughter Elisabeth. Johann Balthasar Diefenbach died 24 Jan. 1820 at his son George's place near Stentaun [Staunton], age 77 y. 16 days. Anna Maria Becker Diefenbach d. 31 Oct. 1810, aged about 60 years."

Their surviving children were:
1. Catharina b. 11 Apr. 1770. She m. Johann Christoph Kirchhoff, a weaver from Germany. They lived in Rockingham co., VA. 8 children.
2. Henrich b. 5 Dec. 1771, in MD. Lived in VA with his parents, studied with Pastor Willy, became a Reformed minister. Lived in Gilford co, NC. Married Anna Maria Albrecht. Later lived in PA, then to Highland co., OH. 9 children.
3. Anna Maria b. 11 Feb. 1773. [Zion Reformed KB, Hagerstown, MD]. She m. Abraham Maurer. 7 children.
   Anna Maria died 11 June 1837 in Goshkton [Coshocton] co., OH.
4. Johannes b. 3 Nov. 1776. [Zion Reformed KB, Hagerstown, MD] He m. Elisabeth Huckmann. They lived in Augusta co., VA, 4 miles from Stantaun [Staunton]. 9 children.
5. Georg b. 26 Jan. 1779. m. Agnes (Nancy) Maurer. 6 children.
6. Jacob b. 27 Feb. 1784; he also became a Reformed Minister. He m. (1) Lidia Juhs (Hews) and had 3 children.
   [Ebenezer Cemetery Records, Lynn twp., Lehigh co.: Lydia Diefenbach nee Hughsin b. 20 Aug. 1789, d 9 July 1812]
   He m. (2) Sarah Andreas in Blumsburg [Bloomsburg], PA. 3 children. He d. in Aspytown, Columbia co., PA, 13 Apr. 1825.

[The *Memorandum Buch* continues with the names of the children in the next generation, and included in many instances where they lived.]

98. DIEFENBACH, CHRISTOPH   Oberseebach=
Emigration date unknown   67160 Wissembourg

EUROPEAN RECORDS

Rott Reformed KB:
Heinrich Tieffenbach of Seebach had a son:
    Christoph conf. 1746 at Rott

[See immigrant Balthaser Dieffenbach, 1764, for additional family data.]

AMERICAN RECORDS

Rev. Henry Diefenbach's *Memorandum Buch,* in the Hinke collection, Philip Schaff Library, Lancaster:
    "Christoph Diefenbach, my father's half-brother, was a stonecutter in Germany, but in America he was a mason.
    He m. Magdalena Neumann from Hanover, in York co., PA. He had a plantation in Frederick co., MD near the town of Westminister. He had 4 children:
    1. Johannes m. Catharina Baumgärtner
    2. Catharina m. Jacob Utz, a saddler in Westminster
    3. Barbara m. ____ Baumgartner and lived in Standing Stone, PA
    4. Maria also m. a Baumgartner and lived in Standing Stone, PA".

Christian Deefenbach of Germany twp., York co., (PA) German, also referred to as Christopher Deefenbach, nat. 7 May 1767 (Colonial MD Naturalizations).

99. DIEMER, ANDREAS   Griesbach=
Phoenix, 1750   67110 Niederbronn-les-Bains
S-H, I: 440
EUROPEAN RECORDS

Gundershoffen Lutheran KB:
Johann Philipps Diemer, son of Christman Diemer, citizen at Gundershoffen, m. 19 Apr. 1712 Maria, daughter of Magnus Mallo, citizen at Griesbach.

Johann Philipps Diemer, citizen and *Gerichtsschöffen* at Griesbach, and wife
Maria *Magdalena* had a son:
  Andreas b. 30 Nov. 1726, bp. 3 Dec. 1726.

AMERICAN RECORDS

St. Paul's (Blue) Lutheran KB, Upper Saucon twp., Lehigh co.:
Andreas Diemer m. (2) __ 1755 Margaretha, daughter of Christian Naumann
from Dryland. Andreas Diemer and wife Christina Margaretha had children:
  1. Elisabeth Barbara b. 5 Dec. 1756, bp. 10 Dec. 1756
     Sp.: Johann Peter Roth & Elisabeth Barbara Schilp
  2. Philip b. 17 Nov. 1758, bp. 12 Apr. 1759
     Sp.: Nicolaus Schall & Elisabeth Barbara Schilp
  3. Johann Peter b. 20 July 1760, bp. 29 Aug. 1760
     Sp.: John Peter Schilp & Anna Magdalena Fuchs

Emmanuel Reformed KB, Moore twp., Northampton co.:
Andrew Diemer and wife Christina Margaret had:
  4. Maria Magdalena b. 31 Dec. 1766, bp. 5 Mar. 1767
     Sp.: Martin Roer & Maria Magdalena

Dryland Lutheran and Reformed KB, Northampton co.:
Andrew Diemer and Christina Margaret had:
  5. Andrew b. 13 Nov. 1764, bp. 7 Apr. 1765
     Sp.: John Christian Neuman & Anna Magdalena Fuchs
  6. Christine b. 17 Dec. 1768, bp. 12 Mar. 1769
     Sp.: Christian Naumann and wife Anna Maria
  7. Maria Margaret b. 29 Apr. 1770, bp. 1 June 1770
  8. Barbara b. 2 June 1772, bp. 30 Aug. 1772
  9. Anna Elisabetha b. 14 Mar. 1777.

Northampton co. Wills:
Andreas Diemer wit. a will in Moore twp. in 1785. Andreas Deemer was
named as a cousin and executor in the will of Joh. Reinhard Bene [q.v.].
Andreas Diemer was co-exr. in 1777, est. of Nicholas Roth of Moore twp.

100. DOCTOR, MARTIN   Stattmatten=
Halifax, 1752   67770 Sessenheim
S-H, I: 482
                              EUROPEAN RECORDS

Sessenheim Lutheran KB:
Martin Dockter, single fisherman at Stattmatten, son of the late Theobald

Dockter, former *Gerichtsschöffen*, m. 2 June 1723 Maria Magdalena, daughter of the late Abraham Krebs, former tailor at Baltenheim [Baldenheim =67600 Sélestat]. They had a son:

> Johann Martin b. 1 Jan. 1742, bp. same day
> Sp.: Adam Theerhammer of Stattmatt; Heinrich, son of Heinrich Buchman; Barbara, wife of Marx Bohn.

AMERICAN RECORDS

Trinity Lutheran KB, Lancaster:
Martin Doctor from Stattmatten near Fort Louis, m. 9 Nov. 1762 Catharina Stampach, single.

101. DORMEYER, JOHANN JACOB   67430 Diemeringen
DORMEYER, ANDREAS
DORMEYER, JACOB
Neptune, 1752
S-H, I: 493

EUROPEAN RECORDS

Diemeringen Lutheran KB & Dehlingen Lutheran KB:
Joh. Jacob Dormeyer and wife Anna Catharina nee Schönenberger had a son:

> Johann Jacob b. 2 Sept. 1703

Johann Jacob Dormeyer, wagoner of Diemeringen, m. 11 May 1734 at Dehlingen Maria Elisabetha Köppel, dau. of Nickel Köppel of Dehlingen. Children, bp. at Diemeringen:

1. **Johann Andreas** b. 18 Feb. 1735
2. **Johann Jacob** b. 10 Sept. 1736
3. Maria Catharina b. 1 Dec. 1738, d. 16 Oct. 1739
4. Johannes b. 4 Sept. 1740, died
5. Johann Georg b. 21 July 1743
6. Johann Conrad b. 19 June 1745, d. 7 July 1747
7. Maria Salome b. 23 Nov. 1748, d. 15 Feb. 1751

Emigration data from 1763 inventory of Nickel Köppel, Notary Public records of Dehlingen, provided by Dr. Bernd Gölzer:
The daughter (of Nickel Köppel) Maria Elisabetha and her husband Jacob Dormeyer are in America.

Records of Saarwerden county office for Berg und Thal:
Dated 10 Apr. 1769, inventory of Nickel Schönenberger of Bern:
Jacob Dormeyer, the son of Joh. Jacob Dormeyer and Anna Catharina
Schönenberger, is in America.

AMERICAN RECORDS

Rev. Daniel Schumacher's records:
Andreas Dormeier [also Dormeyer, Dohrmeyer] and wife Catharina had:
1. Catharina bp. 6 July 1760 in Egypt
   Sp.: Jacob Dormeier; Jacob Wirth; Eva Schneider;
   Dorothea Andressen
2. Maria Susanna bp. 18 Oct. 1762 in Egypt
   Sp.; Samuel Seger; Jacob Wolff; Maria Susanna Seger;
   Catharina Röder; all married
3. Anna Eva bp. 11 June 1764 in Egypt
   Sp.: Christian Seger, a married man; Anna Eva, wife of
   Samuel Seger.

Jacob Dormeyer and wife Magdalena nee Fritnern had:
   Johann Nicolaus b. 2 Feb. 1765, bp. 10 Mar. 1765 in Egypt.
   Sp.: Johann Nicolaus Hertzog: Jürg Dormeier, single; Maria
   Barbara Nelich, wife of Henrich Nelich; Catharina Andressen, single.

Longswamp Reformed KB, Berks co.:
A Jacob Tornmayer and wife [N.N] had a son:
   Joh. Jacob b. 27 Dec. 1784.

102. DORMEYER, PETER   Dehlingen=
Polly, 1764   67430 Diemeringen
S-H, I: 690
   [appears on list as Beter Thormyer]

EUROPEAN RECORDS

Dehlingen Lutheran KB:
Hans Peter Dormeyer, daylaborer at Dehlingen, m. 22 Feb. 1718 Maria
Elisabetha Nehlich, dau. of Mathias Nehlich. They had:
   1. Johann Georg b. 28 Dec. 1718; conf. 1732. He
      m. 9 July 1748 Maria Magdalena Köppel.
   2. Catharina Barbara b. 19 Nov. 1720; conf. 1734.
   3. Carolina Christina b. 3 May 1723; conf. 1737.
      She m. 8 Nov. 1763 Joh. Leonhard Bauer [q.v.]

4. Johann Adam b. 10 July 1725. He m. 7 Apr. 1750
Anna Ottilia Morlang; d. 1 July 1772 at Diemeringen.
5. Catharina Margaretha b. 20 Apr. 1728; conf. 1742.
She m. 15 Apr. 1764 Conrad Friedrich Bauer [q.v.]
6. **Hans Peter** b. 19 Apr. 1731; conf. 1746.
7. Johann Philipp b. 18 Feb. 1734; conf. 1746.
8. Johann Friedrich b. 20 Aug. 1737, d. 1 July 1738.
9. Catharina m. 17 Feb. 1760 Ludwig Benedict.

AMERICAN RECORDS

Hocker, *German Settlers of Pennsylvania:*
Philadelphische Correspondenz, newspaper dated 3 June 1783:
Leonhard Bauer seeks information about his wife's brother, Peter Dormeyer, born in *Diemringer Amt, Dorf Deringer,* who in 1764 came to America, with his sister, Carolina Christina, and her husband, and was indentured. Dormeyer is believed to be in the dry lands near Bethlehem. Notify Jacob Friesz, innkeeper, Salem co., N. J.

AMERICAN RECORDS

Christ Lutheran (Tulpehocken) KB, Stouchsburg, Berks co.:
A Peter Dornmeier and wife Christina had a son:
Peter b. 10 Mar. 1772, bp. 4 May 1772

Longswamp Reformed KB, Berks co.:
A Peter Dormeyer and wife Catharina had a daughter
Maria Magdalena b. 24 Aug. 1775, bp. 26 Mar. 1776
Sp.: David Mertz [q.v.]; Magdalena Klein, single.

103. DÖRRMANN, JOH. GEORG Hunspach=
_____, 1752 67250 Soultz-sous-Forêts

EUROPEAN RECORDS

Birlenbach Lutheran KB:
Hans Willhelm Dürrmann, citizen at Hunspach, and wife had a son:
Johann Georg bp. 7 Jan. 1709

Hunspach Reformed KB:
Joh. Georg Dörrmann, son of the late Wilhelm Dörrmann of Hunspach, m. 9 Jan. 1731 Anna Maria, dau. of the late Samuel Lesser from Gundischwyl, BE [? Gundetswil, ZH or ?CH-5728 Gontenschwil, AG]. Children:

1. Susanna Maria b. 1 Nov. 1731, bp. 2 Nov. 1731

Zweibruecken Manumissions Protocoll, Clee- and Catharinenburg, 1752:
Johann Gorg Doerrmann of Hunspach leaves for America.

104. DRACHSEL, HANS GEORG   Liniehausen,
Sarah, 1764   Langensoultzbach=
S-H, I: 691   67360 Woerth
EUROPEAN RECORDS

Langensoultzbach Lutheran KB:
Melchior Drachsel, *Erbeständer* at Liniehausen, and wife Magdalena nee
Dietz had children:
  1. Johann Ulrich bp. 17 Oct. 1717
  2. Johann Philipp bp. 22 Feb. 1720
  3. Catharina Barbara bp. 5 Nov. 1722
  4. Joh. Georg bp. 20 Feb. 1724
  5. Hans Peter bp. 16 Mar. 1728
  6. **Hans Georg** bp. 8 July 1735

Isolated farms were often tenanted by Swiss who moved
into the area after the defeat of Louis XIV in 1697.

AMERICAN RECORDS

Trinity Lutheran KB, Lancaster:
One Georg Drachsel and wife Margaret had children:
  1. Johann Peter b. 5 Feb. 1764, bp. 20 May 1764
      Sp.: Joh. Peter Funkhauser [?Franckhauser, q.v.] and wife Eva
  2. Johann Georg b. 26 June 1766, bp. 9 Nov. 1766

105. DRACHSEL, PETER age 42
Samuel, 1733
S-H, I: 107, 110, 111, 112
   with Catharina age 30, Peter age 9, Daniel age 7

Katzenthal,
67510 Lembach

EUROPEAN RECORDS

Lembach Lutheran KB:
Peter Traxel, Hoffman in Katzenthal, and wife Juliana Catharina nee Frawhüger had children:
   1. Joh. Jacob b. 16 Feb. 1723
   2. Twin daughter b. 16 Feb. 1723, died
   3. Joh. Peter b. 23 Jan. 1724
   4. Johann Daniel b. 8 Dec. 1725
   5. Leonhard b. 4 Oct. 1727, died
   6. Maria Barbara b. 1 Oct. 1728

AMERICAN RECORDS

Egypt Reformed KB, Lehigh co.:
Peter Traxel, church *censor* of the Reformed congregation here, and wife Juliana Catharina, had children:
   7. David b. 27 July 1734, bp. 23 Sept. 1734
      Sp.: Nicolaus Kern and wife Maria Margaretha
   8. Johannes bp. 26 Oct. 1736
      Sp.: Nicolaus Kern, Johannes Egender and Margaretha Egender
   9. Christian bp. 16 Apr. 1739, conf. 1753
      Sp.: Christian Brengel, Peter Traxel, Salome Gut [for Brengel and Guth, see Burgert, *The Western Palatinate*].
   10. Juliana Margaretha bp. 16 Apr. 1739, conf. 1753
   11. Twin to Juliana M.
      Sp.: Johannes Gertsch [q.v.] Catharina Elisabetha Kern [q.v.], Maria Margaretha Neuhart
   12. Georg Friederich bp. 28 July 1741
      Sp.: Georg Kern; Frederich Neuhart; Salome, wife of Lorentz Gut; Susanna, wife of Georg Ruch.
   13. Margaretha b. 25 Oct. 1744, bp. 21 Dec. 1744

Jordan Lutheran KB, Lehigh co.:
Daniel Trachsel and wife Sophia had:
   Daniel b. 8 Mar. 1749, bp. 6 May 1749

Jordan Reformed KB, Lehigh co.:
Peter Trachsel and wife Anna Maria had:

Susanna b. 9 Mar. 1765, bp. 14 Apr. 1765
Christian b. 6 Dec. 1771, bp. 26 Jan. 1772

Frederick County Will Abstracts in *Western Maryland Genealogy*, vol.2, no.3, 1986. Will Book A I: 213-4:
Peter Troxell of Frederick co. 16 Apr. 1766 - 6 May 1766.
To (wife) Julianah Catherinah: one cow, heifer, and bed, besides her thirds of my moveable estate. Sons Frederick and John exec. Moveable estate to be divided among my 8 children: Peter, Daniel, David, John, Christian, Frederick, Juliana, and Margaretha. /s/ Peter Troxell. Wit: Philip Klingensmith, Adam Rydenower, Peter Schaafer. On 8 May 1766 Thomas Schley translated the will from the "Dutch" language.

Peter Trachsell, Bucks co., nat. 10 Apr. 1742.
Peter Trachsell, Jr., Bucks co., nat. 10 Apr. 1742.
Daniel Traxell, Whitehall twp., Northampton co., nat. Apr. 1761.

106. DREHER, HANS GEORG   Preuschdorf=
Not located in S-H   67250 Soultz-sous-Forêts

EUROPEAN RECORDS

Preuschdorf Lutheran KB:
Hans Dreher, son of Hans Michel Dreher, m. __ Nov. 1725 Maria Barbara Cuntz, daughter of Hans Georg Cuntz, Their son:
        Hans Georg b. 15 Dec. 1727 bp. 17 Dec. 1727

Hans Georg Dreher m. 7 Feb. 1747 Maria Catharina Berri, daughter of Hans Jacob Berri, smith at Lampertsloch [=67250 Soultz-sous-Forêts]. Children:
        1. Catharina Barbara b. 29 Nov. 1749, bp. 1 Dec. 1749
        2. Catharina Elisabetha b. 23 Aug. 1751, bp. 25 Aug. 1751

Notation in KB: "Went to the new land."

107. DRION, JOHANN MICHAEL   67690 Hatten
Janet, 1752
S-H, I: 475
EUROPEAN RECORDS

Hatten Lutheran KB:
Johann Georg Trion, citizen, *balbierer*, and Maria Catharina had a son:
        Joh. Michael b. 11 Nov. 1725, bp. 14 Nov. 1725

Sp.: Hans Jörg son of Ulrich Dietsch; Anna Eva, wife of Melchior Köhlhoffer

AMERICAN RECORDS

Millbach Reformed KB, Lebanon co.:
Michael Driann and wife Elisabetha had:
1. Mary Elizabeth bp. 25 Aug. 1760

Heidelberg Lutheran KB, Schaefferstown:
Mich. Trion and wife had:
Joh. Jacob b. 19 June 1773, bp. 20 June 1773, died

Egle, *History of Lebanon Co: 352*:
Michael Trion, of Heidelberg; d. prior to 1799. At his death he left a wife and children:
1. George; 2. Michael; 3. Frederick; 4. Elizabeth, m. George Leshner; 5. Catharine, m. Peter Moore; 6. Peggy; 7. Barbara; 8. Eva; 9. Polly; 10. Peter; 11. Jonathan; 12. Sally.

108. DROG, HANS DIEBOLT age 41   Merkwiller-Pechelbronn=
Snow *Fox*, 1738   67250 Soultz-sous-Forêts
S-H, I: 231, 232, 233

EUROPEAN RECORDS

Preuschdorf Lutheran KB:
Diebold Trog, son of the late Jacob Trog, former citizen and miller at Merckweiler, m. __ Feb. 1721 Maria Barbara Rech, daughter of Hans Martin Rech [name also appears in records as Reck, Reeg, Reech], citizen at Lampertsloch [=67250 Soultz-sous-Forêts].
Notation in KB by marriage record: "Went to the new land."

Maria Barbara Reech was b. 1703, daughter of Martin Reech and wife Catharina nee Clauss, daughter of Hans Christoph Clauss of Preuschdorf.

Kutzenhausen Lutheran KB:
Johann Theobald Trog [he signed Drog], miller at Merckweiler, and wife Maria Barbara had children:
1. Johann Georg b. 9 Dec. 1721, bp. 14 Dec. 1721
2. Maria Barbara b. 25 Jan. 1723, died
3. Eva Catharina b. 14 July 1725, bp. 16 July 1725
4. Maria Barbara b. 17 June 1727, bp. 19 June 1727

   5. Anna Maria b. 25 Sept. 1729, bp. 29 Sept. 1729
   6. Johann Jacob b. 16 Aug. 1731, bp. 19 Aug. 1731
   7. Maria Dorothea b. 1 Feb. 1733, bp. 5 Feb. 1733
   8. Maria Magdalena b. 10 May 1735, bp. 14 May 1735
   9. Margaretha b. 27 Jan. 1737, bp. 31 Jan. 1737

AMERICAN RECORDS

Philadelphia co. Adm. Book D: 60:
Estate #148 - Letters of Adm. on the estate of Theobald Trog, granted to
Nicholas Löscher, co. of Philadelphia, yeoman. Dated 19 Feb. 1738/9.
Bond to Nicholas Löscher during the minority of five children. Reckoning
to be made by 19 Feb. 1739. Inventory of the est. of Theobald *Troeck*
exhibited 28 Mar. 1739. Two children are bound out. Inventory signed by
Jacob Börstler and Weilhelm Pott. A note added to inventory: "I found here
in Philadelphia one old stillor and one little kettle by the hereonto written
Koopershmitt, (signed) Johannes Söffrens."

Christ Lutheran KB (Mertz's), Bieber Creek, Berks co:
Jacob Trog and wife Magdalena nee Scheurin had a daughter:
      1. Anna Maria b. 15 May 1755, bp. 15 June 1755
         Sp.: Christian Heinrich and wife Anna Maria.

St. Joseph's (Oley Hills) Church, Pike twp., Berks co.:
A family record for the Dry family was inserted in the Oley Hills KB in
1936; it was not a part of the original record. The source of information
concerning the family is not given.
   "Johann Jacob and Hans Georg Troy, now Dry, sons of Dewald Troy of
Alsace, Germany, coming to America Sept. 19, 1732. Settled in Chester co.,
later moved to Berks co. in 1754." The entry continues with a list of 9
children attributed to Hans George Dry.

109. DUCHMANN, HANS ADAM   Gundershoffen=
Polly, 1766   67110 Niederbronn-les-Bains
S-H, I: 712
   [transcribed and indexed in S-H as Duhmann]

EUROPEAN RECORDS

Gundershoffen Lutheran KB:
Hans Adam Tuchmann, single weaver from [67580] Mertzweiler, son of
Hans Adam Tuchmann, m. 27 Jan. 1761 Christina, daughter of the late
Christian Schleichter, former citizen here. They had children:

1. Margaretha Dorothea b. 4 Jan. 1762, bp. 6 Jan. 1762
2. Christina b. 2 Aug. 1763
3. Hans Georg b. 23 Dec. 1764
   Sp.: Johannes Weisgerber; Dorothea, daughter of Meister
   Nicklaus Schliechter; Jacob Gerber, tailor at Niederbronn.
[He signed the baptismal entries as Hans Adam Duchmann; his signature in
the KB is a perfect match with signature on ship list, S-H, II: 817.]

AMERICAN RECORDS

Trinity Lutheran KB, New Holland, Lancaster co.:
Adam Tuchmann and wife A. Christina had:
4. Hannes Jurg b. 23 Oct. 1767, bp. 13 Dec. 1767
   Sp.: Christian Tuchmann and A. Maria
5. Georg b. 29 Aug. [?1768], bp. 4 Oct. [?1768]
   [year given as 1767 but recorded with 1768 baptisms.]
6. Jacob b. 11 Mar. 1770, bp. 15 Apr. 1770
   Sp.: Michel Schmidt and wife

Married 19 Mar. 1793 - Georg Tuchmann and Elis. Schäfer, daughter of
Peter Schäfer.
Conf. 23 May 1779 - Margreta Tuchmannin, age 18.

Hans Adam Tuchmann and wife Christina were sp. in 1767 for a child of
Christian Tuchmann.

Buried 25 February 1782 - Adam Tuchmann, resident of Earl Township,
Lancaster County, Pennsylvania, a member of the congregation at New
Holland, came from Alsace in Germany 15 years before his death, was
married for 21 years to Christina, nee Schlichter, with whom there were five
children, three sons and two daughters, of whom three still live. He was
aged 54 years. He was wounded by a home grinder [Hausreibmühl] and
lived fifteen days after the accident.

DUCHMANN see also TUCHMANN

110. DÜFFORT, PHILIP   Langensoultzbach=
    DÜFFORT, JACOB   67360 Woerth
Robert and Alice, 1738
S-H, I: 212, 214, 216
They did not sign list; appear on A list as Toffer; on B list as Tofort; on C
list as Thiffort.

EUROPEAN RECORDS

Langensoultzbach Lutheran KB:
Hans Philipps Düfforth of Sultzbach and wife Eva nee Anthoni had children:
1. (Probable) Jacob, bp. not located at Sultzbach
2. Anna Clara, bp. not located; m. 31 Jan. 1736
   Joh. Stephan Dürrenberger [q.v.]
3. Johann Georg bp. 28 Oct. 1728
4. Johann Philipp bp. 9 July 1721
5. Johann Georg bp. 2 Feb. 1724
6. Johann Adam bp. __ Nov. 1726
7. Anna Catharina bp. 19 Feb. 1729

Eva nee Anthoni Düffort died 24 July 1732, age 40 y. 2 mo.
Philip Düffort, widower, m. (2) 16 June 1733 in Sultzbach Anna Maria, daughter of Christian Martini, citizen at Bettweiler, *Lützelsteinischen jurisdiction.* They had:
8. Zacharias bp. 22 July 1734
9. Maria Catharina bp. 28 Nov. 1736

AMERICAN RECORDS

Chambers, *Early Germans of New Jersey:* 152-153:
Jacob Dufford leased 200 A in German Valley on 20 May 1747. Jacob Dufford was the son of Philip Tofort or Dufford, who arrived in Philadelphia 11 Sept. 1738. Philip Dufford died ca 1767, his son Jacob possibly predeceased him.

Philip Dufford also had sons Adam, George, and Philip, Jr. [See also Chambers p. 342-344].

New Jersey Archives, First Series, Vol. XXXIII: 439:
Abstracts of Wills:
Tufford, Philip, of Roxbury, Morris co. 15 Feb. 1767- 1 Feb. 1769.
To grandson, Jurrey Staffey Tufford, and to my 2 sons, George and Adam, each 5 shillings. Wife, Catrena, rest of my estate, and, after her death, to go to my daughter, Mary Magdilen. Executors - my wife and Stuffey Derburger. Witnesses - Roelof Roelofson, Elizabeth Roelofson, Lawrance Roelofson. 1769, Jan. 18. Inventory, £67.7.6, made by Roelof Roelofson and John Tackerd.

Stuffey Derberger also called Stephen Terryberry [Stephan Dürrenberger, q.v.] was a son-in-law of Philip Duffort. He leased the tract adjacent to the Duffort lands, a farm of 150 A, in 1747.

Philb. Duford signed the 1749 call to John Albert Weygand, a Lutheran pastor.

St. Michael's Lutheran KB, Germantown, Philadelphia co.:
Stevanus Dofferd m. 23 June 1767 Anna M. Trimmer.
(Chambers, *Early Germans of New Jersey*, p. 537: this is George Stephen Dufford, b. 1741, son of Jacob Dufford, named as grandson in Philip Düffort's will. His wife, Mary Trimmer, was b. 1743, daughter of Matthias Trimmer of German Valley.)

First Reformed KB, Easton, Northampton co.:
Adam Duffart and wife Susanna had a son:
> Philip b. 4 Apr. 1776.

111. DÜRRENBERGER, CHRISTOPF   Gundershoffen=
Phoenix, 1750   67110 Niederbronn-les-Bains
S-H, I: 440
EUROPEAN RECORDS

Gundershoffen Lutheran KB:
Hanns Dürrenberger, son of the late Hanns Dürrenberger, former citizen at Reichersweyler in Canton Basel, Switzerland [?CH-4418 Reigoldswil, BL], m. __ Nov. 1701 Anna, daughter of the late Jacob Eichkorn, former citizen at Ingelh. [possibly Ingenheim=67270 Hochfelden or Ingolsheim=67250 Soultz-sous-Forêts.] They had a son:
> Christophorus b. 27 Sept. 1716

Christoph Dürrenberger, son of the late Joh. Dürrenberger, m. 20 Jan. 1739 Anna Maria, daughter of the late Christoph Jung, former citizen here. They had children:
> 1. Hans Peter b. 7 June 1742
> 2. Catharina Barbara b. 27 July 1744
> 3. Nicolaus bp. 3 Feb. 1746
>   [mother given as Anna Barbara in this one entry]
> 4. Nicolaus b. 1 Apr. 1748, bp 2 Apr. 1748 [mother Anna Maria]

112. DÜRRENBERGER, GEORG   Volksberg=
Phoenix, 1750   67290 Wingen-sur-Moder
S-H, I: 442
[appears on list as Hans Jerg Dieren[berger].

EUROPEAN RECORDS

Mertzweiler Lutheran KB:
Christian Dürrenberger, the younger, and wife Anna Margaretha had children:
1. **Hans Georg** b. 7 Mar. 1709
2. Anna Barbara b. 31 Jan. 1712. She m. (1) Georg Wambach [q.v.]; m. (2) Martin Schröter [q.v.]
3. Anna Margaretha b. 21 Feb. 1715, bp. 24 Feb. 1715
4. Hans Jacob b. 21 Sept. 1717
5. Hans Adam b. 21 Sept. 1720
6. Christian b. 31 July 1724
7. Maria Magdalena b. __ July 1727, bp. 4 July 1727; She m. Joh. Jacob Schock [q.v.]

Died 12 May 1729 - Christian Dürrenberger, aged 48 years.

Georg Dürrenberger, son of Christian Dürrenberger, m. 1 Nov. 1729 Anna Barbara, daughter of Hans Jac. Zebst. [Signed Dierenberger-his signature by marriage entry and bp. entries matches S-H, II: 512] They had children:
1. Joh. Georg b. 8 Mar. 1730
2. Anna Margaretha b. 26 Nov. 1731
3. Anna Magdalena b. 3 Jan. 1733
4. Anna Barbara b. __ June 1734, bp. 5 June 1734
5. Anna _____ b. ?Dom.p.Trin? 1736

Dehlingen Lutheran KB:
Hans Georg Dürrenberger of Volcksburg had a daughter:
6. Anna Elisabetha b. 24 Apr. 1738, bp. 26 Apr. 1738

Waldhambach Lutheran KB:
Johann Georg Dürrenberger of Volksberg and wife Anna Barbara nee Zebst had children:
7. Anna Maria b. 14 Dec. 1741, d. 18 Mar. 1743
8. Anna Christina b. 14 Oct. 1744

Tiefenbach Catholic KB:
Johann Georg Dürrenberger, Lutheran at Volksberg, and wife Anna Barbara had:
9. Johannes b. 23 Sept. 1747

He arrived on the *Phoenix*, 1750. Another passenger on this ship, Johann Jacob Schoch [q.v.] was married to a Dürrenberger. They were also from Volksberg.

113. DÜRRENBERGER, HANS JACOB   Griesbach=
DÜRRENBERGER, HANS MICHEL   67110 Niederbronn-les-Bains
DÜRRENBERGER, STEPHAN
Robert & Alice, 1738
S-H, I: 212, 214, 215

EUROPEAN RECORDS

Mertzweiler Lutheran KB:
Hans Peter Dürrenb.(erger) m. 25 Sept. 1708 Eva Cathar. N. (no name recorded). They had children:
  1. Hans Stephan (Dürrenb.) bp. 25 Jan. 1711
  2. Maria Magdalena b. 7 Dec. 1713
  3. Hans Michel b. 15 Feb. 1716
  4. Hans Jacob b. 15 Nov. 1717, bp. 18 Nov. 1717

Gundershoffen Lutheran KB:
Joh. Stephan, son of Peter Dürrenberger, *Gemeinsschöffen* at G(rie)sb(ach), m. 31 Jan. 1736 Anna Clara, daughter of Philipp Düffort [q.v.], citizen at Langensultzbach [=67360 Woerth]. They had:
  1. Joh. Georg bp. 12 Dec. 1736
      Sp.: Zacharias Weyrauch, *Herrschaffl. Gärtner* at Fröschweiler [=67360 Woerth]; Joh. Georg Bene, citizen at G(ries)b(ach); and Maria Magdalena, daughter of Andreas Schall.

AMERICAN RECORDS

Jordan Lutheran KB, Lehigh co.:
Jacob Dorrenberger m. 28 Sept. 1742 Anna Margaretha Bastian.

Muhlenberg's Journals, II: 360:
Confirmed in New Jersey, 1768: Anna Elisabetha Durreberger, age 16, and Gertraut Durreberger, daughters of Stephan Durreberger.

Chambers, *Early Germans of New Jersey:* 153:
Stephen Terryberry [Stephan Dürrenberger] was a son-in-law of Philip Duffort [q.v.]. Stephan leased the tract of 150 A, adjacent to the Duffort lands in German Valley in 1747.

Michel Direnberger [Terryberry] and Peter Direnberger signed the 1749 call to John Albert Weygand, a Lutheran pastor.

New Jersey Archives, First Series, Vol. XXXIV: 155:
Abstracts of Wills:
[No date.] Durenberger, Stephen, of Roxbury, Morris co., farmer;
Wife, Mary, to have all while she goes by my name. Oldest son, Philip
Durenberger, £8. Sons, Philip and Jury Frederick Durenberger, the farm
where Philip lives. Youngest son, Stephen, horses. My 3 youngest
daughters, Anna Lizabeth, Margaret and Mary, as they arrive to age, an
outset as the rest of the daughters. Executors - wife, Mary, and John Sayger.
Witnesses - John Sayger, Jacob Hager, David Fetter. Proved Jan. 23, 1776.
1776, Jan. 16. Inventory, £290.1.0, made by Anna Mary Dirburger, widow and
John Sager, Executors, and Roelof Roelofson and Christopher Kerns,
appraisers.

114. DÜRRENBERGER, PETER   Gundershoffen=
Diana, 1791   67110 Niederbronn-les-Bains
S-H, III: 43
   with wife Eliza, children: Salome, Philip, Georg Frederich, Hans Jerry.
   [appears on list as Durenburgh]

EUROPEAN RECORDS

Gundershoffen Lutheran KB:
Johann Peter Dürrenberger, citizen and turner here, and wife Maria
Elisabetha nee Müller had children:
   1. Philip Georg b. 19 Mar. 1775
   2. Maria Salome b. 28 May 1777, bp. 30 May 1777
   3. Georg Friederich b. 16 Aug. 1779, bp. 18 Aug. 1779
      Sp.: Jacob Löwenguth, citizen and cooper; Stephan
      Dammeron, Jr.; Maria Elisabetha, daughter of Joh. Peter Bürcky
   4. Hans Georg b. 9 Apr. 1782, bp. 11 Apr. 1782

AMERICAN RECORDS

St. Michael's and Zion KB, Philadelphia:
Buried 15 Apr. 1805: Georg Derreberger, b. 18 Aug. 1779 in Gundershoffen,
Alsace. He m. 1801 Hannah Woodtert. One child.

115. EBERHARD, FRIEDRICH age 40   Durstel=
Samuel, 1737   67320 Drulingen
S-H, I: 169, 171, 172

EUROPEAN RECORDS

Durstel Lutheran KB:
Died 12 Jan. 1714: Hans Jacob Eberhardt, aged 58 y.

Johann Friedrich Eberhard, linenweaver of Durstel, son of the late Jacob Eberhard, m. 21 Apr. 1722 at Durstel Anna Catharina Stambach, daughter of Ulrich Stambach and his wife Eva Catharina nee Gangloff. It is mentioned in the marriage record that Frederich Eberhard's step-mother was Maria Margaretha nee Stauffenberger. Friedrich Eberhard and wife Anna Catharina had children:

1. Anna Catharina Elisabetha b. 24 Mar. 1723. Notation in the KB by her baptism: "went to America with her parents in 1737". Sp.: An. Cath. Dieterich, wife of Georg Joh. Dieterich, the *Steinbacher Hoffmann*; Joh. Nic. Steckel, son of Joh. Jacob Steckel, *Censor* at Lohr; An. Elis. Jung, daughter of Joh. Jac. Jung from Lohr [=67290 Wingen-sur-Moder].
2. Johann Friedrich b. 19 Nov. 1724
3. Anna Elisabetha b. 25 July 1726
4. Maria Eva b. 27 Oct. 1728, d. 20 Feb. 1733
5. Johann Arnold b. 10 Aug. 1732
6. Catharina Barbara b. 11 July 1734
7. Anna Eva b. 30 Nov. 1735

AMERICAN RECORDS

Augustus Evangelical Lutheran KB, Trappe, Montgomery co.:
Johann Bernhard Kuhnz [q.v. Kuntz] m. (no date given) 1745, in the Oley Mountains, Catharina Elisabeth Eberhard(in).

Egypt Reformed KB, Lehigh co.:
Catharina Eberhardt was a sp. in 1743 for a child of Joh. Friederich Schneider [q.v.]

Samuel Seeger, son of Nicolaus Seeger, m. 28 Nov. 1752 Anna Eva, daughter of the deceased Fredrich Eberhard.

Philadelphia Adm. F: 434, 1751, Estate #25:
Will of Fredrick Eberhardt. 16 Nov. 1750 - 13 Dec. 1751
Provides for wife [who is not named in will, but she signed the document:

Cattrin Eberhardt.]   Son Arnold is to have the plantation, and he is to provide for his mother. He is to pay £24 to be paid as follows: £7 to Paul Everhardt in 1758; £7 to Eve in 1759; £7 to Barbara in 1760; £1 to Catharine in 1762; remainder to Arnold. Paul Everhardt to live with his mother until he is 15 years old. Barbara and Eve to remain with mother until of age. If mother remarries, she is to leave the premises. This unusual will was signed by the testator and all of the heirs: Frittrich Eberhardt, Cattrin Eberhardt, Fridterich Eberhardt, Bernhardt Kuntz, Arnold Eberhartt, Paulus Eberhartt (all signed in German script) and Barbara Eberhard and Eva Eberhard made their marks. Wit: Jacob Mückli (his mark), Michel Neuhart (his mark), Jacob Bröckes (his mark), Ulli Fleckinger (his mark).

Adm. Bond to Catherine Everhard, widow, dated 13 Dec. 1751. Registered in Book F: 434. Adm. was granted to Catharine, the widow, and Fredrick Everhardt, eldest son of the deceased.

Estate was valued at £56.17.6. Debts totaled £20.18.2. Dated 28 Apr. 1752.
       Signed: David Karcher, John Nicholas Snider, William (WB) Bast

Rev. Daniel Schumacher's records:
Friderich Eberhard and wife Elisabeth had:
       1. Johann Peter bp. 27 Apr. 1760, 14 days old in Lehigh twp.
          Sp.: Peter Anthony; Bernhard Kuntz; Anna Elisabeth Reiss;
          Anna Magdalena Jung; all married.

Arnold Eberhard and wife Maria Margaretha had:
       1. Catharina bp. 22 June 1760, 5 weeks old, in Salisbury
          Sp.: Frederick Weber and Catharina

Paul Eberhard and Maria had:
       1. Johann Jacob bp. 2 Oct. 1760, Lehigh
          Sp.: Jacob Husson and Magdalena
       2. Johannes b. 31 Aug. 1764, bp. 30 Sept. 1764 in Egypt
          Sp.: Johannes Muffly and Catharina Stambach, single
       3. Johann Henrich b. 30 May 1768, bp. 19 June 1768 in Lehigh twp.
          Sp.: Henrich Rüsly, Barbara Mufflin, single
       4. Christian b. 10 May 1772, bp. 8 June 1772

St. Paul's (Indianland) Lutheran KB, Lehigh twp., Northampton co.:
Friderick Eberhard and wife Elisabeth had:
       Catharina Barbara b. 23 Jan. 1765, bp. 17 Mar. 1765
       Sp.: Bernhard Reis; Frederick Kunz; Catharina Barbara Dorn;
       Catharina Scheürin

Paul Eberhard and wife Maria had:
   Maria Catharina b. 3 Aug. 1770
   Sp.: Michael Reed, single

Williams twp. congregation, Northampton co.:
Arnold Eberhard and wife Anna Margaretha had:
   2. Elisabeth b. 12 June 1770
First Reformed KB, Easton, Northampton co.:
   3. Anna Maria b. 10 Apr. 1778.

116. EBERSOHL, CARL age 21   Berg=
Peggy, 1753   67320 Drulingen
S-H, I: 546, 548, 550

EUROPEAN RECORDS

Berg and Thal Lutheran KB:
Johann Michael Ebersoll of Berg and wife Anna Christina nee Wilhelm had
a son:
   Carl b. 25 Nov. 1732

Verification of this emigrant provided by Dr. Bernd Gölzer from the
compiled records of Dr. Gerhard Hein:
Records of Saarwerden county office for Berg und Thal:
Dated 2 Apr. 1756, inventory of Anna Christina Wilhelm: the eldest son
Carl Ebersoll, a linenweaver, has gone on his travels three years ago and
went to America.

AMERICAN RECORDS

Charles Ebersohl, Berks co. nat. 24 Sept. 1768 at Philadelphia.

117. ECKER, GEORG   Herbitzheim=
Phoenix, 1749   67260 Sarre-Union
S-H, I: 405 [Acker on list; did not sign]

EUROPEAN RECORDS

Herbitzheim Lutheran KB:
Georg Ecker, shephard at Salzbrunn [Saltzbronn, near 57430 Sarralbe] m.
13 Feb. 1748 Anna Margaretha, daughter of Jacob Altmann [q.v.] of
Herbitzheim.

Verification of this emigration supplied by Dr. Bernd Gölzer, from the county records of Nassau-Saarwerden, compiled by Dr. Gerhard Hein:
On 7 Feb. 1747, Georg Ecker, Lutheran, and Maria Nicola Helwig, Catholic, had an illegitimate son Jacob. Records of Saarwerden county office for Keskastel, dated 28 Nov. 1765: the son Jacob Ecker is 18 years old; his father has left for the New Land.

AMERICAN RECORDS

One of the signers on a petition for protection from the Indians, dated 5 Oct. 1757, Forks of the Delaware: Geo. Acker

Egypt Reformed KB, Rev. Daniel Schumacher's records and St. Paul's (Indianland) Lutheran KB, Lehigh co:
Jürg Ecker and wife Anna Margaretha had:
1. Possible son Philip, sp. in Lehigh in 1768, 1771
2. Possible daughter Catharina, sp. in Lehigh 1768, 1770, 1771
3. Georg Nicolaus bp. 6 June 1756 (Egypt- surname Aeckert)
   Sp.: Nicolaus Nehlich; Maria Catharina Altmann;
   Jacob Roth and wife.
4. Maria Christina b. 11 May 1758, bp. 25 June 1758
   (Egypt- surname Eckert). Sp.: Peter Altmann; Peter
   Wannenmacher; Maria Catharina Altmann; Maria Christina
   Schutter
5. Maria Margaretha bp. 25 May 1760 in Lehigh twp.
   Sp.: Peter Altman [q.v.]; Caspar Altman [q.v.];
   Magdalena Ruch, and Christine Schittler, single
6. Maria Catharina b. 3 Jan. 1763, bp. 10 May 1763
   at St. Paul's (Indianland) KB. Sp.: Caspar Altmann
7. Joh. Jacob b. 16 Mar. 1765, bp. 16 Aug. 1763
   Sp.: Jacob Keppel and Eleonora; Nicholas Keppel
   and Anna Maria at St. Paul's (Indianland)
8. Maria Elisabetha bp. 1 Mar. 1767 at St. Paul's
   Sp.: Thomas William (?)
9. Johann Nicolaus b. 21 Apr. (1770), bp. 16 Dec. 1770
   at Lehigh (Schumacher)
   Sp.: Johann Nicolaus Antony and Anna Margaretha Küster, single

118. ECKER, PETER age 40   Hinsingen=
    ECKER, CHRISTIAN age 19   67260 Sarre-Union
    ECKER, PETER JR.
Lydia, 1741
S-H, I: 301, 302, 303

EUROPEAN RECORDS

Keskastel Lutheran KB:
Peter Eckert and wife Veronica had a son bp. at Hinsingen:
1. Hans Peter bp. 7 June 1720, conf. 1734
   [Recorded in Diedendorf Reformed KB].

Diemeringen Reformed KB:
Hans Peter Ecker, swineherder from Ratzweiler, [?CH-3354 Riedtwil, BE or
?Rudswil, BE=CH-3423 Ersigen], Canton Bern, Switzerland, and wife
Veronica had:
2. Christian b. 14 Feb. 1724

AMERICAN RECORDS

First Reformed KB, Lancaster:
Married 23 Nov. 1742 - Peter Ecker, widower of Conestoga, and Margaret
nee Stutter, widow of Jacob Hoschauer [q.v. Hoschar] of Conestoga.

Muddy Creek Reformed KB, Lancaster co.:
Peter Ecker signed the Reformed church doctrine on 19 May 1743.
A Peter *Hecker* and wife Maria Catherine were sp. in 1743 for a child of
Jacob Manny [q.v.] and his wife Catharine [nee Ecker.]

The family moved to Anson co., NC and an extensive genealogy of the
Eakers has been compiled. See Lorena Shell Eaker, *The Shoe Cobbler's Kin,*
Genealogy of the Peter Ecker, Sr. Family. Gateway Press, Baltimore (1976).

Anson co. NC land records:
Grants were made to Christian Eaker in Anson co., NC 15 May 1754 - 302
acres on Waters of Beaver Dam Creek; 10 April 1761 - 300 acres No.
Branch of Long Creek on the So. side of the So. Fork of the Catawba River;
in Tryon co., NC a grant was issued on 14 Nov. 1771 - 100 acres on the
Waters of Beaverdam Creek.

Two grants were made to Peter Eaker, Senior #1477 & #1986 Anson co.,
NC for 246 acres each on 10 Apr. 1761 on both sides of a South branch of
Indian Creek being a So. branch of the So. Fork of the Catawba. Number
1986 reads as follows:
Peter Acre Senr., county of (?) Anson on both sides of a South Branch of
Indian Creek being a So. branch of the So. Fork of the Catawba River by
Larance Kysers land including his own improvements beginning at a white
oak and meanes So. 34 W 200 poles to a hickory No. 56 W 200 poles to a
red oak W 34 E 105 poles to a white oak No 60 E 128 poles to a white oak

and thence So 74 E 144 poles to the beginning - dated 10 Apr. 1761. Arthur Dobbs.

Tyron co. NC Wills:
Christian Aker, dated 25 June 1776, proved July 1777. Wife Eve. Children: Peter, Christian, Daniel, Barbery, Catherine. Exrs: Peter Aker, Sr., Christian H. Carpenter, Sr., John Axer.

Mecklenberg co., NC Land Grants:
24 Nov. 1762 Grantor Book 1, pg. 527, Christian Acre sold 302 acres on Beaver Dam Creek to Peter Acre.

25 Nov. 1762 Grantor Book 1, pg. 528, Christian Acre sold 302 acres on Beaver Dam Creek to Peter Acre.

13 Apr. 1765 Grantor Book 2, pg. 77, Christian Acre and Eve sold 300 acres on Long Creek to William Hager.

13 Apr. 1765 Grantee Book 2, pg 79, Christian Acre purchased 300 acres on Beaver Dam Creek from William and Elizabeth Hager (Heaker).

Lincoln co., NC Wills:
Peter Eaker of Lincoln co., dated 10 Nov. 1797. Wife Barbara. Children: Oldest daughter Barbara (Hillibrand), oldest son John and John's three children (Peter, Michael and Elizabeth), son Peter, son Christopher, son Michl., daughter Catharine, daughter Susanna, daughter Elisabeth, daughter Mary, daughter Faney. Names son-in-law Samuel Carpenter. Exrs: Michael Eaker and Carpenter.

[The full text of both wills, also estate inventories and other valuable data is published in *The Shoe Cobbler's Kin.*]

119. EDELMANN, DAVID age 49   Rott=
    EDELMANN, PHILIP JACOB age 25   67160 Wissembourg
Richard & Elizabeth, 1733   Steinseltz=
S-H, I: 126, 127, 129, 130   67160 Wissembourg
  others on ship: Margaretha Edelman, age 26;
  Anna Maria Edelman, age 54; Baltasar Edelman, age 4].

EUROPEAN RECORDS

Birlenbach Lutheran KB:
Hans David Edelmann, citizen in Rott, and wife Anna Margaretha had

children:
1. Philip Jacob b. ca. 1708
2. Anna Elisabetha bp. 13 May 1713
3. Maria Ursula bp. 6 Sept. 1716
4. A daughter b. 9 June 1718, bp. 11 June 1718

Steinseltz Reformed KB:
Philips Jacob Edelmann, son of Davyd Edelmann of Rott, m. 15 Jan. 1732
Maria Margretha Wenner, dau. of Simon Wenner of Oberhoffen [=67160
Wissembourg].

Zweibrücken Manumissions Protocoll, Cleeburg, 1733:
David and Philipp Edelmann of Steinseltz move with wives and children to
Pennsylvania.

AMERICAN RECORDS

First Reformed KB, Lancaster:
Jacob Edelmann and wife had a son:
John David b. 1 Dec. 1736, bp. 15 May 1737
Sp.: David Edelmann and wife

Matthew Bauser and wife Anna Elis. nee Edelmann had:
l. Anna Margaret bp. 12 May 1739
2. David bp. 12 May 1739

Colonial Maryland Naturalizations:
Philip Edleman, Reformed, Baltimore co., nat. 31 Aug. 1757.

120. EHRHART, CHRISTIAN   Rittershoffen=
Robert & Alice, 1739   67690 Hatten
S-H, I: 264, 267, 271

EUROPEAN RECORDS

Hunspach Reformed KB:
Conf. 1730 - Christian Erhart, son of Daniel Erhart of Retschweiler
[Retschwiller=67250 Soultz-sous-Forêts].

Christian Ehrhardt from Rittershoffen m. (1) 1 Oct. 1734 Anna Barbara,
daughter of Jacob ?Clor of Hunspach [=67250 Soultz-sous-Forêts].

Rittershoffen Lutheran KB:
Christian Ehrhart, citizen and widower here m. (2) 5 May 1738 Susanna,

daughter of the late Jacob Müller, citizen at Oberkutzenhausen [=67250 Soultz-sous-Forêts] and his wife Susanna.
[Christian Ehrhart made his mark by this entry in the KB: (CE), the same mark he used in the ship list].

AMERICAN RECORDS

First Reformed KB, Lancaster:
Christian Erhardt, from Hoffen, Alsace and his wife Susanna nee Müller had children:
1. Susanna b. 17 May 1741, bp. 17 May 1741
   Sp.: Peter Ganther and wife; Susanna Reichert
2. Anna Eva bp. 25 Dec. 1744
   Sp.: Jacob Stambach
3. Christian b. 5 Mar. 1748, bp. 19 May 1748
   Sp.: Jacob Stampach
4. Anna Catharina b. 10 Feb. 1750, Rapho twp, bp. 15 Apr. 1750
   Sp.: Conrad Merck and wife Catharine

1790 Census: Rapho twp., Lancaster co.:
Christian Erhart, 4 males over 16, 4 females.

121. EISENMAN, JOH. GEORG   Herbitzheim=
     EISENMAN, JOH. NICKLAS   67260 Sarre-Union
     EISENMAN, PETER
Phoenix, 1749
S-H, I: 405

EUROPEAN RECORDS

Hirschland Lutheran KB:
Joh. Georg Eisemann, son of Jacob Eisenmann at Herbitzheim m. 3 Feb. 1711 Elisabeta Finck, daughter of Benedick Finck.

Herbitzheim Lutheran and Keskastel Lutheran KB:
Joh. Georg Eisenmann, citizen and inhabitant at Herbitzheim, and wife Anna Elisabetha had:
1. Hans Jacob b. 8 May 1712, d. 11 Aug. 1713 (Keskastel)
1. Joh. Nickel b. 4 May 1714; conf. 1728
2. Anna Elisabeth bp. 24 June 1718 at Herbitzheim (Keskastel)
3. Joh. Peter, bp. 25 May 1720 (Keskastel) conf. 1734
   Sp.: Hans Peter Wannenmacher, tiler; Christian Wampffler, linenweaver
4. Joh. Conrad b. 26 Nov. 1722, bp. 27 Nov. 1722

Sp.: H. Conrad Rippel, schoolmaster; Friedrich Gelbacher,
master butcher; Anna Catharina Eisenmann, single
5. Maria Catharina b. 31 Mar. 1724, bp. 2 Apr. 1724
   Sp.: as above, plus Frau Maria Barbara Gelbach
6. Anna Catharina b. 25 Oct. 1729, conf. 1743.

Hans Nickel Eisemann, son of Georg Eisenmann, citizen and inhabitant at
Herbitzheim, m. 31 Jan. 1748 Elisabetha, daughter of Johannes Westerich,
inhabitant at Gerlingen [Goerlingen = 67320 Drulingen].

Verification of this emigration supplied by Dr. Bernd Gölzer, from the
county records of Nassau-Saarwerden, compiled by Dr. Gerhard Hein:
Dated 27 Mar. 1756: Anna Elisabetha Finck emigrated to America with her
husband Hans Georg Eisenmann about eight years ago (AD Strasbourg 6 E
35, vol. 146.)

AMERICAN RECORDS

Jerusalem Lutheran and Reformed KB, W. Salisbury twp., Lehigh co:
Peter Eysemann and Maria Catharina had:
   Catharina b. 25 June 1755.

Rev. Daniel Schumacher's records:
Hans Nicolaus Eisemann and wife Anna Elisabetha had:
   Nicolaus bp. 9 Nov. 1755, 3 weeks old, in Windsor
   Sp.: Nicolaus Schneider [q.v.]; Nicolaus Wingerth
   and Christina Papsten.

Peter Eisemann and wife Maria Catharina had:
   Andreas b. 16 Apr. 1768, bp. 10 July 1768, Lehigh
   Sp.: Peter Altmann [q.v.] and Christina

Georg Eisemann was sp. in 1769 and 1770 for Keppell [q.v.] children. Jürg
Eisemann, single, was sp. in 1768 for an Altmann [q.v.] child at Lehigh.

Other Eisemanns appear in Schumacher's records:
   A Peter Eisemann was conf. 1768, Lehigh
   Anna Catharina Eisemann, conf. 1770, Lehigh

One of the signers on a petition for protection from the Indians, dated 5
Oct. 1757, Forks of the Delaware:
   Peter Eisseman

St. Paul's (Blue) Lutheran KB, Lehigh co.:
Peter Eisemann and wife Catharina had:

Joh. Georg b. 28 June 1751, bp. 2 Oct. 1751
Sp.: Georg Altman [q.v.] and Anna Keppler [? Anna Köppel, q.v.]

Westmoreland co. Will Abstracts:
One Peter Iseman witnessed the 1787 will of Jacob Kepple [q.v.-Köppel].

Peter Eysenman, Lehi twp., Northampton co. nat. Autumn, 1765.

122. EISENMANN, MICHEL   Herbitzheim=
Bilander *Vernon,* 1747   67260 Sarre-Union
S-H, I: 364 [Eysenman]

EUROPEAN RECORDS

Herbitzheim Lutheran KB:
Joh. Michel Eisenmann m. 27 Jan. 1729   Anna Catharina Spirckebach,
single, from Eisenbach am Glan [Eisenbach-Matzenbach= W-6799
Matzenbach, Pfalz].

Verification of this emigration supplied by Dr. Bernd Gölzer, from the
Archives Départementales at Strasbourg, 6 E 35, vol. 69:
dated 21 Dec. 1746: Michael Eisenmann sells house and lots for he wants to
move to the New Land in Spring, 1747.

AMERICAN RECORDS

Berks co. wills:
Michael Eisenmann, Windsor twp. dated 9 May 1772; prob. 17 Aug. 1772.
Names as his heirs, after his wife Catharina's death, the following: "my
brother's son Nicholas Eisenmann, Peter Eisenmann's children Elisabetha,
now Paul Benninger's wife; Catharina, now Philip Karcher's wife; and Jacob
Bart's children. Exrs: Philip Henchell and Peter Wacks. Wit.: George Müller
and Bastian Kruger.

123. EMIG, JOHANNES   Uttenhoffen=
John and William, 1732   67110 Niederbronn-les-Bains
S-H, I: 102, 104, 105
   with Dorothy Emich, Nicholas, Johannes, Jacob

EUROPEAN RECORDS

Gundershoffen Lutheran KB:
Johannes Emich, nailsmith journeyman, m. 21 Nov. 1717 at Uttenhoffen
Anna Dorothea daughter of Hans Georg Rotter, citizen at Uttenhoffen.
Children:

1. Johan Georg b. 18 June 1718, bp. 20 June 1718
2. Nicolaus b. 24 May 1719, bp. 29 May 1719
3. Joh. Georg b. 7 Mar. 1721, bp. 9 Mar. 1721
4. Johannes b. 14 Mar. 1722, bp. 15 Mar. 1722
5. Anna Maria b. 6 July 1723, bp. 8 July 1723
6. Joh. Daniel b. 6 Feb. 1727, bp. 9 Feb. 1727
7. Magdalena b. 28 Sept. 1731, bp. 30 Sept. 1731

Her parents:
Married 28 Nov. 1690 at Uttenhoffen: Hans Georg Rotter, single son of the
late [n.n.] Rotter, former citizen at Gumprechtshoffen [Gumbrechtshoffen
=67110 Niederbronn-les-Bains] and Anna Maria, daughter of Dorst Völckel,
citizen at Uttenhoffen.

AMERICAN RECORDS

Trinity Lutheran KB, Lancaster:
Johann Emich and wife Dorothea were sp. in 1738 for a child of Georg
Adam Stiess.

Also in 1738, Johannes Moll had a daughter Anna Maria b. 13 Dec. 1738,
bp. 25 Dec. 1738. One of the sp. at her baptism was Anna Maria Emich,
"but on account of her minority, her mother Dorothea Emich stood in her
place."

First Reformed KB, Lancaster:
Nicholas Emig and wife Eva Margaret had:
Eva Barbara b. 17 July 1740, bp. 19 July 1740
Nicholas Emig and wife Eva Marg. nee Rausch were sp. in 1740.

John Ehmig and wife had:
Matthias b. 28 Feb. 1737, bp. 17 Apr. 1737
John Ehmig, son of John Ehmig, m. 15 Dec. 1745 Maria Margaret Crentz,
daughter of Valentin Crentz.
Maria Emig was a sp. in 1741.

Anthony Kobel and wife Anna Maria nee Emig had a son:
John b. 15 July 1742, bp. 4 Oct. 1742.   Sp.: John Emig
[See Burgert, *The Northern Kraichgau,* for Kobel.]

Rev. Jacob Lischy's records, York co.:
Johannes Ehmig and Maria Margreth had:
  1. Valentin bp. 22 Jan. 1749
     Sp.: Valentin Krantz and Elisabeth
  2. Anna Margr. bp. 11 Nov. 1750
     Sp.: Zacharias Schuckert and Anna Margreth
  3. Anna Barbara bp. 8 Apr. 1764

Niclaus Ehmig and wife Eva had:
  1. Johannes bp. 5 July 1753
     Sp.: John Ehmig and Dorothea
  2. Joseph bp. 20 Apr. 1755
     Sp.: Joseph Schmid and Barbara
  3. Friedrich bp. 13 May 1759

Matheus Ehmig and Anna Margreth had:
  1. Eva Dorothea bp. 16 Dec. 1759
     Sp.: Johannes Ehmig, Sr. and Eva Dorothea
  2. Niclaus bp. 4 Jan. 1762
     Sp.: Niclaus Ehmig and Eva Margareth
  3. Elisabeth bp. 20 Nov. 1762
     Sp.: Peter Büdinger and Mary Elisabeth Ehmig

Dewald Ehmig and wife Susanna had:
  1. Maria Elisabeth bp. 15 Feb. 1761
  2. Joh. Philliph bp. 31 July 1763
     Sp.: Phill. Ehmig

John Emig, Manchester twp., York co., nat. 24 Sept. 1762
George Emig, Pikes twp., Chester co., nat. Autumn, 1765.

124. ENES, PHILIP   Hoffen=
Janet, 1751   67250 Soultz-sous-Forêts
S-H, I: 474
                        EUROPEAN RECORDS

Oberseebach Catholic and Lutheran KB:
Joannis Enes and wife Elisabetha, Pietist., had a son:
     Joannes Philippus bp. 14 June 1726
     Sp.: Joes Philippus Probst; Elisabetha Saum.

Hoffen Reformed KB:
Joh. Philipp Enes, son of the late Johannes Enes, former citizen at

Oberseebach [=67160 Wissembourg] m. 8 Nov. 1746 Maria Catharina, daughter of the late Jacob Weimer, citizen and cooper. They had children:
1. Eva Margaretha b. 16 July 1747, bp. 23 July 1747
   Sp.: Michael, son of the late Jacob Weimer; Margaretha, daughter of Lorentz Weimer, church elder at Hofen; Eva, daughter of Abraham König [q.v.].

The Protestant church book at Hoffen starts in 1729. Earlier entries for Hoffen families are found in the Hunspach Reformed KB.

Zweibrücken Manumissions Protocoll, 1751:
Philips Enes of Cleeburg leaves with wife and one child for America. [Actually, as will be seen from the above entries, from Hoffen.]

AMERICAN RECORDS

Lowhill Union KB, Lehigh co.:
List of contributors to Lowhill Church in 1769: Philip Ennes.

125. ENGEL, ANDREAS   Gundershoffen=
Phoenix, 1750   67110 Niederbronn-les-Bains
S-H, I: 441

EUROPEAN RECORDS

Gundershoffen Lutheran KB:
Hanns Georg Engel, citizen, smith and widower here, m. 19 June 1715 Anna
Magdalena Stumpff, daughter of the Pastor Stumpff. They had a son:
    Andreas bp. 1 June 1719

Andreas Engel, widower and locksmith at Guntershoffen, m. 6 May 1749
Anna Magdalena, daughter of the late Marx Vögelin, former citizen at
Rittershoffen [=67690 Hatten], *Hanauischer jurisdiction.*

Signature from KB: Signature from S-H, II: 512:

AMERICAN RECORDS

Trinity Lutheran KB, Reading, Berks co.:
Andreas Engel and wife Maria Magdalena had:
    Jacob b. 11 Feb. 1758, bp. 11 Mar. 1758
    Sp.: Heinrich Hahn and Catharina

Died 1 Feb. 1768: Maria Magdalena Engel, wife of Andreas Engle, aged 39
y. 6 mo. 9 days; lived with her husband 19 y. 10 mo. 5 days. Buried 3 Feb.
1768.

Andreas Engel m. 22 Nov. 1768 Anna Margareth Grissin.

Egle, History of Lebanon co.:
Andreas Engle, shopkeeper of Heidelberg, died before 1793, leaving, among
other children:
    1. Andreas, residing at that time in Orange County, NY.
    2. Michael, residing in Parkin, N.J.

126. ENGEL, PHILIP   Durstel=
Halifax, 1752   67320 Drulingen
S-H, I: 482

EUROPEAN RECORDS

Durstel Lutheran KB:
Philipp Engel, son of the late Philipps Engel, citizen and *censor "auff dem Sch____berg"*, m. 29 Jan. 1715 Anna Margreth, daughter of the late Hans Jacob Eberhard, former citizen at Durstel.
Philipp Engel, linenweaver at Durstel, and wife Maria Margaretha nee Eberhard had a son:
>   Johann Philipp b. 1 Jan. 1716

Johann Philipp Engel, stonemason at Durstel, son of the late Philipp Engel, m. 11 Feb. 1751 Maria Christina Wildermuth, daughter of the late Philip Wildermuth, carpenter at Adamsweiler [=67320 Drulingen].   Maria Christina Wildermuth was b. 9 Sept. 1729 in Adamsweiler, dau. of Philipp Wildermuth and wife Anna Catharina nee Scherer; conf. 1742.

Verification of this emigration supplied by Dr. Bernd Gölzer, from the records compiled by Dr. Gerhard Hein:
According to an annotation in the Durstel Lutheran KB, they went to America. No children are recorded there.

127. ENSMINGER, HANS NICKEL   Weyer=
Neptune, 1754   67320 Drulingen
S-H, I: 621, 623, 625
EUROPEAN RECORDS

Hirschland Lutheran KB:
Hans Nickel Ensminger, *Rothgerber*, from Weyer, and wife Anna Eva had a son:
>   Hans Nickel bp. 21 Mar. 1723
[The father may be the Johann Niclaus Ensminger, b. 4 Oct. 1699 at Durstel, son of Philipp Ensminger and wife Elisabetha. He may also be the immigrant on the ship *Thistle*, 1738, S-H, I: 240. The passenger on that ship is given as Hans Nicolas Ensminger, age 39.]

AMERICAN RECORDS

Raymond Martin Bell, in a mimeographed paper on the Ensminger family, gives 1723 as the birth year for Nickel Ensminger. He further states "Nicholas Ensminger, Jr. is not listed in the 1738 ship list. He may have come to America in 1754. The will of Nicholas Ensminger, Sr., was filed in Lancaster in Oct. 1786. He died at the age of 87. His will named his wife Margaret; oldest son, Nicholas; son, Ludwig, deceased; deceased daughters, Christina, Elizabeth; daughters, Catharine, Mary, Margaret. His son Henry is not mentioned and must have died without heirs."

128. ENSMINGER, PETER age 39   Mattstall=
Samuel, 1733   67510 Lembach
S-H, I: 107, 111, 112
. with Catharina (Hansminger) age 33, Hendrick age 10, Catharina age 8,
Hans Philip age 6, Nicolas age 1

EUROPEAN RECORDS

Matstall Lutheran KB:
Peter Entzminger, single smith, son of Mstr. Phillipp Entzminger, now
inhabitant here, m. 21 Nov. 1719 Maria Catharina, daughter of Christoph
Trautmann, citizen at Mattstall. They had children:
1. Johann Peter b. 13 Apr 1721, bp. 16 Apr. 1721, died
2. Joh. Hennrich b. 7 Apr. 1723, bp. 11 Apr. 1723
3. Susanna Catharina b. 9 Aug. 1725, bp. 12 Aug. 1725
4. Johann Philip b. 20 Nov. 1727
5. Anna Christina b. 17 Apr. 1730, bp. 19 Apr. 1730
6. Johann Niclaus b. 22 July 1732, bp. 25 July 1732

AMERICAN RECORDS

Muddy Creek Lutheran KB, Lancaster co.:
Johann Peter Enssminger, (died) [after 1739] had children:
7. Johann Michael b. 18 Nov. 1735, bp. 30 Nov. 1735
   Sp.: Michael Andreas
8. Catarina Margaretha b. 22 June 1739, bp. 5 July 1739
   Sp.: Joh. Nicolaus Enssminger and wife Maria Margaretha
   and M. Cath. Stöver, wife of Pastor Joh. Caspar Stöver

Susanna Catarina Ensminger m. 29 Apr. 1742 at Muddy Creek, Martin Frey
[q.v.].

Joh. Heinrich Enssminger m. 19 Oct. 1742, at Cocalico, Christina Gaurin.
They had 6 children bp. at Muddy Creek 1743-1751.
Another Joh. Heinrich Enssminger (Jr.) m. 12 Mar. 1744 Maria Barbara
Crantzdorff. They had 2 children bp. at Muddy Creek 1750-1752.

Lancaster co. Deeds, Book A, pg 108:
7 Sept. 1748 - Maria Katharina Ensmonger, widow, sells 200A on branch of
Conestoga Creek to Jacob Hershberger.

Lancaster Orphan's Court, 6 Sept. 1748:
Maria Catherine Ensminger produces an account of sale of the plantation
of her husband, to be distributed to the widow Maria Catherina, the eldest

son and the other children. John Nicholas Ensminger, being upwards of 14 years of age, chose Catherine Ensminger, his mother, as guardian.

Lancaster co. Wills:
Nicholas Ensminger, Lebanon twp. 21 Feb. 1781- 28 June 1781. Exrs: Christopher Zebold and Jacob Phillippi. Wife: Elisabetha. Children: Peter and Daniel.

Nichs. Entsminger, Lebanon, Lancaster co., nat. autumn, 1765.

129. ERHART, PETER   Hirschland=
     ERHART, DIETRICH   67320 Drulingen
Phoenix, 1750
S-H, I: 440

EUROPEAN RECORDS

Hirschland Lutheran KB:
Joh. Peter Erhard from Betborn [Bettborn=57930 Fénétrange] and wife Agnes had children:
      Joh. Diedrich (twin) bp. 30 May 1721
      Sp.: Dietrich Hartman from Helgeringen; Jacob Erhard from
      Betborn; Anna Catharina Biber from Hirschland.

      Daughter (twin) bp. 30 May 1721
      Sp.: Maria Elisabetha Erhard; Anna Martha _____, widow of
      the late Durst.

AMERICAN RECORDS

Trinity Lutheran KB, Lancaster:
Dieterich Erhardt, a bachelor from the congregation and neighborhood, m. 17 Dec. 1751 Anna Maria Hatzin, daughter of Hanss Georg Hatz.

130. ESCHBACHER, ANDREAS   Diedendorf=
Phoenix, 1744   67260 Sarre-Union
S-H, I: 355   Berg=
                   67320 Drulingen

EUROPEAN RECORDS

Diedendorf Reformed KB:
Hans Eschbacher, citizen at Berg und Thal, and wife Anna Maria nee Fähs had children:
      1. Anna Margaretha bp. 4 Nov. 1704

2. Hans Nickel bp. 7 Feb. 1706
3. **Andreas** bp. 4 Sept. 1707
   Sp.: Andreas Fäss at Thal; Hans Jacob Lederman of Steinbach;
   Anna Elisabeth Andres from Berg
4. Anna Maria bp. 8 Mar. 1711
5. Catharina Barbara m. 6 Oct. 1728 Johann Christoph Obel [q.v.]
6. Anna Catharina, conf. 1730

AMERICAN RECORDS

Rev. Daniel Schumacher's records:
Andreas Eschbach and wife Anna Elisabeth had:
1. Andreas b. 24 Jan. 1764, bp. 25 Feb. 1764 in Lowhill
   Sp.: Christopher Obell [q.v.]; Anna Catharina Eulern;
   Johannes Jurg; Maria Eva Knerr, single.

Christopher Obell and Anna Elisabeth Eschbachen, Andreas Eschbach's wife
were sp. in 1764 for a child of Daniel Stedler, bp. in Weisenberg.

Lancaster Will Book C-I: 108:
Andrew Eshbagh, Lebanon twp. 18 May 1772-10 June 1772.
Wife: Ann Eliza Ashbagh. Children: Anna, John, Mary, Adam and Daniel.
Exrs: Ann E. Ashbagh and Philip Greaver.

Andrew Ershbach, Lowhill twp., Northampton co., nat. Autumn, 1765.

131. ETTER, HANS GEORG   Rittershoffen=
Phoenix, 1750   67690 Hatten
S-H, I: 440 [last name on page - his mark (wheel with spokes) on list, S-H,
II: 511, same mark he used in KB]
     ETTER, GEORG HENRICH
Phoenix, 1750
S-H, I: 441 [first name, top of page]

EUROPEAN RECORDS

Rittershofen Lutheran KB:
Joh. Georg Etter, wagoner and *shirmer*, Reformed, son of Joh. Peter Etter
of Oberhofen [67160 or 67240] and wife Anna, m. 8 July 1732 Eva Wein,
daughter of Joh. Jacob Wein and wife Eva nee Süss. Children:
1. Georg Heinrich b. 22 Apr. 1733, bp. 24 Apr. 1733
   Sp.: Georg Heinrich, son of Johannes Späth; Hans Georg,
   son of Michael Ries; Anna, daughter of Valentin Humpert.

2. Anna Eva b. 20 May 1734, bp. 22 May 1734
   Sp.: Hans Georg, son of Jacob Wein; Anna Maria, wife of
   Matthis ?Lehr; Anna Eva, daughter of Martin Knab.

AMERICAN RECORDS

Hocker, *German Settlers of Pennsylvania*, p. 41:
Pennsylvanische Geschicht - Schreiber dated 16 June 1754:
Georg Etter, wheelwright in Rapho twp, Lancaster co, in the White Oak
Land, seeks his son Christian, who was indentured in Philadelphia several
years ago to Wilhelm Müller in the Jerseys.

132. EVA, BARTHEL   Mackwiller=
Halifax, 1752   67430 Diemeringen
S-H, I: 482 [Bartholmae (E) Evar on list]

EUROPEAN RECORDS

Bütten Lutheran KB and Berg und Thal Lutheran KB:
Barthel Eva, Lutheran daylaborer of Mackweiler, son of Johann Adam Eva,
m. 20 July 1747 at Mackweiler Anna Margaretha Scheurer, daughter of the
late Daniel Scheurer, tailor at Thal.   She was b. 12 July 1722 at Thal
[=67320 Drulingen]. Children:
   1. Eva Catharina, illegitimate, b. 5 Apr. 1746 at Thal
   2. Johann Nickel b. 31 Aug. 1748, d. 19 Oct. 1748
      at Mackweiler [Bütten KB].
   3. Johannes b. 6 Oct. 1749 at Mackweiler [Bütten KB].

Verification of this emigrant provided by Dr. Bernd Gölzer from the
compiled records of Dr. Gerhard Hein:
Records of Saarwerden county office for Berg and Thal:
Dated 28 Dec. 1780 (inventory of her sister Anna Dorothea Scheurer): the
sister Anna Margaretha Scheurer and her husband Barthel Eva have moved
to America.
AMERICAN RECORDS

New Hanover Lutheran KB, Montgomery co.:
Bartel Eva and wife Anna [Elisabeth in 1755 record] Margareth had
children:
   4. Jacob, twin b. __ Apr. 1754, bp. 19 Oct. 1755
   5. Maria, twin b. __ Apr. 1754, bp. 19 Oct. 1755
   6. Anna Margareth b. 18 Jan. 1757, bp. 17 Apr. 1757

133. EYER, JOH. MARTIN   Feldbach, Kutzenhausen=
Ann, 1749   67250 Soultz-sous-Forêts
S-H, I: 416
EUROPEAN RECORDS

Kutzenhausen Lutheran KB:
Jacob Eyer, widower and citizen at Feldbach, m. 23 Nov. 1723 Anna
Barbara, daughter of Hennrich Löwenstein, citizen and master shoemaker
at Feldbach. Their son:
> Johann Martin b. 22 June 1729, bp. 24 June 1729
> Sp.: Joh. Martin, son of Johan Herlemann, citizen at
> Merckweiler; Joh. Wilhelm, son of Lorentz Eyer, citizen
> here; Dorothea, daughter of Heinrich Löwenstein, citizen
> at Feldbach.

AMERICAN RECORDS

Tohickon Lutheran KB, Bucks co:
Martin Eyer and Dorothea Beuscher were sp. in 1752 for a child of
Gottfried Schmelcher; also in 1753 they sp. children of James and Mary
Hoepenny; in the Reformed KB in 1753, they sp. a child of Johannes
Wildanger. Martin Eyer and wife Dorothea had a son:
> 1. Johann Adam b. 27 July 1755, bp. 17 Aug. 1755
> Sp.: John Adam Beischer and Anna Barbara.
> He became a schoolmaster and fraktur artist.

The outstanding folk art of Johann Adam Eyer. Private Collection.

See Frederick S. Weiser, *IAE SD, The Story of Johann Adam Eyer (1755-1837) Schoolmaster and Fraktur Artist with a Translation of his Roster Book, 1779-1787,* in the Pennsylvania German Society Volume 14 (1980): 437-506.

Weiser lists the following children of John Martin and Anna Dorothea (Beuscher) Eyer:
1. Johann Adam b. 27 July 1755, d. 29 Dec. 1837, unmarried
2. Johannes m. Margaret
3. Phillip Jacob d. 1833, unmarried
4. Anna Barbara b. ca. Sept. 1762, died young
5. Susanna b. ca. Apr. 1764 m. Philip Dorrand
6. Ludwig b. 8 Jan. 1767, d. 20 Sept. 1814; m. Catharine Long
7. Johann Friedrich b. 5 Mar. 1770, d. 19 Jan. 1827; m. Susanna
8. Philipp Heinrich b. 5 Mar. 1770, d. 26 June 1845;
   m. Elisabeth Rothrock
9. Barbara m. Jacob Wolfinger
10. Anna Catharina b. 3 Jan. 1778, d. 16 Sept. 1806

See the above cited volume for additional detail on the Eyer family.

John Martin Eyre, Bedminster twp., Bucks co., nat. Autumn, 1765.

134. EYERMAN, JOH. GEORG age 37   67510 Lembach
Two Sisters, 1738
S-H, I: 209, 211 [appears on list as Iremann]
   with Maria Margt. Ireman age 32

EUROPEAN RECORDS

Lembach Lutheran KB:
Johan Georg Eyerman, farmer, and wife Margaretha had:
1. Johann Martin b. 25 June 1732, bp. 27 June 1732
   died 1732. Sp.: Martin Dielmann?, Hans Adam
   Schweighard, A. Maria wife of Bern. Trautmann
2. Joh. Georg b. 4 Sept. 1734, bp. 6 Sept. 1734
   Sp.: Bernhard Trautman, Joh. Theobald Motz
   of Lampersloch; Christina wife of Michael Thumm
3. Johann Michael b. 4 July 1736, bp. 8 July 1736
   Sp.: Rudolff Spiri, shoemaker; Michael Thum;
   Maria Barbara, wife of Michael Müller.

135. EYERMAN, JOH. MATTHIAS   Preuschdorf=
Before 1779   67250 Soultz-sous-Forêts
Not in S-H

EUROPEAN RECORDS

Preuschdorf Lutheran KB:
Joh. Georg Eyerman, son of Joh. Henrich Eyermann of Lampertsloch and
wife Catharina nee Rössel, b. 24 May 1719 at Lampertsloch [=67250 Soultz-
sous-Forêts], m. 12 Feb. 1745 at Preuschdorf Anna Maria, daughter of Joh.
Martin Eyer of Feldbach. They had children:
1. Georg Henrich b. 13 May 1746
2. Anna Maria b. 2 Apr. 1749
3. Joh. Michel b. 11 Oct. 1750
4. Joh. Matthias b. 24 Feb 1753, conf. 1769
5. Georg Jacob b. 21 May 1756
6. Catharina Salome b. 15 Feb. 1759 d. 1771
7. Dorothea Barbara b. 10 Feb. 1762
8. Joh. Georg b. 18 June 1764
9. Johanna Elisabetha b. 27 May 1766

AMERICAN RECORDS

Joh. Matthias Eyerman lived in New Hanover, Montgomery co., later in
Easton, where he d. 18 Nov. 1816. He m. Johanna Sneider [Hanna Sibilla
in some records] b. 1749, d. 1843, daughter of Henry and Catharina
Schneider of New Hanover. Children:
1. Hanna Sibilla b. 15 Mar. 1779, bp. 11 June 1779
   Bp. at Falkner Swamp Ref. [surname Eyerman]
2. Susanna Sophia b. 29 Jan. 1781, bp. 1 July 1781
   New Hanover Luth. KB [surname Eiermann]
3. Anna Maria b. 6 Apr. 1782, bp. 16 June 1782
   [surname Eirman]
4. Henry b. 29 Jan. 1784, bp. 16 Apr. 1784
   New Hanover Lutheran [surname Eyermann]
5. Elisabeth b. 19 Nov. 1789 [First Reformed KB, Easton]

St. John's Lutheran KB, Easton, PA:
Died 15 Oct. 1805 - Susanna Sophia Eyerman, daughter of Jacob (? should
be Matthias), age 24 years, 8 months, 14 days, in Easton. Sickness:
Consumption.

136. FAHRINGER, JOH. THEOBALD
Phoenix, 1750
S-H, I: 441 [Debalt (TF) Farringer on list]

Ottwiller=
67320 Drulingen
Keskastel=
67260 Sarre-Union

EUROPEAN RECORDS

Drulingen Lutheran KB:
Heinrich Varinger, cowherd, and wife Barbara had a son:
    Hans Theobald b. 28 July 1718 bp. 31 July 1718
    Conf. 1732 at Bischtroff: Theobald Faringer
    [See Nicolas Fahringer for family record]

Keskastel Lutheran KB:
Joh. Diebold Fahringer, son of the late Hennrich Fahringer, citizen and inhabitant at Wolfskirchen [=67260 Sarre-Union], m. 14 Jan. 1744 Anna Barbara nee Fischer, widow of the late Ludwig Leiser, citizen and tailor here.
[Joh. Ludwig Leiser, tailor, son of Friedrich Leiser of Lorentzen [=67430 Diemeringen] m. 19 Aug. 1738 Anna Barbara, daughter of the late Hans Georg Fischer, citizen and inhabitant at Keskastel. They had children:
    1. Hans Georg Leiser bp. 15 Nov. 1739
    2. Joh. Ludwig Leiser bp. 9 Feb. 1742
These two Leiser children may have emigrated with their mother.]

Diebold Fahringer and Anna Barbara had children:
    1. Maria Catharina bp. 26 July 1744
      Sp.: Diebold Fischer son of the late Nickel Fischer, Maria Margaretha wife of Hans Nickel Reüth? & Catharina daughter of the late Christmann Beer.
    2. Hans Diebold bp. 10 Feb. 1746
      Sp.: Hans Georg Schäffer son of the late Christian Schäffer, wagner here; Hans Nickel Fahringer; & Catharina daughter of the late Diebold Schmid, Keskastel [=67260 Sarre-Union].
    3. Maria Magdalena bp. 10 May 1748

Verification of this emigration supplied by Dr. Bernd Gölzer, from the county records of Nassau-Saarwerden, compiled by Dr. Gerhard Hein:
Records of Saarwerden county office for Keskastel, dated 9 May 1752: Thiebold Fahringer of Keskastel has moved to the New Land one year ago, and had his property auctioned prior to his departure.

AMERICAN RECORDS

Christ "Little" Tulpehocken Lutheran KB, Berks co:
Confirmed 9 May 1761 - Theobald Fahringer, age 15, poor [schlect].
Communicants 9 May 1761: #30 Catharina Fahringerin
        #48 Theobald Fahringer
Communicants at the Northkill, 1762: Theobald Fahringer

A Georg Fahringer and Martin Fahringer appear in the Altalaha Lutheran KB, Rehrersburg, Berks co. records in the 1790s.

137. FAHRINGER, MARTIN   Wolfskirchen=
Halifax, 1752   67260 Sarre-Union
S-H, I: 483   Bischtroff-sur-Sarre=
    [appears on list: Martin (v) Varinger]   67260 Sarre-Union

EUROPEAN RECORDS

Pistorf (Bischtroff) Lutheran KB:
Conf. 1724- Hans Martin Fahringer from Wolffskirchen
[See brother Nicholas Fahringer for other family records.]

Hans Martin Fahringer m. 25 Jan. 1746 Anna Margaretha Isemann. They had children:
    1. Catharina Margretha b. 19 Oct. 1746, bp. 20 Oct. 1746
       Sp.: Daniel, son of the late Daniel Müller of Neusaarwerden;
       Theobald Fahringer [q.v.], the father's brother from Castell
       [Keskastel]; Margretha, wife of Henrich Klein; Maria Elisabetha,
       daughter of Joh. Wampler of Herbitzheim.
    2. Catharina Magdalena b. 19 Apr. 1749, bp. 20 Apr. 1749
       Sp.: Georg, son of Hans Fischer; Carl Friedrich, son of the
       Pastor Textor; Catharina, daughter of Daniel Klein; Maria
       Magdalena, daughter of Herr Daniel Weiss, *Meyer* here.

Anna Margaretha Iseman was b. 5 July 1716, daughter of Johann Nickel Iseman and his wife Anna Magdalena.

AMERICAN RECORDS

St. Michael's Lutheran KB, Germantown, Philadelphia co.:
Martin Vahringer and wife Margaretha had children:
    3. Martin b. 16 Dec. 1758, bp. 26 Aug. 1759.
       Sp.: Martin Schlotterer and Anna Barbara.
    4. Joh. Nicolaus b. 28 Mar. 1761, bp. 10 May 1761; d. 5 Sept. 1767.
       Sp.: Peter Rieb [q.v.- Reeb] and Margaretha Renner.

Died 2 Nov. 1793- Martin Faringer, aged 82 y., 9 mo., 26 days.
Died 3 Dec. 1797- Widow Fahringer, aged 81 y.

The Sarre River at Bischtroff.

138. FAHRINGER, NICHOLAS   Ottwiller=
Halifax, 1752   67320 Drulingen
S-H, I: 484 [Joh. Nicklas (+) Farringer]

EUROPEAN RECORDS

Drulingen & Wolfskirchen Lutheran KB:
Heinrich Varinger (Faringer), herdsman, and wife Barbara had children:
1. Martin [q.v.] b. ca 1710, conf. 1724
2. A son (N.N.) b. 21 Apr. 1714, bp. 24 Apr. 1714
   Sp.: Christoph Sackenreuter, smith; Philip, son of Hans Jacob
   Schmidt, Ottweiler Christina, daughter of Joachim Schmidt,
   church *censor*, all Ottweiler
3. Maria Barbara b. 28 Apr. 1715, bp. 30 Apr. 1715 at Ottweiler
4. Hans Theobald [q.v.] b. 28 July 1718, bp. 31 July
   He was conf. 1732 at Pistorf [=Bischtroff]
   Sp.: Hans Theobald Martzloff, Theobald Wehrung son of Hans
   Theobald Wehrung, Margareta Kastenteich, daughter of the late
   Leonhard Kastenteich
5. **Nicholas** bp. 24 Aug. 1720, Wolfskirchen Lutheran KB.

139. FEUERSTEIN, NICKELL age 40   Thal=
   FEUERSTEIN, NICHOLAS, JR. age 21   67320 Drulingen
Peggy, 1753
S-H, I: 546, 548, 550

EUROPEAN RECORDS

Berg Lutheran KB:
Nickel Feyerstein [also Feuerstein], carpenter at Thal. and wife Anna
Catharina nee Nunnemacher had children:
   1. Anna Catharina b. 23 Aug. 1733, bp. 27 Aug. 1733
   2. **Johann Niclaus** b. 12 Apr. 1735, bp. 19 Apr. 1735
   3. Johann Joseph b. 7 May 1737, bp. 12 May 1737
   4. Eva Catharina b. 3 June 1739, bp. 7 June 1739
   5. Rosina b. 13 Mar. 1742, bp. 16 Mar. 1742
   6. Johann Mathias b. 5 Apr. 1744, bp. 8 Apr. 1744
   7. Maria Dorothea b. 17 Feb. 1747, bp 19 Feb. 1747
   8. Maria Magdalena b. 22 Mar. 1750, bp. 25 Mar. 1750
   9. Johann Theobald b. 3 Aug. 1752, bp. 6 Aug. 1752

AMERICAN RECORDS

Trinity Lutheran KB, Lancaster:
Conrad Stauzenberger, single, m. 3 June 1754 Catharina Feuerstein, single.

Frederick Lutheran KB, Frederick, MD:
Matthis Feuerstein and wife Anna Maria had:
   1. Johannes b. 16 May 1782, bp. 25 Dec. 1782
      Sp.: Jacob Biber and Catharina
   2. Salomon b. 4 May 1786, bp. 4 June 1786
      Sp.: Jacob Medart and Magdalena
   3. Anna Mary b. 9 Oct. 1789, bp. 18 Oct. 1789
      Sp.: John Lieblich and Louisa

Joseph Feuerstein and wife Catharina had:
   1. Magdalena b. 1 May 1783, bp. 25 May 1783
      Sp.: Margreth Macbride

[The surname became Firestone in later generations.]

Nichs. Fierstone, Paradise, York co. nat. 11 Apr. 1763.

140. FISCHER, HANS PETER   Gundershoffen=
    FISCHER, JACOB   67110 Niederbronn-les-Bains
Dragon, 17 Oct. 1749
S-H, I: 423

EUROPEAN RECORDS

Gundershoffen Lutheran KB:
Hans Georg Fischer and Barbara had:
    Johann Peter b. 29 June 1698, bp. 2 July 1698

Peter Fischer, son of Hans Georg Fischer, citizen here, m. (1) 27 Apr. 1719
at Guntershoffen, Magdalena, daughter of the late Jacob Dürrenberger,
former *Hoffmann* at Merzweiler [=67580 Mertzwiller]. Children:
    1. Johann Peter b. 7 Oct. 1722, bp. 9 Oct. 1722
    2. **Johann Jacob** b. 10 July 1725, bp. 13 July 1725
    3. Johann Georg b. 20 Aug. 1730
    4. Abraham bp. 27 Mar. 1733
    5. Maria Salome bp. 2 May 1734
    6. Andreas bp. 10 Jan. 1737
    7. Dorothea bp. 15 Jan. 1738

Johann Peter Fischer, citizen and widower here, m. (2) 15 Nov. 1739 Maria
Elisabetha, daughter of Peter Gassen?, citizen here. They had:
    6. Barbara bp. 11 Mar. 1743
    7. Johannes b. __ Dec. 1747, bp. 28 Dec. 1747

AMERICAN RECORDS

Hocker, *German Settlers of Pennsylvania:* 21:
Sower's newspaper, dated 16 Aug. 1750:
Hansz Peter Fischer and his wife Maria Elisabeth Gasser, who arrived in this
country last autumn, seek her brother Peter Gasser, from Guntershoffen,
Alsace, who came here 12 years ago. They are in Heidelberg twp. on the
Brunenkill at Michael Schauer's place.

141. FISCHER, PHILIPP   Hunspach=
_____, 1752   67250 Soultz-sous-Forêts

EUROPEAN RECORDS

Hunspach Reformed KB:
Joh. Philipp Fischer, son of the late Simon Fischer, former inhabitant at
Drusweiler [?] m. 18 Apr. 1730 Maria Barbara, daughter of the late Michael

Haug, former smith and *Gerichtsschöffen* at Hunspach. They had:
1. Johann Michael b. 22 Dec. 1730, d. 20 Jan. 1740
2. Anna Maria b. 12 Oct. 1732, bp. 19 Oct. 1732
3. Maria Barbara b. ?9 Dec. 1734, bp. ?12 Oct. 1734
4. Maria Eva b. 20 Jan. 1738, bp. 26 Jan. 1738

Maria Barbara Fischer nee Haug d. 29 Jan. 1740, age 42 y. 1 mo.
Philipp Fischer, citizen and widower here, m. (2) 24 May 1740 Anna
Catharina, daughter of the late Antoni Rheinhard, former *Schirmsverwanthen*
at Merckweyler [Merkwiller=67250 Soultz-sous-Forêts]. Children:
5. Johann Georg b. 30 Dec. 1741, bp. 3 Jan. 1742
6. Maria Dorothea b. 20 Aug. 1743, bp. 25 Aug. 1742
7. Maria Catharina b. 15 Dec. 1747, bp. 18 Dec. 1747
8. Maria Catharina b. 22 Sept. 1750, bp. 27 Sept. 1750

Zweibruecken Manumissions Protocoll, Clee- and Catharinenburg,: 1752:
Johann Philips Fischer of Hunspach leaves for America.

142. FISCHER, SIMON   Keskastel=
Hero, 1764   67260 Sarre-Union
S-H, I 698
EUROPEAN RECORDS

Keskastel Lutheran KB:
Hans Nickel Fischer and wife Anna Elisabetha nee Reeb had a son:
Simon bp. 25 Feb. 1721

Simon Fischer, son of the late Hans Nickel Fischer, m. 24 Jan. 1747 Anna
Elisabetha, daughter of the late Marx Völler. They had children:
1. Anna Elisabetha b. 18 Jan. 1748
2. Anna Eva b. 11 Dec. 1753
3. Johann Jacob b. 24 Apr. 1757
4. Johann Georg b. 2 June 1759
5. Johann Christian b. 6 Nov. 1763

Verification of this emigrant provided by Dr. Bernd Gölzer from the
compiled records of Dr. Gerhard Hein:
Records of Saarwerden county office for Keskastel:
Dated 18 May 1773, inventory of Thiebald Fischer of Keskastel. His brother
Simon Fischer "residing in the New Land" is one of the heirs. Dated 21 July
1768: Hans Nickel Fischer, deceased; the son Simon went to Pennsylvania
four years ago.

143. FORSCH, JOHANN ADAM age 22   Niederkutzenhausen,
Halifax, 1753   Kutzenhausen=
S-H, I: 560, 562, 563   67250 Soultz-sous-Forêts

EUROPEAN RECORDS

Kutzenhausen Lutheran KB:
Leonhart Forsch, joiner, son of Caspar Forsch from Markheidenheim,
Anspach Jurisdiction [?W-8824 Heidenheim, Mittelfr.], m. 24 Jan. 1730
Maria Barbara Eyer, daughter of Lorentz Eyer. They had 13 children, of
whom two sons emigrated to America:
    1. Joh. Adam b. 21 Nov. 1731, bp. 22 Nov. 1731
    2. Joh. Martin [q.v.] b. 8 Nov. 1733

AMERICAN RECORDS

Trinity Lutheran KB, Lancaster:
Adam Forsch and wife Barbara were sp. in 1760 for a child of Martin
Brunkhart; they also sp. a child of Valentin Schaeffer in 1760. They also sp.
a child of Martin Forsch in 1763.

144. FORSCH, MARTIN   Niederkutzenhausen,
Richmond, 1763   Kutzenhausen=
S-H, I: 685   67250 Soultz-sous-Forêts

EUROPEAN RECORDS

Kutzenhausen Lutheran KB:
Leonhart Forsch, joiner, son of Caspar Forsch from Markheidenheim, [?W-
8824 Heidenheim, Mittelfr.] Anspach Jurisdiction, m. 24 Jan. 1730 Maria
Barbara Eyer, daughter of Lorentz Eyer. They had 13 children, of whom
two sons emigrated to America:
    1. Joh. Adam b. 21 Nov. 1731 [q.v.]; emigrated 1753.
    2. Joh. Martin b. 8 Nov. 1733, bp. 10 Nov. 1733
        Sp.: Joh. Martin Eyer of Feldbach.

Joh. Martin Forsch, son of the joiner here, m. 4 May 1762 Barbara
Haltemann, daughter of the late Joh. Haltemann, former *Schlossmeyer* at
Hohweiler. One of the witnesses at the marriage was the father Leonhard
Forsch. [Martin Forsch's signature in this marriage record matches his
signature on the ship list, S-H, II: 775.]

AMERICAN RECORDS

Trinity Lutheran KB, Lancaster:
Martin Forsch and wife Barbara had:
  1. Jacob b. 20 Dec. 1763, bp. 29 Jan. 1764
    Sp.: Adam Forsch and wife Barbara.

1790 PA Census:
Martin First, Warrington twp, York co. 1 male over 16; 3 males under 16;
4 females.

145. FRANCKHAUSER, MICHAEL   Langensoultzbach=
Sandwich, 1750   67360 Woerth
S-H, I: 449

EUROPEAN RECORDS

Langensoultzbach Lutheran KB:
Christian Franckhauser of Nähweiler [Nehwiller-pres-Woerth=67110
Niederbronn-les-Bains] and wife Fronica (nee ?Kischer or ?Rauscher) had
a son:
    Johann Michael bp. 28 Jan. 1714

Hans Michael Franckhauser, son of Christian Franckhauser of Nähweiler,
m. 2 Dec. 1734 at Fröschweiler   Anna, daughter of Jacob Krebs of
Liniehausen. (Jacob Krebs *aus d. Schweitz, Berner Geb.*, Reformed religion,
died 22 June 1741 at Liniehausen.)
They had children:
  1. Anna Barbara bp. 17 Feb. 1736
  2. Maria Dorothea bp. 19 Apr. 1737
  3. Catharina b. 26 June 1740
  4. Joh. Michael b. 3 June 1746

AMERICAN RECORDS

Muddy Creek Reformed KB, Lancaster co.:
John Michael Franckhauser and wife Anna had:
    Anna b. 28 Jan. 1753, bp. 25 Feb. 1753
    Sp.: Peter Franckhauser [q.v.] and wife Eva

Trinity Lutheran KB, New Holland, Lancaster co.:
Dorothea Franckenhausserin was sp. in 1759 and 1760.

Michael Frankhauser died 26 Nov. 1799, age about 88 years.

Berks co. wills and adm.:
Michael Frankenhauser, Brecknock twp., on 2 Dec. 1799, adm. granted to
Michael Frankenhauser, only son.

A street of half-timbered houses
in Langensoultzbach with the
centrally located village church.

146. FRANKHAUSER, PETER age 28   Liniehausen,
St. Andrew, 1743   Langensoultzbach=
S-H, I: 349, 350, 351   67360 Woerth
   [Franker on A list, Frankhousen on B list - did not sign]

EUROPEAN RECORDS

Langensoultzbach Lutheran KB:
Peter Fanghauser, [elsewhere in KB: Franckhusser] son of the late Christian
Fanghauser of Nähweiler m. 13 Jan. 1739 at Sultzbach Eva Sichler, daughter
of the late Hans Martin Sichler of Liniehausen. They had a son:
   1. Johann Jacob b. 3 Feb. 1740 at Liniehausen

Buried 11 Nov. 1736 at Nähweiler:
Christian Franckhauser of Nähweiler, aged about 67 years.

AMERICAN RECORDS

Muddy Creek Lutheran & Reformed KB, Lancaster co.:
Joh. Peter Franckhausser had children:
   2. Joh. Peter b. 2 Nov. 1744, bp. 16 Dec. 1744 (Lutheran KB)
      Sp.: Joh. Jacob Wüst [q.v.] and Christina Krebs [q.v.]
   3. Christian bp. 8 Aug. 1746 (Reformed KB)
      Sp.: Christian Krebs and wife Christina
   4. Eva b. 13 May 1748 bp. 22 May 1748 (Lutheran KB)
      Sp.: Christina Krebs
   5. a daughter bp. 30 July 1755 (Reformed KB)
      Sp.: Michael Frankhauser [q.v.] and wife Susanna
   6. a daughter bp. 2 July 1758 (Reformed KB)
      Sp.: Valentin Schneider and Eva Eliza Brucker
   7. a daughter bp. 26 Dec. 1759 (Reformed KB)
      Sp.: Valentin Schneider and wife.

Peter Franckhauser and wife sp. a child of Christian Krebs in 1746, 1747.
Peter Franchausser and wife Eva were sp. for children of Jacob Wüst.

Married 9 June 1767 (Reformed KB):
Peter, son of Peter Franckhauser, single and Anna Barbara, daughter of
Benedict Hirschy [q.v.].

Peter Frankhausser (Jr.) had:
      1. Nicolaus b. 5 May 1765, bp. 27 May 1765
         Sp.: Nicolaus Haller and wife

Married 5 Nov. 1771 (Reformed KB):
Christ Franckhauser, Ref., son of Peter Franckhauser, Ref. and Margaret
Frey, Lutheran, daughter of Martin Frey [q.v.]

Peter Franckhauser was installed as an elder of the Muddy Creek Reformed
Church on 11 Aug. 1771. He died 20 July 1784 at Muddy Creek.

Trinity Lutheran KB, New Holland, Lancaster co.:
Buried 24 Feb. 1804: Eva Frankhauser, aged 82 years, 10 months, 7 days.

147. FRANTZ, ABRAHAM   Schalbach=
[unnamed ship] 20 Oct. 1747   57370 Phalsbourg
S-H, I: 369, 370
                        EUROPEAN RECORDS

Rauwiller Reformed KB:
Peter Frantz, son of Peter Frantz of Schalbach, m. 26 Feb. 1706 Maria Anna
Hahn, daughter of Jacob Hahn of Fleissheim. They had a son:
     Abraham b. 29 Sept. 1729

                        AMERICAN RECORDS

Rev. Daniel Schumacher's records:
Abraham Frantz and wife Catharina had:
     Elisabetha b. 17 Apr. 1769, bp. 28 May 1769 in Lehigh twp.
     Sp.: Jürg Walcker and wife Elisabeth.

148. FRANTZ, DEBALT   Wolfskirchen=
Phoenix, 1750   67260 Sarre-Union
S-H, I: 440
                        EUROPEAN RECORDS

Pisdorf [Bischtroff] Lutheran KB:
Jacob Frantz, born in ?*Ellenbogen in Ketzingerthal, Wirtenbergischer
Herrschaft,* m. 21 Feb. 1719 Anna Maria Dintinger, daughter of the late
Hans Dintinger of Wolfskirchen. Jacob Frantz, carpenter of Wolfkirchen,
and wife Anna Maria had children:
     1. Anna Elisabetha b. 21 Aug. 1720, bp. 25 Aug. 1720
        She m. 11 Sept. 1753 at Diedendorf Anton Braun [q.v.]
     2. **Catharina Barbara** b. 1 Mar. 1723, bp. 4 Mar. 1723
     3. Anna Eva b. 28 Oct. 1725, bp. 30 Oct. 1725

4. **Theobald** b. 1 Jan. 1728, bp. 6 Jan. 1728
5. Gertruda b. ca. 1730 m. 16 Apr. 1765 Jacob Karcher
6. Johann Henrich b. 2 Nov. 1756, bp. 6 Nov. 1756

Verification of this emigration supplied by Dr. Bernd Gölzer, from the county records of Nassau-Saarwerden, compiled by Dr. Gerhard Hein: Notary Public records of Wolfskirchen:
Dated 1 Dec. 1756, inventory of Anna Maria Dintinger Frantz: the daughter Anna Elisabetha, 35 years old, emigrated to America in 1753; the daughter Catharina Barbara, 33 years old, emigrated to America in 1749; the son Theobald has died in America, according to a letter written by his sisters.

149. FRANTZ, HENRICH   Schalbach=
[unnamed ship] 20 Oct. 1747   57370 Phalsbourg
S-H, I: 369, 370
EUROPEAN RECORDS

Rauwiller Reformed KB:
Henrich Frantz from Schalbach m. 21 July 1742 Susanna, daughter of Stephan Balliet. They had children:
    1. Maria Margaretha b. 2 May 1743
    2. Anna Maria b. 14 Sept. 1744
    3. Saara b. 24 Feb. 1746

AMERICAN RECORDS

Philadelphia Adm. G: 401. Estate # 28, 1764:
Estate of Henry Frantz. Adm. Bond dated 5 May 1764.
Peter Frantz of Lynn twp., Northampton co., brother of Henry Frantz, late of the same place, yeoman, deceased, and Philip Miller of Whitemarsh twp., and Christian Schnyder of the City of Philadelphia.
Inventory of the estate of Henry Frantz, late of Heydelberg twp., County of Northampton, appraised 14 Nov. 1763, total £59.3.6. Signed by Ulrich Näff, Jacob Riedy, Adam Räder. Exhibited 5 May 1764.
Account by Peter Frantz, eldest brother and adm. of Henry Frantz, dec'd. Estate totaled £177.14.5½.

Charles Roberts et al, *History of Lehigh County, Pennsylvania,* **Vol. III:**
Henry Franz was killed by the Indians in 1760 (another account says 1764) and his daughter Margaret, age 15, was taken captive (another account says Sept. 1757, along with a girl named Solt). She lived with the Indians for 7 years, until exchanged. She m. 9 May 1769 Joh. Nickel Votring, son of Samuel Wotring [q.v.]. Margaret Frantz' birth date is given in American

records as 8 May 1745. She d. 29 June 1823 and is buried at Unionville, Lehigh Co. Nicholas Wodring and wife Margareth had children:
1. Samuel b. 9 Sept. 1772
2. Johan Peter b. 17 Sept. 1774, d. y.
3. Johan Nicholas, twin, b. 24 Jan. 1776
4. Johan Peter, twin, b. 24 Jan. 1776
5. Johan Henrich b. 9 Nov. 1778
6. Maria Susanna b. 15 Nov. 1780

150. FRANTZ, HENRICH   Diedendorf=
Two Brothers, 1748   67260 Sarre-Union
S-H, I: 378, 380, 381

EUROPEAN RECORDS

Diedendorf Reformed KB:
Michel Frantz and wife Margaretha nee Birin [elsewhere Bury] of Diedendorf had a son:
Henrich bp. 15 Nov. 1716, conf. 1731

Rauwiller Reformed KB:
Henrich Frantz from Diedendorf m. 23 June 1744 Susanna Girading from here [Rauwiller]. They had a son:
1. Peter bp. 16 Sept. 1745

AMERICAN RECORDS

Tohickon Reformed KB, Bucks Co.:
Henry Frantz and Maria Susanna had:
John Jacob b. 3 Aug. 1757, bp. 20 Aug. 1757
Sp.: Jacob Jeradin, Catharine Jeradin

Henry Frantz, Chestnut Hill, Northampton Co., nat. Autumn, 1765.

151. FRANTZ, JOHAN PETER   Schalbach=
[unnamed ship] 20 Oct. 1747   57370 Phalsbourg
S-H, I: 369, 370

EUROPEAN RECORDS

Diedendorf Reformed KB:
Peter Frantz, son of Peter Frantz of Schalbach, m. 26 Feb. 1706 Maria Anna Hahn, daughter of Jacob Hahn of Fleissheim [Fleisheim=57119 Lixheim].

They had a son:
Johann Peter b. 11 Oct. 1727

Rauwiller Reformed KB:
Johan Petter Frantz from Schalbach m. 2 Apr. 1747 Eva Elisabeta Martzlof
from Schalbach.

AMERICAN RECORDS

Muddy Creek Reformed KB, Lancaster co.:
Peter Frantz and wife Eva Elisabeth had children:
1. Catharina b. 25 Aug. 1748
   Sp.: Peter Fuesen; Dorothy Heft, single.
2. John Henry bp. 26 May (1751)
   Sp.: Henry Schlabach and wife
3. John Peter b. 7 Sept. 1753, bp. 21 Oct. 1753
   Sp.: Wolfgang Aachen and Dorothea.

Egypt Reformed KB, Lehigh co.:
Peter Frantz and wife Eva Elisabeth had:
4. Christina Barbara bp. 15 Aug. 1756
   Sp.: Samuel Wotring and wife: Johannes Berret;
   Christina, wife of Jacob Wolf.

Rev. Daniel Schumacher's records:
Peter Frantz and wife Eva Elisabeth had:
5. Anna Margaretha bp. 3 Dec. 1758, 11 weeks old, in Weisenberg.
   Sp.: Jürg Kind; Christina and Sara Koch(in).
6. Eva Magdalena b. 15 June (?1764), bp. 3 Mar. 1765 in Linn twp.
   Sp.: Joseph Gerber and Eva Magdalena.

Philadelphia Adm. G: 401:
Peter Frantz of Lynn twp., Northampton co. was named adm. of his brother
Henry Frantz' estate in 1764. His signature appears on the adm. bond in the
estate papers, est. # 28, 1764.

152. FRANTZ, PAUL age 50   Schalbach=
Samuel, 1737   57370 Phalsbourg
S-H, I: 169, 171, 172

EUROPEAN RECORDS

Rauwiller Reformed KB:
Paulus Franz and wife Anna Maria Harthi ? had sons:
1. Joh. Paul b. 4 June 1733 at Schalbach
2. Johann Jacob b. 11 Mar. 1736

AMERICAN RECORDS

Lower Saucon Reformed KB, Northampton co.:
Paul Frantz (Jr.) and wife Anna Maria nee Schall had children:
1. Nicholas b. 25 Jan. 1756
2. John George b. 10 Feb. 1758. Sp.: George Bender and wife.
3. Michael b. 7 May 1760
4. John b. 1 Apr. 1764
5. Paulus b. 17 Apr. 1762. Sp.: Paulus Frantz, Sr.
[There are two other children listed in the KB, parents not certain, possibly children of this Paul Frantz.]

Northampton co Wills:
Paul Frantz, Lower Saucon twp., dated 3 Dec. 1763, probated 13 Oct. 1766. Wife: Mary. Children: Nicholas, Paul, Ludwig, Susanna (Artman), Catarina (Slough), Madland (Dornblesser), Mary (Hartzell), Barbary (Grove). Wit: Fredk. Gwinner, Johannes Huber, Anna Mar. Huber.

Indiancreek Reformed KB, Montgomery co.:
Buried 14 Aug. 1783 - wife of Paul Franz, aged 49 y., 10 mo.
Buried 1 Feb. 1796 - Paul Franz, died of apoplexy, aged 61 y., 7 mo.
[This is Paul, Jr. His children, bp. at Lower Saucon, appear in this church book; also Johannes Huber and Anna Maria Huber appear in this record (See witnesses to Paul, Sr.'s will). It is interesting to note that the third Paul Frantz, b. 1762, married 28 Jan. 1790 Maria Dames (Thomas). Three generations of men named Paul Frantz, all with wives Maria!]

153. FRAWINGER, JACOB   Katzenthal,
Crown, 1749   67510 Lembach
S-H, I: 393
EUROPEAN RECORDS

Lembach Lutheran KB:
Hans Frauhiger [name also appears as Frawhüger, Frauhüger, Frawthüger, and Frauinger], born in Canton Bern, Switzerland, and his wife Barbara nee Jäcki, also born in Canton Bern, both Reformed, had children:
1. **Hans Jacob,** bp. not located, see m. below.
2. Juliana Catharina b. ca. 1700, first appears in the Lembach record

as a bp. sp. in 1714. She m. Peter Traxel [q.v. Drachsel]
3. Catharina Elisabetha b. 8 Apr. 1703, bp. 15 Apr. 1703
   Sp.: Christian Matti from Canton Bern; Anna Catharina, wife of
   Philip Knoderer, master butcher in Weissenburg [=67160
   Wissembourg]; Anna Christina, wife of Mstr. Caspar Knoderer,
   Lembach; Elisabetha, daughter of Wilhelm Käser, herdsman at
   Buchweiler. She m. 1723 Joh. Georg Kern [q.v.]
4. Maria Margaretha b. 4 Aug. 1707, bp. 11 Aug. 1707
   Sp.: Hans Michael Rosenbaum, Niedersteinbach; Hans Adam, son
   of Georg Weber, Hoffmann at Pfaffenbronn, Reformed; Anna
   Maria nee Hügel, wife of Hans Niclaus Müntzer, butcher;
   Margaretha, daughter of Wilhelm Käser swine herder at
   Buchsweiler [67330 Bouxwiller]. She m. 1727 Georg Friedrich
   Newhard [q.v.]
5. Catharina Dorothea b. 22 Jan. 1710, died 4 Oct. 1713

Hans Jacob Frawthüger, son of the late Hans Fraiwhüger, former Hoffmann
in Katzenthal, m. 24 Jan. 1723 at Lembach Anna Barbara, daughter of the
late Joh. ? Huhri (also appears as Hauri in records), former *Meyer* at *Hoff,
Hochgraffl. Nassau Saarbruckischen Herrschafft.* They had children:
1. Christoph b. 30 Apr. 1725 in Katzenthal, bp. 1 May 1725 in the
   house; died. Sp.: Christoph Hörth; Theobald, son of Joh. Hördt,
   Mattstall; Christian, son of Jacob Draxel, citizen *an der
   Leggen, Berner Geb.* [CH-3775 Lenk im Simmental, BE];
   Catharina Salome, daughter of Johann Görtz [q.v.-Gertsch],
   Hoffmann at Obersteinbach [=67510 Lembach].

Woerth Lutheran KB:
Hans Jacob Frauinger, *Buchischen Meyer,* and wife Anna Barbara, had:
2. Catharina Barbara b. 3 Aug. 1726, died
3. Anna Barbara b. 10 Sept. 1727, died 1728
4. Catharina Dorothea b. 11 June 1729

154. FREY, ANDREAS	Eywiller=
Halifax, 1754	67320 Drulingen
S-H, I: 652, 654	Mackwiller=
[with Jacob Frey, q.v.]	67430 Diemeringen

EUROPEAN RECORDS

Berg und Thal Lutheran KB:
Simon Krug, son of Martin Krug of Mackweiler, m. 26 Jan. 1715 Maria Eva,
daughter of Hans Adam Haffner, also inhabitant at Mackweiler.

Hans Jörg Frey, cartwright at Eyweiler, and wife Christina had children:
1. Hans Nicolaus, sp. in 1732
2. Peter b. 2 Nov. 1714, died
3. Anna Catharina b. 30 Aug. 1716
4. Maria Magdalena b. 13 July 1718
5. Margaretha b. 24 July 1720, died
6. Anna Ottilia b. 29 Oct. 1722, died
7. Margaretha b. 15 May 1724
8. **Joh. Andreas** b. 31 Mar. 1726

Bütten Lutheran KB:
Andreas Frey m. 26 Jan. 1751 at Mackweiler Ottilia Krug, daughter of Simon Krug.

Verification of this emigrant provided by Dr. Bernd Gölzer from the compiled records of Dr. Gerhard Hein:
Records of Saarwerden county office for Mackweiler:
Dated 10 Dec. 1767, inventory of Simon Krug: the daughter Ottilia is married to Andreas Frey of Eyweiler. They moved to America about 1754. One has no definite news on their whereabouts.

155. FREY, ANDREAS age 40									Wingen=
Two Sisters, 1738										67510 Lembach
S-H, I: 209, 210, 211

EUROPEAN RECORDS

Wingen Lutheran KB:
Jacob Frey and wife Anna Maria nee Schaub had a son:
Andreas b. 7 Nov. 1698
[See 1733 immigrant Peter Frey for a more complete family record.]

Lembach Lutheran KB:
Andreas Frey, single son of the late Jacob Frey of Wingen, was a sp. in 1732 for a child of his brother Henrich Frey [q.v.]

AMERICAN RECORDS

Muddy Creek Lutheran KB, Lancaster co:
Andreas Frey had a daughter:
1. Anna Maria b. 24 June 1740, bp. 25 July 1740
Sp.: Heinrich Schmidt [q.v.] and wife.
Andreas Frey and wife sp. a child of Heinrich Schmidt in 1743.

156. FREY, HEINRICH   Eywiller=
_____, 1741   67320 Drulingen

EUROPEAN RECORDS

Berg und Thal Lutheran KB:
Heinrich Frey, son of Balthasar Frey, *Herrschaffl. Meyer* at Eyweiler, m. 29
Oct. 1715 Anna Eva, daughter of Frantz Walther, farmer there, after three
proclamations. They had children:
1. Anna Catharina b. 13 June 1716
2. Lorentz b. 3 Feb. 1719, died
3. Joh. Jacob b. 23 Nov. 1720, died
4. Anna Christina b. 1 Mar. 1722, died
5. Anna Margaretha b. 21 Mar. 1725, died
6. Johann Georg b. 22 Feb. 1728
7. Christina Margaretha b. 12 Feb. 1732
8. Johann Peter b. 18 July 1733
9. Maria Frantzel b. 23 Nov. 1737
[The father may have died on the voyage, since he is not in the ship's lists.
The children were under 16, and do not appear in the lists.]

AMERICAN RECORDS

Hocker, *German Settlers of Pennsylvania:*
Sower's newspaper, dated 16 Mar. 1748:
Georg Frey, Peter Frey and their sister Maria arrived in this country six
years ago last autumn and were indentured in Conestoga (Lancaster
County). Their sister, Anna Margretha Freyin, seeks them. Notify Jacob
Weyermann, Hatfield Township, Philadelphia County (now Montgomery).
Newspaper dated 16 Oct. 1749:
Georg Frey, Conestoga (Lancaster County), with Bastian Reyer, seeks his
sister, Christina Margaretha Freyin, and his brother Peter, and also Maria
Frantze Freyin.

Newspaper dated 1 June 1750:
Relatives seek Maria Frantza Freyin, who was indentured to the wife of
Friedrich Hob.

157. FREY, JACOB   Eywiller=
Halifax, 1754   67320 Drulingen
S-H, I: 652, 654

EUROPEAN RECORDS

Berg und Thal Lutheran KB:
Peter Frey, son of Balthasar Frey, *Herrschaffl. Meyer* at Eyweiler, m. 1 June 1719 Anna Maria, daughter of the late Haman Geck, former inhabitant at Thrulingen [Drulingen]. Children:
1. Maria Christina b. 21 Aug. 1720
2. Johann Niclaus b. __ Sept. 1722
3. Johann Peter b. 7 dec. 1724
4. **Johann Jacob** b. 30 Nov. 1731

He arrived with his cousin, Andreas Frey [q.v.].

158. FREY, JOH. HENNRICH   Wingen=
[possibly died on voyage-   67510 Lembach,
was likely a passenger on   Trautbronn
Two Sisters, 1738 with
2 sons-in-law and other children]
Children on list: Hendrick age 12; Martha [likely Martin] age 9; Jacob age 6; Maria age 5, Anna age 4. Note that the ages are incorrect on this ship list.

EUROPEAN RECORDS

Wingen Lutheran KB:
Joh. Jacob Frey and wife Anna Maria nee Schaub had a son:
Joh. Heinrich b. 17/27 ?June or ?July 1693 [See 1733 immigrant Peter Frey for a more complete family record].

Lembach Lutheran KB:
Hans Hennrich Frey, from Wingen, son of the late Jacob Frey, m. 23 Apr. 1715 at Lembach Maria Dorothea Rummel, daughter of Hans Michael Rummel, citizen at Lembach. They had children:
1. Maria Barbara b. 13 June 1715, bp. 16 June 1715
   She m. 1737 Joh. Peter Brücker [q.v.]
2. Eva Catharina b. 9 Sept. 1717, bp. 12 Sept. 1717
   She m. 1735 Hans Georg Brendel [q.v.]
3. Anna Dorothea b. 19 Nov. 1719, bp. 22 Nov. 1719
4. Joh. Hennrich b. 25 Dec. 1722, bp. 28 Dec. 1722
5. Joh. Martin b. 29 Oct. 1724
6. Sybilla Magdalena b. 13 Sept. 1727
7. Joh. Jacob b. 21 Apr. 1729, bp. 24 Apr. 1729
8. Maria Margretha b. 5 Jan. 1732, bp. 6 Jan 1732
   Sp.: one of the sp. at her baptism was Andreas Frey, single son of Jacob Frey, former citizen at Wingen.
9. Anna Catharina b. 6 Aug. 1734, bp. 8 Aug. 1734

Died 25 Mar. 1737 in Trautbrunnen-
Anna Catharina Rümel, nee Motz, widow of the late Hans Michael Rümel,
age about 73 years. This burial entry was witnessed by her son-in-law
Heinrich Frey. [H= his mark].
It is the last entry in the KB for this family.

AMERICAN RECORDS

Muddy Creek Lutheran KB, Lancaster co., PA:
Martin Frey sp. in 1741 a child of Georg Brendel. Maria Dorothea Frey sp.
in 1742 a child of Christoph Schaub.
Marin Frey m. 29 Apr. 1742 Susanna Catarina Ensminger. They had
children:
1. Dorothea b. 14 June 1743, bp. 10 July 1743
   Sp.: Joh. Heinrich Enssminger and Dorothea Frey
2. Maria Catarina b. 1 June 1746, bp. 12 July 1746
3. Maria Margaretha b. 29 Sept. 1748, bp 24 Oct. 1748
4. Johann Martin b. 13 Feb. 1751, bp. 24 Feb. 1751
5. Susanna Catarina b. 16 Apr. 1753, bp. 30 Apr. 1753
6. A daughter b. __ Oct. 1755, bp. 9 Nov. 1755

Maria Sybilla Frey m. 16 Dec. 1744 Joh. Philip Martzeloff.
Margaretha Frey m. 20 May 1750 Johannes Rupp

Trinity Lutheran KB, New Holland, Lancaster co.:
Buried 14 Mar. 1806: John Martin Frey, age 83 years, 4 months, 12 days.

159. FREY, PETER age 44   Wingen=
Samuel, 1733   67510 Lembach
S-H, I: 106,
   with Barbella Fry age 37, Valentin Fry age 12, Eve age 10, Anna Maria
age 8, Hans Peter age 4, Christian 2

EUROPEAN RECORDS

Wingen Lutheran KB:
Joh. Jacob Frey, citizen here, m. 11/21 Oct. 1688 Anna Maria, daughter of
the late Matthias Schaub "à Lange dic Ursula." Jacob Frey and wife Anna
Maria had:
1. **Joh. Peter** b. 27 Sept. 1689
2. Joh. Heinrich b. 17/27 June or July? 1693 [q.v.]
3. Anna Cleophe b. 27 Apr. 1696 "Anno 1732 went to Pennsylvania
   with her husband Christman Low" [q.v.]

4. Andreas b. 7 Nov. 1698 [q.v.]
5. Maria Barbara b. 21 Apr. 1701 She m. Conrad Low [q.v.]
6. Anna Catharina b. 10 Jan 1704

Married 18 Feb. 1716- Peter Frey and Anna Barbara, daughter of the late
Theobald Schmidt. They had:
1. Maria Margretha bp. 22 Nov. 1716
2. Anna Eva bp. 1 Jan. 1719
3. Joh. Valentin b. 9 May 1721, bp. 11 May 1721
4. Anna Barbara b. 7 Sept. 1723
5. Anna Maria b. 7 Apr. 1726
6. Joh. Peter b. 13 Nov. 1729
7. Christian b. 22 Dec. 1731

Hanns Diebolt Schmit and wife Maria had a daughter:
Anna Barbara b. 5 Apr. 1696

The earliest mention of Frey in the KB is a Rudolff Frey from Switzerland.

AMERICAN RECORDS

Muddy Creek Moravian KB:
Peter Frey, born in Wingen in Sickingen territory in Lower Alsace. [Wingen,
Alsace, France] 27 Sept. 1689, baptized 1 Oct. 1689. His wife Anna Barbara,
nee Schmidin, was born there, too, 5 Apr. 1696, and baptized thereafter on
the 8th of the same. Were m. 18 Feb. 1716. Their children are:

1. Maria Margaretha, b. 20 Nov. 1716, bp. 22 Nov. 1716
   Maria Margaretha Frey m. 1736, Muddy Creek, Michael Kapp
2. Anna Eva, b. 30 Dec. 1718, bp. 1 Jan. 1719
   Anna Eva Frey m. 1736, Muddy Creek, Georg Högie
3. Johann Valentin, b. 9 May 1721, bp. 11 May 1721
4. Anna Barbara, bp. 7 Sept. 1723, bp. the Sunday thereafter
   Anna Barbara Frey m. 1741, Muddy Creek, Michael Lauer
5. Anna Maria, b. 7 Apr. 1726, bp. 9 Apr. 1726
6. Johann Peter, b. 13 Nov. 1729, bp. 17 Nov. 1729
7. Christian, b. 22 Dec. 1731, bp. 26 Dec. 1731 St. Stephen's Day
8. Juliana, b. at end of Feb. 1735 on the Muddy Creek, bp. 8 weeks
   thereafter
9. Johann Georg, b. at beginning of Dec. 1740 on the Muddy Creek,
   bp. Jan. 1741

Valentin Frey, eldest son of Peter Frey in Muddy Creek. Anna Barbara, his wife nee Binckele, had to her first husband Matthes Meyer the following two daughters:
1. Anna Catharina Meyerin, b. Sept. 1739,
2. Elisabeth Meyerin, b. Jan. 1741

Valentin Frey married Anna Barbara (nee Binckele) Meyer in Muddy Creek in May 1742. Children:
1. Anna Barbara, b. 6 Mar. 1743, bp. Apr. 1743
2. Hans Michel, b. 8 Jan. 1745, bp. Feb. 1745
3. Johann Peter b. 23 Sept. 1746, bp. 4 Nov. 1746
4. Valentin, b. 18 Mar. 1748, bp. 21 Mar. 1748
5. Anna Maria b. 27 Oct. 1749, bp. 26 Nov. 1749
6. Henrich, b. Mar. 1751
7. Johannes, b. 25 Dec. 1752

Heidelberg Moravian KB, Berks co:
The family register of this congregation names the same children for Peter Frey and wife Anna Barbara as given in the Muddy Creek register.

Johann Valentin Frey's family also includes the first 7 children as given in the Muddy Creek register. In this record, his wife is named Anna Maria Barbara, nee Pinckel, widow Meyer, and mentions that she was b. Whitsunday 1722. These additional children appear in the Heidelberg records:
8. Maria Margretha b. 18 Sep. 1755 in Heidelberg, bp. same day
   Sp.: Elisabeth Wagner, Barbara Frey; Christina Bökel;
   Maria Margretha Meyer; Barbara Stöhr; Catharina Brendel.
9. Anna Rosina b. 27 Aug. 1757, bp. 28 Aug. 1757
10. Christina b. 22 Nov. 1759 bp. same day
11. A son died shortly after birth 23 Aug. 1762
12. Tobias b. 10 Jan. 1764, bp. 12 Jan. 1764

In 1765, Peter and Valentin Frey, with their families, moved from here to NC; a total of 21 persons.

Reichel, *The Moravians in North Carolina,* Philadelphia, 1857; reprinted Baltimore, 1968: 182:
Peter Frey, born in 1689 in Alsace, Germany; came to NC in 1765; died in 1766 in Friedberg.

See also Clifford R. Canfield, *My German (Swiss) Ancestors II,* p. 105-114 for additional Frey data from Wingen, and illustrations of entries from the KB there.

160. FRIEDLI, HANS GEORG age 25   67580 Mertzwiller
Britannia, 1731
S-H, I: 48, 50, 52, 53
  with Solomia, age 24, Hans Georg age 15 days, Lawrence age 2

EUROPEAN RECORDS

Mertzweiler Lutheran KB:
Hans Georg Friedli, son of Hans Georg Friedli, citizen and farmer at Zöppegs? Basler Gebiets, Reformed religion, m. 16 Jan. 1729 Maria Salome, single daughter of Hans Jacob Blattner, daylaborer at Schweighaus [Schweighouse=68610 Lautenbach], Lutheran religion.
[Friedli made his mark (H) in the KB, and used the same mark on the ship list].

Maria Salome was b. 19 Aug. 1708, daughter of Hans Jacob Plattner and Anna Catharina. This couple from Schweighaussen were married 31 Jan. 1708.

161. FRUTSCHI [FRUSCHTHI], JOHANN FRIEDRICH   Asswiller=
Priscilla, 1749   67320 Drulingen
S-H, I: 398
EUROPEAN RECORDS

Assweiler Lutheran KB:
Johannes Frutschi, Reformed, joiner at Assweiler and wife Appolonia (Antonia) had a son:
      Johann Friedrich b. 12 Sept. 1724

Details of this emigrant were provided by Dr. Bernd Gölzer from *Info-Dienst der AG für Saarländische Familienkunde,* (Apr. 1984) No. 71, p. 15:
A letter dated 10 Aug. 1749: Joh. Henrich Geiger [q.v.] of Saanen, Switzerland [CH-3792 Saanen, BE] and Joh. Friedrich Frutschi were together tenants of the *Steincallenfels'ian* farm in Assweiler. They brought a substitute tenant to replace them, and emigrated to Pennsylvania.

AMERICAN RECORDS

Tohickon Reformed KB, Bucks co.:
Frederick Frutschy and wife Anna Margaret had:
     1. Sibylla Margaret b. 25 Feb. 1757, bp. 6 Mar. 1757
        Sp.: Matthew Gorth and Sibylla
     2. John b. 4 Jan. 1759, bp. 7 Jan. 1759

Sp.: John Lerch, Eliza Freyman

Frederick Frutschy's wife d. 6 Jan. 1761, buried 7 Jan. 1761.
Frederick Frutschy m. (2) 24 Nov. 1761 Catharine Gettert.

Lower Saucon Reformed KB, Northampton co.:
Frederick Frutchy and wife Anna Maria had:
    Anna Maria b. 11 Nov. 1773

Northampton co. Will Abstracts:
Frederick Frutschie, Lower Saucon, 20 Jan. 1779 - 1 Mar. 1779.
Wife: Ann Maria, Exr. Children: eight children, some minors.
Names Sons: Frederick and John, Exrs: ?sons William and Jacob.
Wit: Anthony Lerch, Jr., Christopher ?Cllick, Adam Hartman, John Ludwig.

Williams twp. Congregation, Northampton co.:
Friederich Frutchi and wife Anna Maria had:
    Johann Peter b. 22 Jan. 1776, bp. 17 Mar. 1776
    Sp.: Peter Pfeiffer and wife Anna Maria

    Sybilla b. 6 Oct. 1778, bp. 8 Nov. 1778
    Sp.: Mattheus Grub and wife

162. FUCKEROTH, HANS ADAM age 48   67360 Woerth
Samuel, 1733
S-H, I: 107, 111, 112
    with Juliana age 43, Maria age 16, Philip age 15, Eleanor age 9, Jerick age
    7, Jacob age 3, Godfrey age 1.

EUROPEAN RECORDS

Woerth Lutheran KB:
Hans Adam Fuckroth from [W-7900] Ulm, former soldier in the
Elsässischen Regt., and linenweaver, m. 29 Oct. 1714 Juliana Catharina
Erhardt, daughter of the late Hans Georg Erhardt, *gerichtseltesten.* Children:
    1. Maria Barbara b. 27 Dec. 1715
    2. Philipp b. 17 Oct 1717
    3. Maria Magdalena b. 23 Feb. 1720, d. 1723
    4. Joh. Georg b. 15 Jan 1722, d. 1724
    5. Maria Magdalena b. 11 Oct. 1724
    6. Joh. Georg b. 20 Oct. 1726 bp. 23 Oct. 1726
    7. Joh. Jacob b. 24 May 1730
    8. Gottfried b. 27 July 1732

AMERICAN RECORDS

Williams Township Congregation, Northampton co:
Adam Fückeroth and Juliana Catharina Fückeroth were sp. in 1748 for a
child of Heinrich and Maria Magdalena Lück.

St. Michael's and Zion Lutheran KB, Philadelphia:
Jacob Vockerodt and wife Anna Christina had children:
1. Elisabeth b. 7 July 1759, bp. 12 Aug. 1759
   Sp.: Elisabeth Adams(in)
2. Georg Henrich b. 22 Oct. 1761, bp. 22 Nov. 1761
   Sp.: Johann Georg Schultz and Catharina

Buried 28 May 1772- Joh. Adam Vockerod b. 17 Dec. 1684 in Reichstadt
Ulm; m. 25 Oct. 1714 Juliana Catharina and had 5 sons and 3 daughters, 39
grandchildren and 7 great-great-grandchildren. Served as *vorsteher* in the
Zion's congregation at Readington in Jersey, then for 10 years at Franckfurt,
6 mi. from Philadelphia. Died the 27th, age 87 y. 5 mo. 10 d., leaving three
sons and two daughters and the 80 year old widow.

Buried 6 Sept. 1776- Catharina Vogerod b. in W___(Woerth) in Unter
Elsass in 1689. Was married 57 y. to Johann Vokerod who died 4 years ago.
3 sons and 2 daughters living. Age 87 years. Has 60 grandchildren.

St. Michael's and Zion Communicant lists- 1734-1735
   Juliana Cath. Fuckerroth
   Maria Barb Fuckerrothin

St. Michael's Lutheran KB, Germantown:
Philipp Vackerodt and Maria Barbara had a son:
1. Jacob b. 4 Apr. 1746, bp. 8 June 1746
   Sp.: Jacob von der Weide and wife Salome

Died 15 Apr. 1785: Catharina Barbara Folkrothin, buried in Frankfurt; aged
67 y., 9 mo., 11 days.

Jacob Fuckeroot, Oxford twp., Philadelphia, nat. Apr. 1764

Geo. Fuckrodt, Oxford twp., Philadelphia, nat. Apr. 1764

Philip Fackeroth, Oxford twp., Philadelphia, nat. 10 Apr. 1765

163. FÜHRER, JOHANN CASPAR   Berg=
Bilander *Vernon,* 1747   67320 Drulingen
S-H, I: 363
[appears on list as Hans Caspar (H) Feerer]

EUROPEAN RECORDS

Berg Lutheran KB:
Johann Caspar Führer, son of Benedict Führer, inhabitant at Alleweiler
[Allenwiller=67310 Wasselone], m. 26 Feb. 1737 Catharina, daughter of the
late Jacob Dintinger, weaver at Berg.
Caspar Führer, farmer at Berg, and wife Catharina had:
  1. Johann Joseph b. 17 Nov. 1737
  2. Anna Elisabetha b. 14 Sept. 1740, bp. 18 Sept. 1740
  3. Catharina b. 30 July 1744, bp. 2 Aug. 1744

Catharina Führer sp. in 1746 a child of Johann Henrich Startzman.
[Führer was a brother-in-law of Heinrich Reitenauer [q.v.] and Heinrich
Startzman [q.v.].

164. FUHRMAN, PAULUS age 60   Goerlingen=
      FUHRMAN, PAULUS, JR. age 18   67320 Drulingen
Europa, 1741
S-H, I: 317, 318, 319

EUROPEAN RECORDS

Diedendorf Reformed KB:
Johann Paulus Fuhrman from Görlingen m. 8 May 1722 Maria Elisabetha,
daughter of Johann Petter Ochs.

Paulus Fuhrman, citizen at Görlingen and wife Anna Elisabetha nee
Ochs(in) had children:
  1. **Paulus** bp. 7 Apr. 1723
     Sp.: Paulus Girardin, citizen at Görlingen; Lorentz Fournier,
     son of David Fournier, citizen at Helleringen; Maria Frantz,
     single; A daughter of Joh. Peter Witersheim, Görlingen;
     Anna Susanna, daughter of Peter Welschans, Kirburg.
  2. Maria Elisabetha bp. 30 May 1726
     Sp.: Paulus Brod, *Rothgerber* at Lixheim; Joh. Jacob, son of
     Joh. Peter Witersheim, Görlingen; Maria Fuhrman, wife of
     Joh. Jacob Salm *aus Hessenland;* A. Maria, daughter of Jacob
     Welshhans, Görlingen.

Rauwiller Reformed KB:
   3. Anna Elisabeth bp. 16 Sept. 1730

AMERICAN RECORDS

Rev. John Waldschmidt's records, Lancaster co.:
Paul Fuhrmann and wife Barbara had:
   Elisabeth b. 1 Jan. 1754, bp. 27 Jan. 1754
   Sp.: Andreas Hollsbaum and wife Fronica

Nicolaus Losser, son of Nicolaus Losser, m. 11 Apr. 1780 Maria, daughter
of Paul Fuhrmann.

Peter Fuhrmann, son of Paul Fuhrmann, m. 19 Apr. 1783 Juliana, daughter
of Jost Reitel.

Reiher's Reformed KB, near Ephrata, Lancaster co:
Paul Fuhrmann, Reformed, m. 14 Feb. 1775 Philippina Weber, Lutheran.

165. FÜNFROCK, MICHAEL   Schwabweiler=
Sandwich, 1750   67660 Betschdorf
S-H, I: 450
EUROPEAN RECORDS

Oberbetschdorf Lutheran KB:
Daniel Fünfrock, citizen at Schwabweiler, son of Joh. Georg Fünfrock and
his wife Eva nee Heitz, married Maria Margaretha Greiner. They had a son:
   Hans Michel bp. 17 May 1716

Johann Michael Fünffrock of Schwabweiler, son of Daniel and Margaretha
nee Greiner Fünffrock, m. 29 Apr. 1738 Barbara, daughter of the late Jacob
Wegeling, former citizen and carpenter at Hohweyler [Hohwiller=67250
Soultz sous Forets]. They had children:
   1. Joh. Theobald b. 11 Mar. 1739, bp. 12 Mar. 1739
   2. Joh. Jacob b. 15 Feb. 1741, died 1742
   3. Georg Heinrich b. 12 Feb. 1743, bp. 13 Feb. 1743
   4. Joh. Michael b. 11 Oct. 1745, bp. 13 Oct. 1745
   5. Joh. Georg b. 16 Mar. 1748, bp. 17 Mar. 1748

Signature from KB: Signature from S-H, II:

[See also Michael Fünfrock, Sr. and Jr., 1770 emigrants from Merckweiler and Kutzenhausen.]

AMERICAN RECORDS

Muddy Creek Lutheran KB, Lancaster co.:
Michael Fünffrock, Muddy Creek, had a son:
    Joh. Jacob b. 4 Oct. 1751, bp. 3 Nov. 1751
    Sp.: Johannes Beck.

Trinity Lutheran KB, New Holland, Lancaster co.:
Conf. 1765: Theob. Fün*fort*, age 25.
Theobald Fünfrock, son of Michael Fünfrock, m. 17 Sept. 1765 Rosina Rau; married in the church. They had children:
    1. J. Henrich bp. 12 Apr. 1773, age 1 year.
    2. J. Michael b. 13 Mar. 1780, bp. 25 June 1780
    3. Georg b. 12 Feb. 1790, bp. 28 Mar. (Trinity Luth., Lancaster)
    4. Susanna b. 16 Mar. 1792, bp. 4 June (Trinity Luth., Lancaster)

Henrich Fünfrock and wife Catharina had children:
    1. A. Christina b. 25 Mar. 1773, bp. 2 May 1773
      Sp.: Georg Fünfrock & Catharina Miller, both single.
    2. Henrich b. Dec. 1774, bp. 22 Jan. 1775
      Sp.: Adam Tuchman [q.v.] and Christina
    3. Johannes b. 12 Aug. 1776, bp. 29 Sept. 1776
    4. Cath. Margret b. 20 Aug. 1779, bp. 10 Oct. 1779
      Sp.: Jacob Fünfrock and Margareta Fünfrock

Georg Fünfrock and wife Christina had children:
    1. Marg. Ursula bp. 11 May 1777, age 4 months
    2. Johannes b. 24 Dec. 1778, bp. 11 Apr. 1779
    3. Georg b. 30 Apr. 1780, bp. 11 June 1780

PA, Third Series, Vol. 18: 24, 113, 212, 345, 471:
Michael Finfrock appears on the 1767 tax list of Carnarvon twp., Berks co. with 100A. In 1780, the following appear on this township tax list:
    Jacob Finfrock 120A; Dewald Finfrock 50A;
    Mich'l Finfrock, no acres listed; Mich'l Finfrock, Jr., no acres listed

1790 Census:
Theobald Finfrock, Manheim twp., Lancaster co:
    1 male over 16, 5 males under 16, 4 females.

166. FÜNFROCK, MICHAEL   Merkwiller-Pechelbronn=
FÜNFROCK, MICHAEL, Jr.   67250 Soultz-sous-Forêts
FÜNFROCK, STEPHAN
Minerva, 1770
S-H, I: 730
[The two sons signed the ship list, and their signatures match entries in the KB; the father appears on the ship list as Mich. (H) 5 Rock!; his mark, H, is also the same mark he used in the church records.]

EUROPEAN RECORDS

Kutzenhausen Lutheran KB:
Johann Michael Funffrock, son of Philipp Funffrock, former *Schirmsverwandten* here, m. 2 Mar. 1734 at Merckweiler, Maria Barbara, widow of Johannes Nonnenmacher, former citizen at Merckweiler. [She was a daughter of Jacob Stammbach of Oberkutzenhausen, and m. (1) 25 Nov. 1721 Johannes Nonnenmacher. There were 5 daughters to this first marriage.]
Johann Michael Funfrock and wife Maria Barbara had children:
    1. **Johann Michael** b. 4 Apr. 1735, bp. 6 Apr. 1735
    2. Johann Jacob b. 1 Dec. 1736, bp. 4 Dec. 1736
    3. Rosina b. 25 May 1738, bp. 27 May 1738
    4. Johann Niclaus b. 28 July 1740, bp. 30 July 1740
    5. **Johann Stephan** b. 19 Nov. 1742, bp. 22 Nov. 1742
        Sp.: Johann Stephan Behni, citizen at Griesbach;
        Nicolaus Nonnenmacher, citizen at Merckweiler;
        Anna Margretha, wife of Georg Bär
    6. Susanna b. 18 Feb. 1745, bp. 20 Feb. 1745
    7. Georg Heinrich b. 11 Apr. 1748, bp. 12 Apr. 1748

Joh. Michael Fünfrock, son of Joh. Michael Fünffrock, citizen and farmer at Merckweiler, m. 21 Aug. 1769 Margaretha Senn, daughter of the late Jacob Senn, former *Herrschafflichen Förster* at Merckweiler. They had one child there, the father being listed in the baptismal record as a citizen and daylaborer at Feldbach:
    1. Maria Eva b. 29 Nov. 1769, bp. 1 Dec. 1769
        Sp.: Johann Jacob Schneider, tailor at Rötschweiler;
        Anna Eva, wife of Claus Fünfrock at Merckweiler;
        Anna Maria Mardel, single, from Oberkutzenhausen.

[The father's signature by this baptism matches his signature on the ship list, S-H, II: 884.]

Joh. Stephan Fünfrock, son of Hans Michel Fünfrock, citizen and farmer at Merckweiler, m. 10 Oct. 1768 Anna Catharina Nonnenmacher, daughter of Niclaus Nonnenmacher. Joh. Stephan's occupation is given as weaver in bp. record. They had a daughter:
    1. Catharina b. 9 Feb. 1769, bp. same day
       Sp.: Hans Georg Trog, citizen at Merckweiler;
       Catharina, wife of Hans Georg Müller, weaver at Merckweiler;
       Maria Salome, wife of Michel Nonnemacher, citizen and farmer.
       [His signature in these KB entries matches S-H, II: 884.]

AMERICAN RECORDS

St. Michael's and Zion KB, Philadelphia:
Buried 2 Dec. 1771- Anna Catharina Fünfrock, wife of _____ Funfrock, aged 34 years; in this land for a little over one year.

Stephanus *Finckforth*, widower, m. 28 Jan. 1771/2? Maria Catharina Müller, widow.

PA, Third Series, Vol. 21: 13, 184, 369, 496, 677, 678:
Manchester twp., York co., tax lists, 1779-1782:
    Michael Finfrock
    Stephen Finfrock

Manchester twp. list for 1783:
    Michael Finfrock, no acres listed, 6 inhabitants
    Stephan Finfrock, 150 A, 9 inhabitants.

1790 Census:
Georg Finfrerk, Manchester twp., York Co: 1 male over 16; 3 males under 16; 5 females.

167. GALLMANN, JACOB   67690 Hatten
Janet, 1751
S-H, I: 475

EUROPEAN RECORDS

Hatten Lutheran KB:
Hans Jacob Gallmann and wife Catharina nee Bornstätter had a son:
Joh. Jacob b. 17 Aug. 1724

AMERICAN RECORDS

Frederick, MD, Lutheran KB:
Jacob Galmann was a sp. in 1754 for a child of Joseph Eckhardt.

Colonial Maryland Naturalizations:
Jacob Gallman, Alsatian, Lutheran in Frederick town, nat. 13 Sept. 1758.

168. GANTHER, JACOB   Keffenach &
John and Elizabeth, 1754   Ingolsheim=
S-H, I: 667. 669, 671   67250 Soultz-sous-Forêts
      [Gander on list]

EUROPEAN RECORDS

Hunspach Reformed KB:
Nicklaus(!) Ganther from Keffenach, a soldier in the *Königl. Frantzösischen Regiment Fersene,* m. 30 Apr. 1750 Maria Margaretha, daughter of Johannes Dörredinger [q.v.], citizen and *Gerichtsmann* at Ingelsheim.
[Note by compiler: This is a good example of an error in a primary source document. The entry should probably read: Jacob, son of Nicklaus Ganther from Keffenach. In all other records, including the baptismal records, mamumission record, and PA records, he is named Jacob.]

Joh. Jacob Ganther, soldier in the *Regiment Versen*, and wife Maria Margaretha nee Dörredinger had a son:
      1. Johann Michael b. 15 July 1750, bp. 19 July 1750
         Sp.: Joh. Michael Frey; Joh. Martin Hüller;
         Magdalena, wife of Johannes Jundt of Ingelsheim.

Zweibrücken Manumissions Protocoll, 1754:
Jacob Ganther of Keffenach leaves with his wife for America.
[See also her father Johannes Därendinger; both families in cabin #69 on the ship.]

AMERICAN RECORDS

First Reformed KB, Lancaster:
Jacob Ganther and wife Maria Margaretha had children:
  2. Elizabeth bp. 1 Feb. 1756
  3. Susanna Catharina b. 7 May 1758, bp. 18 June 1758
  4. Maria Margaretha b. 17 Feb. 1760, bp. 18 May 1760
  5. Jacob b. 17 Dec. 1761, bp. 31 May 1762
  6. Margaretha b. 9 Jan. 1766, bp. 8 May 1766

Conf. 1766: Michael Gander
Conf. 1771: Elizabeth Ganther age 15; Susanna Ganther age 14.

169. GANTHER, WILLHELM age 30   Keffenach=
Peggy, 1753   67250 Soultz-sous-Forêts
S-H, I: 546, 547, 549

EUROPEAN RECORDS

Birlenbach Lutheran KB:
Nicolas Ganther, son of Wilhelm Ganther, former citizen at Guntershoffen
[=67110 Niederbronn-les-Bains] m. 24 Jan. 1708 Anna Margaretha, widow
of Hans Ulrich Burchardt of Keffenach.

Hunspach Reformed KB:
Conf. 1738 - Willhelm, son of Nicklaus Ganther, citizen at Keffenach.
[He was a brother of Jacob Ganther, q.v.]

AMERICAN RECORDS

First Reformed KB, Lancaster:
William Gander and wife Anna Catharina had:
      1. Joh. Casper b. 17 Dec. 1756, bp. 19 May 1757
      2. Elisabetha b. 15 Apr. 1758, bp. 18 June 1758
      3. Barbara b. 2 July 1759, bp. 23 Sept. 1759
      4. Georg Peter b. 22 Nov. 1760, bp. 30 Apr. 1761
      5. Barbara b. 8 Apr. 1762, bp. 30 May 1762

William Gander m. (2) 4 July 1765 Margaret Fey. Children:
      6. Eleonora b. 5 Dec. 1765
      7. William b. 20 Mar. 1767
      8. Jacob b. 10 Sept. 1768, bp. 9 Mar. [?1769]
      9. Christian b. 30 Nov. 1771, bp. 11 Nov. 1773
     10 Abraham b. 15 Nov. 1780, bp. 1 Jan. 1789

170. GARTNER, HANS PETER age 26   Rittershoffen=
Britannia, 1731   67690 Hatten
S-H, I: 48, 49, 52, 53
  with Margerita age 26

EUROPEAN RECORDS

Rittershoffen Lutheran KB:
Christian Farni, Reformed herdsman, and wife Catharina had a daughter:
Margretha b. 17 Nov. 1707, bp. 20 Nov. 1707
    Sp.: Hans Jacob Arbogast, Margretha, daughter of Theobald Wahl
    and Catharina, daughter of Valentin Knab.

Hans Peter Gartner, master smith, son of the late Diebold Gartner of
Niedermodern [=67350 Pfaffenhoffen] m. 24 May 1729 Margretha Farni,
daughter of the late Christian Farni of Rittershoffen. They had:
    1. Catharina, b. 11 Feb 1730 bp. 12 Feb. 1730
        Sp.: Hans Georg, son of Philipp Knab; Catharina, wife of Hans
        Jacob Wuncherer; Catharina, daughter of Hans Georg Götzmann.
Notation in the KB: "Went to the new land."

AMERICAN RECORDS

Trinity Lutheran KB, Lancaster, PA:
Peter Gärtner (York Register) had children:
    1. Joh. Peter b. 19 Feb. 1734, bp. 28 Apr. 1734
        Sp. Joh. Peter Knobel and wife Anna Ursula
    2. Joh. Adam b. 23 Mar. 1735, bp. 30 Mar. 1735
        Sp.: Joh. Philipp Schütz and wife Elisabetha
    3. Catarina b. 2 Apr. 1737, bp. 1 Aug 1737
        Sp.: Martin Weigel and wife Maria Juliana
    4. Heinrich b. 12 Jan. 1739, bp. 20 Apr. 1739
        Sp.: Heinrich Bahn and wife Eva
    5. Joh. Michael b. 4 Mar. 1741, bp. 28 Oct. 1741
        Sp.: Michael Beyerle and wife
    6. Joh. Georg b. 8 June 1743, bp. 19 June 1743 (York KB)

Heinrich Gärtner, single, from York co., m. 6 May 1766 Catharina Barbara
Bolz, single.

Michael Gardner of York co. m. 13 Dec. 1763 Catharina Kuntz, spinster.

Christ Lutheran KB, York:
Peter Gärtner, Jr. m. 26 June 1760 Louisa Erb, by liscense.

Adam Gartner, son of Peter Gartner, m. 19 Aug. 1762 Elisabeth Amendt, daughter of Georg Amendt.

Peter Gardner, Lancaster co., nat. Apr. 1744

171. GASSER, HANS ADAM age 32   67350 Pfaffenhoffen
Loyal Judith, 1732
S-H, I: 89, 90, 92

EUROPEAN RECORDS

Pfaffenhoffen Lutheran KB:
Hans Adam Gassert, widower and *Marckschäff* here, m. 24 July 1725 Anna Maria, widow of the late Philipps Greiner, *Herrschaffl. Stubenhitzer.*

There are two possibilities for this immigrant:
1. Michael Gassert, citizen, and wife Anna Maria, had a son:
        Hans Adam bp. 1 Apr. 1699

OR

2. Hans Adam Gassert and wife Anna Elisabetha, had a son:
        Hans Adam bp. 30 July 1701

AMERICAN RECORDS

Trinity Lutheran KB, Lancaster:
Joh. Adam Gasser, widower, from Pfaffenhofen in Alsace, m. 23 Jan. 1757 Anna Maria Benkingerin, widow.

172. GASSER, PETER   Gundershoffen=
Ship Unknown, ca. 1738   67110 Niederbronn-les-Bains

EUROPEAN RECORDS

Gundershoffen Lutheran KB:
Peter Gass[er], son of the late Henrich Gass, m. 17 Nov. 1699 Barbara Dorothea, daughter of Magnus Mallo, citizen at Griesbach.

Peter Gasser, nailsmith apprentice, son of Peter Gasser, citizen here, m. 13 Jan. 1728 Magdalena, daughter of the late Jacob Springer, former citizen at Uttenhoffen [=67110 Niederbronn-les-Bains]. Children:
        1. Johann Jacob b. 3 Dec. 1728

2. Maria Elisabetha b. 13 Dec. 1729
3. Peter b. 31 Jan. 1733
4. Anna Magdalena b. 5 May 1736

AMERICAN RECORDS

Hocker, *German Settlers of Pennsylvania:* 21:
Sower's newspaper, dated 18 Aug. 1750:
Hansz Peter Fischer and his wife, Maria Elisabeth Gasserin, who arrived in this country last autumn, seek the latter's borther, Peter Gasser, from Gunters-Hoffen, Alsace, who came here twelve years ago. Fischer and his wife are in Heidelberg twp., "an der Brunen Kehr," on Michel Schauer's place.

173. GASSMANN, BENJAMIN   Birlenbach =
Betsey, 1765   67160 Wissembourg
S-H, I: 706

EUROPEAN RECORDS

Birlenbach Lutheran KB:
Michael Gassmann m. 1 July 1738 Apollonia Ehrstein, daughter of Jacob Ehrstein, miller at Birlenbach.
Michael Gassmann, the younger, and Apollonia his wife had a son:
   Benjamin b. 24 June 1745, bp. 27 June 1745; conf. 1759.
   Sp.: Mstr. Benjamin Woog, citizen and butcher in Weissenburg;
   Caspar Furstenhausser, citizen in Sultz; Catharina Elisabetha
   Haller wife of Joh. Jacob Haller, Ev. Schoolmaster at Wörth.

AMERICAN RECORDS

St. Michael's and Zion KB, Philadelphia:
Benjamin Gasman m. 17 Oct. 1769 Maria Esswein, single persons in Philadelphia.

1790 Census, Northern Liberties, Philadelphia co.:
Benjamin Gossman, 2 males over 16, 3 males under 16, 2 females.

174. GEIGER, JOHAN HEINRICH   Asswiller =
Priscilla, 1749   67320 Drulingen
S-H, I: 398

EUROPEAN RECORDS

Assweiler Lutheran KB:
Johann Heinrich Geiger, Reformed, joiner at Assweiler, and wife Anna
Maria had children:
>   1. Anna Maria b. 8 Feb. 1745
>   2. Anna Margaretha b. 6 Aug. 1746

Details of this emigrant were provided by Dr. Bernd Gölzer from *Info-Dienst
der AG für Saarlandische Familienkunde,* (Apr. 1984), No. 71:15:
A letter dated 10 Aug. 1749: Joh. Henrich Geiger of Saanen, Switzerland
[CH-3792 Saanen, BE] and Joh. Friedrich Frutschi [q.v.] were together
tenants of the *Steincallenfels'ian* farm in Assweiler. They brought a
substitute tenant to replace them and emigrated to Pennsylvania.

AMERICAN RECORDS

Henry Geiger was a wit. to eight wills in Northampton Co. from 1761 to
1788; many of the testators were residents of Heidelberg twp. [now Lehigh
co.] Heinrich Geiger was a member of the Heidelberg Reformed
congregation and signed the church agreement in 1757. The early Reformed
KB for this congregation is either lost or did not exist.

Rev. Daniel Schumacher's records:
Maria Geiger, daughter of Henrich Geiger, was sp. in 1762 for a child of
Jacob Bender, in Heidelberg. Maria Geiger, wife of Heinrich Geiger, was
a sp. in 1766 for a ch. of Frederich Schleich in Heidelberg.

One Henry Geiger, Heidleburgh, Northampton co., nat. 10/11 Apr. 1761.

175. GEIST, GOTTLIEB   Mitschdorf=
Hamilton, 1767   67360 Woerth
S-H, I: 717   Goersdorf=
                                                  67360 Woerth
EUROPEAN RECORDS

Preuschdorf Lutheran KB:
Ludwig Geist and wife Anna nee Hirscheyer [Hirschiger, Hirschicher in
other records] had a son:
>   Joh. Gottlieb b. 27 Feb. 1739

Gottlieb Geist, day laborer at Görsdorff, and wife Maria Margretha nee
Berling had a daughter:
>   1. Maria Margretha b. 2 Sept 1766, bp. 3 Sept. 1766, emergency
>   baptism signed by the sponsors: Barbara, daughter of Jacob

Heinrich Müller; Philipps Jacob of Preuschdorf; Eva Catharina daughter of Joh. Michael Kieffer of Görsdorff.
Entry also witnessed by the following:
Maria Salome Kieffer, the midwife; Anna Maria Berling, the mother-in-law; Anna Maria Geist, the child's grandmother.
[Father's signature by bp. matches signature in S-H, II: 825].

Entries for the families of Goersdorf appear
in the Preuschdorf Lutheran parish registers.

AMERICAN RECORDS

Frederick Lutheran KB, Frederick, MD:
Gottlieb Geist and wife Margaretha had:
    2. Johann Michael b. 10 Oct. 1768, bp. 16 Oct. 1768
        Sp.: Johann Michael Stocker [q.v.] and wife

3. Philipp b. 8 Oct. 1771, bp. 3 Nov. 1771
   Sp.: Philipp and Maria Eva Kullmann
4. Catharina Barbara b. 12 Dec. 1773, bp. 10 Apr. 1774
   Sp.: Jacob and Catharina Barbara Staehli.

176. GELBACH, FRIDRICH   Kirrberg=
GELBACH, FRANZ   67320 Drulingen
GELBACH, FRIEDERICH
Christian, 1749
S-H, I: 399
EUROPEAN RECORDS

Herbitzheim Lutheran KB:
Friderich Gelbach and wife Maria Barbara had children:
   1. Johanetta Dorothea b. 4 Dec. 1723
   2. Anna Elisabetha b. 9 Aug. 1725
[In one record at Herbitzheim, his full name is given as Joh. Friedrich Jacob
Gelbach.]

Friedrich Gelbacher, master butcher, and Mrs. Maria Barbara Gelbach were
sp. in 1722, 1724 for children of Joh. Georg Eisenmann [q.v.]

Rauwiller Reformed KB:
Friederich Gelbach of Kirberg and wife Maria Barbara nee Rüger [also
Rieger in some records] had:
   1. Johann Franciscus b. 1 Dec. 1729
   2. Maria Susanna b. 17 Aug. 1732
   3. Johann Friederich bp. 18 Jan. 1735
   4. Johann Georg b. 24 Mar. 1737
   5. Maria Catharina b. 27 Nov. 1739

AMERICAN RECORDS

First Reformed KB, Lancaster, PA:
Peter Liwig m. 20 May 1754 Susanna Gelbach.

Frederick Gelbach m. 28 Nov. 1758 Anna Rudolph.

Christian Hunter m. 29 Dec. 1767 Magdalena Gehlbach.

Frederic Gelbach and wife Anna had children:
   1. John b. 28 Oct. 1759, bp. 18 Nov. 1759
   2. Catharina b. 14 Aug. 1761, bp. 18 May 1762

Peter Libig, Lybig, Liebich and wife Susan had:
1. Elisabeth b. 8 Apr. 1755, bp. 18 May 1755
2. Mary Barbara b. 4 July 1756, bp. 15 Aug. 1756
3. John b. 14 Oct. 1758, bp. 28 Nov. 1758
4. Susan b. 19 June 1761, bp. 7 Aug. 1763

Lancaster co. Wills:
Book J-I:73:
Frederich Gelbach, Maytown, 16 Dec. 1796- 14 Mar. 1797
Exrs: Frederich Gelbach & James Mackey. Wife: Anna. Children: Frederick, Catharina, Barbara, and John. Son-in-law: James Mackey (wife not stated).
Book G-I: 85:
John Gelbaugh or Galbough, Maytown, 8 Apr. 1797- 17 Apr. 1797
Exrs: Anthony Haines and Christian Rountz. Wife: Mary.
Brother: Friderick Galbough; sister: Barbara, wife of ____ Garnon.

177. GEMBERLING, JACOB   Asswiller=
    GEMBERLING, JACOB   67320 Drulingen
Polly, 1765
S-H, I: 704 [two together on list]

EUROPEAN RECORDS

Assweiler Lutheran KB:
Samuel Gemberling and wife Eva (Maria) Magdalena nee Hahn had a son:
    Johann Jacob b. 17 Oct. 1738; he sponsors in 1756 and 1764.
    [see his brothers Carl and Joh. Paul Gemberling
       for additional family data.]

Assweiler Lutheran KB:
Hans Henrich Gemberling, Reformed, at Assweiler, and wife Maria Anna nee Brodt had children:
1. **Johann Jacob** b. 10 July 1739, conf. 1754 at Burbach, age 15.
   [Burbach = 67260 Sarre-Union]
2. Anna Catharina b. 26 Mar. 1743, conf. 1757 at Burbach, age 15.
   Notation in KB "Emigrated to Pennsylvania."

Hans Henrich Gemberling died in 1779 and it is mentioned in his obituary that one son and one daughter are in America. [This data kindly supplied from the Assweiler records by Dr. Bernd Gölzer.]

AMERICAN RECORDS

Heidelberg Reformed KB, Schaefferstown, Lebanon co.:
Jacob Gemberling and wife Catharina were sp. in 1769 for a child of Paul
Gemberling [q.v.]

Jacob Gemberling and wife Catharina had:
    Mary Magdalena b. 14 June 1784, bp. 5 Sept. 1784

See Charles A. Fisher, *Snyder County Pioneers,* pg. 29 for additional data on
the Jacob Gemberling (b. 1738, son of Samuel). This work names his wife
as Catharine Wolfensberger and indicates that he was a non-resident land
owner in Penn twp., Snyder co. as early as 1774. He was taxed in Heidelberg
twp., Lancaster co. (now Lebanon co.) in 1779, and in 1782 he was listed as
a farmer and tavernkeeper in Schaefferstown. He was residing in Penn twp.
by 1785.

Snyder co. Probate records:
Letters of Adm. on the estate of Jacob Gemberling of Penn twp. were
granted 11 Aug. 1826 to Peter Hackenberg.

Snyder co. Wills:
Jacob Gemberling, Penn twp., 10 Oct 1821 - 17 May 1824.
Wife: Catherine Wolfsberger. Children: Elizabeth (wife of Philip Morr);
Jacob; Philip; George B.; Samuel; Sarah (wife of Jacob Moyer); Mary (wife
of Fred. Esterline); Mary Elizabeth (wife of Joseph Walter).

First Reformed KB, Lancaster:
The other 1765 immigrant Jacob Gemberling may be the Jacob who appears
in this record.
Jacob Gemberling and wife Susan had:
    1. Jacob b. __ Sept. 1780; bp. 26 Dec. 1784
    2. Susan b. 1778, bp. 1 Jan. 1789

178. GEMBERLING, JOH. PAUL   Asswiller=
        GEMBERLING, CARL   67320 Drulingen
Neptune, 1754
S-H, I: 621, 623, 625

                        EUROPEAN RECORDS

Assweiler Lutheran KB:
Samuel Gemberling, shoemaker at Assweiler, m. 9 May 1726 Eva (Maria)
Magdalena Hahn, Reformed, from Fleissheim [Fleisheim= 57119 Lixheim].
They had children:

1. **Carl Johann Samuel** b. 18 May 1727, conf. 1740
   at Burbach [= 67260 Sarre-Union]
2. Catharina Margaretha b. 13 Dec. 1728
3. Maria Magdalena b. 24 Apr. 1730, d. 25 Apr. 1730
4. Johann Henrich b. 4 June 1731, conf. 1745, Burbach
5. Samuel b. 4 Nov. 1732
6. **Hans Paulus Friedrich** b. 13 May 1734, conf. 1749, Burbach
7. Johann Philipp b. 18 Feb. 1736, conf. 1750, Burbach
8. Johann Jacob b. 17 Oct. 1738 [q.v., em. 1765]
9. Anna Magdalena b. 17 June 1740
10. Johann Christian b. 20 Nov. 1743, d. 8 Mar. 1748
11. Anna Christina b. 6 Mar. 1746

Samuel Gemberling d. 22 Mar. 1782. In his obituary if is mentioned that he had 11 children, 4 were deceased, 3 sons and 1 daughter went to Pennsylvania. 2 sons and one daughter lived in Assweiler. [This data kindly supplied by Dr. Bernd Gölzer from the Assweiler records.]

AMERICAN RECORDS

First Reformed KB, Philadelphia:
Carl Gemperlin from Ossweyler [Assweiler] and wife Magdalena nee Steinmetz had children:
1. Catharine bp. 20 May 1759 [surname Gaemperli]
   Sp.: Frederick Steinmetz and Sibylla
2. Maria Magdalena bp. 3 Nov. 1760 [surname Gaemperli]
3. Carl bp. 6 Feb. 1763, 16 days old [Gemperlin]
4. Susanna bp. 28 July 1765, 14 days old [Gemberling]
5. Sarah b. 24 Apr. 1769, bp. 17 May 1769 [Gambestein]
6. Elizabeth b. 25 Mar. 1771, bp. 1 Apr. 1771 [Gamberlein]
7. Esther bp. 23 May 1773 [Gemberling]
   Sp.: Parents for children 2-7.

Heidelberg Reformed KB, Schaefferstown, Lebanon co.:
Paul Gemberling and wife Elisabetha had:
1. Joh. Philip b. 17 Nov. 1766, bp. 23 Nov. 1766
   Sp.: Justice Mr. DeHaas and wife
2. Anna Elisabetha b. 18 Aug. 1769, bp. 12 Sept. 1769
   Sp.: Jacob Gemberling and wife Catharina

See Charles A. Fisher, *Snyder County Pioneers,* p. 29 for additional Gemberling family data.

Paul Gimberling, Heidleberg, Lancaster co. nat. Fall, 1765.

179. GERBER, CHRISTMAN age 46   67110 Niederbronn-les-Bains
Charming Nancy, 1738
S-H, I: 245, 246, 247

EUROPEAN RECORDS

Niederbronn Lutheran KB:
Christman Gerber and wife Christina had children:
1. Johan Jacob b. 5 Apr. 1716, d. 5 Jan. 1717
2. Maria Elisabetha b. 25 Oct. 1717
3. Johan Christman b. 1 Nov. 1719
4. Johannes b. 26 Dec. 1721
5. Joh. Jacob b. 24 Jan. 1724
6. Eva Catharina b. 17 May 1727
7. Nicolaus b. 13 July 1729
8. Christina b. 14 Apr. 1731
9. Joh. Adam b. 7 Dec. 1732
10. Maria Magdalena b. 15 May 1735
11. Andreas b. 26 Nov. 1737

Archives du Bas-Rhin, Document E 4367:
Christmann Gerber is listed in this document, on a list of emigrants from
Niederbronn in 1738.
AMERICAN RECORDS

St. Joseph's (Oley Hills) Church, Pike twp., Berks co.:
Johann Gerber b. 26 Dec. 1721, son of Christman Gerber *"aus dem Elsass"*
and his wife Christina. He came to America in 1738 with his parents. He
m. 27 Jan. 1747 Anna Magdalena Elisab., b. 12 Mar. 1721, daughter of
Johann Forch from Haasenthal in the Pfalz, and his wife Anna Elisabetha.

Communicants lists, 8 Sept. 1754; 14 Dec. 1755; 30 May 1756:
      Johann Gerber and Anna Magdalena, his wife.
Adam Gerber and wife Anna Maria had:
      1. Conrad b. 28 Apr. 1760, bp. 1 June 1760
         Sp.: John Schleicher and Margretta
      2. Anna C. b. 14 Dec. 1765, bp. 28 Jan. 1766. Sp.: Anna Schleiger.

New Hanover Lutheran KB, Montgomery co.:
Johannes Gerber d. 12 July 1795, aged 73 y. 6 mo. 2 weeks

Trappe Lutheran KB, Montgomery co.:
Johannes Gerber and Magdalena were sp. in 1749 for a child of Joh. Carl
Weiss and Eva Gerber.

Conf. 7 Apr. 1751 - Christina Gerber, daughter of the widow Gerber, age 20. Lived in service in the past and was neglected.

180. GERBER, HEINRICH   67110 Niederbronn-les-Bains
died on voyage
probably on *Charming Nancy*, 1738

EUROPEAN RECORDS

Niederbronn Lutheran KB:
Heinrich Gerber and wife Anna Catharina had children:
   1. possibly Joh. Jacob b. __ ___ 1724 (page torn)
   2. Maria Catharina b. 11 Aug. 1725
   3. Maria Salome b. 13 Aug. 1727
   4. Anna Dorothea bp. 16 Jan. 1730
   5. Benedict b. 13 Oct. 1732

Archives du Bas-Rhin, Document E 4367:
Heinrich Gerber is listed in this document, on a list of emigrants from Niederbronn in 1738.

AMERICAN RECORDS

Philadelphia Administration Book D:
Pg. 43, #113 Letters of Administration to John Cunrads, co. of Philadelphia, cordwainer, adm. of Henderick Kererver [Gerber] dec'd (during minority of Dorothy and Benedictus Kererver, daughters [children?] of said deceased, 11 Nov. 1738.

Muhlenberg's Journals, III: dated 21 Oct. 1777:
Muhlenberg mentions a visit to an unnamed woman, who was critically ill. He describes her as follows:
   "She was born of evangelical parents in December, 1729, in Niederbrunn, Alsatia, was baptized and sent to school, set out for America in 1738 with her father, mother, grandfather, and four brothers and sisters, but had the misfortune to lose, by death at sea, her parents, grandfather, and three brothers and sisters, and thus she arrived as a poor nine-year-old orphan with a six-year-old brother. Here the Lord revealed himself as a father of orphans and showed that none of His creatures is too small or insignificant for His gracious providence and oversight. When the little children arrived in this strange land, divine providence brought it to pass that an honorable Mennonite in Germantown bought the two sick children and drove them

home in his cart. In this family they were brought up respectable and decently, were made to work, and were provided with food and clothing. Now and then they were also permitted to go to the Lutheran church in Germantown to hear the late Pastor Brunnholz, etc. When the two children had completed their years of service and were free, she went on her own initiative to Pastor Brunnholz for instruction and confirmation, while her brother reported to me in Providence, received instruction and confirmation, and became an inhabitant of Providence and a faithful parishioner. At the age of twenty she was properly married to a Christian man and settled in the neighborhood of Shippach, some nine miles from the Providence church."

Muhlenberg then adds that she lived with her husband for 28 years and 6 months, and had 10 children, 9 of whom were living. She died after contracting dysentery from a poor woman she had nursed. For 13 days she was bedridden, and died in her 48th year.

A search of all of the available records failed to produce her marriage record, but the preponderence of evidence would indicate that she was Dorothea, wife of Joh. Philip Sperr. A partial list of their children:
1. Leonhard b. 11 Apr. 1750, Trappe Luth. KB
2. Anna Christina bp. 20 May 1755 at Skippach
   Sp.: Benedict Gerber and Christina Heilman, both single.
3. Daniel m. 20 Feb. 1787 Rosina Bayer, daughter of the late
   Andreas Bayer, both residing in Worcester twp., Montgomery co.
   [Muhlenberg's Journals, III: 731]
4. Possible Henry, wit. at the above marriage.
5. Jacob b. 8 Mar. 1771 at Wentz's Reformed KB,
   Worcester twp., Montgomery co.

Egle, *Notes and Queries,* annual vol. 1899, pg. 44-45:
Benedict Garber, b. 18 Oct. 1732; d. 12 June 1817. He came to America from Alsace, Germany in 1741 (sic) when a lad, with his parents, who died on shipboard. He settled in Upper Providence, now Montgomery co., two and a half miles south of the Trappe. He married 12 Nov. 1758 Dorothea Loreht (Loreth).

Trappe Lutheran KB, Montgomery co.:
Benedict Gerber, single, was a sp. in 1755 for a child of Johann Philip Sperr and Dorothea.
Benedict Gerber m. 12 Nov. 1758 Dorothea Loreth. Wit: Johannes Loreth, Philip Sperr.
Benedict Gerber and wife Dorothea had:
        1. Joh. Heinrich b. 3 Feb. 1759
        2. Jacob b. 3 July 1761

3. Johan Carl b. 12 July 1762
4. Catarina b. 4 July 1765
   Sp.: Philip Sperr and wife Dorothea
5. Johannes b. 4 July 1767
6. Benjamin, bp. not located, named in an article in *Notes and Queries,* annual vol. 1899.
7. Joseph died 20 Feb. 1773, age 11 mo., 3 weeks, and 3 days.

181. GERBER, JOH. JACOB   67110 Niederbronn-les-Bains
died on voyage
probably on *Charming Nancy,* 1738

EUROPEAN RECORDS

Niederbronn Lutheran KB:
The emigrating Jacob Gerber who left Niederbronn in 1738 was the father of Heinrich Gerber [q.v.] who also left the village in 1738 with his family, and died on the voyage. There is a major gap in the Niederbronn KB for the years when his children were born, and there are no marriage records available on microfilm. He appears to be the Joh. Jacob Gerber with wife Dorothea who had a son Joh. Philip b. 8 Jan. 1712. There are no further entries for this couple, and this was probably their youngest child.

Archives du Bas-Rhin, Document E 4367:
Joh. Jac. Gerber is listed in this document, on a list of emigrants from Niederbronn in 1738.

AMERICAN RECORDS

See Muhlenberg's Journal, Vol. 3, pg 89, for his grandaughter's obituary, mentioning her grandfather and parents who died on the voyage to America. See also Heinrich Gerber for family data.

182. GERI, HANS ADAM [Keere on list]   Hirschland=
Robert & Alice, 1739   67320 Drulingen
S-H, I: 264, 268, 271
   with Jacob Kerre, Gerrhy

EUROPEAN RECORDS

Hirschland Lutheran KB:
Rudolph Gera (Switzer) and wife Elisabetha, both Reformed, had:
   Joh. Adam b. 6 Nov. 1718

Anna Magdalena b. 22 Feb. 1720
notation in KB: "auch abgerecht"

Johann Rudolf Geri of Hirschland was a sp. in 1718 at Diedendorf.

AMERICAN RECORDS

Longswamp Reformed KB, Longswamp twp., Berks co.:
Adam Göry was a sponsor in 1748 for a child of Theobald Carl [q.v.].

Zion's Lutheran KB, Upper Macungie, Lehigh co.:
Johann Adam Göry, shoemaker, single, m. 8 May 1758 Magdalena, daughter
of Matthai Heinli.

New Goshenhoppen Reformed KB, Montgomery co.:
Buried in the year 1786: Adam Geri, b. 6 Nov. 1718, aged 68 years.

Berks co. Adm: Adam Gery, Longswamp; adm. granted 28 Nov. 1786 to
Adam Helwig and John Haas, friends and neighbors.

Berks co. Orphan's Court records:
Dec. 27, 1786. Adam Gerry (above 14), son of Adam Gerry of Longswamp,
yeoman, deceased, chooses Samuel Butz for guardian.
Barbara Gerry (above 14) chooses Adam Helwig for guardian.
Dec. 14, 1790. Petition of Adam Gehry eldest son of Adam Gehry, late of
Longswamp, dec'd. Petitioner states that his father died intestate leaving
five children: Adam (the petitioner); Magdalena, wife of John Lithweiler
(elsewhere Leitweiler); Elisabeth, wife of Jacob Danner; Margaret, wife of
John Keiser; Barbara, wife of David Long. The intestate died seized of a
tract of land in Longswamp containing 150 A. Prays for partition or
valuation. Property valued at £537. Confirmed to Adam Gehry, eldest son.

Philadelphia co. Tax Lists:
1774:   Adam Gearey   83 acres.
1783:   John Geary   75 acres.
         Jacob Geary   75 acres.

New Goshenhoppen Reformed KB, Montgomery co.:
List of members in the congregation of Rev. G. M. Weiss: Jacob Gery.
Jacob Göry and wife had children:
    1. Anna Maria bp. 25 Oct. 1746
    2. Catharina bp. 30 July 1749
        Sp. for both: Valentin Griesemer and wife.

Jacob Geri had a son:
    Joh. Michaelus b. 13 July 1771. Sp.: Joh. Cunius and wife.

Johannes Hellicas, son of Jacob Hellicas of New Goshenhoppen, m. 3 Mar. 1767 Anna Maria Geri, daughter of Jacob Geri.
Michael Hillicas, son of Adam Hillicas of New Goshenhoppen, m. 10 Nov. 1767 Catharina Geri, daughter of Jacob Geri.
Conf. 1769: Joh. Adam Geri, aged 17 years.
Johannes Keri, son of Jacob Keri of New Goshenhoppen, m. 11 May 1784 Susanna Wigner, daughter of the late Georg Wigner.
Joh. Adam Geri, son of Jacob Geri, m. 11 June 1776 Barbara Weiller, daughter of Andreas Weiller of New Goshenhoppen.

1790 Census: Montgomery co.:
Jacob Gery   3 males over 16; 2 females.
Jacob Gery, Jr. 1 male over 16; 3 males under 16; 1 female.
John Gerry   2 males over 16; 1 male under 16; 4 females.

Montgomery co. Wills:
Jacob Gehry, Upper Hanover twp. 24 Oct. 1797 - 13 Apr. 1808.
Wife Gertrude. Children: Jacob; Peter; Michael; Adam, deceased; Catharine, wife of John Wagener; Elisabeth; Rebecca; Anna Maria, late wife of John Hillegas, dec'd. Grandchildren: children of daughter Anna Maria; children of daughter Catharine, wife of John Wagener, to her first husband Michael Hillegas, dec'd; children of son John Adam Gehry, dec'd.
Exrs: sons Jacob and John. Wit: Casper Yeakel, Baltzer Schultz.

183. GERLACH, BALSER   67510 Lembach
John & William, 1732
S-H, I: 102, 104, 105
  with Maria Gerloch
                    EUROPEAN RECORDS

Lembach Lutheran KB:
Joh. (in one record Görg) Balthaser Gerlach and wife Rosina Barbara nee Newmeyer had children:
    1. Maria Catharina b. 21 June 1722, bp. 24 June 1722, died
    2. Joh. Balthasar b. 17 Feb. 1724, bp. 20 Feb. 1724, died
    3. Georg Balthasar b. 6 ?June 1728, died
    4. Georg Michael b. 21 Aug. 1731, bp. 22 Aug. 1731

Balser Gerlach arrived with several others from Lembach, all listed together on the ship list.

AMERICAN RECORDS

Balsar Gerlach was a trustee of the Old Goshenhoppen Lutheran Church in
1744.

Berks co. wills:
George Baltzer Gerlach, Upper Salford, Philadelphia co., dated 7 Apr. 1744;
prob. 2 May 1767. To wife Maria Sibilla and my 3 step-children, George,
Peter, and Susanna Hail, all my estate in 4 equal shares. To daughter Eliza
Barbara Goot one English shilling, "she did not do well to me". Wife Maria
Sibilla and son George Hail, exrs. Letters to Hail, the wife being deceased.
Wit.: Daniel Hiester, Jacob Nuss and Henry Keller.

One Baltzer Erlach nat. 10 Apr. 1758 (no location mentioned).

184. GERRET, PETER   Herbitzheim=
Phoenix, 1749   67260 Sarre-Union
S-H, I: 405
                        EUROPEAN RECORDS

Herbitzheim Lutheran KB:
Peter Gereth, day laborer at Herbitzheim, and Elisabetha, his wife, had:
1. Johann Wilhelm b. 27 June 1745, bp. 29 June 1745
   Sp.: Wilhelm Haldy; Johann Nickel son of Christian Hochstädter;
   Justina Catharina, wife of Daniel Eichacker; Catharina
   Margretha daughter of the late Christoph Jesel.
2. Maria Barbara b. 10 Jan. 1748 bp. 11 Jan. 1748
   Sp.: Ludwig, son of Samuel Haldy; Johannes Wampfler;
   Anna Maria, wife of Ulli Hochstätler; Barbara Christina,
   daughter of Christian Hochstätler [q.v.].

AMERICAN RECORDS

St. David's (Sherman's) KB, York co.: (early records published in *Der
Reggeboge,* Vol. 11, No. 2 (1977):
Peter Gehret and wife Maria Elisabeth had:
   Maria Eva b. 7 Mar. 1753, bp. 24 Mar. 1753
   Sp.: Nicholaus Hochstätter [q.v.];
   Maria Eva Warnerin, both single.

William Gerret and Maria Margaret had:
   Maria Margaret b. 24 Mar. 1783, bp. 18 Apr. 1783
   Sp.: Jacob Nonnemacher and Maria Margaret.

Henry b. 30 July 1794, bp. 11 Sept. 1795
Sp.: Michael Steffan and Christine.

A Christian Gehret also appears in these later records (1787-1802).

Rev. Jacob Lischy's records, York co.:
Peter Gerrott and wife Elisabeth had a son:
Joh. Peter bp. 1 June 1760
Sp.: Peter Schweitzer; Catharina Hochstätterin.

185. GERSCHHEIMER, JOHANN PHILIPP   Waldhambach=
Britannia, 1764   67430 Diemeringen
S-H, I: 693
EUROPEAN RECORDS

Waldhambach Lutheran KB:
Johann Matthias Gerschheimer and wife Anna Barbara nee Quirin had:
Johann Philipp b. 11 Jan. 1728

Johann Philipp Gerschheimer, weaver at Waldhambach, son of Matthias
Gerschheimer, m. 23 Nov. 1751 in Volksberg, Maria Magdalena Meder,
daughter of Johann Nicolaus Meder of Volksberg. They had children:
1. Eva Christina b. 15 Jan. 1753
2. Catharina Barbara b. 21 Nov. 1754
3. Maria Elisabetha b. 8 July 1757
4. Child b. 11 Apr. 1760, died.
5. Johann Philipp b. 7 July 1761, d. 20 Dec. 1762
6. Johann Jacob b. 22 Sept. 1763

Notation in the *Familienbuch Waldhambach:*
Johann Philipp Gerschheimer left this land in 1764.

186. GERTSCH, JOHANNES   Neunhoffen=
Thistle, 1738   67110 Niederbronn-les-Bains
S-H, I: 221, 222, 224   Obersteinbach=
                                                    67510 Lembach
EUROPEAN RECORDS

Langensoultzbach Lutheran KB:
Johannes Gertsch, Hoffmann at Neunhoffen, and wife Salome had a
daughter:
Eva Barbara b. 29 Feb. 1716

Sp.: Eva wife of Velten Naas; Peter Gertsch, brother of
Johannes Gertsch, Susanna Barbara, daughter of Hans ?Ferari,
Hoffmann at Philippsburg [Philippsbourg = 57230 Bitche].

See Burgert, *The Western Palatinate,* p. 138-139 for additional data on this
immigrant.

Hans Gertsch, Hoffman at Obersteinbach, sp. a child of Hans Michael
Lugenbiel in 1722.

AMERICAN RECORDS

Egypt Reformed KB, Lehigh co.:
Johannes Gertsch sp. a child of Peter Trachsel [see Drachsel] in 1739.

187. GIEBELHAUS, ERHARD   Preuschdorf=
Minerva, 1768   67250 Soultz-sous-Forêts
S-H, I: 722
EUROPEAN RECORDS

Preuschdorf Lutheran KB:
Erhard Giebelhaus, single *Wollentuchmacher,* son of the late Justus
Hartmann Giebelhaus, former *Wollentuchmacher* at [W3558] Franckenberg
in Hessen, m. 5 Feb. 1765 Maria Barbara Müntzer, daughter of Jacob
Müntzer, citizen and tailor at Preuschdorf.
[His signature by this marriage entry matches the immigrant's signature in
S-H, II: 832.]
Erhard Giebelhaus, soldier in the Regiment Boccard and inhabitant at
Preuschdorf, and wife Maria Barbara nee Müntzer had children:
  1. Catharina Elisabetha b. 14 Nov. 1765
  2. Georg Friedrich b. 5 Jan. 1768
     [Notation in the KB by this bp.: "this child and parents left
     here for the New Land."]

188. GIESS, JOHANN CHRISTIAN   Volksberg=
possibly on *Phoenix,* 1750   67290 Wingen-sur-Moder
with Johannes & Georg Claus [q.v.]
S-H, I: 442
EUROPEAN RECORDS

Waldhambach Lutheran KB:
Johann Christian Giess, son of Johann Henrich Giess of Struth, Vogtei

Schönau [Struth=67290 Wingen-sur-Moder] m. 20 May 1748 in Volksberg Christina Sophia Clauss, daughter of Johannes Clauss of Volksberg. They had:
>   1. Johann Conrad b. 1 Oct. 1749

AMERICAN RECORDS

St. Paul's (Blue) Lutheran KB, Upper Saucon, Lehigh co.:
Christian Gies and wife Christina Sophia had:
>   Christian b. 13 July 1753

Rev. Daniel Schumacher's records:
Christian Kiess and wife Christina Sophia had:
>   Johann Philipp bp. 24 May 1761, 4 weeks old, Salisbury.
>   Sp.: Philipp Böhm; Maria Margaretha Clauss.

Moravian Cemetery Records, Bethlehem, PA:
Christina Sophia Giese, maiden name Clauss, b. 1724, d. 1814, from Volzburg, near Zweibrücken, Germany. She married Christian Giese.

Williams Township Congregation, Northampton Co.:
Christian Giesi and wife Christina Sophia had:
>   Maria Eva b. 14 July 1758, bp. 5 Nov. 1758
>   Sp.: Johann Claus and Maria Eva Lorentz

189. GIRARDIN, JACOB   Rauwiller=
Two Brothers, 1748   67320 Drulingen
S-H, I: 378, 380, 381
>   with Peter Girardin, only on A list

EUROPEAN RECORDS

Diedendorf and Rauwiller Reformed KB:
Jacob Girarding [b. 21 Feb. 1706, son of Jacob Girardin] from Rauweiler, m. 3 Feb.1726 Maria Francisca Wiedersheim [also appears as Wittersheim] from Görlingen [=67320 Drulingen]. Children:
>   1. Maria Susanna b. 19 Mar. 1727; she m. 23 June 1744 Henrich
>   Frantz [q.v.].
>   2. Johannetta b. 17 Oct. 1728
>   3. Possibly Peter b. ca 1732 or earlier, bp. not located;
>   appears as a bp. sp. in 1745.
>   4. Paulus b. 24 Dec. 1730
>   5. Jacob bp. 1 Jan. 1735

6. Maria Magdalena b. 27 Mar. 1739
7. Maria Catharina b. 19 Mar. 1741

Maria Francisca Wiedersheim Girardin d. ca. 1742.

Verification of this emigrant provided by Dr. Bernd Gölzer from the compiled records of Dr. Gerhard Hein:
Records of Saarwerden county office for Görlingen:
Dated 1748, inventory of Peter Widdersheim: the daughter Maria Francisca is dead. Her husband Jacob Girardin took five of their six children with him to America; the son Paulus stayed in Görlingen.

AMERICAN RECORDS

Delong's (Bowers) Church, Cemetery, Maxatawny twp., Berks co.: Tombstone inscriptions:
Jacob Schirardin, born in Rauweiler, Europe in Jan. 1735, d. 14 July 1820, age 85 years 6 mo.
Margaret Schirardin, nee Haag, b. 15 Feb. 1735, died ___, age 72 y. 11 mo. 15 days.
Abraham Schirardin b. 25 July 1766, d. 29 Dec. 1818.
Jacob Schirardin b. 8 Jan. 1761, d. 9 Jan. 1822

Christ Lutheran KB (Mertz's), Bieber Creek, Berks co:
Paulus Charetin [Girardin] was a sp. in 1756 for a child of Johannes Biber [q.v.].

1780 Tax Lists:
Paul Sheradine, East District twp., Berks co.
Abraham Sharadin, Pikeland twp., Chester co.
Henry Sharadin, Vincent twp., Chester co.
Jacob Sharadine, Maxatawny twp., Berks co.

Jacob Girardin, Longswamp twp., Berks co., nat. 10 Apr. 1755.

190. GIRARDIN, PAULUS   Rauwiller=
Edinburg, 14 Sept. 1753   67320 Drulingen
S-H, I: 522, 524
   [appears on list as Schirardin]

EUROPEAN RECORDS

Rauwiller Reformed KB:
Jacob Girardin of Rauweiler and wife Maria Francisca nee Wiedersheim had
a son:
> Paulus b. 24 Dec. 1730

See Jacob Girardin, 1748 immigrant, for additional family data.

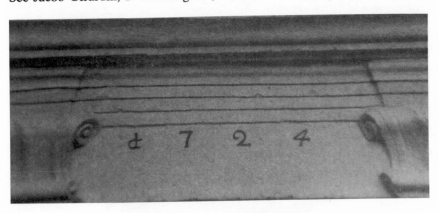

Ornate doors decorate the homes in this area,
and sometimes include the date of construction.
This portal in Rauwiller is dated 1724.

Records of Saarwerden county office for Görlingen:
Dated 1748, inventory of Peter Widdersheim: the daughter Maria Francisca
is dead. Her husband Jacob Girardin took five of their six children with him
to America; the son Paulus stayed in Görlingen.

AMERICAN RECORDS

Christ Lutheran KB (Mertz's), Bieber Creek, Berks co:
Paulus Charetin [Girardin] was a sp. in 1756 for a child of Johannes Biber
[q.v.].

191. GRAFF, JACOB   Leiterswiller=
Peggy, 1754   67250 Soultz-sous-Forêts
S-H, I: 641 [Sick on board]   Kuhlendorf=
                                          67660 Betschdorf

EUROPEAN RECORDS

Oberbetschdorf Lutheran KB:
Joh. Philip Graff, citizen at Dorf Leitersweiler, died 1772 in Kühlendorf,
Reformed. He and his wife Catharina nee Stüdin had a son :
> Joh. Jacob

Joh. Jacob Graff, single son of Joh. Philipp Graff and his wife Catharina nee
Stüdin of Leitersweiler, m. 12 Oct. 1745 Maria Eva Herrmann, daughter of
the late Joh. George Herrmann, former citizen at Kühlendorff and his wife
Catharina nee Fuchs. Witnesses at the marriage were Philbs Graff, Johann
Georg Fuchs, Beter Hermann. Joh. Jacob Graff and Maria Eva nee
Herrmann had children:

    1. Joh. Jacob b. 27 Mar. 1746, bp. 30 Mar. 1746
    2. Joh. Georg b. 7 Oct. 1747, bp. 8 Oct. 1747
    3. Joh. Martin b. 8 June 1749, bp. 11 June 1749
    4. Maria Eva b. 30 Nov. 1752, bp. 2 Dec. 1752

Typical half-timbered, canopied Alsatian house in Leitersweiler.

AMERICAN RECORDS

Egypt Reformed KB, Lehigh co.:
Georg Graf and wife Barbara had:
    1. Magdalena b. __ Oct. bp. 15 Dec. 1771
      Sp.: Jacob Neuhart and Maria Kohler

2. Maria Barbara b. 30 Apr. bp. 31 May 1773
   Sp.: Peter Kohler and Barbara, wife of Jacob Kohler

PA, Sixth Series, Vol. 6: (End notes to Egypt Reformed KB): P. 140
George Graff was a son of Jacob Graff and was born in Killendorf, Lower
Alsace, Germany, on 11 Oct. 1747. He arrived at Philadelphia with his
parents, a brother and sister, on 16 Oct. 1754. On 8 Oct. 1763 he had a
narrow escape from Indians who burned the home of Nicholas Marx, with
whom he lived. He served as a captain in the Revolutionary War, then as
Collector of Excise for Northampton co., Sheriff of Northampton co. from
1787 to 1790, and Member of the Legislature from 1793 to 1796. He was
Burgess of Allentown in 1814. He died in Allentown, 2 Feb. 1835, aged
eighty-seven years. He married 1 May 1770 Barbara Kohler, daughter of
Jacob Kohler, who was b. 6 Feb. 1750, and d. 8 Feb. 1826. Their children
were, Barbara, wife of Peter Rhoads, Jr., Magdalena, wife of John Rhoads,
Joseph, George, Sara, wife of Dr. Ferdinand Miller, Hanna, wife of Tobias
Groh, Catharina and Anna, wife of Daniel Leisenring.

Egypt Reformed KB, Lehigh co.:
Martin Graf and wife Anna Barbara had:
1. Solomon b. 14 Aug., bp. 18 Sept. 1774
   Sp.: Peter Stoeckli and wife Elisabeth
2. Johann Georg b. 14 Feb., bp. 10 Mar. 1776
   Sp.: Nicolaus Saeger and Anna Margreth Siegfried
3. Magdalena b. 9 July, bp. 7 Sept. 1777
   Sp.: Jacob Flickinger and wife Maria Elisabeth
4. Peter b. 25 Sept., bp. 28 Oct. 1780
   Sp.: Peter Siegfried and Eva Catharina Graf

PA, Sixth Series, Vol. 6: pg. 141:
Martin Graff, son of Jacob Graff and brother of Capt. George Graff, was
born in Alsace in 1748. He settled in North Whitehall twp., where he died
in 1797, leaving a widow and seven children.

1790 Census: Northampton co., Salisbury twp.:
George Graf 1 male over 16, 2 males under 16, 7 females

192. GRÄSSEL, PETER   67510 Lembach
   GRÄSSEL, MATTHIS
Hamilton, 1767
S-H, I: 715 (Peter Krassle on list - did not sign.)
S-H, I: 717 (Matthis Grässel - signed)

EUROPEAN RECORDS

Lembach Lutheran KB:

Hans Wolff Gräsel, son of Christian Gräsel, former shoemaker at the *Glashütt* by Mattstall, m. 30 May 1684 Margretha, daughter of Hans Müller. They had a son:

    Johann Peter b. 30 Aug. 1701, bp. 2 Sept. 1701; conf. 1718.

Johann Peter Grässel, citizen and farmer here, and wife Susanna Catharina nee Hördt had children:

1. Johannes Leonhardt b. 7 Sept. 1737, bp. 8 Sept. 1737
2. Susanna Margaretha b. 16 May 1739, bp. 19 May 1739
   [the father made his mark (handzeichen) by this
   baptism; the same mark is used on the ship list in 1767.]
3. Maria Catharina b. 25 Apr. 1741, bp. 26 Apr. 1741
4. Johann Peter b. 18 Aug. 1742
5. Maria Catharina b. 7 July 1745, bp. 9 July 1745, died
6. **Matthias** b. 7 Jan. 1748, bp. 9 Jan 1748
7. Joh. Peter b. 1 Dec. 1749, bp. 4 Dec. 1749, died
8. Joh. Fridrich b. 25 Dec. 1750, bp. 27 Dec. 1750
9. Susanna Dorothea b. 11 Oct. 1758

AMERICAN RECORDS

St. Michael's and Zion KB, Philadelphia:

Died 28 Sept. 1771 - Peter Grassel, born 1700 in Lembach in Elsass. Came 14 (or ?4) years ago to this land. Had 12 children, 7 are living. Died 27 Sept. 1771 age 71 years.

Indianfield Lutheran KB, Montgomery co.:

Matthias Graessel m. 23 Oct. 1774 Anna Maria Fischer, daughter of Nicholas Fischer. They had children:

1. John b. 12 May 1776, bp. 18 May 1776
   Sp.: Nicholas Fischer and Elisabetha Catharina
2. Maria Elisabeth b. 18 Aug. 1777, bp. 22 Aug. 1777
   Sp.: Henry Nees and Maria Elisabeth Fischer
3. Mary Catharina b. 3 Sept. 1778, bp. 4 Oct. 1778
   Sp.: John Georg Nees and Maria Catharina
4. Joh. Peter b. 23 Feb. 1780, bp. 27 Mar. 1780
   Sp.: Joh. Peter Franck and Eva Margaret Fischer
5. Susanna b. 6 May 1781, bp. 3 June 1781
   Sp.: John Nees and Susanna Fischer
6. Anna Maria b. 14 July 1782, bp. 18 Aug. 1782
   Sp.: Thomas Edtman and Anna Maria Eva Fischer
7. Magdalena b. 18 Sept. 1783, bp. 12 Oct. 1783

8. Abraham b. 30 Apr. 1785, bp. 12 June 1785
9. Susanna b. 1 Sept. 1786, bp. 8 Oct. 1786
10. Maria Barbara b. 12 May 1788, bp. 8 June 1788
11. Maria Eva b. 15 June 1791, bp. 7 Nov. 1791.

193. GRÄSSLE, CHRISTOPH   Bütten=
Shirley, 1751   67430 Diemeringen
S-H, I: 454

EUROPEAN RECORDS

Bütten Lutheran KB:
Christophel Gräsel, Lutheran, daylaborer of Bütten, and wife Anna Barbara
nee Schneider had children:
1. Child b. before 1742 (1742 census of Bütten)
2. Child b. before 1742 (1742 census of Bütten)
3. Anna Maria b. 29 Jan. 1741
4. Johann Adam b. 6 Sept. 1743, d. 28 Aug. 1744
5. Johann Michael b. 25 Oct. 1745

Verification of this emigration supplied by Dr. Bernd Gölzer, from the
county records of Nassau-Saarwerden, compiled by Dr. Gerhard Hein:
1742 Census of Bütten: Christophel Gräsel, daylaborer, *Beysass,* aged 40
years, 3 children, Lutheran, fortune bad. Annotation in Bütten KB: "this
man has moved to the so-called New Land". The pastors mailed him
certificates of baptism and burial.

AMERICAN RECORDS

First Reformed KB, Philadelphia:
Christopher Graesel and wife were sp. in 1753 for a child of Arnold
Kraemer.

St. Michael's and Zion KB, Philadelphia:
Christophel Graessel was a witness to the 1758 marriage of Michael
Dormeyer and Cathrina Ebernacher.

194. GREBER, LEOPOLD   Weyer=
Robert and Alice, 1739   67320 Drulingen
S-H, I: 264, 268, 271

EUROPEAN RECORDS

Diedendorf Reformed KB:
Leopoldt Greber, son of Hans Jacob Greber of Sumiswald, Canton Bern [CH-3454] m. 29 Jan. 1706 at Diedendorf, Elisabetha, daughter of Niclaus Christ from Rockwill, Arwangen, Canton Bern [CH-4914 Roggwil, BE]. Children:
1. Anna Maria bp. 4 Ma. 1708
2. Anna Magaretha bp. 24 May 1711
   Sp.: Michel Büche, son of Peter Büche, miller at Burbach; Anna Maria, daughter of Melchior Fischer, Wolffskirchen; Anna Margaretha, daughter of Peter Bader of Burbach.
3. Anna Eva bp. 26 Dec. 1712
   Sp.: Hans Scheürer, citizen in Weyer; Anna Eva Mäul, wife of Isaac Freyermuth, citizen and *censor* at Weyer; Anna, wife of Jacob Palliet.
4. A daughter (N.N.) bp. 18 Apr. 1715, recorded in **Hirschland Lutheran KB;** the father is mentioned as a cowherder in Weyer, both parents are Reformed religion.
   Sp.: Anna Maria Altmeyer, wife of the shoemaker; Anna Magdalena Tussinger; Joseph Freyermuth; Joh. Adam Schneider, all from Weyer.
5. Johann Jacob bp. 7 Mar. 1717
   Sp.: Joh. Jacob Gruber, citizen and shoemaker at Wolfskirchen; Johannes, son of Ulrich Wirth; Catharina Schlosser, wife of Philip Müller, residing at Wolffskirchen.

Leopold Greber, widower m. (2) 15 Sept. 1736   Anna Maria Weiss of Hirschland.

AMERICAN RECORDS

Longswamp Reformed KB, Longswamp twp., Berks co:
Leobolt Greber and wife Anna Maria were sp. for a daughter of Theobald Carl [q.v. - Carle] in 1744.

195. GREBIEL, ANDREAS   Dehlingen=
    GREBIEL, PETER   67430 Diemeringen
Polly, 1764
S-H, I: 690
                              EUROPEAN RECORDS

Dehlingen Lutheran KB:
Joh. Friedrich Grebiel and wife Anna Catharina nee Sent had sons:
    Peter bp. 27 Dec. 1727
    Andreas bp. 1 Jan. 1731

Andreas Grebiel, weaver of Dehlingen, son of Joh. Friedrich Grebiel, m.
5 Feb. 1754 Anna Magdalena Gurtner, daughter of Carl Gurtner of
Dehlingen. Children:
   1. Maria Margaretha bp. 25 Jan. 1755
   2. Hans Peter bp. 31 May 1756, d. 13 Nov. 1756
   3. Johann Paulus bp. 20 Sept. 1757
   4. Johann Peter bp. 31 *Erntemonat* 1759, d. 26 Jan. 1760
   5. Elisabetha Catharina bp. 9 Feb. 1761
   6. Maria Elisabetha bp. 25 Dec. 1762

Data on this immigrant family provided by Dr. Bernd Gölzer, from the
compiled records of Dr. Gerhard Hein.

AMERICAN RECORDS

1790 Census, Manheim twp., Lancaster co.:
One Peter Graybill, 2 males over 16, 1 male under 16, 2 females.
1790 Census, Harrisburg, Dauphin co.:
One Peter Grebill, 1 male over 16, 2 females.
1790 Census, Dauphin co.:
One Peter Greybill, 1 male over 16, 1 male under 16, 5 females.

196. GREINER, ANDREAS   67430 Diemeringen
Phoenix, 1749
S-H, I: 404 [Andereas (O) Creiner on list]

EUROPEAN RECORDS

Diemeringen Lutheran KB:
Daniel Greiner, widower (son of Daniel Greiner), m. 3 Feb. 1729 Catharina
Dorothea, daughter of the late Henrich Schöneberger, tilemaker at
Dehlingen.
Daniel Greiner and wife Dorothea had a son:
      Johann Andreas b. 15 Nov. 1729, bp. 19 Nov. 1729
      Sp.: Andreas Schönberger; Hans Görg Heusser; Elisabetha, wife of
      Jacob Jani, innkeeper; Dorothea, wife of Dieterich _____?.
   Conf. 1746, Joh. Andreas Greiner, son of the late Daniel Greiner.
A marginal note in the confirmation record: "this Greiner went to America
in 1749 with his step-father Ludwig Strauss."

Daniel Greiner died and his widow married (2) Joh. Ludwig Strauss [q.v.]
who arrived on the same ship.

AMERICAN RECORDS

Fredrich Krebs," Pennsylvania Dutch Pioneers", *The Pennsylvania Dutchman.* (1954-1956) Translated by Don Yoder:
From Kleinbundenbach (Kreis Zweibrucken):
Maria Catharina Gerlinger, daughter of Philipp Jacob Gerlinger of Kleinbundenbach and his wife Agnes Kaercher, married to Andreas Greiner (born in Diemeringen in Alsace), emigrated (before 1752) to America. Both were living in Whitemarsh Township, Philadelphia County, Pennsylvania.

197. GRETER, JACOB   Gumbrechtshoffen=
before 1738   67110 Niederbronn-les-Bains
[one Jacob Croiter age 38
on *Virtuous Grace*, 1737
S-H, I: 176, 177,178
did not sign; Croiter on A list, Croyter on B & C list]

EUROPEAN RECORDS

Engwiller Lutheran KB:
Jacob Greter, born in Hammerstein in the Brisgau [=W-7842 Kandern], son of ? Felten Greter, mine worker [bergarbeiter], m. 24 Jan. 1702 Maria Magdalena, daughter of Caspar Holler. They had:
    1. Maria Magdalena b. 11 Oct. 1702
    2. Anna Catharina b. 22 July 1706
    3. Friderich b. 1 Apr. 1708

Gumbrechtshoffen Lutheran KB:
Hans Jacob Greter, citizen at Gumprechtshoffen, and wife Maria Magdalena had:
    4. Hans Jacob b. 3 Mar. 1712, bp. 7 Mar. 1712
       Sp.: Henrich Haller [q.v.] young man from Wogenhaussen, Canton Zürich, now tilemaker in Zinsweyler; Magdalena Wingerlin, daughter of the late Matthias Wingerlin of Zinsweyler; Peter Lewenguth, single son of Peter Lewenguth.

AMERICAN RECORDS

Muddy Creek Lutheran KB, Lancaster co:
Jacob Greter m. 7 Nov. 1738 Maria Barbara Hartin

Heidelberg Moravian KB, Berks co:
Jacob Greter from Gumbartshoffen in Lower Alsace [Gumbrechtshoffen]

was born in 1708. He married Barbara Hert, widow, from Preuschdorf in
Alsace. They were m. 12 Sept. 1737 [sic] by Caspar Stöver in a private
house at Muddy Creek. She was b. 18 Nov. 1702 and died 1757. Children:
1. Johann Georg b. 22 Sept. 1739 at Muddy Creek, bp. by Stöver,
   23 Oct. 1739 (also recorded Christ "Little" Tulpehocken)
   Sp.: Johan Georg Heft and Maria Barbara Stör
2. Johann Heinrich b. 7 Feb. 1742, bp. 21 Feb. 1742, d. 8 Sept. 1743
   Christ "Little" Tulpehocken KB, Berks co.
   Sp.: Heinrich Gruber and wife Maria Rosina
   (this child not listed in Moravian records)
3. Abraham b. 13 Feb. 1745 bp. by Jacob Lischy at Heidelberg.
   Sp.: Andreas Bayer and his wife Maria. Abraham d. 17 May 1758.

Barbara Greter d. 24 Oct. 1757. Her first husband was Jacob Hert [q.v.]
Jacob Greter m. (2) at Oley 11 Apr. 1758 Maria Catharina Moll, widow of
Martin Moll. She had four children by her first marriage. Children of
second marriage:
4. Elisabeth b. 12 Jan. 1759, bp. 14 Jan. 1759
5. Catharina Barbara b. 15 Apr. 1762, bp. 18 Apr. 1762;
   she d. 26 Feb. 1766
6. Jacob b. 16 Apr. 1764, bp. 20 Apr. 1764
On 6 May 1767 Jacob Greter's family with four children left for North
Carolina.

Reichel, *The Moravians in North Carolina,* 1857; Reprinted Baltimore, 1968:
183: Jacob Greter died in 1788 in Friedberg.

198. GRINEUS, SIMON CONRAD   Postroff=
[unnamed ship], 20 Oct. 1747   57930 Fénétrange
S-H, I: 370
                    EUROPEAN RECORDS

Hirschland Lutheran KB:
The pastor at Hirschland, Joh. Jacob Lucius and his wife Martha Margretha
had a daughter:
       Anna Regina bp. 28 Oct. 1707
       By her baptism, he later recorded the following:
       "Ist auch mit Simon Conrad Gryneus in Americam."
Pastor Lucius served this parish for 56 years and made many emigration
notations in his record. His handwriting stops in 1750 and he died on 18
May 1754, age 89 y. and 2 months.

Anna Regina Lucius m. (1) Johannes Junker. Children of first marriage:

1. Anna Catharina Junker b. 13 Oct. 1726 at Postorf; conf. 1739
2. Anna Magdalena Junker b. 29 June 1732 at Postorf; conf. 1745

Simon Conrad Gryneus and Anna Regina, daughter of Pastor Lucius were
not married in this parish, but had several children bp. in Postroff:
1. Anna Christina bp. 24 Apr. 1737, d. 16 Oct. 1738
2. Joh. Jacob bp. 13 Aug. 1739, d. 11 Jan. 1741
3. Dorothea bp. 7 Mar. 1742

Simon Gryneus is specifically mentioned in these records as son-in-law of
the pastor, and his occupation is given as stocking weaver.

The Lutheran families of Postroff are recorded in the Hirschland
parish records. Today, there are two churches in Postroff.

Verification of this emigration supplied by Dr. Bernd Gölzer, from the
county records of Nassau-Saarwerden, compiled by Dr. Gerhard Hein:
Records of Saarwerden county office for Hirschland, dated 31 Mar. 1754:
inventory of Joh. Jacob Lucius: his daughter and her husband moved to the
so-called New Land.

AMERICAN RECORDS

Old Goshenhoppen Lutheran KB, Montgomery co:
Magdalena Juncker, daughter of Johann Juncker, deceased, was a sp. in 1755 for a child of Peter Bickler.
Communicants lists:
3 Dec. 1752: Anna Regina Gruenyous, wife of Simon Gruenyous, Reformed.
15 Apr. 1753: Anna Magdalena Juencker, daughter of Johann Juencker, dec'd, at Crinius'. She also appears on the lists for 25 Dec. 1754, 30 Nov. 1755, 11 Apr. 1756.
13 July 1753 & 31 Mar. 1754: Anna Regina Crinius, wife of Simon Crinius.
30 Nov. 1755: Dorothea Crinius, single daughter of Simon Crinius.
6 June 1756: Anna Regina, wife of Simon Crinius.
19 Mar. 1758: Anna Regina Crinius and Dorothea, her daughter.

Conf. 30 Mar. 1755: Dorothea Crinius, age 13, daughter of Simon Crinius.
Conf. 22 Apr. 1759: Maria Christina Crineus, daughter of Simon Crineus, age 14. Scharlotta Crineus, daughter of Simon Crineus, age 13.

Conrad Crineus and wife Regina were sp. in 1759 for a child of Philip Philman.

Old Goshenhoppen Reformed KB, Montgomery co:
Simon Conrad Grineus m. 19 June 1760 Anna Margaretha Rab.
Simon Crineus, widower at Old Goshenhoppen, m. 21 Nov. 1769 Margaretha Klapper, widow, Old Goshenhoppen.

199. GROSSMAN, MICHAEL age 26   Hirschland =
Lydia, 1741   67320 Drulingen
S-H, I: 301, 302, 303

EUROPEAN RECORDS

Hirschland Lutheran KB:
Joh. Paulus Grossmann m. 10 Nov. 1705 Anna Maria Biber. Children:
  1. Anna Catharina bp. 14 Oct. 1706; conf. 1720
     She m. 1734 Peter Tussing [q.v.]
  2. A son, bp. 14 Apr. 1708
  3. Joh. David bp. 27 Sept. 1711
  4. **Joh. Michel** bp. 2 Sept. 1714
     Sp.: Joh. Michel Schmitt, citizen and church *censor* at
     Hirschland; Joh. Wettstein, schoolmaster; Christina Bachman

of Hirschland.
5. Hans Nickel bp. 11 Dec. 1716
6. Eva Maria bp. 12 Dec. 1719

AMERICAN RECORDS

Emanuel [Warwick] Lutheran KB, Elisabeth twp., Lancaster co.:
Michael Grossmann had:
1. Maria Barbara b. 11 Sept. 1742, bp. 16 Oct. 1742
   Sp.: Peter Tussing [q.v.] and Maria Barbara Greiner(in)

Rev. John Casper Stoever's Records:
Michael Groszman (Warwick) had:
2. Sophia b. 18 Nov. 1744, bp. 4 Dec. 1744
   Sp.: Michael Beattly; Sophia Ber(in)
3. Maria Barbara b. 5 Sept. 1746, bp. 9 Nov. 1746
4. John Michael b. 22 Jan. 1748, bp. 4 Sept. 1748
   Sp.: For #3 and #4 were Casper Schnaebele and wife
5. John Nicolaus b. 5 Feb. 1751, bp. 4 Mar. 1751
   Sp.: John Nickel Jost and wife

Lancaster Will Book L-I: 111:
Michael Grossman, 1 Oct. 1810 - 18 Oct. 1810 (May be Jr. b. 1748)
Ex.: John and George Grosman. Warwick twp.
Wife: Mary. Children: John and George.

200. GRÜNEWALD, JACOB age 18   Diedendorf=
Lydia, 1741   67260 Sarre-Union
S-H, I: 301, 302, 303

EUROPEAN RECORDS

Diedendorf Reformed KB:
Joh. Georg Grünewalt of Diedendorff, son of Michel Grünewalt, m. 12 Jan.
1718 Anna Magaretha, daughter of Michel Matti, from Erlenbach, Vogtey
Wimmis, Canton Bern [CH-3762 Erlenbach in Simmental, BE]. Children:
1. Maria bp. 2 July 1718. She d. 13 Apr. 1730.
2. Samuel bp. 21 May 1720
   Sp.: Samuel Müller; Nicolaus Schneider; Anna Maria Magnus,
   all of Diedendorf; Eva Martzloff from Seeweiler.
3. **Johann Jacob** bp. 22 Feb. 1722; conf. 1736.
   Sp.: Jacob Allemang, son of Christian Allemang, *Hoffmann in*

Schloss Diedendorff; Samuel, son of Michael Grünewalt, *Gerichtsschöffen* in Diedendorf; Maria Magdalena, daughter of Pastor von Peroudet; Thorothea, daughter of Christian Haldi of Diedendorff.

The chateau at Diedendorf was constructed in 1577. In the eighteenth century, several Swiss families were tenant farmers at Schloss Diedendorf.

Jacob Grünewald, son of the late Georg Grünewald, last appears in the KB in 1739, as a sp. for a child of Jacob Huber. Earlier Grünewald in the KB were from Zweisimmen, [CH-3770] Ober-Simmenthal and Boltigen [CH-3766], Canton Bern.

AMERICAN RECORDS

Weisenberg Lutheran and Reformed KB, Weisenberg Twp., Lehigh Co.:
Jacob Grünewaldt, Sr. appears on a list of elders in 1754.
Jacob Grünewalt and wife Catharine had:
>   Abraham bp. 15 Apr. 1759
>   Sp.: Abraham Schellhammer and Anna Maria

Jacob Grünewald and Dorothea had:
    Cathar. Elisabeth bp. 22 Jan. 1764
    Anna Barbara b. 16 May 1766, bp. 3 Aug. 1766
    Sara bp. 30 Oct. 1768, Allemangel (Schumacher's record)

Margaretha Grünewalt, single, was a sp. in 1768 for a child of Jürg Braucher.

Mertz' Lutheran Church, Bieber Creek, Rockland Twp., Berks Co.:
Jacob Grünewald and wife Maria Catharina nee Fillhauer had a son:
    Johann Georg b. 16 Nov. 1754, bp. 31 Aug. 1755
    Sp.: Matthaeus Kleber and wife Mar. Eva.

Jacob Greenwalt, Weisenberg, Northampton Co., nat. Autumn, 1765.

201. GRÜNEWALD, JACOB   Diedendorf=
      GRÜNEWALD, ANNA   67260 Sarre-Union
    ca. 1747
                   EUROPEAN RECORDS

Diedendorf Reformed KB:
Heinrich Grünewald, son of Jacob Grünewald of Zweisimmen, Canton Bern
[CH-3770], herdsman at Kirberg, m. 24 July 1716 Barbara Rubi, daughter of
Peter Rubi from Vogtei Blankenburg, Canton Bern [CH-3771 Blankenburg,
BE]. They had children:
    1. Catharina, bp. not located, m. Jacob Dietrich.
    2. Nickel, conf. 1732; d. 4 Apr. 1742, aged 24 y.
    3. **Jacob,** bp. not located
    4. **Anna,** bp. sp. in 1744
    5. Johann Georg b. 22 Dec. 1726; conf. 1741.

Verification of this emigrant provided by Dr. Bernd Gölzer from the
compiled records of Dr. Gerhard Hein:
Records of Notary Public for Diedendorf:
Dated 19 Nov. 1772, inventory of Catharina Grünewald, widow of Jacob
Dietrich; they had no children. Listed among the heirs were her two siblings,
Jacob Grünewald and Anna Grünewald, who both emigrated to America 25
years ago [ca. 1747]. In the 18 Jan. 1749 cession of Henrich Grünewald,
three children are mentioned: Catharina, Jacob (to America), and Anna.

[This may be the Jacob Grünewald who arrived in 1741, see above; or there
may have been two immigrants with the same name, with only one appearing
in the lists. Therefore, data on both is presented here.]

202. HAAS, PETER   Mattstall=
Brigantine *John*, 1736   67510 Lembach
S-H, I: 167, 168
EUROPEAN RECORDS

Mattstall Lutheran KB:
Peter Haas, linenweaver, and Barbara, his wife, had:
>   1. Anna Maria b. 13 Apr. 1733, bp. 15 Apr. 1733
>   Sp.: Jacob Knobel; Anna Maria, single daughter of Peter Knobel;
>   Anna wife of Peter Kohl of Sultzbach [q.v.].
>   2. Catharine Barbara b. 16 Apr. 1736, died.
>   Sp.: Johannes Herr [q.v.], single, linenweaver; Maria Barbara,
>   wife of Jacob Knobel; Anna, wife of Peter Kohl of Sultzbach.

Peter Kohl and Johannes Herr, sp. of the above children both appear on the
ship list.

AMERICAN RECORDS

A Peter Haas nat. 24 Sept. 1759 (residence not given).

Berks co. Wills and Adm:
One Peter Haas, Union twp.- Adm. granted 16 June 1770 to Margaret Haas,
widow. Berks OC petition dated 16 Feb. 1771 names 10 children and gives
his occupation as tavernkeeper.

Another Peter Haas, Heidelberg twp. will dated 12 Mar. 1777-7 June 1777
Wife: Anemilla; Son Lawrence; daughter Catharine Killean; daughter
Elisabeth; daughter Christina.
Exr: Son Lawrence. Wit: John Ludwig, John Wm. Bohn.

Annathila Haas, Heidelberg twp; will dated 8 Mar. 1782-8 Apr. 1782.

St. Paul's Lutheran KB, Upper Hanover twp., Montgomery co.:
Another Peter Haas and wife Catharina had:
>   Johannes b. 29 May 1745. Sp.: Johann Doerr; Anna Maria Bitting.

Jordan Lutheran KB, Lehigh co.:
Peter Haass and wife Catharina had:
>   Johann Peter b. 11 Dec. 1748, bp. 18 June 1748
>   Sp.: Peter Simon.

Peter Haass sp. in 1742 a child of Philip Schmeyer.

203. HAHN, DAVID   Diedendorf=
Edinburg, 14 Sept. 1753   67260 Sarre-Union
S-H, I: 522, 524   Fleisheim=
                                                   57119 Lixheim

EUROPEAN RECORDS

Diedendorf Reformed KB and Rauwiller Reformed KB:
Johann Jacob Hahn from Fleisheim, son of Jacob Hahn, m. 12 May 1722
Anna Maria, daughter of Nicolaus Schweitzer, citizen at Schalbach.
Jacob Hahn and Anna Maria nee Schweitzer had a son:
          David bp. 21 Nov. 1733 at Fleisheim
          [see Jacob Hahn, 1751 immigrant, for more data.]

Verification of this emigrant provided by Dr. Bernd Gölzer from the
compiled records of Dr. Gerhard Hein:
Records of Saarwerden county office for Eyweiler:
Dated 27 Feb 1764, 3 Mar. 1764: David Hahn of Fleissheim, now a resident
of Pennsylvania, presents himself in Eyweiler, Saarwerden county, and with
letters of authorization fetches the shares of Georg Bieber [q.v.] and for
Theobald Bieber's widow and children [q.v.].

AMERICAN RECORDS

Egypt Reformed KB, Lehigh co.:
David Hahn m. Eva Wotring, daughter of Abraham Wotring [q.v.]. They
had children:
          1. Jacob b. 15 Feb. 1768
          2. Christian b. 5 Feb. 1772
          3. Daniel b. 7 Jan. 1774
          4. Nicholas b. 16 Dec. 1775
          5. John b. 30 Dec. 1776
          6. Eva Catharina b. 19 Mar. 1779

Charles Roberts et al, *History of Lehigh County, Pennsylvania,* **Vol. III:**
The Wotring family history indicates that the Hahns moved to Kentucky.

204. HAHN, JACOB   Diedendorf=
Possibly on *Janet,* 1751   67260 Sarre-Union
S-H, I: 475   Fleisheim=
                                                   57119 Lixheim

EUROPEAN RECORDS

Diedendorf Reformed KB and Rauwiller Reformed KB:
Johann Jacob Hahn from Fleisheim, son of Jacob Hahn, m. 12 May 1722
Anna Maria daughter of Nicolaus Schweitzer, citizen at Schalbach.
Children:
1. Maria Magdalena b. 11 July 1723
2. Margaretha b. 27 Dec. 1724
3. Elisabeth b. 6 July 1727
4. Anna Maria b. 9 Oct. 1729
5. Jacob b. 29 Nov. 1731
6. David b. 21 Nov. 1733 [q.v.]
7. Maria Susanna bp. 7 Feb. 1736
8. Maria Elisabetha b. 29 June 1740

Another Jacob Hahn of Fleisheim and Maria Balliet had:
Maria Catharina b. 29 Apr. 1738

AMERICAN RECORDS

Eva, daughter of Abraham Wotring [q.v.], married David Hahn. They had
6 children.

Egypt Reformed KB, Lehigh co.: Footnotes in published record:
Christian Saeger, son of John Nicholas Saeger, was born 26 Jan. 1731, and
d. 30 Nov. 1800. He married Maria Susanna Hann, who was b. 6 Feb. 1736
and d. 6 Mar. 1800. The children surviving were Nicholas, Jacob, Daniel,
Magdalena, Catharina, Barbara, Christina and Margaret.

205. HALLER, HEINRICH Age 44   Mattstall=
Samuel, 1733   67510 Lembach
S-H, I: 107, 109, 111, 112
   with Catharina Holler, age 40, Peter Holler, age 18, Christina age 16,
Hendrich age 13, Catharina age 7, Dorothea age 3

EUROPEAN RECORDS

Wolfersweiler Reformed KB:
Hennrich Haller from Wogenhausen [CH-8260 Wagenhausen, TG], Zürich,
Switzerland, m. 7 Jan 1714 Anna Cathrina, daughter of Christian Carle of
Diemptig, Bern [CH-3753 Diemtigen, BE].

Lembach Lutheran KB:
Hennrich Haller of Wobenhausen, Zürich, and wife Anna Catharina nee
Carler had children:

1. Peter b. 8 Aug. 1715 in Mattstall, bp. 11 Aug. 1715
2. Anna Christina b. 15 Feb. 1717 [parents both Reformed, mother's maiden name Carli].

Matstall Lutheran KB:
Hennrich Haller and wife Catharina had:
  3. Johann Henrich b. 2 Sept. 1719
  4. Anna Maria Elisabetha b. 7 Aug. 1722, d. 21 Apr. 1723
  5. Anna Catharina b. 29 July 1724
  6. Johann Daniel B. 9 Mar. 1727, d. 13 Apr. 1728
  7. Elisabeth Dorothea b. 6 May 1730
  8. Maria Ursula b. 28 Feb. 1733, bp. 3 Mar. 1733
     Sp.: Peter Frey from Wingen [q.v.] Maria Catharina, wife of
     Peter Ensminger [q.v.], Anna Ursula, wife of Peter Knobel [q.v.]

AMERICAN RECORDS

Muddy Creek Lutheran KB, Lancaster co.:
Heinrich Haller and wife Anna Catharina were sp. in 1737 for achild of Abraham Kern [q.v.]

Joh. Heinrich Haller had:
  9. Joh. Nicolaus b. 15 Dec. 1735, bp. 20 Jan. 1736

Dorothea Haller sp. a child of Michael Bünckely in 1747.

Muddy Creek Reformed KB, Lancaster co.:
Two Heinrich Hallers signed the 1743 Muddy Creek Reformed Church doctrine.

Peter Haller and wife had one son and two daughters bp. 19 June 1755. Given names not listed in record.

Nicholas Haller and wife had a son bp. 30 Sept. 1760.

The financial accounts of the church indicate that Heinrich Haller served as treasurer of the congregation from 1749-1760.

Muddy Creek Moravian KB, Lancaster co:
Heinrich Haller, Jr., from Mazstall in Alsace, [Mattstall, Alsace, France] born 2 Sept. 1719. His wife Anna Maria, nee Hundsickerin from Zweybrücken territory, born 2 Sept. 1719, the same as her husband. Children:
  1. Catharina, twin, b. 20 Aug. 1741, bp. 28 Aug. 1741

  2. Charlotta, twin, b. 20 Aug. 1741, bp. 28 Aug. 1741
     Sp.: Peter Hundsicker
     [See Burgert, *Western Palatinate* for this Hundsicker family].
  3. Abraham b. 29 Dec. 1743, bp. 1 Jan. 1744
     Sp.: Abraham Hundsicker
  4. Elisabeth, b. 21 Apr. 1746, bp. 29 Apr. 1746
     Sp.: Mrs. Ronnerin and Mrs. Münsterin

Peter Haller moved to what is now Shenandoah co., VA before 1761. He
died there testate in 1799.

206. HAMMER, HANS GEORG   Preuschdorf=
Lydia, 1749   67250 Soultz-sous-Forêts
S-H, I: 421
                        EUROPEAN RECORDS

Preuschdorf Lutheran KB:
Hans Georg Hammer, from Bischoffsheim, [=67210 Obernau] son of Hans
Hammer, citizen and tailor, m. 9 July 1720 Anna Margaretha Pfeifer,
daughter of the late Joh. Martin Pfeifer, former citizen at Preuschdorf.
Children:
  1. Joh. Georg b. 24 Apr. 1719, illegitimate
  2. Maria Dorothea b. 17 Oct. 1721, d. 1728
  3. Joh. Michel b. 21 Mar. 1724, d. 1729
  4. Johannes b. 10 Dec. 1726, bp. 12 Dec. 1726
  5. Anna Maria b. 2 Aug. 1730, bp. 3 Aug. 1730

Notation in KB by marriage entry: "Went to the new land."

                        AMERICAN RECORDS

Chalkley's Chronicles, I: 97:
George Hammer received certificate for naturalization 18 May 1762,
Augusta co., VA.

Chalkley's Chronicles III: 129:
George Hammer qualified as exr. of the est. of George Capliner, 18 May
1773, Augusta co., VA.

Augusta Co. Deed Book 9: 458:
29 May 1760, George Hammer purchased 114 A. for £19.17, part of 350 A.
pat. to Robert Green 12 Jan. 1746.

207. HANAUER, JOH. JACOB   67110 Niederbronn-les-Bains
_____, 1784
Not in S-H

EUROPEAN RECORDS

Niederbronn Lutheran KB:
Maria Catharina Korn, wife of Joh. Georg Hanauer, had a son:
    Joh. Jacob b. 5 Feb. 1763

A note in KB: "dieser Johann Jacob Hanauer ist gestorben in Friedrichs Stadt in Maryland in America 17 Dec. 1788."

AMERICAN RECORDS

Frederick, MD, Lutheran KB, burials:
Buried 20 Dec. 1788 - Johann Jacob Hanauer, Christian Remsperger's former servant, born 6 Feb. 1763 in Niederbronn in Nieder Elsass. Came to this land in 1784. Died 19 Dec., aged 25 years, 10 months, 13 days.

208. HARR, MICHAEL   Rott=
_____, 1752   67160 Wissembourg

EUROPEAN RECORDS

Rott Lutheran KB:
Michael Harr, son of Johann Jacob Harr, citizen and smith at Rott, m. 15 Nov. 1745 Maria Magdalena Edelmann, dau. of the late ?_____Edelmann, former citizen here. Married in the church at Birlenbach. Children:
    1. Maria Juliana b. 28 Dec. 1746, bp. 30 Dec. 1746
        Sp.: Jacob Harr, grandfather; Maria Juliana, wife of Johannes Orth, cooper at Rott; Petronella, wife of Phil. Jacob Pfänder, schoolmaster at Petschdorff [Betschdorf].
    2. Maria Magdalena b. 6 Mar. 1749, bp. 10 Mar. 1749.

Zweibruecken Manumissions Protocoll, Clee- and Catharinenburg,, 1752:
Michel Harr of Rott with wife and one child leaves for America [a group of 17 families].

209. HASCHAR, CHRISTIAN age 21   Kirrberg=
    HASCHAR, ABRAHAM age 18   67320 Drulingen
Lydia, 1741
S-H, I: 301, 302, 303

EUROPEAN RECORDS

Diedendorf Reformed KB:
Jacob Haschar from Kirberg and wife Anna Apolonia nee Gantzmüller had children:
1. **Johann Christian** bp. 18 Dec. 1718
2. **Abraham** bp. 17 Nov. 1720
3. Johann Georg bp. 21 Feb. 1723
4. Joh. Samuel bp. 15 Apr. 1725
5. Johann Heinrich [q.v] bp. 16 June 1726
6. Johann Theobald bp. 15 Aug. 1728
7. Johann David bp. 11 Nov. 1729

Verification of this emigration supplied by Dr. Bernd Gölzer, from the county records of Nassau-Saarwerden, compiled by Dr. Gerhard Hein: Records of Saarwerden county office for Kirberg: 4 Dec. 1749, inventory of Anna Appolonia Gantzmüller Haschar: the eldest son Christian is in America; the second son Abraham is in America.

AMERICAN RECORDS

First Reformed KB, Lancaster:
Abraham Hascher was a sp. in 1742 for a child of Jacob Welschhans [q.v.] and his wife Elisabetha, nee Schleppi.

Northampton co. Wills:
Abraham Hashar, Williams twp., dated 4 Nov. 1755. Brother Henry Hashar; brother Christian Hashar, had a son named Peter. Wit: Johannes Berger, Jacob Kochert, Hans George Cleiss and Wendel Schenk. Adm. granted 26 Apr. 1756 to Henry Hashar, and Jacob Kochert, yeoman, Lower Saucon.

210. HASCHAR, HEINRICH age 26   Kirrberg=
Peggy, 1753   67320 Drulingen
S-H, I: 546, 548, 550

EUROPEAN RECORDS

Diedendorf Reformed KB:
Jacob Haschar of Kirberg and wife Anna Apolonia, nee Gantzmüller, had a son:
　　　Johann Heinrich bp. 16 June 1726
　　　Sp.: Joh. Heinrich, son of Abraham Welchans of Kirberg;
　　　Jacob Kühnert, son of Michael Kühnert of Rauweiller;

[Rauwiller=67320 Drulingen]; Margaretha nee Welchans, wife of Christian Frölich of Görlingen [Goerlingen=67320 Drulingen]; Anna Margaretha, daughter of Friederich Rohr, Kirberg. [See his brothers Christian and Abraham Haschar, 1741 immigrants for additional family data.]

Rauwiller Reformed KB:
Henrich Haschard m. 10 Nov. 1750 at Rauweiler Johanetta Jamais, daughter of Jacob Jamais of Kirberg. She was b. 19 Jan. 1725, daughter of Jacob Jamais and his wife Elisabetha nee Welschhans.

Verification of this emigration supplied by Dr. Bernd Gölzer, from the county records of Nassau-Saarwerden, compiled by Dr. Gerhard Hein: Records of Saarwerden county office for Kirberg: dated 4 Dec. 1749, inventory of his mother Anna Appolonia Ganzmüller: the son Henrich is in the Royal French Swiss Regiment Wittmar as a soldier. 1753: Henrich Haschar(d) wants to emigrate to America, sells his property to his sister. Dated 22 July 1758, cession of Elisabetha Welschans Jamais: the daughter Johanneta and her husband are in America 3 years ago.

AMERICAN RECORDS

Northampton co. Wills:
Henry Hashar is named in his brother's will: Abraham Hashar, Williams twp., dated 4 Nov. 1755. Adm. of the est. was granted on 26 Apr. 1756 to Henry Hashar, and Jacob Kochert, yeoman, of Lower Saucon.

One Henry Hasher, Heidelberg twp., Berks co., nat. Fall, 1765. [Note that Theobald Hoschar also had a son Heinrich].

211. HAUCK, BLASIUS   Ingolsheim=
     HAUCK, BÄRNHARDT   67250 Soultz-sous-Forêts
Ann, 1749
S-H, I: 416
     HAUCK, HANS MICHEL
S-H, I: 417
                         EUROPEAN RECORDS

Hunspach Reformed KB and Birlenbach Lutheran KB:
Blasius Hug, son of Burckardt Hug of Cleeburg, m. 8 Nov. 1712 in the church at Hunspach, Margaretha, daughter of Jacob Vogler of Ingelsheim. [Surname also Haug, Hauch in records]. Children:
     1. Anna Barbara b. 28 July 1713, bp. in the church at Hunspach,

recorded in the Birlenbach KB. She m. Martin Hüller [q.v.]
2. Joh. Martin, b. 15 July 1716, bp. 19 July 1716, conf. 1731 [q.v.]
3. **Hans Michel** b. 5 July 1719, bp. 9 July 1719
4. Hans Jörg b. 25 Mar. 1723, d. 1725
5. Anna Margaretha b. 10 June 1725, recorded in Birlenbach KB
6. **Joh. Bernhard** b. 3 Mar. 1728, conf. 1742

Blasius Haug, citizen and widower at Ingelsheim, m. (2) 20 July 1745
Magdalena, widow of the late Jacob Weimer, citizen and cooper at Hoffen.

AMERICAN RECORDS

Rev. Jacob Lischy's Records, York co.:
Michel Hauck and Magdalena had children:
1. Michael bp. 26 May 1751
2. Petrus bp. 29 Oct. 1752
3. Joh. Georg bp. 4 May 1755
4. Barbara bp. 1 May 1757
5. Maria Margreth bp. 16 Dec. 1759

Bernhard Haug and wife Catharina Barbara had:
1. Maria Magdalena bp. 24 July 1760
   Sp.: Michel Haug and Maria Magdalena
2. Maria Elisabetha bp. 23 May 1762
   Sp.: Michel Vogel and Elisabetha Haughin
3. Joh. Niclaus bp. 15 July 1764

Görg Haug and Catharina had:
1. Joh. Jacob bp. 10 Oct. 1761

St. Jacob's (Stone) KB, York co.:
Bernhardt Haug and wife Barbara had:
4. Johan Peter bp. 17 May 1767
   Sp.: Peter Becker and wife Christina.

212. HAUCK, JOH. DIEBOLD   67690 Hatten
Hamilton, 1767
S-H, I: 717 [Appears on list as Joh. Lieb. Hauck]

EUROPEAN RECORDS

Hunspach Reformed KB:
Werle Hug, born in Lubsigen, Canton Basel [probably CH-3251 Lobsigen,

BE], Switzerland, and wife Barbara nee Birgen, had a son:
   Hans Diebolt b. 3 Aug. 1723, bp. 9 Aug. 1723 in Hunspach.
   Conf. 1738.

Hatten Lutheran KB:
Diebold Hauck, daylaborer at Hatten, and his wife Barbara, nee Schindler,
daughter of Johannes Schindler, geeseherder at Niederbetschdorf, had
children:
   1. Johann Diebolt b. 27 Jan. 1758, bp. 29 Jan. 1758
      Sp.: Jacob Gallmann, citizen and joiner here; Anna Maria,
      daughter of Johannes Schlosser, citizen at Betschdorf.
   2. Maria Magdalena b. 1759, d. 1760
   3. Maria Barbara b. 3 Jan. 1760, d. 1763
   4. Johann Heinrich b. 22 Jan. 1762, bp. 24 Jan. 1762; father
      named in this entry as *Rosshirt und Stundenruffer.*
   5. Maria Eva b. 9 Feb. 1764
   6. Georg b. 16 May 1766, bp. 18 May 1766.

Signature from KB: Signature from S-H, II: 825:

AMERICAN RECORDS

Michael Tepper, ed., *Emigrants to Pennsylvania,* Baltimore, 1975, p. 261:
[Excerpted from *Pennsylvania Magazine of History and Biography*, Vol.
XXXIII, no. 4, p. 501, 1909]
The following list of German families arrived at Philadelphia, appears in an
advertisement in Henry Miller's *Staats Bote* of Feb. 9, 1758. [Note by
compiler: this date of the newspaper is obviously in error, and should be
1768. See corrected list in Appendix B of this volume].
"The following German families, and a couple of unmarried persons, are
now in the city; all held for their passage from Holland, and desiring to bind
themselves out for same ......" Among those named in this list are:
Johan Derbald Hauck, a farmer, born in the Zweybrücken jurisdiction,
village of Hunbach [Hunspach]; his wife Barbara Schunckel, from the village
of Hassen [Hatten].

St. Michael's and Zion KB, Philadelphia:
Joh. Theobald Hauck and wife Barbara (newcomers) had:
      7. Maria Catharina b. 18 Mar. 1768, bp. 20 Mar. 1768
         Sp.: Daniel ?Gusky and Maria Catharina.

213. HAUCK, MARTIN   Ingolsheim=
St. Andrew, 1752   67250 Soultz-sous-Forêts
S-H, I: 484

   [appears on list as Hans Martin (HMH) Hang or Haug; did not sign]

EUROPEAN RECORDS

Hunspach Reformed KB:
Blasius Hug [Haug, Hauck, q.v.] and wife Anna Margretha of Ingelsheim had
a son:
   1. Hans Martin b. 15 July 1716, bp. 19 July 1716

Joh. Martin Hauck, son of Blasius Hauck, citizen at Ingelsheim, m. 14 Apr.
1739 Maria Magdalena Billmann, daughter of the late Theobald Billmann,
former citizen at Ingelsheim. Children:
   1. Maria Margaretha b. 9 Oct. 1740, bp. 16 Oct. 1740
   2. Maria Elisabetha b. 14 Dec. 1742, bp. 16 Dec. 1742
   3. Johann Adam b. 18 Dec. 1746, bp. 21 Dec. 1746
   4. Johann Michael b. 29 Dec. 1749, bp. 1 Jan. 1750

Zweibruecken Manumissions Protocoll, Clee- and Catharinenburg, 1752:
Martin Hauck with wife and two children, Martin Hüller with wife and four
children, Theobald Billman, Johann Köhler with wife and one child, all of
Ingolsheim, leave for America. [Hans Mardin Ziller, whose last name could
be Hiller, Hans Martin (HMH) Hang or Haug, and H. Dewalt (XX)
Billman, arrived together on the ship *St. Andrew,* 1752. Martin Hüller and
Dewalt Billmann were both brothers-in-law of Martin Hauck.]

AMERICAN RECORDS

Rev. Jacob Lischy's records, York co.:
Martin Haug and wife Magdalena had:
      Maria Margreth bp. 16 Dec. 1759
      Sp. Görg Ziegler and Margretha.

214. HAUDENSCHILD, HANS MICHEL   Langensoultzbach=
   HAUDENSCHILD, HANS MICHEL   67360 Woerth
Dragon, 17 Oct. 1749
S-H, I: 423

   [A Henry (X) Heydersh appears on the list between the 2 Michels,
   possibly the Joh. Henrich Haudenschild b. 1732]

EUROPEAN RECORDS

Langensoultzbach Lutheran KB:
Hans Michael Haudenschild, son of the late Diebold Haudenschild, shepherd at Niederbr__ [?Niederbronn] m. 11 Jan. 1724 at Sultzbach Anna Margaretha, daughter of Hans Adam Ruch, shepherd at Sultzbach. Children:
1. Johann Georg bp. 25 Jan. 1725, d. 15 Nov. 1727
2. Eva Elisabetha bp. 23 Jan. 1727, d. 11 Nov. 1727
3. **Johann Michael** bp. 17 May 1729; he m. 1749 Dorothea, daughter of Joh. Seitel of Preuschdorf
4. **Joh. Henrich** bp. 19 June 1732
5. Joh. Jacob bp. 1 June 1736
6. Anna Regina bp. 5 May 1739
7. Maria Barbara b. 9 May 1742
8. Hans Diebold b. 17 Aug. 1745

AMERICAN RECORDS

Frederick Lutheran KB, Frederick, MD:
Jacob Hautenschild and wife Elisabetha had;
1. Anna Maria b. 2 Oct. 1772, bp. 20 Oct. 1772
   Sp.: Jacob Baarb and Anna Maria
2. Johannes b. 10 Aug. 1774, bp. 28 Sept. 1774. Sp.: Parents.

Michael Hautenschild and wife Maria Dorothea had:
Adam b. 8 Nov. 1772, bp. 10 Dec. 1772.

Schreiner-Yantis and Love, *The 1787 Census of Virginia:* **61, 310, 697:**
Loudoun co., VA, personal property tax, 1787:
Michael Howdershell
John Howdershell
Lawrance Howdershell
Jacob Howdershell

Lincoln co., KY, personal property tax, 1787:
Jacob Howdershell

Culpeper co., VA, personal property tax, 1787:
Henry Houdeshel

Davidsburg Lutheran and Reformed KB, New Market, VA:
George Haudischilt and wife Susan nee Zirkel had 5 children bp. from 1803 to 1811. Sp. at one of the baptisms were Michael and Mary Haudischilt.

215. HAUER, DANIEL   Diedendorf=
_____, 1770   67260 Sarre-Union
[No ship arrival recorded in S-H for Jan. 1770]

EUROPEAN RECORDS

Diedendorf Reformed KB:
Otto Hauer and wife Catharina nee Guth had a son:
        Daniel bp. 24 Mar. 1748
[See his brother, Johann Nicklaus Hauer, 1754 immigrant, for additional
family data.]

Verification of this emigration supplied by Dr. Bernd Gölzer, from the
county records of Nassau-Saarwerden, compiled by Dr. Gerhard Hein:
Records of Saarwerden county office for Diedendorf: dated 11 Apr. 1776,
inventory of Otto Hauer: the son Nickel is in America without manumission
as a craftsman; the son Daniel is in America without manumission as a
craftsman; both have renounced their shares of the inheritance by means of
a letter dated 15 July 1771.

AMERICAN RECORDS

Maryland Historical Magazine, Vol. 10, No. 1, p. 81:
"Jacob Englebrecht says in his diary for July 6, 1827 that Daniel Hauer told
him that he (Hauer) was born in Lothringer [sic], Germany, Mar. 24, 1748,
left London for America, Aug. 24, 1769, Baron De Kalb being a passenger
on the same ship, arrived in Philadelphia January, 1770. He came to
Frederick about the year 1771. He died August 11, 1831."

See Charles C. Hower, "The European Ancestors of Barbara Fritchie, born
Hauer", in *Maryland Historical Magazine* (1793), pg. 94-103, for more
detailed information.

Frederick Reformed KB, Frederick, MD:
Daniel Hauer and wife Catharina had:
        1. Nicolaus b. 16 Sept. 1771, bp. 3 Oct. 1771; conf. 1789, age 17
                Sp.: Nicolaus Hauer and Catharina
        2. Magdalena b. 28 Feb. 1775, bp. 23 Apr. 1775
                Sp.: Maria Hauer
        3. Anna Margaretha b. 28 Nov. 1785, bp. 8 Mar. 1786
                Sp.: Nicolaus Hauer and Catharina

Died 18 Aug. 1831, buried 20 Aug. 1831: Daniel Hauer, age 85 y. 5 mo.
Buried 24 July 1834: Widow Hauer, age 91 years.

The Reformed parish at Diedendorf has records dating from 1698
and contain hundreds of entries for Swiss families residing in the region.

216. HAUER, JOHANN NICKLAUS   Diedendorf=
Neptune, 1754   67260 Sarre-Union
S-H, I: 622, 625

EUROPEAN RECORDS

Diedendorf Reformed KB:

Peter Hawer [elsewhere Hauer], master tailor at Diedendorf, and wife
Catharina nee Bürge had a son:

    Otto Eberhard bp. 24 Nov. 1701

Otto Hauer, son of Peter Hauer of Diedendorf, m. 27 Jan. 1727 Catharina,
daughter of Ulrich Guth of Neusaarwerden.

Otto Hauer, church elder and hat maker, and wife Catharina, had children:

    1. Dorothea Maria bp. 13 June 1728, conf. 1742

    2. Anna Christina bp. 20 Nov. 1729, conf. 1743

3. Joh. Felix Daniel bp. 20 July 1731, d. 1732
4. **Johann Nicolaus** bp. 6 Aug. 1733, conf. 1747
   Sp.: Jacob, son of the late Peter Hauer of Diedendorf;
   Johann Nicolaus, son of Thieboldt Juncken, Diedendorf;
   Maria Dorothea, daughter of Ulrich Guth, Neusaarwerden;
   Christina, daughter of the late Jonas Vomar, former citizen
   at Vingstingen [=57930 Fénétrange].
5. Anna Catharina bp. 16 Sept. 1737, conf. 1750, d. 1764.
6. Johann Elias bp. 12 Feb. 1741, conf. 1755, d. 1762.
7. Anna Susanna bp. 1 May 1744, d. 1765
8. Johan Christian bp. 3 Apr. 1746, d. 1746
9. Daniel [q.v.] bp. 24 Mar. 1748, conf. 1761
10. Johann Jacob b. 16 May 1751, bp. 20 May 1751

[See Daniel Hauer for verification of emigration.]

Ulrich Guth, grandfather of Joh. Nicolaus Hauer, is mentioned in the
records as Herr Ulrich Guth, *"des Artzney, Wohl erfahrnen"* son of Christian
Guth of Diemeringen; his wife was Susanna daughter of the late N. Storcker,
innkeeper at Buchsweiler. Ulrich Gutt of Neusaarwerden m. (2) 26 July
1713 Johannetha, daughter of Simon Brod, butcher at Lixheim.

AMERICAN RECORDS

First Reformed KB, Lancaster:
Nicolaus Hauer and wife Catharina had children:
1. Catharina b. 16 Oct. 1760; conf. 1777
2. Jacob b. 12 Mar. 1762
3. Maria Elisabeth b. 16 Mar. 1765; conf. 1779
4. Barbara b. 3 Dec. 1766; conf. 1782, Frederick
   Reformed KB, Frederick, MD. She m. Casper Fritchie.

Frederick Lutheran KB and Frederick Reformed KB, Frederick, MD:
5. Daniel b. 11 Nov. 1768
6. Joh. Ludwig b. 25 Nov. 1770; buried 20 June 1800;
   (Frederick Reformed KB).
7. Margaret, conf. 1790 age 17
8. Johannes b. 14 Mar. 1775, bp. 23 Apr. 1775
   Sp.: Daniel Hauer [q.v.] and wife Catharina

There are possibly other children in this family:
   A Magdalena Hauer was conf. 1773 (Frederick Reformed KB).
   A Maria Hauer was conf. Jan. 1775.

The John Nicholas Hauer family Bible is on display in the Fritchie House in Frederick, MD. It contains the following inscription: "This Bible belongs to me, Nicholas Hauer, born in Germany in Dildendorf situated in district Nassau, Saarbrücken in German Lothringen, born anno domini 1733 on the 6th of August. Left my native land the 18th of May, 1754, arrived here and lived in Bentztown, Frederick, MD from the 8th of October."

For additional data see Charles C. Hower, "The European Ancestors of Barbara Fritchie, born Hauer" in *Maryland Historical Magazine* (1971) p. 94-103.

Frederick Reformed KB, Frederick, MD:
Buried 11 Dec. 1799: Nicholas Hauer, age 66 y. 4 mo. 3 da.

Nicholas Hauer, Lancaster, Lancaster co. nat. 5 Aug. 1764.

217. HAUSER, MARTIN   Lampertsloch=
Molly, 1727   67250 Soultz-sous-Forêts
S-H, I: 13
EUROPEAN RECORDS

Woerth Lutheran KB:
Martin Hausser, single apprentice carpenter, son of the late Hans Gerg Hausser, former butcher at Reichenweyer [=68340 Riquewihr] m. 3 Feb. 1722 Margretha, daughter of Hans *Nicol* Schäfer, former citizen at Lampertsloch.

Preuschdorf Lutheran KB:
Martin Hausser, schirmer and carpenter at Lampertsloch and Anna Margreth, his wife, had:
    1. Johann Martin b 30 Dec. 1725, bp., __ Jan. 1726
       Sp.: Hans Jacob Cronmüller, carpenter at Lampertsloch
       Johann Martin ?Beri, *schirmer* at Lampertsloch; Maria
       Margretha, wife of Hans Jacob Stepp, citizen and tailor
       at Mitschdorff.

Maria Margaretha Schäffer was b. 3 Nov. 1702 in Lampertsloch, daughter of Joh. *Michel* Schäffer and wife Maria Barbara nee Geiger. A note by her bapt. in another hand "died in Amerika 12.1.1775."

AMERICAN RECORDS

Moravian Archives, Winston Salem, NC:
Martin Hauser and wife Margaretha nee Schaefer came to America, living first in PA, then MD. In 1753 they moved to NC, on the banks of the Yadkin River. They moved to Bethabara and then to Bethania, NC in 1759. They had seven sons, one who died on the journey to America, and one daughter. Children:
1. Martin, born in Europe, died on voyage to America
2. Georg, b. 8 Feb 1730 Goshenhoppen, PA
   d. 28 Feb. 1801 Bethania, NC
3. Michael, b. 29 Sept. 1731, d. 24 Apr. 1789 Bethania
4. Martin, b. 16 Oct. 1733, Skippack twp. (twin)
   d. 9 Nov. 1794, Bethania, NC
5. Jacob b. 16 Oct. 1733, Skippack twp. (twin)
   d. 20 Jan. 1806 Hope, NC
6. Unknown daughter b. ca 1735
7. Georg Peter b. 30 May 1740 on the Canawago, PA
   d. 21 Mar 1802 Bethania, NC
8. Daniel b. 11 Mar. 1744 Skippack, PA

218. HEBEL, JOHANNES   Langensoultzbach=
Anderson, 1750   67360 Woerth
S-H, I: 436
                        EUROPEAN RECORDS

Langensoultzbach Lutheran KB:
Johannes Hebel, former coachman in Strassburg, *Schirmer* and daylaborer here, m. 18 Feb. 1738 Anna Elisabetha, daughter of Joh. Martin Karst, citizen and farmer here. Children:
1. Johann Henrich b. 14 Apr. 1740
2. Salomon b. 23 Sept. 1742
3. Johannes b. 1 May 1745, d. 21 Mar. 1746
4. Johann Georg b. 22 Jan. 1747
5. Johann Friedrich b. 15 June 1748
[The father's signature by this last bp. entry in the KB is a perfect match with the signature in S-H, II: 504.]

Anna Elisabetha Karst was bp. 18 Mar. 1714, daughter of Joh. Martin Karst and wife Anna Margaretha nee Jung.

                        AMERICAN RECORDS
1790 Census:
One John Hebble in Conestoga twp., Lancaster co., 1 male over 16; 2 males under 16; 4 females.

219. HECHLER, HANS GEORG age 46   Ingolsheim=
   HECHLER, MARTIN age 19   67250 Soultz-sous-Forêts
Barclay, 1754
S-H, I: 595, 596, 597, 599
   [name on A List: Eygler, Heighler; B List: Yerrick (X) Eyler;
   C List: Martin (o) Hechler, H. Georg (H) Hechler]

EUROPEAN RECORDS

Birlenbach Lutheran KB:
Jacob Hechler and wife Margaretha of Birlenbach had a son:
   Hans Georg b. 14 Apr. 1708, bp. 15 Apr. 1708

Georg Hechler and wife from Ingolsheim had:
   1. Hans Martin bp. 27 Jan. 1735 in the church at
   Hunspach; Conf. 1749, Rott Reformed KB.

Rott Lutheran KB:
Georg Hechler, Lutheran, inhabitant and daylaborer at Ingelsheim, and wife
Susanna, Reformed, had children:
   2. Samuel b. 27 July 1739, bp. 4 Aug. 1739
      Sp.: Joh. Martin Hiller; Samuel Hauck of Hunspach;
      Anna Maria Roth.
   3. Johann Jacob b. 8 June 1741, bp. 11 June 1741
   4. Johann Georg b. 13 June 1743, bp. 16 June 1743
   5. Johann Michael b. 20 Feb. 1747, bp. 24 Feb. 1747.

Hunspach Reformed KB:
Died 30 July 1741- Anna Maria, daughter of Joh. Georg Hechler, citizen at
Ingelsheim, age 8 years.
Conf. 1746- Barbara, daughter of Georg Hechler of Ingelsheim.
Conf. 1750- Elisabetha, daughter of Georg Hechler of Ingelsheim.

Zweibrücken Manumissions Protocoll, 1754:
Georg Hechler of Ingelsheim leaves with his five children for America.

AMERICAN RECORDS

First (Trinity) Reformed KB, York:
Johann Georg Frey and wife Elisabeth nee Hechler had children:
   1. Susanna b. 20 Sept. 1760, bp. 29 Mar. 1763
      Sp.: Johann Georg Hechler and Elisabeth Peter
   2. Anna Maria b. 13 Mar. 1762, bp. 29 Aug. 1763
      Sp.: Johann Jacob Hechler and Catharina Klein

York co. unrecorded wills:
George Heckler, dated 12 Apr. 1773, probated 31 Jan. 1774.
"To wife Susanna the cow, bed, all my household furniture, linen and what she needs of all my implements; also £30.
Exrs.: wife and youngest son Jacob.
Wit.: Andreas Klein, Peter Schaffer, Ludwig Staudenhauer.
[Original in German; trans. by Geo. Lewis Lefler, 1774].

Christ Lutheran KB, York:
Joh. Martin Hechler and wife Barbara had:
  1. John George b. 31 Apr. 1761, bp. 19 sept. 1761
     Sp.: Joh. George, son of Nicholas Vogel and the single daughter of Conrad Stuck.

Zion Reformed KB, Hagerstown, MD:
Martin Hechler and wife Anna Barbara were sp. in 1774 for a child of Georg Fogler.

220. HECK DANIEL   Burbach=
Halifax, 1754   67260 Sarre-Union
S-H, I: 654
                        EUROPEAN RECORDS

Diedendorf Reformed KB & Rauwiller Reformed KB:
Joh. Peter Heck, cooper, son of Hans Heck of Burbach, m. 24 Feb. 1727 Anna Maria Vautrin of Vinstingen [57930 Fénétrange]. They had children:
  1. Maria Catharina, bp. not located, d. 13 Mar. 1728 [Diedendorf]
  2. **Daniel,** bp. not located, b. ca. 1729, conf. 1742 at Burbach.
  3. Johann Peter b. 29 Oct. 1730

Joh. Peter Heck, the father, d. 1732. He was b. 22 Oct. 1702, son of Hans Heck [Hegg] and Anna Maria nee Marc. His widow Anna Maria nee Vautrin m. (2) Sebastian Klein, cooper at Burbach.

Verification of this emigrant provided by Dr. Bernd Gölzer from the compiled records of Dr. Gerhard Hein:
Records of Saarwerden county office for Burbach:
Peter Heck died in or before 1732 leaving a widow and two sons. A county office record dated 3 Mar. 1737 mentions the son Daniel as seven years old. Later records in 1764 and 1766 mention the son Daniel is in Pennsylvania and is married there. His emigration was with permission.

221. HECK, DANIEL   Burbach=
Edinburg, 14 Sept. 1753   67260 Sarre-Union
S-H, I: 522, 524
EUROPEAN RECORDS

Diedendorf Reformed KB:
Hans Hegg, son of Hans Heg from Buchsen, Canton Bern, m. 9 Feb. 1700
Maria Marc, daughter of Jean Marc [also appears in the records as Marx],
kirchenpfleger at Burbach.
Died 12 Nov. 1699 - Johann Heg, citizen at Burbach, born at Buchsel?,
Canton Bern. [Another member of the Heck family is given in this same
church record from Minchenbuchsee, today CH-3053 Münchenbuchsee, BE].
Hans Heck and wife Maria had a son:
  Joh. Nicolaus Heck, b. ca. 1701, citizen at Burbach, and his wife Maria
  Catharina Lentz had a son:
        Johann Daniel bp. 31 July 1727
        Sp.: Joh. Daniel Blais; Joh. Jost, son of Joh. Nicolaus Backer;
        Maria Elisabetha, wife of Henrich Juncker, all of Burbach;
        and Maria, daughter of Joh. Nicolaus Pailiet, church *censor* at
        Rauweiler.

Hans Heck (Jr.) died 11 Mar. 1707 at Burbach and his widow Maria nee
Marc [Marx] m. (2) 8 May 1708 Durst Lantz, son of the late Melchior Lantz
of Kilchberg, Canton Bern [?CH-4496 Kilchberg, BL or ?CH-8802
Kilchberg, ZH].

Verification of this emigrant provided by Dr. Bernd Gölzer from the
compiled records of Dr. Gerhard Hein:
Records of Saarwerden county office for Burbach:
Dated 6 Aug. 1758, marriage contract for Nickel Heck's third marriage: the
son Daniel Heck from the first marriage to Catharina Lanz is 30 years old,
and moved to the New Land five years ago. Dated 14 Jan. 1774, inventory
of Nickel Heck: the son Daniel is 45 years old, moved to the New Land 21
years ago.

AMERICAN RECORDS

First Reformed KB, Philadelphia:
Daniel Heck and wife Elisabeth had:
        1. Daniel bp. 11 May 1761, 7 months old.
        Sp.: Jacob Euler and Maria Philippina
        2. Joh. David bp. 19 Apr. 1762
        Sp.: Joh. David Schaefer [q.v.] and Maria Catharina

Daniel Heck, Philadelphia, nat. Autumn 1767.

222. HECKENDORN, JACOB   Retschwiller=
Patience, 1750   67250 Soultz-sous-Forêts
S-H, I: 426

EUROPEAN RECORDS

Kutzenhausen Lutheran KB:
Jacob Heckendorn, citizen at Rötschweyler and wife Anna Barbara nee Jung
had a son:
1. Johann Jacob b. 22 July 1744
   Sp.: Joh. Georg Anstätt, citizen at Rötschweyler; Martin Ohm,
   citizen at Sultz; Maria Eva, daughter of Joh. Georg Jung,
   Rötschweyler.

[father's signature matches list 146C].

AMERICAN RECORDS

Colonial Maryland Naturalizations:
Jacob Heckendoon, communion at Lutheran Church "on the mittel end of
Thames Creek", nat. 15 Apr. 1761.

223. HECKMANN, CATHARINA   Steinseltz=
Widow of **HENRICH HECKMANN**   67160 Wissembourg
_____, 1754   Ingolsheim=
[probably on *John and*   67250 Soultz-sous-Forêts
Elizabeth, 1754 with father, Johannes Därendinger]

EUROPEAN RECORDS

Hunspach Reformed KB:
Henrich Heckmann, son of Martin Heckmann, *Gerichtsmann* at Steinseltz,
m. 11 Jan. 1746 Catharina, daughter of Johannes Dörredinger [q.v.]
Gerichtsschöffen at Ingelsheim.

Steinseltz Reformed KB:
Henrich Heckmann, of Steinselz, and wife Catharina had children:
1. Christian b. 29 Oct. 1746, bp. 2 Nov. 1746
2. Catharina (twin) b. 29 Oct. 1746, bp. 2 Nov. 1746

3. Magdalena b. 28 Jan. 1748, bp. 2 Feb. 1748
4. Maria Margretha b. 24 May 1749, bp. 26 May 1749
5. Maria Juliana bp. 11 Nov. 1751, daughter of Anna
   Catharine, widow of Henrich Heckmann

Henrich Heckmann's parents: Johan Martin Heckmann, son of Peter
Heckmann of Steinseltz, m. 10 May 1706 in the parsonage in Rott, Maria
Catharina, daughter of Joh. Georg Klein.

Zweibrücken Manumissions Protocoll, 1754:
Catharina, widow of Henrich Heckmann of Steinseltz, leaves with her four
children for America.

AMERICAN RECORDS

First Reformed KB, Lancaster:
John Roth m. 10 ?Jan 1768 Juliana Heckman.

Stephen Lutz m. 1 Nov. 1789 Catharine Heckman.

224. HELL, JOH. JACOB   Hellering=
    HELL, JACOB   57930 Fénétrange
Minerva, 1768
S-H, I: 721

EUROPEAN RECORDS

Rauwiller Reformed KB:
Joh. Jacob Hell, of Helleringen, m. 12 Nov. 1765 Susanna Fichter, daughter
of Paulus Fichter. They had a daughter:
    1. Catharina Elisabetha b. 4 May 1767

Joh. Jacob Hell was b. 31 Oct. 1720 in Pirmasens, son of Joh. Jacob Hell
and wife Margaretha.

Verification of this emigrant provided by Dr. Bernd Gölzer from the
compiled records of Dr. Gerhard Hein:
Records of Saarwerden county office for Kirberg:
Dated 22 Apr. 1790, inventory of Jacob Grosjean of Kirberg and his wife
Judith nee Fichter, who had no children. Among the heirs of Judith Fichter
was her sister Maria Susanna Fichter of Helleringen who is in America with
her husband Jacob Hell.

225. HENNINGER, HANS MICHEL, age 32   Rittershoffen=
Britannia, 1731   67690 Hatten
S-H, I: 48, 52, 53
   with Anna Maria age 26, Conrad age 9

EUROPEAN RECORDS

Rittershofen Lutheran KB:
Hans Conrad Henninger, shopkeeper from [W-6800] Mannheim, now
residing in Rittershofen, Lutheran, and wife Anna Rosina, Calvinist, had
children:
1. Susanna Margretha b. 11 Feb. 1695, bp. 13 Feb. 1695
2. Joh. Michel b. 21 Dec. 1697, bp. 4 Advent 1697
   Sp.: Diebold Wahl; Michael ___?, shopkeeper at Sultz; and
   Maria Catharina, wife of Joh. Fried. Kampmann, Pastor here.

Hatten Lutheran KB:
Joh. Conrad Henninger, shopkeeper, (b. ca Feb. 1642; d. 19 June 1712) and
wife Anna Rosina nee Gräber, Reformed, had children:
1. Susanna Margaretha (see bp. above) m. (1) 14 Jan. 1715 Joh.
   Jacob Dietsch. He d. 8 Feb. 1728. She m. (2) 1730 Joh. Jacob
   Humpert.
2. **Hans Michel,** (see above), first mentioned in Hatten KB as a
   single sp. in 1717.
3. Anna Catharina, first mentioned as a single sp. in 1716
4. Catharina Rosina, first mentioned as a single sp. in 1720
5. Maria Magdalena m. (1) 5 Feb. 1725 Hans Michael Tschantz, son
   of Benedict Tschantz of Steffisberg, BE, Switzerland. She m.
   (2) 1735 Joh. Jacob Wolf, weaver
6. Joh. Martin, weaver, married Anna Catharina Fuchs. They had
   a son Joh. Georg b. 10 Apr. 1737 [q.v.]

Johann Michael Henninger, master tailor, son of the late Hans Conrad
Henninger, former citizen and shopkeeper here, m. 18 Feb. 1721 Anna
Maria, daughter of Jean Pary, *Herrschafftl Wachtmeister* (Sergeant) here.
They had a son:
1. Joh. Conrad bp. 14 May 1722
   Sp. Conrad R___?, citizen and potter, Hans Wahl, citizen at
   Rittershoffen, Maria Catharina, widow of Hans Martin Humpert.

AMERICAN RECORDS

Rev. John Caspar Stoever's records:
John Michael Henninger (Maxatawny) had children:

2. Maria Rosina b. 21 Nov. 1731, bp. 27 Nov. 1731
3. John Michael b. 30 Sept. 1736, bp. 29 Oct. 1736.
Michael Henninger and wife Anna Maria sp. a child of Thomas Gowringer
in 1736.

Moselem Lutheran KB, Berks co.:
Conrad Henninger and wife Catharina nee Kutz had:
    1. Johannes b. 3 Sept. 1747
    2. child (n.n.) b. ____1749
    3. Anna Catharina bp. 27 Jan. 1751
    4. Conrad b. 2 Feb. 1755

Michael Henninger and wife Eva Maria had:
    1. Eva Maria b. 4 Feb. 1766
    2. Joh. Georg b. 3 May 1768
    3. Maria Elisabetha b. 8 Sept. 1771

Other Henningers appear in this record:
Georg Henninger and wife Catharine first appear in 1769;
Jacob Henninger and wife Eva first appear in 1772.

Berks County Will Abstracts:
Michael Henninger, Jr., Maxatawny. 29 Dec. 1770 - 11 Feb. 1771.
All estate to be sold wife (not named) to have £20 and afterwards her 1/3
part, and what remains shall go to the children "but the mother shall keep
the 3 small children with her." Letters to wife Eva and Sebastian Levan.
Witness: Antony Schreter and George Henninger. Translation.

Michael Henninger, Maxatawny. 9 Feb. 1763 - 29 Oct. 1774.
Provides for wife Anna Maria "as son Conrad hath the mill of his father
£100 cheaper, so shall all the children have equal shares of my inheritance".
Wife Anna Maria, executor. Letters to Martin Kinkinger and Maria Rosina,
his wife, only daughter of the deceased. Witness: Adam Reichbacher and
Daniel Dorne. Translation.

Berks County Orphans Court:
11 Dec. 1775. On motion of Mr. Burd, ordered that Martin Kinkinger and
Rosina his wife, Admr's. of Michael Henninger are ordered to appear before
William Reeser, Benjamin Pearson and Henry Haller to answer complaint
of Conrad Henninger one of he heirs of deceased, and to render an account.

St. Peter's Lutheran KB, Rocky Hill, Frederick co., MD:
Conf. 1768: Catharina Henninger, age 17, daughter of Conrad Henninger.

Johannes Henninger, son of Conrad Henninger, was a sp. in 1767.
Johannes Henninger and wife Maria Louisa had:
1. Joh. Jacob bp. 12 Oct. 1771
   Sp.: Nicolaus Kappel and Barbara
2. Conrad b. 20 July 1773, bp. 21 Sept. 1773
   Sp.: Conrad Henninger, single.

226. HENNINGER, JOH. GEORG   67690 Hatten
Chance, 1763
S-H, I: 686

EUROPEAN RECORDS

Hatten Lutheran KB:
Joh. Martin Henninger, weaver, son of Joh. Conrad Henninger, and wife
Anna Catharina nee Fuchs had a son:
   Joh. Georg b. 10 Apr. 1737, bp. 11 Apr. 1737

[See Hans Michel Henninger, 1731 immigrant, for additional data.]

AMERICAN RECORDS

Moselem Lutheran KB, Berks co.;
Georg Henninger and wife Catharina had:
1. Anna Maria b. 6 Sept. 1766, bp. 15 Oct. 1766
   Sp.: Benjamin Weiser and Maria Geiger
2. Christian b. 4 Sept. 1768, d. 9 Oct. 1841
   [data from TS at Grimsville, Berks co.]
3. Jacob Friederich b. 15 Nov. 1771, bp. 22 Dec. 1771
   Sp.: Jacob Henninger and Eva Hill

They sp. a child of Geo. Graff and Maria Eva in 1771, 1772.

Grimsville Cemetery Records, Berks co.:
Georg Henninger, b. 13 Apr. 1737 in "Haffen in Elsas" [Hatten], married
Catharina Levan and had 12 children, 6 sons and 6 daughters; d. 14 July
1815. Aged 78 y., 3 m., and 1 day.

Catharine Henninger, wife of Georg Henninger; she was born in Maxschany,
(?Maxatawny) Berks co., 15 June 1748; d. 25 May 1822, aged 73 y., 11 mo.,
10 days.

Berks co. Wills and Adm.:
George Henninger, Albany twp., 7 Aug. 1715, Adm. to Catharine, the widow,

and George and Christian Henninger, sons.

Catharine Henninger, widow of George Henninger, Albany twp. will dated 13 June 1818- prob. 21 May 1822. Children: Susanna, George, Christian, Frederick, John, Maria Hetler, Catharine Shankweiler, Elizabeth Hammel, Magdalena Schmidt, and Eva Hartman. Exr: Son Christian. Wit: Adam Dietrich and Jacob George.

227. HERMANN, HEINRICH   Kuhlendorf &
Betsey, 1765   Niederbetschdorf=
S-H, I: 706   67660 Betschdorf
                    EUROPEAN RECORDS

Oberbetschdorf Lutheran KB:
Joh. Georg Herrmann, son of Hans Jacob Herrmann, carpenter at Kühlendorf, m. 1713 Christina Memminger, daughter of Durst Memminger of Oberhoffen. Their son:
          Georg Heinrich b. 27 Mar. 1718

Alsatian canopied houses in Betschdorf with the architecture typical of this region.

Georg Heinrich Herrmann, single, smith from Kühlendorf, son of Joh. Georg Herrmann, m. 24 Nov. 1739 Catharina Ernst, daughter of Joh. Michael Ernst, shoemaker at [67770] Sessenheim. She died 1745. They had children:
> 1. Philip Heinrich b. 27 Jan. 1742, bp. 2 Feb. 1742
> 2. Margretha Dorothea, b. 7 Sept. 1744, bp. 13 Sept. 1744
>   at Niederbetschdorf.

AMERICAN RECORDS

Hocker, *German Settlers of Pennsylvania:*
Pennsylvanische Staatsbote, dated 15 Jan. 1771:
Philipp Henrich Haerman, tailor, from Betschdorf in Alsace, came here six or seven years ago. His sister Margaretha Dorothea arrived 30 Sept. 1770. She is married to Jacob Paulus, tailor, and seeks her brother. She may be found at Metzner's German apothecary in Philadelphia.

228. HERMANN, JOH. HENRICH   Weitersweiler =
Betsy, 1768   67340 Ingwiller
S-H, I: 725

EUROPEAN RECORDS

Weitersweiler Lutheran KB:
Joh. Georg Hermann, tailor at Weitersweiler, and wife Maria Magdalena nee Ziebig had a son:
> Joh. Henrich b. 23 Aug. 1748, conf. 1762

Verification of this emigration supplied by Dr. Bernd Gölzer, from the county records of Nassau-Saarwerden, compiled by Dr. Gerhard Hein:
The obituary of the father, Joh. Georg Hermann, on 12 July 1775, mentions that the son Joh. Henrich went to America a couple of years ago.

229. HERMANN, WENDEL   Kuhlendorf =
Sandwich, 1750   67660 Betschdorf
S-H, I: 450

EUROPEAN RECORDS

Hoffen Reformed KB:
Johann Wendel Hermann, son of the late Lorentz Hermann at Kühlendorff, m. 8 Nov. 1746 Eva, daughter of the late Jacob Weimer, citizen and cooper here. They had a son:
> 1. Heinrich b. 31 July 1747, bp. 2 Aug. 1747 in the church at Hoffen

[this baptism recorded in the Rott Lutheran KB; the father's trade
is given in this record as *holtzmacher* in the Hagenau Forest.]
[His wife Eva was a sister of Maria Catharina Enes. See Philip Enes, 1751
emigrant.]

Hunspach Reformed KB:
Died 22 Feb. 1748: Maria Eva, wife of Joh. Wendel Herrmann, daylaborer.
Her age was 23 years.

Rott Lutheran KB:
Hans Wendel Herrmann from Kiehlendorf [Kuhlendorf], widower, m. (2) 18
Nov. 1748 Anna Maria, daughter of Hans Jacob Salade, daylaborer at
Hunspach. [Anna Maria Salade was b. 18 Mar. 1723, daughter of Hans Jacob
Salade; see also immigrant Peter Salathe].

Oberbetschdorf Lutheran KB:
Lorentz Hermann, son of Lorentz Hermann, m. 1701 Catharina Sebastian,
daughter of Hans Jacob Sebastian, of [67690] Hatten. Their son Joh. Wendel
was b. in 1721.

230. HERR, JOHANNES   Mattstall=
Brigantine *John,* 1736   67510 Lembach
S-H, I: 167, 168
                              EUROPEAN RECORDS

Matstall Lutheran KB:
Johannes Herr, single linenweaver, was a sp. at the bp. of Catharina Barbara,
daughter of Peter Haas [q.v.] and wife Barbara, on 16 Apr. 1736. Peter Haas
and Johannes Herr appear together on this ship list dated 19 Oct. 1736.
Peter Kohl [q.v.] also appears on the same list; his wife Anna sp. two
children of Peter Haas, linenweaver.

                              AMERICAN RECORDS

Rev. John Casper Stoever's Records:
John Herr and Maria Elisabetha Haussahn [See immigrant Johannes Husam
from Langensoultzbach] were sp. in 1741 for a child of Frederick Ohnselt.

Peggy S. Joyner, *Abstracts of Virginia's Northern Neck Warrants and Surveys,
Frederick County:* 158:
Frederick Unsult, assignee of Jacob Hood, no warrant, date from survey: 21
Sept. 1750 - 19 Nov. 1750; 163 a. on Back Creek at North Mountain, adj.
John Harr [Herr].

231. HERTZOG, HANS NICKEL   Schopperten=
Two Brothers, 1751   67260 Sarre-Union
S-H, I: 465

EUROPEAN RECORDS

Keskastel Lutheran KB:
Hans Nickel Hertzog, single weaver, son of the late Hans Theobald Hertzog, citizen at Domfessel, m. 26 Oct. 1741 Maria Elisabeth, daughter of Heinrich Zinck, citizen at Schopperten. Children:
1. Maria Margaretha bp. 16 Dec. 1743
2. Hans Nickel bp.11 Dec. 1743
3. Anna Christina bp. 28 Apr. 1745
4. Maria Elisabetha bp. 23 Jan. 1747

Verification of this emigrant provided by Dr. Bernd Gölzer from the compiled records of Dr. Gerhard Hein:
Records of Saarwerden county office for Schopperten:
1770 inventory of Henrich Zinck: daughter Maria Elisabetha married N. Hertzog; her children Christmann, Margaretha, and Hans Nickel Hertzog are in America. [She d. 23 Jan. 1747, age 33].

Hans Nickel Hertzog and second wife Maria Catharina nee Bach had:
5. Hans Jacob bp. 19 Mar. 1748
6. Daniel bp. 6 Sept. 1749

AMERICAN RECORDS

Rev. Daniel Schumacher's records:
Hans Nicholas Herzog and wife Maria Catharina had:
Anna Maria bp. 11 Feb. 1760, 3 weeks old in Egypt [Lehigh co.]
Sp.: Christopher Bähr; Anna Maria Wirths; Johannes Schad; Catharina Wedderholten.

Margaretha Hertzog, single, was sp. in 1760 at Egypt for a child of Samuel Seger. Johann Nicolaus Hertzog was sp. at Egypt in 1765 for a child of Jacob Dormeyer and wife Magdalena nee Fritner. Johann Dewald Hertzog was a sp. at Lehigh in 1770 for a child of Christopher Feitner.

Conf. 1760 in Egypt, Whitehall twp.: Christina Hertzagin.
Conf. 1765 in Egypt: Catharina Hertzagin.
Conf. 1768, across the Lehigh: Dewald Hertzog
Conf. 1767 at Egypt: Magdalena Hertzog.

232. HESS, DANIEL   Oberbronn=
Patience, 1751   67110 Niederbronn-les-Bains
S-H, I: 456

EUROPEAN RECORDS

Oberbronn Lutheran KB:
Daniel Hess, citizen and hatmaker here and wife Anna Barbara nee Dick
had children:
    1. Joh. Jacob b. 26 July 1722, bp. 28 July 1722
       Sp.: Joh. Jacob Handwercker, Joh. Philip Haus, Jr., Ursula
       daughter of Joh. Jacob W____?
    2. **Daniel** b. 26 Jan. 1725 bp. 29 Jan. 1725, conf. 1741
       Sp.: Johan Valentin Haus, Hanns Jacob Metz, Jr., Anna Barbara
       Winter
    3. Johann Christian b. __ Oct. 1727, bp. 8 Oct 1727
    4. Johann Christoph b. __ July 1730, bp. 25 July 1730
    5. Mathias b. __ Apr. 1732, bp. 3 Apr. 1732
    6. Catharina b. 12 Dec. 1734, bp. 13 Dec. 1734

AMERICAN RECORDS

Germantown Lutheran KB:
Daniel Hess, a single hatmaker from Oberbrun in Elsass, m. 13 Apr. 1755
Gertrauda Schmitt, a single person from Walgendorff in the Nassau region.

Philadelphia Will Book R: 238:
Daniel Hess, Germantown, Philadelphia co., Hatter. 23 July 1779 - 4 Dec.
1779. Wife: Gertrude. Children: Andrew, Christian, Rosina, Catharina.
Exrs. Wife and Andrew Hess. Wit: Thomas Rose, John Fry, Thomas
Watterman.

233. HETZEL, HANS MICHEL   67510 Lembach
Bennet Gally, 1750
S-H, I: 429

EUROPEAN RECORDS

Lembach Lutheran KB:
Hans Hetzel, citizen here, and wife Maria Catharina nee Metz had:
    1. **Hans Michel** b. 29 Aug 1726 bp. 1 Sept. 1726
       Sp.: Hans Michel Müller, Hans Michel ? Thum or Thurn, and
       Anna Maria nee Hügelin widow of the late Joh. Nicolaus Müntzer
    2. Andreas b. 26 Apr. 1729, bp. 28 Apr. 1729
    3. Christophorus b. 17 Sept. 1732, bp. 21 Sept. 1732

AMERICAN RECORDS

Germantown Lutheran KB, Philadelphia co:
Johann Michael Hetzel, single smith, born in Lembach in Alsace m. 8 May 1755 Anna Maria Walcher, single daughter of Georg Walcher, born in Mesenigen in Tübinger Weid in Mechlenberg.

Michael Hetzell, Northern Liberties, Philadelphia, nat. Sept. 1764

234. HIRSCHI, BENEDICT   Diedendorf=
before 1733   67260 Sarre-Union
Not in lists

EUROPEAN RECORDS

Diedendorf Reformed KB:
Benedictus Hirschi was conf. in 1715 in Diedendorf.

AMERICAN RECORDS

Muddy Creek Moravian KB, Lancaster co.: in *Der Reggeboge,* Vol. 10, No. 3-4 (1976):
Benedict Hischy, from Ephrata [Cloister], his wife Judith, nee Hienigen, her father Thomas Hiening. She was born not far from Manheim. Her mother was named Barbara. Their children:
1. Jacob b. 22 Sept. 1733
2. Barbara b. 1735. She m. 9 June 1767 Peter, son of Peter Franckhauser [q.v.]. (Muddy Creek Ref.)
3. Andreas b. July 1737
4. Peter b. Apr. 1740
5. Johannes b. July 1744, bp. 12 Aug. 1744 at Muddy Creek Ref. Sp.: Maria Magdalena Wissenandt
6. Esther b. 18 Apr. 1747

Ephrata Cloister burial records:
Brother Bens Hirschi died 1761, no other date given.

Lancaster Intestate records:
Benedict Hershey 1762 (No. vol. or pg. no.)

235. HIRT, MARIA age 39 [widow of Jacob Hördt]   67510 Lembach
Snow *Two Sisters,* 1738   Preuschdorf=
S-H, I: 209, 210   67250 Soultz-sous-Forêts
    with Hann Martha [Martin] Hirt age 10

EUROPEAN RECORDS

Lembach Lutheran KB:
Jacob Hördt, citizen and tailor at Lembach, son of the late Wendel Hörth,
m. 25 Jan. 1729 at Preuschdorf **Maria Barbara,** daughter of Hans Michel
Dräher, citizen and *Gerichtsmann* at Preuschdorf. Children:
    1. **Johann Martin** b. 23 Nov. 1729, bp. 30 Nov. 1729
    2. Anna Elisabetha Barbara b. 2 Nov. 1731, bp. 4 Nov. 1731
    3. Georg Ludwig b. 26 Feb. 1734, bp. 1 Mar. 1734
    4. Maria Magdalena bp. 26 Nov. 1736

Preuschdorf Lutheran KB:
Maria Barbara Dreher was b. 18 May 1703, daughter of Hans Michel Dreher
and his wife Maria nee Biebel.

AMERICAN RECORDS

Muddy Creek Reformed KB, Lancaster co.:
Jacob Greter m. 7 Nov. 1738 Maria Barbara Hartin.
[See Jacob Greter for additional family data.]

Bethlehem Moravian Marriages:
Martin Hirt, b. 1729; from *Lein*bach, Alsace; a farmer; came to America with
parents; d. 1760 in Bethlehem. He married 20 Apr. 1757 Anna Barbara
Beroth, (?Maria Joanna), b. 7 Aug. 1732, in Oppa, Palatinate, of Reformed
parentage; in 1738 came to Pennsylvania; d. 15 Sept. 1813, in Bethlehem.
She m. (2) 1779 at Nazareth, Hermanus Loesch, who d. 1791 in Bethlehem.

Cherub from Johann Adam Eyer *Fraktur.* Private Collection.

236. HOCH, GEORG   67510 Lembach
Hamilton, 1767
S-H, I: 716

EUROPEAN RECORDS

Birlenbach Lutheran KB:
Hans Georg Hoch, widower, m. 25 June 1737 Catharina Elisabetha Brick, daughter of the late Nicolaus Brick, former carpenter.
Johann Georg Hoch, swineherder here, and wife Elisabetha had a son:
  Johann Georg b. 23 Aug. 1740, bp. 18 Aug. 1740; conf. 1755.
  [see brother Joh. Leonhard Hoch for further data]

Lembach Lutheran KB:
Andreas Bauer and wife Eva Margaretha had a daughter:
  Maria Dorothea b. 3 Dec. 1733, bp. 6 Dec. 1733

Johann Georg Hoch, single son of Georg Hoch, swineherder here and his wife Maria Elisabetha nee Brück, m. 4 Jan. 1763 Maria Dorothea Baur, daughter of the late Andreas Baur, former citizen and farmer here and his wife, the deceased Eva Margaretha nee Dillmann. They had children:
  1. Susanna b. 8 Nov. 1764, bp. 11 Nov. 1764
     Sp.: Joh. Jacob Zimmer; Eva Christina, wife of Joh. Valentin Jung; Susanna, daughter of Joh. Georg Hoch, herdsman at Keffenach [=67250 Soultz-sous-Forêts]
  2. Catharina Magdalena b. 18 June 1766, bp. 19 June 1766
     Sp.: Joh. Jacob Zimmer, citizen and master cooper; Susanna, daughter of Joh. George Hoch and Christina Elisabetha Neuschwander, daughter of Joh. Peter Neuschwander [q.v.].

AMERICAN RECORDS

Michael Tepper, ed., *Emigrants to Pennsylvania,* **Baltimore, 1975, p. 261:**
[Excerpted from *Pennsylvania Magazine of History and Biography*, Vol. XXXIII, no. 4, p. 501, 1909]
The following list of German families arrived at Philadelphia, appears in an advertisement in Henry Miller's *Staats Bote* of Feb. 9, 1758. [Note by compiler: this date of the newspaper is obviously in error, and should be 1768. See corrected list in Appendix B of this volume].
"The following German families, and a couple of unmarried persons, are now in the city; all held for their passage from Holland, and desiring to bind themselves out for same ......" Among those named in this list are:
Johann Georg Hoch, a farmer, born in the Zweybrücken jurisdiction, village of Bürlebach, and wife Maria Dorothea Baur, born in Alsace, village of Lembach.

St. Michael's and Zion KB, Philadelphia:
Georg Hoch and wife Dorothea had a son
    Georg b. 7 Apr. 1772, bp. 17 Apr. 1772
    Sp.: Peter Rieb and wife Catharina

1790 Census: Moyamensing and Passyunk twps., Philadelphia co:
    George High, 2 males over 16, 1 male under 16, 2 females

237. HOCH, JOHAN LEONHARD   Birlenbach=
Hamilton, 1767   67160 Wissembourg
S-H, I: 716
                        EUROPEAN RECORDS

Birlenbach Lutheran KB:
Joh. Georg Hoch m. (1) Margaretha Schlosser. Hans Georg Hoch, widower,
m. (2) 25 June 1737 Catharina Elisabetha Brick, daughter of the late
Nicolaus Brick, former carpenter here. Joh. Georg Hoch, swineherder at
Birlenbach, later mentioned as herdsman at Keffenach [=67250 Soultz-sous-
Forêts] and wife Elisabetha, had children:
    1. Susanna b. 30 June 1738; conf. 1752. She m. 1 July 1766 at
       Lembach Joh. Jacob Frey, son of the late Philip Frey of Wingen.
    2. Joh. Georg b. 23 Aug. 1740 [q.v.]
    3. Georg Jacob b. 30 June 1743
    4. **Johann Leonhard** b. 10 Dec. 1745, bp. 12 Dec. 1745;
       conf. 1764 as Johann Hoch
    5. Joh. Peter b. 20 Jan. 1749 [Rott Lutheran KB]
    6. Johannes b. 19 Apr. 1750 [Rott Lutheran KB]
    7. Johann Michael b. 12 Jan. 1753; conf. 1767
    8. Catharina Magdalena b. 3 Feb. 1756; conf. 1770

Lembach Lutheran KB:
Joh. Georg Hoch, widower and swineherder here, m. (3) 28 Apr. 1761
Elisabetha Margaretha nee Ebbrecht, widow of Joh. Andreas Bey, former
herdsman in Sultzthal.

[See brother Joh. Georg Hoch, also on the *Hamilton,* 1767].

                        AMERICAN RECORDS

1790 Census: Moyamensing and Passyunk twps., Philadelphia co:
    Leonard High, 1 male over 16, 3 males under 16, 3 females.

238. HOCHSTÄTTER, CHRISTIAN   Herbitzheim=
HOCHSTÄTTER, NICKLAUS   67260 Sarre-Union
Phoenix, 1749
S-H, I: 407

EUROPEAN RECORDS

Keskastel Lutheran KB:
Christian Hochstetter, *des Melcker* at ?Euch, son of Ulrich Hochstetter, *Melcker* at Herbisheim, m. 24 ?Apr. 1724   Gertrudt, daughter of Jean Vautrin, miller here.

Herbitzheim Lutheran KB:
Christian Hochstädter, *bestander* at the Hoff, and his wife Gertrud had:
  1. Christian b. 5 Jan. 1741 bp. in house; [no sp. given]
  2. Joh. Samuel b. 29 Jan. 1742, bp. 1 Feb. 1742
     Sp.: Joh. Nichol Kabele, Saarbockenheim; Samuel Haldy; Justina Catharina, wife of Daniel Eichacker; Johanna Catharina Elisabetha, wife of Joh. Ernst Demuth.
  3. Joh. Christian b. 17 May 1744, bp. 20 May 1744
     Sp.: Joh. Christian Wampffler, master weaver here; Joh. Michael Heintz, tanner; Anna Maria wife of Joh. Peter Würtz; Anna Maria, wife of Ulrich Hochstädter, *melcker* at Witterwald.
  4. Maria Gertrud b. 13 Mar. 1746
     Sp.: Daniel Eichacker; Wilhelm Haldy; Maria, wife of Samuel Haldy; Susanna, wife of Michael Heintz.

AMERICAN RECORDS

First Reformed KB, Philadelphia:
Christian Hoffstetter sp. in 1749 a child of fellow passenger Ulrich Mischler.

St. David's (Sherman's) KB, York, co., published in *Der Reggeboge,* Vol. 11, No. 2 (1977):
Nicholaus Hochstätter was a sp. in 1753 for a child of Peter Gehret [q.v.].

Rev. Jacob Lischy's records, York co.:
Niclaus Hochstätter and wife Magdalena had a son:
     Joh. Niclaus bp. 1 June 1760
     Sp.: Benedict Kautzman and Margreth Kähner.

239. HOCHSTRASSER, CATHARINA ELISABETHA   Harskirchen=
---------, unknown, [Perhaps with   67260 Sarre-Union
husband Johannes Fuchs (one on *Sandwich,*
1750 and another on the ship *Union,* 1774)].

EUROPEAN RECORDS

Neu Sarrwerden Lutheran KB and Harskirchen Lutheran KB:
Peter Hochstrasser, herdsman, son of Burkhart Hochstrasser, herdsman at
Zollingen, m. 24 Feb. 1727 Johannetta Michel.   Lived 1716-1730 in
Zollingen, 1733-1741 at Harskirchen.   Peter Hochstrasser d. 12 Mar. 1741.
His obituary in the Harskirchen Lutheran KB mentions that he had been a
herdsman at Harskirchen for 10 years, and died leaving a pregnant wife
Nannet and five children. His obituary also mentions that they had planned
to go to the New Land.   He d. aged 40 y. 8 mo. 14 d.   His wife also died
there 23 Apr. 1770, aged 68 y.   Of their eight children, 3 were bp. at
Zollingen and 5 were bp. at Harskirchen. One of the daughters was:
  Catharina Elisabetha bp. 18 Apr. 1730 at Zollingen.

AMERICAN RECORDS

Trinity Lutheran KB, Reading, Berks co:
Died 21 Dec. 1790: Catharina Elisabetha Fuchs, nee Hochstrasser, native
of Harschkirchen, Province of Saar Bockenheim, aged about 63 y. She was
a widow since 25 June [1790]. She was buried here 23 Dec. 1790.

Died 25 June 1790: Johannes Fuchs, blacksmith, native of Saargemunde,
Loraine, aged 72 y. 6 mo. 3 weeks less 1 day. Buried here 26 June 1790.

240. HOCHSTRASSER, PAULUS   Schalbach=
Edinburg, 14 Sept. 1753   57370 Phalsbourg
S-H, I: 523, 525
EUROPEAN RECORDS

Diedendorf Reformed KB:
Samuel Hochstrasser, citizen at Schalbach, and wife Elisabetha nee Rosin
[elsewhere Rossi, Rosee] had a son:
  1. Johann Paulus bp. 18 May 1725 [Recorded with the March bp.]
     Sp.: Paulus Schweitzer; Jacob Allemand, son of Jacob Allemand;
     Dorothea Margar. Kurtz, wife of Conrad Mochel; and Maria
     Catharina, daughter of Abraham Rosee, all of Schalbach.
  2. Jacob [q.v.] b. 11 Nov. 1728, bp. at Rauwiller

Friedrich Krebs, "Annotations to Strassburger and Hinke's Pennslyvania German Pioneers", in *The Pennslyvania Genealogical Magazine,* **Vol. 21 (1960):**
"Paul Hochstraser, son of the town official Samuel Hochstraser at Brenschelbach, district of Homburg, in the Saar, and his wife Elisabetha. He established himself as a tailor in Philadelphia. (Deposition 18 April 1761.) According to a power of attorney which Paul Hochstraser and his sister Catharina signed 23 Jan. 1764 at Albany, Province of New York, they were living there. "Paul Hochstraser" arrived 14 Sept. 1753 in ship *Edinburg.* In the year 1763 a Jacob Hochstraser emigrated to America, presumably he was a brother of Paul, for local records show that Paul had a brother of that name."

AMERICAN RECORDS

St. Michael's and Zion KB, Philadelphia:
Paulus Hochstrasser and wife Elisabetha had:
     Samuel b. 21 Oct. 1757, bp. 30 Oct. 1757
     Sp.: Samuel Mauss and Elisabetha

241. HOCHSTRASSER, JACOB   Schalbach=
Hamilton, 1767   57370 Phalsbourg
S-H, I: 715
EUROPEAN RECORDS

Diedendorf Reformed KB:
Samuel Hochstrasser and wife Elisabetha nee Rosee of Schalbach had a son:
     Jacob b. 11 Nov. 1728
     [See also Paulus Hochstrasser]

AMERICAN RECORDS

Friedrich Krebs, "Pennsylvania Dutch Pioneers", in *The Pennsylvania Dutchman* **(1954-56):** From Brenschelbach (Kreis Homburg, Saar):
" Hochstraser, Paul - son of Samuel Hochstraser of Brenschelbach and his wife Elisabetha, "who has now established himself as master tailor in Philadelphia" (Document dated 18 Apr. 1761). But according to a letter of Attorney dated 23 Jan. 1764, Paul Hochstraser, breeches maker, with his sister Catharina, was resident in the city of Albany, province of New York. [Paulus Hochstrasser, Ship *Edinburg,* 14 Sept. 1753.] The Jacob Hochstrasser who emigrated in 1767 was perhaps a brother of Paul's since the latter had a brother by that name."

242. HOFFMANN, HANS MICHAEL   Liniehausen,
John and William, 1732   Langensoultzbach=
S-H, I: 102, 104, 105   67360 Woerth
    with Eva [name on list in error: Hausman]

EUROPEAN RECORDS

Langensoultzbach Lutheran KB:
Hans Michael Hoffmann, son of Claus Hoffmann citizen from ?Vestlenheim
m. 6 May 1732 Eva Catharina, daughter of Johannes Jacki, joiner in
Liniehausen.

Eva Catharina Jacki was b. 4 Aug. 1714 at Lembach, a daughter of Johannes
Jäcki [q.v.-Jägi] and his wife Catharina nee Draxel, both parents Reformed
from Canton Bern in Switzerland. They had 3 children bp. at Lembach,
while residing in Katzenthal. They next appear in the Langensoultzbach KB
in 1717, residing in Liniehausen, where they had 5 more children.
Catharina, wife of Johannes Jacki, joiner at Liniehausen, died 15 Mar. 1727,
age 40 y. 2 mo. Johannes Jacki m. (2) 9 Sept. 1727 Anna Maria, daughter
of Johannes ? Drosch, citizen and farmer at ? Gutschberg, Switzerland. One
of the sp. at the bp. of Eva Catharina Jäcki was Anna Julianna Catharina,
daughter of Hans Frawhüger, *Hoffmann* in Katzenthal.   This sp. later
married Peter Traxel [Drachsel] and they also emigrated.

AMERICAN RECORDS

Egypt Reformed KB, Lehigh co.:
Michael Hoffman and wife Eva Catharina had:
    1. Catrina Lisabeth bp. 22 Mar. 1739
       Sp.: Peter Traxel [q.v.] and Catrina Lisabeth Kern, wife of
       Georg Kern [q.v.].
    2. Joh. Michael b. 27 Mar 1752, bp. 3 Oct. 1752
       Sp.: Adam Deshler and Michael Neuhard, of Egypt; Maria
       Margaretha, wife of Georg Jacob Kern; and Magdalena,
       wife of Johannes Draxel.

PA, Sixth Series, Vol., pg. 135:
Michael Hoffman settled on a tract of 250A in Whitehall twp. He died in
1786, leaving two sons, John and Michael, and four daughters, Maria
Magdalena, Catharina Elisabetha, Juliana and Maria Barbara.

Northampton co. Will Abstracts:
Michael Hoffman, Whitehall, yeoman, (20 Jan. 1777 - 12 Jan. 1787)
Children: John; Michael; Maria Magdalena, wife of Theobald Kennel [q.v.];

Catharina Elisabeth, wife of Peter Bear of Heidelberg; Juliana, wife of Henry Smith of Heidelberg; Maria Barbara, wife of Samuel Wotring of Whitehall. Exr: Son John. Wit: Adam von Erd, J. Okely and William Boehler.

Rev. Abraham Blumer's records:
Buried 8 Dec. 1786 - Michael Hoffman, age 77 years.

Michael Hoffman, Bucks co., nat. Apr. 1743.

243. HONIG, NICKLAS   Kutzenhausen=
Robert and Alice, 1739   67250 Soultz-sous-Forêts
S-H, I: 264, 270
                        EUROPEAN RECORDS

Kutzenhausen Lutheran KB:
Niclaus Honig, single, weaver from Lusan [possibly Lobsann= 67250 Soultz-sous-Forêts], m. 17 Nov. 1733 in Niederkutzenhausen Catharina, widow of the late Johannes Stambach, former citizen here. [See her son Jacob Stambach for complete list of her children of this earlier marriage.]
Niclaus Honig and wife Catharina had children:
  1. Anna Maria b. 26 Nov. 1734, d. 1738
  2. Johannes b. 3 June 1736, bp. 5 June 1736

A Hof located near the church in the center of Kutzenhausen.

AMERICAN RECORDS

Trinity Lutheran KB, Lancaster:
Nicolaus Honig m. 25 Dec. 1739 Maria Eliesabetha Fischerin.

York County Wills:
Nichlaus Honing, dated 18 Feb. 1751- probated 11 June 1752:
Wife: Mary Elisabeth; children: John (minor). Exrs: Jost Wagner,
Conrad Law [q.v.- Löw]. Wit: Henry Wert and Michael Danner.

244. HORN, HANS GEORG   67360 Woerth
    HORN, GEORG FRIEDRICH
Bennet Gally, 1750
S-H, I: 429
EUROPEAN RECORDS

Woerth Lutheran KB:
Joh. Georg Horn, tailor at Woerth, and wife Anna Eva had children:
    1. Georg Jacob b 26 July 1722, d. 1731
    2. Joh. Philipp b. 25 Nov. 1723, d.
    3. Eva Dorothea b. 26 Nov. 1725
    4. Joh. Philipp b. 31 Dec. 1726, bp. 2 Jan. 1727
    5. **Georg Friedrich** b. 20 Jan. 1731, bp. 22 Jan. 1731
    6. Ludwig Friedrich b. __ Aug. 1735, d. 1738
    7. Joh. Georg b. 24 Aug. 1738, d. 1741

AMERICAN RECORDS

St. Michael's and Zion Lutheran KB:
Friedrich Horn m. 14 Oct 1755 Anna Maria Dutin.
Witness: Hans Jurg Horn, Joh. Hin. Krauss

Hans Jurg Horn m. 21 May 1751 Cathrina Weise
Witness: Johann Michael Swab, Anna Cathrina Rheinin, Maria Eva Kuntzin.
They had a son:
    1. Jurg Heinrich b. 16 Aug. 1752, bp. 16 Aug. 1752
Johan Georg Horn and wife Catharina were sp. in 1751 for a child of Joh.
Christ. Fried. Wolf [q.v.]

Christ Lutheran KB, York:
Frederick and Anna Maria Horn, both Lutherans, had a daughter:
        Anna Maria b. 29 June 1761, bp. 16 Jan. 1762
        Sp.: Peter and Susan Lau [see Löw].

245. HORN, HANS GEORG
Polly, 1766
S-H, I: 712

Rittershoffen=
67690 Hatten
Hoelschloch=
67250 Soultz-sous-Forêts

EUROPEAN RECORDS

Kutzenhausen Lutheran KB:
Joh. Georg Horn, son of the late Heinrich Horn, citizen and carpenter at Rittershoffen, m. 1 Feb. 1762 Maria Magdalena Gartenmann, daughter of Christoph Gartenmann, citizen at Hölschloch. They had no children there. The bridegroom signed this entry in the KB, and his signature is a close match with the immigrant's signature on list 261 C.

AMERICAN RECORDS

1790 Census:
There are four George Horns listed in the 1790 census:
One Geo. Horn in Robeson twp., Berks co.:
1 male over 16; 2 males under 16; 1 female.
Another George Horn in East Nantmill twp., Chester co:
1 male over 16; 1 male under 16; 1 female.
Another George Horn in Montgomery co:
1 male over 16; 2 males under 16; 5 females.
Another George Horn in Macungie twp., Northampton co:
1 male over 16; 1 male under 16; 4 females.

246. HORNBERGER, JOH. HEINRICH
Minerva, 1770
S-H, I: 730

Froeschwiller=
67360 Woerth
Merkwiller-Pechelbronn=
67250 Soultz-sous-Forêts

EUROPEAN RECORDS

Fröschweiler Lutheran KB:
Joh. Heinrich Hornberger, master tailor, m. 17 Feb. 1766 Eva Rosina, daughter of Joh. Philipp Graff, master smith in Jägerthal [=67110 Niederbronn les Bains].

Joh. Heinrich Hornberger, widowed tailor, m. 17 Nov. 1767 Maria Magdalena S____?, daughter of the late Jacob S____? former *Herrschaffl. Förster* at Merckweiler.

A unique structure in Froeschwiller. The ruling family in 1721 was
Johann Philipp Freyherrn von Zyllehardt, Herrn zu Rhod u. Widdern.
His wife was Catharina Maria Sophia nee Eckbrecht, Freyfrauen von Durkheim.

Kutzenhausen Lutheran KB:

Joh. Jacob Senn, *Herrschaffl. Förster* at Merckweiler and wife Maria
Catharina had daughters:

1. **Maria Magdalena** b. 26 July 1731, bp. 29 July 1731
2. Anna Margaretha b. 18 June 1738; She m. 1769 Joh.
   Michael Fünfrock, Jr. [q.v.], who arrived on the same
   ship.

AMERICAN RECORDS

St. Michael's and Zion KB, Philadelphia:

Buried 8 Sept. 1771: the wife of Joh. Heinrich Hornberger, aged 39 years,
came to America in 1770. Daughter of Johannes *Sehns, Herrschafflichen
Förster, Merckweiler Amts, in Unter Elsass.*

Marriage records, dated 14 Jan. 1772-

"We the subscribers of this do certify that there is no impediment at all by reason of precontract consanguinity or any such cause whatsoever, why Henry Hornberger, widower, and Magdalena Behlin may not lawfully be joined together in Holy Matrimony, and therefore we the said subscribers bind ourselves in the sum of £200, lawful PA money to be paid unto Christoph Kunze or his heirs, exrs, or Adm. to keep indemnified the said Christian Kunze in the city of Philadelphia (Cleric?) if there should appear afterwards one or more of the said impediments or else this shall be of none effect."   In witness our hands [signed in German script:]
Philip Jacob Cuntzman
Johan Heinrich Hornberger.

247. HOSCHAR, JACOB   Altwiller =
Emigration data not located   67260 Sarre-Union
Not in S-H
EUROPEAN RECORDS

Diedendorf Reformed KB:
Jacob Hoschar from Altweiller, son of Paulus Hoschar, citizen there, m. 6 May 1720 Margaretha, daughter of Johannes Studer from Nieder Rieth, Canton Bern, [CH-3853 Niederried b. Interlaken, BE or Niederried b. Kallnach = CH-3283 Kallnach]. They had:

    1. Anna Catharina b. 18 July 1723
        Sp.: Johann Peter Keller, citizen and master tailor at
        Altweiller; Johann Jacob Singerich, *Herrschafft. Melcker*
        at Pittingen; Catharina, daughter of Joh. Nicolaus
        Schmid, citizen at Choperten [Schopperten = 67260
        Sarre-Union]; Catharina, daughter of Melchior Stam,
        citizen and church censor at Altweiller.

AMERICAN RECORDS

First Reformed KB, Lancaster:
Married 23 Nov. 1742 - Peter Ecker [q.v.], widower, of Conestoga and Margaret nee Stutter, widow of Jacob Hoschauer of Conestoga.

248. HOSCHAR, THEOBALT   Altwiller =
     HOSCHAR, HANS PETER   67260 Sarre-Union
     HOSCHAR, HENRICH
Phoenix, 1749
S-H, I: 407

EUROPEAN RECORDS

Diedendorf Reformed KB:
Joh. Theobald Hochar from Altweiller, son of Paulus Hochar, citizen there, m. 12 Oct. 1724 Anna Barbara, daughter of Heinrich Wieder, also citizen at Altweiler.

Died 17 Jan. 1726 - Paulus Hoschar, citizen in Altweiler. His widow, Anna Elisabeth, nee Schulz, died in Altweiler on 29 Sept. 1738. They were married for 36 years and had 3 sons and one daughter, 22 grandchildren and 2 great grandchildren. She was aged 80 years and 6 months.

AMERICAN RECORDS

Joh. Theobald Hoschar and wife Barbara had children:
1. Johan Peter b. 17 Mar. 1729, d. 15 Dec. 1802 in Berks co.; married Barbara _____, and had 8 children.
2. Henrich, birth not located, d. Oct. 1814 in Shenandoah co., VA; m. (1) Anna Stuckey, m. (2) Margaret Keller, m. (3) Elizabeth Bidleman. 12 children.
3. Anna Barbara m. Michael Stolz
4. Catharina, named in will.
5. Margretha, named in will.
6. Elisabeth, named in will.
7. Friedrich, b. 6 Mar. 1753; m. 19 Nov. 1775 Christina Kreinert. 8 children. Lived in PA until 1788, then in Shenandoah co., VA; later in Mason co. (West)VA; and Green co., OH, where they died.

Lancaster co. Wills:
Theobald Hoschar, prob. Apr. 1785.
Children: Peter, Henry, Barbara, Cattarine, Margretha, Elisabeth, Fridrig (Friedrich), and a son-in-law William Sneider.

Rev. John Waldschmidt's Records, PA, Sixth Series, Vol. VI:
Heinrich Hoshaar's wife bp. 1750

Heinrich Hosschauer and wife Anna had children:
1. Heinrich b. 17 Apr. 1764, bp. 27 May 1764
   Sp.: Heinrich Ache and wife Anna
2. Johan Heinrich b. 30 Apr. 1768, bp. 4 May 1768.

The mother died 6 May 1768.

Heinrich Hoschaar, widower, m. 7 June 1768 Margaretha, daughter of Martin Keller. They had:
>   Anna b. 12 Mar. 1777, bp. 27 Apr. 1777

Johannes, son of Heinrich Hoschaar, m. 17 Apr. 1781 Eva, daughter of the late Johann Jost Walter.

Friedrick Hoschaar, son of Dewald Hoschaar, m. 19 Nov. 1775 Christina, daughter of Andreas Kreinert. They had:
>   Johann Peter b. 21 Dec. 1780, bp. 11 Mar. 1781
>   Catharina b. 4 Nov. 1783, bp. 12 Apr. 1784

Conf. at Allegene 11 Apr. 1779:
>   Maria Margretha, daughter of Peter Hoschaar

Conf. Allegene, 30 Apr. 1780:
>   Wilhelm, son of Peter Hoschaar
>   Catharina, daughter of Peter Hoschaar

Allegheny Reformed KB, Berks co.:
John Peter Hoshour b. 17 Mar. 1729, d. 15 Dec. 1801, buried Allegheny Church Yard.

Elisabeth Schweitzer, nee Hoschauer, wife of Peter Schweitzer, b. Mar. 1741, died 15 Dec 1838 at Alleghenyville, age 97 years.

Berks co. Wills:
Barbara Hoshaar, widow, Brecknock twp., dated 5 Apr. 1824, prob. 15 June 1824. Estate divided among children: William, Margaret, Catharine, Barbara, Anna, Elizabeth, Peter, Henry and James. Exr: John Kessler, Sr. Letters of Adm. to Abraham Ziegler, the Exr. renouncing. Wit: John Becher and Samuel Bowman.

249. HUBACKER, JACOB   Liniehausen,
Sally, 1770   Langensoultzbach=
S-H, I: 732   67360 Woerth
                     EUROPEAN RECORDS

Langensoultzbach Lutheran KB:
Johann Jacob Hubacker, *Erbbeständer* and *Ackermann* in Liniehausen, and wife Elisabetha nee Kiefer had a son:
>   Johann Jacob b. 19 Nov. 1766, bp. 21 Nov. 1766

Sp.: Valentin Paul, citizen and carpenter, Liniehausen;
Maria Clara wife of Heinrich Egert, citizen and
Ochsenwirths at Jägerthal [=67110 Niederbronn-les-Bains];
Georg Friedrich Pilger, citizen and tailor, Liniehausen;
Salomea nee Mattern wife of Joh. Georg Hanauer, Jägerthal.

The father signed this entry in bapt. record and his signature matches the
immigrant's signature on S-H, II: 847.

250. HÜGEL, JOHANNES   Herbitzheim=
Priscilla, 1750   67260 Sarre-Union
S-H, I: 444

EUROPEAN RECORDS

Herbitzheim Lutheran KB:
Johannes Hügel, *hoffmann* and widower at the Kuderbacher Hoff, m. 22 Oct.
1736 Barbara Hirtzel, widow of the late Johannes Bürgy from *Harteren aus
dem Kirschspiel Liess lot. Berner Cantons.* [Hardern, BE = CH-3250 Lyss].
Children:
    1. Joh. Conrad b. 4 Mar. 1737
    2. Maria Magdalena b. 4 Mar. 1737, twin
    3. Stephan b. 26 Dec. 1738
    4. Catharina Margaretha b. 13 Nov. 1740

AMERICAN RECORDS

Hocker, *German Settlers of Pennsylvania:*
Newspaper dated 16 May 1752:
Friedrich Eschbach and Johannes Hugel are going to Germany after the
harvest. They will take letters if forwarded to Johannes Eschbach or
Johannes Hugel, Falckner Swamp (Montgomery co.).

251. HÜGEL, LUDWIG   67510 Lembach
John & William, 1732
S-H, I: 102, 105

EUROPEAN RECORDS

Lembach Lutheran KB:
Hans Hügel, inhabitant and widower, m. 21 Jan. 1688 Anna Christina,
daughter of Johannes Rothschmitt, citizen and inhabitant at Bruchweiller.
Their son:
    Johann Ludwig bp. 3 Dec. 1699 at Lembach

He arrived with several others from Lembach, listed together on the ship list.

AMERICAN RECORDS

St. Michael's and Zion KB, Philadelphia:
Christina Hegelin was a witness at a marriage in 1751.

St. Michael's Lutheran KB, Germantown:
Died 28 Feb. 1773- Johann Ludwig Hugel, age 73 y., 2 mo., 24 days.

252. HÜLLER, MARTIN   Ingolsheim=
_____, 1752   67250 Soultz-sous-Forêts

[It is possible that this immigrant is the Hans Martin Ziller who arrived on the ship *St. Andrew*, 1752 with Dewalt Billman [q.v.]; both Rupp and Hinke translate the name as Zeller, but the signature on S-H, II: 575 appears to be Ziller and may be Hiller.]

EUROPEAN RECORDS

Birlenbach Lutheran KB:
Michel Hüller and wife Anna of Ingelsheim had a son:
   Hans Martin b. 17 Apr. 1708, bp. 19 Apr. 1708 at Hunspach.

Hans Martin Hüller, son of Michael Hüller of Ingelsheim, m. 15 Feb. 1735 at Hunspach, Anna Barbara, dau. of Bläss Hauck of Ingelsheim.

Hunspach Reformed KB and Rott Lutheran KB:
Johann Martin Hüller of Ingelsheim and wife Barbara had children:
   1. Anna Elisabetha bp. not located, d. 1737
   2. Maria Margaretha b. __ Apr. 1738
   3. Johann Michael b. 27 Jan. 1741 [Rott Lutheran KB]
   4. Maria Eva b. 25 Oct. 1744, bp. 1 Nov. 1744
   5. Johann Michael b. 25 July 1747 [Rott Lutheran KB]
   6. Maria Dorothea b. 18 Nov. 1751, bp. 21 Nov. 1751

Zweibruecken Manumissions Protocoll, Clee- and Catharinenburg, 1752:
Martin Hueller with wife and four children, of Ingolsheim, leaves for America.

AMERICAN RECORDS

New Goshenhoppen Reformed KB; Montgomery co.:
Marty Hiller, son of Marty Hiller of Limerick twp., m. 13 Oct. 1772 Anna
Roeder, dau. of Michael Roeder of New Goshenhoppen.

253. HUMBERT, ADAM   67690 Hatten
Hamilton, 1767
S-H, I: 716
EUROPEAN RECORDS

Hatten Lutheran KB:
Joh. Georg Humbert, citizen and juror here (commonly called "Bottenjörg"),
and his wife Maria Barbara nee Kuntz had a son:
  Joh. Adam b. 3 Mar. 1727, bp. 4 Mar. 1727

Joh. Adam Humbert, son of Joh. Georg Humbert, m. 10 Aug. 1747 Maria
Barbara, daughter of Hans Georg Wagner. Children:
  1. Maria Magdalena b. 7 Oct. 1748, bp. 8 Oct. 1748
  2. Maria Eva b. 29 Oct. 1750, bp. 31 Oct. 1750
  3. Eva Catharina b. 20 Feb. 1753
  4. Joh. Georg b. 17 Aug. 1755, bp. 18 Aug. 1755
  5. Maria Barbara b. 23 June 1758, bp. 24 June 1758
  6. Rosina b. 7 Apr. 1761, d. 1764
  7. Anna Margaretha b. 16 Dec. 1763, d. 22 Apr. 1767

Adam Humbert's signature in the KB, pg. 179 matches perfectly with his
signature in S-H, II: 824.

254. HUMBERT, JOH. BERNHARD   67690 Hatten
    HUMBERT, PHILIP
ca. 1773
Not in S-H.
EUROPEAN RECORDS

Hatten Lutheran KB:
Joh. Bernhard Humbert, son of Joh. Georg Humbert, and his wife Dorothea
nee Bastian had children:
  1. Joh. Bernhard b. 5 May 1748, died.
     In this entry the father of the child was serving as *Sergeant
     bey dem Fürstl. Nassauischen Infantrie Regiment.* The entry was
     witnessed by Joh. Georg Humbert, the grandfather "in the name
     of the father, my son, who is absent."
  2. **Joh. Bernhard** b. 6 Feb. 1750, d. 1793 in St. Augustine,

Florida. Father's occupation listed as baker.
3. **Christian Philipp** b. 9 Aug. 1752
4. Joh. Georg Gotthard b. 22 Mar. 1754, d. 1757
5. Maria Salome b. 18 Feb. 1756
6. Georg Friedrich b. 21 Apr. 1757
7. Eva Margaretha b. 18 Mar. 1759
8. Joh. Jacob b. 22 Oct. 1761. Father is listed as *Ochsenwirth.*
9. Eva Dorothea b. 22 Sept. 1763
10. Anna Maria b. 24 Sept. 1765, d. 1771
11. Georg Heinrich b. 23 Oct. 1767

AMERICAN RECORDS

Hocker, *German Settlers of Pennsylvania:*
Wochentlicher Pennsylvanischer Staatsbote, dated 4 Apr. 1775:
Bernhard Humbert, St. Augustine, East Florida, seeks his brother Philip, born at Haetten, Lower Alsace, near Cronweissenburg, who came to America in 1773 and is believed to be in Maryland.

255. HUMBERT, JOH. GEORG   67690 Hatten
Brothers, 1754
S-H, I: 610, 612
EUROPEAN RECORDS

Hatten Lutheran KB:
Hans Georg Humpert, son of the Innkeeper at the Grunenbaum, and his wife Barbara nee Bisch, had children:
1. Joh. Georg b. 23 Sept. 1733, died
2. **Joh. Georg** b. 24 Aug. 1735 bp. 25 Aug. 1735
3. Anna Maria b. 5 Dec. 1736, bp. 9 Dec. 1736
4. Christina Sophia b. 14 Sept. 1737, bp. 15 Sept. 1737
5. Friedrich b. 30 Mar. 1739
6. Georg Jacob b. 1 Apr. 1742
7. Maria Eva b. 17 July 1744

Hans Georg Humpert died in 1754. There is a marginal note by the bp. record of child #6: "the mother, with her children, has gone away."

AMERICAN RECORDS

Frederick Lutheran KB, Frederick, MD:
Buried 16 Oct. 1771 - Barbara Humbertin, Johann Georg Humbert's surviving widow, died the 14th, in her 60th year.

Buried 29 May 1772 - Sophia, wife of Johannes Usselden, nee Humbertin, born in Alsace, died May 28 in childbirth; left 3 sons and 3 daughters, aged about 31 years.

Philipp Kullmann m. 21 May 1771 Maria Eva Humbert .

Georg Humbert and wife Eva had:
1. Anna Maria b. 26 Aug. 1766, bp. 25 Dec. 1766

Jacob Humbert and Maria Elisabetha had:
1. Susanna Margretha b. 18 Sept. 1771, bp. 13 Oct. 1771
2. Maria Barbara b. 13 Sept. 1773, bp. 10 Oct. 1773
   Sp.: Philipp and Maria Eva Kuhlmann
3. Georg Daniel b. 30 Dec. 1775, bp. 3 Feb. 1776
4. Catharina b. 8 Jan. 1779, bp. 1 Apr. 1779
   Sp.: Fridrich and Margreth Humbert

Trinity Lutheran KB, New Holland, Lancaster co.:
Friedrich Humbert, son of the late Joh. Georg Humbert, m. 28 Jan. 1761 Margaretha Meyer, daughter of Georg Meyer of Manackessen (Monocacy, Frederick co., MD). *In casu impregnationis.*

St. Peter's Lutheran KB, Rocky Hill, Frederick, co., MD:
Friedrich Humpert and Margaretha had:
1. Anna Margaretha b. 27 Mar. 1773, bp. 27 July 1773
2. Johann Georg b. 12 Aug. 1775, bp. 27 Nov. 1775, twin
3. Georg Jacob b. 12 Aug. 1775, bp. 27 Nov. 1775, twin
   Sp.: Georg Meyer, widower; Sophia Robbin;
   and Georg Jacob Humpert.
4. Solomon b. 10 Sept. 1779, bp. 24 Apr. 1780, twin
5. Susanna b. 10 Sept. 1779, bp. 24 Apr. 1780, twin

Moselem Lutheran KB, Berks co:
Georg Humbert and wife Eva (in other records Eva Maria, Maria Eva, Eva Hanna) had children:
1. Maria Eva b. 15 Aug. 1772, bp. 20 Sept. 1772
2. Esther b. 25 Dec. 1774, bp. 12 Feb. 1775
3. Johann Gottfried b. 28 Dec. 1776, bp. 4 May 1777
4. Johann Gottfried b. 8 Dec. 1777, bp. 10 Jan. 1778
5. Maria Christina b. 14 Sept. 1779, bp. 17 Oct. 1779

George Humber, German, nat. MD 3 May 1768.

256. HUMBERT, PHILIP JACOB   67690 Hatten
HUMBERT, JOH. FRIEDRICH
Janet, 1751
S-H, I: 475
EUROPEAN RECORDS

Hunspach Reformed KB:
Johann Georg Humbert, organist and *Gastgeber zum Ochsen (Innkeeper),* son of Joh. Phillipps Humbert, former citizen, butcher and *Gastgeber zum Ochsen* in Hatten, m. 8 Sept. 1722 Maria Margaretha, daughter of M. Bernhard Hermann, Pastor at Hunspach.

Hatten Lutheran KB:
Hans Georg Humpert and wife Margaretha nee Hermann had children:
   1. Joh. Bernhard b. 9 July 1723
   2. Anna Maria b. 17 Feb. 1725
   3. Joh. Georg b. 11 Feb. 1727, died
   4. Joh. Georg b. 4 Mar. 1728
   5. **Philipp Jacob** b. 20 June 1732
   6. **Joh. Friedrich** b. 9 Jan. 1735
   7. Susanna Margaretha bp. 21 Apr. 1737

AMERICAN RECORDS

Trinity Lutheran KB, Lancaster:
Philipp Jacob Humbert, a young man recently arrived in this land, died 2 Nov. [1751] and was buried 3 Nov. 1751, aged 19 years.

257. HUMMEL, MICHEL   Birlenbach=
_____, 1753   67160 Wissembourg
EUROPEAN RECORDS

Birlenbach Lutheran KB:
Michel Hummel, inhabitant at Birlenbach, and wife Anna Catharina, had a son:
   Johann Michel b. 3 Oct. 1716, bp. 6 Oct. 1716

Hans Michel Hummel m. 7 Apr. 1739 Maria Magdalena Krebs from Keffenach. They had:
   1. Georg Heinrich b. 17 Dec. 1740, bp. 21 Dec. 1740
   2. Maria Elisabetha b. 6 Oct. 1748, bp. 8 Oct. 1748
      both at Keffenach.

Michael Hummel from Birlenbach and wife Catharina Louisa nee Burckherr had a son:
>   Johann Peter b. 1 Aug. 1752, bp. 6 Aug. 1752

Zweibruecken Manumissions Protocoll, Clee- and Catharinenburg, 1753:
Michel Hummel of Birlenbach leves for America with his wife.

258. HUNTZIGER, JOHANNES   Schalbach=
Two Brothers, 1748   57370 Phalsbourg
S-H, I: 378, 379, 381
[Appears on A list as Holsecker, B list and C list as Huntzeker; did not sign.]

EUROPEAN RECORDS

Diedendorf Reformed KB:
Ullerich Huntziger, son of Rudolff Huntziger at Schalbach, m. 12 Nov. 1720, Sara, daughter of Johannes Dilger (elsewhere Deller, Tiller), inhabitant at Schalbach. They had a son:
>   Johannes bp. 24 Aug. 1721
>   Sp.: Stephan Paillet; Jacob Tiller; Veronica Bläsin,
>   all from Rauweiler.

Johannes Ulerich Hontziger from Schalbach and wife Sara Tiller had:
>   Johannes bp. 24 Aug. 1722, conf. 1730
>   Sp.: Stephan Baillet; Jacob Tiller, both citizens at Schalbach;
>   Veronica Huntziger, wife of Petter Bless of Rauweiller.

Ullerich Huntziger died and his widow Sara married (2) Joseph Kennel [q.v.]. The next name on the ship list is Jacob Kendel, a son of her second marriage.

Rauwiller Reformed KB:
Johannes Huntzinger of Schalbach m. 30 Apr. 1743 Magdalena Bieren (elsewhere in record: Bierson). They had:
>   1. Joh. Theobald b. 24 Jan. 1744

[see her brother Joh. Philip Birson (Bierson, Pierson) for additional data.]

AMERICAN RECORDS

A certificate was brought to America by the Hunsicker family, dated 27 May 1748, signed by the Reformed pastor at Rauweiler. It states that Dewalt (Theobald) Hunsicker was bp. 24 Jan. 1744 in the church at Rauweiller,

Duchy of Nassau, and his parents were Johannes Hunsicker from Schallbach and his wife Maria nee Pierson.

Johannes Hunsicker settled in Heidelberg twp., then Bucks co., now Lehigh co.; Land warrant dated 18 May 1750 for 43 A southeast of the present village of Saegersville.

Tohickon Reformed KB, Bucks co.:
Conf. 2 Apr. 1756 in Heidelberg: Dewalt Hunzicker.

Children of Johannes and Magdalena Hunsicker were:
1. Johann Theobald bp. 24 Jan. 1744
2. Jacob bp. not located
3. Johannes b. 25 Oct. 1755
4. Magdalena b. 28 Dec. 1757. She m. Wilhelm Peter.
5. Casper b. ca. 1759
6. Anna Maria b. ca. 1760
7. Joseph bp. 9 May 1762 by Rev. Daniel Schumacher.
   Sp.: Dewald Kendell; Anna Maria Müller, both single.
8. Heinrich b. ca. 1763
9. Peter b. 1 May 1771

Northampton County Will Abstracts:
John Hunsicker, prob. 17 Dec. 1800.
Exrs: Casper and Jacob Hunsicker.
Wit: George Bloss, Jacob Peter, George Horn.

see **Charles Roberts et al,** *History of Lehigh County, Pennsylvania,* **Vol. II:** 593: for a complete transcript of will, and additional family data.

Jno. Heintzicker, Heidelberg twp., Northampton co., nat. Autumn, 1765.

259. HUSAM, JOHANNES   Langensoultzbach=
John and William, 1732   67360 Woerth
S-H, I: 104, 105
  with Maria Hausman
                        EUROPEAN RECORDS

Langensoultzbach Lutheran KB:
Johannes Husahmmen (Husam) and wife Maria Elisabetha Engel had:
1. Maria Salome bp. 15 Feb. 1729
2. Johannes bp. 8 Feb. 1730
3. Johann Adam bp. 20 Jan. 1732

AMERICAN RECORDS

Muddy Creek Lutheran KB, Lancaster co.:
Johannes Husam was a sp. in 1742 for a child of Peter Schmidt [q.v.]

Joh. Haussahm and his wife were sp. in 1742 for a ch. of Jacob Kissinger.

Maria Eliesabetha Hausahm(in) was a sp. in 1741 for a child of Friederich Ohnsellt.

Trinity Lutheran KB, New Holland, Lancaster co.:
Johannes Husam had children:
> 4. Elisabetha b. 12 Oct. 1733, bp. 28 Dec. 1733
>   Sp.: Lorenz Hörchelrodt and wife Maria Elisabetha
> 5. Eva Dorothea b. 30 Jan. 1733, bp. 30 Mar. 1735
>   Sp.: Johannes Heckmann and wife Eva Dorothea

260. HUSER, JOHAN JACOB   Gundershoffen=
Edinburgh, 1751   67110 Niederbronn-les-Bains
S-H, I: 460

EUROPEAN RECORDS

Gundershoffen Lutheran KB:
Johann Jacob Huser, son of the late Peter Huser, m. 11 Jan. 1746 Anna Barbara, daughter of the late Hans Georg Dürrenberger, former citizen in Mertzweiler [67580]. Children:
> 1. Johann Peter b. 11 Mar. 1747, bp. 12 Mar. 1747
>   Sp.: Diebold Fischbach; Peter Hausser; Salome Kyburtz, widow, all from here.
> 2. Anna Barbara d. 17 July 1749, infant.
> 3. Maria Salome b. 11 Jan. 1751, bp. 13 Jan. 1751

[The father's signature by these baptisms in KB, matches the immigrant's signature in S-H, II: 540].

AMERICAN RECORDS

One Jacob Hauser, Tredeffrin, Chester co. nat. autumn, 1765.
Another Jacob Hauser, Linn twp. Northampton co. nat. autumn, 1765.

261. HUSSONG, JOH. JACOB   Waldhambach=
one on *Phoenix,* 1754   67430 Diemeringen
S-H, I: 629, 632, 635 (but see comment below).

EUROPEAN RECORDS

Waldhambach Lutheran KB:
Joh. Jacob Hussong, weaver of Waldhambach, son of Joh. Nicolaus Hussong, schoolteacher at Ratzweiler, m. 14 May 1743 Anna Margaretha Meder, daughter of Joh. Anton Meder of Waldhambach. She was b. 31 Oct. 1719, daughter of Joh. Anton Meder and wife Anna Eva Sämann. Children:
1. Hans Adam b. 10 Oct. 1744
2. Johann Michael b. 4 Dec. 1747, d. 16 Feb. 1749
3. Johann Jacob b. 26 Nov. 1749

Verification of this emigration supplied by Dr. Bernd Gölzer, from the county records of Nassau-Saarwerden, compiled by Dr. Gerhard Hein: Dr. Hein quotes a "Familienbuch Waldhambach": Joh. Jacob Hussong "moved to the New Land." Dr. Gölzer adds a comment: "He may not be the man aboard the *Phoenix,* 1754, the latter being more likely born 31 Mar. 1733 in Bliesdalheim. (W. Bohrer, Walsheim records, p. 48.)

AMERICAN RECORDS

Rev. Daniel Schumacher's records:
Jacob Husson and wife Magdalena were sp. in 1760 for a child of Paul Eberhard [q.v.] and wife Maria in Lehigh.

Zion Reformed KB, Allentown:
Jacob Husson and wife Magdalena had:
    Elisabetha b. 26 Apr. 1766.

262. ISCH, PETER   Pfalzweyer=
Phoenix, 1749   67320 Drulingen
S-H, I: 405   57119 Lixheim
EUROPEAN RECORDS

Diedendorf Reformed KB:
Johann Jacob Isch from Pfaltzweyer, Litzelsteiner Herrschafft, son of Durst Isch, m. (1) 10 Oct. 1719 Maria Magdalena, daughter of Jacob Kreup of Lixheim. Children:
1. **Johann Peter** bp. 15 May 1725
2. Elisabetha b. 25 Aug. 1733 (Rauwiller KB)

Rauwiller Reformed KB:
Joh. Jacob Isch, shoemaker m. (2) 24 Feb. 1740 Ottillia, daughter of Joh. Nicklaus Balliet, church *vorsteher* at Rauwiller.

Joh. Jacob Isch of Lixheim and wife Uttilia nee Balliette had a son:
Joh. Jacob b. 29 Dec. 1740

AMERICAN RECORDS

Peter Ish, Lancaster, Lancaster co., nat. 24 Sept. 1763.

263. JACK, KILIAN   Gundershoffen=
Phoenix, 1750   67110 Niederbronn-les-Bains
S-H, I: 441
[appears on list as Killian (+) Jaac].

EUROPEAN RECORDS

Gundershoffen Lutheran KB:
Kilian Jacke, son of Kilian Jake, citizen here, m. (1) 11 Jan. 1714 Anna
Margretha _____? daughter of the deceased cooper at Engweiler [Engwiller
= 67350 Pfaffenhoffen]. Children:
    1. Johann Georg b. 4 Apr. 1716, bp. 5 Apr. 1716
       He m. 1735 Christina, daughter of the late Joh. Peter Mallo.
    2. Maria Magdalena b. 7 Nov. 1718, bp. 10 Nov. 1718
       She m. 1740 Jacob Jung.
    3. Anna Dorothea b. 23 Sept. 1721, bp. 25 Sept. 1721
    4. Eva Elisabetha b. 28 Feb. 1724, bp. 3 Mar. 1724
       She m. 1745 Joh. Peter Voltz [q.v.]
    5. Anna Margretha b. 7 Aug. 1728, bp. 11 Aug. 1728
       She m. 1752 Georg Michael Trautner, and it is recorded in the
       marriage entry that she was a daughter of Kilian Jack, formerly
       a citizen here who has gone to America.
    6. Anna Maria b. 22 Apr. 1729, bp. 25 Apr. 1729
       She m. 1754 at [67340] Rothbach, Joh. Adam Schmidt
    7. Catharina Barbara b. 10 Apr. 1731, bp. 12 Apr. 1731
       She m. 1750 Jerg Voltz [q.v.]

Kilian Jacke, widower and citizen here, m. 24 Jan. 1736 Anna Barbara,
daughter of Jacob Voltz, citizen here. Kilian Jacki and Anna Barbara had
children:
    8. Maria Elisabetha bp. 5 Mar. 1741
    9. Maria Catharina bp. 4 Mar. 1743
    10. Christina b. __ Sept. 1746, bp. 15 Sept. 1746

AMERICAN RECORDS

Christ "Little Tulpehocken" Lutheran KB, Berks co:
Communicant 9 May 1761 - Kilian Jack
Communicant 13 Sept. 1761 - Anna Barbara Jackin
Communicant 24 Apr. 1761 - Maria Catharina Jackin
Communicant 30 May 1762 - Kilian Jack and A. Barbara Jackin
Communicant 30 Oct. 1762 at Northkill - Kilian Jack

Conf. 9 May 1761 - Catharina Jackin, age 17 years.

264. JACOB, HANS GEORG   Lampertsloch=
     JACOB, GEORG HENRICH   67250 Soultz-sous-Forêts
Minerva, 1769
S-H, I: 727
EUROPEAN RECORDS

Preuschdorf Lutheran KB:
Hans Georg Jacob, citizen and master shoemaker here, son of Martin Jacob, m. 23 Nov. 1746 Anna Catharina, dau. of Hans Jacob Kronmüller of Lampersloch. [She signed the marriage entry Gronmüllerin. The groom's signature, Hans Georg Jacob, in the Preuschdorf marriage record, matches the signature of the immigrant on S-H, II: 839. The groom's father also signed the entry as Hans Marx Jacob.] Children:
    1. Joh. Georg b. 22 July 1747, d. 1747
    2. Georg Heinrich b. 29 Dec. 1748, bp. 31 Dec. 1748
    3. Catharina Barbara b. 28 Jan. 1751
    4. Catharina Elisabetha b. 8 Mar. 1753
    5. Anna Margaretha b. 26 May 1755
    6. stillborn son 4 Jan. 1758
    7. Maria Rosina b. 16 Apr. 1759
    8. Joh. Georg b. 7 Mar. 1762, d. 12 Mar. 1765
    9. Georg Michel b. 12 Aug. 1764, d. 3 hours after birth
    10. Maria Dorothea b. 13 Oct. 1765
    11. Anna Maria b. 25 Aug. 1768, died.

AMERICAN RECORDS

Hocker, *German Settlers of Pennsylvania:*
Staatsbote, newspaper dated 9 Aug. 1774:
Johann Georg Jacob, Race St., between Second and Third St., Philadelphia, is going to Germany. He was born in Alsace.

St. Paul's Lutheran KB, Upper Hanover twp., Montgomery co.:
Georg Henrich Jacob and wife Elisabetha had:

1. Margaretha b. 8 Oct. 1788, bp. 26 Apr. 1789
   Sp.: Margaretha Martin
2. Friederich b. 22 July 1794, bp. 13 Sept. 1794
   Sp.: Johan Staut and Juliana

Died 23 Feb. 1795 - Georg Heinrich Jacob, born in Lampresloch in Europe, aged 47 y. 2 mo.

265. JACOB, HEINRICH   Preuschdorf=
Dragon, 17 Oct. 1749   67250 Soultz-sous-Forêts
S-H, I: 423

EUROPEAN RECORDS

Preuschdorf Lutheran KB:
Joh. Heinrich Jacob, single son of Johann Jacob of Preuschdorf, m. (1) __
Jan. 1718 Anna Margaretha, daughter of Durst Capler, citizen at Preuschdorf. Their son:

> Heinrich b. 27 Dec. 1725, bp. 29 Dec. 1725
> Sp.: Michael Clauss; Hans Clauss, son of Hans Clauss;
> Anna Margretha, wife of Martin Jacob, all of Preuschdorff.
> Notation by his bp. record: "went to the New Land."

Anna Margaretha, wife of Joh. Heinrich Jacob, died in 1731. He m. (2) 9 Feb. 1734 Anna Dorothea (no surname given) from [W-6661] Hornbach in Zweibrücken.

AMERICAN RECORDS

Hocker, *German Settlers of Pennsylvania:*
Sower's newspaper, dated 8 Jan. 1757:
Henrich Jacob, Warwick twp., Lancaster co., near Henrich Voltz, two miles from Michel Mayer.

266. JÄGI, JOHANN   Liniehausen,
John and William, 1732   Langensoultzbach=
S-H, I: 104, 105   67360 Woerth

EUROPEAN RECORDS

Lembach Lutheran KB:
Johannes Jäcki, joiner, b. in Canton Bern, Switzerland, and wife Catharina nee Drachselin, both Reformed, had children:

> 1. Johann Michael b. 29 Mar. 1712, bp. 1 Apr. at Katzenthal

2. Anna Catharina Barbara b. 27 Mar. 1713, died
3. Eva Catharina b. 4 Aug. 1714. She m. 1732 Michael Hoffmann
[q.v.]. One of the sp. at her bp. was Anna Juliana Catharina,
daughter of Hans Frawhüger, *Hoffmann* in Katzenthal, who later
married Peter Drachsel [q.v.].

Langensoultzbach Lutheran KB:
Johannes Jacki, *Schirmer* at Liniehausen, and wife Catharina nee Drachsel
had children:
4. Maria Catharina bp. 1 Feb. 1717
5. Anna Magdalena bp. 27 Nov. 1718
6. Juliana bp. 6 July 1721, d. 17 Jan. 1727
7. Johann Jacob bp. 22 Apr. 1724, d. 27 Mar. 1724
8. Johann Daniel bp. 23 Sept. 1725, d. 3 Sept. 1727

Died 15 Mar. 1727: Catharina, wife of Johannes Jacki, joiner in Liniehausen,
aged 40 y., 2 mo.

Johannes Jacki, widower, m. (2) 9 Sept. 1727 Anna Maria, daughter of
Johannes ?Drosch [Drescher in bp. records], citizen and farmer in
?Gutschberg in Switzerland. They had:
9. Maria Dorothea bp. 5 Nov. 1730

Johann Jägi arrived on the same ship as his daughter and son-in-law Michael
Hoffmann [q.v.].

267. JAUCHZI, BERNHARD   Hoffen =
Robert & Alice, 1739   67250 Soultz-sous-Forêts
S-H, I: 264, 267, 271
    [did not sign; appears as Youtzee, Yonser, Jauzy]

EUROPEAN RECORDS

Hunspach Reformed KB:
Bernhard Jauchzi, son of Ulerich Jauchzi of Hofen, m. 15 Aug. 1719 Anna
Maria, daughter of Benedict Erhard, *Schirmsverwanden.* They had:
        Hans Jorg b. 17 Oct. 1723, bp. 24 Oct. 1723
        Hans Peter b. 10 Aug. 1726, bp. 11 Aug. 1726
    [in this entry the father is mentioned as *Gemeiner Hirt* at Hofen]

He arrived with Christian Erhardt [q.v.] next name on ship list.

268. JOHO, JOHANNES age 37   67510 Lembach,
Snow *Two Sisters*, 1738   Sultzthal
S-H, I: 209, 210, 211
  with Susanna Joho, age 44

EUROPEAN RECORDS

Lembach Lutheran KB:
Johannes Joho, single *Holtzschuhmacher* (maker of wooden shoes) in
Sultzthal, son of the late Joh. Michael Joho, former butcher, m. 1 Mar 1735
Susanna Catharina, daughter of Theobald Lau, smith at Sultzthal. They had:
  1. Maria Christina b. 20 Oct. 1735
      Sp.: Friederich Boh, son of Philip Boh; Maria Catharina wife of
      Joh. Jacob Bender, Sultzbach; Anna Christina, daughter of Joh.
      Heinrich Zehender, *des Jäger von der Hard.*
  2. Eva Catharina b. 18 June 1737

AMERICAN RECORDS

Rev. John Casper Stoever's records:
Johannes Joho (Conewago) had children:
  3. Maria Christina b. 14 Mar. 1740, bp. 22 May 1740
      Sp.: Janeslaus Wuchtel and Maria Christina Baumann
  4. Eva Catharina b. 26 May 1749, bp. 25 June 1749
      Sp.: Wentzel Buchtrueckel and wife.

Rev. Jacob Lischy's records, York co:
Johannes Joho and wife Anna Maria had:
  5. Anna Maria bp. 9 Sept. 1750. Sp.: Peter Lau and Susanna.

269. JONELE, VERONICA age 40   67110 Niederbronn-les-Bains
[widow of Ulrich Christian Jonele]
    JONELE, CHRISTIAN age 20
    JONELE, ELISBAT age 19
Hope, 1733
S-H, I: 116, 118,
  with Johanes Junliey, age 14, Hans Raynart Junliey, age 9.

EUROPEAN RECORDS

Niederbronn Lutheran KB:
Ulrich Christian Jonele, shoemaker, and wife Veronica had children:
  1. probably Christian

2. probably Elisabetha
3. Joh. Jacob. b. 6 July 1716
4. Joh. Georg b. 12 Jan. 1719
5. Joh. Reinhard b. 27 Nov. 1721
6. Johannes b. 9 Dec. 1725
7. Johannes b. 10 July 1727

Another Joneli is mentioned in the Uhrweiler KB in 1725, from Obersimmenthal, BE, Switzerland.

AMERICAN RECORDS

Philadelphia Wills and Adm.:
One Mary Yonely, Adm. Book H: 89. Estate # 112, 1776.

270. JUNCKER, JACOB   Wolfskirchen=
Halifax, 1752   67260 Sarre-Union
S-H, I: 483
    [with Nickel Quierin, Nickel Fahringer and others]

EUROPEAN RECORDS

Wolfskirchen Lutheran KB:
Johannes Juncker and wife Dorothea nee Neubecker had children:
    1. Anna Christina b. __ June 1721
    2. Johannes b. 26 Apr. 1742
    3. Joh. Georg b. 15 Dec. 1726
    4. Anna Elisabetha b. 25 Feb. 1730
    5. **Joh. Jacob** b. 3 Feb. 1732
    6. Maria Elisabetha b. 16 Dec. 1738

Verification of this emigration supplied by Dr. Bernd Gölzer, from the county records of Nassau-Saarwerden, compiled by Dr. Gerhard Hein: Records of the Notary Public for Wolfskirchen: Dated 27 Feb. 1765 and 17 Mar. 1772, inventory of Dorothea Neubecker Juncker: the son Johann Jacob is married, in America.

AMERICAN RECORDS

Emanuel [Warwick] Lutheran KB, Elisabeth twp., Lancaster co.:
Jacob Juncker had children:
    1. Joh. Jacob b. 9 Aug. 1752, bp. 1 Oct. 1752
       Sp.: Jacob Wolff and Margaretha Hoffin

2. Christoph (No dates given)
   Sp.: Christoph Wieder
3. Ana Ellisabetha b. 5 Feb. 1759, bp. 1 Apr. 1759
   Sp.: Johannes Simmon and Ana Elisabeth Retter

271. JUNDT, HANS GEORG age 40   67110 Niederbronn-les-Bains
JUNDT, JACOB age 16
Britannia, 1731
S-H, I: 48, 50, 52, 53
   others on ship: Anna Maria Gunt age 40; Hans Georg, age 12; Johanis, age 8; Maria Elizabeth, age 6.

EUROPEAN RECORDS

Niederbronn Lutheran KB:
Hans Georg Jundt and wife Anna Maria had children:
1. Johann Jacob b. 8 Oct. 1714
2. Johann Heinrich b. 15 Jan. 1716, died July 1716
3. Maria Margaretha b. 1 May 1717, died 21 Mar. 1726
4. Johann Georg b. 11 Mar. 1719
5. Maria Elisabetha b. 18 Apr. 1721
6. Johannes b. 23 Apr. 1723
7. Johann Daniel b. 4 Dec. 1728, died 10 Dec. 1728
Died 4 Feb. 1723 - Anna Ursula, widow of the late Mr. Johannes Jund, age 67 years.

AMERICAN RECORDS

Jordan Lutheran KB, Lehigh co.:
Johannes Diether, widower, m. 3 July 1749 Elisabeth Jundt.

Jacob Jundt was a sp. in 1748 for a child of Henerich Egener. Jacob Jundt and wife Dorothea had:
1. A son (n.n.) b. 29 July 1748, bp. 9 Oct 1748
   Sp.: Jacob Schreiber [q.v.]; Magdalena Schreiber; Henrich Ebener; Johannes Jundt

Northampton co. Adm.:
Jacob Yount, Whitehall twp., Adm. 16 May 1760 to Dorothy Yount, widow, and John Yount. Inventory 9 May 1760; settlement 31 May 1765.

Northampton co. Will Abstracts;
Dorothea Yund, widow of Jacob Yund of Whitehall, dated 16 Mar. 1780.

Children: George, Daniel, Abraham, Mary, Peter (eldest), Jacob. Mentions son's wife Eva Catharine. Exrs: Son Daniel and Philip Jacob Schreiber. Wit: Michael Kolb and Stephan Schnyder.

Rev. Abraham Blumer's records:
Buried 21 Mar. 1780 - Catharina Dorothea Jundt, age 60 years.

George Yund, Earl twp., Lancaster co., nat. Apr. 1761.
John Junt, Upper Salford, Northampton co., nat. Autumn, 1765.

272. JUNG, GEORG   Gundershoffen=
possibly on the   67110 Niederbronn-les-Bains
Adventure, 1754
S-H, I: 601, 602, 603
or on the *Recovery,* 1754
S-H, I: 660

EUROPEAN RECORDS

Gundershoffen Lutheran KB:
Michael Jung, son of the late Michael Jung, m. 10 Feb. 1708 Maria Ursula, daughter of Hans Jacob Lichtenthaler. They had a son:
    Georg Wilhelm b. 13 Mar. 1730 bp. 16 Mar. 1730
    Sp.: Joh. Jacob Duchmann; Georg Wilhelm Duchmann;
    Anna Margretha, wife of Hans Stephan Duchmann

AMERICAN RECORDS

St. Michael's and Zion KB, Philadelphia:
Buried 9 Sept. 1769 - Georg Jung, b. 16 Mar. 1730 in Gundershoffen; came to America 14 years ago. Was married two times. Aged 39 years.

273. JUNG, JACOB   Ingolsheim=
1752   67250 Soultz-sous-Forêts
to Broadbay, Maine

EUROPEAN RECORDS

Hunspach Reformed KB:
Hans Jacob Jung and wife Eva nee ?Blösch had a son:
    Hans Jacob b. 23 Jan. 1715 at Hofen; bp. 24 Jan. 1715

Jacob Jung, citizen and tanner at Ingelsheim and wife Anna, had children:
   1. Susanna Catharina b. 8 Mar. 1738, bp. 11 Mar. 1738
   2. Jacob b. 24 Nov. 1740, bp. 27 Nov. 1740
      Sp.: Joh. Valentin Schuler, baker at Cleeburg; Joh. Georg,
      son of Joh. Georg Jung of Bischweiler; Margaretha, wife of David
      Burger.
   3. Johann Michael b. 5 Jan. 1743, bp. 6 Jan. 1743
      Sp.: Jacob Herr, *Anwaldt* at Ingelsheim, Joh. Michael, son of
      Benedict Ruby of Neuhoffen; Maria Margaretha, wife of Gabriel
      Billmann of Ingelsheim.

Zweibrücken Manumissions Protocoll, 1752:
Jacob Jung of Ingolsheim leaves with wife and two children for America.

AMERICAN RECORDS

Lititz Moravian Burials:
Johann Michael Jung, unmarried; came with parents to Broadbay, Maine ca.
1751. Lived there until 1767, then moved to Bethlehem; became Moravian.
Died in Lititz, 1826. He served as a missionary among the Indians for 28
years. Retired in Lititz in 1813.

274. KARCHER, JOHANN JOST   Bischtroff-sur-Sarre=
Patience, 1751   67260 Sarre-Union
S-H, I: 456

EUROPEAN RECORDS

Pisdorf [Bischtroff] Lutheran KB:
Johann Georg Karcher of Wolfskirchen m. 4 Sept. 1714 Elisabetha, nee
Bieber, widow of the late Johannes Schneider of Hirschland. They had a
son:
>Johann Jost b. 31 July 1722, bp. 2 Aug. 1722
>Sp.: Jacob Schmidt of Hirschland; Jost Stroh, Jr.;
>Anna Margaretha Wagner; Catharina Magdalena Weiss

Verification of this emigrant provided by Dr. Bernd Gölzer from the
compiled records of Dr. Gerhard Hein:
Records of Saarwerden county office for Pisdorf:
Dated 16 Feb. 1753 inventory of Anna Elisabetha Bieber Karcher: the son
Jost is absent for 1 ½ years, and one has heard that he moved to the New
Land.

275. KENNEL [KENDAL], JACOB   Schalbach=
Two Brothers, 1748   57370 Phalsbourg
S-H, I: 378, 379, 381
[with half brother Johannes Huntzinger]

EUROPEAN RECORDS

Diedendorf Reformed KB:
Sara Teller and her first husband, Ullrich Huntzinger, had a son Johannes
Huntzecker [q.v.]. Her first husband died, and she m. (2) Joseph Kenell
[q.v.] [Also Kennel]. Their oldest son was:
>Joh. Jacob b. 21 Nov. 1733
He emigrated with his half brother in 1748, and the rest of the family
followed in 1751.

AMERICAN RECORDS

Rev. Abraham Blumer's records, Lehigh co.:
Buried 20 Apr. 1787: Jacob Kendel, age 53 years.

276. KENNEL (KENELL), JOSEPH   Schalbach=
Brothers, 1751   57370 Phalsbourg
S-H, I: 463

EUROPEAN RECORDS

Diedendorf Reformed KB:
Hans Deller from Schallbach and wife Maria nee Paillet had a daughter:
    Sara bp. 4 Mar. 1700
    Sp.: Jacob Toussin from Weyer; Hans Nickel, son of Jacob
    Paillet of Schalbach; Mrs. Sara Schweitzer, Schalbach; and
    Elisabeth, daughter of Jacob Anton.

Sara Deller [also Teller] m. (1) Ulrich Huntziger and had a son Johannes
Huntziger [q.v.].

Joseph Kennel and wife Sara, nee Teller, had children:
    1. Anna Maria bp. 13 Apr. 1725 at Schalbach
       Sp.: Heinrich Kennel; Joh. Jacob Teller; Maria Kennel;
       Anna Maria, daughter of Stephan Paillet, all of Schallbach.
    2. Johanetta bp. 15 Feb. 1727
    3. Maria Barbara bp. 1 June 1732

Rauwiller Reformed KB:
    4. Joh. Jacob bp. 21 Nov. 1733 [q.v.]. He arrived on the ship
       Two Brothers, 1748 with his half-brother, Johannes Huntzecker.
    5. Joseph bp. 29 Mar. 1736
    6. Theobald bp. 11 Jan. 1738
    7. Joseph bp. 15 May 1742
    8. Johann Peter bp. 11 Nov. 1744

AMERICAN RECORDS

Egypt Reformed KB, Lehigh co.:
Joseph Kennel and wife Sara of Egypt were sp. in 1752 for a child of
Johannes Schneider [q.v.] and his wife Anna Margaretha [nee Wotring -
q.v.].

Maria, single daughter of Joseph Kennel, was sp. in 1752 for a child of
Paulus Baillet [q.v.].

Maria Barbara, daughter of Joseph Kennel, was sp. in 1753 for a child of
Jacob Peter in Heidelberg.

Hocker, *German Settlers of Pennsylvania:*
Pennsylvanische Geschicht-Schreiber, dated 9 July 1757:
Last Friday Joseph Kendel of Limerick was killed when his wagon upset while attempting to cross the Perkiomen.

Philadelphia Adm. G: 91: dated 29 July 1757:
Letters of Adm. granted to Joseph Kendel on the est. of Joseph Kendel, deceased. Inventory to be exhibited 29 Aug. 1757 and before 30 July 1758.

Charles Roberts et al, *History of Lehigh County, Pennsylvania,* **Vol. III:**
pg. 1420:
Theobald Kennel was born 11 Jan. 1737, and died 26 Sept. 1808. He m. (1) Maria Magdalena Hoffman [daughter of Michael Hoffman, q.v.]; she died between 1775 and 1782; He m. (2) Elizabeth Erdman.

Rev. Abraham Blumer's records:
Buried 20 Apr. 1787 - Jacob Kendel age 53 years.
Buried 13 Dec. 1775 - Peter Kendel, son of Theobald Kendel, age 17 days.
Buried 27 Dec. 1775 - Magdalena Kendel, wife of Theobald Kendel, age 30 years.

Dewald Kendel m. (2) 18 June 1776 Elisabeth Erdmann.

Joseph Kendell, Whitehall twp., Northampton co., nat. Autumn 1765.
Theobald Kendell, Whitehall twp., Northampton co., nat. Autumn 1765.

277. KENNEL, PETER   Schalbach=
[unnamed ship] 20 Oct. 1747   57370 Phalsbourg
S-H, I: 369, 370
                    EUROPEAN RECORDS

Diedendorf Reformed KB:
Barbara Kenel, widow of the late Heinrich Kenel, had a son:
    1. Joh. Peter bp. 16 Mar. 1726 at Schalbach
      Sp.: Peter Frantz; Jacob Utter; Eva, wife of Abraham Frantz;
      Elisabeth, daughter of Joh. Adam Dürmeyer all of Schallbach.

278. KERN, ABRAHAM age 28   Kirrberg=
Britannia, 1731   67320 Drulingen
S-H, I: 48, 52, 53   Langensoultzbach=
  with Katherina age 22 &   67360 Woerth
  Elizabeth Kern age 55

EUROPEAN RECORDS

Diedendorf Reformed KB:
Hans Kern from *Brunsthoch, Fürstl. Ohnspachischer Jurisdiction* [?W-8801 Brunst Post Dombühl, near W-8800 Ansbach], son of Georg Kern, m. 24 Sept. 1706 Elisabetha, daughter of the late Ulrich Gruber from Betterchingen, Berner Geb. [CH-3315 Bätterkinden, BE].

Hirschland Lutheran KB:
Hans Kern (also Johannes) b. in Hochfurstl Anspach, now residing in Kirburg, Ev. Lutheran Religion, and Elisabetha nee Gruber, Reformed Religion, born in Switzerland, had a son:
    Abraham bp. 16 July 1708
    Sp.: Abraham Brion from Kirburg; Jacob Bilarich from Kirburg; Catharina Gruber; Barbara Nägel.

Langensoultzbach Lutheran KB:
Abraham Kern, son of Hans Kern born in the *Hochfurst. Anschbachischen,* and former citizen at Kurburg, *Nassauischen Graffschafft,* m. 18 Feb. 1731 at Sultzbach Catharina, daughter of Conrad Müller, former schoolmaster at Lehmbach.

AMERICAN RECORDS

Muddy Creek Lutheran KB, Lancaster co.:
Abraham Kern had children:
    1. Joh. Christophel b. __ Feb. 1735, bp. 26 May 1735
       Sp.: Joh. Christophel Steinle
    2. Heinrich b. 24 Sept. 1737, bp. 21 Dec. 1737
       Sp.: Heinrich Haller [q.v.] and wife Anna Catharina
    3. Maria Catharina bp. 19 July 1743 (Muddy Creek Reformed KB)
    4. Anna Catharina b. 14 Apr. 1746, bp. 19 May 1746
       Sp.: Andreas Gansert and wife Margaretha
    5. Joh. Peter b. 1 Aug. 1749, bp. 1 Aug. 1749
       Sp.: Peter Tritt and wife

Muddy Creek Reformed KB, Lancaster co.:
Abraham Kern signed the 1743 Muddy Creek Reformed church doctrine. Abraham Kern's wife is named Maria Catharina in this record.

Trinity Lutheran KB, New Holland, Lancaster co.:
Abraham Kern, of Muddy Creek, m. 26 Nov. 1764 Anna Barbara Brendel of Brecknock, were married in Henrich Brendel's house.

Abraham Kern, Brecknock twp., Lancaster co., nat. Sept. 1751.

279. KERN, JACOB   Wolfskirchen=
St. Andrew, 1749   67260 Sarre-Union
S-H, I: 396
EUROPEAN RECORDS

Diedendorf Reformed KB:
Jacob Kern, woolenspinner of Niederstinzel [=57930 Fénétrange], son of
Jacob Kern from [CH-8200] Schaffhausen, Switzerland, m. 3 Mar. 1718
Barbara Schreyer, daughter of Durst Schreyer of [CH-4500] Solothurn,
Switzerland. Their oldest daughter Philippina Sophia b. 15 Jan. 1719, m. 11
Feb. 1749 at Neusaarwerden Joh. Heinrich Becker. It is mentioned in the
marriage record in the Neusaarwerden Lutheran KB that her father Jacob
Kern has emigrated to Pennsylvania.
On 2 Sept. 1734 Jacob Kern of Wolfskirchen m. the widow Eicher of
Wolfskirchen. This could be a second marriage of this Jacob Kern.
Data on this family provided by Dr. Bernd Gölzer.

Children of Jacob Kern and Barbara (Schreyer):
1. Philippina Sophia b. 15 Jan. 1719
2. Dorothea Catharina b. 9 June 1720
3. Johann Georg b. 28 Dec. 1726
4. Anna Magdalena b. 16 Dec. 1727
5. Christina Margaretha b. 13 Sept. 1730

AMERICAN RECORDS

One Jacob Kern, York twp., York co. nat. 11 Apr. 1763.

280. KERN, WIDOW OF JACOB   Rott=
KERN, HENRICH   67160 Wissembourg
KERN, BALTHASER
_____, 1752
Not in S-H.
EUROPEAN RECORDS

Birlenbach Lutheran KB:
Hans Jacob Kern, citizen at Rott, and wife Susanna had sons:
1. Johann Henrich bp. 15 Dec. 1712
2. Johann Baltsar b. 15 May 1716

Zweibruecken Manumissions Protocoll, Clee- and Catharinenburg, 1752:
Jacob Kern's old widow of Rott leaves for America. Balthaser Kern of Rott,
his wife and three children leave for America. Henrich Kern with wife and

three children, from Rott, leave for America.

AMERICAN RECORDS

Frederick Reformed KB, Frederick, MD:
Balthasar Kern and wife Magdalena had children:
    A child b. 11 May 1755, no sp. given.
    Valentin bp. 20 Aug. 1758

281. KERN, JOH. GEORG   67510 Lembach
St. Andrew Galley, 1737
S-H, I: 178, 180, 183

EUROPEAN RECORDS

Lembach Lutheran KB:
Joh. Georg Kern, son of Christoph Kern, citizen and *Gerichtsmann* and
church elder at [6749] Rumbach, *Pfalz Zweybruckischen* m. 2 Feb. 1723 at
Niedersteinbach [=67510 Lembach] Catharina Elisabetha, daughter of the
late Jacob Frawhüger, former *Hoffmann* in Katzenthal.
[See brothers-in-law Jacob Frawinger, Georg Friedrich Newhard and Peter
Traxel for more Frawhüger data.]

Zweibrücken Manumissions Protocoll, 1737
Georg Kern and Friederick Neuhard of Rumbach move with wives and
children to America.

[See Dennis A. Kastens, *Ancestors and Descendants of Wilhelm Neuhart, Sr.
and Caroline nee Weber,* (1980), p. 145 for additional Kern data from
Rumbach].

AMERICAN RECORDS

Georg Kern and his brother-in-law George Frederick Newhart [q.v.] took
out a warrant for 400A on the Coplay Creek in Whitehall twp. (now Lehigh
co.) on 1 Feb. 1743. This tract was divided between them on 30 Nov. 1744.

Egypt Reformed KB, Lehigh co.:
Georg Kern and wife Catharina Elisabetha had:
        Catharina Elisabetha bp. 28 July 1741; conf. 1753
        Sp.: Peter Traxel, church *censor* here [q.v.-Drachsel];
            Roland Schmidt; Maria Barbara wife of Michael Neuhart;
            Luce, wife of Ulrich Flickinger.

Georg Kern, Philadelphia co., nat. Apr. 1747.
George Jacob Karn, Whitehall twp., Northampton co., nat. 10 Apr. 1755.

282. KIEFER, JACOB   Goersdorf=
Edinburgh, 1752   67360 Woerth
S-H, I: 480
   [appears on list as Jacob (H) Küber; should read Küfer]

EUROPEAN RECORDS

Preuschdorf Lutheran KB:
Joh. Melchior Kiefer of Goersdorf, son of Hans Jacob Kiefer, m. 12 July
1707 Catharina Schnepp, daughter of the late Martin Schnepp, shepherd at
Görsdorf. Their son:
   Joh. Jacob b. 6 May 1718, bp. 8 May 1718

Hans Jacob Kieffer, son of Melchior Kieffer, m. 20 Nov. 1742 at Goersdorf
Dorothea, daughter of the late Peter Hoffman, citizen at ?Lusen.
[His mark (H) by his marriage entry is the same mark in the ship list.]
One of the witnesses at the marriage was Elisabeth Hoffmann, the bride's
mother.

Hans Jacob Kieffer and Dorothea had:
   1. Hans Georg b. 12 Aug. 1745, bp. 14 Aug. 1745
      Sp.: Jacob Mosser; Magdalena, wife of Hans Georg Weber, miller;
      Hans Jörg Brücker, son of Peter Brücker.

AMERICAN RECORDS

Bindnagel's Lutheran KB:
Jacob Kiefer b. 6 May 1717 at Gersdorf, Alsace; m. (1) in Germany and
lived in matrimony nine years when he emigrated to America in 1750; m. (2)
Catharina Altman. He d. Aug. 1804.

283. KIRSCHENMANN, JOHAN CHRISTIAN   67690 Hatten
Hamilton, 1767
S-H, I: 715

EUROPEAN RECORDS

Hatten Lutheran KB:
Christian Kirschmann, citizen and tailor, and Catharina nee Gütelmann had:
   1. Catharina Barbara b. 27 Dec. 1762, bp. 29 Dec. 1762

Sp.: Catharina Barbara wife of Adam Humbert; Jacob Dangle
from Betschdorff; Cath. Scheer daughter of Martin Scheer of
Rittershoffen.
2. Joh. Georg b. 26 Feb. 1764
3. Johann Heinrich b. 7 July 1766, d. y.?

Signature from KB: Signature from S-H, II: 823:

284. KLEIBER, GEORG   Niederbetschdorf=
   KLEIBER, HENRICH   67660 Betschdorf
Sally, 5 Oct. 1767
S-H, I; 714

EUROPEAN RECORDS

Oberbetschdorf Lutheran KB:
Joh. Georg Kleiber of Niederbetschdorf, and wife Maria Elisabetha nee
Gerber or Gerwig (appears with both spellings in KB), had children:
   1. Maria Elisabetha b. 11 Jan. 1732, bp. 14 Jan. 1732
   2. Anna Maria b. 7 Dec. 1733
   3. Joh. Georg b. 19 Oct. 1734, died 1738
   4. Joh. Martin b. 15 Aug. 1737
   5. **Joh. Georg** b. 9 Oct. 1740, bp. 12 Oct. 1740
   6. Joh. Jacob b. 8 Dec. 1743, died
   7. Margaretha b. 5 Jan. 1745, died
   8. Joh. Jacob b. 28 Mar 1746
   9. **Joh. Heinrich** b. 10 Dec. 1749

AMERICAN RECORDS

Trinity Lutheran KB, Reading, Berks co:
Joh. Georg Kleiber, second son of the deceased Georg Kleiber of
Niederbetschdorf, Alsace, m. 17 Dec. 1770 Rosina Margareth Weber, oldest
daughter of Joh. Nicolaus Weber from Wintersburg in Zweibrücken [W-6551
Winterburg]. Bern twp.

1790 Census, Northumberland co:
   Henry Cliver 1 male over 16, 3 males under 16, 5 females.
   George Cliver 2 males over 16, 1 male under 16, 4 females.

285. KLEIN, BERNHARD Age 30   Postroff=
Lydia, 1741   57930 Fénétrange
S-H, I: 300, 301, 303

EUROPEAN RECORDS

Hirschland Lutheran KB:
Mauritius Klein, son of Sebastian Klein of Steinsel, m. 19 Oct. 1706 Anna
Catharina, daughter of Joh. Theobald Marzloff of ?Postoff. Their son:
  1. Johann Bernhard b. 29 Nov. 1707; "in Americam Gereist"
  [See immigrant Moritz Klein for more family data].

Bernhard Klein m. 23 Feb. 1734 Anna Elisabetha, widow of Christoph Biber.
They had:
  1. Laurentius b. 15 Feb. 1735

Christoph Biber m. 18 July 1719 Anna Elisabetha N.N. from Eyweiler. [Her
name is given as Ludmann in other records.] They had children:
  1. Maria Elisabetha bp. 2 Apr. 1720, 14 years old in 1734.
  2. Johannes bp. 19 Feb. 1722, 14 years old in 1734. He m.
     23 Oct. 1742 at Eyweiler Anna Magdalena Heckel and emigrated
     to PA in 1751 [q.v.].
  3. Johannes bp. 21 Nov. 1724, d. 22 Mar. 1728
  4. Agnes bp. 19 Aug. 1727, d. 12 Dec. 1728
  5. a son, n.n., d. 30 Sept. 1729
  6. Matthias, listed as 3½ in 1734.

Christoph Biber d. 28 June 1733, age 31.

Verification of this emigrant provided by Dr. Bernd Gölzer from the
compiled records of Dr. Gerhard Hein:
Records of Saarwerden county office for Hirschland:
Dated 15 Feb. 1734, inventory of Christoph Bieber: the widow has married
Bernhard Klein of Postorf. Three children of Christoph Bieber are alive.
Records of Saarwerden county office for Eyweiler:
Dated 5 Feb. 1761, inventory of her brother, the mayor Peter Ludmann of
Eyweiler: the sister Anna Elisabetha, married to Bernhard Klein of
Hirschland; they moved to America 20 years ago with their children.

AMERICAN RECORDS

Christ Lutheran (Mertz's) KB, Bieber Creek, Berks co:
Bernhard Klein and wife Elisabetha sp. a child of Johannes Biber and
Magdalena nee (Heck or Haegel) [Heckel].

Jerusalem Church Cemetery, Western Salisburg, Lehigh co:
Lorenz Kline, Sr.
b. 5 Feb. 1735, d. 6 July 1819
Age 84 y. 40 mo. 21 days

Eva Kline nee Stettler, wife of Lorenz Kline, Sr.
b. 25 Dec. 1740, d. 21 Nov. 1821
Age 84 y. 4 mo. 27 d.

A Peter Kline, b. 13 Dec. 1741, d. 22 Dec. 1819, m. 1763 Margaret Stettler, sister of Eva Stettler, wife of Lorentz Kline. Children were Margaret, Lorentz, Jacob, Jonathan, Henry, Maria wife of Michael Acker, and Mrs. George Smith. Several of their children were bp. at Jordan Lutheran and Jerusalem Lutheran Church, Lehigh co.

Jordan Lutheran KB and Jerusalem Lutheran KB, W. Salisbury twp., Lehigh co.:
Lorentz Klein and wife Eva had children:
        Christoph b. 1 June 1765
        Catharine b. 28 Nov. 1772
        Henrich b. 16 Aug. 1775
        Magdalena b. 3 Mar. 1779

Rev. Daniel Schumacher's Records:
Lorentz Klein and wife Eva had:
        Maria Elisabeth bp. 22 Nov. 1767, 3 weeks old, in the Schmaltzgass
        Sp.: Johannes Ritter and Apollonia Stedlerin, single

Johann Peter Klein and Margaretha had:
        Margaretha b. 10 Apr. 1768, bp. 1 May 1768, in Schmaltzgass
        Sp.: Christopher Stettler and Margaretha.

Lorentz Klein, Lowhill twp., Northampton co., nat. Autumn, 1765.
Peter Klein, Maccungy twp., Northampton co., nat. Autumn, 1765.

286. KLEIN, JOHANNES   Postroff=
Several in lists   57930 Fénétrange
One on S-H, I: 666, 668, 670

                          EUROPEAN RECORDS

Hirschland Lutheran KB:
Johannes Klein from Postroff m. 21 Apr. 1722 Anna Margretha Gangloff,

daughter of the *Nassauischen Meyer* (notation in KB: sind in Americam). They had children:
1. Joh. Sebastian bp. 29 Jan. 1723, d. 18 Feb. 1723
   [There is an emigration notation by this baptismal record; either that notation or the death entry is an error. See also Joh. Sebastian, son of Moritz Klein, who may be the one for whom the em. note was intended].
2. Joh. Nickel bp. 5 Feb. 1724. "sind auch in Americam gezogen"
3. A son (n.n.) bp. 14 June 1725; emigration notation
4. Johannes bp. 17 Sept. 1727; emigration notation
5. Hans Theobald bp. 9 Apr. 1733; emigration notation
6. Anna Catharina bp. 16 Sept. 1734; emigration notation
7. Hans Görg bp. 21 July 1740; emigration notation.

AMERICAN RECORDS

Berks co. Wills and Adm.:
Theobald Klein, Longswamp. On 20 July 1759, adm. was granted to Peter Klein and wife Christina, who was the widow of said intestate.

Theobald Kline and George Kline, Longswamp twp., Berks co., nat. Autumn, 1765.

287. KLEIN, MARX age 45   Wingen=
Samuel, 1733   67510 Lembach
S-H, I: 107, 109, 111, 112
   with Elizabeth Clyne age 42, Juliana Clyne age 13, Elizabeth Clyne age 1 (should be age 11), Catharina age 10, Dorothea age 8, Marks age 4.

EUROPEAN RECORDS

Wingen Lutheran KB:
Marcus Klein, weaver, m. (1) 9 June 1716 Anna Margretha daughter of Rudolph Schaffner at Wingen. They had:
1. Maria Juliana bp. 29 Mar. 1718

Anna Margretha Schaffner Klein d. 28 Aug. 1719, age 23 years.

Marcus Klein, Reformed citizen and weaver at Wingen, m. (2) 30 Apr. 1720 Anna Elisabetha Deckenberger. They had:
2. Maria Elisabeth bp. 24 Jan. 1721
3. Maria Catharina bp. 4 Jan. 1722
4. Joh. Valentin b. 15 Jan. 1723, died 1730

5. Anna Margaretha b. 28 May 1724
6. Maria Dorothea b. ___ Aug. 1726
7. Joh. Marx b. 8 Jan. 1728, bp. 11 Jan. 1728
8. Joh. Adam b. 18 June 1731, died 26 June 1731

Half-timbered houses in Wingen, without the canopies found in other Alsatian villages.

AMERICAN RECORDS

Muddy Creek Reformed KB, Lancaster co.:
Marx Klein signed the 1743 Muddy Creek Reformed Church doctrine.
Marx Klein and wife had:
> Anna Margaret bp. 31 July 1751
> Sp.: A. Margaret daughter of Peter Klein

Muddy Creek Lutheran KB, Lancaster co.:
Maria Juliana Klein, daughter of Marx Klein, was a sp. 13 Apr. 1735 for
Maria Juliana Frey, daughter of Peter Frey [q.v.].

Rev. John Waldschmidt's Records:
Marx Klein had a daughter:
> Anna Maria bp. 22 Apr. 1753
> Sp.: Friedrich Muller and wife.

288. KLEIN, MATTHIS   Rexingen=
_____, 1754   67320 Drulingen

EUROPEAN RECORDS

Drulingen Lutheran KB:
Matthias Klein of Rexingen and his wife (Maria Margaretha in another entry) had a son:

Hans Matthias b. 4 Mar. 1708, bp. 9 Mar. 1708
Sp.: Caspar Springer of Rexingen; Nicolaus Heckele, son of the late Hans Theobald Heckele of Thal; Anna Elisabetha, daughter of Philipp Andreas of Berg.

Berg Lutheran KB:
Matthis Klein, son of Matthis Klein, formerly a farmer at Rexingen, m. 24 Nov. 1739 Eva Elisabetha, daughter of Hans Georg Frey, citizen and inhabitant at Eyweiler. They had children:

1. Johann Niclaus b. 1 June 1741, bp. 4 June 1741
2. Johann Theobald b. 3 Jan. 1743, bp. 6 Jan. 1743
3. Johann Andreas b. 15 Feb. 1744, bp. 18 Feb. 1744
4. Anna Magdalena b. 17 Aug. 1746, bp. 19 Aug. 1746
5. Eva Christina b. 10 Apr. 1750, bp. 13 Apr. 1750
6. Johann Georg b. 21 Sept. 1752, bp. 24 Sept. 1752

AMERICAN RECORDS

Hocker, *German Settlers of Pennsylvania:*
Newspaper dated 1 May 1755:
Matheus Klaen arrived in America last autumn from Rexingen, Nassau, and indentured two boys -- Hansz Michael Klaen, 14 years old, and Andreas Klaen, 12 years old. Mattheus Klaen was sick at the time and received no indenture papers nor does he know the names of the masters. He died, and his widow seeks her sons. Information may be sent to David Schaefer, Philadelphia.

One Nichs. Klein, Northern Liberties, Philadelphia, nat. autumn 1765.
One Andrew Cline, Lancaster, nat. 24 Sept. 1762.

289. KLEIN, MORITZ   Postroff=
    KLEIN, JACOB   57930 Fénétrange
Phoenix, 1749
S-H, I: 405

EUROPEAN RECORDS

Hirschland Lutheran KB:
Mauritius Klein, son of Sebastian Klein of Steinsel, [Nieder or Ober Stinzel = 57930 Fénétrange] m. 19 Oct. 1706 Anna Catharina, daughter of Joh. Theobald Marzloff of Borstorff (Postorff).

Moritz Klein from Steinsal, citizen at Postorff, and wife Anna Catharina had children:
1. Johann Bernhard bp. 29 Nov. 1707 [q.v.]; to America.
2. A son (n.n.) [?Jacob] bp. 8 Oct. 1713
   Sp.: Nickel Schmitt; Joh. Jacob Klein.
   Notation in KB: "went to America with wife and children"
3. Joh. Sebastian bp. 17 June 1716
   (One Bastian em. 1739); no emigration notation; however, there is an em. note by the bp. of another Joh. Sebatian Klein who died there 18 Feb. 1723.
4. a son (n.n.) and
5. a daughter(n.n.), twins, bp. 20 Feb. 1719. To America.
   Sp.: Joh. Adam Durrmeyer; Theobald Bachmann; Maria Barbara Klein; Anna Margretha Gangloff
6. Hans Michael bp. 27 May 1725. To America.
   [He might be the Johann Michael Klein who arrived on the ship *Friendship,* 1744 with the Biebers, S-H, I: 357; or the Hans Mickel Klein on the unnamed ship 20 Oct. 1747 with others from Hirschland and Postorff, S-H, I: 370.]
7. Johannes bp. 16 Nov. 1727. To America.
8. Joh. Theobald bp. 4 Jan. 1732

AMERICAN RECORDS

Christ Lutheran KB (Mertz's), Bieber Creek, Berks co:
Michael Klein, unmarried son of Moritz Klein, m. 17 June 1750 Catharina Schufert, single daughter of Joh. Georg Schufert. Children:
1. Christina Magd. b. 13 Apr. 1751, bp. 12 May 1751
   Sp.: Michael Biber and Jacob Biber; Christian Klein; Anna Mar. Schufert.

A. Campbell Cline, *Descendants of Michael Klein.* Charlotte, NC: Crabtree Press, Inc. 1973:
Michael Klein died 1792 in Cabarrus co., NC. His wife Catharine nee Schuffert died 11 Mar. 1798 and was buried in Coldwater. They had 14 children, of whom seven were living in 1798. They also had 54 grandchildren and eight great-grandchildren (in 1798). From the diary of Rev. Adam Marcard, Pastor of St. John's and Coldwater Lutheran Churches, Cabarrus co., NC.

The will of Michael Klein was recorded in Mechlenberg co., NC, Will Book D:126. Dated 1 Dec. 1784. Children were: Christina, Barbel, Mary Magdalena, Anna Mary, George, Anna ELisabeth, Anna Margaret, Medlina, Samuel, John, Catharine.

Today there are two churches in Postroff. In the eighteenth century, the Lutheran records were entered in the Hirschland parish register.

290. KLEIN, SEBASTIAN   Postroff=
Robert and Alice, 1739   57930 Fénétrange
S-H, I: 264, 268, 271

EUROPEAN RECORDS

Hirschland Lutheran KB:
Moritz Klein from Steinsal, [Niederstinzel=57930 Fénétrange] citizen at
Postroff and wife Anna Catharina had eight children, and all appear to have
emigrated to America [See Moritz Klein for additional family data]. One of
his sons was:
        Joh. Sebastian b. 17 June 1717; conf. 1730.
        [There are emigration notations by all of the other 7 children in this
family; no note by this baptism. Perhaps this emigration note was entered
in error by the baptismal record of another Joh. Sebastian Klein, son of
another emigrant Johannes Klein; this other Sebastian was born in Jan.
1723, and died there in Feb. 1723.]

AMERICAN RECORDS

A. Campbell Cline, *Descendants of Michael Klein.* Charlotte, NC: Crabtree
Press, Inc. 1973:
"Bastian" Klein was a brother of Michael Klein. He settled in Lincoln co.,
NC.

291. KLINGENSCHMIT, DANIEL   Tieffenbach=
Robert & Alice, 1738   67290 Wingen-sur-Moder
S-H, I: 213, 215
EUROPEAN RECORDS

Waldhambach Lutheran KB:
Joh. Daniel Klingesmitt, widower and *Potashbrenner* from Lützingen,
Wuertemberg, m. - Jan. 1718 at Tieffenbach Anna Christina, daughter of
Claus Reitenauer. [She was sister of Johannes Reitenauer, q.v.]
They had:
        1. Maria Catharina b. 7 Oct. 1720

AMERICAN RECORDS

St. Paul's Lutheran KB, Upper Hanover twp., Montgomery co.:
Daniel Klingenschmidt and wife were sp. in 1744 for a child of Christian
Cassel.

Philip Klingenschmidt and wife Maria Elisabetha had:
Anna Christina b. 23 June 1753
Sp.: Christian Cassel.

292. KNOBEL, PETER age 43
Samuel, 1733
S-H, I: 107, 111, 112
with Ursula Knoble age 43, Anna Maria age 16.

Mattstall=
67510 Lembach

EUROPEAN RECORDS

Lembach Lutheran KB:
Johann Peter Knobel, carpenter from Canton Bern, Switzerland and his wife
Anna Catharina (nee Müller as given in the Langensoultzbach records) had
a son:
Johann Peter b. 25 Jan. 1691 in Mattstall.

Johann Peter Knobel m. 27 Apr. 1717 Anna Ursula nee Frahr, widow of
Nicholas Blind. They had a daughter:
1. Anna Maria b. 21 Nov. 1717

Died 1 May 1735 - Magdalena, widow of Peter Knobel, former citizen of St.
Stephan an der Molten, Canton Bern, Switzerland. Age 80 years.

AMERICAN RECORDS

Peter Knobel was a contributor to the Germantown Lutheran Church in
1738.

Trinity Lutheran KB, Lancaster:
Anna Maria Knobelin and Joh. Caspar Schaffner were sp. on 3 Nov. 1735
for a child of Joh. Peter Balspach.

Anna Maria Knobelin m. 30 Dec. 1735 Joh. Caspar Schaffner.

293. KNOBELLOCH, JORG FRIEDERICH
Hamilton, 1767
S-H, I: 716

Birlenbach=
67160 Wissembourg

EUROPEAN RECORDS

Birlenbach Lutheran KB:
Joh. Friederich Knobloch, single linenweaver, son of the late Valentin

Knobloch, former citizen at Langencandel [=W-6744 Kandel, Pfalz] m. 15 Jan. 1765 Anna Catharina, widow of the late Joh. Friedr. Straub, former tailor and citizen at Drachenbrun [=67160 Wissembourg].

Her first m: Georg Friedrich Straub, widower and *Lehnsmann* from _____ *ckerthal in Freyherrl. Turckheimischer Herrschafft,* m. 11 Nov. 1755 Catharina Sailer daughter of the late Matthai Sailer, former citizen and church *censor* at Birlenbach. Children:
   1. Anna Maria died 3 May 1761 age 1 yr. less 22 days
   (no children listed for second marriage)

AMERICAN RECORDS

Michael Tepper, ed., *Emigrants to Pennsylvania,* **Baltimore, 1975, p. 261:**
[Excerpted from *Pennsylvania Magazine of History and Biography,* Vol. XXXIII, no. 4, p. 501, 1909]
The following list of German families arrived at Philadelphia, appears in an advertisement in Henry Miller's *Staats Bote* of Feb. 9, 1758. [Note by compiler: this date of the newspaper is obviously in error, and should be 1768. See corrected list in Appendix B of this volume].
"The following German families, and a couple of unmarried persons, are now in the city; all held for their passage from Holland, and desiring to bind themselves out for same ......" Among those named in this list are:
Johann Kobbeloch, linenweaver, born in the Zweybrücken jurisdiction, village of Langenkandel; his wife (nee) Seyler, from the village of Börlebach.

294. KNÖRR, ABRAHAM age 24   Diedendorf=
Lydia, 1741   67260 Sarre-Union
S-H, I: 300, 301, 303

EUROPEAN RECORDS

Diedendorf Reformed KB:
Confirmed 1733 Abraham Knör.
The confirmation record does not give a village of residence, and this is the only Knörr (Knerr) entry in the KB. It is likely the family was transient through the area. He did not marry there, but came as a single young man. However, association with others from this area after his arrival in PA would seem to indicate that this is the man confirmed at Diedendorf in 1733. The 1733 confirmation date also fits with his age on the ship list.

AMERICAN RECORDS

Jordan Lutheran KB; Lehigh co. and Lowhill KB, Lehigh co:
Abraham Knerr and wife Maria Eva had children:
  1. Christopher b. 8 Oct. 1742, bp. 28 Oct. 1742
     Sp.: Joh. Christoph Ebel [see Obel]; Catharina Margaretha
Stettler
  2. Catharina Barbara b. 20 Aug. 1744, bp. 16 Sept. 1744
     Sp.: Christoph Stettler and wife Catharina; Barbara Obel [q.v.]
  3. Maria Eva b. 9 Apr. 1746, bp. 25 May 1746
     Sp.: Philip Klein; Andreas Eschbach [q.v.]; Regina Ber.
     Maria Eva m. Philip Fenstermacher [tombstone at Lowhill
     Church, Lehigh co.]
  4. Johannes, tombstone at Lowhill gives dates b. 11 Aug. 1745,
     d. 12 June 1823. Wife Magdalena nee Hartmann [tombstone
     at Lowhill]
  5. Anna Barbara (named in will), wife of Joh. Adam Geiss
  6. Abraham b. ca. 1750 d. 12 May 1777, age 27
     (Rev. Abraham Blumer's records.) He and wife Eva Elisabetha
     had children bp. at Lowhill.
  7. Susanna (named in will), wife of Peter Hartmann
  8. Dorothea m. 5 Oct. 1779 Philip Stettler [Blumer's records]
  9. Andrew (named in will)

Northampton co. Wills:
Abraham Knerr, Lowhill twp., 2 Feb. 1790 - 3 May 1793
Children: "daughters yet living, Barbara Horner; Maria Eva Fenstermacher;
Anna Barbara Geiss; Susanna Hartman; Dorothy Stettler; two sons: John
Knerr and Andrew Knerr. Mentions grandchildren: (Children of eldest son
Christopher, dec'd.): Andrew, Barbara, Susanna, Maria Eva; (Children of
dec'd. son Abraham): Abraham, Anna, Elizabeth, Susanna.
Exrs: Jacob Horner, Philip Stettler. Wit: P. Kocher.

295. KOBER, ADAM   Oberbronn-Zinswiller=
  KOBER, CHRISTIAN   67110 Niederbronn-les-Bains
  KOBER, JOH. ADAM
Edinburgh, 1751
S-H, I: 461
                        EUROPEAN RECORDS

Oberbronn Lutheran KB:
Joh. Adam Kober, son of the late Hans Martin Kober, former citizen at
Dirmstein in *Bischthumb Wormbs* [=W-6722 Dirmstein] m. 21 Sept. 1728
Anna Maria, daughter of Joh. Heinrich Port, citizen here. They had

children:
1. Maria Catharina b. 2 July 1729
   Sp.: Mr. Bernhard Diemer; Ottilia, wife of Niclaus Plari;
   Maria Barbara, wife of Joh. Phil. Lambs
2. Henrich Christian b. __ Aug. 1730, bp. 6 Aug. 1730
   Sp.: Georg Heinrich Mader, Jr.; Margaretha Elisabetha
   Kübler; Dorothea Francisca Röderer, wife of Joh. Jacob Röderer;
   Christian Weller.
3. Johann Adam b. 23 Mar. 1733
   Sp.: Joh. Georg Marzolff; Joh. Christoph Fischer [q.v];
   Anna Maria Heidler.
4. Philipp Jacob b. 27 Apr. 1737, bp. 29 Apr. 1737
5. Andreas b. 17 Aug. 1739, bp. 19 Aug. 1739
   Sp.: Andreas Geissler; Henrich Neumann; Andreas Diemer [q.v.];
   Catharina Dorothea, wife of Daniel Baur.

Hans Adam Kober's mark **A Ko** from KB:

Adam Kober's mark **A Ko** from S-H, II: 542:

296. KOCH, PETER   Diedendorf=
[unnamed ship] 20 Oct. 1747   67260 Sarre-Union
S-H, I: 369, 370

EUROPEAN RECORDS

Diedendorf Reformed KB:
Benedict Koch, shepherd, and wife Margaretha nee Huber had a son:
   Johann Peter b. 20 June 1724, conf. 1738

Died 28 Dec. 1742 Benedict Koch from Riegerten, Bern [possibly CH-
Aegerten, BE], age 59 years.

AMERICAN RECORDS

St. Michael's and Zion KB, Philadelphia:
Peter Koch and wife Anna Catharina had:
   Anna Catharina b. 2 Apr. 1748, bp. 11 Apr. 1748.

Rev. Daniel Schumacher's records:
Johann Peter Koch and wife Catharina had:
> Johann Peter bp. 25 Nov. 1759, 4 weeks old at Lehigh Church.
> Sp.: Carl Kress [q.v.] and Juliana Drachseln.

297. KOHL, PETER   Langensoultzbach=
Brigantine *John*, 1736   67360 Woerth
S-H, I: 167, 168

EUROPEAN RECORDS

Langensoultzbach Lutheran KB:
Peter Kohl, citizen and stocking weaver at Sultzbach, and wife Anna nee Lentz had children:
> 1. Joh. Jacob bp. 7 Oct. 1724
> 2. Maria Catharina bp. 18 June 1726
> 3. Maria Eva bp. 13 Nov. 1728, d. __ Nov. 1730
> 4. Maria Eva bp. 16 Jan. 1731
> 5. Johann Philip b. 12 Mar. 1733

AMERICAN RECORDS

Muddy Creek Lutheran KB, Lancaster co.:
Philip Kohl and wife had a daughter:
> Elizabeth bp. 18 Mar. 1756. Sp.: Andrew Ganser and wife.

Muddy Creek Reformed KB, Lancaster co.:
John Kohl and wife Christina had:
> John b. 8 Oct. 1777. Sp.: Jacob Bricker

298. KÖHLER, GEORG FRIEDRICH   Preuschdorf=
Mary, 1733   67250 Soultz-sous-Forêts
S-H, I: 131, 133, 134
  with Elisabeth
EUROPEAN RECORDS

Preuschdorf Lutheran KB:
Georg Friederich Köhler, citizen at Preuschdorf, m. __ May 1726 Elisabetha Kessler, daughter of the late Marx Kessler, former inhabitant at ?Glichan in Switzerland.
Notation in KB, by marriage record: "Went to the new land."

AMERICAN RECORDS

Emmaus Moravian KB, Lehigh co.:
Georg Fried. Koehler and wife Anna Maria had a daughter:
Maria Magdalena b. 26 Nov. 1759.

299. KOHLER, JACOB   Ingolsheim=
_____, 1752   67250 Soultz-sous-Forêts

EUROPEAN RECORDS

Hunspach Reformed KB:
Elias Kohler, daylaborer at Hunspach, and wife Christina had:
Hans Jacob b. 18 Feb. 1705, bp. 22 Feb. 1705

Joh. Jacob Kohler, son of the late Elias Kohler, *Schirmsverwanthen* at
Hunspach, m. 22 Nov. 1729 Maria Barbara, daughter of the late Jost Eby,
former inhabitant at Ingelsheim.
 1. Leonhart (twin) b. 15 Dec. 1730, d. 29 Dec. 1730
 2. Elias (twin) b. 15 Dec. 1730 d. 2 Jan. 1731
 3. Joh. Jacob b. 23 July 1732
 4. Maria Margaretha b. 1 July 1734
 5. Maria Barbara b. 17 Sept. 1737
 6. Joh. Jacob b. 5 Feb. 1741
 7. Maria Elisabetha b. 17 Nov. 1742
 8. Susanna Maria b. 5 Aug. 1745

Johann Jacob Kohler, citizen and widower at Ingelsheim, m. (2) 2 May 1751
[recorded in KB with 1752 marriages] Maria Margaretha, widow of Theobald
Weiss, former citizen at Hunspach.

Zweibrücken Manumissions Protocoll, Clee- and Catharinenburg, 1752:
Jacob Kohler of Ingelsheim leaves for America.

300. KÖHLER, JOHANNES age 24   Ingolsheim=
possibly on: *Barclay,* 1754   67250 Soultz-sous-Forêts
S-H, I: 596, 598, 599

EUROPEAN RECORDS

Hunspach Reformed KB:
Johannes Kohler, son of Peter Kohler, former *Gemeinsmann* at Lutzelfluh, Canton Bern [CH-3432 Lützelflüh, BE] m. 13 Jan. 1750 Magdalena, daughter of the late Jacob Weimer, former citizen at Hofen. They had:
1. Johann Michael b. 18 Feb. 1751
    Sp.: Samuel Niess; Joh. Michael, son of Jacob Biegler of Ingelsheim;, Eva, daughter of Michael Wütterich, citizen at Ingelsheim.

Zweibrücken Manumissions Protocoll, 1752:
Johann Koehler, with wife and one child, of Ingolsheim, leaves for America. [Note: Although he was listed in the 1752 manumission list, he does not appear on the ships with other emigrants that year (see Mart. Haug and H. Dewalt Billman). He may have been manumitted in 1752, and emigrated in 1754. Others on the *Barclay* in 1754 appear in this KB.]

301. KÖHLHOFFER, BENJAMIN [KELHOVER]   67690 Hatten
Bennet Gally, 1750
S-H, I: 429
EUROPEAN RECORDS

Hatten Lutheran KB:
Heinrich Köhlhoffer and wife Margaretha nee Schwitzgäbel had:
    Benjamin b. 26 Jan. 1729, bp 27 Jan. 1729
    Sp.: Georg Jacob, son of Hans Jacob Dech; Michael Henninger [q.v.] citizen and tailor; Maria Magdalena daughter of Hans Georg Humpert. [Only living son of this couple; they had 11 daughters, and 3 other sons who died young.]

AMERICAN RECORDS

Friesburg Lutheran KB, Salem co., N.J.:
Benjamin Gelloper [also Gellhoefer; this is possibly a misspelling of the Köhlhoffer name] and wife Maria had children:
1. Andreas b. 1 Nov. 1757, bp. 26 feb. 1758
    Sp.: Andreas Brandner and wife Susanna
2. Johannes b. 13 Oct. 1760
    Sp.: Johannes Lotz and wife Maria
3. Benjamin b. 17 Dec. 1762
    Sp.: Adam Mensch and wife Barbara
4. Maria Barbara b. 2 July [1765]
    Sp.: Adam Mansch and wife Maria Barbara.

302. KÖHLHOFFER, FRIDRICH   67690 Hatten
Minerva, 1770
S-H, I: 729 [appears on list as Hehlhoffer]

EUROPEAN RECORDS

Hatten Lutheran KB:
Joh. Michel Köhlhofer, son of the late Melchior Köhlhofer, m. 27 Jan. 1722
Maria Elisabetha, daughter of the late Jacob Humbert. They had a son:
Friedrich b. 10 Apr. 1728

Friedrich Köhlhoffer and wife Eva nee Rörig had children:
1. Eva b. 27 Aug. 1754, d. 1755
2. Barbara b. 16 Nov. 1755, bp. 17 Nov. 1755
3. Maria Magdalena b. 23 Aug. 1757, bp. 24 Aug. 1757
4. Eva b. 15 July 1759, bp. 16 July 1759
5. Joh. Friederich b. 20 Mar. 1761, bp. 21 Mar. 1761
6. Philipp Heinrich b. 19 Jan. 1763, bp. 20 Jan. 1763
7. Johann Michael b. 2 Dec. 1765
8. Maria Salome b. 17 July 1768

Eva Rörig, wife of Friedrich Köhlhoffer, was b. 31 May 1733, daughter of
Hans Michel Rörig, linenweaver, and wife Salome nee Eppelin.

Fridrich Köhlhoffer signed several of these church book entries, and
consistently made his *K* like an *H*:

Signature from KB: Signature from S-H, II: 844:

AMERICAN RECORDS

St. Michael's Lutheran KB, Germantown:
Jacob Müller, widower from Upper Milford, Northampton co., m. 25 Sept.
1776 Barbara Köhlhöfer of Springfield twp., Philadelphia co.

Died 13 May 1775: Elisabetha Köhlhofferin, age 2 y., 8 mo., 24 days.
Died 11 Apr. 1780: Friederich Köhlhoffer, aged 54 y.

Philadelphia Wills, Book R: 484
Frederick Kohlhoffer, Springfield twp., 20 Nov. 1779 - 27 Nov. 1780.
Wife, Eva. Children: Eldest son Frederick, Henry, Barbara, Magdalena, Eva,
Sally. Legacy of £10 to the Lutheran Church in Germantown. Also £10 to

the poor. Exrs: Wife Eva and Jacob Miller, son-in-law. Wit: Frederick Smith and Jacob Welker.

St. Michael's and Zion KB, Philadelphia:
Buried 1 Nov. 1804: Magdalena Sänders, daughter of Friederich and Eva Köhlhöfer, born in Alsace in 1757; m. (1) Henrich Schmidt and had two children: m. (2) Elisa (sic) Sanders.

303. KÖNIG, ABRAHAM   Hoffen=
Janet, 1751   67250 Soultz-sous-Forêts
S-H, I: 474
                        EUROPEAN RECORDS

Hunspach Reformed KB:
Abraham König, son of Abraham König of Bischweiler [=67240 Bischwiller] m. 9 May 1724 Anna Maria, daughter of Hans Adam Weymert [Weimer], former *Gemeinsmann* at Hofen.
Abraham König, tailor at Hofen, and wife Anna Maria nee Weymer, had children:
1. Hans Adam b. 12 Mar. 1725, bp. 18 Mar. 1725; conf. 1739 at Hoffen
2. Maria Eva b. 17 Jan. 1728, bp. 25 Jan. 1728; conf. 1741 at Hoffen.

Hoffen Reformed KB:
Abraham König and Anna Maria had:
3. Maria Magdalena b. 10 Mar. 1730, bp. 12 Mar. 1730; conf. 1744
   Sp.: Joh. Jacob Weimar, the cooper; Anna Barbara, wife of Johann Jung; Magdalena, daughter of Andreas Postetter.
4. Abraham b. 11 Jan. 1733, bp. 15 Jan. 1733; conf. 1747
   Sp.: Joh. Jacob Niess, citizen at Hoffen; Martin Weimer, son of Martin Weimer; Maria Barbara, daughter of Valentin Spindler.
5. Barbara b. 17 June 1735, bp. 19 June 1735; died 6 Feb. 1736
   Sp.: Maria, wife of Jacob Schwob, citizen and carpenter here; Johannes Prefried, master tailor here; Barbara, daughter of Jacob Weimer, citizen and cooper here.
6. Maria Barbara b. 27 Jan. 1738, bp. 2 Feb 1738
   Sp.: Andreas Weimer, weaver; Maria Anna, daughter of Michel Niess; Anna Maria, ?wife of Jacob Schwob, carpenter.
7. Joh. Georg b. 17 Aug. 1740, bp. 21 Aug. 1740
   Sp.: Georg Niess, mayor; Georg Niess the younger; Maria Magdalena, wife of Joh. Jacob ?Weimer, the Reformed

schoolteacher here.
8. Maria Elisabeth b. 28 Sept. 1745, bp. 3 Oct. 1745
   Sp.: Joh. Michael Weimer, citizen here; Elisabetha, widow of
   Johannes Brefried, former master tailor at Rittershoffen;
   Anna Maria, daughter of Christian ?Fahens from Rittershoffen.

Zweibruecken Manumissions Protocoll, Clee- and Catharinenburg, 1751:
Abraham Koenig of Hooffen [Hofen] leaves with his family, wife and six
children for America.

AMERICAN RECORDS

York co. Will Abstracts:
Abraham King, dated 28 Feb. 1766, probated 13 June 1766.
Exr: George King. Wife (name not given); Children: George; Eve, wife of
Thomas Fisher; Abraham; Mrs. Stephan Wible; Mrs. Reinhart Replogle.
[Resided in Kingsdale, south of Littlestown.]

Adams co. Will Book B:
Abraham King (son of immigrant), Germany twp. dated 3 Sept. 1807,
probated May 1813. Wife: Margaret. Sister: Marillis (Maria Elisabeth), wife
of Stephen Wyble. Brother: George King. Legacy to former wife's two
daughters.

George King, Germany twp. dated 20 Feb. 1810, probated May 1816.
Wife: Fronica. Children mentioned but not named. (There are 5 children
listed in the Christ Church, Littlestown, Adams co. records.)

A biographical sketch of the family of Reinhard Replogle and wife Barbara
is found in *The Brethren Encyclopedia.*

304. KÖPPEL, ANDREAS   Dehlingen=
Boston, 1764   67430 Diemeringen
S-H, I: 702

EUROPEAN RECORDS

Dehlingen Lutheran KB:
Joh. Clemenz Köppel, smith at Dehlingen, and wife Anna Barbara nee Reb
had:
   Andreas b. 3 Oct. 1732, conf. 1744.
   Christina Elisabetha b. 30 July 1741, conf. 1754.

Verification of this emigration supplied by Dr. Bernd Gölzer, from the
county records of Nassau-Saarwerden, compiled by Dr. Gerhard Hein:

Records of the notary public for Dehlingen:
Dated 7 July 1773, inventory of Clemenz Köppel: The son Andreas is in America; the daughter Christina Elisabetha moved to America and allegedly died there. Dehlingen Deed book, record dated 20 Apr. 1776: Andreas Köppel and Christine Elisabetha Köppel, both since 12 years in America, are heirs of Clemenz Köppel.

AMERICAN RECORDS

Emanuel Church, Petersville, Moore twp., Northampton co.:
Andrew Keppel and wife Anna Maria had:
1. Anna Margaret b. 31 Dec. 1768
2. Maria Verona b. 27 Feb. 1771, bp. 31 Mar. 1771
   Sp.: Joseph Nehlig; Maria Verona Müller.
3. Joh. Christian b. 12 Sept. 1772, bp. 8 Nov. 1772
   Sp.: Christian Miller and Anna Margaret.

305. KÖPPEL, MICHEL   Herbitzheim=
    KÖPPEL, JOH. NICKEL   67260 Sarre-Union
    KÖPPEL, JACOB
Phoenix, 1749
S-H, I: 405
EUROPEAN RECORDS

Herbitzheim Lutheran KB:
Michel Köppel m. 6 Apr. 1723 Anna Bentz, daughter of Herr Joh. Bentz, former Evang. schoolteacher here. They had:
1. Joh. Nickel b. 26 Feb. 1724, bp. 28 Feb. 1724; conf. 1739
   Sp.: Nickel Hemmerth, smith at Dehlingen [=67430
   Diemeringen]; Joh. Adam ?Erdter; Catharina Hausswald, single
2. Gustavus b. 21 Oct. 1725, bp. 24 Oct. 1725, d. 1728
3. Maria Elisabetha b. ca. 1727; conf. 1741
4. Maria Catharina b. 19 June 1729, bp. 21 June 1729; conf.1743
5. Joh. Jacob b. 1 Jan. 1732, bp. 3 Jan. 1732

AMERICAN RECORDS

One of the signers on a petition for protection from the Indians, dated 5 Oct. 1757, Forks of the Delaware:
    Michael Keppel

St. Paul's (Indianland) Lutheran KB, Lehigh co.:

Jacob Keppel and wife Elenora; and Nicholas Keppel and wife Anna Maria were sp. in 1765 for a child of Georg Ecker [q.v.]

Rev. Daniel Schumacher's records:
Jacob Keppell and Leonora had:
  1. Johann Jacob bp. 21 Dec. 1759, 4 weeks old at Lehigh
     Sp.: Parents
  2. Johann Georg b. 18 Jan. 1770, bp. 29 Mar. 1770
     father is Elder of the Lehigh congregation
     Sp.: Jürg Eisemann and Margaretha Küster, both single
  3. Ludewigh b. 21 Aug. 1772, bp. 11 Oct. 1772
     Sp.: Ludewigh Küster and Anna Cath. Eisemann, single

Johann Nicolaus Keppell and Anna Maria had:
  1. Jürg Peter bp. 21 Dec. 1759, 8 weeks old; bp. in Lehigh church
  2. Georg Nickolaus b. 12 July 1769, bp. 22 Aug. 1769, Lehigh twp.
     Sp.: Georg Eisemann [q.v.]; Catharina daughter of Jost Treisbach
  3. Johannes b. 28 Sept. 1772, bp. 22 Nov. 1772 across the Lehigh in
     the new church.   Sp.: Abraham Frantz and Catharina.

Tohickon Reformed KB, Bucks co.:
Nicholas Keppel m. 28 Sept. 1756 Maria Williams.

Emanuel Reformed KB, Moore twp., Northampton co.:
Jacob Keppel and wife Eleonora had twins:
     John Henry, twin, b. 22 Oct. 1767, bp. 1 Nov. 1767
     Catharina, twin, b. 22 Oct. 1767
     Sp.: Nicholas Keppel & Magdalena; Peter Eisenman & Maria
     Catharina.

Westmoreland co. Will Abstracts:
Jacob Kepple, South Hempfield twp., 14 Apr. 1787- 8 May 1787. Wife:
Elenor; Children: Jacob, Peter, Henry, George, Lewis, Lucy Altman, Mary
Elizabeth, Catharine, Margaret, and Magdalena.
Exrs: Wife Elenor and Jacob Macklin.
Wit: Anthony Lutze, Peter Iseman, N. Swope.

306. KÖPPEL, PAULUS   Herbitzheim=
KÖPPEL, HENRICH   67260 Sarre-Union
KÖPPEL, PETER
Phoenix, 1749
S-H, I: 405

                          EUROPEAN RECORDS

Herbitzheim Lutheran KB:
Paulus Köppel and wife Anna Elisabetha had:
1. Johan Henrich b. 24 Feb. 1726, bp. 26 Feb. 1726; conf. 1739
   Sp.: Johan Henrich Köppel, Christian Letzler;
   Mrs. Elisabetha Reiff and Regina Mugel, single.
2. Joh. Nickel b. 17 Aug. 1728. He died 6 Jan. 1729.
3. Joh. Peter b. 28 Apr. 1731, bp. 29 Apr. 1731; conf. 1745
4. Maria Catharina b. 3 Aug. 1736, bp. 5 Aug. 1736; conf. 1747

AMERICAN RECORDS

Old Goshenhoppen Lutheran KB, Montgomery co:
Communicants, 1751: Anna Elisab., widow of Paulus Keppel, Maria
            Catharina, daughter of Paul Keppel, deceased.
Communicants, 1752: Peter Keppel, son of the late Paul Keppel.
Communicants, 1754: Henrich Keppel, Margr. Elis., his wife, and
      and 1755: Maria Cathar., single, his sister.
Communicants, 1756: Peter Keppel; Anna Elisabetha Keppel, his mother;
            Elisabetha, wife of Peter Keppel; Anna Maria Keppel,
            single, daughter of Paul Keppel, deceased.

Jacob Müller, from Zoll in Wuertenberg, single, m. 28 Feb. 1760 Maria
Catharina *Kepler*, single, b. in Closter Herbesheim of the Nassau Region.

307. KREBS, CHRISTIAN age 33   Liniehausen,
Samuel, 1733   Langensoultzbach=
S-H, I: 106, 110, 112   67360 Woerth
[appears on list as Krobs, Krapts]
   with Christina Krapts age 24, Maria Crete age 4, Anna Percy age 1/2

EUROPEAN RECORDS

Langensoultzbach Lutheran KB:
Died 22 June 1741 Jacob Krebs, Ref., from Canton Bern, Switzerland, age
72 years.
Christian Krebs and wife Catharina nee Sichler had children:
   1. Maria Margarethe bp. 8 Nov. 1729 at Liniehausen
   2. Christian bp. 7 Dec. 1731
   3. Possible a daughter born during the journey; see ship list.

Christian Krebs, widower of Liniehausen, m. (2) in Fröschweiler 4 July 1732
Christina Margaretha, daughter of the late Hans Bischoff of Schönechen
Ampt.

314   EIGHTEENTH CENTURY EMIGRANTS

Hans Bischoff, age 52, of Jägerthal, was buried in Sultzbach 7 Oct. 1729.

AMERICAN RECORDS

Trinity Lutheran KB, Lancaster:
Christian Krebs had children:
4. Maria Magdalena b. 24 June 1735, bp. 14 Oct. 1735
5. Johannes b. 15 Jan. 1738, bp. 25 Feb. 1738

Muddy Creek Lutheran KB, Lancaster co.:
6. Joh. Georg b. 26 Feb. 1743, bp. 10 Apr. 1743
7. Joh. Jacob b. 13 Aug. 1744, bp. 21 Oct. 1744
   Sp.: Joh. Jacob Wüster [see Wüst] and wife
8. John Peter bp. 2 Feb. 1746 (Reformed KB)
9. Eva bp. 7 June 1747 (Reformed KB)

A Susanna Krebs was sp. in 1741 for a child of Joh. Heinrich Brendel.
Christian Krebs and wife were sp. in 1742 for a child of Althans Frantz.
Christina Krebsin was sp. in 1748 for a child of Joh. Peter Franckhausser.
Christian Krebs and Eva Franckhausser were sp. in 1746 for a child of Jacob
Wüst [q.v. Franckhauser and Wüst].

Muddy Creek Reformed KB, Lancaster co.:
Christian Krebs, Elder, signed the Muddy Creek Reformed Church doctrine
in 1743.
Conf. 30 Mar. 1746 - Maria Margaret Krebs

It will be noted that the son Christian Krebs b. 1731 does not appear on the
ship list. It is possible that he remained behind when the family emigrated.
One Christian Krebs arrived on the ship *Peggy* in 1753, S-H, I: 546, 548, 550.

St. Michael's and Zion KB, Philadelphia:
Buried 10 Mar. 1776 - Joh. Christian Krebs, b. 1732 in Elsass. Aged 43 years,
5 months.

308. KREBS, PETER   67770 Sessenheim
ca. 1752
Not in S-H.
EUROPEAN RECORDS

Sessenheim Lutheran KB:
Joh. Peter Krebs, son of the late Peter Krebs, m. 2 Jan. 1732 Maria
Magdalena, daughter of Joh. Georg Krebsstein. They had a son:

Petrus b. 11 Sept. 1740, bp. 12 Sept. 1740
Sp.: Joh. Jacob Wolff; Margaretha, daughter of Matthaus Jung.

AMERICAN RECORDS

Hocker, *German Settlers of Pennsylvania:*
Pennsylvanische Geschichts-Schreiber, dated 10 June 1758:
Peter Krebs, his wife Magdalena and their family, arrived at Philadelphia five years ago last Autumn. Their daughter, Anna Maria, was indentured in Lancaster to English people, who removed to Charlestown, MD, then to Williamsburg, VA. Maria was freed and is now in Baltimore, with Samuel Hook, and she seeks her mother.

New Holland Lutheran Cemetery records:
Peter Krebs, b. 29 Sept. 1740 in "Sesnem in Elsasz", d. 24 Mar. 1798.

309. KRESS, JOHANNES   67430 Diemeringen
    KRESS, HENRY (on Board)
    KRESS, CASPAR
    KRESS, CARL(S)
Neptune, 1752
S-H, I: 493

EUROPEAN RECORDS

Diemeringen Lutheran KB:
Johannes Kress, hatmaker at Diemeringen, first appears in the records there in 1734. His wife Maria Salome died 28 July 1749, aged 50 y. 4 mo., 23 days. Their children appear in the confirmation records:

    1. Johannes, conf. 1737. Notation by his confirmation record:
      "This young Kress went to America and died there in 1752;
      The father with his family to America in 1752."
    2. Barbara, conf. 1737 "Zog 1752 in American."
    3. Joh. Friedrich, conf. 1744; d. 2 Sept. 1759,
      single, age 33 years in Diemeringen.
    4. Joh. Henrich, conf. 1747
    5. Margaretha, conf. 1747
    6. Joh. Carl, b. 20 Nov. 1734, conf. 1750
    7. Johanna Christina b. 18 Aug. 1739
    8. Johanna Maria b. 5 June 1743

AMERICAN RECORDS

St. Michael's Lutheran KB, Germantown, Philadelphia co.:
Buried 5 Oct. 1752 - Johannes Kress, the hatmaker, died 4 Oct., aged 30
years. [This would be the son Johannes, conf. 1737. He died on the day of
the ship's arrival in Philadelphia]. It is possible that he preceded the other
family members to America. A Johannes Gress arrived on the [unnamed
ship] on 20 Oct. 1747 with others from the area (S-H, I: 369, 370).
At Germantown, Johannes Kroess, hatmaker, and wife Anna Magdalena, had
a daughter:
>   Anna Magdalena b. 14 July 1752, bp. 21 Aug. 1752
>   Sp.: Paulus Gensel and wife Anna Maria, Reformed.

Hocker, *German Settlers of Pennsylvania:* newspaper dated 1 Jan. 1755:
Johannes Kresz, on the Great Lehigh at Egypt, hatmaker; wife Catharina,
widow of Friedrich Eberhart [q.v.].

Rev. Daniel Schumacher's records:
Carl Kress and Juliana Drachsel sp. a child of Johann Peter Koch in 1759
at Lehigh Church.

Carl Kress and wife Catharina Margaretha had:
>   1. Elisabeth bp. 2 Oct. 1768; 12 weeks old, bapt. at Lehigh
>   Sp.: Philipp Ecker & Apollonia Dreisbach
>   2. Catharina Margaretha b. 11 Mar. 1770; bp. 17 June 1770, Lehigh
>   Sp.: Valentin Sterry, Catharina Ecker

Philadelphia Will Book K: 19:
Johannes Gress, Germantown, Phila. co. 20 Aug. 1752 - 9 Nov. 1752
Wife: Anna Magdalena. Children: Elizabeth and Anna Magdalena.
Exrs. & Guardians: Wife and John Zachary, tanner at Germantown.
Wit: George Herger and John Theobald Ent.

310. KUHN, CHRISTOPH age 48   67690 Hatten
  KUHN, ADAM SIMON age 19
Hope, 1733
S-H, I: 116, 118, 119, 120, 121 Signed Cunn
  [Surname appears in lists as Kown, Kon, Kan, Cumm!]
  with Margrita Kon age 43, Efa Barbra Kan age 13, Anna Maria Kan age 9.

EUROPEAN RECORDS

Hatten Lutheran KB:
Joh. Christoph Kuhn, herdsman and *Schirmer*, Reformed, and wife
Margaretha nee Ruch, from Switzerland, had children:

1. Adam Simon b. ca 1714
2. Anna Rosina b. ca 1716, d. 21 June 1722, age 6 y., less 5 weeks.
3. Eva Barbara b. 8 Aug. 1719, bp. 10 Aug. 1719
4. Anna Maria b. 13 Dec. 1722, bp. 16 Dec.1722
5. Maria Margaretha b. 24 Aug. 1725, bp. 26 Aug. 1725
6. Maria Catharina b. 16 July 1728, bp. 18 July 1728
7. Maria Magdalena b. 29 Dec. 1731, bp. __ Feb. 1732
    Sp.: Georg Kuntz [q.v.], citizen and linenweaver;
    Margaretha, daughter of Joh. Heinrich Christ [q.v.]

AMERICAN RECORDS

Augustus Ev. Lutheran KB, Trappe, Montgomery co.:
Johan Adam Simon Kun m. 11 Dec. 1740 Anna Maria Sarina [?Sabina]
Schrack, youngest daughter of Hans Jacob Schrack and Euphrosina.

Moselem Lutheran KB, Berks co.:
Conrad Maneschmid, single son of Christian Maneschmid, m. 13 Mar. 1744
Anna Maria Kuhn, single daughter of Christoph Kuhn.

Paul Kepplinger, single son of Leonard Kepplinger, m. 23 Apr. 1750 Maria
Catharina Kuhn, single daughter of Christoph Kuhn. Children:
    1. Johann Christoph b. 19 June 1750, bp. 29 July 1750
    2. Maria Catharina b. 11 Dec. 1751, bp. 26 Dec. 1751
    3. Anna Maria b. 13 June 1754

Georg Kramer and Eva Barbara nee Kuhn had children:
    1. Joh. Christoph b. 26 Mar. 1744
        Sp.: Conrad Maneschmidt and Anna Maria
    2. Maria Barbara b. 11 Feb. 1746, bp. 23 Feb. 1746
        Sp.: Adam Simon Kuhn and Margaret Kuhn
    3. Maria Eva b. 26 Aug. 1748, bp. Dom. 20 Trin. 1748
        Sp.: Simon Adam Kuhn and Margaret Kuhn
    4. Anna Maria b. 17 Jan. 1752, bp. Cantate 1753

Berks County Adm.:
Christopher Kuhn, Maidencreek twp.: adm. granted on 6 Feb. 1754 to
Margaret Kuhn, the widow, and Adam Simon Kuhn, Esq. of Lancaster, the
eldest son.

Trinity Lutheran KB, Lancaster:
Dr. Adam Simon Kuhn and wife Maria Sabina had:
    1. Eva b. 8 Oct. 1744 bp. 14 Oct. 1744
        (Nyberg's records, Lancaster Moravian KB)

2. Johann Friederich b. 24 Aug. 1748, bp. 4 Sept. 1748
3. Daniel b. 14 Nov. 1750 bp. 18 Nov. 1750
4. Maria Sabina b. 18 Sept. 1755, bp. 5 Oct. 1755
5. Joh. Jacob b. 30 Oct. 1757, bp. 6 Nov. 1757
6. Hanna b. 13 Nov. 1761, bp. 22 Nov. 1761

311. KUNTZ, GEORG   67690 Hatten
Pennsylvania Merchant, 1732
S-H, I: 66, 67, 69, 70
    with Catharina Conce, Hans, Eva, and Catharine Conce

EUROPEAN RECORDS

Hatten Lutheran KB:
Meister Georg Kuntz, citizen and linenweaver, m. 11 June 1720 Catharina
Jäger, daughter of the late Johannes Jäger, former citizen at Rittershoffen
[Catharina Jäger was b. 1690, daughter of Hans Jäger and his wife Anna nee
Sommer.] They had children:
    1. Joh. Georg b. 15 Sept. 1722, d. 1724
        Sp.: Hans Georg Sebastian; Joh. Jacob Humpert; Catharina, wife
        of Christian Arn of Rittershoffen.
    2. Anna Eva b. 15 June 1724, bp. 18 June 1724
        Sp.: Hans Jacob Humpert, weaver; Catharina, wife of Christian
        Arn, Rittershoffen; Anna Eva nee Suter, wife of Hans Georg
        Sebastian.
    3. Johannes b. 22 July 1726, bp. 25 July 1726
        Sp.: Hans Henrich Christ; Hans Jörg Claus; Catharina,
        daughter of Valentin Humpert.
    4. Maria Catharina b. 26 Jan. 1729, bp. 27 Jan. 1729
        Sp.: Christoph Kuhn; Maria Catharina, wife of Jacob Gallmann;
        Maria Catharina, daughter of Conrad Ramiger, potter here.

AMERICAN RECORDS

Maryland Commission Book, 82, in *Maryland Historical Magazine,* **XXVI:
1931 and XXVIII: 1932:**
George Coontz, Planter of Baltimore Co., native of High Germany, nat. 4
June 1738, and his children John, Eva and Catharine.

Pennsylvania German Society, Sources and Documents, Vol. IV:
Notes on families:
Maria Eva Kuntz, daughter of Joh. Georg and Catharina Kuntz, m. 18 June
1739 Philip Morgenstorn, son of John and Juliana Morgenstern.

Adam Hubert (Huppert) ca. 1715-1781, arrived on the *Glasgow,* 1738, and m. 24 June 1744 Maria Catharina Kuntz (ca.1728-1812). His 150 A tract near Hanover was a gift from his father-in-law in 1745.

York co. Wills:
Catharine Coons, widow of John George Coons, dec'd. 9 June 1755-2 Feb. 1758. Heidelberg twp.; Children: John, dec'd; Eve Morningstar; Catherine Hoopert; Julianna, Francina, and Catherine, children of dec'd son John.
Exrs: Philip Sawer, George Ungafare.
Wit: Thomas M. Carney, Ludwig and Anne Mary Schriber.

St. Matthew's Lutheran KB, Hanover, York co.:
John Kuntz had children:
1. Juliana b. 2 Mar. 1747
    Sp.: Juliana Elisabetha Morgenstern
2. Frantzina b. 26 Apr. 1749, bp. 13 May 1749
    Sp.: Philipp Sauer and wife
3. Catharina Elisabeth b. 1751
    Sp.: Henry Büdinger and Elise Schreider
4. Louisa b. 25 Feb. 1753, bp. 12 Mar. 1753
    Sp.: Georg Spanseiler and wife

York County, Unrecorded Wills:
Johannes Kuntz [Original in German; two contemporary translations]
Dated 21 April 1753. Johannes Kuntz of Heidelberg Township. The child that marries first shall have the 150 acres of land at Pipe Creek, but the children shall be held equal in the judgment of impartial men. Wife shall continue housekeeping with servants and cattle and in everything as before. Wife can stay on this plantation whether she remains a widow or remarries. Cattle that wife raises shall be divided into four shares, one quarter for her and each child a quarter. If one of my youngest children or both should marry on the place and the men or women can not agree, then it shall be divided according to law. As to my mother's situation, things shall remain as my father ordered it in his will. All outstanding debts shall be collected and both the places paid off with that money. When the children marry, the household goods shall be divided as it seems good. Executors of my children: Philip Sower, George Ungefehr, and Ludwig Schreiber. Witnesses: Niclaus Hacken and Martin Ungefehr. Testator marked. Probated 1 June 1753, with witnesses making oath before George Stevenson, Deputy Register. [One translation by Geo. Lewis Leffler and other by Jno. Meem].

For additional data on this family, see Frederick S. Weiser, "John George Kuntz and the Conewago Settlement" in *Maryland Magazine of Genealogy,* 2(1979): 11-21.

312. KUNTZ, JOH. JACOB   67690 Hatten
Minerva, 1770
S-H, I: 729

EUROPEAN RECORDS

Hatten Lutheran KB:
Joh. Jacob Kuntz, linenweaver, son of Adam Kuntz m. __ ___ 1746 Anna
Eva Bastian, daughter of Hans Georg Bastian. They had children:
1. Maria Magdalena b. 31 Aug. 1747, died 1749
2. Joh. Jacob b. 18 Dec. 1748, died 1757
3. Joh. Heinrich b. 20 Jan. 1753
4. Maria Eva b. 20 Oct. 1754
5. Georg Jacob b. 19 Feb. 1758
6. Joh. Georg b. 19 Sept. 1760
7. Joh. Michel b. 2 Dec. 1763, died 1766

AMERICAN RECORDS

Salem Lutheran KB, Lebanon:
Buried 3 Feb. 1796- Jacob Kuns, born in Elsass, Germany in June 1718; bp.,
conf., and married twice, the first m. to Eva Bastian; by this marriage there
were three children. He m. (2) the widow Stupp. By this 2nd marriage
there were 3 more children born, 2 are living (1796).   Sickness:
Consumption. Aged 77 years, 7 months.

313. KUNTZ, JOHAN JACOB age 42   67110 Niederbronn-les-Bains
     KUNTZ, JOHAN JACOB age 21
Charming Nancy, 1738
S-H, I: 245, 247, 248

EUROPEAN RECORDS

Niederbronn Lutheran KB:
Johann Jacob Kuntz and wife Anna Margretha had children:
1. Joh. Jacob b. 3 June 1719
2. Joh. Bernhard b. 3 Dec. 1723
3. Christina b. 1 May 1727
4. Maria Catharina b. 13 Jan. 1730
5. Joh. Georg b. 10 Mar. 1734
6. Johannes bp. 8 Dec. 1736

Died 11 Jan. 1731 - Anna Catharina, widow of the late Johann Georg Cuntz,
citizen and *Gerichtsschöffen;* age 73 years less 25 weeks and 4 days.

Archives du Bas-Rhin, Document E 4367:
Jacob Kunz is listed in this document, on a list of emigrants from Niederbronn in 1738.

AMERICAN RECORDS

St. Joseph's (Oley Hills) Church, Pike twp., Berks co.:
Johann Jacob Kuntz, b. 19 Feb. 1692, son of the late Johann Georg Kuntz, a surgeon and barber of Niederbronn, and his wife Catharina, deceased, a daughter of the late Jacob Muller. In 1719 married Anna Margaretha, b. 22 Sept. 1695. She was a daughter of John Jacob Paltzgraff and his wife Greta; she died on the sea in 1738. In 1738 he came to America. They had children:
1. Jacob
2. Bernhard
3. Christina
4. Maria Cathar.
5. Anna Barbara [? not in Niederbronn record]
6. Joh. Georg
In 1742 he m. (2) Susanna b. __ 1711, daughter of Joh. Jacob Klein, linenweaver from Hangeweiler [Hangviller = 57370 Phalsbourg] in Alsace, and his wife Anna Catharina. She came to America 13 years ago without her parents [1754].

The daughter Maria Catharina Kuntz, b. 13 Jan. 1730, m. Cantate Sunday 1748 Johann Michel Klein, b. 1715, son of Jacob and Anna Catharina Klein from Hangeweiler [Hangviller=57370 Phalsbourg]. His first wife was Anna Maria, daughter of Joh. and Elisabeth Steinmann. They were m. in 1740, and came to America in 1741. Children of his first marriage:
1. Daniel, died at sea, age 3 weeks, 2 days.
2. John b. Oct. 1742
3. Daniel b. 5 June 1744
Anna Maria nee Steinmann Klein d. 1747.
Children of the second marriage to Maria Catharina Kuntz:
4. Maria Magdalena b. 28 Aug. 1749
5. Maria Christina b. 3 days before Simon Judae 1751
6. Susanna b. 23 Dec. 1754
  Sp.: George Kuntz, single; Christina, single daughter of Jacob Müller[q.v.]; Christina, single daughter of Conrad Böhm.
7. Joh. Michael b. 6 Nov. 1757
8. Joh. Georg b. 24 Feb. 1760

George Kuntz and wife Elizabeth Greta had children:
1. Maria Barbara b. 13 Apr. 1757, bp. 27 May 1757
  Sp.: Joh. Bernt Kuntz; and Maria Barbara,

wife of Michael Neuhart, grandmother.
2. Friedrich b. 25 Sept. 1765, bp. 27 Oct. 1765
   Sp.: Friedrich Neuhard; Simon Stauch; Magdalena Klein.

Communicants list, 8 Sept. 1754:
John Jacob Kuntz, wife Susanna, son John George.

New Hanover Lutheran KB, Montgomery co.:
Conf. 1744: Maria Catharina Kuhnz, Catharina Barbara Kuhnz, Johann
Jacob Kuhnz's daughters.

Trappe Lutheran KB, Montgomery co.:
Johann Bernhard Kuhnz m. 1745, in the Oley Mountains, Catharina
Elisabeth Eberhard(in) [q.v.].

Jordan Lutheran KB, Lehigh co.:
Bernhard Kuntz and wife Anna Catharina had:
1. Johann Friedrich b. 16 Nov. 1745
2. Joh. Philipp b. 1 Apr. 1747
3. Anna Catharina b. 17 June 1749

For additional data on this Kuntz family, see:
Frieda Krueger Ewing, "Kuntz/Cuntz of Niederbronn, Alsace" in *The Palatine Immigrant*, Vol. XV no. 4 (winter 1990-91), p. 179-182.

Bernard Kuhns, Lehi twp., Northampton co., nat. Autumn 1765.

KUNTZ see also CUNTZ

314. KUNTZMAN, LORENTZ   67110 Niederbronn-les-Bains
Edinburgh, 1751   Gundershoffen=
S-H, I: 460   67110 Niederbronn-les-Bains

EUROPEAN RECORDS

Niederbronn Lutheran KB:
Lorentz Kuntzman, weaver, and wife Anna Barbara had children:
1. Joh. Philip bp. 10 Mar. 1712
2. Philip Jacob bp. 10 May 1714
3. probably Lorentz (bp-Jan) 1725 [page torn]

Gundershoffen Lutheran KB:
Lorentz Cuntzmann, single, *Weberknapp* from Niederbronn, son of the late

Lorentz Cuntzmann, former citizen and weaver there, m. 11 Feb. 1749 Eva Barbara, daughter of Niclaus Lindemann [q.v.], citizen at Griesbach.

315. KUNTZMAN, PHILIP JACOB   Windstein=
Britannia, 1767   67110 Niederbronn-les-Bains
S-H, I: 716
EUROPEAN RECORDS

Niederbronn Lutheran KB:
[There are no marriages available on micorfilm for Niederbronn, but an entry in the Langensoultzbach KB indicates that Reinhard Cuntzmann's wife was Anna Margaretha nee Leininger, and describes him as a linenweaver from Niederbronn.]
Reinhard Cuntzman and wife Margaretha had children:
1. Joh. Jacob b. 21 Nov. 1730
2. Johannes b. __ Feb. 1732
3. **Ph(ilip)s Jacob** b. 14 Apr. 1734
4. Maria Margretha b. 27 Feb. 1737
5. Johannes b. __ Oct. 1738, bp. 14 Oct. 1738

Langensoultzbach Lutheran KB:
Philipp Jacob Cuntzmann, tailor and *Erbestander auff dem Windstein* and his wife Maria Catharina nee Kyburt had children:
1. Margaretha Elisabetha b. 28 Apr. 1759, bp. 1 May 1759
2. Maria Barbara b. 3 June 1762
     Sp.: Joh. Georg Gütinger, Jägerthal; Georg Ludwig Schwally, son of Peter Schwally of Grünthal; Maria Barbara, daughter of the late Reinhard Cuntzmann, linenweaver at Niederbronn; Esther Elisabetha Breysach, daughter of Ludwig Breysach of Leizelthal.
3. Maria Catharina (twin) b. 19 Aug. 1765
4. Maria Salome (twin) b. 19 Aug. 1765, d. 28 Feb. 1766
     One of the sponsors of the twins was Maria Cleophe nee Herzog, wife of Johann Daniel Kyburt, day laborer *auf dem Windstein.*

AMERICAN RECORDS

St. Michael's and Zion KB, Philadelphia:
Philip Jacob Cuntzman and Maria Catharina had:
5. Maria Salome b. 6 July 1767 (Rec. with Feb. 1768 bp.)
     bp. 19 July 1767 at sea
     Sp.: Maria Salome Newschwender [q.v.]; Peter Schind; Maria Margreth Rimelin
6. Philip b. 16 Aug. 1771, bp. 15 Sept. 1771. Sp.: Parents

Buried 27 June 1795: Philip Jacob Kunsman, b. 15 Apr. 1734 at Niederbronn-les-Bains, son of Joh. Reinhard and Margaretha Kunsman. Married
Maria Catharina and had eight children.

316. KÜSTER, LUDWIG   Durstel=
Neptune, 1752   67320 Drulingen
S-H, I: 493   Oberbronn=
also on ship: Jerg Phillips Küster[q.v.]   67110 Niederbronn-les-Bains

EUROPEAN RECORDS

Oberbronn Lutheran KB:
Johannes Küster, citizen and master shoemaker, and wife Susanna had a son:
    Johann Ludwig b. 1 Dec. 1688, bp. 3 Dec. 1688

Durstel Lutheran KB:
Johann Ludwig Kister m. 1717 Maria Susanna Schneider from Asswiller
[=67320 Drulingen]. Ludwig Kister d. 12 July 1747 in Durstel. His widow
Maria Susanna d. 12 Aug. 1770. They had children:
    1. A son (no further record)
    2. Johann Jacob bp. 16 Feb. 1721, m. 13 May 1751 Maria Catharina,
       daughter of Joh. Philip Entzminger of Adamswiller [= 67320
       Drulingen]
    3. **Johann Ludwig** b. 18 Sept. 1723, bp. 19 Sept. 1723, conf. 1740
    4. Maria Christina bp. 29 Dec. 1728, conf. 1742
    5. Maria Elisabeth bp. 31 Mar. 1731
    6. Georg Philip b. 25 Sept. 1733, bp. 27 Sept. 1733.
       Conf. 1747 [q.v.]
    7. Johann Martzloff b. 26 Aug. 1737, bp. 28 Aug. 1737

Ludwig Kister, shoemaker, son of the late Ludwig Kister, former shoemaker
at Durstel, m. 4 Nov. 1748 Eva Christina, daughter of the late Caspar
Antoni, wheelwright at Betschweiler [?68620 Bitschwiller or Bettwiller].
They had a son:

    1. Johann Georg Philip b. 8 Feb. 1749, bp. 9 Feb. 1749
       in the Bettwiller Church [Bettwiller = 67320 Drulingen].

Waldhambach Lutheran KB:
Ludwig Küster, shoemaker at Volksberg, and wife Eva Catharina (Christina
in some records) nee Anthoni had children:
    2. Maria Margaretha b. 29 July 1750
    3. Johann Ludwig b. 18 Jan. 1752

AMERICAN RECORDS

Rev. Daniel Schumacher's records:
Martzeloff Küster and wife Rahall had a son:
> Johann Ludewig b. 3 Mar. 1769 bp. 26 Mar. 1769, "across the
> Lehigh". Sp.: Ludewigh Küster and Elisabeth Dieterin,
> both single.

Ludewig Küster and wife Catharina had:
> Susanna b. 24 Mar. 1769, bp. 16 Apr. at Lehigh
> Sp.: Johannes Sylvius and wife Anna

> Johann Georg b. 30 Jan. 1771, bp. 24 Mar. 1771, Lehigh
> Sp.: Jürg Anthon and Catharina Eckern, single

Margaretha Küster, single, and Jurg Eisemann [q.v.] sp. a child of Jacob
Keppell [q.v.] in 1770 in Lehigh. She also sp. a child of Jurg Ecker [q.v.] in
1770.

Ludewigh Küster and Anna Catharina Eisemann, single, sp. a child of Jacob
Keppell in 1772, Lehigh.

Confirmed 29 Apr. 1770, across the Lehigh in the church on Indian land,
Lehigh twp: Peter Küster and Eva Christina Küstern

Rev. Daniel Schumacher's records:
Ludewigh Kuster and Eva Christina had:
> Jürg Jacob b. __ Feb. 1760

Indianland (St. Paul's) Lutheran KB, Lehigh twp.:
Ludwig Küster and wife Eva Christina had:
> Maria Salome bp. 12 Jan. 1764
> Sp.: Peter Altman and ?Susanna; Maria Salome Neihart

Northampton co. Wills:
Ludwig Kuester, Lehigh twp., yeoman, 11 Dec. 1786- 29 Jan. 1787.
Wife: Catharina. Exrs: Peter Anthony, Jr. and Conrad Herman, of Lehigh
twp., yeoman. Wit: Conrad Herman and P. Anthony, Sr.

The will indicates a large family by two wives, including children by the
second wife Catharine who are yet under age of 14. His estate is to be
leased to his son Johann Nicholas. Another son George is also named in
the will. The Exrs. named in the will renounced their right to administer

and sons Johann Nicholas and Peter were named as adm. The estate accounts name the following additional children: Philip, Ludwig, Jacob, Margaret, Christina, and Salome.

At least three of these children settled in Westmoreland co. The oldest son (Johann George Philip, b. 1749 in Bettwiller) was commonly known as Philip. Philip Köster and wife Elisabetha have several children bp. in Westmoreland co. from 1779-1789 (see Paul Miller Ruff, *The German Church Records of Westmoreland County, PA,* 1772-1791, Vol. 1 (1979). Ludwig Köster and wife Catharina Margaretha also appear in these records, having children bp. 1775-1787. Salome Köster had two children baptized in Westmoreland co.

317. KÜSTER, JERG PHILLIPS   Durstel=
Neptune, 1752   67320 Drulingen
S-H, I: 493

EUROPEAN RECORDS

Durstel Lutheran KB:
Johann Ludwig Kister and wife Maria Susanna nee Schneider had a son:
      Georg Philip b. 25 Sept. 1733, bp. 27 Sept. 1733. Conf. 1747
      [See his brother Ludwig Küster for additional family data].

AMERICAN RECORDS

Old Goshenhoppen Lutheran KB, Montgomery co.:
Philip Kister, Lutheran, single, born 1733, father: Ludwig Kister, deceased; mother: Susanna, from Dorstel in Alsace, 14 hours from Strasburg. Came to America in 1752, servant at Rudolph (Herbe?) at Skippack. Married Anna Maria, single, Lutheran, 25 years of age, father: Philip Tetisman, deceased; came to America 1731, was servant at John Schneiders. Banns published: 1) 5 Oct. in Old Goshenhoppen; 2) 12 Oct. in Oley Hills; 3) 19 Oct. in Old Goshenhoppen. Married 30 Oct. 1755.

318. LAMBERT, JACOB   67510 Lembach
Sally, 5 Oct. 1767
S-H, I: 715

EUROPEAN RECORDS

Lembach Catholic KB:
Jacobus Lambert, son of Joseph Lambert, citizen and *Fabrilignarii,*
(carpenter) and his deceased wife Apoloniae nee Hugler, m. 6 Apr. 1751
Maria Schraeckler, daughter of the late Ottmann Schraeckler and his wife
Christina Knoblin. Wit: Michael Habach, *incola* (inhabitant) in Lembach,
Christianus Sambtmann, *Sartor* Josephus Rehm.
   [signature in S-H, II: pg 821 matches signature in KB by marriage].

Joseph Lambert d. in Nov. 1762.

AMERICAN RECORDS

1790 Census, Bedford co.:
One Jacob Lambert, 1 male over 16.
1790 Census, Cumru twp., Berks co.:
Another Jacob Lampert, 2 males over 16, 3 males under 16, 3 females.

319. LANGENECKER, PETER   67110 Niederbronn-les-Bains
probably died on voyage
possible on *Charming Nancy,* 1738

EUROPEAN RECORDS

Niederbronn Lutheran KB:
Ulrich ?Langenecker, born in Aschen in Bern [? CH 3549 Aeschau, BE or
?CH 3703 Aeschi] d. 21 Jan. 1730, age 30 years less 22 weeks and 1 day.

Joh. Peter Langenecker and wife Anna Eva had children:
   1. Joh. Jacob b. 20 Jan. 1725
   2. Maria Salome b. 13 Oct. 1727
   3. Catharina Barbara b. 7 Jan. 1732

Archives du Bas-Rhin, Document E 4367:
Peter Langenecker is listed in this document, on a list of emigrants from
Niederbronn in 1738.

AMERICAN RECORDS

Philadelphia Adm. Book D, pg. 84, #37 - Letters of Adm. to Barbara
Longacre, widow, county of Philadelphia, adm. of Peter Longacre, deceased.
18 May 1739.

A Jacob Longacre of Coventry twp., Chester co., nat. 11 Apr. 1763.

320. LAU, JOH. PETER   67510 Lembach
   LAU, DAVID
before 1749
Not in S-H
EUROPEAN RECORDS

Lembach Lutheran KB:
Diebold Lau and wife Margaretha had a son:
        Hans Peter b. 11 Apr. 1701, bp. 14 Apr. 1701

Hans Peter Law, single tailor, son of Hans Theobald Law, *Hoffman* at
Sultzthal, m. 5 May 1721 Maria Elisabetha, daughter of the late Samuel
Guthman, former citizen and baker at Strassburg [67000 Strasbourg].
Children, surname Lau in baptismal records:
        1. Johann Jacob b. 14 Dec. 1722, bp. 16 Dec. 1722
        2. Joh. David b. 7 Jan. 1724
        3. Maria Elisabetha b. 7 May 1725, bp. 10 May 1725
        4. Hans Peter b. 9 Feb. 1727, bp. 11 Feb. 1727
        5. Maria Catharina b. 31 Dec. 1727, died young
        6. Margaretha b. 11 Mar. 1731, bp. 13 Mar. 1731
        7. Joh. Peter b. 8 Feb. 1736, bp. 10 Feb. 1736
        8. Catharina Elisabetha b. 9 Sept. 1738

Langensoultzbach Lutheran KB:
Joh. Peter Lau, day laborer at Cappenwoog, and wife Maria Elisabetha nee
Gutmann had:
        9. Maria Magdalena b. 12 Jan. 1741
           [Marginal note in KB by her bp: "Went to Pennsylvania"
           - no year given]

AMERICAN RECORDS

Christ Lutheran KB, York:
David Lau was a sp. in 1749.

Maria Elisabetha Lau m. 26 May 1749 Georg Albrecht.

One Peter Lau also appears in the York records in 1749; he may be a son of one of the earlier Low emigrants.

Dover Lutheran KB, York co.:
Georg Philip Gensler m. 17 Nov. 1767 Maria Magdalena, daughter of Peter Lau.

St. David's (Sherman's) KB, York co: in *Der Reggeboge* Vol. II, No. 2 (1977) David Lau and wife Anna Maria were sp. in 1752 for a child of Johan Nicholas Wolfgang.

David Lauh and Anna Maria had:
1. A son died 1753
2. Maria Magdal(ena) b. 25 Mar. 1753, bp. 23 Apr. 1753
   Sp.: Jacob Hauck, Cath. Götzin, both single
3. Samuel bp. 6 Apr. 1755, aged 3 days
   Sp.: Hans Georg Vogelmann, Catharine Götz

Catharina Elisabetha Lawin was a sp. in 1755 for a child of Joh. Nicolaus Wolfgang.

In 1752, David Lau obtained a MD warrant for a tract called *Long Hill* just south of Sherman's Church.

David Law, Orange co., N.C., nat. in PA 10/11 Apr. 1761.

321. LAZARUS, MARTIN   Ingolsheim=
Sandwich, 1750   67250 Soultz-sous-Forêts
S-H, I: 450 [appears on list as Nazarus - did not sign]
  Arrived with stepfather Peter Schmidt.

EUROPEAN RECORDS

Birlenbach Lutheran KB, Rott Lutheran KB, and Hunspach Reformed KB:
Philip Lazarus from Guntershoffen [Gundershoffen = 67110 Niederbronn-les-Bains] m. 27 Jan. 1728 Anna Barbara Bürger from Ingelsheim. They were married at Hunspach. Children:
1. **Johann Martin** bp. 24 Oct. 1728
   Sp.: Hans Martin Hüller; Martin Rott; Catharina Gucker.
   [Birlenbach]
2. Hans Georg bp. 30 Jan. 1730: [Birlenbach];
   conf. 1743 [Rott Lutheran KB].
3. Anna Maria b. 21 Feb. 1731, bp. 25 Feb. 1731

[Hunspach Ref. KB]; conf. 1744
4. Maria Barbara b. 28 May 1732; bp. 1 June 1732;
   conf. 1746 [Hunspach Ref KB].

Johann Peter Schmidt [q.v.], widower from Niederrodern [= 67470 Seltz],
m. 19 Feb. 1743 Anna Barbara, widow of the late Philip Lazarus, former
citizen at Ingelsheim.

Zweibruecken Manumissions Protocoll, Clee- and Catharinenburg, 1750:
Peter Schmidt of Ingelsheim leaves with wife and 6 children for America.

AMERICAN RECORDS

Rev. Daniel Schumacher's records:
Martin Lazarus and wife Christina had:
   1. Leonhard bp. 14 June 1761, age 1½, in Salisbury.
      Sp.: Parents

Dryland Lutheran and Reformed KB, Nazareth twp., Northampton co.:
Martin Lazaras and wife Christina had:
   2. Catharina Barbara b. 13 Sept. (?1763), bp. 22 Apr. 1764
      Sp.: John Claus and Catharina

Northampton co. Wills:
Martin Lazarus, Allen twp. __ July 1797 - 20 July 1797.
Exrs: Leonora [?Leonhard] Lazarus, George Ehret.
Wit: Casper Ritter, John Daniel Young

Martin Lazarus is mentioned as a stepson in the will of Peter Schmit [q.v.]

322. LEDERMAN, DIEBOLD   Mattstall= 67510 Lembach
James Goodwill, 1727
S-H, I: 10, 11
   [6 in family]
EUROPEAN RECORDS

Lembach Lutheran KB:
Hans Theobald Ledermann of Mattstall and wife Anna Maria nee Engler
had children:
   1. Hans Peter b. 18 Sept. 1711 [q.v.]
   2. Maria Ursula b. 17 Apr. 1714, died
   3. Twin - stillborn daughter b. 17 Apr. 1714
   4. Catharina Barbara b. 25 Jan. 1716

Langensoultzbach Lutheran KB:
Hans Diebold Lederman and wife Maria nee Engel had:
  5. Hans Daniel bp. 6 Nov. 1718
  6. Johann Melchior bp. 23 Apr. 1721
  7. Anna Catharina bp. 17 May 1723

Dehlingen Lutheran KB:
Hans Theobald Lederman, linenweaver *aus der Elsass*, and wife Maria Engel
had a son:
  8. Johann Nickel bp. 7 Sept. 1724

AMERICAN RECORDS

Rev. John Casper Stoever's Records, (unpublished early records):
Theobaldt Ledermann in Falckner Schwamm had a son:
  8. Johann Christian b. 27 Aug. 1730, bp. 4 Oct. 1730
     Sp.: Christian Muller and wife Veronica

One Peter Lederman, Heidelberg twp., Lancaster co., nat. 24 Sept. 1762.
[see also Jacob Lederman of Kirberg who also had a son Peter.]

323. LEDERMANN, HANS PETER age 18   Mattstall=
Britannia, 1731   67510 Lembach
S-H, I: 48, 52, 53

EUROPEAN RECORDS

Mattstall Lutheran KB:
Hans Theobald Ledermann, [q.v.] weaver in Mattstall, and wife Anna Maria
nee Engler had children:
  1. **Hans Peter** b. 16 Sept. 1711, bp. 20 Sept. 1711
     Sp: Nicolaus Hertzog son of Hans Michel Hertzog, citizen at
     Schweichhausen [=67590 Schweighouse-sur-Moder] Hans Peter
     Knobell son of Mstr. Peter Knobell of Mattstall, Reformed
     religion, and Christina Schleber daughter of Hans Hennrich
     Schleber, of Mattstall
  2. Maria Ursula b. 18 (month faded) 1714; died 1714
  3. Stillborn child, twin to Maria Ursula
     Sp: Hans Theobald Hördt; Anna Ursula wife of Hans Wittmar,
     herdsman there; Maria Barbara, daughter of Peter Knobell,
     citizen and Zimmermann there.
  4. Catharina Barbara b. 25 Jan. 1716, bp. 28 Jan. 1716
     Sp: Hans Hennrich Trautmann single son of Hennrich
     Trautmann, citizen and innkeeper of Mattstall; Maria Barbara

Knobel, daughter of Peter Knobel, carpenter; Maria Catharina, daughter of Christoph Trautmann, citizen here.

324. LEDERMAN, JACOB age 32   Kirrberg=
Lydia, 1741   67320 Drulingen
S-H, I: 301, 302, 303

EUROPEAN RECORDS

Diedendorf Reformed KB:
Hans Ulrich Lederman from Ruffshaussen, Canton Bern [possibly CH-3204 Rosshäusern, BE], son of Hans Jacob Lederman, m. 4 Feb. 1705 Elisabeth, daughter of the late David Forny from Heilgeringen [Hellering= 57930 Fénétrange].
Hans Ulrich Lederman, carpenter from Rauwiller, and wife Elisabetha Fournier had a son:
    Jacob bp. 21 Aug. 1707
    Sp.: Paul Girardin, Rauwiller; Christoffel Keller;
    Rachel Gyllemin and Maria Fournier.

Ulrich Lederman d. 21 Mar. 1739 in Kirberg, age 69 y.

Rauwiller Reformed KB:
Jacob Lederman of Kirberg and wife Anna Maria nee Schneider had children:
    1. Joh. Peter bp. 14 Aug. 1729
    2. Joh. David bp.6 Jan. 1731
    3. Anna Maria bp. 24 Nov. 1737

Verification of this emigration supplied by Dr. Bernd Gölzer, from the county records of Nassau-Saarwerden, compiled by Dr. Gerhard Hein:
Records of Saarwerden county office for Kirberg: dated 17 May 1743, inventory of Joseph Schneider, linenweaver of Kirberg: the daughter Anna Maria and her husband have moved to America with permission of the government in the year 1741.

AMERICAN RECORDS

Berks County Wills:
Jacob Lederman, Tulpehocken, 10 Aug. 1762- 2 Oct. 1762.
Wife: Maria to have 1/3 of personal estate. All real estate to son Peter and son-in-law Jacob Walter in equal shares. Exr: Jacob Walter.
Wit: Benjamin Spycker and George Schissler.

Peter Lederman, Tulpehocken, 4 June 1801- 17 Aug. 1801.
Wife: Catharine Elisabeth. Exr. to sell plantation and est. divided into 5 shares for children: deceased son Peter's children, Peter, John and Catharine; daughter Barbara wife of Andrew Braucher; daughter Catharine wife of Thomas Gerhart; daughter Margaretha wife of John Braucher; daughter Christina wife of Adam Wolf. Exr: son-in-law Andrew Braucher.
Wit: George Laux and Leonard Seltzer.

Peter Lederman, Heidelberg twp., Lancaster co., nat. 24 Sept. 1762.

325. LEHMANN, PHILIP JACOB   Hunspach=
_____, 1752   67250 Soultz-sous-Forêts
                        EUROPEAN RECORDS

Hunspach Reformed KB:
Philip Jacob Lehemann, son of the late Nicklaus Lehemann from Niederhorbach [= W-6749 Niederhorbach] m. 18 Apr. 1741 *Anna* Barbara, daughter of the late Bernhardt Zimmermann.

Conf. 1734 - Anna Barbara, dau. of Bernhard Zimmermann, citizen here.

The Hunspach church, south of Wissembourg, has Reformed records from 1681.

Philip Jacob Lehemann and *Maria* Barbara had:
1. Maria Salome b. 11 Apr. 1742, bp. 15 Apr. 1742
2. Johann Adam b. 18 May 1744, bp. 20 May 1744
3. Johann Bernhardt b. 21 Jan. 1747, bp. 22 Jan. 1747

Zweibrücken Manumissions Protocoll, Clee- and Catharinenburg, 1752:
Philips Jacob Lehmann of Hunspach leaves for America.

AMERICAN RECORDS

Frederick Reformed KB, Frederick, MD:
Confirmations, undated list, probably 1756:
  Salome Leman, age 15.

Philip Jacob Lehmann and wife Barbara had:
    4. Susanna, bp. (no specific date) 1753
       Sp.: Johan Neef and Susanna
    5. Clara bp. 21 Oct. 1759; conf. 1776
       Sp.: Friedrich Holtzmann and wife Clara
    6. Jacob b. 21 Mar. 1764, bp. 22 Apr 1764; conf. 1781
       Sp.: Jacob Froschauer and wife.

Colonial Maryland Naturalizations:
Jacob Leahman of Frederick Co., German, a member of Reformed Church,
Fredericktown, nat. 28 Sept. 1762.

326. LEININGER, HANS JACOB   Griesbach=
Phoenix, 1750   67110 Niederbronn-les-Bains
S-H, I: 441

EUROPEAN RECORDS

Gundershoffen Lutheran KB:
Hanns Georg Leininger and wife Maria Ursula had:
    Johann Jacob b. 10 Mar. 1722, bp. 12 Mar. 1722

Hans Jacob Leininger, son of Hans Georg Leininger, citizen at Griesbach,
m. 4 Jan. 1742 Anna Elisabetha, daughter of Diebold Amman. Children:
    1. Hans Georg bp. 11 Dec. 1742
    2. Michael bp. 7 Sept. 1744
    3. Maria Elisabetha bp. 18 Mar. 1746
    4. Joh. Michael b. 13 Apr. 1748, bp. 15 Apr. 1748
[the father's signature by this last baptismal entry is a perfect match with the
immigrant's signature in S-H, II: 512.]

AMERICAN RECORDS

Christ Tulpehocken Lutheran KB, Berks co.:
Jacob Leininger and wife Elisabeth had:
     5. Joh. Stephanus b. 3 Oct. 1751, bp. 13 Oct. 1751
       Sp.: Joh. Georg Mallo [q.v.] and wife.

Jacob Leuninger(in) [sic] sp. a child of Joh. Georg Mallo in 1752.

Stephen Leininger, single son of Jacob Leininger, m. 26 Feb. 1771 Philippine
Specht, daughter of Martin Specht. Both from Heidelberg twp.
Wit: Ludwig Fisher, Sr., after proclamation.

Johannes Leininger, son of Jacob Leininger in Heidelberg twp., Berks co.,
m. 24 Dec. 1776 Margreth Miller, daughter of Pet. Miller in Heidelberg twp.,
Lancaster co.

Peter Leininger, single son of Jacob Leininger, m. 23 June 1778 Christina
Wenrich, daughter of Matheus Wenrich.

Christian Schenckel, single son of Carl Schenckel from Heidelberg twp., m.
8 Aug. 1780 Maria Magdalena Leininger, single daughter of Jacob Leininger.

Berks co. Wills & Adm.:
Jacob Leininger, Heidelberg. 11 Nov. 1797 - 2 Nov. 1802.
Provides for wife and divides estate among eight children, none named
except Peter to whom he had sold his plantation. Son-in-law John Palm,
Exr. Wit: Daniel Groff, William Wood.

St. Daniel's Cemetery, Heidelberg twp., Berks co.:
Catharina nee Leininger
b. 11 Mar. 1760, d. 18 Oct. 1820
Married to John Palm.

Peter Leininger
b. 21 Sept. 1766, d. 11 Sept. 1835

Berks Wills:
Jacob Leininger, Womelsdorf. 31 May 1812 - 13 June 1812.
Wife: Elisabeth. Children, who are not named. Wife and son Peter, Exrs.
Wit: John Smith, George Ulrich.

Stephen Leininger, Bern twp., Adm. 10 Aug. 1820 to son George and
Michael Nunemacher, son-in-law, the widow renouncing.

327. LEISER, BENEDICT   Burbach=
    LEISER, HANS MICHAEL   67260 Sarre-Union
    LEISER, NICHOLAS
Robert & Alice, 1739
S-H, I: 264, 267, 268, 271

EUROPEAN RECORDS

Diedendorf Reformed KB:
Benedict Leiser from Burbach, and wife Barbara nee Isch first appear in the
Diedendorf KB in 1719. They had children born elsewhere before their
arrival in Burbach. There is a Benedict Leiser, herdsman at Pistorff, who is
mentioned as having been born in Schünenberg, Canton Bern [there are
three Schönenbergs in Switzerland]. His wife is named Barbara nee Jacki.
They may be identical.
Benedict Leiser and wife Barbara nee Isch had sons:
1. Nickel, bp. not located there, mentioned as a sp. at a baptism
   in 1738, occupation tailor.
2. Benedict, bp. not located there, conf. 1730
3. Johann Michael bp. 22 Jan. 1719, conf. 1734
   Sp.: Herr Michael Marx, innkeeper at Burbach; Johann Nicolaus
   Marx; Anna Maria, daughter of Melchior Guth, *Hoffman* at Berg.
4. Anna Elisabetha bp. 20 June 1723
5. Johannetta Anna bp. 25 Sept. 1725
6. Philipp Jacob b. 16 Dec. 1727
7. Maria Barbara b. 4 Feb. 1731
8. Anna Eva b. 26 Aug. 1736

AMERICAN RECORDS

St. Joseph's Lutheran KB, Oley Hills, Berks Co.:
Benedictus Leser and wife Margaretha were sp. in 1756 for a child of
Friedrich Bats.

Michael Lieser and wife Maria Elisabetha were sp. in 1765 for a child of
George Rorbag [Rohrbach] and wife Elizabeth .

Berks County Wills:
Benedict Leeser, Hereford, 19 Feb. 1772- 12 Aug. 1772.
Wife Margaretha to have all estate until youngest child is 21 then all shall
be sold, and after provision for wife, all children to have equal shares, of
whom eldest son Joseph only is named. Brother Samuel Leeser and friend
Michael Bower, executors. Witness: Balthaser Zimmerman and Christopher
Schultz.

Berks County Wills:
Michael Leeser, Hereford, 28 May 1774- 9 Aug. 1774.
Wife Elisabeth to have the direction of all estate until the youngest child is
of age, when eldest son, Benedict shall have land at appraisal value, except
26 acres of the lower part that the youngest son, John, shall have as
appraised; son Benedict shall provide for son Philip who is blind.   All
children to have equal shares. Wife Elisabeth and son Benedict executors.
Witness: Jacob Miller and Balzer Simmerman.

328. LENTZ, JOH. SEBASTIAN   Postroff=
Edinburg, 14 Sept. 1753   57930 Fénétrange
S-H, I: 522, 524

EUROPEAN RECORDS

Hirschland Lutheran KB:
Hans Petrus Lens [elsewhere Lentz] and wife Anna Magdalena from Postorff
had a son:
    Joh. Sebastian b. 26 Aug. 1735
A notation by his baptismal record: "went to America 1753"

AMERICAN RECORDS

St. Joseph's (Oley Hills) Lutheran KB, Pike twp., Berks co.:
Bastian Lentz and wife (not named) had a daughter:
    Anna Catharine bp. 15 Aug. 1776

Christ Lutheran KB (Mertz's), Bieber Creek, Berks co:
Bastian Lentz and wife Marcretha had children:
    1. Peter b. 29 Mar. 1762, bp. 8 Apr. 1762
       Sp.: Peter Klein and Catharina Bechtel
    2. Dewald b. 26 June 1766, bp. 20 July 1766
       Sp.: Dewald Lentz and Maria Klein
    3. Adam b. 2 May 1768, bp. 22 May 1768
       Sp.: Adam Hartmann and wife Gertraut.

Dewald Lentz and wife Elisabetha had:
    1. Anna Marcretha b. 10 Jan. 1768, bp. 13 Jan. 1768
       Sp.: Marcretha Lentz.

Bastian Lentz, Rockland twp., Berks co., nat. Autumn, 1765.

329. LEYENBERGER, FRANTZ   Kirrberg=
Robert and Alice, 1739   67320 Drulingen
S-H, I: 263, 267, 270

EUROPEAN RECORDS

Diedendorf Reformed KB and Rauwiller Reformed KB:
Frantz Leyenberger, schoolmaster at Kirberg, and wife Elisabeth Quarter
[also Quartner] had children:
1. Joh. Conrad bp. 26 Apr. 1722
2. Maria Elisabetha bp. 15 Aug. 1725 Kirberg
3. Joh. Georg bp. 5 Jan. 1727
4. Nikolaus bp. 31 Oct. 1728
5. Maria Susanna bp. 1 May 1730
6. Johannes bp. 2 Sept. 1731
7. Maria Elisabeth bp. 2 May 1733
8. Maria Eva bp. 22 Mar. 1735
9. Joh. Jacob bp. 9 Dec. 1736
10. Moritz bp. 17 Dec. 1738

AMERICAN RECORDS

Host Reformed KB, Berks co.:
Franz Layenberger was a sp. in 1748 for a child of Christoph Heddrich.

F. G. Livingood, *Eighteenth Century Reformed Church Schools.* **Proceedings of the Pennsylvania German Society, Vol. 38 (1930): 82:**
Host (Tulpehocken) Reformed church school: the first schoolmaster referred to by name is Francis Layenberger who served during Boehm's second ministry, 1735-1744.

Rev. John Casper Stoever's Records:
John Frantz Leyenberger and wife were sp. in 1750 for a child of Jacob Schopff (Northkill).

Nicolaus Leyenberger was sp. in 1751 for a child of Michael Aver (Altalaha) and also in 1751 for a child of Joh. Nicolaus Fringer (Tulpehocken).

330. LIEBENGUTH, HANS JACOB age 39   Schalkendorf=
Richard and Elizabeth, 1733   67350 Pfaffenhoffen
S-H, I: 127, 129, 130 [Lebegut on list]
Other passengers on ship: Margaretha age 40, Joh Jacob 10, Anna Gretha 10, Anna Catharina 3 ½

EUROPEAN RECORDS

Ringendorf Lutheran KB:
Hans Georg Artzt, single linenweaver, son of Hans Georg Artzt, *Gerichts and Marckschöffen* m. 22 Nov. 1681 Anna Rosina, daughter of the late Georg Vogel, former linenweaver. They had a daughter:
Anna Margaretha bp. 6 Apr. 1688

Obermodern Lutheran KB:
Hans Peter Liebenguth, son of the late Hans Liebenguth, former citizen at Schalkendorff [=67350 Pfaffenhoffen], m. 24 Nov. 1695 Margaretha, daughter of Hans Caspar Quirin, citizen at Rothbach [=67340 Ingwiller]. Their son:
1. Hans Jacob bp. _ Jan. 1698

Hans Jacob Liebenguth, son of Hans Peter Liebenguth m. 30 Jan. 1720 Anna Margretha, daughter of the late Hans Georg Artzt of Ringendorff. They had:
1. Elisabetha b. 28 Jan. 1721; died 1721
2. Anna Margaretha b. 5 May 1722
3. Anna Barbara b. 6 Nov. 1723, bp. 9 Nov. 1723

Johann Jacob Liebengutt, citizen and widower here, m. 15 May 1725 Margaretha, daughter of Andreas Götz, citizen at Gries [=67240 Bischwiller]. Children of second marriage:
4. Johann Jacob b. 18 Mar. 1727
5. Anna Catharina b. 7 Oct. 1728
6. Johannes b. 8 Mar. 1731
7. Johann Peter b. 3 June 1732

AMERICAN RECORDS

Berks co. Wills:
Jacob Lewengut, Tulpehocken. 2 Dec. 1749 - 29 Apr. 1758.
To only son Jacob all estate on condition that he provide for wife Margred during her life and pay to daughter Anna Margreda Fehler £10 and to daughter Anna Barbara £5. Exr.: son Jacob.
Wit.: William Parson, Conrad Weiser, Jacob Rith. Translation.

Christ Lutheran KB, Stouchsburg, Berks co.:
Jacob Lewegud and wife Catharina had children:
1. a child (n.n.) b. 26 Jan. 1752, bp. 30 Jan. 1752
   Sp.: Jacob Lewegud and wife, parents of the father
2. Catharina b. 19 Nov. 1753, bp. 2 Dec. 1753

3. Anna Margretha b. 29 May 1755, bp. 8 June 1755
   Sp.: Jacob Lewegut, Sr. and wife
4. Anna Catharina b. 23 Feb. 1758, bp. 5 Mar. 1758
5. Joh. Jacob b. 15 July 1760, bp. 27 July 1760
6. Joh. Peter b. 25 Mar. 1763, bp. 17 Apr. 1763
7. Eva Elisabetha b. 5 Sept. 1765, bp. 6 Oct. 1765
8. Johannes b. 23 Nov. 1768, bp. 25 Dec. 1768

Jacob Lewegood, Tulpohoccon, Berks co., nat. 11 Apr. 1763.

331. LIEBENGUT, HANS JACOB   Gumbrechtshoffen=
LIEBENGUT, HANS JACOB, JR.   67110 Niederbronn-les-Bains
LIEBENGUT, PETER (Beter on list)   67580 Mertzwiller
Phoenix, 1750
S-H, I: 441

EUROPEAN RECORDS

Mertzweiler Lutheran KB:
Hans Jacob Löwengut, son of Hans Jacob Löwengut of Gumprechtshoffen
[=67110 Niederbronn-les-Bains], m. 9 Dec. 1720 Margaretha Schäfer
daughter of Hans Adam Schäfer of Ringendorf [=67350 Pfaffenhoffen].
Maria Margaretha Schäfer was bp. 2 July 1694 at Ringendorf, daughter of
Hans Adam Schäfer and Anna Maria.

Gumbrechtshoffen Lutheran KB:
Hans Jacob Löwengut, Jr. and wife Anna Margaretha had children:
1. Anna Catharina b. 17 Mar. 1721, bp. 20 Mar. 1721
   Sp: Ottilia, Peter Löwengut's wife; Catharina, daughter of the
   late Hans Adam Schäfer, Ringendorf; and Hans Jacob Schneider,
   citizen here.
2. Anna Margretha b. 22 Aug. 1722, bp. 25 Aug. 1722
3. Maria Barbara b. 29 June 1724, bp. 2 July 1724
4. Maria Magdalena b. 3 Jan. 1726, bp. 5 Jan. 1726
   She m. Georg Schnepp [q.v.]
5. **Johann Jacob** b. 10 June 1728, bp. 2 Trinity 1728
   Sp: Daniel Weber, Agatha wife of Georg Schneider & Hans Peter
   Baltersperger.
6. Johannes b. 25 May 1730, bp. 28 May
7. **Johann Peter** b. 16 Dec. 1733, bp. 20 Dec.
8. Anna Catharina b. 27 Nov. 1735, bp. 30 Nov.
[The father first made his mark in the early bp. records; by the birth of the
third child, he signed his name.]

AMERICAN RECORDS

New Hanover Lutheran KB, Montgomery co.
Jacob Libegut and Christina had:
    1. Elisabeth b. 21 Jan. 1763, bp. 3 Sept. 1763
       Sp: Michael Brand & wife

Peter Liebegut and Eva had:
    1. Magdalena b. 4 Dec. 1756, bp. 20 Mar. 1757
       Sp: Jacob Bauer & Magdalena Schnep
    2. Peter b. 3 Mar. 1759, bp. 29 Apr. 1759
       Sp: George Schnep and wife
    3. Maria Margaretha b. 3 Sept. 1763, bp. 6 Nov 1763
       Sp: George Sneb and wife

332. LIEBENGUT, ULRICH age 45
    LIEBENGUT, JOHAN PETER age 16   Hunspach=
Charming Betty, 1733   67250 Soultz-sous-Forêts
S-H, I: 134, 135, 136   Langensoultzbach=
    with Susanna Leebegoot age 36, Adam age 13,   67360 Woerth
    Jacob age 10, Anna age 5, Maria age 5.

EUROPEAN RECORDS

Hunspach Reformed KB:
Ulrich Leibegut, born in Melchnau in der Landvogtey Arwangen, Berner
Geb. [CH-4917 Melchnau, BE], m. 19 Mar. 1715 in the church at Hunspach,
Anna, daughter of Michel Henni, born in Homberg, Steffenberg in der
Landvogtey Theun? [CH-3611 Homberg b. Thun, BE], Berner Geb.

Langensoultzbach Lutheran KB:
Ulrich Liebegut and wife Anna, nee Henni, had children:
    1. Hans Peter bp. 12 July 1716
    2. Hans Adam bp. 6 Jan. 1719
    3. Hans Jacob bp. 8 June 1721
    4. Anna Margaretha bp. 15 Oct. 1723
    5. Maria Catharina bp. 4 July 1726
    6. Albrecht bp. 5 Apr. 1729, died 1732

AMERICAN RECORDS

Falkner Swamp Reformed KB, Montgomery co.:
Conf. 1752: Herman, son of Ulrich Liebegut, age 18.

Philadelphia Adm. Book F: 407:
1 July 1751- Adm. on the estate of Ulrich Levergood, deceased, granted to his son Jacob Levergood of Philadelphia co., the widow renouncing.

Berks co. Orphan's Court records, dated 11 May 1768:
Petition of Christina Liebenguth, Admrx. of Peter Liebenguth, of Douglass, Yeoman, deceased. That said intestate lately died, leaving a widow (the petitioner) and 9 children, to wit: John, aged 18, Jacob 17 years, Peter 13 years, Daniel 9 Years, Adam 2 years, Catharina (the wife of John Becker) Anna Maria of 20 years, Christina aged 15 years and Elizabeth of 7 years and possessed of a messuage and tract of land in Douglas twp., of 75 acres. Personal estate insufficient to pay debts, and prays for an order to sell real estate. Ordered.
Dated 30 Dec. 1771. Petition of John Levergood of Douglass twp., eldest son of Peter Levergood, deceased. That his father died intestate about 4 years past, being seized of two plantations in said twp. one containing 200 acres, the other containing 40 acres - that said intestate left a widow and 8 children, to wit: John (the petitioner), Jacob, Peter, Daniel, Adam, Catharine (wife of John Baker), Mary (wife of Henry Bitting), Christina (Wife of William Mayberry), and Elizabeth. That Adam died soon after his father, in his minority, unmarried and without issue. Prays court to award an inquest to partition or value. So ordered.

Trappe Lutheran KB, Montgomery co.:
John Adam Liebegut m. 4 Jan. 1750 Christina Gansert.

New Hanover Lutheran KB, Montgomery co.:
Adam Liebegut and wife Christina had:
>   Matthias b. 22 Dec. 1753, bp. 31 Dec. 1753
>   Sp.: Matthias Reichert and wife

Montgomery co. Will Book 2: 325
Adam Liebenugh dated 16 Feb. 1804, proved 27 Apr. 1804
Wife: Christina; Children: Jacob, Mathias, John, Peter, Elizabeth wife of Charles [Carl] Neiman; children of daughter Catharine wife of William Kepner.

Falkner Swamp Reformed Church, cemetery records; New Hanover, Montgomery co.:
Elisabeth Newmann, wife of Carl Newmann
b. 30 Oct. 1757 - d. 25 May 1831
Carl Neumann, husband of Elisabeth Liebenguth
b. 9 Feb. 1751 - d. 5 Feb. 1833

Adam Liebenguth, b. in Alsace, Germany in 1718; married to Christina for 60 years; d. 4 Apr. 1804, age something less than 86 years.

Falkner Swamp Reformed KB, Montgomery co.:
Jacob Liebgut m. 9 Nov. 1748 Christina Brand. Children:
1. Anna Margaret bp. 18 Feb. 1750
2. Joh. Philip b. 20 Nov. 1751, bp. 23 Feb. 1752
3. Catharina b. 12 Sept. 1757, bp. 9 Apr. ____?
4. Christina b. 28 May 1766, bp. 2 Oct. 1766

Conf. 1766: John Liebegut, son of Peter Liebegut, age 17.

Berks County Will Book B:
Jacob Liebenguth - Douglas twp. 6 Dec. 1783 - 17 Feb. 1784
Provides for wife Christina. To son Philip, my plantation where I now dwell in Douglas, con't 225 acres, paying to son John when he is 21, £330. To son Jacob my plantation in Amity and Douglass, con't 105 acres and ½ of meadow. To son Peter, 100 acres of a plantation con't 117 acres 120 per. in Douglass, he paying £250 to sons Jacob & John. To son Henry £450 when 21. To son John £450 as mentioned above. To daughter Catharine £400 in trust for her children if she should have any. Exrs to sell land in New Hanover twp., Phila. co. Sons Philip & Jacob exrs. Wit. by John Becker, John Richards & Adam Liebenguth.

Peter Lebengut, Douglass twp., Berks co., nat. 24 Sept. 1762.
Adam Lubengut, Newhanover twp., Philadelphia co., nat. 24 Sept. 1762.
Jacob Libegut, Frankford and New Hanover, Philadelphia co., nat. 10 or 11 Apr. 1761.

See article by Donald J. Martin, Jr. "Ulrich Liebengut" in the *Pennsylvania Genealogical Magazine,* Vol. XXIX, no. 4 (1976) p. 253-255. Additiond and corrections in *PGM*, Vol. XXX, pg. 54.

333. LINDEMANN, GEORG   Gundershoffen=
Phoenix, 1750   67110 Niederbronn-les-Bains
S-H, I: 440

EUROPEAN RECORDS

Gundershoffen Lutheran KB:
Nicolaus Lindemann of Griesbach and wife Veronica had a son:
Johann Georg b. 28 Nov. 1696, bp. 10 Nov. 1696

Georg Lindenmann, son of Nicolaus Lindenmann, citizen at Griesbach, m. 5 Sept. 1717 at Griesbach, Anna Barbara, widow of the late Christian Springer. (She m. (2) Christian Springer 17 Apr. 1714 as the widow of Henrich Bürger, former citizen of Mertzheim by Landau [Mörzheim=W-6740 Landau]). Georg Lindermann and Barbara had:

1. Joh. Michael b. 27 Sept. 1719, bp. 29 Sept. 1719
2. Anna Catharina b. 23 Apr. 1721, bp. 26 Apr. 1721
3. Anna Barbara b. 27 July 1723, bp. 29 July 1723
   m. 1747 Jacob Baur [q.v.]
4. Joh. Georg b. 25 May 1725, bp. 26 May 1725
5. Maria Salome b. 6 June 1727, bp. __
6. Maria Salome b. 22 Mar. 1729, bp. same day in house
7. Anna _____? bp. 22 Mar. 1731
8. Jacob bp. 18 July 1735

Died _ Aug. 1748: Anna Barbara, wife of Johann Georg Lindemann, citizen at Griesbach; aged 60 years.

Johann Georg Lindenmann, widower in Griesbach, m. 21 Nov. 1748 Maria Catharina widow of the late Johan Georg Pfeiffer.

His mark from KB: His mark from S-H, II: 511:

334. LINDEMANN, NICHOLAS   Griesbach=
Edinburgh, 1751   67110 Niederbronn-les-Bains
S-H, I: 461

EUROPEAN RECORDS

Gundershoffen Lutheran KB:
Nicolaus Lindemann and wife Veronica had :
          Joh. Nicolaus b. 20? Mar. 1698, bp. 26 Mar. 1698

Nicolaus Lindenmann, son of Nicolai Lindenmann of Griesbach, m. 19 Jan. 1723 at Griesbach Anna Dorothea, daughter of Hans Jacob Duchmann, citizen at Niedermottern [Niedermodern = 67350 Pfaffenhoffen].

AMERICAN RECORDS

St. Michael's Lutheran KB, Germantown, Philadelphia co.:
Nicolaus Lindemann m. 8 July 1759 Catharina Scheier? of Cheltenham.

Died 29 Mar. 1772: Elisabetha, daughter of Nicolaus Lindermann, age 11 y., 10 mo., 4 days.

Died 24 May 1775: Mar. Magdalena, daughter of Nicolaus Lindermann, age 2 y., 8 mo., 19 days.

Jacob Löster m. 22 Jan. 1765 Elisabetha Lindemann.

Philadelphia Adm. I: 12; estate # 49, 1778:
Nicholas Linderman, bond taken out 15 Sept. 1778. Admrs: John Fry and George Ritter; Godlip Fry and Peter Hay of Germantown, Philadelphia. Inventory of Nicholas Lindermann, late of Germantown, Husbandman, appraised 16 and 19 Jan. 1778, totaled £ 597.1.6. Inventory by John Rex and Sebastian Müller.

Nichs. Linderman, Cheltenham, Philadelphia co., nat. Autumn, 1765.

335. LISCHER, PHILIP JACOB   Morsbronn-les-Bains=
ca. 1781   67360 Woerth

EUROPEAN RECORDS

Morsbronn Lutheran KB:
Johann Philipp Lischer, farmer, and wife Maria Salome nee Mercker had:
1. Philip Jacob b. 7 Aug. 1745, bp. 10 Aug. 1745
2. Maria Salome b. 3 June 1748, died 1752

AMERICAN RECORDS

St. Michael's and Zion Lutheran KB, Philadelphia:
Buried 27 Aug. 1798 - Philip Jacob Lischer, son of Philip Jacob Lischer and wife Salome; b. 10 Aug. 1745 in Morsbron in Unter Elsass; m. (1) The widow Faster; m. (2) Catharina Louise [? Linner or Binner]. Children are all dead.

Hocker, *German Settlers of Pennsylvania*:
Philadelphische Correspondenz, Oct. 24, 1781:
Philip Jacob Lischer, with Conrad Hess, Race street, Philadelphia, seeks his mother's brother, Paulus Maerker, a miller, born at Langen Sulzbach, Lower Alsace, who came to America about thirty years ago.

336. LÖSCHER, JACOB   Uhrwiller=
Mary, 1733   67350 Pfaffenhoffen
S-H, I: 131,133,134
   with Catharina Löscher (woman) and children: Hans Georg age 14,
Catharina age 17 ½, Barbara age 16, Margaretha age 9.

EUROPEAN RECORDS

Obermodern Lutheran KB:
Married at Schalckendorff 28 Feb. 1713, Jacob Löscher, son of the late Peter
Löscher, citizen at Uhrweyler, and Catharina Barbara Weissgerber, daughter
of the late Jacob Weisgerber, citizen and *Gerichtsschöffen* at Schlackendorff.
They had children, bp. recorded in **Uhrwiller Lutheran KB:**
   1. Catharina Elisabetha bp. 5 Feb. 1714
      Sp.: Jac., son of Joh. Marzolff, Schalckendorf; Catharina,
      daughter of Joh. Zwilling; Elisabetha, daughter of Joh.
      Georg Richart.
   2. Barbara bp. 18 Apr. 1716
      Sp.: Georg, son of Jacob Zeuter; Catharina, daughter of
      Hans Jerg Zeuter; Elisabetha, daughter of Hans Jerg Richart
   3. Joh. Georg bp. 2 Oct. 1718
      Sp.: Melchior Höttinger; Hans Jerg, son of Jac. Läuffer;
      Elisabetha, daughter of Joh. Georg Richart
   4. Anna Margaretha bp. 17 May 1722
      Sp.: Marcus Kieffer; Ottilia, daughter of Peter Striegel;
      Anna Margaretha, daughter of Joh. Georg Zebst.
   5. Eva bp. 16 Apr. 1725
      Sp.: Marcus Kieffer; Margaretha, wife of Joh. Lang;
      Eva, wife of Joh. Georg Richart, Jr.
   6. Eva Margaretha b. 18 Dec. 1729, bp. 20 Dec. 1729
      in *Gumbrechtshoffen Lutheran KB*.
      [The father signed this entry in KB and his signature matches
      the immigrant's in S-H, II: 122]

AMERICAN RECORDS

St. Michael's and Zion KB, Philadelphia:
1734 Communicants lists: Joh. Georg Lescher, Cathrina Loscherin, Cathrina
Loscherin, Jr., Jacob Loscher, Barbara Loscherin.
1735 Communicants lists: Jacob Loscher, Joh. Georg Lescher, Christina
Lescherin, Cathrina Loscherin.

Lancaster Moravian Burials:
Buried 19 Dec. 1800- Catharina Albrecht, widow, b. __ Dec. 1713 in

Uhrweiler in Alsace, nee Loescher. She m. 1738 Anton Albrecht. Had 6 children, 3 sons and 3 daughters. One daughter died before her. Of those surviving, she lived to see 36 grandchildren and 19 greatgrandchildren.

Jacob Loescher, Lower Dublin twp., Philadelphia co., nat. Autumn, 1765.

337. LOW, CHRISTMAN
Pink *John & William,* 1732
S-H, I: 102, 103, 104, 105
Wingen &
Mattstall=
67510 Lembach, Sulzthal

   with Conrad Low [q.v.] Anna Gluf Lowein, Philip Lowein, Christian Lowein, Barbara Lowein, Margaret Lowein

EUROPEAN RECORDS

Wingen Lutheran KB:
Joh. Jacob Frey, citizen here, m. 11/21 Oct. 1688 Anna Maria daughter of the late Matthias Schaub "à Lange dic Ursula". [See immigrant Joh. Peter Frey for complete list of children]. Their daughter:
   Anna Cleophe b. 27 Apr. 1696. Marginal note in KB by her
   bp. record: "Anno 1732 mit ihrnen Mann Christmann Low in
   Pennsylvanien gereisset."

The village of Wingen.   Photo by C. Canfield.

Lembach Lutheran KB:
Joh. Christmann Low and wife Anna Cleophe nee Frey had children:
1. Joh. Philipp b. 29 Mar. 1722
2. Catharina Juliana b. 8 Oct. 1724 bp. 10 Oct. 1724
   [also entered in Mattstall Lutheran KB, where the
   father listed as *Hoffman* at Sulzthal]
   Sp.: Philipp ?Hoch; Anna Cath. wife of Hans ?Kächel;
   Juliana Catharina nee Frawinger, wife of Peter Droxel [q.v.]
   Hoffmann in Katzenthal [=67510 Lembach].
3. a son b. 19 Feb. 1727 died
4. Joh. Peter b. 19 Mar. 1728
5. Hans Jacob b. 11 Dec. 1730, bp. 13 Dec. 1730

AMERICAN RECORDS

Christ Lutheran KB, York, PA (also in Trinity Lutheran KB, Lancaster):
Christmann Lau had:
6. Anna Margaretha b. Nov. 1733, bp. 23 Feb. 1735
   Sp. Joh. Georg Schwab. Jr. and Anna Maria Eberdt
7. Joh. Michael b. 30 Oct. 1735 bp. 6 Nov. 1735
   Sp. Joh. Michael Eberdt and M. Magdal. Schwab
8. Anna Maria b. 17 Apr. 1737, bp. 20 June 1737
   Sp. Joh. Georg Schwab, Jr. and A. Maria Eberdt
9. Maria Magdalena b. 5 Sept. 1739, bp. 14 Nov. 1739
   Sp. Michael Ebert and M. Magdal. Schwab

Christmann Lau and wife Anna Cleva Lau were sp. in 1736 and 1739 for two
children of Joh. Nicholaus Koger.

Peter Lau and wife Susan had:
1. Mary Magdalena b. 22 Aug. 1749, bp. 12 Nov. 1749
2. Andrew b. 7 Oct. 1751, bp. 3 Nov. 1751
3. Joh. Georg b. 18 Jan. 1754, bp. 17 Feb. 1754
4. Anna Eva b. 29 Apr. 1760, bp. 27 May 1760

Buried 10 Jan. 1801: Susanna Lau, aged 68 y., 7 mo.; buried at Wolffs.

Philip Lau and Magdalen had:
Gertrude b. 17 Mar. 1761, bp. 24 Mar. 1761

Philip Lau, Manchester twp., York co., nat. 24 Sept. 1763

338. LOW, CONRAD   67510 Lembach, Sultzthal
Pink *John and William*, 1732
S-H, I: 102, 103, 104, 105
   with Christman Low [q.v.] Anna Gluf Lowein, Philip Lowein, Christian
Lowein, Barbara Lowein, Margaret Lowein

EUROPEAN RECORDS

Lembach Lutheran KB:
Conrad Low, son of Hans Theobald Low, *Hoffmann* in Sultzthal, m. 25 Feb.
1721 Maria Barbara daughter of the late Jacob Frey, citizen in Wingen. (She
was b. 21 Apr. 1701 in Wingen, daughter of Jacob Frey and Anna Maria, See
1733 immigrant Joh. Peter Frey for full record).
They had children:
   1. Maria Catharina b. 28 Nov. 1722
   2. Maria Barbara b. 14 May 1724
   3. Hans Peter b. 26 Sept. 1725, died
   4. Anna Barbara b. 24 July 1727, bp. 27 July 1727
      (Recorded **Oberbronn Lutheran KB**)
   5. Anna Maria b. 18 Mar. 1729
   6. Johann Peter b. 19 Jan. 1731

AMERICAN RECORDS

Christ Lutheran KB, York, PA:
Cunradt Lau had children: (also in Trinity Lutheran KB, Lancaster)
   7. Johann Peter b. Nov. 1733 bp. 15 Feb. 1735
      Sp.: Jacob Ziegeler
   8. Maria Barbara b. 28 Dec. 1736, bp. 14 Jan. 1737
      Sp.: Philipp Ziegler and M. Barb Wittmer
   9. Johann Friederich b. 9 Oct 1739, bp. 14 Nov 1739
      Sp.: Joh. Friederich Tranberg and his fiancee
         Maria Eva Wittmer.

339. LÖWENSTEIN, MICHEL   Schwabweiler=
Betsey, 1765   67660 Betschdorf
S-H, I; 706   Kutzenhausen=
                                               67250 Soultz-sous-Forêts

EUROPEAN RECORDS

Kutzenhausen Lutheran KB:
Johann Heinrich Löwenstein, *Herrschaffl. Amptsbotten* here, and wife Maria
Dorothea nee Hirlemann had a son:
    Johann Michael b. 4 Feb. 1739, bp. 6 Feb. 1739

Michel Löwenstein, citizen and farmer at Schwabweiler, was a sp. 18 Oct.
1763 for a child of Joh. Jacob Schlee of Niederkutzenhausen and his wife
Dorothea nee Löwenstein.

Oberbetschdorf Lutheran KB:
Joh. Michel Löwenstein of Schwabweiler, son of Heinrich Löwenstein citizen
and *Amtsboten* at Niederkutzenhausen and his wife Dorothea nee Hirleman,
m. 13 Sept. 1763 at Schwabweiler Maria Magdalena, daughter of Hans Adam
Gack, citizen at Schwabweiler and his wife Barbara nee Maurer. They had
a daughter:
    Eva Dorothea b. 6 Aug. 1764, bp. 7 Aug. 1764
    Sp.: Johann Gottfried Meyer, citizen and weaver here;
    Dorothea, wife of Jacob Schleh, citizen and mason at
    Niederkutzenhausen; Eva Maurer, daughter of the late Jacob
    Maurer, citizen at Schwabweiler.

Signature from KB: Signature from S-H, II: 808:

340. LUTTER (LUTHER), HENRICH   Herbitzheim=
Phoenix, 1749   67260 Sarre Union
S-H,I: 406
    [Appears on list as Henrich Lutter]

EUROPEAN RECORDS

Herbitzheim Catholic KB:
Henrich Luther, Catholic, tailor at Herbitzheim, and wife Anna Maria nee
Müller had children:
    1. Thiebold b. 22 May 1732
    2. Maria Catharina b. 28 Aug. 1734
    3. Peter b. 4 Aug. 1737
    4. Anna Elisabetha b. 12 Mar. 1741

Verification of this emigrant provided by Dr. Bernd Gölzer from the compiled records of Dr. Gerhard Hein:
Records of Saarwerden county office for Herbitzheim:
Dated 23 Dec. 1757: Anna Maria nee Müller and her husband Henrich Lutter escaped to the New Land in 1749.

AMERICAN RECORDS

Pennsylvania Marriage Licenses, in *Pennsylvania Vital Records* (Baltimore, 1983), Vol I: 679:
10 Sept. 1763: Josiah Harper and Catherine Luter.

Rev. Daniel Schumacher's records:
Henrich Lutter and wife Anna Maria were sp. in 1769 at Lehigh for a child of Melchert Sold and his wife Philippina. Henrich Lutter was a sp. in 1769 at Lehigh for a child of Nicolaus Scheuer.

Lovisa Lutter, single, was a sp. at Lehigh for a child of Melcher Sold in 1770. Louisa Lutter was prepared for Holy Communion at Indianland, Lehigh twp. on 5 May 1771.

341. MACHOLT, JOH. NICOLAUS   Burbach=
  MAKHOLD (x) NICKLAS (2 on ship)   67260 Sarre-Union
Crown, 1749   W-6660 Zweibrücken
S-H, I: 393
EUROPEAN RECORDS

Pisdorf [Bischtroff] Lutheran KB:
Johann Nicolaus Magholdt [Magholt, Magold], schoolmaster at Burbach and wife Maria Catharina had:
  1. Johann Nickel b. Bartholomaus Day 1724, bp. 27 Aug. 1724
     Sp.: Nicolaus Teutsch; Hans Nickel Bader the younger;
     Susanna Margaretha Blais.
  2. Johann Peter b. 1 Nov. 1725, bp. 4 Nov. 1725
  3. Georg Rudolph b. 16 Nov. 1727, bp. same day

Zweibrücken Lutheran KB:
Johann Nicolaus Machold, tailor, son of the Lutheran schoolteacher at Lorentzen [67430], m. 12 July 1743 Sophia Margaretha Leissmann from Völlerdingen [67430 Voellerdingen] in the *Graffschafft* Saarwerden.

Dehlingen Lutheran KB:
Niclaus Machhold of Lorentzen had a son:

EIGHTEENTH CENTURY EMIGRANTS

1. Johann Georg b. 1 Oct. 1743
   Sp.: Joh. Georg Seiffert of Lorentzen; Joh. Niclaus Machhold,
   schoolmaster at Lorentzen; Maria Sophia Rheinhard.

AMERICAN RECORDS

Christ Lutheran KB, York:
Buried 25 Sept. 1752: Nicolaus Machold. age 27 y; d. 24 Sept. 1752, buried
in the city.

342. MAHLER, FRIEDERICH   Langensoultzbach=
Betsy, 1768   67360 Woerth
S-H, I: 724

EUROPEAN RECORDS

Langensoultzbach Lutheran KB:
Master Friederich Mahler, mason and stonecutter, and wife Eva Margaretha
nee Benckler had:
1. Johann Friedrich b. 15 Oct. 1748, bp. 19 Oct. 1748
   Sp.: Friedrich Sattler; Anna Eva nee Bender, wife of Michael
   Cuntz; Joh. Georg Stambach; Maria Magdalena, nee Kyburt,
   wife of Andreas Grunder.
2. Catharina Elisabetha b. 20 June 1751
3. Georg Peter b. 10 Feb. 1754

Joh. Friedrich Mahler (Sr.) d. 1755 at Sultzbach. He was from Württemberg.
His wife Eva Margaretha nee Benckler was from Minfeld [W-6741 Minfeld].
She d. 1764. The bp. of their son Conrad is not in the Langensoultzbach
KB, nor is their marriage there.

AMERICAN RECORDS

Hocker, *German Settlers of Pennsylvania:*
Wochentlicher Pennsylvanischer Staatsbote, dated 11 June 1771:
Conrad Mohler, carpenter, near Lancaster, seeks his brother, Friedrich, born
in Sulsbach, Alsace, who arrived in America two years ago last Autumn.
Conrad, who is now free, is employed with Georg Eberle, Lancaster.

The brother Conrad Mahler arrived on the *Hamilton,* 1767 with others from
the area.

343. MALLO, JOH. GEORG   Griesbach=
Phoenix, 1750   67110 Niederbronn-les-Bains
S-H, I: 441
  [appears on reconstructed list as Malle;
  signature not available.]

EUROPEAN RECORDS

Gundershoffen Lutheran KB:
Hanns Dieboldt Mallo, son of Michael Mallo, citizen at Griesbach, m. 9 May 1713 Anna Catharina, daughter of the late Hans Jacob Voltz, citizen at Griesbach. They had children:
  1. Joh. Georg b. 22 Mar. 1714
  2. Joh. Peter b. 26 Feb. 1716
  3. Joh. Jacob b. 20 Mar. 1718
  4. Joh. Michael [q.v.] b. 8 Oct. 1720
  5. Joh. Diebold b. 28 Mar. 1723
  6. Anna Catharina b. 19 July 1725
  7. **Joh. Georg** b. 22 Dec. 1727
  8. Anna Margretha b. 15 July 1730

AMERICAN RECORDS

Christ Lutheran KB, Stouchsburg, Berks co.:
Joh. Georg and Anna Barbara Mallo had a son:
  Joh. Georg b. 17 Mar. 1752, bp. 30 Mar. 1752
  Sp.: Georg Conrad [q.v.]; Jacob Leuningerin [q.v.- Leininger].

Joh. Georg Mallo and wife were sp. for the following children:
in 1751, a child of Friederich and Anna Margaretha Winter.
in 1751, a child of Jacob and Elisabetha Leininger [q.v.]
in 1752 and 1753, children of Joh. Georg and Anna Barbara Fols [q.v. Voltz]

Chalkley's Chronicles:
Augusta Co. Deed Book 11: 802, dated 9 Mar. 1765:
Tewalt Harman and Sarah to George Mallow for £30, 50 A between Peeked Mountain and Shanandore (River), devised to Teawalt Harman by his father Jacob Harman. Delivered: George Mallow, May, 1776.
Deed Book 11: 804, dated 9 Mar. 1765:
Peter Harmon and Margaret to Geo. Mallow £60, 104 A, same location, devised to Peter by his father Jacob by will dated 18 Sept. 1761. Delivered: Same.

344. MALLO, JOH. MICHAEL   Griesbach=
Phoenix, 1749   67110 Niederbronn-les-Bains
S-H, I: 405

EUROPEAN RECORDS

Gundershoffen Lutheran KB:
Hanns Dieboldt Mallo, son of Michael Mallo, citizen at Griesbach, m. 9 May
1713 Anna Catharina, daughter of the late Hans Jacob Voltz, citizen at
Griesbach. They had a son:
    Johann Michael b. 8 Oct. 1720, bp. 10 Oct. 1720

    [See immigrant Joh. Georg Mallo for more family data].

AMERICAN RECORDS

Christ Lutheran KB, Stouchsburg, Berks co.:
Joh. Michael Mallo and wife Anna Margretha had:
    1. Anna Maria b. 19 Oct. 1749, bp. 22 Oct. 1749
        Sp.: Joh. Ramler, single; Anna Maria Moser.

Chalkley's Chronicles:
Augusta co. adms: Dated 18 May 1758 - Michael Mallow's bond as Adm. of
Peter Moser. His estate was settled 28 June 1758 by Michael Mallow.
Michael Mallow also settled Georg Mouse's estate on 28 June 1758.
Michael Mallow also appraised several estates, including John Conrad in
1759, Ludwick Foalkes in 1760, Andrew Smith in 1765, Valentine Giles in
1766.

16 Mar. 1773 - Adam Mallow and Fred. Keester's bond (with Henry Stone,
John Skidmore) as Adm. of Michael Mallow. Mallow's estate was appraised
8 Apr. 1773.

Augusta Co. Deed Book 14: 481, dated 16 May 1768:
Michael Mallo to Wm. Mountgomery for £50, 470A on the mountain
between South Fork of South branch of Potowmac, line of Jacob Sybert's
survey.

Deed Book 18: 398, dated 18 Aug. 1772:
George Shaver, eldest son and heir apparent of Paul Shaver, deceased and
Elizabeth Shaver, widow of Paul, to Michael Mallow, 200 A on Licking
Creek, a branch of South Branch of Potowmac.

345. MANNI, JACOB age 50   Altwiller=
MANNI, JOST age 19   67260 Sarre-Union
MANNI, HANS ADAM age 16
Lydia, 1741
S-H, I: 301, 302, 303 [see also Jacob Manni (Jr.)]

EUROPEAN RECORDS

Keskastel Luthern KB and Diedendorf Reformed KB:
Jacob Manni, carpenter in Altweiler, m. 25 Aug. 1716 Anna Maria Werli.
[Keskastel KB]. Children:
1. Hans Jacob [q.v.] bp. 20 Feb. 1717 at Altweiler [Keskastel KB]
2. A child (n.n.) bp. 11 June 1719, [Diedendorf KB]
3. Johann Jost bp. 10 Dec. 1722
     Sp.: Lorentz Baur, dairy farmer; Joh. Jost, son of Sebastian
     Müller; Christian Stamm's wife; and the daughter of the late
     Ulrich Bertholdi. [Keskastel KB].
4. Johann Adam bp. 3 Dec. 1724
     Sp.: Jacob Bruner; Johann Adam, son of Moses Alter; Anna
     Maria, wife of Joh. Peter Georg Müller, all of Altweiler;
     Anna Elisabetha, daughter of Johannes Heügel of Neüsaarwerden.
     [Diedendorf KB].

Died 18 Mar. 1725 - Jacob Manny from [CH-3293] Dotzigen, Canton Bern,
citizen in Altweiler. [He is possibly the father of the immigrant].

Died 7 Mar. 1725 - Jacob Werly from Dolen, Canton Bern, Jacob Mani's
father-in-law.

AMERICAN RECORDS

Northampton co. Wills:
Jacob Manni, carpenter, Williams twp., 2 Jan. 1764 - 10 June 1765.
Names wife Anna Maria and mentions children. Also mentions three
children of deceased son Jost. Exr: Friend Mathias Bruch.
Wit.: Henry Miller, John Moer, Johann Georg Maisch.

Williams twp. KB, Northampton co.:
Adam Mani and wife Maria Dorothea had children:
1. Maria Margaretha b. 13 Aug. 1750
2. Johann Phillip b. 10 Jan. 1752.

346. MANNI, JACOB age 24   Mackwiller=
Lydia, 1741   67430 Diemeringen
S-H, I: 301, 302, 303   Altwiller=
                                                 67260 Sarre-Union
EUROPEAN RECORDS

Keskastel Lutheran KB:
Jacob Manni [q.v.], carpenter in Altweiler, m. 25 Aug. 1716 Anna Maria
Werli. Their first child was:
   1. Hans Jacob bp. 20 Feb. 1717 at Altweiler.
   [A notation in the KB that his record was extracted 7 Aug. 1740].
[See Jacob Manni (Sr.) for more family data.]

Bütten Lutheran KB:
Jacob Manny, of Mackweiler, and wife Catharina nee Ecker had a son:
   1. Johann Valentin bp. 15 Oct. 1740
   Sp.: Otto Bärcki, Diemeringen; Valentin Horn, shepherd at
   Mackweiler; Anna Barbara, wife of Theobald Hoshar of Altweiler;
   Anna Catharina, daughter of Jacob Manny of Altweiler, all Ref.

AMERICAN RECORDS

Muddy Creek Reformed KB, Lancaster co.:
Jacob Manni (Jr.) signed the Muddy Creek Reformed Church doctrine in
1743.

Jacob Manny and wife Catharina had:
   2. Jacob bp. 29 May 1743
   Sp.: Peter Hecker [possibly Ecker, q.v.] and Maria Catharina

North Carolina land records:
Jacob Maney was granted 200 A on the First Broad River, NC, on 25 Apr.
1760.
Valentin Maney and wife Catharina received 370 A on the north side of
Indian Creek on 23 Nov. 1762.

347. MARCK, MICHAEL age 45   Burbach=
Europa, 1741   67260 Sarre-Union
S-H, I: 317, 318, 319

EUROPEAN RECORDS

Diedendorf Reformed KB:
Michael Marc (Marck), innkeeper at Burbach, son of Jean Marc of Burbach, m. 30 Apr. 1715 Elisabetha Werthmüller, daughter of Andreas Werthmüller at the Berlinger Obermühl. Children:
1. Elisabetha bp. 19 Sept. 1716
2. Sophia Susanna bp. 1 Jan. 1718
3. Maria Elisabetha bp. 9 Feb. 1720
4. Johann Michael bp. 23 Nov. 1721; conf. 1735
5. Anna Catharina b. 14 Feb. 1724 at Burbach [Pisdorf KB]

Michael Marck, Reformed, of Burbach and wife Maria Magdalena nee Klein, Lutheran, had:
6. Magdalena bp. 7 Dec. 1727
7. Anna Maria b. 19 Jan. 1729 [Pisdorf KB]
8. Johann Peter bp. 25 June 1730
9. Johann Georg bp. 3 Jan. 1732
10. Maria Elisabetha b. 15 Mar. 1734 [Pisdorf KB]
11. Catharina Salome b. 23 Mar. 1737 [Burbach KB]

Verification of this emigrant provided by Dr. Bernd Gölzer from the compiled records of Dr. Gerhard Hein:
Records of Saarwerden county office for Berg und Thal:
12 Dec. 1744: According to a letter dated 26 Oct. 1742 written by Michel Marck "*am Fluss Leesau auf der Insel Philadelphia*" to Burbach, Lorentz Feuerstein of Thal died on the journey at sea.

AMERICAN RECORDS

Rev. Abraham Blumer's records, Lehigh co:
Died 16 Sept. 1773 - Michael Marx (no age given).

348. MARTIN, JACOB
Windsor, 1753
S-H, I: 556, 557, 558

Bütten=
67430 Diemeringen

EUROPEAN RECORDS

Bütten Lutheran KB:
Jacob Martin, son of Jacob Martin of Bütten, conf. 1743.

Jacob Martin, lumberman of Bütten, m. 1 Feb. 1752 at Berg Anna Dorothea Fäss, daughter of Andreas Fäss. She was b. 3 Mar. 1725 at Berg, daughter of Andreas Fäss and wife Anna nee Eichenberger, Reformed; conf. 1739,

Reformed, at Diedendorf.

Verification of this emigration supplied by Dr. Bernd Gölzer, from the county records of Nassau-Saarwerden, compiled by Dr. Gerhard Hein: Records of Saarwerden county office for Berg und Thal: Dated 26 June 1766, inventory of Anna Eichenberger Fäss: the daughter Anna Dorothea Fäss and her husband Jacob Martin have moved to America twelve years ago with permission of the government.

AMERICAN RECORDS

One Jacob Martin, Cocalico, Lancaster co., nat. without oath 10/11 Apr. 1761.

349. MARX, NICKLAUS   Hirschland=
ship data not located   67320 Drulingen

EUROPEAN RECORDS

Wolfskirchen Lutheran KB:
An illegitimate son Johann Nicolaus was born 27 Jan. 1731 to Anna Eva Wagner. The father is Joh. Nickel Marck, son of Jean Marck from Burbach.

Hirschland Lutheran KB:
Nicklaus Marx, linenweaver at Hirschland, and wife Anna Eva had a son:
    Nicolaus bp. 25 Nov. 1736
    Sp.: Johannes Schaad; Samuel Burger; Anna Elisabetha Schmid; and Anna Magdalena Gerin.
[This entry is crossed out and an emigration notation is entered, indicating that they went to "*Preusische Littan.*"].

AMERICAN RECORDS

Egypt Reformed KB, Lehigh co.:
Joh. Nickel Mark [also Marx] and wife Eva had:
    Catharina b. 25 Sept. 1766
    Eva b. 8 Nov. 1771
    Johann Peter b. 15 Jan. 1775
    Daniel b. 12 Dec. 1778

Charles Roberts et al, *History of Lehigh County, Pennsylvania,* **Vol. I: 108:**
Petition to the Assembly dated 15 May 1765. Petition from Nicholas Marks, next friend and brother-in-law to Magdalena and Dorothy Schneider,

daughters of John Schneider, of Whitehall township in the county of Northampton, deceased, both being minors, was presented to the House. The petition states that on the 8 Oct. 1763, the said John Schneider, his wife, and three children, were most cruelly murdered by the Indians, at their dwelling house in Whitehall twp., one of the children was taken captive; the two girls named above were wounded, one scalped and left for dead. One of the girls, Magdalena, through the skill of the surgeons who attended her, has happily recovered; but the other, Dorothy, is still in a languishing condition. Medical expenses were attached to the petition, which the estate of their deceased father is insufficient to pay. The petition requested financial assistance. On 18 May, funds for the medical expenses were granted. [See also Johannes Schneider].

350. MATHES, HANS JACOB age 29   Gundershoffen=
Samuel, 1733   67110 Niederbronn-les-Bains
S-H, I: 106, 108, 110, 112
  with Maria Crete age 24

EUROPEAN RECORDS

Gundershoffen Lutheran KB:
Johan Jacob Matthis, appr. cartwright, son of the late Hans Jacob Matthis, former citizen at Schweighausen [67590 Schweighouse-sur-Moder], m. 25 Jan. 1729 Anna Margretha, daughter of the late Michael Jung, former citizen at Guntershoffen.

AMERICAN RECORDS

Trinity Lutheran KB, Lancaster:
Joh. Jacob Mattheis (later Monocacy) and wife (n.n.) had:
    1. Anna Margaretha b. 11 June 1734, bp. 23 June 1734
    2. Anna Magdalena b. 15 Sept. 1735, bp. 28 Apr. 1736
    3. Joh. Georg b. 30 Mar. 1737, bp. 10 June 1737
    4. Cathrina b. 20 May 1738, bp. 7 June 1738

Grace Tracey and John Dern, *Pioneers of Old Monocacy* (Baltimore, 1987): pg. 205-207 contains extensive family detail, and names the wife of Johann Jacob Matthias as Margaretha Jung and gives the year of marriage as 1729; the source of this information is not given.

Frederick Lutheran KB, Frederick, MD:
Jacob Matheus is named as a wagoner in the KB, 1747. Children:

5. Anna Maria b. 28 Feb. 1742, bp. 4 Oct. 1742
6. Maria Barbara b. 26 Mar. 1744, bp. 27 Mar. 1744

Jacob Matthias d. 7 May 1782, aged 77 years.
His wife Margaret d. 12 Oct. 1788 and is buried at Apple's church.

Jacob's will, indexed under the anglicized surname Matthews, dated 2 Apr. 1776, names children: Conrad; George; Henry; Philip; John; Margaret Valentine; Magdalena Feeror; Catharina Stull; Mary Flower; Barbara Ambrose.

351. MERCKEL, MARTIN   Lampertsloch=
Peggy, 1754   67250 Soultz-sous-Forêts
S-H, I: 638, 639, 641

EUROPEAN RECORDS

Preuschdorf Lutheran KB:
Hans Martin Merckel, son of Hans Martin Merckel of Lampersloch, m. __ Feb. 1728 Maria Eva nee Gack, daughter of Leonhardt Gack from Reymersweyl [Reimerswiller = 67660 Betschdorf].
    1. Maria Margaretha b. 23 Nov. 1728
    2. Joh. Heinrich b. 5 Oct. 1732, bp. 8 Oct. 1732
    3. Maria Barbara b. 27 Apr. 1736, she d. 1738
    4. Catharina b. 3 Apr. 1738
Mother is also marked deceased (in 1738?).

AMERICAN RECORDS

His (HM) mark in the ship list, S-H, II: 734, is the same as his mark in the Preuschdorf KB.

352. MERCKER, GEORG PAUL   Froeschwiller=
Ship unknown, 1752   67360 Woerth
EUROPEAN RECORDS

Langensoultzbach Lutheran KB:
Hans Georg Mercker, potter at Froeschweiler, and his wife Barbara, nee Rebenach, had children:
    1. Velten, d. 4 Sept. 1727, age 4 years
    2. **Georg Paul** b. 31 Aug. 1727, conf. 1742
    3. Johannes bp. 15 Jan. 1730, d. 16 June 1732

4. Maria Margaretha, conf. 1747, age 14
5. Catharina Barbara bp. 3 July 1735, d. 11 Apr. 1738

The main street in Froeschwiller.

AMERICAN RECORDS

"Diary of Christian Streit", in William E. Eisenberg, *This Heritage, the Story of Lutheran Beginnings in the Lower Shenandoah Valley*, (Winchester, 1954): 344: Georg Paul Mercker b. in Alsace in 1727; died 11 Dec. 1786, aged 59. Came to America 1752; married aboard ship; Three children survive, all living and married. Sick for 2 weeks. Buried 13 Dec. 1786.

353. MERCKER, PAUL   Preuschdorf=
Brothers, 1751   67250 Soultz-sous-Forêts
S-H, I: 463

EUROPEAN RECORDS

Preuschdorf Lutheran KB:
Joh. Philip Mercker, miller at Preuschdorf, son of Joh. Heinrich Mercker, miller at Wördt [Woerth] m. (1) __ Sept. 1702 Anna Catharina, daughter of the late Joh. Diebold Tielmann.
Joh. Philip Mercker, widower, m. (2) __ May 1707 Susanna Zinck, daughter of Joh. Jacob Zinck, citizen and weaver at Preuschdorf. Among their children were:

Maria Margaretha b. 21 Mar. 1717, bp. 23 Mar. 1717
Joh. Paul b. 2 July 1720, bp. 5 July 1720
Maria Salome b. 1 Jan. 1723, bp. 3 Jan. 1723
Joh. Georg b. __ May 1725

Paul Mercker from Preuschdorf, son of the late Philipps Mercker, former master miller, m. 26 Jan. 1745 at Mitschdorf, Maria Elisabetha Wetzel, daughter of the late Niclaus Wetzel, former master miller at the Brechmühl. Notation by the m. entry: "Went to the new land." Children:

1. Joh. Georg b. 9 May 1747, bp. 10 May at Mitschdorf
2. Joh. Jacob b. 18 Sept. 1750 at Langensoultzbach
   [father mentioned as master miller in bp. records and *untern müller* at Sultzbach in 1750.]

Paul Mercker's signature on pg. 38 of the Preuschdorf marriage records matches the signature in S-H, II: 545.

AMERICAN RECORDS

Hocker, *German Settlers of Pennsylvania:*
Philadelphische Correspondenz, dated 24 Oct. 1781:
Philip Jacob Lischer, with Conrad Hess, Race street, Philadelphia, seeks his mother's brother, Paulus Maerker, a miller, born at Langen Sulzbach, Lower Alsace, who came to America about thirty years ago. [See Philip Jacob Lischer].

One George Merker, Philadelphia, nat. Autumn 1765.

354. MERTZ, DAVID age 44   Hangviller=
Richard and Elizabeth, 1733   57370 Phalsbourg
S-H, I: 126, 127, 129
  with Veronica age 40, Joh. Nicholas age 18, Joh. Peter age 13 3/4, Christina age 3 3/4

EUROPEAN RECORDS

Diedendorf Reformed KB:
David Mertz from Hangenweiller [Hangviller] and wife Frena [Veronica] nee
Schneider had a son:
> Johannes bp. 20 Sept. 1722
> Sp.: Johannes Scheürer, citizen and master tailor at Weyer;
> Lorentz Teüschen, shepherd at Bärlingen; Eva, wife of Nicolaus
> Schneider [q.v.], schoolmaster at Rauweiller; Catharina, daughter
> of Ludwig Morel from Sieweiller [Siewiller = 67320 Drulingen].

Abraham Vautrin's wife (same ship) was nee Mertz from Hangenweiller.

Verification of this emigration supplied by Dr. Bernd Gölzer, from the
county records of Nassau-Saarwerden, compiled by Dr. Gerhard Hein:
Records of Saarwerden county office for Kirberg: dated 18 Oct. 1764,
contempory table of descendants of Joseph Schneider of Diedendorf,
originally from Melchnau, BE. Veronica Schneider, wife of David Mertz, was
a daughter of Joseph Schneider. David Mertz of Hangweiler and wife
Veronica have moved to the New Land with three children:
> 1. Hans Nickel
> 2. Hans Peter
> 3. Christina.

AMERICAN RECORDS

Longswamp Reformed KB, Longswamp twp., Berks co.:
A David Mertz with wife Catharina was sp. in 1764 for a child of Adam
Hener.

355. METTAUER, JOHANNES age 25   Keskastel=
Lydia, 1741   67260 Sarre-Union
S-H, I: 301, 302, 303

EUROPEAN RECORDS

Erckartsweiler Lutheran KB:
Samuel Mettauer, single linenweaver from Zopfingen, Canton Bern,
[possibly CH-4800 Zofingen, AG or CH-3052 Zollikofen, BE] Switzerland,
m. 30 Oct. 1714 Magdalena Wampfler.

Keskastel Lutheran KB:
Samuel Mettauer and wife (not named) had a son Johannes bp. 18 Feb. 1717
at Kastel [the church book indicates that the record was extracted 6 May
1741].

Samuel Mettauer, citizen and widower, linenweaver, m. (2) 5 Mar. 1726 at Keskastel, Anna Maria, widow of Christian Birki, former *Hoffmann* at Luderbach.

Verification of this emigration supplied by Dr. Bernd Gölzer, from the county records of Nassau-Saarwerden, compiled by Dr. Gerhard Hein:
Records of Saarwerden county office for Keskastel, dated 10 June 1757: Johannes Mettauer, son of Samuel Mettauer, has moved to the New Land 16 years ago. Dated 22 Jan. 1785: Johannes Mettauer resided in Frederic County, Maryland. An authorized translation of his will existed. He left everything to his sister Maria Eva, wife of Johannes Krebs of Keskastel.

AMERICAN RECORDS

Rev. John Waldschmidt's records:
Conf. at Cocalico, 20 Mar. 1761: Jacob and Johannes Meddauer, two sons of Johannes Medauer.

Muddy Creek Reformed KB, Lancaster co.:
A Magdalena Mettaur was a sp. in 1763 for a child of Henry Reich.

John Mettauer, Cocalico twp., Lancaster co. nat. 10/11 Apr. 1761.

356. MEURER, JOH. PHILIP   67340 Ingwiller
Snow *Catharine*, 1742
S-H, I: 320, 321, 322
[This is the Moravian "First Sea Congregation"; John Philip Meurer was listed with the single men.]

EUROPEAN RECORDS

Ingweiler Lutheran KB:
Hans Adam Meurer, citizen and potter here, and first wife Anna Maria had children:
    1. Elisabetha Margretha b. 23 Jan. 1701
    2. Anna Maria, twin, b. 23 Jan. 1701
    3. Catharina Elisabetha b. 25 Feb. 1702

Hans Adam Meurer, citizen and master potter, and second wife Catharina Esther had:
    4. **Johann Philipps** b. 24 Mar. 1708, bp. 29 Mar. 1708
      Sp.: Johann Philipps Engelhard, son of the late Herr Albrecht
      Christoph Engelhard, former *Kirschschaffner* here; Anna Maria,

daughter of Philipp Schwenck, shoemaker at Buchsweyler, Herr Joh. Jacob Itzstein, citizen and Innkeeper at the Crown Inn.

AMERICAN RECORDS

Bethlehem Moravian marriages:
Johann Philipp Mäurer, b. 1708 in Ingweiler, Alsace, m. 24 Apr. 1744 Christiana Kraft from Württemberg.

Old Moravian Cemetery of Bethlehem, PA:
John Philip Meurer, 1708-60, originally a shoemaker from Ingweiler, Alsace. He arrived with the first "Sea Congregation" on the snow *Catharine*. Wife Christiana, nee Kraft. He was ordained at Tulpehocken and had charge of a Lutheran congregation until 1746. Later he served in the [Moravian] churches at Donegal, Lebanon, Swatara and York.

357. MEYER, JOHANN SIMON   Wolfskirchen=
Snow *Squirrel*, 1761   67260 Sarre-Union
S-H, I: 683
EUROPEAN RECORDS

Wolfskirchen Lutheran KB:
Daniel Schmidt of Wolfskirchen and wife Catharina had a daughter:
Eva Rosina b. 30 Mar. 1738. She m. Simon Meyer.

Verification of this emigration supplied by Dr. Bernd Gölzer, from the county records of Nassau-Saarwerden, compiled by Dr. Gerhard Hein:
Records of notary public of Wolfskirchen:
Dated 16 May 1771, inventory of Daniel Schmidt: the daughter Eva Rosina and her husband Simon Meyer emigrated to America 13 Years ago. Her property will fall to her only sister Anna Christina after five years, if nothing is heard from Eva Rosina.

358. MISCHLER, ULLRICH   Keskastel=
Phoenix, 1749   67260 Sarre-Union
S-H, I: 407
EUROPEAN RECORDS

Keskastel Lutheran KB:
Ulrich Missler, *Hoffmann auff dem Roderhoff* by Saarbrucken, son of the late Hans Missler from Ober? Ruchy aus der Schweitz [?Oberscherli, BE = CH-3145 Niederscherli], m. 9 Mar. 1745 at Keskastel Eleonora Magdalena,

daughter of Samuel Müller, citizen, inhabitant and linenweaver at Keskastel [notation in KB: record was extracted 12 Feb. 1749].

Verification of this emigration supplied by Dr. Bernd Gölzer, from the county records of Nassau-Saarwerden, compiled by Dr. Gerhard Hein: Records of Saarwerden county office for Keskastel, dated 30 Oct. 1755: Samuel Müller of Keskastel is deceased; his heirs are his daughters. The daughter Eleonora Magdalena is married to Ulrich Mischler and they moved to the New Land in 1749.

AMERICAN RECORDS

First Reformed KB, Philadelphia:
Ulrich Mischler and wife Eleonora nee Müller, from Schwarzenburg, Bern, [CH-3150 Schwarzenburg, BE] had a daughter:
>   Maria Louisa b. 17 Aug. 1749 on the sea, bp. 27 Sept. 1749
>   Sp.: Christian Hoffstetter [q.v.]
Ulrich Meashler, warrant #676, Warwick twp., Lancaster co., 21 Aug. 1751; patent 26 May 1762 to George Hocker.

Frederick Reformed KB, Frederick MD:
Ulrich Mistler and wife Eleonora had:
>   Johannes bp. 15 Apr. 1758, Sp.: Parents

Colonial Maryland Naturalizations:
Ulrich Misler, German, Reformed, nat. 25 Oct. 1756.

359. MOOS, JOHANNES   67160 Wissembourg
before 1782
Not in S-H
EUROPEAN RECORDS

Saint Jean Lutheran KB, Wissembourg:
Johann Henrich Moos, single, baker, son of Joh. Heinrich Moos, stocking weaver, m. 11 Aug. 1733 Christina Margaretha, duaghter of Bernhard Foltz, citizen and butcher. Children:
>   1. Johann Heinrich b. 16 July 1734
>   2. Maria Catharina b. 25 Jan. 1737
>   3. Johann Caspar b. 12 Feb. 1739
>   4. Johann Philipp b. 9 Oct. 1741
>   5. Johannes b. 23 May 1744
>   6. **Johannes** b. 20 Oct. 1746, bp. 21 Oct. 1746
>   Sp.: Johannes Klein and wife Anna Rosina

7. Rosina Margaretha b. 10 Oct. 1753

AMERICAN RECORDS

St. Michael's and Zion KB, Philadelphia:
Buried 25 Feb. 1782 - Johann Moos, born in Weissenburg in 1746. Died 24 Feb. [1782], aged 36 years.

360. MOSER, JOHANN PAUL   Zittersheim =
_____, 1729   67290 Wingen-sur-Moder
[not in S-H]

EUROPEAN RECORDS

Wingen Lutheran KB:
Nicolaus Moser from Zedersheim, *Leining. Weserburgischen Herrschafft,* [Zittersheim = 67290 Wingen-sur-Moder], m. 3 July 1692 Anna Elisabeth Stielin from Busweyler, [Buswiller=67350 Pfaffenhoffen] *Lutzelsteinischen Herrschaft.* [bp. of son Joh. Paul not located in this KB]

AMERICAN RECORDS

St. Joseph's (Oley Hills) Church, Pike twp., Berks co.:
Johann Paul Moser, b. 29 Mar. 1697, a son of Nicholas Moser and his wife Maria Elizabeth, from Kohlthal near Wingen. He came to America in 1729. In 1723 he was married in Germany to Maria Barbara, b. 1 May 1702, daughter of Wilhelm Cassel and Maria Catharina from Zittergen [Zittersheim = 67290 Wingen-sur-Moder]. Children:
1. Maria Elisabeth b. Nov. 1724
2. Franciscus b. 14 days before St. John's Day, 1733
3. Maria Christina b. 19 Apr. 1740
4. Johann Michael b. July 1743, d. 27 July 1754

Communicants list, 14 Apr. 1754
Hans Pauli Moser, Cath. Barb. his wife, son Frantz, daughter Christina.

John Franc Moser, son of Paul and Catharina Barbara Moser, m. 20 Apr. 1756 Maria Elizabeth Busch, single daughter of Jacob Busch. Children:
1. Catharina b. 7 Jan. 1757, bp. 6 Feb. 1757
2. Johannes b. 16 Oct. 1758, bp. 22 Oct. 1758
   Sp.: Johannes Gerber and Magdalena
3. John Michael b. 19 Dec. 1760, bp. 28 Dec. 1760
4. John George b. 1 Jan. 1763, bp. 9 Jan. 1763
   Sp.: John Gaerber; George Kuhns

5. Franciskus b. 19 Mar. 1765
6. Magdalena b. 8 Mar. 1772
7. Daniel b. 21 Aug. 1774
8. Barbara b. 5 Apr. 1779
9. Christina b. 4 Dec. 1782

Other later Mosers in this KB.

361. MOTZ, HANS JACOB   Lampertsloch=
Polly, 1766   67250 Soultz-sous-Forêts
S-H, I: 712

EUROPEAN RECORDS

Preuschdorf Lutheran KB:
Hans Michael Motz of Lampertsloch and wife Maria Barbara nee Cuntz had a son:
    Hans Jacob b. 17 June 1739 [entry faded].

Hans Michel Motz, citizen and wagoner in Lampertsloch, and wife Anna Catharina had a son Joh. Jacob b. 18 Apr. 1761. One of the sp. at his baptism was **Hans Jacob Motz**, single son of Hans Michael Motz, citizen at Lampertsloch. The signature of this sp. by the bp. entry matches the signature of the immigrant in S-H, II: 817.

362. MOTZ, HANS MICHEL age 24   Lampertsloch=
Britannia, 1731   67250 Soultz-sous-Forêts
S-H, I: 48, 49, 52, 54   Preuschdorf=
    with Anna Maria Moths age 22   67250 Soultz-sous-Forêts

EUROPEAN RECORDS

Preuschdorf Lutheran KB:
Hans Martin Motz, of Lampertsloch, son of the late Michel Motz of Mitschdorf, m. 18 Jan. 1701 Anna Catharina, daughter of the late Hans Adam Perlin [her maiden name also given as Berling in other records], *Gerichtsschöffen* at Görstorff [Goersdorf = 67360 Woerth]. Children:
    1. Anna Catharina b. 20 Oct. 1701, bp. 22 Oct. 1701
       She m. 1723 Matthias Näss [q.v.]
    2. Hans Michel b. __ Sept. 1704
    3. Joh. Georg [q.v.] b. 6 Jan. 1708, bp. 9 Jan. 1708
       He m. 1727 Rosina Klein, emigrated 1728
    4. Susanna b. 7 Mar. 1712

5. Catharina b. __ Sept. 1714
6. Joh. Jacob b. ?4 ?Sept. 1717 (faded)
7. Joh. Heinrich b. 17 July 1720

Hans Michel Motz, son of the late Hans Martin Motz, former citizen at Lampersloch, m. 27 May 1727 Anna Maria Klein, daughter of Hs. Diebold Klein, former citizen at Schalckendorf [= 67350 Pfaffenhoffen]. [See immigrant Joh. Georg Motz for additional Klein data.] Notation in KB by marriage record: "went to the new land".

AMERICAN RECORDS

Philadelphia Adm. H: 106, 1772, estate # 68:
Inventory of the est. of Michael Motz, deceased, filed 1 Dec. 1772.
Inventory by Theowald Nees; personal est. sold at vendue 22 Nov. 1771.
Renunciation of Catharine Motz, widow of Michael Motz, dec'd, dated 28 Oct. 1772. Adm. bond to Dewald Nease, principal creditor of Michael Motz, dec'd. Signed: Dewald Ness, John (H) Hornecker, Nicolaus Neess.
Account of Dewald Nease, adm. of the est. of Michael Motz, dec'd, totaled £ 199.4.0; signed Dewald Nes, 26 Oct. 1773.

363. MOTZ, JOHANN GEORG   Lampertsloch=
Albany, 1728   67250 Soultz-sous-Forêts
S-H, I: 20, 21   Preuschdorf=
   [Jerick Moots on A list]   67250 Soultz-sous-Forêts

EUROPEAN RECORDS

Preuschdorf Lutheran KB:
Johann Georg Motz, son of the late Johann Martin Motz, former citizen at Lampertsloch. m. __ Sept. 1727 Rosina, daughter of the late Theobald Klein, *Gerichtsschöffen* at Schalckendorf.
Notation in KB by marriage record "went to the new land." [See immigrant Hans Michel Motz for additional family data.]

Obermodern Lutheran KB:
Diebold Klein and wife Anna Maria of Schalkendorf [=67350 Pfaffenhoffen] had children:
    1. Anna Margaretha Klein bp. 3 Oct. 1700
    2. Catharina Klein bp. 7 Nov. 1702
    3. Rosina Klein bp. 8 Feb. 1704
      Sp.: Wilhelm, son of Hans Schneberger of Modern; Catharina, wife of Hans Martzolff; Marta, daughter of Jacob Weissgerber,

Schalckendorf [= 67350 Pfaffenhoffen].
4. Anna Maria Klein bp. 27 Jan. 1706; she m. 1727 Hans Michael Motz [q.v.] and emigrated 1731.
5. Lorentz Klein bp. 30 Jan. 1709
6. Eva Klein bp. 28 Apr. 1711
7. Hans Georg Klein bp. 7 Feb. 1714
8. Johannes Klein bp. 4 Oct. 1716
9. Anna Barbara Klein bp. 9 Aug. 1719

AMERICAN RECORDS

Emmaus Moravian KB, Lehigh co:
Rosina Moz was born in "Kalkendorf" in Alsace on February 8, 1703. Her father was Dewald Klein, a farmer and her mother was Anna Maria Marzolf. On 19 Nov. 1728 she m. Georg Mozer who is now deceased. She came to Pennsylvania with her husband in 1729. She died 27 Feb. 1760 in her 57th year. They had 11 children:
1. Martin Moz; 2. Johann Georg Moz; 3. Mattheus Moz; 4. Maria Barbara Moz; 5. Magdalena Moz; 6. Catharina Moz; 7. Anna Maria Moz; 8. Elizabeth Moz; 9. *Maria* Catharina Moz, b. 26 Sept. 1736; 10. Maria Margaretha Moz, b. 12 May 1743; 11. Sabina Moz.

Anna Catharina Hahn, nee Motz, was b. 26 Sept. 1736 in Upper Milford; m. Geo. Adam Hahn. They had 6 children.

364. MÜLLER, ANDREAS   67510 Lembach
Edinburgh, 1750
S-H, I: 429
EUROPEAN RECORDS

Lembach Lutheran KB:
Lorentz Müller, *Schurer,* and wife Catharina nee Mercker, at the Glasshutt, had a son:
Johann Andreas b. 25 Dec. 1717, bp. 29 Dec. 1717
Sp.: Andreas Bawer, son of Hans Theobald Bawer, *Schultheis* at Obersteinbach; Hans Michel Bey, son of the late Hans Peter Bey; Anna Catharina, wife of Hans Peter Krämer.

AMERICAN RECORDS

Trinity Lutheran KB, Lancaster:
Andreas Miller from Lehmbach in Alsace, m. 14 Oct. 1760 Elisabet Odenwalder from Frickefeld. Children:

1. Elisabet b. 27 Aug. 1761, bp. 11 Oct. 1761
   Sp.: Michael Eccart and wife Eva
2. Johannes b. 2 Feb. 1764, bp. 1 Apr. 1764. Sp.: Parents.
3. Joh. Heinrich b. 18 Jan. 1766, bp. 30 May 1766. Sp.: Parents.

365. MÜLLER, GEORG   Merkwiller-Pechelbronn=
Minerva, 1770   67250 Soultz-sous-Forêts
S-H, I: 730
                        EUROPEAN RECORDS

Kutzenhausen Lutheran KB:
Johann Jacob Müller, citizen and weaver at Merckweiler, and wife Eva nee
Lorentz from Widbruch [Weitbruch = 67500 Haguenau] had a son:
   Johann Georg b. 24 Oct. 1739, bp. 27 Oct. 1739

Joh. Georg Müller, son of Joh. Jacob Müller, weaver at Merckweiler, m. 18
Jan. 1757 Maria Catharina Heinrich, daughter of Joh. Jacob Heinrich,
schoolmaster at Oberkutzenhausen. [She was a sister of Hans Georg Schill's
[q.v.] wife.] Children:
   1. Joh. Jacob b. 11 Aug. 1758, bp. 14 Aug. 1758
   2. Joh. Michel b. 25 Sept. 1760, bp. 28 Sept. 1760
      Sp.: Joh. Michael Fünffrock [q.v.], son of Joh. Michel Fünffrock
      of Merckweiler; Joh. Georg, son of Joh. Georg Herlemann; Anna
      Maria, daughter of Joh. Jacob Knobel of Mattstall.
   3. Maria Barbara b. 17 Oct. 1763

[Note: There were two Georg Müllers on the Minerva; this immigrant
appears to be the seventh passenger listed; he signed his name *Goerg* in the
KB and on the ship list.]

366. MÜLLER, JACOB age 43   67110 Niederbronn-les-Bains
  MÜLLER, JACOB age 19
Charming Nancy, 1738
S-H, I: 246, 247, 248
                        EUROPEAN RECORDS

Niederbronn Lutheran KB:
Johann Jacob Müller and wife Maria Magdalena had children:
   1. Joh. Jacob b. 19 Dec. 1719
   2. Eva Catharina b. 8 Feb. 1721, d. 28 May 1723
   3. Dorothea b. 13 Apr. 1723, d. 25 July 1724
   4. Maria Barbara b. 22 June 1725

5. Maria Elisabeth b. 1 May 1728
6. Christoph b. 12 July 1730
7. Johannes b. 10 Jan. 1733
8. Joh. Jacob b. 5 Nov. 1734
9. Maria Magdalena b. 7 Oct. 1737

Died 7 Dec. 1731 - Joh. Jacob Müller age 69 y. less 26 weeks and 6 days.

Died 9 Dec. 1740 - Anna Margaretha Müller, widow of the late Joh. Jacob Müller, former citizen and *Gerichtsschöffen*, age 80 years.

Archives du Bas-Rhin, Document E 4367:
Joh. Jacob Müller is listed in this document on a list of emigrants from Niederbronn in 1738.

AMERICAN RECORDS

St. Joseph's (Oley Hills) Church, Pike twp., Berks co.:
Johan Jacob Müller, b. 1695, a son of Jacob Müller and his wife Margaretha from Niederbronn. In 1738 he came to America.
In the Year 17__, he was married with Maria Magdalena, b. 20 Sept. 1697, daughter of Joh. Christmann Gerber [q.v.] and Anna Maria.

Communicants list, 8 Sept. 1754:
Joh. Jacob Müller, wife Maria Magdalena, son Johann, daughter Christina

Communicants, 18 May 1755:
Hannes Müller, single, Christina, single, children of Jacob Müller

Hannes Müller, single son of Jacob Müller and Maria Magdalena, Lutheran, m. 23 Mar. 1756 Maria Magdalena Linck, daughter of the late Joh. Jacob Linck and the deceased wife Anna Magdalena from Grossgartach [=W-7105 Leingarten]. They came to America in 1733. Maria Magdalena Linck was b. in 1731. Children:
    1. Johann Jacob b 17 Dec. 1756, bp. 6 Feb. 1757
    2. Johannes b. 24 Apr. 1759
    3. Johann Adam b. 8 Sept. 1761
    4. Johann Georg b. 7 Nov. 1763
    5. Anna Catharina b. 14 Feb. 1768
    6. Johan Daniel b. 11 Apr. 1772
    7. Abraham b. 21 July 1778

Frederick Lutheran KB, Frederick, MD:
Buried 18 May 1786 - Maria Elisabeth, wife of Adam Linck, b. 10 May 1727

in Niederbrunn, Elsass.   Parents: Jacob Müller and his wife Maria Magdalena. Married her surviving widower 3 Feb.1748, and had 10 children, 6 sons and 2 daughters living in 1786. Died 16 May, aged 59 years, 6 days.

367. MÜLLER, MARIA BARBARA   Langensoultzbach=
Ship Unknown, 1763   67360 Woerth
                         EUROPEAN RECORDS

Langensoultzbach Lutheran KB:
Johann Jacob Müller, farrier at Sultzbach, and wife Maria Barbara nee Pfeiffer, had a daughter:
> Maria Barbara b. 10 Jan. 1745, bp. 12 Jan. 1745
> [Marginal note by her baptism: "is in the New Land 1763"]

The Lutheran Church in Wolfskirchen.

368. MÜLLER, MATHIAS, sick on board   Wolfskirchen=
?Halifax, 1752   67260 Sarre Union
S-H, I: 483 [with Nickel Quirin]

EUROPEAN RECORDS

Wolfskirchen Lutheran KB:
Mathias Müller m. 5 Apr. 1736 Catharina Elisabetha Gabelin from
Zweybrücken. They had:
1. Barbara Catharina b. 27 Dec. 1737
2. Christina Elisabetha b. 15 Nov. 1741
3. Joh. Philipp b. 24 Dec. 1743

AMERICAN RECORDS

St. Michael's and Zion KB, Philadelphia:
Died 11 May 1787: Catharina, b. 1739 in Wolfskirchen, in Nassau-
Saarbrucken, daughter of Matthias Müller and Catharina. Married Jacob
Henriegel. They had 2 sons and 1 daughter.

369. MUTSCHLER, FRIEDRICH   67360 Woerth
      MUTSCHLER, VALENTIN
Duke of Bedford, 1751
S-H, I: 459
EUROPEAN RECORDS

Woerth Lutheran KB:
Andreas Mutschler, widower and linenweaver, m. 13 May 1715 Anna
Margretha Sattler, daughter of Jonas Sattler, citizen and tailor at
Langensultzbach [=67360 Woerth]. Two of their children were:
        Joh. Friedrich b. 17 Mar. 1724
        Joh. Valentin b. 27 June 1731

AMERICAN RECORDS

First Reformed KB, Easton, Northampton co:
Buried 31 Aug 1794 - Friedrich Mutschler in Greenwich (N.J.), age 70 years

Buried 15 Mar. 1803 - Elizabeth Mutschler, Greenwich, age 35 years, 3
months, 28 days

Samuel Mutschler m. 10 Aug. 1788 Maria Fischer

370. NAGEL, JOHANNES   67510 Lembach
John and William, 1732
S-H, I: 102, 103, 104, 105
  with Maria Nagelin

EUROPEAN RECORDS

Lembach Lutheran KB:
Conf. 1721: Hans Nagel, son of the late Johannes Nagel.

Johannes Nagel, son of the late Johann Nagel, former *Dragoner unter der Compagni des ?Hohlche Regiment --- von Leiningen*, m. 21 Jan. 1731 at Lembach Maria, daughter of Hans Sprecher, citizen here. They had:
  1. Maria Dorothea b. 30 Nov. 1731, bp. 31 Nov. 1731
      Sp.: Leonhart Treiber; Susanna, wife of Gorg Bauer;
      Maria, wife of Heinrich Hört of Mattstall.

The mother of Johannes is probably the Catharina Spreakering who also arrived on the *John and William* in 1732. Catharina nee Hügelin, widow of the late Johann Nagel, former *Dragoner unter Churpfaltzischen Truppen*, m. 24 Nov. 1720 at Lembach Hans Sprecher, widower. [See also his son of first marriage, Hans Georg Sprecher].

AMERICAN RECORDS

Rev. John Casper Stoever's Records:
Johannes Nagel (Germantown) had children:
  2. John b. 16 Apr. 1734, bp. 19 May 1734
      Sp.: John Ulrich Beckle and Susanna Margaretha Weipent
  3. Maria Margaretha b. 16 June 1736, bp. 28 June 1736
      Sp.: Susanna Margaretha Weipent(in).

371. NÄSS, [NÖSS] MATHIAS, SR age 58   Mitschdorf=
  NÄSS, MATHIAS, JR age 27   67360 Woerth
Britannia, 1731   Lampertsloch=
S-H, I: 48, 49, 50 [Nehs on list]   67250 Soultz-sous-Forêts
  with Maria Barbara Nehs, age 60; Anna Katherine Nehs, age 28; Magdalena Nehs, age 7; Hans Jacob Nehs, age 5; Katharine Nehs, age 2. See also Michel Näss. Also on ship: Jacob Nehs, age 31; Johannes Nehs, age 26; Dewald Nehs, age 24; Hans Georg Nehs, age 21.

EUROPEAN RECORDS

Preuschdorf Lutheran KB:
Matthis Näss, son of Matthis Näss, citizen, smith and *Gerichtsschöffen* at
Mitschdorff, m. 6 Jan. 1723 Anna Catharina Motz, daughter of the late Hans
Martin Motz, former citizen at Lampersloch. Notation in KB: "went to the
New Land." They had children:
1. Maria Magdalena b. 26 Dec. 1723, bp. 29 Dec. 1723
2. Hans Jacob b. 25 July 1726, bp. 27 July 1726
   Sp.: Johann Jacob Näss, single son of Matthias Näss, the smith
   at Mitschdorff. [This sp. is probably the Jacob Nehs, age 31,
   who also arrived on the *Britannia*, 1731].
3. Anna Catharina b. 25 Apr. 1729, bp. 27 Apr. 1729

AMERICAN RECORDS

Rev. John Casper Stoever's Records:
Mattheis Naesz m. 28 Nov. 1733 Maria Barbara Hoerdter, Skippach.

Philadelphia Wills F: 276, 1741, Estate #252:
Mathias Nasse (Nees on estate file folder) of Sulford (Salford) twp.,
Philadelphia co., blacksmith, will dated 31 Jan. 1741/2. Wife Mary Barbary
to have all est. during widowhood or until youngest child is 15 years old.
Then she is to have 1/3 part of all est. The other 2/3 to be divided between
two children: John Henery Nasse and Johan Owldrick (?Ulrich) Nasse.
Exrs: wife Mary Barbery and son Dewalt Nasse.
Wit: John Isaac Klein, Henrich Dänig, William Nash.

Inventory of Mattes Nees, dated 27 Feb 1741/2, includes among other items,
improvement on 150 acres of land and five books. His estate totaled
£138.10.2. The inventory was taken by Jan Jansen and Jacob Reiff.

Dewalt Ness and Jacob Ness, who also arrived on the Britannia, appear in
the Indianfield Lutheran KB, Franconia twp., Montgomery co., along with
children of Michael Nees [q.v. - Näss].

Christ Lutheran KB, York:
Jacob Nees, son of Mathew Nees, m. 22 Nov. 1748 Mary Magdalen Yoh.
[Her name is given as Josi elsewhere].

From Family Bible & Taufscheine:
Johan Jacob Ness, b. 25 July 1726, and wife (page torn) had the following
children:
1. Margaretha b. 31 Dec. 1753
2. Michael b. 23 Sept. 1755
3. Magdalena b. 20 Sept. 1758

Sp.: for all three were Michael Gieselmann and wife Margaretha
4. Wilhelm. b. 13 July 1761
   Sp.: Wilhelm Ehrhard and wife Catharina
5. Johann Jacob b. 26 May 1766
   Sp.: Peter Ness and wife
6. Susanna b. 20 Apr. 1769
   Sp.: Peter Lau and wife Susanna
7. Johannes b. 30 Sept. 1771
They lived in Shrewsbury twp., York co.

Christ Lutheran KB, York:
George Nees and wife Anna Maria had:
        Maria Barbara b. 10 Feb. 1753, bp. 18 Feb. 1753
        Sp.: Philip and Anna Maria Mueller

Matheus Nees, Philadelphia co., nat. 1740.

372. NÄSS [NESS] HANS MICHEL age 30   Mitschdorf=
Britannia, 1731   67360 Woerth
S-H, I: 48, 49, 50   Preuschdorf=
                                                  67250 Soultz-sous-Forêts

  with Dorothea Neahs, age 27; Michel Nehs, age 1.
See also Mathias Näss.
Also on ship: Jacob Nehs, age 31; Johannes Nehs age 26, Dewald Nehs
age 24, and Hans Georg Nehs, age 21.

EUROPEAN RECORDS

Preuschdorf Lutheran KB:
Hans Michel Näss, smith, son of Mathis Näss, citizen here, m. 3 Feb. 1728
at Mitschdorff Anna Dorothea, daughter of the late Hans Martin Pfeiffer,
citizen at Preuschdorf. Notation in KB: "Went to the new land." They had:
        1. Maria Margretha b. 11 Jan. 1729, bp. 12 Jan. 1729, died.
        2. Hans Michel b. 12 July 1730, bp. 13 July 1730

AMERICAN RECORDS

Philadelphia Wills & Adm.:
Michael Ness, Philadelphia Adm. F:32, 1745, Estate #55.
Letters of Adm. granted 22 Feb. 1745 to Dorothy Nees of the county of
Bucks, widow of Michael Nees, deceased, and to Christopher Trube.
Inventory to be exhibited on or before 22 Mar. 1745 and before 20 Feb.
1746.

Indianfield Lutheran KB, Franconia twp., Montgomery co.:
Michael Neas, (Jr.) m. 6 Mar. 1753 Margaretha Zirkle - left for Virginia.
Conf. 1753 - Jacob Nees, age 14½, son of the late Michael Nees.
George Nees, son of the late Michael Nees, m. 20 Nov. 1753 Maria
Catharina, dau. of Adam Bender.

Mickel Neace, Bucks co., nat. by Act of Assembly, 19 May 1739.

373. NEUFER, SALOME   Hunspach=
Emigration date unknown   67250 Soultz-sous-Forêts
                                                            Hoffen=
                                               67250 Soultz-sous-Forêts

EUROPEAN RECORDS

A combined house-barn structure in Hunspach.

Hunspach Reformed KB:
There are two possibilities for this immigrant:
1. Johann Neufar, citizen at Hunspach, and wife Margareta had a daughter:
      Maria Salome b. 26 May 1730, bp. 28 May 1730, conf. 1744
      Sp.: Hans Martin, son of Georg Reedy; Margareta, wife
      of Hans Martin Lehmann; Maria Salome, dau. of Nickel Haug.

OR:
2. Joh. Georg Neufer, citizen and tailor here, and wife Maria
Catharina had a daughter:
Maria Salome b. 2 Sept. 1754

**Friedrich Krebs, "18th Century Emigrants from the Palatinate, Lower
Alsace, and Rheinhessen" in Don Yoder, ed. *Rhineland Emigrants*
(Baltimore, 1981): 67:**
The property left behind by Salome Neufer, who had gone to America from
Hofen, Lower Alsace, was confiscated for the treasury by decree of the
Zweibrücken Government dated July 14, 1778. At the same time the
request of her brothers and sisters for the release of the property was
denied.

374. NEÜSCHWENDER, PETER   67510 Lembach
     NEÜSCHWENDER, PETER
Hamilton, 1767
S-H, I: 716
   [one signed Neischwenter; one signed Neüschwender]

EUROPEAN RECORDS

Lembach Lutheran KB:
Hans Neuwischwander, son of the late Peter Neuwischwander from
Langenauw in der Schweitz [CH 3550 Langnau im Emmental, BE] m. 23
Nov. 1717 in Lembach, Maria Zimmermann, daughter of the late Joseph
Zimmermann, former citizen at *Zumeswald, Berner Gebiets* [CH-3454
Sumiswald, BE]. They had a son:
   Hans Peter b. 9 Oct. 1718, bp. 12 Oct. 1718

Johann Peter Neuschwanger, son of the late Johannes Neuschwanger, citizen
here, m. 23 Jan. 1742 Anna Eva, daughter of the late Johann Adam Götz,
former *potaschbrenner*. Both 23 years old. They had children:
   1. Maria Elisabetha b. 19 Feb. 1743, bp. 21 Feb. 1743
   2. Maria Barbara b. 15 Oct. 1744, bp. 18 Oct. 1744
   3. Johann Peter b. 14 Nov. 1746, bp. 16 Nov. 1746
   4. Christina Elisabetha b. 30 June 1749, bp. 2 July 1749
   5. Johann Martin b. 1 May 1751, died
   6. Johann Conrad b. 21 Apr. 1753, bp. 24 Apr. 1753

[The father signed each entry in the KB: Neischwenter; the signature
matches S-H, II: 823.]

Hatten Lutheran KB:
Adam Götz, *potaschbrenner*, and wife Anna Maria had a daughter:
Anna Eva b. 19 Apr. 1718, bp. 21 Apr. 1718.

AMERICAN RECORDS

First Reformed KB, Philadelphia:
Buried 9 Oct. 1783, Peter Neuschwanger, aged 65 years.

St. Michael's and Zion KB, Philadelphia:
Buried 27 Aug. 1785- Eva Neischwender, widow of Peter Neischwender. She
was b. in 1718 in [67690] Hatten, Alsace. She d. 25 Aug. 1785, age 67 years.
Peter Neuschwander m. 31 May 1773 Eva Velt.
Heinrich Petz m. 28 Sept. 1773 Barbara Neuschwander.

St. Michael's Lutheran KB, Germantown:
Died 29 Oct. 1782: Peter, son of Peter Neischwenner, age 6 y., 3 mo., 11
days.

Trinity Lutheran KB, Lancaster:
Conrad Neuschwender and wife Sybilla had a son:
Michael b. 5 May 1781, bp. 11 May 1781

1790 Census, Brunswick & Manheim twps. Berks co.:
Conrad Newswender   1 male over 16, 2 males under 16, 4 females
Peter Neuswender   2 males over 16, 2 males under 16, 2 females

375. NEWHARD, GEORG FRIEDRICH   67510 Lembach
St. Andrew Galley, 1737
S-H, I: 179, 181, 183
EUROPEAN RECORDS

Lembach Lutheran KB:
Georg Friedrich Newhard m. 22 Apr. 1727 at Schonau [W-6781 Schönau,
Pfalz] Maria Margaretha, daughter of the late Hans Frawhüger.
[See brothers-in-law Joh. Georg Kern, Peter Traxel and Jacob Frawinger,
for more Frawhüger data.]

Zweibrücken Manumissions Protocoll, 1737:
Georg Kern and Friederich Neühard of Rumbach move with wife and
children to America.
[See Dennis A. Kastens, *Neuhart Chronicle*, Vol. II, pg. 21-22 for a list of
their children, and additional Newhard ancestry and descendants.]

AMERICAN RECORDS

Egypt Reformed KB, Lehigh co.:
Friederich Neuhart and wife Margaretha had:
Joh. Michael Lorentz bp. 23 Sept. 1740
Sp.: Lorentz Guth; Michael Neuhardt; Juliana Catharina, wife of
Peter Traxel [q.v. Drachsel]; Engel, daughter of Simon Trumer.
[See Burgert, *The Western Palatinate* for Guth and Drumm.]

PA, Sixth Series, Vol. 6: p. 135:
Frederick Newhard died 29 Nov. 1765 and is buried in Allentown. He had
9 children. His son Lorentz Newhard died in Allentown on 1 Aug. 1817.

Northampton co. Will Abstracts:
Frederick Neihart, Whitehall. 1 Jan. 1764 - 14 May 1766.
Wife: Maria Margaretta. Children: Frederick, Lawrence, Peter, Christopher,
Daniel, Juliana wife of Stephen Schneider of Whitehall, Salome, Elizabeth
Barbara, Sophia.
Wit: George Knauss, George Jacob Kern.
[See *History of Lehigh County,* Vol. III, p. 950 for complete transcript of will]

Frederick Newhard nat. 10 Apr. 1755.

376. NIESS, THEOBALD   Hoffen=
_____, 1752   67250 Soultz-sous-Forêts

EUROPEAN RECORDS

Hunspach Reformed KB:
Hans Jacob Niess and wife Anna Maria of Hofen had a son:
Hans Diebolt b. 3 Mar. 1715, bp. 6 Mar. 1715.

Hoffen Reformed KB:
Theobald Niess, son of Jacob Niess, m. 13 Sept. ?1745 or ?1746, Elisabetha,
daughter of Jacob Hechler, former citizen at Hunspach. They had:
1. Maria Dorothea b. 20 Aug. 1747, bp. 22 Aug. 1747
Sp.: Joh. Jacob Mathes, citizen and wagoner here; Maria
Dorothea, wife of Michel Newiger; Rosina, wife of Theobald
Riedel, Oberseebach.

Zweibrücken Manumissions Protocoll, Clee- and Catharinenburg, 1752:
Theobald Niess of Hoffen leaves for America.

377. NIPPERT, EVA   Goersdorf=
after 1738   67360 Woerth
                        EUROPEAN RECORDS

Preuschdorf Lutheran KB:
Hans Michel Nippert, widower, m. 5 Jan. 1729 Anna Eva Lazarus from
Guntershoffen [Gundershoffen = 67110 Niederbronn-les-Bains]. They had:
    1. Johann Michael b. 21 Dec. 1729, bp. 24 Dec. 1729
    2. Theobald b. 18 June 1731, died 1733
    3. Maria Magdalena b. 25 June 1733, died 1734
    4. Eva Barbara b. 12 Nov. 1734, bp. 15 Nov. 1734

Eva nee Lazarus from Guntershofen, widow of the late *Meister* Hans Michel
Nippert, had a son:
    5. Johann Georg b. 13 Jan. 1737, died 1738.
    Notation in the KB: "this *Frau* went to the New Land".

378. NONNEMACHER, ABRAHAM   Rexingen=
Phoenix, 1749   67320 Drulingen
S-H, I: 405
                        EUROPEAN RECORDS

Berg und Thal Lutheran KB:
Andreas Nonnemacher, daylaborer at Rexingen, and wife Anna Maria, had
a son:
        Abraham b. 12 Oct. 1716

Abraham Nunnemacher, linenweaver, son of Andreas Nunnemacher, former
inhabitant and farmer at Rexingen, m. 14 Apr. 1739 Anna Christina,
daughter of Hans Adam Otto, former inhabitant and cartwright at
Lorentzen. They had children:
    1. Catharina Christina b. 26 Dec. 1739
    2. Johann Nickel b. 17 Dec. 1740
    3. Eva Catharina b. 24 Jan. 1743
    4. Anna Margaretha b. 15 Mar. 1744
    5. Georg Philipp b. 16 Aug. 1747

                        AMERICAN RECORDS

PA, Third Series, Vol. XXI: 171, 332, 648, 667:
Abram Nunnemacher appears on the York Town tax lists for the years 1780,
1781, 1782, 1783.

York co. Wills:
Abraham Nunnamacher, York (Boro). 19 Aug. 1791- 12 Sept. 1791.
Wife: Christiana. Children: Anna, wife of Henry Lochner; Nicholas.
Exr: Henry Lochner.

379. NONNEMACHER, HANS EMERICH age 45   Weyer=
    NONNEMACHER, REINHART age 20   67320 Drulingen
    NONNEMACHER, HENRY age 16
Lydia, 1741
S-H, I: 301, 302, 303
                    EUROPEAN RECORDS

Hirschland Lutheran KB:
Conf. 23 May 1706 - Hans Emrich Nonnemacher from Weyer.

Joh. Emmerich Nonnemacher, son of Nicklaus Nonnemacher from Weyer
m. 26 Jan. 1717 Barbara Gösler from Zielingen [possibly Zollingen = 67260
Sarre-Union]. Emigration notation by marriage record that both went to
America [no children listed in KB].
Nickel Nonnemacker d. 4 Sept. 1726, age 82 years. He had 58 grandchildren
and 13 great-grandchildren.

                    AMERICAN RECORDS

St. Michael's and Zion KB, Philadelphia:
Hans Emerich Nonnemacher was sp. in Apr. 1754 for a child of Mathias
Schütz and wife Anna Barbara.

Matheus Schütze m. 9 Feb. 1748 Anna Barbara Nonnemacher.
Wit: Mathews Schütze, Joh. Emerich Nonnemacher, David Kercher,
Nicolaus Leiser, Wilhelm Tauber.

Indianfield Lutheran KB, Montgomery co:
Daniel Nonnemacher, widower, son of John Emmerich Nonnemacher, m. 26
Nov. 1754 Henrietta Niel, servant of Jacob Leyde.

Charles Price, *A History of Christ Reformed Church at Indian Creek
(Indianfield),* **Montgomery co., PA (Telford, 1966): 93-97:**
 John Emrich Nunnemacher, b. in Germany ca. 1696; d. in Rockhill twp. in
1777. He purchased a tract of land in Rockhill twp., Bucks co., just east of
the Bucks and Montgomery co. line.
 "Emrich Nunnemacher died in 1777, but his estate was not settled until 10
Dec. 1793; therefore, the land was still in his name when Jacob Cressman

purchased the land in 1788, and is the homestead fram where he probably died. He was naturalized in Philadelphia on 24 Sept. 1762, having taken the Sacrament on 6 Sept. 1762. We find him listed on the Deacons' Collection Lists of 1768, 1772, and 1776.

The Bucks county Recorder of Deeds records show that on 11 Nov. 1767 Emrich Nunnemacher loaned his son, John Nunnemacher, 600 Pounds on a second mortgage on a farm he purchased in Plumstead Township, Bucks county, which was recorded 8 May 1768. This farm amounted to 178 acres and was purchased by John Nunnemacher on 8 Dec. 1763, and he sold it to Francis Titus of Plumstead township on 2 June 1773. These transactions have the appearance that son, John, may not have progressed too well on this Plumstead township farm.

In Emrich Nunnemacker's will we see that he had married Judith _____ late in life, as he mentions that Judith was to have the plantation she possessed before they were married, which was in Durham twoship. He divided the balance of the estate into seven parts among his seven children or their heirs. The settlement was made on 10 Dec. 1793, and the Settlement total for personal estate was £ 438 and the balance left for distribution was £ 107. The will gives his occupation as a "Joiner," a carpenter or cabinet maker. The will was written by Abraham Stout, with a neighbor George Nase, a blacksmith, and his son Henry as Executors.

On 28 Aug. 1779 Judith Nunnemacher, widow of John Emrich Nunnemacher sold her plantation situated in Tinicum Township containing 100 A, bordering along the Delaware River and the mouth of Tinicum Creek, for £ 1700 to Colonel George Wall. This is not the plantation mentioned in the Emerich Nunnemacher Will, as the deed records that it was purchased by James Wilson on 6 June 1779 and sold to Judith Nunnemacher on 22 June 1779. The Will mentions certain things she is to have since she brought them with her whey they married. This would, therefore, appear that his farm was one she may have received from possibly her first husband, or at least from her side of the family."

The known children of Joh. Emrich Nunnemacher were:
1. Daniel, birth date unknown. He married as a widower, son of John Emmerich Nonnemacher, 26 Nov. 1754 Henrietta Niel. He does not appear on the ship list, and is possibly the Daniel Nonnemacher who arrived on the *Ann* Galley in 1752 [S-H, I:486]. They had children bp. at Indianfield Lutheran Church.
2. Reinhart b. ca 1721
3. Henry b. ca 1725, m. Elisabeth ----? Lived in Rockhill twp., and several children appear in the Tohickon Lutheran KB.
4. Jacob, sp. at Tohickon, m. Catharine ---?; d. 3 Aug. 1803 at Tohickon; lived in Salisbury twp., Northampton co.
5. Solomon, b. ca 1737, conf. 1753, age 16, son of Emmerich N. He m. Anna Maria ---? and had children bp. at Indianfield KB.

6. Johannes Nunemacher m. 20 July 1746 at Trappe Lutheran KB, Maria Müller, living in Indianfield. Children listed in the Indianfield Lutheran KB.
7. Barbara
8. Anna Maria, single sp. in 1752, Tohickon KB.
9. Possibly Sarah, who sp. a child of Solomon N. in 1765, at Indianfield.

Embrick Nonemaker, Cushhohoppen, Philadelphia co., nat. 24 Sept. 1762.

380. NONNEMACHER, A daughter of **JOHANNES**   Weyer=
Emigration date unknown   67320 Drulingen

EUROPEAN RECORDS

Hirschland Lutheran KB:
Johannes Nonnemacher m. 27 Oct. 1705 Anna Sibilla Funck from Weyer. They had:
1. **A daughter (n.n.)** bp. 11 July 1706
   Notation by baptism that she went to America.
   Sp.: Anna Catharina Schneider and Anna Maria Bircker
2. Anna Eva b. 26 May 1720, bp. crossed out, but
   no emigration notation.

381. NONNENMACHER, JOH. MICHAEL   Merkwiller-Pechelbronn=
Minerva, 1770   67250 Soultz-sous-Forêts
S-H, I: 730
EUROPEAN RECORDS

Kutzenhausen Lutheran KB:
Joh. Niclaus Nonnenmacher and wife Susanna had a son:
   Johann Michael b. 24 May 1736, bp. 26 May 1736

Johann Michael Nonnenmacher, son of Nicolaus Nonnenmacher, citizen and farmer at Merckweyler, m. 11 Jan. 1763 Maria Salome, daughter of Johann Georg Hirlemann, also citizen and farmer there. They had children:
1. Dorothea b. 5 Dec. 1763
   Sp.: Michel Senn, forester at Merckweiler; Salome Dorothea Marx nee Rieth, of Feldbach; Dorothea Trautmann, single, from Oberkutzenhausen.
2. Georg Heinrich b. 15 July 1766
   Sp.: Michel Greiss of Höllschlach [Hoelschloch]; Georg

Heinrich, son of Georg Hirlemann; Susanna, wife of Georg Trog.
3. Nicolaus b. 5 Dec. 1768, bp. 6 Dec. 1768
Sp.: Michel Senn, *Herrschaffl. Förster*; Daniel Weiss,
citizen and farmer at Merckweiler; Maria Barbara, wife of
Georg Heinrich Trautmann of Oberkutzenhausen.

[Joh. Michael Nonnenmacher's signature in the church book by these baptisms matches his signature on the ship list, S-H, II: 843.]

AMERICAN RECORDS

1790 Census:
Michl. Nunneymaker, German twp., Fayette co:
2 males over 16; 1 male under 16; 5 females.

382. OBEL, CHRISTOFEL   Altwiller=
Robert and Alice, 1739   67260 Sarre-Union
S-H, I: 264, 267, 270

EUROPEAN RECORDS

Keskastel Lutheran KB:
Christoph Obel, single butcher, son of Adam Obel from Saarwerden
[Sarrewerden=67260 Sarre-Union], m. (1) 16 Nov. 1723 at Altweiler, Anna,
daughter of Michel Gele.

Diedendorf Reformed KB: [Also recorded Rauwiller Reformed KB].
Christofel Obell from Altweiller, m. (2) 6 Oct. 1728 Catharina Barbara,
daughter of Johannes Eschbach from Berg [=67320 Drulingen].

[No children listed in either KB].

AMERICAN RECORDS

Jordan Lutheran KB, South Whitehall twp., Lehigh co.:
Catharina Barbara Obel was sp. in 1744 for children of Henrich Christmann
and Abraham Knerr [q.v.].

Christoph Obel and Catharina Barbara were sp. in 1748 for a child of Jacob
Dannert.

Hocker, *German Settlers of Pennsylvania:*
Pennsylvanische Geschicht-Schreiber, dated 1 June 1749:

Imanuel Schneider, with Christophel Obel, Macungie (now Lehigh co.) seeks his two sons, Hansz Henrich, 23 years old, and Philip, 25 years old.

Lancaster Will Book Y-2: 48:
Christopher Obel, Lebanon twp. 20 Oct. 1767-11 July 1768.
Wife: Catharine Obel. Exrs: Philip Gerber and Andrew Eshbach [q.v.].

Christopr. Oble, Lowhill twp., Northampton co., nat. Autumn 1765.

Several old buildings in Altwiller still have the water pump in the yard.

383. OBERSTEG, MARTIN   Lorentzen=
Phoenix, 1749   67430 Diemeringen
S-H, I: 407

EUROPEAN RECORDS

Lorentzen Lutheran KB:
Martin Obersteg, Reformed, miller of Lorentzen, and wife Christina nee Friedrich had children:
>   1. Catharina Elisabetha b. 9 Aug. 1724, conf. 1738
>   She m. 25 May 1745 at Lorentzen Peter Rebenack.
>   2. Johann Nicolaus b. 19 Nov. 1725, d. 21 Nov. 1726
>   3. Johann Friedrich b. 4 Nov. 1728

Martin Obersteg, Reformed, miller at Lorentzen and wife Catharina Eva had a daughter:
> Louisa bp. 29 Jan. 1749 at Lorentzen

Verification of this emigrant provided by Dr. Bernd Gölzer from the compiled records of Dr. Gerhard Hein:
Records of Saarwerden county office for Mackweiler: [Mackwiller = 67430 Diemeringen]   15 July 1758, inventory of Hans Henrich Friedrich of Mackweiler, who died single, leaving no issue; his sister Christina nee Friedrich is deceased. Her husband Martin Obersteg of Lorentzen has moved to the New Land.
1742 Census of Lorentzen: Martin Obersteg, miller, 60 years old. [hence b. ca. 1682].

AMERICAN RECORDS

First Reformed KB, Philadelphia:
Joh. Martin Obersteg and wife Catharina Eva had:
> Johanna Maria Henrietta b. 22 Sept. 1750, bp. 30 Sept. 1750
> Sp.: Henry Basler and wife

Died 16 Mar. 1762 - Martin Obersteig, aged 77 years.

St. Michael's and Zion KB, Philadelphia:
Martin Obersteg and wife Cathrina had a son:
> Johannes b. 29 Sept. 1753, bp. 6 Oct. 1753

Adam Feberetz m. 5 Aug. 1762 Anna Catharina Obersteg(in), widow.

384. OBERSTEG, PETER   Lorentzen=
Phoenix, 1749   67430 Diemeringen
S-H, I: 407

EUROPEAN RECORDS

Lorentzen Lutheran KB:
Hans Martin Obersteg of Lorentzen and wife Anna Margaretha had a son:
> **Peter** bp. 10 Aug. 1714

Peter Obersteg, Reformed, miller at Lorentzen, and wife Anna Elisabetha [her name also given as Margaretha in records] had children:
> 1. Johann Peter bp. 16 Dec. 1743
> 2. Johann Jacob bp. 14 Mar. 1745, d. 17 June 1745
> 3. Johann Christian bp. 10 Apr. 1746
> 4. Louisa Catharina bp. 14 Feb. 1748

AMERICAN RECORDS

First Reformed KB, Philadelphia:
Joh. Peter Obersteg and wife Anna Maria nee Regelsperger had:
A child (N.N.) b. 2 Dec. 1750 bp. _ Dec. 1750
Sp.: John Opp and Elisabetha Catharina Mischler

385. OFFENBACH, ANDREAS   Froeschwiller=
      OFFENBACH, JACOB   67360 Woerth
Minerva, 1770
S-H, I: 730

EUROPEAN RECORDS

Langensoultzbach Lutheran KB:
Andreas Offenbach m. 21 May 1737 Susanna Barbara Hermann from Hirschthal.

Andreas Offenbach, citizen and tailor at Fröschweiler, and Susanna Barbara nee Hermann had:
1. Philip Jacob b. 19 Aug. 1742
2. Andreas b. 10 Apr. 1747, bp. 13 Apr. 1747
   Sp.: Joh. Jacob Becker; Maria Catharina, nee Ruthi, wife of Jacob Meyer; Johann Philipp Schweitzer; Catharina Spielmann, daughter of Hans Diebold Spielmann.

AMERICAN RECORDS

St. Michael's and Zion KB, Philadelphia:
Philip Jac. Offenbach m. 2 Feb. 1777 Catharina Schnerr.

386. OSTERROTH, JUSTES   67430 Diemeringen
Pennsylvania Merchant, 1733
S-H, I: 122, 125, 126

EUROPEAN RECORDS

Diemeringen Lutheran KB:
Bartholomeus Osterroth, schoolteacher at Diemeringen, and wife Ottilia nee Dionysius had a son:
Johann Gustav b. 1 Sept. 1707, conf. 1722

Verification of this emigration supplied by Dr. Bernd Gölzer, from the county records of Nassau-Saarwerden, compiled by Dr. Gerhard Hein: Records of the Notary Public for Diemeringen: 14 Mar. 1741, inventory of Ottilia Dionysius: her son Johann Gustav Osterroth is in America.

387. OTZ, WILHELM   Herbitzheim=
Bilander *Vernon*, 1747   67260 Sarre-Union
S-H, I: 364

EUROPEAN RECORDS

Herbitzheim Lutheran KB:
Wilhelm Otz (Ott in one record), daylaborer at the Hoff, and wife Anna Elisabetha had children:

1. Louisa Catharina b. 26 July 1742, bp. 29 July 1742
   Sp.: Christian Hochstädter, *Melcker* at the Hoff; Justina
   Catharina, wife of Daniel Eichacker, *Hoffman*; Joh. Adam Matt
   from Ermingen [67970 Oermingen]; Maria Louisa, wife of Mr.
   Joh. Philipp Grishile.
2. Maria Margaretha b. 21 Dec. 1744, bp. 24 Dec. 1744.
   She d. 28 Jan. 1745.
   Sp.: Joh. Nickel, son of Joh. Georg Eisemann [q.v.],
   Gerichtsmann; Georg, son of Christian Wampfler [q.v.],
   master weaver here; Maria Catharina, daughter of the late
   Andreas Ingold, citizen and potter at [67430] Diemeringen;
   Anna Margaretha Wägelin from Burbach [=67260 Sarre-Union].
3. Andreas b. 7 Dec. 1745, bp. 9 Dec. 1745.

AMERICAN RECORDS

Trinity Lutheran KB, New Holland, Lancaster co.:
Wilhelm Ots, Reformed, and wife Anna Elisabetha, Lutheran, had:

4. Johann Lorentz b. 21 Oct. 1748, bp. 23 Oct. 1748
   Sp.: Lorenz Maier and wife Margaretha.

388. PETER, HEINRICH age 26   67360 Woerth
Samuel, 1733
S-H, I: 107, 109, 111, 112
   with Catharina age 32 and Henry age 1

EUROPEAN RECORDS

Woerth Lutheran KB:
Heinrich Peter, son of Jacob Peter, pig herdsman at Wörth, m. 17 Jan. 1731
Maria Catharina Enssminger, daughter of Philip Enssminger, *Schirmer* at
Mättingen, Herrschaft Finstingen. [possibly Metting=57370 Phalsbourg].

AMERICAN RECORDS

Hocker, *German Settlers of Pennsylvania*, p. 13:
Pennsylvanische Geschicht-Schreiber, 16 Apr. 1749:
Henrich Peter, dyer, Falckner Swamp, near Jan Neisz, Jacob Mayer,
Waldoerffer and Philip Hahn (Montgomery co).

One Henrich Peters, Philadelphia co., nat. 1740
One Henry Peter, York twp, York co., nat. 1762
One Henry Peters, Lebanon twp, Lancaster co., nat. 1765

389. PETERSOHN, JOH. CHRISTIAN   67690 Hatten
[unnamed ship], 20 Oct. 1747
S-H, I: 369, 370
EUROPEAN RECORDS

Hatten Lutheran KB:
Christian Petersohn, hatmaker, and wife Susanna Maria nee Schmitt had a
son:
    1. **Joh. Christian,** his bp. not located at Hatten

The father Christian Petersohn m. (2) 1741 Catharina Elisabetha
Reichardeau, daughter of Gabriel Hericourt of [25200] Montbeliard. They
had two children there, both died young.

Joh. Christian Petersohn, son of Joh. Christian Petersohn, citizen and
hatmaker here, was a sp. 8 Apr. 1738 for a child of Ulrich Huffschmitt.
Petersohn's signature in the KB by this baptismal entry matches the
signature of the immigrant in S-H, II: 401.

390. PFEIFER, FRIEDRICH   Mitschdorf=
Thistle of Glasgow, 1730   67360 Woerth
S-H, I: 31, 33, 34   Preuschdorf=
                                      67250 Soultz-sous-Forêts

EUROPEAN RECORDS

Preuschdorf Lutheran KB:
Hans Martin Pfeiffer, son of Hans Balthaser Pfeiffer of Preuschdorf, m. 25 Nov. 1692 Anna Maria Motz, daughter of the late Michel Motz of Mitschdorf. Hans Martin Pfeiffer died 27 Sept. 1706, aged 42 y, after being mistreated by a soldier between Fröschweiler and Wörth. Children:
    1. Maria Barbara bp. 15 Dec. 1693. She m. 1718 Hans Georg Bellman [q.v.].
    2. Anna Margaretha bp. 24 Aug. 1695. She m. 1720 Hans Georg Hammer [q.v.].
    3. Hans Heinrich b. 20 Jan. 1698, bp. 21 Jan. 1698
    4. Georg Friedrich b. 15 Apr. 1699, bp. 17 Apr. 1699
    5. Maria Catharina b. 25 Nov. 1700, bp. 28 Nov. 1700
    6. Anna Dorothea b. 17 Nov. 1702. She m. 1728 Hans Michel Näss [Nehs, q.v.].
    7. Hans Martin b. 1 Mar. 1706 [Entry crossed out - possibly died].

(Georg) Friedrich Pfeifer, son of the late Martin Pfeifer, citizen at Mitschdorf, m. (1) __ Jan. 1720 Maria Elisabetha, daughter of Hans Michel Stocker of Mitschdorf. Children:
    1. Anna Catharina b. __ Sept. 1720, bp. 10 Sept. 1720; she d. 1722
    2. Maria Barbara b. 13 July 1723, bp. 15 July 1723

Maria Elisabetha, wife of Friedrich Pfeifer, d. 13 Feb. 1725, age 27 years.

Georg Friedrich Pfeifer m. (2) __ Oct. 1725 Christina Schaffer, daughter of the late Balthasar Schaffer, citizen at Preuschdorf.
[His first wife was a sister-in-law of Schram and Stiefel, who also arrived on the *Thistle of Glasgow,* 1730. His second wife was a sister-in-law of Heinrich Acker and half-sister of Friedrich Schäfer, both 1732 immigrants.]

391. PHILIPPI, JOHANNES   Volksberg=
PHILIPPI, JOHANNES, JR.   67290 Wingen-sur-Moder
PHILIPPI, ANDREAS
PHILIPPI, CHRISTIAN
Phoenix, 1750
S-H, I: 441
  another Johannes Philippi also arrived on the *Phoenix,* 1750 and appears on S-H, I: 442 as Johannes Filipipi [did not sign].

EUROPEAN RECORDS

Waldhambach Lutheran KB:
Johannes Philippi, nailsmith at Volksberg, and wife Maria Christina nee

Cleiss, had children:
1. Johannes, conf. 1735
2. Andreas, conf. 1738
3. Christian, bapt. sponsor in 1748
4. Eva Christina b. 13 Jan. 1730, conf. 1743
5. Anna Maria b. 16 Aug. 1733, d. 26 Aug. 1733
6. Anna Elisabetha b. 31 Oct. 1734, conf. 1749
7. Johann Jacob b. 9 Dec. 1737

The other Johannes Philippi who arrived on the same ship might be the following:
Johann Georg Philippi m. 26 ___ 1723 in Volksburg Anna Barbara Roth. They had a son:
Johannes b. 9 Oct. 1728, conf. 1745; he last appears in the record in 1748 as a bp. sponsor.

AMERICAN RECORDS

Muddy Creek Moravian KB, Lancaster co.:
Johannes Philippi, a nailsmith, was m. in Muddy Creek 17 Sept. 1751 to Juliana Riehm, youngest daughter of Johann Eberhardt Riehm. They had:
1. Johannes b. 25 July 1752 in Readingtown, bp. 1 Nov. 1752 in his father's arms. Sp.: Eberhardt Riehm, grandfather.

Rev. Daniel Schumacher's records:
2. Juliana bp. 29 Dec. 1754
Sp.: Jürg Schultze and wife Maria Juliana.

Rev. John Casper Stoever's Records:
Christian Philippy m. 12 Dec. 1752 Anna Maria Ensminger, Cocalico. They had children:
1. Johannes b. 5 May 1755, bp. 25 May 1755, Muddy Creek Lutheran KB. Sp.: Joh. Ludwig Ensminger and wife Christina
2. Anna Maria b. Aug. 1757, bp. 8 Oct. 1757
Sp.: John Nicolaus Ensminger, Jr. and Anna Maria Nef.

John Ludwig Ensminger m. 12 Dec. 1752 Eva Christina Philippi, Cocalico. They were sp. at Muddy Creek Lutheran Church for a child of Valentin Schneider in 1752.

John Nicolaus Ensminger m. 18 May 1754 Christ. Elisab. Philippi, Cocalico. They were sp. at Muddy Creek Lutheran Church for a child of Joh. Ludwig Ensminger in 1753.

Another Johannes Philippy m. 2 Aug. 1757 Maria Eva Barbara Eichelberger, Warwick. Johannes Philippi was a sp. at Muddy Creek Lutheran Church for a child of Joh. Jacob Juncker in 1751. They had children, bp. at
Emanuel Lutheran KB, (Warwick), Elizabeth twp., Lancaster co.:
1. Maria Barbara b. 25 July 1758, d. 29 Aug, 1758
   Sp.: Leonhardt Miller and wife Barbara
2. Johannes b. 20 Jan. 1760, bp. 3 Feb. 1760. Same sp.
3. Anna Elisabeta b. 15 Nov. 1764
4. Christoph b. 29 Dec. 1762, Eichelberger Sp.
5. Christina Barbara b. 12 Dec. 1763, Eichelberger Sp.
6. Sophia Barbara b. 29 Dec. 1765
7. Christina Catharina b. 1 Feb. 1767
8. Maria Margaretha b. 17 Jan. 1769.

Salem Lutheran KB, Lebanon, burials:
Daniel Ensminger d. 24 Aug. 1802, age 45 yrs. less 13 days. He was a son of Nicolaus and Elisabeth Ensminger, b. 5 Sept. in Lancaster County. Baptized and confirmed. On 24 June 1795 he m. Christiana Fahring (Fahrny). They had no children. Sickness, consumption. He was sick a long time.

Christina Elisabeth Ensminger (nee Philippi) d. 15 May 1803, age 68 yrs. 9 mos. 28 days. She was a daughter of Johannes Philippi and wife Christina, b. 3 Nov. 1734 in Vollsperg in Alsace. Baptized and confirmed. Came to this country in her 15th year with her parents and lived in Muddy Creek. In May 1754 she m. Nicolaus Ensminger. They had nine children, six are living. Her husband died 1 Apr. 1782. She was ill a long time.

Lancaster Wills:
Nicholas Ensminger, Lebanon twp., 21 Feb. 1781- 28 June 1781.
Wife: Elisabeth. Children: Peter and Daniel.
Exrs.: Christopher Zebold and Jacob Phillippi.

Jacob Phillippi, Heidelberg twp., Berks co., nat. Autumn, 1765
Christian Philippi, Cocalico twp., Lancaster co., nat. Autumn, 1765
John Phillippi, Elizabeth twp., Lancaster co., nat. Autumn, 1765.

392. PHILIPPI, JÖRG FRANTZ   Volksberg=
Phoenix, 1749   67290 Wingen-sur-Moder
S-H, I: 404
                        EUROPEAN RECORDS

Waldhambach Lutheran KB:
There are two possibilities for this immigrant:
Johann Nicolaus Philippi, citizen at Volksberg, son of Georg Hans Philippi, *Kirchschaffner der Grafschaft Lützelstein,* m. 27 Feb. 1716 in Waldhambach, Anna Eva Hauptmann, daughter of Johann Jacob Hauptmann of Weinburg. Their son:

> George Franz b. 24 May 1733, conf. 1748.

OR

George Frantz Philippi, son of Johannes Philippi, former citizen and church *censor* at Vollsberg, m. 27 Nov. 1725 in Tieffenbach, Anna Magdalena, daughter of Johann Michael Reitenauer of Tieffenbach. They had a son:

> Georg Frantz b. 1 Oct. 1726, conf. 1740.

The next name on the ship list is Hans Goerg Weidenauer who is probably Hans Georg Reidenauer [q.v.; the signature on the ship list, S-H, II: 451, could very well be Reidenauer.]

Houses with canopies in the distinctive Alsatian
architecture in the picturesque village of Seebach.

393. PROBST, PHILIP JACOB (sick)   Oberseebach=
John and William, 1732   67160 Wissembourg
S-H, I: 102, 103
   with Cathrina Proops, Michael Proops, Felder Proops

EUROPEAN RECORDS

Oberseebach Catholic and Protestant KB:
(All records combined together in one KB; entries in Latin):
Philippi Jacobi Probst and wife Anna Catharina, Lutheran, had children:
   1. Joannes Michael bp. 28 Aug. 1721
   2. Joannes Valentinus bp. 18 Feb. 1724
      Sp.: Joannes Valentinus Christ; Anna Elisabeth Aenes
   3. Joannes Martin bp. 29 Dec. 1726
   4. Anna Maria bp. 8 Mar. 1731
      Sp.: Anna Maria Köbel; Jacobus Christ.

AMERICAN RECORDS

Rev. Daniel Schumacher's records:
Michel Probst and wife Maria Elisabeth had:
   1. Eva Rosina bp. 3 Aug. 1755 in Allemangle
      Sp.: Jacob Driess and Eva Catharina Probst, single
   2. Valentin b. 2 May 1764, bp. 13 May 1764 in Allemangel
      Sp.: Valentin Probst, a married man and his sister
      Dorothea Probst
   3. Christian b. 14 Sept. 1767, bp. 25 Oct. 1767 in Allemangel
      Sp.: Christian Hechler and Maria

Conf. 1757 in Albany twp: Jürg Probst
Conf. 1761 in Weisenberg Church: Philipp Jacob Probst

Martin Probst, single, was a sp. in Allemangel in 1767.

Berks co. Wills and Adm:
Philip Brobst, Philadelphia County (Phila. County when will was written,
Albany township, Berks County, when will was probated). Dated 1747- 21
Mar. 1760. Provides for wife, Cerene (Name ?). To son Michael 100 acres
of land, grist mill and implements of husbandry. To daughter Anamary £50
when she is of age. To daughter Eve Catrena £50; To daughter Dority £50
when of age. Son Feltea (Valentine) to have 100 acres "that is the old
settlement haus". Son Marte also mentioned. (This will is very confused
and difficult to understand). Letters c.t.a. to Michael Brobst. Wit. Erhard
Fosselman and Wm. Farmer.

Michael Brobst, Albany twp., 15 July 1771: adm. to Henry Brobst, eldest son, the widow renouncing.

Berks co. Wills and Adm:
Valentin Probst, Albany twp., 3 July 1775 - 16 Oct. 1775.
Wife: Catharina. "To Jacob Probst, son of my deceased brother Michael, the plantation I bought of Jacob Gortner at the price I gave for it." Mentions brothers and sisters: deceased brother Martin Probst, and his daughter Catharina Stein; sister Dorothea Federolff, wife of Jacob Federolff, and their son Johannes; Exrs: Wife Catharine and brother-in-law Frederick Kill (Hill?) and nephew Henry Probst.
Wit: Philip Stambach and George Kistler.

Martin Probst, Albany, Berks co., nat. 24 Sept. 1762
Michael Probst, Albany, Berks co., nat. 24/25 Sept. 1761
Valentin Probst, Albany, Berks co., nat. 24/25 Sept. 1761

394. QUIRIN, NICKEL   Wolfskirchen=
Halifax, 1752   67260 Sarre-Union
S-H, I: 484
EUROPEAN RECORDS

Wolfskirchen Lutheran KB, Family Book:
Pritius Quirin died 1719, age 71. His wife Rosina died 1712. They had:
1. Daniel Quirin m. 1693 Anna Catharina Schaffer
2. Johannes Quirin, was schoolmaster in Schopperten
3. Nickel Quirin *"ist ins Neue Land gezogen"*.

Johannes Nicolaus Quirin, son of Briccius Quirin of Wolffskirchen, m. 27 Jan. 1711 Maria Magdalena daughter of Daniel Fischer of Pistorff.
Joh. Nickel Quirin and wife Maria Magdalena had:
1. Johann Mathias b. 23 Feb. 1712, conf. 1725 at Wolfskirchen.
2. Maria Louisa b. 21 June 1714
3. Maria Elisabetha b. 24 May 1716
4. Anna Christina b. 14 Sept. 1718
5. Catharina Margaretha b. 17 Feb. 1721
6. Margaretha Elisabetha b. 4 Mar. 1723
7. Maria Magdalena b. 15 Aug. 1725

Diedendorf Lutheran KB:
Nickel Quirin and wife Maria Magdalena nee Fischer had:
8. Catharina Elisabetha b. 11 Feb. 1729
9. Johann Henrich b. 4 June 1731

AMERICAN RECORDS

Christ Lutheran KB (Mertz's), Bieber Creek, Berks co:
Philip Mertz m. 29 May 1764 Catharina Quierin.

Nicolas Bieber and Catharina Quierin were sp. in 1761 for a child of Michael Bauer.

An Elisabetha Quierin was sp. in 1759 for a child of Jacob Schirner.

Nicolaus Quirin and wife Margretha nee Baur had:
　　1. Christina b. 9 July 1757, bp. 31 July 1757
　　　　Sp.: Joh. Mich. Schaefer & Christina Steinbrenner
　　2. Johann Henrich b. 6 Jan. 1760, bp. 29 Feb. 1760
　　　　Sp.: Johann Henrich Mertz and Anna Maria.

Nichs. Quierin, Maxatawny twp., Berks co., nat. Autumn, 1765.

Title page of the Lutheran KB at Diedendorf.

395. REBMANN, ANNA MARIA   Uttenhoffen=
before 1740   67110 Niederbronn-les-Bains

EUROPEAN RECORDS

Gundershoffen Lutheran KB:
Hans Jacob Rebmann, pig herder at Griesbach, and wife Anna Maria had children:
  1. Johannes b. 22 June 1713, bp. 23 June 1713
     [He might be the Johannes Rebmann, age 19, who arrived on the *Loyal Judith*, 1732].
  2. Anna Maria b. 7 June 1715 at Uttenhoffen
     Sp.: Hanns Jacob Reinhard, son of Hanns Jacob Reinhard from Uttenhoffen; Anna Maria, daughter of Rudolph Erb; Veronica, wife of Hans Conrad of Mitisheim [Mietesheim].

AMERICAN RECORDS

York Moravian KB, York co.:
Johann Daniel Votrin [q.v.-Johannes Votrin], b. 24 June 1711 in Helleringen, Reformed, m. (2) __ Apr. 1740 Anna Maria nee Rebmann, b. 10 June 1715 in Utenhofen in Elsass, Reformed.
[See Johannes Votrin for additional data].

396. REEB, GUSTAVUS   Pistorff today=
Halifax, 1754   Bischtroff-sur-Sarre=
S-H, I: 652,654   67260 Sarre-Union

EUROPEAN RECORDS

Bischtroff Lutheran KB:
Peter Reeb, innkeeper from Pistorff, and wife Anna Margretha Guth had a son:
             Gustavus bp. *Domin. Reminiscere* 1699
             Sp.: Gustavus Herrnschmidt from Pistorff (Pastor), Herr Joh. Nickel Braun from Bockenheim (=67260 Sarre-Union)

Gustavus Reeb m. 14 June 1718 Anna Margretha Stroh, daughter of *Herr* Jost Stroh, now *Landmeyer* in the *Graffschafft Saarwerden*. Gustavus Reeb is mentioned in the later records as *Herr Handelsmann*. They had children:
  1. Anna Margretha b. 27 Mar. 1719, bp. 30 Mar. 1719
  2. Susanna Magdalena b. 20 Feb. 1720, bp. 22 Feb. 1720
  3. Elisabetha Barbara b. 9 Feb. 1722

4. Christina Dorothea b. 13 June 1723
5. Joh. Peter [q.v.] b. 6 Sept. 1724
   Sp.: Hans Peter Bader, the old church *censor;* Theobald Stroh
   from Wiebersweiler; the Pastor's wife Louisa Salome Houssdorff.
6. Johann Jacob b. 18 Nov 1726, bp. 22 Nov 1726
7. Johann Georg b. 17 Mar. 1729, bp. 20 Mar 1729
8. Johann Henrich b. 8 Jan 1731, bp. 12 Jan 1731
9. Susanna Magdalena b. 20 Dec. 1732, bp. 23 Dec. 1732
10. Joh. Gustavus b. 10 Dec. 1734, bp. 15 Dec. 1734
   Sp.: Herr Peter Endross, Diedendorff [=67260 Sarre-Union];
   Philipp Heinrich Becker, miller; Anna Eva, wife of Daniel
   Weiss; Maria Elisabetha, wife of Mstr. Hans Nickel Weidmann
11. Rosina b. 25 Mar. 1737, bp. 27 Mar. 1737
12. Joh. Nicolaus b. 12 Apr. 1739
13. Joh. Michael b. 31 May 1741
14. Joh. Friedrich b. 29 Aug. 1743, bp. 1 Sept. 1743
15. Anna Christina b. 21 Mar. 1746
16. [After the death of Gustavus Reeb, his widow had:]
    Joh. Jacob b. 16 Dec. 1748

House-barn structure in Bischtroff.

Verification of this emigration supplied by Dr. Bernd Gölzer, from the county records of Nassau-Saarwerden, compiled by Dr. Gerhard Hein: Records of Saarwerden county office for Pisdorf, dated 25 Aug. 1748, inventory of Gustavus Reeb: son Gustav is 13 years old. Dated 13 Oct. 1758: son Gustav, 23 years old, smith, has moved to the New Land.

397. REEB, PETER   Pistorff today=
Halifax, 1752   Bischtroff-sur-Sarre=
S-H, I: 482,483,484   67260 Sarre-Union

EUROPEAN RECORDS

Bischtroff Lutheran KB:
Peter Reeb, innkeeper from Pistorff, and wife Anna Margretha Guth had a son:
> Gustavus bp.*Domin. Reminiscere* 1699

Gustavus Reeb, m. 14 June 1718 Anna Margretha Stroh, daughter of Herr Jost Stroh, *Landmeyer in the Graffschafft Saarwerden.* [See immigrant Gustavus Reeb for a list of their children]. Their fifth child was:
> Joh. Peter b. 6 Sept. 1724
> Sp.: Hans Peter Bader, the old church *censor.* Theobald Stroh from Wiebersweiler and the Pastor's wife Louisa Salome Houssdorff.

Verification of this emigration supplied by Dr. Bernd Gölzer, from the county records of Nassau-Saarwerden, compiled by Dr. Gerhard Hein: Records of Saarwerden county office for Pisdorf: dated 25 Aug. 1748, inventory of Gustavus Reeb: the son Peter, 23 years old, coppersmith, single. Dated 13 Oct. 1758: son Peter, 33 years old, has moved to Pennsylvania several years ago. One has no news.

398. REIDENAUER, PETER   Tieffenbach=
Boston, 1764   67290 Wingen-sur-Moder
S-H, I: 702

EUROPEAN RECORDS

Tieffenbach Lutheran KB:
Joh. Jacob Reutenauer of Tiefenbach and wife Maria Christina nee Gerber had a son:
> Johann Peter b. 5 June 1744, conf. 1759

AMERICAN RECORDS

Hocker, *German Settlers of Pennsylvania:* Newspaper dated 1 May 1792: Peter Ridenauer, Heidelberg twp., Northampton Co. (now Lehigh) intends leaving on May 27 for Germany. He was born at Dieffenbach, Littel, Steiner-Amt. [Tieffenbach, Lützelstein].

399. REIFF, HANS JACOB   Kirrberg=
Robert and Alice, 1739   67320 Drulingen
S-H, I: 263, 267, 270

EUROPEAN RECORDS

Diedendorf Reformed KB:
There are two possibilities for this immigrant:
  1. Johann Jacob Reiff, son of the late Benedict Reiff, former inhabitant at Rotschweiler [possibly Retschwiller=67250 Soultz-sous-Forêts or this might be a place in Switzerland] m. 30 Apr. 1715 Maria Elisabetha, daughter of Bernhard Bollinger, citizen and farrier at Stinsel.
Johann Jacob Reiff from Kirberg and wife Maria Elisabetha nee Bolinger had children:
  1. Johann Adam bp. 19 Apr. 1716, d. 22 Mar. 1717
  2. Maria Barbara bp. 6 Mar. 1718
     Sp.: Joh. Jacob Bachman [q.v.] from Hirschland; Maria Barbara wife of Mathäus Klein, Niederstensel; Veronica, daughter of Rudolph Bratsche from Leng, Obersiebenthal, Canton Bern [CH-3775 Lenk in Simmental, BE].
  3. Maria Christianna bp. 17 Sept. 1719
     Sp.: Joh. Nicolaus Bolinger, Niederstensel; Joh. Jacob Bachman, Hirschland; Margaretha Gassert, Heillering[en]; Anna Christina Martzloff, Hirsland [Hirschland].
  4. Christina Catharina bp. 26 July 1722?
  5. Susanna Magdalena bp. 4 Oct. 1722?
     [Perhaps an error in dates in the KB; both children are recorded as daughter of Jacob Reiff and wife Maria Elisabetha Bollinger.]
  6. Anna Maria bp. 28 Mar. 1726

The second possibility for this immigrant is:
Heinrich Reiff, carpenter in Vinstingen [57930 Fénétrange], and wife Magdalena, nee Stucki, had a son Johann Jacob bp. 15 Aug. 1715.

AMERICAN RECORDS

Rev. Jacob Lischy's records, York co.:
Maria Elisabetha Reiff sp. a child of Joseph Welschans [q.v.] in 1746.

A Jacob Reiff and wife Anna Elisabeth had a son:
1. Johann Jacob bp. 9 Nov. 1757.
    Sp.: Georg Michael Kann and Anna Barbara

Strayer's (Salem) Reformed KB, York co.:
Jacob Reiff and wife Anna Elisabetha had:
2. Anna Magdalena bp. 17 Aug. 1760
    Sp.: Anna Magdalena Welschhans

400. REITENAUER, HANS BALTHASAR   Rexingen=
Robert & Alice, 1738   67320 Drulingen
S-H, I: 213, 214, 216
    [Baltzer Reydenauer on list]

EUROPEAN RECORDS

Waldhambach Lutheran KB:
Clauss Reitenauer and wife Susanna nee Windstein had a son:
    Johann Balthasar b. 18 May 1696; conf. 1711.

Johann Balthasar Reutenauer, son of Clauss Reutenauer, *schindeldecker,* m.
22 Feb. 1718, in Tiefenbach, Maria Elisabetha Zenss, daughter of Joh. Jacob
Zenss of Puberg [=67290 Wingen-sur-Moder]. They had a son:
    Adam bp. 26 Feb. 1731 at Puberg.

AMERICAN RECORDS

New Hanover Lutheran KB, Montgomery co.:
Adam Reitenauer and wife Wilhelmina had:
    1. Anna Maria Ursula b. 13 Dec. 1755, bp. 25 Jan. 1756
        Sp.: Maria Ursula Reitenauer

Philadelphia Adm F: 230, Est. # 99, 1749:
Baltzer Reidenover. Bond dated 31 Mar. 1749 taken out by Henry Daring
of Hanover twp., yeoman, and Ludwich Filling of Colebrookdale for £200.
George Reidenover, yeoman, son of Baltzer R., late of same place.
Inventory of est. of Baltzer Reidenour of McCalls Manor in county of
Philadelphia. Signed by Adam Wartman and Casper Richman ? or Rieman.

New Hanover Lutheran KB, Montgomery co.:
(Hans) George Reitenauer and wife Juliana had:
1. Johannes b. 3 Aug. 1750
2. Elisabeth b. 10 Nov. 1753
3. Elisabetha bp. 9 Feb. 1755

Abraham Reitenauer and Elisabeth had:
1. Joh. Jacob b. 27 Nov.1756, bp. 8 Apr. 1757

Christopher Reitenhauer and Margretha had:
1. Georg Adam bp. 25 Nov. 1746

Frederick Lutheran KB, Frederick, MD:
Adam Reitenauer and wife Wilhelmina had:
    Christina b. 7 Apr. 1763, bp. 8 May 1763
    Sp.: Valentin Kreiger and wife Christina

401. REITENAUER, JOHANNES age 40   Tieffenbach=
    REITENAUER, JOHANNES, JR. age 16   67290 Wingen-sur-Moder
Lydia, 1739
S-H, I: 273, 274

EUROPEAN RECORDS

Waldhambach Lutheran KB:
Johannes Reitenauer, son of Claus Reitenauer, citizen and *Schindeldecker* at
Tieffenbach, m. 21 Apr. 1716 Maria Catharina, daughter of the late Nicolaus
Lendler, former citizen at Rossteig [Rosteig=67290 Wingen-sur-Moder].
They had children, bp. at Tieffenbach:
1. Johannes b. 11 Apr. 1717, bp. 15 Apr. 1717; d. 9 May 1721.
2. Joh. Georg, b. 18 Nov. 1718, conf. 1733. He is probably the
    Hans *Georg Weidenauer* who arrived on the ship *Phoenix*, 1749
    [S-H, I: 404, with Jörg Frantz Philippi, q.v.].
3. Johann Nicolaus b. 26 Feb. 1720
    Sp.: Joh. Nicolaus Gerber of Durstel [=67320 Drulingen];
    Daniel Klingeschmidt [q.v.] of Tieffenbach; Hans Martin, son
    of Diedrich Gartner; Johannetta, wife of Philips Gartner;
    Maria Elisabetha, wife of Hans Nicolaus Scherrer;
    Anna Magdalena, daughter of Michael Reitenauer.
4. Maria Margretha b. 12 Jan. 1722
5. **Johannes** b. 20 Dec. 1723
6. Johann Jacob b. 10 Nov. 1725; died.
7. Catharina Barbara b. 24? Aug. 1727

8. Anna Christina b. 20 Oct. 1729
9. Johann Christoph b. 29 Mar. 1731
10. Maria Elisabetha b. 3 Apr. 1733

AMERICAN RECORDS

St. Joseph's (Oley Hills) Church, Pike twp., Berks co., family register:
Hannes Reitenauer, b. 3 Mar. 1690, son of Nicolaus Reitenauer and his wife
Susanna, from Tieffenbach in Lower Alsace. In 1716, he married Maria
Catharina, b. 5 June 1696, daughter of Nicholas *Lehnhard* [note: Lendler in
Waldhambach KB] and his wife Anna Barbara from ?*Rorthal* [note: Rosteig
in KB] in Alsace. In 1739, about Christmas, he came to America. They had:
1. Hannes b. Apr. 1717, died in May 1721.
2. Johann George bp. 26 Dec. 1718. He married Elizabeth
   Kissinger and lives in Conegetsick [MD].
3. Nicolaus b. 28 Feb. 1720, lives abroad.
4. Margaret b. 1722 married Joh. Nicol. Philips.
5. Johannes b. Dec. 1723. Married Elizabeth Herb.
6. Johann Jacob b. 6 Nov. 1725, d. 14 Nov. 1727.
7. Catharina Barbara b. St. Bartholomew Day 1728. She m. Peter
   Hohl in 1746, son of Hannes and Elizabeth Hohl.
8. Christina b. 14 Oct. 1729. She m. 1748 John Adam
   Forch, son of Hannes and Maria Forch.
9. Christoph bp. 1 Apr. 1732
10. Maria Elizabeth bp. 7 Apr. 1733. She m. 1756 Conrad Schmid.
11. Maria Albertina Christina b. Mar. 1735, d. Feb. 1740
12. Elizabeth b. St. Bartholomew's Day 1737, d. 1739
13. Anna Ursula b. St. John's Day 1746. [Note: St. Paul's Luth. KB,
    Red Hill, Montgomery co. gives her birth and baptism in 1741].

Died 3 Nov. 1755: Johannes Reitenauer, son of Nicolaus Reitenauer and his
wife Susanna, from Tieffenbach. Came to America, 1739. Was b. 3 Mar.
1690. Buried 5 Nov. 1755. Aged 65 years, 8 months.

Communicants list 14 Dec. 1755:
Maria Catharina Reitenauer widow of John Reitenauer, deceased, her son
Christopher and daughter Ursula.

Johannes Reitenauer, b. 1723, son of Hannes and Maria Catharina, came to
America with his parents in 1739. He m. 1751 Johanna Elisabeth,
Reformed, b. Nov. 1732, daughter of the late Johann Herb and Judita.
Children:
1. Maria Elisabeth b. 17 May 1752
2. Maria Susanna

3. Maria b. 18 Feb. 1755, bp. 16 Mar. 1755
4. Catharina Barbara b. 15 Aug. 1756, bp. 12 Sept. 1756
5. Joh. Daniel b. 30 Apr. 1758, bp. 21 May 1758
6. Johannes b. 3 Dec. 1759, bp. 16 Dec. 1759
7. Elisabeth b. 5 July 1765, bp. 7 July 1765

Catharina Barbara Reitenauer, b. 1728 and Peter Hohl had children:
1. Maria Barbara Hohl b. Nov. 1748, d. 1751
2. Maria Catharina Hohl b. Nov. 1748
3. Elizabeth Hohl b. Jan. 1750, died aged 8 days.
4. Maria Magdalena Hohl b. 1753, died on Pentecost.
5. Maria Christina Hohl b. Aug. 1755

Christina Reitenauer, b. 1729, and John Adam Forch had:
1. Johann Forch b. Mar. 1749
2. Johann Adam b. 1751, d. 1754
3. Christoph b. 1753, d. 1754

402. REITENAUER, JOH. HENRICH   Rexingen=
Robert & Alice, 1738   67320 Drulingen
S-H, I: 213, 214, 216
  [with Peter]
                          EUROPEAN RECORDS

Berg und Thal Lutheran KB:
Hans Nickel Reutenauer, farmer at Rexingen, and wife Anna Magdalena nee
Arnet had a son:
        Johann Heinrich b. 29 SEpt. 1713

Johann Heinrich Reutenauer, single tailor from Rexingen, son of Nickel
Reütenauer, m. 9 July 1737 at Berg [=67320 Drulingen] Anna Catharina
Führer, daughter of the late Benedict Führer, farrier at Allenweiler
[Allenwiller = 67310 Wasselonne]. [No further records in KB].

Verification of this emigrant provided by Dr. Bernd Gölzer from the
compiled records of Dr. Gerhard Hein:
Records of Saarwerden county office for Rexingen:
22 July 1745, cession of Benedict Führer's widow Catharina Gehrin: The
daughter Catharina and her husband Henrich Reutenauer have moved to the
New Land 10 years ago.

                          AMERICAN RECORDS

Frederick Lutheran KB, Frederick, MD:
Henrich Reitenauer had a son:
>   Mattheus b. __ Jan. 1749, bp. 31 May 1749
>   Sp.: Mattheus Reitenauer and Anna Catharina Ruchin, single

Henrich Reitenauer and wife Catharina were sp. in 1750 for a child of
Henrich Störtzmann [q.v. - Startzmann].

Henry Reidenhauer nat. MD, April term, 1753.

403. REITENAUER, PETER   Rexingen=
Robert and Alice, 1738   67320 Drulingen
S-H, I: 213, 215, 216

EUROPEAN RECORDS

Waldhambach Lutheran KB:
Clauss Reütenauer, *schindeldecker* in Tiefenbach, and wife Susanna had a
son:
>   Johann Nicolaus, conf. 1698

Drulingen Lutheran KB and Berg Lutheran KB:
Hans Nicolaus Reitenauer of Rexingen and wife Anna Magdalena nee Arnet
had children:
>   1. Joh. Philipp b. 23 Dec. 1708 [Drulingen KB]
>   2. Joh. Nicolaus b. 14 Feb. 1711 [Drulingen KB]
>   3. Johann Heinrich b. 29 Sept. 1713 [q.v.]
>   4. Anna Margretha b. 6 Apr. 1716
>   5. Anna Catharina b. 7 Aug. 1718
>   6. Johann Daniel b. 6 Mar. 1721, died
>   7. **Johann Peter** b. 21 July 1723
>   8. Johann Matthias bp. 25 Oct. 1725
>   9. Anna Elisabetha b. 29 June 1728

AMERICAN RECORDS

Frederick Lutheran KB, Frederick, MD:
Peter Reitenauer had children:
>   1. Elisabetha b. 26 July 1748, bp. 31 May 1749
>   Sp.: Elisabetha Heger
>   2. Maria Magdalena b. 2 July 1750, bp. 29 June (sic) 1750
>   Sp.: Nicolaus Reitenauer and wife

Mattheus Reitenauer was a sp. in 1749 for a child of Henrich Reitenauer [q.v.].

404. RIEHL, ADOLPH   Mulhausen=
Bennet Gally, 1750   67350 Pfaffenhoffen
S-H, I: 428

EUROPEAN RECORDS

Pfaffenhoffen Lutheran KB:
Adolph Riehl, weaver at Mühlhausen, m. 22 Apr. 1732 Anna Maria, daughter of Peter Götz, *Herrschafft. Förster* at Niedermothern. [Niedermodern = 67350 Pfaffenhoffen.]

Mühlhausen Lutheran KB:
Adolph Riehl and wife Anna Maria nee Götz had children:
1. Johann Michel b. 16 June 1738, bp. 19 June 1738
2. Joh. Jacob b. 8 Apr. 1740, bp. same day
3. Maria Catharina b. 6 Oct. 1741, bp. 9 Oct. 1741
4. Adolph b. 8 Feb. 1744, bp. 10 Feb. 1744
5. Johann Michael b. 20 Nov. 1745, bp. 23 Nov. 1745; died 1747.
6. Anna Maria b. 3 Jan. 1749

Signature from KB: Signature from S-H, II: 490:

AMERICAN RECORDS

St. Michael's and Zion KB, Philadelphia:
Adolph [Reele] Riel and wife Anna Maria had:
7. Johan Heinrich b. 12 Oct. 1752, bp. 4 Feb. 1753
8. Johannes b. 11 June 1757, bp. 21 Aug. 1757; d. 30 Aug. 1757.

Jacob Riel m. 9 Dec. 1762 Christina Sophia Wolff.
Wit: Christ. Fried. Wolff [q.v.], Adolph Riel, Johannes Kuhn, Ludw. Wirth, Johannes Weismann, Georg Thürmer.

Buried 2 Feb. 1767 - Michael Riel from Muhlhausen near Bussweiler. Buried gratis.

Buried 14 Nov. 1767 - Catharina Jones, wife of Charles Jones (English). She was a daughter of Adolph Riel, b. 1741 at Mühlhausen in Alsace near

Busweiler. Came to America 1750; conf. by Pastor Handschuh. Married 1761. Aged 26 years, 1 month.

Buried 31 Dec. 1769 - Adolph Riehl, b. 6 Nov. 1705 in the *Herrschaft Rottenburg in Elsass;* m. 1729 Anna Maria nee Goetz; had 14 children, 3 sons and 1 daughter living; to America 1750. Aged 64 y., 7 mo., 4 days.

Buried 5 Feb. 1825 - Widow Margretha Riehl from Bischweiler, aged 90 y., 9 mo., 14 days.

405. RIPPEL, PHILIPP	Herbitzheim=
Betsy, 1768	67260 Sarre-Union
S-H, I: 725 [with Andreas Bach, q.v.]	

EUROPEAN RECORDS

Herbitzheim Lutheran KB:
Johann Conrad Rippel, schoolteacher, and wife Maria Catharina had a son: Georg Philip b. 16 June 1725, bp. 18 June 1725; conf. 1739.

Catharina Margaretha Jesel, daughter of Christophel Jesell of Bockenheim and Maria Dorothea, was conf. 1739.

Georg Philip Rippel, master stockingweaver, m. 2 Aug. 1746 Catharina Margaretha Jesel, born in Bockenheim. He died 5 Dec. 1757, age 32 y. 5 mo. 2 weeks, 3 days. His widow m. (2) Peter Bauer and (3) Andreas Bach [q.v.] who also arrived on the *Betsy,* 1768.

Georg Philipp Rippel, stockingweaver, and wife Margaretha had:
    1. Catharina Margaretha b. 22 Dec. 1747, bp. 25 Dec. 1747; conf. 1762
    2. Johann Philipp b. 22 May 1749; conf. 1762
       Sp.: Wilhelm Haldy; Peter Jesel; Anna Maria, wife of Peter ____?; Maria Margaretha, wife of Georg Bauer.
    3. Johann Ludwig b. 4 June 1751; conf. 1765
    4. Maria Catharina b. 20 June 1756

Verification of this emigration supplied by Dr. Bernd Gölzer, from the county records of Nassau-Saarwerden, compiled by Dr. Gerhard Hein: Records of the Notary Public for Dehlingen: 25 Apr. 1782, inventory of Anna Margaretha Bauer: Among the heirs are listed two children of Peter Bauer who are reported as living in America.

AMERICAN RECORDS

Salem Reformed KB, Hagerstown, MD:
Johann Philip Ripel and wife Engel had:
   Johan Philip b. 6 Mar. 1774, bp. 10 May 1774
   Sp.: Daniel Schneid and wife Anna

St. John's Lutheran KB, Hagerstown, MD:
Philipp Ripel and wife Angelica had:
   Katharina b. 13 Nov. 1775, bp. 1 Feb. 1776.

406. ROSER, LORENTZ   Windstein=
John and William, 1732   67110 Niederbronn-les-Bains
S-H, I: 102   Langensoultzbach=
   [Laurence Rosier, sick and Dorothy Rosar]   67360 Woerth

EUROPEAN RECORDS

Langensoultzbach Lutheran KB:
Lorentz Roser, son of Hans Roser, *Erbestander* at Windstein, m. 8 Jan. 1726
at Sultzbach Maria Dorothea Günter, daughter of the *Fuhrknecht* in
Jägerthal. Children:
   1. Catharina Barbara bp. __ Jan. 1727
   2. Maria Magdalena bp. 19 Jan. 1729
   3. Maria Dorothea bp. 28 Jan. 1731

AMERICAN RECORDS

Augustus Lutheran KB, Trappe, Montgomery co.:
Jacob Früh, widower, m. 17 Aug. 1748 Maria Dorothea Roser(in).

Rev. John Casper Stoever's Records:
Leonhardt Faber m. 30 Oct. 1748 Catarina Barbara Roesser, Swatara.

407. ROTH, DANIEL age 30   Gundershoffen=
Hope, 1733   67110 Niederbronn-les-Bains
S-H, I: 116, 119, 121
   with Margrita age 30
EUROPEAN RECORDS

Gundershoffen Lutheran KB:
Daniel Roth, son of Christian Roth, *Erbeständer auf dem Reichsacker,* m. 18

Jan. 1729 Margretha, daughter of Adam Weis, *Erbeständer auf dem Ingelhoff.*
They had children:
  1. Joh. Daniel b. 4 Feb. 1730 [Niederbronn Lutheran KB]
     Sp.: Christoph Weber; Joh. Jacob Hanauer; Anna Margretha,
     daughter of _____?
  2. Margaretha bp. 5 Sept. 1731 [Gundershoffen Lutheran KB]
  3. Joh. Peter b. 30 Dec. 1732 [Gundershoffen]
     Sp.: Joh. Peter Staub; Joh. Jacob Hanauer from Niederbronn;
     Anna Barbara, daughter of Bernhard Hooff of Niederbronn.

The related families of Roth and Schreiber left Niederbronn on 4 May 1733,
and arrived in Pennsylvania on the ship *Hope*, 28 August 1733.

AMERICAN RECORDS

Roberts, *History of Lehigh Co., PA:*
Daniel Roth, b. 1703, came to PA in 1733 with his wife and children and
sister Anna Magdalena, and her husband John Jacob Schreiber [q.v.] having
left Niederbronn on 4 May 1733, where his sister had been married on 28
Apr. 1733. The Roth and Schreiber families lived for some time in Skippack
twp., Montgomery co., but in 1737 removed to Whitehall twp., where Daniel
Roth applied for a warrant for a tract of 150A on the Jordan Creek, where
the village of Sherersville is now located. He died before the warrant was
granted, in Apr. 1737, in the same hour in which his son, Peter, was born.
The warrant, dated 25 May 1737, was granted to his widow. She d. 25 Feb.
1757, aged about 54 years. Daniel Roth and Peter Rhoads, only surviving
issue of Daniel Roth, released their rights to this tract on 25 June 1761 to
Gottfried Knauss.
Daniel Roth and wife Anna Margaret had 3 children:
> 1. Daniel
> 2. Jacob, conf. 1753 at Egypt Reformed, d. before 1761
> 3. Peter b. __ Apr. 1737, conf. 1754 at Egypt
> ------------

Daniel Roth, nat. 10 Apr. 1761

[See Roberts et al, *History of Lehigh County, Pennsylvania,* vol. 3: 1082-1083
for additional family data.]

408. ROTH, MARIA EVA   Goersdorf=
probably on *St. Andrew Galley,* 1737   67360 Woerth
  with stepfather Heinrich Schmid [q.v.]

EUROPEAN RECORDS

Preuschdorf Lutheran KB:
Hans Georg Stocker of Goersdorf and wife Anna Maria nee Fischer had a
daughter:
> Anna Maria b. __ __ 1698

Johannes Roth, apprentice stonecutter, son of Ewald Roth, former citizen
at Kleinamstatt in *Churpfaltz, Hessen-Darmstadt Gemeinschafftl. Ort* [Klein-
Umstadt=W-6114 Gross-Umstadt] m. 20 Feb. 1725 Anna Maria Stocker,
daughter of Hans Georg Stocker, citizen and *Gerichtsschöffen.* They had
children:
> 1. Joh. Georg b. 3 May 1726, d. 1728
> 2. Joh. Adam b. 22 Mar. 1728

3. Maria Eva b. 29 Aug. 1729, bp. 30 Aug. 1729
   after her father's death.

Lembach Lutheran KB:
Johann Heinrich Schmid, widower and *Hoffman* in Trautbrunnen m. 7 July 1733 at [67510] Lembach Anna Maria, widow of the late Joh. Roth, former citizen at Gerstorff.

AMERICAN RECORDS

Muddy Creek Moravian KB, Lancaster co.:
Johann Heinrich Schmid from Wingen and his second wife Anna Maria nee Stockerin, widowed Roth, brought a girl with her, namely Maria Eva Roth b. 19 Aug. 1729 in Preuschdorf, Alsace.

409. RUBB, JOH. JACOB   Oberhoffen =
_____, 1752   67160 Wissembourg

EUROPEAN RECORDS

Kutzenhausen Lutheran KB:
Johannes Nonnenmacher of Merckweyler [Merkwiller = 67250 Soultz-sous-Forêts] m. 25 Nov. 1721 Maria Barbara Stambach, daughter of Jacob Stambach of Oberkutzenhausen [=67250 Soultz-sous-Forêts]. Children:
   1. **Maria Barbara** b. 17 Nov. 1722, bp. 19 Nov. 1722;
      m. 1746 Joh. Jacob Rubb
   2. Anna Eva b. 21 Apr. 1724; d. 1733
   3. Anna Maria b. 2 Jan. 1727, bp. 5 Jan. 1727
   4. Christina b. 31 Dec. 1730, bp. 3 Jan. 1731;
      m. 1750 Joh. Michel Werner
   5. Margaretha b. 10 Mar. 1733, bp. 12 Mar. 1733

The mother, Maria Barbara, m. (2) 2 Mar. 1734 Joh. Michael Fünfrock [q.v.]. She d. 1768; he emigrated to PA in 1770.

Steinseltz Reformed KB:
Jacob Rupp, the younger, of Oberhoffen, and wife Barbara had children:
   1. Johann Jacob b. 22 Dec. 1747, bp. 26 Dec. 1747
   2. Johann Michel b. 6 Apr. 1749, bp. 11 Apr. 1749
   3. Johann Martin b. 6 Mar. 1751, bp. 12 Mar. 1751
      [This entry crossed out in KB; line drawn through the name
      of the child.]

Zweibruecken Manumissions Protocoll, Clee- and Catharinenburg, 1752:
Jacob Rubb with wife and three children, from Oberhoffen, leaves for
America.

AMERICAN RECORDS

Colonial Maryland Naturalizations:
Jacob Rup, German, nat. 12 Apr. 1771.

Langensoultzbach appears in the eighteenth century records as Sultzbach.

410. RUHLMAN, JACOB age 35   Langensoultzbach=
Hope, 1733   67360 Woerth
S-H, I: 117, 120, 121
   with Aplon Rollman age 36; Hans Jan, age 9; Maria age 7

EUROPEAN RECORDS

Langensoultzbach Lutheran KB:
Hans Christman Rhulmann and wife Catharine had a son:
Johann Jacob bp. 5 Feb. 1696 at Sultzbach

Hans Christman Rhulmann d. 17 Aug. 1741, age 78 y. 9 mo. 2 weeks and 3 days. Catharina, widow of Hans Christman Rhulmann, d. 11 Nov. 1742, age 75 y. 9 mo. and 3 weeks.

Hans Jacob Ruhlman, son of Hans Christman Ruhlman, citizen at Sultzbach, m. 16 Feb. 1719 Apollonia, daughter of Hans Jacob Herkel, citizen of Roth, [Rott=67160 Wissembourg] *Zweybruckischen Hertzogthumbs*. They had children:
1. Johann Jacob bp. 3 Mar. 1720, d. 18 Apr. 1732
2. Hans Georg bp. 7 Nov. 1721
3. Maria Catharina bp. 16 Dec. 1723
4. Maria Magdalena bp. 11 Nov. 1725
5. Johann Peter b. 22 Dec. 1728 at Rott, bp. at Birlenbach Reformed KB.
6. Johannes bp. 24 June 1731

AMERICAN RECORDS

Muddy Creek Lutheran KB, Lancaster co.:
Joh. Jacob Ruhlmann of Muddy Creek had twins:
7. Joh. Jacob b. 15 May 1735, bp. 20 July 1735
Sp.: Joh. Jacob Dambach and wife
8. Maria Appolonia b. (15 May 1735)
Sp.: Joh. Wingertman and Maria Eliesabetha Wentzel

Maria Magdalena Ruhlmännin and Heinrich Frey [q.v.] were sp. in 1741 for a child of Philipp Wick.

Joh. Caspar Eckhardt of Cacusi m. 29 Nov. 1743 Maria Catarina Ruhlmann. Georg Ruhlman and Eva Maria Schmidt were sp. for their child bp. 1745.

Muddy Creek Reformed KB, Lancaster co.:
George Rullman and Maria Catharine had a daughter:
Anna Maria bp. 29 Aug. 1747
Sp. Peter Schab and Anna Maria Fisser

Chalkley's Chronicles, III: 126: Augusta co., VA estates;
17 Nov. 1772, Christian Roleman and Henry Stone's bond (with John

Skidmore, George Kile) as adm. of Jacob Roleman.
p. 128: Jacob Roleman's estate appraised 1 Dec. 1772.
p. 157: 21 Mar. 1780, Jacob Ruleman's estate settled.
p. 399: Augusta Co. Deed Book no. 11: 261:
21 June 1763, Jacob Rollman and wife Margaret and Christian Rollman to
Henry Black for £60, 280 A. on Howell's branch of Bever Creek.

411. SALATHE, PETER   Hunspach=
Sandwich, 1750   67250 Soultz-sous-Forêts
S-H, I: 449   Hoffen=
                                               67250 Soultz-sous-Forêts
                        EUROPEAN RECORDS

Hunspach Reformed KB:
Hans Jacob Salathe and wife Anna Maria nee ?Gischler had a son:
    Hans Peter b. 2 May 1715, bp. 5 May 1515, conf. 1730

Hoffen Reformed KB:
Joh. Peter Salathe, son of Joh. Jacob Salathe, inhabitant at Hunspach, m. 13
Jan. 1739 Maria Barbara, daughter of Andreas Müller. They had children:
    1. Maria Eva b. 4 Sept. 1740, bp. 7 Sept. 1740
       Sp.: Lorentz, son of Lorentz Weimer; Eva, daughter of Georg
       König; Barbara, daughter of Joh. Jacob Jung
    2. Maria Barbara b. 19 Oct. 1745, bp. 25 Oct. 1745
       Sp.: Jacob Niess, citizen and shoemaker; Barbara, daughter of
       the late H. Georg Bruckner of Rittershoffen; Maria Catharina,
       daughter of the late Jacob Weimer, cooper; She d. 8 Sept. 1748.
    3. Maria Barbara b. 5 Sept. 1748, bp. 8 Sept. 1748
       Sp.: Jacob Niess, shoemaker; Barbara, daughter of Georg Brucker,
       Rittershofen; Magdalena, daughter of Abraham König

Conf. 1733- Maria Barbara, daughter of Anderas Müller, citizen at Hoffen.

                        AMERICAN RECORDS

Frederick Reformed KB, Frederick, MD:
Buried 2 June 1794 - Peter Salethe, age 79 years.

412. SALING, JOHAN PETER   Struth=
Pennsylvania Merchant, 1733   67290 Wingen-sur-Moder
S-H, I: 122, 125, 126
[with Maria Saling, woman, & children Catrina & Elizabeth Saling]

EUROPEAN RECORDS

Waldhambach Lutheran KB:
Johann Peter Saling, a hunter from Struth, son of Franz Saling of Wildengut, [Wildenguth is today Reipertswiller = 67340 Ingwiller], m. 9 Nov. 1728 in Tieffenbach, Anna Maria Vollmar, daughter of Georg Michael Vollmar of Struth. Children:
1. Anna Catharina b. 29 Aug. 1729
2. Margaretha Magdalena b. 21 Oct. 1731, d. 3 Nov. 1731

Georg Michael Vollmar of Struth d. 1 Nov. 1724, aged 52 y. 6 mo. 3 days. His wife is named Anna Sabina Barbara in the records in 1722, 1728. An Adam Vollmer who arrived on the *Pennsylvania Merchant*, 1733, with Johan Peter Saling, is possibly a member of this family from Struth.

AMERICAN RECORDS

Muddy Creek Lutheran KB, Lancaster co.:
Joh. Peter Sailing had a son:
Georg Adam b. 9 Feb. 1736, bp. 29 Feb. 1736
Sp.: Adam Vollmar; George Michael Koch; Anna Catharina Ergebrecht.

Klaus Wust, *The Virginia Germans* (Charlottesville, 1969) pg. 38:
"In 1740 John Peter Saling settled in the first fork of James River below Natural Bridge."
Pg. 40-41:
"John Peter Saling made a notable contribution to the knowledge of the English authorities about the western country at a time of growing conflict with France over the possession of trans-Allegheny lands. Saling landed in Philadelphia with his wife and two daughters in September 1733. His first American home was on 250 acres of land along Conestoga Creek in Lancaster County, Pennsylvania, which were surveyed for him in November 1735. Five years later Saling was occupying what was then the southernmost habitation west of the Blue Ridge, a cabin on a fork of James River. It became a favorite stopping place for people venturing into the Southwest. In March 1741/42 John Howard, commissioned by the governor "to go upon discoveries on the Lakes and Rivers of Mississippi," stopped at Saling's and persuaded the German to go along with him and three others on this expedition. The party set out on an adventurous journey down the New, Coal, Kanawha, and Ohio rivers to the Mississippi. After three and a half months of traveling, they were apprehended by the French, who transferred them to jail in New Orleans. Here Saling remained imprisoned for more than two years until he made a successful escape in October 1744. A

tedious journey of nearly seven months fraught with dangers and mishaps brought him back to Virginia and his home in May 1745. His copious notes taken during the expedition were lost, so he sat down to write from memory a detailed account which was eagerly studied by the authorities. Joshua Fry made a transcript of Saling's notes, adding information "personally had from Salley himself," and Fry's transcribed version was incorporated by Acting Governor Lewis Burwell in the "Report on the Back Settlements of Virginia" which was sent to London in 1751. Saling had faithfully reconstructed the entire trip, giving the colonial authorities a first authentic glance at the conditions in the territory west of the frontier. The important early maps of Fry and Jefferson (1751) and John Mitchell (1755) relied heavily on Saling's account."

(The original transcript of Saling's report, entitled "A Brief Account of the Travels of John Peter Salley, A German Who Lives in the County of Augusta in Virginia," is in the Colonial Office Papers, 5/1327, fol. 383-400, Public Records Office, London. It was first published without comment as an appendix to William M. Darlington (ed.), *Christopher Gist's Journals* (Pittsburgh, 1893), 253-60.

Chalkley's Chronicles, Vol. I: 311: Augusta County Court Judgments, August 1754 - Elizabeth Sally, an infant by John Peter Sally, her father and next friend vs. Abraham Dungleberry. Action for breach of promise of marriage. Marriage was to have been performed 15 Aug. 1753. Decl. filed Nov. 1753.

Vol. II: 216; Augusta County, VA Court Records:
Salling vs. Salling--O.S. 287; N.S. 101--Patent, 6 July 1741, to John Peter Salling (Salley), 400 acres in that part of Orange called Augusta in first Fork of James. Will of George Salling of Rockbridge. Wife, Hannah; son, Henry (infant); son, Peter; son, George; son, John; six daughters; daughter, Agnes; daughter, Peggy. Recorded in Rockbridge, 2 Dec. 1788.

Vol. III: 38; Augusta Co. Will Book 2, pg 92:
25 Dec. 1754. John Peter Salling's will, farmer--To daughter, Catherine Fooler, 1 shilling; to daughter Mary Elizabet Burton, 1 shilling; to John Salling, son of daughter Catherine that she had soon after she married Henry Fooler, 100 acres known as the Meadow entry; to sons, George Adam and John Salling; to son, John tract testator lives on, and also tract Peter Crotingal lives on, and horse bought from Joseph Burton, and a horse running at Hart's Bottom. John is infant. Executors, George Adam Salling. Teste: Jos. Bryan (Ryan), James Randal, Richard Borland (is this Borland? Burton? Boston?). Proved, 19 Mar. 1755, by Ryan and Randal.

Vol. III: 364; Augusta Co. Deed Book 9; pg 25:
26 Sept. 1760. George Adam Salling, of Cumberland County, North
Carolina, and John Salling, of Orange County, North Carolina, to John
Paxton, £120, 200 acres, part of 400 patented to John Peter Salling,
deceased, 6 July 1741, and bequeathed in his will to grantors in the first fork
of James, cor. Geo. Adam Salling. Delivered: John Paxton, Dec. 1762.

413. SATTLER, JOH. FRIEDRICH   Langensoultzbach=
Hamilton, 1767   67360 Woerth
S-H, I: 715
                        EUROPEAN RECORDS

Oberbronn Lutheran KB:
Jonas Sattler, widower and nailsmith at Langensultzbach, m. 9 Feb. 1730
Maria Margaretha, daughter of Joh. Ulrich Menguss, master tailor and
citizen at Oberbronn.

Langensoultzbach Lutheran KB:
Jonas Sattler, the younger, master nailsmith, and wife Margaretha nee
Menges had a son:
        Johann Friedrich b. 8 Aug. 1741

[See his sister Maria Barbara Sattler for more family data]

                        AMERICAN RECORDS

Trinity Lutheran KB, Reading, Berks co.:
Friedrich Sattler and wife Barbara had:
        Elisabetha b. 7 Nov. 1773, bp. 3 Apr. 1774
        Sp.: Johannes Bapp & Catharina Gersand

1790 Census:
One Fred(rich) Sadler, Hopewell twp., York co., 2 males over 16, 6 females.

414. SATTLER, MARIA BARBARA   Langensoultzbach=
Ship Unknown, 1763   67360 Woerth
                        EUROPEAN RECORDS

Langensoultzbach Lutheran KB:
Jonas Sattler, the younger, master nailsmith, and wife Margaretha nee
Menges (Mengüss in other records) had children:
        1. Maria Margaretha b. 23 Jan. 1731

2. Maria Eva b. 20 Jan. 1732
3. Maria Dorothea b. 24 Feb. 1733
4. Maria Ursula b. 3 Apr. 1735
5. **Maria Barbara** b. __ Nov. 1736
   [Marginal note by baptism: "is in Pennsylvania 1763"]
6. Maria Christina b. 21 Mar. 1738, d. 15 Feb. 1746
7. Maria Elisabetha b. 18 Mar. 1740, d. 1740
8. Johann Friedrich [q.v.] b. 8 Aug. 1741
9. Johann Ludwig b. 29 Nov. 1744
10. Johann Jacob b. 30 July 1746
11. Anna Catharina b. 19 Jan. 1748

AMERICAN RECORDS

Reading Lutheran KB, Berks co.:
Johann Lippert, son of Jacob Lippert, m. 21 July 1765 Maria Barbara Sattler, fourth daughter of Jonas Sattler.

Reading Reformed KB, Berks co.:
Buried 10 Apr. 1813 - Barbara Lippert, age 76 y., 5 months, 8 days; buried at Preisstown.

415. SCHAAF, FRIEDRICH   Mackwiller=
Halifax, 1752   67430 Diemeringen
S-H, I: 483
EUROPEAN RECORDS

Bütten Lutheran KB:
Timotheus Schaaf, farmer of Mackweiler, and wife Christina nee Friedrich, had nine children, including two sons who emigrated:
  1. Henrich, conf. 1748 [q.v.]
  2. Friedrich, conf. 1745

Verification of this emigrant provided by Dr. Bernd Gölzer from the compiled records of Dr. Gerhard Hein:
Records of Saarwerden county office for Mackweiler:
Dated 22 Oct. 1773, inventory of Timotheus Schaaf: the son Friedrich moved to America 25 years ago without manumission. According to a letter of 1768 he is married there.

AMERICAN RECORDS

Hocker, *German Settlers of Pennsylvania:*
Sower's newspaper, dated 16 Dec. 1752: Henrich Schaaf, living with Christophel Heumacher, on the Little Lehigh, "in der Schmaltzgass", had his brother come to America this year, and he finds in the Philadelphia mayor's book that the brother, Friedrich Schaaf, was indentured to Johannes Baumann, whose place of residence is not given. Henrich Schaaf seeks information about Baumann.

416. SCHAAF, HENRICH   Mackwiller=
Phoenix, 1749   67430 Diemeringen
S-H, I: 405
EUROPEAN RECORDS

Bütten Lutheran KB:
Timotheus Schaaf, framer of Mackweiler, and wife Christina nee Friedrich, had nine children, including two sons who emigrated:
  1. Henrich, conf. 1748
  2. Friedrich, conf. 1745 [q.v.]

Verification of this emigrant provided by Dr. Bernd Gölzer from the compiled records of Dr. Gerhard Hein:
Records of Saarwerden county office for Mackweiler:
Dated 22 Oct. 1773, inventory of Timotheus Schaaf: the son Henrich moved

to America 27 years ago without manumission. Nothing has been heard about him since then.

AMERICAN RECORDS

Rev. Daniel Schumacher's records:
Henrich Schaaf and wife Margaretha Barbara had:
    Anna Catharina bp. 25 Jan. 1759, 3 weeks old, in Linn.
    Sp.: Burchard Mosen; Anna Catharina Haus, single

Conf. 1762 in Allemangel: Henrich Schaaff's wife Anna.

417. SCHÄFER, FRIEDERICH age 19   Preuschdorf=
Loyal Judith, 1732   67250 Soultz-sous-Forêts
S-H, I: 89, 91, 92
EUROPEAN RECORDS

Preuschdorf Lutheran KB:
Hans Baltzer Schäfer, son of the late Hans Georg Schäfer of Preuschdorf, m. (1) 7 Feb. 1704 Maria Magdalena, daughter of the late Hans Michael Fick from Buchsweiler [=67330 Bouxwiller]. Children of first marriage:
    1. Maria Christina b. __ Mar. 1705. She m. 1725 Georg Friedrich
        Pfeifer [q.v., 1730 immigrant]
    2. Joh. Georg b. 21 Apr. 1707, died. The mother of the child also
        died 3 weeks after childbirth, 7 May 1707, age 19 years.

Johann Balthasar Schäfer, widower at Preuschdorf, m. (2) __ Mar. 1708 Anna Catharina, daughter of Hans Stepp, citizen at Preuschdorf. Children:
    3. Anna Catharina b. 4 Mar. 1711, bp. 8 Mar. 1711
        She m. 1728 Hans Heinrich Acker [q.v.-1732 immigrant]
    4. Johann Balthasar b. 30 Sept. 1712, died 1712
    5. **Georg Friedrich** b. 1 Oct. 1713, bp. 3 Oct. 1713
    6. Margaretha b. __ June 1715, died.
    7. Eva b. 16 Nov. 1716, bp. 20 Nov. 1716

Georg Frederick Scheffer, Rockland twp., Berks co., nat. Autumn 1765.

418. SCHÄFER, HANS MICHEL   Lampertsloch=
Duke of Bedford, 1751   67250 Soultz-sous-Forêts
S-H, I: 458   Goersdorf=
          67360 Woerth
EUROPEAN RECORDS

Preuschdorf Lutheran KB:
Hans Michel Schäfer, son of Hans Georg Schäfer, citizen and farmer at Lampertsloch, m. 6 Nov. 1737 Elisabetha, daughter of Joh. Michel Stocker of Goersdorf. Notation in KB by marriage record: "went to the new land." They had a son:
> Hans Michel b. 21 Dec. 1738 [Entry in bp. record crossed out]

[Hans Michel Schäfer's signature by his marriage entry in the KB matches his signature in S-H, II: 537.]

AMERICAN RECORDS

One Mich*uae*l Scheaffer, Rockland twp., Berks co., nat. Autumn, 1765.
One Michael Shaffer, Williams twp., Northampton co., nat. 24 Sept. 1762.

419. SCHÄFFER, JOH. DAVID   Hirschland=
Robert and Alice, 1739   67320 Drulingen
S-H, I: 263, 267, 270
[There are 2 David Schäffers on ship; this appears to be the one who signed.]

EUROPEAN RECORDS

Hirschland Lutheran KB:
Bernhard Schäffer, master smith and citizen at Hirschland, and wife Anna Margretha had children:
> 1. Johannes b. not located, d. 20 Apr. 1700
> 2. Johann Georg bp. 7 Aug. 1701
> 3. Anna Magdalena bp. 2 Aug. 1705; conf. 1718
> 4. Johann Georg [q.v.] bp. 24 Apr. 1707; conf. 1720.
>   [He married in 1728; emigration notation by marriage record.]
> 5. Anna Elisabetha bp. 25 Nov. 1708; d. 4 July 1709
> 6. A child b. June 1710, died. [This appears to be Hans Nickel who died 14 Apr. 1712, age 2 years less 10 weeks.]
> 7. Joh. Henrich bp. 11 Feb. 1712; conf. 1728
> 8. Joh. Michael bp. 17 Nov. 1713
> 9. Petrus bp. 31 May 1716
> 10. **Joh. David** bp. 21 Nov. 1717
>   Sp.: Mstr. David Schmitt; Theobald Schmitt, shopkeeper here; Anna Magdalena Schäffer.
>   [Although there are emigration notations scattered throughout this KB, there is no such notation entered by this baptism, nor is the entry crossed out.]

Bernhard Schäfer, smith in Hirschland, d 18 Feb. 1742, age 73 y. 6 months.

AMERICAN RECORDS

St. Michael's and Zion KB, Philadelphia:
David Schäfer m. 17 Apr. 1746 Maria Catharina Schneider, in the Philadelphia Lutheran Church. She was b. in Dec. 1723 in Feil by Creutznach [W-6550 Bad Kreuznach], daughter of Wilhelm Schneider and his wife Maria Catharina nee Wagner.

David Schäfer and wife Catharina had children:
1. David b. 25 Mar. [probably 1747, year not given, recorded with 1748 baptisms, but see daughter below b. 1748]; conf. 1761, age 15.
2. Anna Maria b. 1 Oct. 1748, bp. 9 Oct. 1748; conf. 1762
   Sp.: Johannes Stellwangen and wife Anna Maria (Ref.)
3. Catharina b. 29 Oct. 1750; bp. 18 Nov. 1750
   She m. 15 Oct. 1771 Frederick Augustus Conrad Muhlenberg
4. Johannes b. 4 Jan. 1752, bp. 19 Jan. 1752; conf. 1766
5. Johan Diedrich b. 10 July 1753, bp. 29 July 1753
   Sp.: Joh. Diedrich Heinzelman; Sarah Elisabetha Makin; conf. 1766
6. Joh. Georg b. 14 Mar. 1758, bp. 27 Mar. 1758
   Sp.: Joh. Georg Schaeffer and wife Ottilia
7. Bernhard b. 13 Nov. 1763, died 16 Nov. 1763

Buried 12 May 1787 - Joh. David Schaffer, born in Hirschland, 21 Nov. 1717, son of Bernhard and Anna Margareta Schaffer.

Muhlenberg's Journals, III: 741:
May 10, 1787: In the afternoon my son Fr[iedrich] Aug[ustus] reported to me that his father-in-law, Mr. David Schäffer, Senr., died today in the Lord after being sick only two days. He is survived by a pious widow, four sons, and two daughters.
May 11, 1787, Friday: Early in the morning Fr[iedrich] Aug[ustus] and his wife set out on their journey to Philadelphia to attend her father's funeral.

May 12, 1787, Saturday: Early this afternoon our relative by marriage, Mr. David Schäffer, was buried in Philadelphia. He was born in Germany in 1719.

Charles Glatfelder, *Pastor and People*, Vol. I: 93, 94:
"Frederick Augustus Conrad Muhlenberg. Lutheran. Born 1 Jan. 1750 at Trappe, Pennsylvania. Son of Henry Melchior and Anna Maria Muhlenberg.

At the age of thirteen years, sent with brothers Peter and Henry to study in the Halle Institutions and at Halle University. Returned with brother Henry and John C. Kunze arriving in New York September 22, 1770. Ordained by the ministerium at Reading on October 25, 1770.

Married 15 Oct. 1771 Catharine Schaefer (1750-1835), daughter of a Philadelphia sugar refiner. They had seven children.

Was the first register of wills and recorder of deeds for Montgomery county (1784-1789).

Became increasingly convinced that both federal and state consitutions needed revising. Was elected to the special convention called to consider ratification of the United States Constitution (1787), serving as its president. Was a member of Congress (1789-1797), and served as Speaker of the House (1789-1791, 1793-1795). Was unsuccessful candidate for governor at various times between 1790 and 1796. Served as receiver general of the Pennsylvania Land Office (1800-1801).

Died 4 June 1801 at Lancaster and was buried there."

David Schaeffer is mentioned frequently throughout Muhlenberg's journals. He served as a trustee of St. Michael's & Zion Congregation for many years. He was also elected an overseer of the German Society when it was founded in 1764.

For additional data on some of the children of David Schaeffer, see: Paul A. W. Wallace, *The Muhlenbergs of Pennsylvania* (Philadelphia, 1950): 286-287.

David Shaffer nat. 10 Apr. 1757.

420. SCHÄFFER, JOH. DAVID   Hirschland=
Robert and Alice, 1739   67320 Drulingen
S-H, I: 264, 267, 270

[There were 2 David Schäffers on this ship; this appears to be the second one on the list; he did not sign.]

EUROPEAN RECORDS

Hirschland Lutheran KB:
Joh. Jacob Schäffer, son of the dairy farmer, m. 10 Jan. 1708 Anna Maria nee Biber of Hirschland. They had:
1. Catharina bp. 22 Nov. 1708
2. Joh. Petrus bp. 6 Jan.1710
3. Joh. Henrich bp. 20 Oct. 1711; conf. 1724
4. **Johann David** bp. 22 Jan. 1713

Sp.: David Schmith, weaver here, Martinus Biber; Eva Schmid.
5. Anna Maria bp. 12 May 1715
6. Anna Christina bp. 21 Feb. 1717
7. Anna Magdalena bp. 6 July 1719
8. Anna Catharina bp. 15 Mar. 1722

Anna Maria, wife of Jacob Schäffer, d. 3 Dec. 1722, aged 38 years. He m. (2) 20 July 1723 Maria Catharina, daughter of Theobald Biber.

AMERICAN RECORDS

Christ Lutheran KB, York:
Joh. David Schafer m. 13 Mar. 1743 Anna Catharina Simon. They had:
    1. Maria Elisabetha b. 16 Jan. 1744, bp. 17 Mar. 1744

Rev. Jacob Lischy's records, York co.:
David Schäffer and wife Catharina had:
    2. Johann Philipph bp. 23 May 1745
      Sp.: Johan Philliph Simon
    3. Magdalena bp. 19 Oct. 1751
      Sp.: Joseph Welschhans [q.v.] and Magdalena.

David Shaefer, Strewsbury twp., York co., nat. 24 Sept. 1763.

421. SCHÄFFER, JOH. GEORG   Hirschland=
[unnamed ship], 20 Oct. 1747   67320 Drulingen
S-H, I: 370

EUROPEAN RECORDS

Hirschland Lutheran KB:
Bernhard Schäffer and Anna Margretha of Hirschland had:
    Johann Georg bp. 24 Apr. 1707, conf. 1720

Joh. Georg Schäffer, son of Bernhard Schäffer of Hirschland, m. 26 Oct. 1728 Anna Utilia Schneider, daughter of Michel Schneider. Notation in KB: "Moved to America". They had children:
    1. Anna Elisabeth bp. 11 Nov. 1729, "sind in Americam gezogen"
    2. Hans Georg bp. 8 Mar. 1731
    3. Maria Magdalena bp. 28 Oct. 1732 (no emigration notation)
    4. (No name recorded) bp. 13 Sept. 1735 "ist in Americam"
    5. Hans Georg bp. 23 Feb. 1742 "ist in America"
    6. Johann Henrich bp. 19 Nov. 1744

Verification of this emigrant provided by Dr. Bernd Gölzer from the compiled records of Dr. Gerhard Hein:
Records of Saarwerden county office for Eyweiler: dated 12 June 1760, the daughter of Michael Schneider and Anna Maria nee Bieber is Anna Ottilia, wife of Hans Georg Schäfer; they moved to the New Land 14 years ago.

AMERICAN RECORDS

Christ Lutheran KB (Mertz's), Bieber Creek, Berks co:
Georg Schaeffer and Elisabetha Quierin were sp. in 1759 for a child of Jacob Schirner.
Georg Schaefer, master joiner, son of Johann Schaefer, m. 17 Sept. 1751 Maria Catharina Ruhl, daughter of Johannes Ruhl.

Georg Scheefer, Jr. and wife Eva Barbara had:
>   Maria Barbara b. 27 Dec. 1765, bp. 12 Jan. 1766
>   Sp.: Henrich Scheefer and Maria Bader

Jacob Sterner, son of Caspar Sterner, m. 27 Nov. 1749 Anna Catharina, daughter of Joh. Georg Schaefer. [Note: his will names her as Elisabetha.]

Berks Co. Wills:
George Scheffer, Rockland. 6 Dec. 1771- 7 Jan. 1772
To son Michael my dwelling place and improvements, and pay to both his sisters Elisabeth and Margaretha their equal shares of my estate and provide for his parents while they live. To my sons John George and Henry, my land lying beyond the Blue Mountains and the £113 which I received for the improvement sold to son Michael. Remainder to children in equal shares; the 4 children of daughter Elisabetha late wife of Jacob Sterner, to wit, Jacob, Michael, Barbara and Elizabeth, to have their mother's share. Wife Anna Ottilia and son Michael, Executors. Witness Conrath Menges and Charles Bernhardt.

422. SCHÄFFER, NICKLAUS   Lampertsloch=
Hamilton, 1767   67250 Soultz-sous-Forêts
S-H, I: 715
EUROPEAN RECORDS

Preuschdorf Lutheran KB:
Niclaus Schäffer, son of Hans Georg Schäffer, inhabitant at Lampersloch, m. 21 Apr. 1750 at Lampersloch Maria Elisabetha Biebel, daughter of Hans Georg Biebel. Notation in KB: "Went to the New Land." Children:
>   1. Catharina Elisabetha b. 15 June 1751

The father's signature by this bp. entry in the KB
matches the signature of the immigrant on S-H, II: 823.
2. Johann Georg b. 30 Dec. 1752, d. 1753
3. Johann Georg b. 28 Feb. 1754, bp. 22 Mar. 1754
4. Anna Margaretha b. __ Nov. 1755, bp. 22 Nov. 1755
5. Catharina Barbara b. 14 Sept. 1757
6. Maria Salome b. 5 Nov. 1760
7. Georg Heinrich b. 14 July 1764
8. Johann Michael b. 7 Sept. 1766
[Notations by several baptisms that the family went to America]

Maria Elisabetha Biebel was a daughter of Hans Georg Biebel of Goersdorf
and his wife Maria Eva nee Burckhardt. She was a sister of Joh. Adam
Biebel [q.v.], 1750 immigrant.

423. SCHÄFFER, THEOBALD   Hirschland=
Robert and Alice, 1738   67320 Drulingen
S-H, I: 212, 214, 215

EUROPEAN RECORDS

Hirschland Lutheran KB:
Conf. 1706 - Theobald Schäffer from Hirschland.
Joh. Theobald Schäffer m. 18 Feb. 1716 Martha Margretha Schmid, both
from Hirschland. They had children:
  1. Hans Michael b. 6 Jan. 1724 "in Americam gereist"
  2. Still born child 25 July 1729
  3. a son [?Conrad] b. 24 Sept. 1730
  4. Anna Margretha b. ?20 Sept. 1735

Johannes Schmitt of Hirschland and wife (n.n.) had a daughter:
  Martha Margretha bp. 4 Jan. 1699
  Margin note: Went to America

AMERICAN RECORDS

Christ Lutheran KB (Mertz's), Bieber Creek, Berks co:
A Joh. Mich. Schaefer sp. a child of Nicolaus Quirin [q.v.] in 1757. He is
possibly a son of Joh. Georg Schäffer [q.v.], 1747 immigrant from
Hirschland.

One Michuael Scheaffer, Rockland twp., Berks co., nat. Autumn, 1765.

424. SCHAUB, CHRISTOFFEL   W-6749 Rumbach
St. Andrew Galley, 1737   Wingen=
S-H, I: 179, 181, 183   67510 Lembach

EUROPEAN RECORDS

Rumbach Reformed KB:
Matthias Schaub and his wife Anna Barbara nee Kochert, daughter of Hans and Elisabeth Kochert, had a son:
>   Christophel b. 22 Nov. 1702

The father, Matthias Schaub, was a brother of Anna Maria Schaub who m. in Wingen Jacob Frey. Five of the Frey children emigrated to PA. [See Frey and Löw].

AMERICAN RECORDS

Muddy Creek Lutheran KB, Lancaster co.:
Christoph Schaub had a daughter:
>   Maria Dorothea b. 18 May 1742, bp. 7 June 1742
>   Sp.: Maria Dorothea Frey

Muddy Creek Reformed KB, Lancaster co.:
Christoph Schaub, Elder of the Muddy Creek Reformed congregation, signed the Reformed Church doctrine in 1743.

Joh. Peter Schaub and Catharine, daughter of Christopher Schaub, were sp. in 1754 for a child of Daniel Zuber.

Christopher Schaub sp. in 1755 a child of Georg Heft.

Peter Schaub and wife have several children recorded in the Lutheran and Reformed KB. They sp. in 1762 a child of Jacob Frey . Peter Schaub appears on the new communicants list in 1747.

Christopher Schaub was buried 13 Apr. 1769, aged 66 y., 5 mo., & 20 d.

Christopher Schaub, Cocalico, Lancaster co., nat. Apr. 1761.

425. SCHEIB, JOHANNES   67160 Wissembourg
Minerva, 1770
S-H, I: 730
EUROPEAN RECORDS

St. Jean [John] Lutheran KB, Weissenburg [Wissembourg]:
Johannes Scheib, citizen and cooper, and wife Anna Elisabetha nee Hock, had children:
    1. Christina Rosina b. 2 Sept. 1754, bp. 3 Sept. 1754
    2. Maria Salome b. 29 Apr. 1756, bp. 30 Apr. 1756
    3. Maria Sophia b. 17 May 1759, bp. 18 May 1759
    4. Johann Caspar b. 30 Sept. 1762, bp. 2 Oct. 1762

[The signature of Johannes Scheib in the churchbook matches his signature on List 281C, S-H, II: 844.]

AMERICAN RECORDS

St. Michael's and Zion KB, Philadelphia:
Buried 16 Feb. 1777 - Johann Scheib, born in Cron Weissenburg. Married Anna Elisabeth Hock. Aged 55 years.

426. SCHEIB, PETER   Steinseltz=
_____, 1733   67160 Wissembourg
EUROPEAN RECORDS

Steinseltz Reformed KB:
Joh. Peter Scheib, son of the late Conrad Scheib of Steinseltz, m. 27 Jan. 1722 Maria Juliana Beyerfalck, daughter of Joh. Michael Beyerfalck. They had:
    1. Maria Catharina bp. 4 Apr. 1723

Joh. Peter Scheib, widower, m. (2) 11 Nov. 1727 Anna Catharina, daughter of the late Herr Joh. Wendel Weiss, former _Schultheiss_ of Appenheim, Churpfaltz [W6531 Appenheim]. Children:
    2. Jacob b. 26 July 1729, bp. 28 July 1729

Zweibrücken Manumissions Protocoll, Cleeburg, 1733:
Peter Scheib of Steinseltz moves with wife and children to Pennsylvania.

427. SCHERER, HANS age 30 [signed Schürer]   Diedendorf=
Richard and Elizabeth, 1733   67260 Sarre-Union
S-H, I: 127, 129, 130
    [with Maria Magdalena Sherer, age 22; Veronica, 4 mo.]

EUROPEAN RECORDS

Diedendorf Reformed KB:
Johannes Scheurer, citizen and tailor at Weyer, [=67320 Drulingen] was a baptismal sponsor in 1722. He first appears in this KB in 1703 with wife Veronica nee Schuck. Hans, b. ca. 1703, is possibly a son born before the family came to this area. Maria Magdalena Christ was conf. 1724.

Neither bp. was located in the Diedendorf KB; they arrived with Jacob Christ [q.v.] and his wife Magdalena nee Schwab, whose marriage is recorded at Diedendorf in 1709. Maria Magdalena, b. ca. 1709/1710, is possibly their daughter.

AMERICAN RECORDS

Moselem Lutheran KB, Berks co:
Johannes Scheurer and wife Maria Magdalena nee Christ had a daughter:
Anna Margaret b. 28 Feb. 1744, bp. Rogate 1744
Sp.: Nicolaus Werner and Anna Maria Haas.

This child was bp. the same day as a child of Marcus Christ [q.v.], who was a son of Jacob Christ and Magdalena, nee Schwab.

428. SCHERER (SCHEURER), JACOB   Weyer=
Two Brothers, 1748   67320 Drulingen
S-H, I: 378, 379, 381
(appears on A list as Johann Sherer; B & C lists as Jacob Scherer)

EUROPEAN RECORDS

Diedendorf Reformed KB:
Johannes Scheurer, tailor, son of Hans Scheurer of Weyer, m. 6 Feb. 1703 at Diedendorf Veronica Schuck, daughter of Heinrich Schuck from Wolsen, ZH. [?CH 8304 Wallisellen, ZH]. They had 4 daughters bp. at Diedendorf. Johannes Scheurer citizen and tailor at Weyer m. (2) 30 Sept. 1719 Anna (nee Schneider) widow of Jacob Reichert (Reichhardt) former inhabitant at Bist, Vinstingen Herrschafft [Büst=67320 Drulingen]. They had one child:
Johann Jacob b. 31 Aug. 1722

AMERICAN RECORDS

Christ Lutheran KB (Mertz's), Bieber Creek, Berks co:
Jacob Scheurer and wife Anna Elisabetha nee Schlichter had a son:
[see also Schlichter]
Johann Nicolaus b. 4 Nov. 1755, bp. 24 Jan. 1756
Sp.: Johann Nicolaus Schlichter and wife Anna Barbara.

429. SCHLANG, GOTTFRIED   67340 Ingwiller
Crawford, 1768
S-H, I: 722

EUROPEAN RECORDS

Ingweiler Lutheran KB:
Joh. Henrich Schlang, tanner, born in Zweybrücken, son of the late H.
?Haeynin Schlang, *Hochfürst. Zweyb. Baumeister,* m. 27 Jan. 1718 Anna
Gertdrud, daughter of Herr Joh. Jacob Itzstein, citizen and Innkeeper at the
Crown Inn here in Ingweyler. Children:
  1. Johann Henrich b. 1 Nov. 1720
  2. Anna Elisabeth b. 4 Jan. 1722
  3. Joh. Jacob b. 20 Oct. 1724
  4. **Johann Gottfried** b. 13 Jan. 1728
  5. Johann Christian b. 30 Dec. 1732
  6. Philipp Henrich b. 14 May 1735; conf. 1749

AMERICAN RECORDS

St. Michael's and Zion KB, Philadelphia:
Buried 16 Apr. 1783 - Gottfried Schlang, b. 1724 in Ingeweiler. Aged 59
years, 3 days.

430. SCHLEPI, ADAM age 46   Herbitzheim=
Lydia, 1741   67260 Sarre-Union
S-H, I: 300, 301, 302

EUROPEAN RECORDS

Diedendorf Reformed KB:
Adam Schleppi, son of Jacob Schleppi, citizen and *Saltzpeterseider an der
Lenck, Berner Gebiet* [CH-3775 Lenk im Simmental, BE], m. 6 Jan. 1718
Magdalena, daughter of the late Christian Pfundt.

Herbitzheim Lutheran KB:
Adam Schleppi and wife Magdalena had:
    Catharina Magdalena b. 28 Oct. 1721
    Sp.: Stephan Hari; Bernhard Rubenthal; Magdalena Beller;
    Catharina Bitsche.

Rauwiller Reformed KB:
Elisabetha, daughter of Adam Schlepi, m. 27 Oct. 1740   Joh. Jacob
Welschans [q.v.] son of Abraham Welschans, Kirberg.

AMERICAN RECORDS

First (Trinity) Reformed KB, York:
Adam Schlaeby signed the York Reformed list of members in 1754.
Magadalena Schleppi sp. a child of Abraham Welschhans [q.v.] in 1745.

Rev. Jacob Lischy's records, York co.:
Adam Schleppi and wife Barbara had:
    1. Anna Maria bp. 26 July 1760. Sp.: Niclaus Ziegler and Catharina
    2. Elisabetha bp. 26 Oct. 1762. Sp.: Jacob Hedrich and Elisabeth

St. Jacob's (Stone) KB, York co.:
Adam Schleppi and wife Barbara nee Schehrer(in) had:
    3. Johann Jacob b. 5 Apr. 1765, bp. Ascension Day
       Sp.: Jacob Schehrer and wife Maria Barbara
    4. Eva Elisabeth bp. 7 Aug. 1768
       Sp.: Christian Neukommer & Eva Elisabeth Welschans(in)
    5. Helena b. 12 Jan. 1771, bp. 3 Mar. 1771

Adam Schleby signed Lischy's Constitution 17 Mar. 1745.

York co. unrecorded Wills:
Adam Schleby, dated 16 Sept. 1774, prob. 9 Jan. 1775
"my wife shall keep the plantation with the children which she yet has. If the children should leave her, plantation to be sold. Wife to have thirds. Children shall have equal shares, those of first wife and those of latter. Exrs: Jacob Zech and John Ulrich Hess. Wit: George Beck and George Weller. [Original in German; trans. by John Morris.]

431. SCHLIGTER, JOHANNES   Diedendorf=
Thistle, 1738   67260 Sarre-Union
S-H, I: 221, 222, 224

EUROPEAN RECORDS

Diedendorf Reformed KB:
Johannes Schlichter, son of Peter Schlichter, *Herrschaffl. Hoffman* at Rixingen? m. 3 Apr. 1714 Magdalena Alimann, daughter of Hans Aliman, *Ober halbthun ?* from St. Stephan, BE [CH-3771 St. Stephan, BE].

Johannes Schlüchter, *Hoffmann* at Diedendorff and wife Magdalena Alemand had children:
    1. Catharina Elisabetha bp. 30 Mar. 1727, d. 1 Feb. 1728

Sp.: Joh. Nicholaus Bollinger, Niederstinsel; Carle Magnus, citizen at Diedendorff; Catharina Elisabetha, wife of Otto Hauer, Diedendorff; Ursula, daughter of Michael Frantz, church *censor*, Diedendorff.

2. Nickolaus, died 1 Feb. 1728, son of Johannes Schlichter
3. Johann Peter (surname Schlichter) bp. 5 May 1728
   Sp.: Jacob Huber, Diedendorf; Peter Gassert, Hellgeringen; Christina, wife of Nickolaus Bolinger, Niederstinsel; Catharina Roth, wife of Ullrich Schneider, Diedendorf.
4. Anna Elisabetha bp. 15 Apr. 1731
   Sp.: Samuel de Perroudet, Pastor in Diedendorff; Samuel Lipp, Neusaarwerden; Barbara nee Stroh, wife of Jost Schlosser in Wolffskirchen; Elisabetha nee Meyer, wife of Johannes Giesling.

AMERICAN RECORDS

New Goshenhoppen Reformed KB, Montgomery co.:
Jacob Wiant, son of Jost Wiant, deceased, m. 17 Apr. 1770 Catharina Schlichter, daughter of John Schlichter, both of New Goshenhoppen.

Christ Lutheran KB (Mertz's), Bieber Creek, Berks co:
Jacob Scheurer [q.v.] and wife Anna Elisabetha nee Schlichter had a son:
1. Johann Nicolaus b. 4 Nov. 1755, bp. 24 Jan. 1756
   Sp.: Joh. Nicolaus Schlichter and wife Anna Barbara.

John Schlichter, Philadelphia co., without oath, 10/11 Apr. 1746.

432. SCHLOSSER, GUSTAVUS   Bischtroff-sur-Sarre=
Hero, 1764   67260 Sarre-Union
S-H, I: 697

EUROPEAN RECORDS

Pistorf (Bischtroff) Lutheran KB:
Georg Schlosser of Wolffskirchen [=67260 Sarre-Union] and his wife Magdalena nee Karcher had a son:
   Johann Gustavus b. 11 Feb. 1735, bp. 13 Feb. 1735
   Sp.: Herr Gustavus Reeb from here Joh. Heinrich Karcher from Pistorff, single; Mrs. Eva Schlosser; Miss Gertrud Schlosser.

433. SCHLOSSER, JOSEPH   67510 Lembach
Hamilton, 1767
S-H, I: 716

EUROPEAN RECORDS

Lembach Catholic KB:
Joseph Schlosser, son of the late Theobald Schlosser, former citizen in Lembach, and wife Catharina ?Rohin, m. 6 June 1763 Anna Maria Herdt, daughter of Adam Herdt and his deceased wife Margaretha Lorentz.
Wit: Joh. Henrich Walder, Wingen; Adam Herdt, Lembach; Georg Theobald Schlosser, Lembach; Gabriel Schlosser, Lembach.
Theobald Schlosser d. __ Jan. 1763 (no age given)

[Joseph Schlosser's signature in the church record is the same signature as S-H, II: 824.]

AMERICAN RECORDS

Goshenhoppen Catholic Register:
Baptisms in Allemengel, in the house of Christian Henrich:
Joseph Schlosser and wife Anna *Margaret* (probably Maria) had a daughter:
    M. Margaret b. 1 May 1773, bp. 16 May 1773
    Sp.: Michael Morloch and wife Magdalena.
Joseph Schlosser and wife Anna Maria had a son:
    George b. 19 Oct. 1774, bp. 20 Nov. 1774
    Sp.: Joseph Lorenz and Anna Maria.

Joseph Schlosser and wife Anna Maria were sp. in 1779 and 1783.
Christian Eckenroth m. __ Apr. 1784 Catharina Anna Schlosser.
Christian Eckenroth and wife Anna had a daughter:
    Elisabeth b. 25 Feb. 1785, bp. 13 Mar. 1785.
    Sp.: Joseph Schlosser, grandfather, & Margaret Eckenroth.

Berks co. Wills:
Joseph Schlosser, Ruscombmanor; 22 Dec. 1820 - 22 Nov. 1821:
Small legacy to children George, John, Jacob, Magdalena Flower, Maria Eckroth, and Margaret Swartz, each having already received advances. Remainder of estate to son Joseph, who is also exr. Wit.: Daniel Bachman and Benjamin Parks.

434. SCHMID, HEINRICH   Wingen=
     SCHMID, FREDERICH   & Trautbrunnen=
St. Andrew Galley, 1737   67510 Lembach
S-H, I: 179, 181, 183

EUROPEAN RECORDS

Wingen Lutheran KB:
Joh. Georg Schmidt and wife Anna Maria had children:
1. Matthaus b. 4 Feb. 1687
2. **Joh. Heinricus** b. 9/19 Dec. 1688
3. Joh. Jacob b. 22 Nov./2 Dec. 1691
4. Apollonia b. 21/31 May 1694
5. Hans Georg b. 18 Jan. 1696
6. Hans Diebold b. 6 Mar. 1698.

Johann Henrich Schmidt, son of Georg Schmidt, m. 27 Aug. 1715 Maria Magdalena, daughter of Conrath Frey. They had children:
1. Johann Georg bp. 13 Sept. 1716, d. 1717
2. Joh. Georg Michael bp. 20 Mar. 1718
3. **Joh. Frederich** b. 17 Apr. 1722
4. Maria Sophia b. 18 Oct. 1724. She m. 2 Feb. 1743 in Wingen Joh. Georg Frey, age 20 years. It is mentioned in the marriage record that she is 18 years old, and a daughter of Joh. Heinrich Schmidt former citizen here, now inhabitant in Carolina."
5. Maria Christina b. __ Oct. 1727, d. 16 July 1730
6. Joh. Balthasar b. 27 July 1730

Lembach Lutheran KB:
7. Johann Heinrich b. 4 July 1732, bp. 6 July 1732

Johann Heinrich Schmid, widower and *Hoffman* in Trautbrunnen, m. (2) 7 July 1733 at Lembach Anna Maria, widow of the late Joh. Roth (see Roth), former citizen at Gerstorff. They had:
8. Joh. Michael b. 5 Apr. 1734, bp. 16 Apr. 1734
9. Joh. Jacob b. 15 June 1736, bp. 18 June 1736

AMERICAN RECORDS

Muddy Creek Moravian KB, Lancaster co.:
Johann Heinrich Schmid from Wingen in Alsace (born Dec. 19, 1688, and married to Maria Magdalena, Conrad Frey's daughter). Children:
1. Johann Friedrich, born April 17, 1722, bp. the 19th by Röderer. Died Sept. 3, 1747.
2. Johann Heinrich, born July 4, 1732; bp. the 6th at Lembach in Alsace.

With his second wife Anna Maria, nee Stockerin, widowed Rothin [q.v., Roth] who brought a girl with her, namely:
Maria Eva Rothin, b. August 29, 1729 at Preuschdorf in Alsace, he had more children:
3. Johann Jacob, b. June 15, 1736, bp. the 18th at Lembach
4. Maria Dorothea, born August 1743.

Heidelberg Moravian KB, Berks co., PA:
The same information given in the Muddy Creek KB is repeated in the family register at this church. Johann Heinrich Schmidt d. 26 Feb. 1765, aged 76 years 2 months and 27 days.
Anna Maria Schmidt, b. 3 Mar. 1698 in Preuschdorff in Upper Alsace, d. 5 Oct. 1757.

Jacob Schmidt, son of Heinrich and Anna Maria Schmidt, m. 27 Sept. 1759 Catharina Fischer, daughter of Johannes and Anna Sybilla Fischer.

435. SCHMIDT, HANS GEORG Goersdorf=
after 1738 67360 Woerth
Several in S-H
EUROPEAN RECORDS

Preuschdorf Lutheran KB:
Hans Georg Schmidt, son of Hans Stephan Schmidt, citizen and linenweaver at Bechingen [W-6741-Böchingen], m. 7 Nov. 1737 at Görschdorff [Goersdorf] Christina Stocker, daughter of Hans Georg Stocker, citizen and *Gerichtsschöffen*. Notation in KB: "went to the New Land." They had a son:
1. Hans Georg b. 24 Aug. 1738, bp. 27 Aug. 1738

Several George Smith's naturalized in PA and MD.

436. SCHMIDT, JOACHIM Ottwiller=
Halifax, 1752 67320 Drulingen
S-H, I: 482
[Surname appears on list as Schmiet]

EUROPEAN RECORDS

Drulingen Lutheran KB:
Joachim Schmidt of Ottweiler and wife Susanna nee Fischer, Reformed, had a son:
Hans Joachim b. 17 May 1728

Verification of this emigrant provided by Dr. Bernd Gölzer from the compiled records of Dr. Gerhard Hein:
Records of Saarwerden county office for Ottweiler:
Dated 25 Aug. 1763; cession of Joachim Schmidt: the son Joachim has been in America for 11 years; one has no news whether he is alive or dead.
1742 census of Ottweiler: Joachim Schmidt (father of emigrant), farmer, 43

years old, 8 children, ½ house, garden, meadow, acreage, acreage elsewhere, 3 horses, 2 oxen, 1 cattle, debts: 500; fortune bad.

437. SCHMIDT, JOHANN JACOB   Hirschland=
one age 20 on *Hampshire,* 1748   67320 Drulingen
another Jacob Schmit on
Phoenix, 1749, S-H, I: 406
with others from area.

EUROPEAN RECORDS

Hirschland Lutheran KB:
Hans Michel Schmitt m. 19 Mar. 1726 Utilia Brua. Joh. Michel Schmitt and wife Utilia of Hirschland had a son:
> Joh. Jacob bp. 22 Feb. 1728
> (Entry crossed out, and emigration notation in margin by bp. entry.)

AMERICAN RECORDS

Emanuel [Warwick] Lutheran KB, Elisabeth twp., Lancaster co.:
One Jacob Schmidt and his wife (not named) were sp. in 1750 for a child of Peter Tussing, also from Hirschland.

438. SCHMIDT, JOHANN JACOB   Weyer=
Robert & Alice, 1739   67320 Drulingen
S-H, I: 263, 267, 270

EUROPEAN RECORDS

Hirschland Lutheran KB:
Joh. Jacob Schmitt from Helgeringen, m. 28 Apr. 1722 Maria Catharina, daughter of Joh. Jacob Biber of Hirschland. Children:
> 1. Maria Catharina bp. 26 Sept. 1723; conf. 1737
>   Sp.: Catharina Schneider; Juliana Biber;
>   Joh. Theobald Schmitt, shopkeeper in Hirschland.
>   Notation by bp: "*Diese sind auch in Americam gezogen*"
> 2. Johannes bp. 16 Trin. 1725, d. 24 Apr. 1728
> 3. Hans Petrus bp. 12 Sept. 1728 in Weyer
>   Notation in KB: "*ist mit allen in Americam gezogen*"
> 4. Ottilia bp. 25 Jan. 1732 in Weyer
> 5. Anna Magdalena bp. 1 Feb. 1739 in Weyer

439. SCHMIDT, PETER   Ingolsheim=
   SCHMIDT, JACOB   67250 Soultz-sous-Forêts
Sandwich, 1750
S-H, I: 450   [Peter (H) Shmit on list]
   Step-son Martin Lazarus [q.v.] also on ship;
   his surname appears as Nazarus.

EUROPEAN RECORDS

Hunspach Reformed KB, and Birlenbach Lutheran KB:
Johann Peter Schmidt, widower from Niederrodern, m. 19 Feb. 1743 Anna
Barbara, widow of the late Philip Lazarus, former citizen at Ingelsheim.
Peter Schmidt of Ingelsheim and wife *Maria* Barbara had:
   1. Daniel b. 13 Feb. 1744, Bp. 15 Feb. 1744
   2. Johann Michael b. 28 Apr. 1746, bp. 1 Mary 1746
   3. Dorothea b. 21 Jan. 1748, bp. 26 Jan. 1748
Conf. 1745 - Joh. Jacob, son of Peter Schmidt, citizen at Ingelsheim.
[Hunspach KB].

Philip Lazarus from Guntershoffen [Gundershoffen = 67110 Niederbronn]
m. 27 Jan. 1728 Anna Barbara Bürger from Ingelsheim. They were married
at Hunspach, recorded in the Birlenbach Lutheran KB. They had 4 children,
including Joh. Martin, b. 1728 [See Martin Lazarus for more data.]

Zweibrücken Manumissions Protocoll, 1750:
Peter Schmidt of Ingelsheim leaves with wife and 6 children for America.

AMERICAN RECORDS

Northampton County Will Abstracts:
Peter Schmit, Allen twp., yeoman; 10 Feb. 1771 - 25 Mar. 1771.
Wife: Anna Barbara. Children: Jacob; Henry; Catharina, wife of Georg
Hagenbuch. Mentions step-son Martin Lazarus. Mentions Peter Funck.
Exrs: Neighbors Georg Henry Hertzel, Nicholas Sterner.
Wit: Mathias Shoener, Peter Kockert.

One Peter Smith, Weisenburg, Northampton co. nat. Autumn, 1765.

440. SCHMIDTEKNECHT, JOHANN MICHEL   Keskastel=
   Phoenix, 1749   67260 Sarre-Union
S-H, I: 405
EUROPEAN RECORDS

Keskastel Lutheran KB:
Johann Michel Schmiedeknecht, tailor, son of Johann Georg Schmiedeknecht, *Schultheissen* in ?Apffelstadt [?CH-6053 Alpnachstad, OW] in ?Schweitz m. 23 Nov. 1728 in Keskastel Anna Maria Dormeyer, widow of the late Hans Georg Fischer, former citizen and innkeeper here.
[Her first marriage: Hans Georg Fischer, son of Jost Fischer, m. 14 Feb. 1702 in Keskastel Anna Maria, daughter of ?Ernst Dietrich Dornmeyer, citizen at Lorentzen.]

AMERICAN RECORDS

Trinity Lutheran KB, Lancaster:
Johann Michael Schmiedeknecht, widower, m. (2) 15 May 1750 Anna Catharina Reinhardt(in). Children:
1. Catharina Christina b. 3 Oct. 1751, bp. 20 Oct. 1751
   d. 7 Sept. 1752
2. Margaretha Friderica b. 4 Feb. 1753
3. Maria Christina b. 11 Aug. 1754
4. Anna Maria b. 13 Feb. 1757, d. 14 July 1759

Anna Catharina Schmidknecht d. 19 Feb. 1758, aged 36 years.
He m. (3) 16 Apr. 1759 Cath. Elisabet Bodin from Osterrode.
Joh. Michael Schmideknecht, a married man, d. 13 Feb. 1760, aged 59 years.

Communicants list, 1750: Johann Michael Schmiedeknecht, schoolmaster among the Mennonites.

441. SCHMITT, CARL (CHARLES)   Hirschland=
[unnamed ship], 20 Oct. 1747   67320 Drulingen
S-H, I: 370 [with Simon Gruneus]

EUROPEAN RECORDS

Hirschland Lutheran KB:
Carolus Schmitt from Helgeringen, [Hellering-lès-Fénétrange = 57930 Fénétrange], m. 13 Jan. 1739 Utilla Bruah, daughter of Theobald Brua [q.v.], smith at Hirschland. They had:
1. Joh. Adam b. 11 Nov. 1739
2. Utilia b. 15 Sept. 1745
   "In America" notations by both baptisms.

AMERICAN RECORDS

Emanuel [Warwick] Lutheran KB, Elisabeth twp., Lancaster co.:
Charles Schmidt had a daughter:
>   3. Maria Barbara b. 10 Oct. 1749, bp. 15 Dec. 1749
>   Sp.: Maria Barbara Motz; Margaretha Oberlin.

Rev. John Casper Stoever's Records:
Carl Schmidt (Bethel) had:
>   4. Eva b. 17 Dec. 1752, bp. 25 Feb. 1753
>   Sp.: Lorentz Hautz and wife.
>   5. Susanna b. 27 Oct. 1754, bp. 3 Nov. 1754
>   Sp.: Peter Klein and Susanna Grossman.

One Adam Smith, Tulpehoccon, Berks co. nat Autumn, 1765.
One Adam Smith, Macungie twp., Northampton co., nat. Autumn, 1765.
A Charles Smith, Bern twp., Berks co., nat. Autumn, 1765.

442. SCHMITT, EBERHART   Hirschland =
SCHMITT, DAVID   67320 Drulingen
Edinburg, 14 Sept. 1753
S-H, I: 522, 524

EUROPEAN RECORDS

Hirschland Lutheran KB:
Conf. 1742 - Eberhard Schmitt from Hirschland.

One Joh. David Schmitt of Helgeringen appears briefly in this record; he and his wife Agnes had one child bp. at Hirschland:
>   Christina bp. 10 Mar. 1715

Verification of this emigrant provided by Dr. Bernd Gölzer from the compiled records of Dr. Gerhard Hein:
Records of Saarwerden county office for Hirschland: Dated 21 Jan. 1761: Eberhard Schmidt has been in America since 9 years.

AMERICAN RECORDS

Rev. Daniel Schumacher's records:
Margareth Schmidth, wife of Eberhard Schmidth, sp. a child of Michael Biber in Weisenberg in 1763.

Eberhard Smidth and Margaretha, in name of their daughter Christina, as parents, were sp. in 1773 for a child of Henrich Kätterer in Bern twp.

Weisenberg Lutheran KB, Lehigh co:
Eberhardt Smidt, elder of the Lutheran congregation, m. 19 Sept. 1758
Margaretha Scheurer, old Johannes Scheurer's single daughter.

Eberhard Schmidt, elder of the Lutheran congregation, and wife Margaretha
had:
Johann Dewaldt bp. 1 Jan. 1761, 3 days old
Sp.: Dewald Keppele and Elisabeth Scheuer, single
Christina b. 5 Feb. 1764, bp. 12 Feb. 1764
Sp.: Johann Nicholas Bieber and Barbara, wife of Michael Bieber.

443. SCHMITT, FRIEDRICH   Hirschland=
Davy, 1738   67320 Drulingen
S-H, I: 234
                    EUROPEAN RECORDS

Hirschland Lutheran KB:
Friedrich Schmitt m. 21 Nov. 1736 Johanna, Grogeans daughter from
Helgeringen [Hellering-lès-Fénétrange = 57930 Fénétrange]. Notation in
KB: "*sind in American gereist.*"

One Fred. Smith, Haycock twp., Bucks co., nat. Autumn, 1765.

444. SCHNEIDER, JOHANNES   Ottwiller=
Robert & Alice, 1738   67320 Drulingen
S-H, I: 212, 214, 216
   [appears on list as Johann (A) Sneyder; did not sign. Another Johannes
   Schneider [q.v.], age 24 arrived on the *Lydia*, 1741, was his nephew,
   from Diedendorf.]

                    EUROPEAN RECORDS

Diedendorf Reformed KB:
Johannes Schneider of Ottweiler, son of Joseph Schneider of Büst, from
Melchnau [CH-4917 Melchnau, BE] m. 15 Nov. 1704 Anna Amalia nee
Hofmann, widow of the late Nickel Wucher. No children in KB.

Verification of this emigrant provided by Dr. Bernd Gölzer from the
compiled records of Dr. Gerhard Hein:
Records of Saarwerden county office for Kirberg:
A contemporary table of descendants of Joseph Schneider, dated 18 Oct.
1764: the son Johannes resided at Ottweiler and moved without children to

the New Land. It is not known whether he is alive or dead. He is a brother-in-law of David Mertz [q.v.] of Hangweiler and Büst.

445. SCHNEIDER, JOHANNES age 24   Diedendorf=
Lydia, 1741   67260 Sarre-Union
S-H, I: 301, 302, 303

EUROPEAN RECORDS

Diedendorf Reformed KB:
Hans Ulrich Schneider from Melchenau, Canton Bern [CH-4917 Melchnau, BE], son of Joseph Schneider, now inhabitant at Seewiler [Siewiller], m. 13 Sept. 1701 Anna Catharina, daughter of the late Peter Rohr. In later records, Ulrich Schneider is mentioned as a weaver in Diedendorf; later he is the *Almossenpfleger* at Diedendorf. Children:
1. Johannes Nicolaus [q.v.] bp. 10 Apr. 1703
2. Christin bp. 13 Sept. 1705
3. Josephus bp. 12 Jan. 1707
4. Otto Johann bp. 9 Dec. 1708
5. Christian bp. 12 Dec. 1711
6. Judith Maria bp. 8 Jan. 1713
7. Margaretha bp. 14 Jan. 1714
8. Johann Fridrich [q.v.] bp. 8 Sept. 1715, conf. 1730
9. **Johannes** bp. 14 Aug. 1718, conf. 1732
10. Maria Magdalena bp. 11 May 1721
11. Anna Ottilia bp. 5 Nov. 1724
12. Maria Esther bp. 18 Dec. 1727, conf. 1741
13. Johann Daniel [q.v.] bp. 1 Mar. 1731, conf. 1743

Ulrich Schneider, linenweaver and *Allmossenpfleger,* d. 23 Feb. 1743, age 73 y. 5 mo. 3 days. Born in Melchenau, Canton Bern.

Catharina nee Rohr, widow of Ulrich Schneider, d. 13 Mar. 1744, age 66 y. 10 days.

Verification of this emigrant provided by Dr. Bernd Gölzer from the compiled records of Dr. Gerhard Hein:
Records of Saarwerden county office for Kirberg, dated 18 Oct. 1764, a contemporary table of the descendants of Joseph Schneider: Ulrich Schneider and his wife had five children who are referred to as "emigrated to America": Johann Nicolaus, Johann Friedrich, **Johannes**, Maria Esther, and Johann Daniel Schneider.

AMERICAN RECORDS

Egypt Reformed KB, Lehigh co.:
Johannes Schneider lived a short distance NW of Egypt church. He sp. a son of his brother Joh. Friederich Schneider [q.v.] in 1743.

John Schneider and wife Anna Margaretha nee Wotring [b. 20 Oct. 1725 daughter of Abraham Wotring, q.v.] lived in what is now North Whitehall twp., Lehigh co. His name appears in the settlement of Abraham Wotring's estate. The Schneiders had five known children, three of whom were murdered by the Indians on 8 Oct. 1763:

1. Eva
2. Sarah b. 16 Aug. 1752, bp. at Egypt Reformed KB
   Sp.: Joseph Kennel [q.v.] and wife Sara
3. Magdalena
4. Dorothea
5. Susanna bp. 12 Apr. 1763, Egypt Reformed KB
   Sp.: Peter Burckhalter; Susanna Seger

Frontier Forts of Pennsylvania, Vol, I: 171-174:
The account of this massacre was given in the Pennsylvania Gazette, being an extract from a letter from Bethlehem dated Oct. 9 [1763].

"[from Mickley's] they went to Hans Schneider's and the Mark's plantations, and found both houses on fire, and a horse tied to the bushes. They also found said Schneider, his wife and three children, dead in the field, the man and woman scalped; and on going further, they found two others wounded, one of whom was scalped."

Charles Roberts et al, *History of Lehigh County, Pennsylvania*, Vol. I: 108:
Petition to the Assembly dated 15 May 1765. Petition from Nicholas Marks, next friend and brother-in-law to Magdalena and Dorothy Schneider, daughters of John Schneider, of Whitehall township in the county of Northampton, deceased, both being minors, was presented to the House. The petition states that on the 8 Oct. 1763, the said John Schneider, his wife, and three children, were most cruelly murdered by the Indians, at their dwelling house in Whitehall twp., one of the children was taken captive; the two girls named above were wounded, one scalped and left for dead. One of the girls, Magdalena, through the skill of the surgeons who attended her, has happily recovered; but the other, Dorothy, is still in a languishing condition. Medical expenses were attached to the petition, which the estate of their deceased father is insufficient to pay. The petition requested financial assistance. On 18 May, funds for the medical expenses were granted.

446. SCHNEIDER, (JOHANN) DANIEL   Diedendorf=
Two Brothers, 1748   67260 Sarre-Union
S-H, I: 378, 380, 381

EUROPEAN RECORDS

Diedendorf Reformed KB:
Ulrich Schneider, *Almossenpfleger* in Diedendorf, and Catharina nee Rohr
had:
> Johann Daniel bp. 1 Mar. 1731
> [See his brothers Nicolaus, Johannes, and
> Friederich Schneider for more family data.]

Verification of this emigrant provided by Dr. Bernd Gölzer from the
compiled records of Dr. Gerhard Hein:
Records of Saarwerden county office for Kirberg, dated 18 Oct. 1764, a
contemporary table of the descendants of Joseph Schneider: Ulrich
Schneider and his wife had five children who are referred to as "emigrated
to America": Johann Nicolaus, Johann Friedrich, Johannes, Maria Esther,
and **Johann Daniel Schneider.**

AMERICAN RECORDS

Egypt Reformed KB, Lehigh co.:
Daniel Schneider (and wife, n.n.) had a daughter:
> Maria Barbel bp. 5 Oct. 1755
> Sp.: Heinrich Huber(?); Maria Barbel Burghalter;
> Catharina Schneider.

Rev. Abraham Blumer's records:
Buried 5 Aug. 1778 - Daniel Schneider, age 47 years, 5 months and 2 days.

Daniel Snyder, Whitehall, Northampton co., nat. Fall 1765.

447. SCHNEIDER, JOHANN FRIEDRICH   Diedendorf=
Robert and Alice, 1738   67260 Sarre-Union
S-H, I: 212, 214, 216

EUROPEAN RECORDS

Diedendorf Reformed KB:
Hans Ulrich Schneider, linenweaver at Diedendorf, and wife Anna Catharina
nee Rohr had a son:

Johann Fridrich bp. 8 Sept. 1715, conf. 1730
[See his brother Johannes Schneider for complete
  family data.]

Verification of this emigrant provided by Dr. Bernd Gölzer from the
compiled records of Dr. Gerhard Hein:
Records of Saarwerden county office for Kirberg, dated 18 Oct. 1764, a
contemporary table of the descendants of Joseph Schneider: Ulrich
Schneider and his wife had five children who are referred to as "emigrated
to America": Johann Nicolaus, **Johann Friedrich**, Johannes, Maria Esther,
and Johann Daniel Schneider.

AMERICAN RECORDS

Egypt Reformed KB, Lehigh co.:
Friederich Schneider and wife Anna Maria had:
  1. Georg Jacob bp. 28 July 1741
     Sp.: Georg Jacob, son of Georg Kern; Anna Barbara, daughter
     of Nicolaus Seger
  2. Johann Samuel b. 20 Nov. 1742, bp. 6 Mar. 1743
     Sp.: Johannes Schneider; Samuel Seger; Catharina Eberhardt.

448. SCHNEIDER, JOHANN NICHOLAUS   Rauwiller=
Robert & Alice, 1738   67320 Drulingen
S-H, I: 212, 214, 216

EUROPEAN RECORDS

Diedendorf Reformed KB and Rauwiller Ref. KB:
Ulrich Schneider, weaver in Diedendorf and Anna Catharina nee Rohr had:
     Johannes Nicolaus bp. 10 Apr. 1703
     [see his brother Johannes for a complete family record]

Johannes Nicolaus Schneider, son of Johann Ullerich Schneider, citizen and
weaver at Diedendorf, m. 10 Sept. 1720 Eva, daughter of the late Adam
Martzluff, shepherd at Sieweiller.

Nicholaus Schneider, schoolteacher at Rauweiler, and Eva nee Marzloff had:
     1. Stephanus b. 31 Aug. 1725 [Diedendorf KB]
     2. Maria Margaretha b. 2 Nov. 1727
     3. Johann Nicklaus bp. 20 Jan. 1730
     4. Maria Susanna bp. 6 July 1732
     5. Maria Magdalena bp. 8 Feb. 1737

Signature of Johann Nicolaus Schneider from Rauwiller records:

Signatures of Johann Nicolaus Schneyder and Johann Friederich Schneider from the ship list, S-H, II: 220:

Eva, wife of Nicolaus Schneider, schoolmaster at Rauweiller, was a sp. 20 Sept. 1722 at bp. of child of David Mertz [q.v.] from Hangenweiller [Hangwiller] and his wife Frena Schneider.

Verification of this emigrant provided by Dr. Bernd Gölzer from the compiled records of Dr. Gerhard Hein:
Records of Saarwerden county office for Kirberg, dated 18 Oct. 1764, a contemporary table of the descendants of Joseph Schneider: Ulrich Schneider and his wife had five children who are referred to as "emigrated to America": **Johann Nicolaus**, Johann Friedrich, Johannes, Maria Esther, and Johann Daniel Schneider.

AMERICAN RECORDS

Egypt Reformed KB, Lehigh co.:
Johann Nicolaus Schneider and wife Eva had:
>   6. Maria Barbara bp. 23 Sept. 1740
>   Sp.: Peter Traxel [q.v.]; Paulus Paillet [q.v.]; Maria Margaretha, wife of Nicolaus Kern; Anna Barbara, daughter of Nicolaus Seger
>   7. Julianna Catharina b. 1 May 1742, bp. 8 Sept. 1743
>   Sp.: Joh. Adam Doeschler; Juliana Cath. Traxel; Barbara Seger
>   8. Peter b. 13 Aug. 1744, bp. 13 Dec. 1744

In 1758, Stephan Schneider was a sp. for a child of George Jacob Kern.

Zion Reformed KB, Allentown, Lehigh co.:
Nicholas Schneider [probably Jr.] and wife Elisabeth ahd children:
    John Peter b. 26 Dec. 1764, bp. 31 Mar. 1765
    Two of the sp. were Peter Schneider and Juliana Schneider.

Stephan Schneider and wife Juliana had:
    Daniel b. 1 Feb. 1766, bp. 31 Mar. 1766
    Jacob b. 25 Jan. 1772, bp. 29 Mar. 1772

449. SCHNEIDER, NICLAUS   Herbitzheim=
Phoenix, 1749   67260 Sarre-Union
S-H, I: 405

EUROPEAN RECORDS

Herbitzheim Lutheran KB:
Nicol Schneider and wife Anna Catharina had children:
    1. Catharina Margaretha b. 13 Nov. 1723
    2. Catharina Elisabetha b. 15 Jan. 1726
    3. Maria Christina b. 9 Oct. 1728
    4. Anna Elisabetha b. 4 Dec. 1730
    5. Joh. Ludwig b. 13 Mar. 1733
    6. Eva Elisabetha b. 13 Aug. 1735
    7. Maria Justina b. 12 June 1741
        She died 29 Apr. 1742 age 10 m., 2 weeks, 1 day
    8. Anna Eva b. 2 Dec. 1743, died 8 Dec. 1743

AMERICAN RECORDS

One of the signers on a petition for protection from the Indians, dated 5
Oct. 1757, Forks of the Delaware:
    Nich's Schneider
    Another Nich's Schneider also signed [see 1738 immigrant].

St. Paul's (Blue) Lutheran KB, Lehigh co.:
One Nicolaus Schneider and wife Catharina had:
    1. Johannes b. 9 Mar. 1750, bp. 21 Mar. 1750
        Sp.: Johann Appel and Elisabeth Catharina
    2. Johann Jacob b. 9 Oct. 1751, bp. 15 Nov. 1757
    3. Lorentz b. 20 Apr. 1753, bp. 25 May 1753
    4. Johannes Henrich bp. 4th Sun. p. Epiph. 1756

450. SCHNEPP, GEORG   Gumbrechtshoffen=
Phoenix, 1750   67110 Niederbronn-les-Bains
S-H, I: 441 [Georg (O) Shep on list]

EUROPEAN RECORDS

Gumbrichtshoffen Lutheran KB:
Georg Schnepp, single shephard, son of Joh. Schnepp, shephard at Imbsheim
[=67330 Bouxwiller], m. 14 Aug. 1749 Maria Magdalena, daughter of Jacob
Löwenguth, citizen here.

AMERICAN RECORDS

New Hanover Lutheran KB, Montgomery co. PA:
Hans Georg Schneb (also Jörg Snep) and wife Magdalena had:
   1. Johan George b. 25 Mar. 1752 at Oley Hills
      Sp: Joh. Cloosheim and Catharina
   2. Anna Magdalena b. 27 Mar. 1756, bp. 16 May 1756
      Sp: Peter Long and Magdalena Köhler
   3. Joh. Peter b. 23 Feb. 1758, bp. 19 Mar. 1758
      Sp: Joh. Peter Liebegut and wife
   4. Eva b. 31 Dec 1761, bp. 28 Mar. 1762
      Sp: Peter Liebegut and wife, Reformed
   5. Anna Margareth b. 13 Feb. 1766, bp. 20 July 1766
      Sp: Stephan Krumrein and Catharina

George Schnep (also spelled Sneb) and wife Magdalena sponsor several
children of her brother Peter Liebegut (see Löwengut) at New Hanover.

Northern Neck of Virginia Surveys, State Archives, Richmond, VA:
George Snapp warranted 400 a. in Frederick co., VA on 2 May 1767. The
survey was dated 15 May 1767 and the land was assigned to George Helm
on 12 Dec. 1775. This tract adjoined land of John Snap, a member of an
earlier immigrant Schnepp family. George Snapp made his mark on the
assignment document to George Helm. He used a small **O**, the same mark
used on the ship list in 1750. (see S-H, II: 512).

Peggy Joyner, *Abstracts of Virginia's Northern Neck Warrants & Surveys,*
Frederick Co., Vol. II: 157: George Snapp also warranted an adjacent tract
of 400 a. on the Little North Mt., 26 Feb. 1773, assigned to Michael
Tomlaiar (or Tomlauer?).

George Snapp, his wife, and some of his children moved to Nicholas Co.,
KY, where he died leaving a will that was probated in 1808.

Nicholas Co., KY, Will Book A: 116. In addition to the five children bp. at New Hanover, PA, the following children were named in his will: Catharina, Elisabeth, Adam and Hannah.

[Schnepp, Snapp data graciously provided by Cleta Smith, Silver Spring, MD.]

451. SCHNEPP, JOHANNES age 37   Duntzenheim=67270 Hochfelden
Samuel, 1733   Printzheim=
S-H, I: 107, 109, 111, 112   67490 Dettwiller
   with Barbara, age 34; Johannes, age 12; Laurence, age 10; Barbara, age 3.
[Surname Snapp on A list].

EUROPEAN RECORDS

Pfaffenhoffen, Alteckendorf, Duntzenheim, etc., Lutheran KB:
The Schnepps were shepherds and moved freely throughout the area. Extensive research has been done on this family by Cleta Smith, who has researched more than a dozen churchbooks to document the family. She generously shared her findings:
Lorentz Schnepp was bp. 20 May 1669 in [67350] Pfaffenhoffen, son of Hans Schnepp and Maria. Catharina Haber was bp. 7 Mar. 1670 at Eckendorf [Alteckendorf KB], daughter of Hans Haber and Anna Barbara nee Hans. Lorentz Schnepp m. (1) 13 Sept. 1689 at Alteckendorf Catharina Haber. They had eleven children. She died 29 Oct. 1725 at Geisswiller [Printzheim KB].
Lorentz Schnepp m. (2) 10 Apr. 1728 at Hatten Anna Barbara Stöckel. They had two children.
Two sons of the first marriage emigrated:
       Johannes b. 1 Dec. 1695 at Duntzenheim; conf. 1709 at Printzheim
       Lorentz [q.v.] bp. 16 Aug. 1711 at Wickersheim [Ringendorf KB].

Johannes Schnepp married Barbara prior to emigrating and their first three children were born in Europe.

AMERICAN RECORDS

Johannes Schnepp and wife Barbara had children:
       1. Johannes b. ca. 1721; nat. Frederick Co., VA on 5 Nov. 1746.
          Wife: Catharine. He d. 1786 in Frederick Co., VA.
          [Will Book 5: 152].
       2. Lorentz b. ca. 1723; nat. Frederick co., VA on 5 Nov. 1746.
          Wife: Margaret. He d. 1782 in Shenandoah co., VA.
          [Will Book A: 420].

3. Barbara b. ca. 1730; m. 19 Nov. 1751 Philip Peter Becker.
   She d. Jan. 1783 in Shenandoah co., VA.
4. Anna Catharina b. 28 Sept. 1734 (Opequon) [Stoever's Records].
   She m. Nicholas Pitman.
5. Christina b. 15 May 1737 (Opequon) [Stoever's Records].
   She m. before 1761 John Lewis Beard. To Rowan co., NC.
6. Margaret m. before 1761 Henry Messersmith.
7. Salomy m. before 1761 John Wisecarver.

Johannes Schnepp d. 19 Mar. 1762, aged 66 y. 3 mo., 3 weeks and a few days
in Frederick co., VA. His wife Barbara d. 20 Nov. 1758 in Frederick co., VA.
Frederick Co., VA Will Book 3:35:
John Snap of Frederick co., 30 Nov. 1761 - 6 Apr. 176(2)
Wife: Barbara. Children: John; Lawrins; Barbara Bakear; Catrin Pitman;
Christian Beard; Margrate Mesorsmith; Salomy Wiscarvar. Bible to son
John. Exr: Lawrins [Lawrence] Snap.
Wit: Joseph Fawcett, John Fawcett, Richard Fawcett.

452. SCHNEPP, LORENTZ age 21   Wickersheim=
Samuel, 1733   67270 Hochfelden
S-H, I: 107, 111, 112

EUROPEAN RECORDS

Ringendorf Lutheran KB:
Lorentz Schnepp and wife Catharina had a son:
        Lorentz bp. 16 Aug. 1711 at Wickersheim
        [See his brother Johannes Schnepp for additional data.]

AMERICAN RECORDS

York co. Deed Book F: 510:
Lawrintz Schnep at the Atkin [Yadkin] River in North Carolina and
Elizabeth, his wife, one of the daughters of Conrad Eyler, late of Lancaster
Co., PA, deceased for ten shillings paid by Valentine Eyler of Manheim twp.,
York co., their share of a tract of land which was granted to Conrad Eyler
by Warrant on 3 Oct. 1738 on the west side of Susquehanna River, cont.
200A. Dated 2 Jan. 1764. Wit: John Lewis Beard; Michael Karli; Christina
Bentz.

Rev. John Casper Stoever's Records:
Lorentz Schnepp, Obecken (Opquon)had:
        1. Johannes b. 12 Aug. 1739, bp. 29 Apr. 1739

Sp.: Johannes Schnepp and wife
2. Lorentz b. 29 Feb. 1740, bp. 29 Apr. 1740
3. Catharina   [bp. not located for these daughters,
4. Anna Margaretha   named in father's will]
5. Barbara
6. Elisabeth
7. Christina

Rowan co., NC Will Book A: 154-156:
Lawrence Snap of the Parish of Saint Luke, Rowan co. 27 Nov. 1768 - __
Feb. 1771. Children: Son Lawrence; daughter Elizabeth; daughter Chris*tian*;
daughter Catharine Real; daughter Margaret Rintleman; daughter Barbara
Barringer. Exrs: George Bruner, Michal Murr, John Dunn.
Wit: John Lewis Beard, Barbara ?Bruner or Beard; James Bradley.
His will disposes of large tracts of land and a few slaves. He owned over
3000A at the time of his death.

453. SCHOCH, JACOB   Volksberg=
Phoenix, 1750   67290 Wingen-sur-Moder
S-H, I: 441
                        EUROPEAN RECORDS

Waldhambach Lutheran KB:
Johann Jacob Schoch, mason at Volksberg, and wife Anna Maria nee
Wasserfall, had children:
        1. Anna Magdalena, conf. 1738, m. 28 Jan. 1749
           Carl Ensminger. son of Joh. Nicolaus Ensminger.
        2. **Johann Jacob,** see below.
        3. Maria Christina b. 14 Sept. 1728.

Johann Jacob Schoch, son of Johann Jacob Schoch, mason at Volksberg, m.
22 Nov. 1746 Maria Magdalena Dürrenberger, daughter of the late Christian
Dürrenberger of Mertzweiler [67580 Mertzwiller]. They had:
        1. Anna Barbara b. 18 Mar. 1748

                        AMERICAN RECORDS

Keller's Lutheran KB, Bucks Co.:
Jacob Schock and wife Maria Magdalena had:
        Catharine b. 3 Nov. 1757, bp.6 Nov. 1757
        Sp.: Henry Junghenn and Catharina
        Jacob bp. in schoolhouse 15 Mar. 1761
        Sp.: Jacob Beudesman & Catharine, daughter of Stephen Ackerman

Rudolph, twin, b. 19 Feb. 1764, bp. 21 Feb. 1764
Eva Catharina, twin, b. 19 Feb. 1764, bp. 21 Feb. 1764

Jacob Schock, Haycock twp., Bucks Co., nat. Autumn, 1765.

454. SCHORR, HANS GEORG   Herbitzheim=
Bilander *Vernon*, 1747   67260 Sarre-Union
S-H, I: 364
                        EUROPEAN RECORDS

Keskastel Lutheran KB:
Hans Georg Schorr, son of the late Jacob Schorr, former citizen at Buchsweiler [67330 Bouxwiller], m. 19 Aug. 1719 at Ehrmingen, Maria Catharina daughter of the late Hans Wilhelm Hauser former schoolmaster at ?Thrulingen [67320 Drulingen].

Herbitzheim Lutheran KB:
Johann Georg Schorr, *strohschneider*, and wife Catharina had:
1. Hans Georg bp. 28 Apr. 1720 at Ehrmingen
   [Keskastel Lutheran KB]
2. Joh. Martin bp. 22 May 1721
   Sp.: Georg Phil. Beer; Hans Martin Schupffer; Jfr. Margar. Bauer
3. Joh. Henrich b. 14 Dec. 1722, bp. 16 Dec. 1722
   Sp.: Henrich Koppel, Oermingen; Herr Johann Wurtz;
   Maria Catharina, wife of Marx Feller; Anna Catharina,
   wife of Carl Bauer.
4. Joh. Peter b. 19 Apr. 1724, bp. 23 Apr. 1724
   Sp.: Peter Wannemacher; Cunrad Fuhrer; Anna Elisabetha Bentz;
   Maria Catharina Rippel.

455. SCHRAM, CHRISTIAN   Mitschdorf=
Thistle of Glasgow, 1730   67360 Woerth
S-H, I: 31, 33, 34
                        EUROPEAN RECORDS

Preuschdorf Lutheran KB:
Joh. Christian Schram, son of Jacob Schram of Landau, Waldeck Herrschaft [Landau, Waldeck = W-3548 Arolsen] m. __ Jan. 1718 Anna Maria Stocker, daughter of Michael Stocker of Mitschdorf. Children:
1. Maria Magdalena b. 6 Oct. 1718, bp. 9 Oct. 1718
   [Kutzenhausen Lutheran KB]
2. Susanna Maria b. 4 Aug. 1720, died

3. Joh. Michel b. 28 May 1722, bp. 31 May 1722 at Mitschdorff
4. Anna Maria b. __ Mar. 1725
5. Christian b. 20 Jan. 1728 at Climbach, [Wingen Lutheran KB].

Schram's wife was a sister of Hans Jacob Stiegel's wife, also a passenger on the *Thistle of Glasgow,* 1730. She was also a sister of Michel Stocker who came on the *Britannia,* 1731.

456. SCHREIBER, JOH. JACOB age 34   67110 Niederbronn-les-Bains
Hope, 1733
S-H, I: 117, 120, 121
  with Ana Scraybrin (!) age 30

EUROPEAN RECORDS

Oberbronn Lutheran KB:
Johann Philipp Schreiber and wife Barbara had a son:
        Johann Jacob b. 14 Mar. 1695, bp. 18 Mar. 1695
        Sp.: Johann Martin Lips (signed Leubs); Maria Catharina, widow
        of Willhelm Schutz; Johan Peter, son of Wendel Lips (signed Liebs.)

[This *might* be the above named immigrant; his age on the ship list indicates a birth in 1699 - no bp. records exist for Niederbronn in that period.]

Niederbronn Lutheran KB:
Died 7 Sept. 1715 - Joh. Phs. Schreiber, age 56 years.

AMERICAN RECORDS

Roberts, *History of Lehigh County,* pg 1169-1170:
John Jacob Schreiber was born in Niederbronn, Alsace, in 1699. In a record written by himself, it is stated that he married Anna Magdalena Roth on 28 Apr. 1733, and left Niederbronn on 4 May 1733. In company with his wife's brother, Daniel Roth [q.v.] and his family, they arrived on the ship *Hope* in 1733. Resided first in Skippack, Montgomery co.; then moved to what is now Lehigh co. He died before 3 Oct. 1752. The biographical sketch in the Lehigh Co. History names the following children:
        1. Philip Jacob b. 13 June 1735 in Skippack
        2. Catharina Maria Magdalena b. 6 Jan. 1737 in Skippack.
           She m. ca. 1755 John Peter Troxell.
        3. John George b. 6 Dec. 1739, bp. 2 Apr. 1740 at Jordan
           Lutheran Church, Lehigh co.
           Sp.: George Ruch; Eva Catharina, wife of Michael Hoffman [q.v.].

Philip Jacob Schreiber, b. 13 June 1735, d. 5 Apr. 1813, buried at Egypt, Lehigh co. He married 1 May 1759 Catharina Elisabeth Kern, daughter of George Kern [q.v.]. The history continues with their eleven children.

457. SCHRÖTER, MARTIN   67580 Mertzwiller
Dragon, 17 Oct. 1749
S-H, I: 423
   [with step-son Georg Wambach, q.v.]

EUROPEAN RECORDS

Mertzweiler Lutheran KB:
Martin Schröter from Klein Hochstätten, Canton Bern, Switzerland [Kleinhöchstetten, BE=CH-3113 Rubigen], son of the late ?____Schröter, m. 27 Apr. 1723 Anna Barbara, daughter of Joseph ?Bigerlin or ?Gigerlen, former citizen here. They had children:
   1. Christina b. 27 Mar. 1724
   2. Hans Martin b. 28 Feb. 1727
   3. Maria Elisabetha b. 7 May 1731

Died 25 Mar. 1747: Anna Barbara, wife of Martin Schröter, linenweaver, aged 54 years less 3 days.

Martin Schröter, widower, and linenweaver here, m. 16 May 1747 Anna Barbara, widow of Georg Wambach, the younger. They had children:
   1. Anna Barbara, twin b. 7 Feb. 1748, bp. 8 Feb. 1748
   2. Maria Salome, twin, b 7 Feb. 1748, bp. 8 Feb. 1748
[See also Wambach, Dürrenberger, Anstatt for additional data].

AMERICAN RECORDS

Hocker, *German Settlers of Pennsylvania:*
Pennsylvanische Geschichts-Schreiber, newspaper dated 1 June 1750:
Martin Schroeter, with Johannes Schneider, Lancaster, indentured his four children last autumn, and wants to know what became of them. They are: daughters, Christina and Elisabeth; stepsons, Hansz Georg Wambach and Peter Wambach. He also seeks his brother-in-law, Johannes Anstert.

458. SCHUBAR, JOHANNES   Hunspach=
_____, 1752   67250 Soultz-sous-Forêts

EUROPEAN RECORDS

456   EIGHTEENTH CENTURY EMIGRANTS

Hunspach Reformed KB:
Johannes Schubar, citizen and shoemaker here, m. 27 June 1735 Utilia, daughter of Nickel Lehemann, former *Gemeinsmann* at Niederhorbach. Children:
1. Maria Juliana b. 23 July 1736
2. Johann Bernhard b. 3 Sept. 1737
3. Maria Barbara b. 14 Aug. 1739
4. Johann Michael b. 24 Dec. 1743

Zweibrücken Manumissions Protocoll, Clee- and Catharinenburg, 1752:
Johannes Schubar of Hunspach leaves for America with wife and one child.

459. SCHUSTER, LUDWIG age 34   Rexingen=
Barclay, 1754   67320 Drulingen
S-H, I: 596, 597, 599

EUROPEAN RECORDS

Berg und Thal Lutheran KB:
Johannes Schuster, single apprentice carpenter from Wancken in the Dukedom of Würtemberg [several Wangens], son of Jacob Schuster, m. 6 Feb. 1720 Anna Catharina, daughter of the late Heinrich Arnet, former Ev. Lutheran schoolmaster at Rexingen.
Johannes Schuster of Rexingen, and wife Anna Catharina Arneth had a son:
    Johann Ludwig b. 7 Sept. 1721

Johann Ludwig Schuster, daylaborer of Rexingen, son of Johannes Schuster, m. 25 July 1743 at Berg [=67320 Drulingen] Catharina Margaretha Klein, daughter of the late Abraham Klein, farmer of Rexingen. Children:
1. Catharina Margaretha b. 1 Apr. 1743, before marriage
    She d. 12 Apr. 1743 at Rexingen.
2. Johann Peter b. 3 Apr. 1744, d. 11 Aug. 1744
3. Catharina Margaretha b. 8 Sept. 1745, d. 19 Feb. 1746
4. Susanna Sophia b. 3 Mar. 1747
5. Johann Jacob b. 15 July 1749
6. Maria Magdalena b. 6 Oct. 1751
7. Maria Christina b. 19 Oct. 1753

Verification of this emigrant provided by Dr. Bernd Gölzer from the compiled records of Dr. Gerhard Hein:
Records of Saarwerden county office for Rexingen:
17 May 1764, inventory of Eva Fritsch who m. (1) Abraham Klein, m. (2) Caspar Reutenauer. Mentions among the children of the first marriage:

Catharina Margaretha Klein, who with her husband Ludwig Schuster moved to America 10 years ago.

AMERICAN RECORDS

New Hanover Lutheran KB, Montgomery co.:
Conf. 1764 - Lovia [probably Sophia], Loduwig Schuster's daughter, 17 years.
Conf. 1773 - Christina Schuster, Ludewig's daughter, age 18.
Conf. 1777 - Johann Schuster, son of Ludwig, age 14.
Conf. 1781 - Catharina, daughter of Ludwig Schuster, age 19.

Ludwig Shuster and wife Catharina Margareth had:
        8. Maria Christina b. __ Dec. 1755, bp. 7 Mar. 1756
           Sp.: Michael Kiele and wife.

460. SCHWANGER, JACOB   Hellering-lès-Fénétrange=
[unnamed ship] 20 Oct. 1747   57930 Fénétrange
S-H, I: 369, 370

EUROPEAN RECORDS

Rauwiller Reformed KB:
Jacob Schwanger and wife Maria nee Leyenberger, of Hellgering, had children:
        1. Johann Peter b. 29 May 1740
        2. Maria Magdalena b. 1 Jan. 1742
        3. Jacob b. 5 May 1743
        4. Isaac b. 25 Nov. 1744
        5. Catharina b. 19 Oct. 1746

AMERICAN RECORDS

Host Reformed KB, Berks Co.:
Jacob Schwanger had: (wife not named)
        Anna Maria bp. 22 Oct. 1749
        Sp.: (Anna Maria) Meerman and husband

Jacob Schwanger and wife Mary Susanna had:
        Eva Elisabeth b. 26 Aug. 1751, bp. 4 Nov. 1751
        Sp.: Eva Elisab. wife of John Trautman
        Abraham b. 16 Feb. 1757, bp. 20 Mar. 1757
        Sp.: Abraham Lauck and Anna Margaretha

461. SCHWEICKERT, JOH. MARTIN   67510 Lembach
Union, 1774
S-H, I: 759

SCHWEICKERT, EVA MARGARETHA, and
SCHWEICKERT, ELISABETHA, 1767
[possible on the ship *Hamilton,* 1767, with others from the area]

EUROPEAN RECORDS

Lembach Lutheran KB:
Johann Georg Schweickert, citizen and daylaborer here, and Maria Barbara
nee Baur, had children:
    1. Johann Michael b. 5 Oct. 1742
    2. **Eva Margaretha** b. 28 Oct. 1744, bp. 30 Oct. 1744
    3. Joh. Georg b. 16 July 1747
    4. **Maria Elisabetha** b. 9 Oct. 1749
    5. **Johann Martin** b. 12 Dec. 1752

AMERICAN RECORDS

Michael Tepper, ed., *Emigrants to Pennsylvania,* **Baltimore, 1975, p. 261:**
[Excerpted from *Pennsylvania Magazine of History and Biography,* Vol.
XXXIII, no. 4, p. 501, 1909]
The following list of German families arrived at Philadelphia, appears in an
advertisement in Henry Miller's *Staats Bote* of Feb. 9, 1758. [Note by
compiler: this date of the newspaper is obviously in error, and should be
1768. See corrected list in Appendix B of this volume].
"The following German families, and a couple of unmarried persons, are
now in the city; all held for their passage from Holland, and desiring to bind
themselves out for same ......" Among those named in this list are:
Eva Schleichart, seamstress, born in Alsace, village of Lembach (single).

Hocker, *German Settlers of Pennsylvania:*
Newspaper dated January 31, 1775:
Johann Martin Schweickart, serving with Henrich Eckel, Bucks County,
thirty miles from Philadelphia, seeks his sisters, Eva Margaretha and
Elisabeth, who came from Alsace to Pennsylvania seven years ago and were
servants six miles from Lancaster, in Warwick Township.

462. SCHWEYER, NICKLAUS   Uttenhoffen=
Neptune, 1752   67110 Niederbronn-les-Bains
S-H, I: 493

EUROPEAN RECORDS

Gundershoffen Lutheran KB:
Niclaus Schweier [signed entries Schweyer], from Uttenhoffen, and wife
Maria Barbara had children:
    1. Hans Georg bp. 16 Nov.1743
    2. Joh. Jacob bp. 10 Nov. 1745
    3. Peter bp. 24 Feb. 1748
    4. a son (?Theo)bold b. __ May 1750
[The signature of Nichlaus Schweyer by these baptisms matches his signature
in S-H, II: 588.]

AMERICAN RECORDS

Berks co. Wills:
Nicholas Sweyer, Maxatawny. 4 June 1799 - 5 Oct. 1802.
Provides for wife Catharine. To son George £5 in full, to son Jacob 5
shillings, son Peter £10, son Christian £10, to granddaughter Judith of son
Henry £10, to wife's grand-daughter Catharina Roush a cow, to grandson
Nicholas, son of Nicholas, my family Bible. Remainder in 4 equal shares to
son Henry, to son Nicholas, one share to the children of daughter Elizabeth
wife of Valentine Miller, and remaining share to daughter Barbara
Shoemaker's children (deceased). Exrs: son Henry and friend John Beaver.
Wit.: Fred. Axe, Jacob Knorr. This will appears to have been presented for
probate Aug. 6, 1800 and contested by Peter Sweyer, and citations issued
Sept. 5, 1800 for a hearing before the Register.

George Sweyer, Windsor. 22 Oct. 1807 - 15 Feb. 1808.
To wife Barbara, plantation and other estate as long as she lives. After her
decease the plantation shall go to youngest sons William and Jacob.
Children George, John, Susanna and Nicholas shall have 10 shillings each
in addition to what they have received. Daughter Elizabeth shall have £25
and described outfit when she marries. Exrs: wife Barbara and friend John
Rishel. Letters to widow, Rishel renouncing. Wit.: Henry Herber and Peter
Staiger.

Jacob Sweyer, Maxatawny. 11 Apr. 1809 - 25 Apr. 1809.
To sons Samuel and Jacob the plantation where I live (100 acres) and also
2 tracts of 16 and 25 A. Samuel paying £1500 and Jacob £500 to six
children, viz, Mary wife of Jacob Winck, Susanna wife of John Levan,
Elizabeth w. of Daniel High, Margaret married to Philip Brobst, Catharine
and Isaac. Provides for wife Elizabeth. Land held in partnership with
Samuel Ely to be sold. Sons Jacob and John, Exrs. Wit.: Solomon
Breyfogel and Casper Schmeck.

St. John's Burial ground, Kutztown, Berks co.:
Nicholas Schweyer
b. 18 Oct. 1721, d. 25 Mar. 1800

Jacob Schweyer
b. 8 Dec. 1745
[stone sunken - date of death underground]

Elisabeth Schweyer nee Kutz
wife of Jacob Schweyer
b. 3 Sept. 1750, d. 1 Nov. 1824

Peter Schweyer
b. 1758 [?1748], d. 3 Dec. 1828
Married Barbara Bayer

Jacob Schweiger, Maxatawny, Berks co., nat. autumn, 1765.
George Schweiger, Maxatawny, Berks co., nat. autumn, 1765.

An article on the "Kuntz/Cuntz of Niederbronn, Alsace" by Frieda Krueger Ewing, published in *The Palatine Immigrant*, Vol. XV, No. 4 (Winter 1990-91), page 181, indicates that Maria Barbara, wife of Nicholas Schweyer, was born 14 Apr. 1720, daughter of Johann Jacob Kuntz of [67110] Niederbronn-les-Bains and his wife Maria Salome.

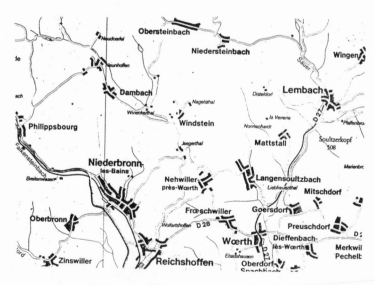

Modern map of Niederbronn-les-Bains area.

463. SEGÄSSER/SENSINGER, ULRICH   Rosenwiller=
Thistle, 1738   67490 Dettwiller
S-H, I: 222, 223, 225

EUROPEAN RECORDS

This immigrant from Wolfersheim [=W-6653 Blieskastel] was presented in Vol. 2: *The Western Palatinate* as two immigrants; #445 Segässer, Ulrich, and # 448 Sensinger, Ulrich. He appeared in the Walsheim a. Blies Reformed KB as both Segässer and Sensinger. He appeared in the Zweibrücken Manumissions Protocoll in 1738 as Seegässer. He appeared in Lehigh co. records always as Sensinger. Dr. Bernd Gölzer has kindly shared the information that the names Segässer and Sensinger are the same names.

Dettwiller Lutheran KB:
Jacob Segisser [also appears in records as Saegeser and Segeser], the younger, of Rasseweiler [Rosenwiller], and wife Barbara, had a son:
    1. Hans Ulrich bp. 9 Mar. 1693
        Sp.: Ulrich Erny?, *Reebmann* here; Jacob Zinck of Rastenweiler; Anna, wife of Hans Kocher.

See Burgert, *The Western Palatinate,* pg. 302-303 for the marriage record of this immigrant and the baptisms of his children at Wolfersheim. A discussion of the dialectic influence on place names and surnames appears on pg. 349-350 of that volume.

Additional American data on the Sensinger family is found in Roberts, et at, *History of Lehigh County, Pennsylvania,* Vol. III.

464. SEIBERT, GEORG FRIEDRICH   Preuschdorf=
not located in S-H   67250 Soultz-sous-Forêts
[A Jurig Sibert, age 25, arrived on the
Winter Galley, 1738; signed Georg Seiberth]

EUROPEAN RECORDS

Preuschdorf Lutheran KB:
Georg Friedrich Seibert, son of Lorentz Seibert, now schoolmaster here, m. 27 Jan. 1733 Anna Catharina Klein from Schalckendorff.
Notation in KB by marriage record: "went to the New Land".

465. SEIDEL, [SEYTEL] HENRICH   Preuschdorf=
Brothers, 1751   67250 Soultz-sous-Forêts
S-H, I: 463

EUROPEAN RECORDS

Preuschdorf Lutheran KB:
Hans Seidel of Preuschdorf, (step-son of Hans Schäfer of Lampertsloch)
[=67250 Soultz-sous-Forêts] m. (1) Anna Rosina Stambach. She d. 1722.
Hans Seidel m. (2) 23 Nov. 1723 Barbara Dreher, daughter of Andreas
Dreher of Alteckendorf [=67270 Hochfelden]. A child of the 2nd marriage:
     Joh. Heinrich b. 31 Mar. 1732 bp. 2 Apr. 1732
     [Note by baptism: "Went to the new land"].

AMERICAN RECORDS

Bern Reformed KB, Berks co.:
Henry Seitel and wife had:
     1. Anna Mary bp. 3 Apr. 1774. Sp.: Michael Arbogass and wife
     2. Joh. Jacob bp. 29 Dec. 1776. Sp.: Jacob Albrecht
     3. A child (n.n.) bp. 23 May 1779. Sp.: Philip Hehn and wife

Hocker, *German Settlers of Pennsylvania:*
Philadelphische Correspondenz, dated 24 Feb. 1784:
Henrich Seytel, Bern twp., Berks co., near the Reformed Church, is going to
Germany in March. He is a native of Breischdorf, Alsace. [Preuschdorf].

Bern Cemetery records, TS inscriptions:
Michael Seydel   Catharina Seidel nee Zunbroh
b. 28 Oct. 1761   wife of Michael Seidel
d. 24 Feb. 1837   b. 8 Mar. 1765
                        d. 29 Nov. 1830

Berks co. Wills:
Henry Seydel, Maidencreek; 12 Aug. 1801 - 16 Sept. 1801. Wife: Catharine;
Children: Michael, Henry, John, Daniel, Jacob, Philip, Margaret, Maria.
Mentions land sold to son Daniel; son John to have the land on which he
lives. Exrs: Sons Henry and John. Wit: Henry Rieser and Adam Gilbert.

Daniel Seydel, Maidencreek; 18 Aug. 1801 - 15 Sept. 1801. Wife: Maria;
Children mentioned but not named. Exrs: Nicholas Grett and brother Jacob
Seydel. Wit: Daniel Rieser and Jacob Detweiler.

Henry Seidell, Bern twp., Berks co., nat. Autumn, 1765.

466. SEYFRIT, PHILLIP   Volksberg=
Minerva, 1769   67290 Wingen-sur-Moder
S-H, I: 727

EUROPEAN RECORDS

Waldhambach Lutheran KB:
Hans Georg Seyfried, son of Hans Philip Seyfried, tailor of Rossteig, [Rosteig=67290 Wingen-sur-Moder], m. 30 Nov. 1719 Anna Maria, daughter of Johannes Hinckel, citizen and *Gerichtsmann* at Lichtenberg [=67340 Ingwiller]. They had a son:
Philipp b. 7 Sept. 1723, conf. 1737

Johann Philipp Seyfried of Volksberg, son of Johann Georg Seyfried, miller at Rossteig, m. 21 Dec. 1749 Anna Catharina Fischer, daughter of Christian Fischer of Volksberg. They had children:
1. Catharina Margaretha b. 2 July 1750, conf. 1763
2. Christina Sophia b. 18 Oct. 1752, conf. 1766
3. Johann Nicolaus b. 24 Oct. 1754, conf. 1768
4. Catharina Barbara b. 11 Dec. 1756, d. 13 May 1758

Anna Catharina Fischer was a daughter of Christian Fischer, glassmaker at Volksberg and his wife Maria Catharina nee Philippi.

AMERICAN RECORDS

St. Michael's and Zion KB, Philadelphia:
Buried 30 Oct. 1769 - Christina Sophia Seyfried, daughter of newcomer Joh. Philip Seyfried from Grafschaft Lützelstein, her age 17 years.

Schoeneck Moravian Graveyard, Northampton Co.:
Philip Seyfried b. 16 Sept. 1723, d. 15 Dec. 1804

Susan Seyfried "late Ehrenhard", b. at Emaus 17 Jan. 1759, d. 15 Sept. 1830

For additional data on this Seyfried family see:
John T. Humphrey, *Early Families of Northampton County, Pennsylvania*, Vol. I: Frack/Seyfried. Pages 63-98.
[This work includes a complete transcript of the will of Nicholas Seyfried, probated 23 Oct. 1832, and the complete inventory of his estate.]

467. SEYLER, HEINRICH   67160 Wissembourg
     SEYLER, CHRISTOPH
Hamilton, 1767
S-H, I: 716

EUROPEAN RECORDS

St. John's Lutheran KB, Wissembourg:
Johann Andreas Seyler, clockmaker here, and wife Anna Maria nee Breisach
had children:
    1. Margaretha Louisa b. 6 Nov. 1785
    2. Margaretha Magdalena b. 10 June 1787

A Michael Seiler, who was also a locksmith and clockmaker, appears in the
record, having six children from 1758 to 1772. Heinrich and Christoph
Seyler do not appear in the records; therefore it seems likely that Johann
Andreas Seyler, who remained in Europe when his father Heinrich
emigrated, may have been apprenticed to Michael Seiler (perhaps a relative).

AMERICAN RECORDS

St. Michael's and Zion KB, Philadelphia:
Henrich Seiler and wife Cathrina Margretha (newcomers) had a daughter:
    Cathrina Margretha b. 17 Oct. 1767 on the Delaware;
    bp. 9 Nov. 1767. Sp.: Conrad Rais (A Johann Conradt Reyss on
    ship); Catharina Margretha Methardtin (A Heinrich Medart on
    ship).

Salem Lutheran KB, Lebanon:
Joh. Heinrich Seyler and wife Catharina appear as sp. in 1773 to 1783.

Dauphin county Wills:
Henry Seiller, Town of Lebanon. 14 June 1785 - 7 July 1785. Locksmith.
To wife Catharina, house and household goods and lot and outlots in
Lebanon town for her natural life so long as she remains a widow.
Remainder to be sold and money put in trust, the interest to be paid to
widow. At wife's decease the estate to be divided as follows: to the three
eldest children of my brother Christopher Seiller £30 to be divided equally.
To the Lutheran congregation in Lebanon £10. Remaining estate to be
divided into two equal parts, ½ to son Andreas, living in the town of
Weisenburg in *Under Elsatz* in Germany. The other half to the heirs of wife
Catharina. If wife remarries all estate to be sold and she gets 1/3. If wife
Catharina should be inclined to go to Germany, estate to be sold, above
legacies paid and ½ of estate given to wife. Wife Catharina, brother
Christopher Seiller, friend Henry Baylor (or Buchler?) exrs. Wit. by John

Gloninger, David Krause.

Dauphin co. Deed Book D-I: 443:
Dated 7 July 1790. Reinhard Loeffler, of the city and state of New York, to Henry Buchler and Christopher Seiler, Exrs. of Henry Seiler, late of the town of Lebanon, locksmith, deceased. Consideration £211. Henry Seiler devised ½ of his estate to his son Andreas Seiler, living in Weisenburg in *Under Elsatz* in Germany, who by his letter of attorney dated 14 July 1788 appointed Reinhard Loeffler to receive monies _ _ . Release in estate except for unpaid sums due from Peter Miller who bought the house and lot in Lebanon Town from executors.

468. SEYLER, JACOB   Birlenbach=
_____, 1752   67160 Wissembourg
EUROPEAN RECORDS

Birlenbach Lutheran KB:
Mathias Seyler, citizen and church *censor* at Birlenbach, and wife Anna Catharina had a son:
        Johann Jacob bp. 26 Dec. 1719

Johann Jacob Seyler, cooper, son of Matthai Seyler, citizen and church *censor* at Birlenbach, m. 16 July 1743 Dorothea Schaff from Retschweiler [Retschwiller= 67250 Soultz-sous-Forêts]. Children:
        1. Johann Philipp b. 1 May 1744, bp. 3 May 1744
        2. Maria Magdalena b. 24 Jan. 1746, bp. 26 Jan. 1746
        3. Maria Catharina b. 29 Sept. 1747, bp. 1 Oct. 1747
        4. Johann Jacob b. 8 Apr. 1749, bp. 13 Apr. 1749
        5. Johann Georg b. 1 June 1751, bp.6 June 1751

Zweibrücken Manumissions Protocoll, Clee- and Catharinenburg, 1752:
Jacob Seyler of Birlenbach, with wife and five children, leaves for America.

469. SIMON, JACOB   Liniehausen,
Sandwich, 1750   Langensoultzbach=
S-H, I: 449   67360 Woerth
EUROPEAN RECORDS

Langensoultzbach Lutheran KB:
Jacob Simon, *Erbständer* and carpenter at Liniehausen, and wife Anna Magdalena nee Wüst, had children:
        1. Maria Magdalena b. 21 Feb. 1747, d. 16 Apr. 1747

2. Maria Barbara b. 4 Apr. 1748
   [father's signature in this bp. entry is a perfect
   match with signature in S-H, Vol. II: 524]
3. Maria Magdalena b. 15 Feb. 1750
   Sp.: Christoph Wüst, Erbständer; Joh. Georg Brecheisen,
   Ertzgräber at Nähweiler; Anna Barbara, daughter of Michael
   Franghauser, *Erbständer* at Liniehausen [q.v.]; and Maria
   Rosina, daughter of Jacob Ägerter, *Erbständer* at Nähweiler.

F. Krebs, "Eighteenth Century Emigrants from the Lower Alsace, and
Rheinhessen" in D. Yoder, *Rhineland Emigrants*:
        "By decree of 17 June 1760, the property of Johann Jacob Simon of
Birlenbach, Lower Alsace, was confiscated on account of illicit emigration.
According to a report by the district bailiff *Keller* of Kleeburg, Simon "had
gone to America some nine years ago, after he had secretly married in the
Dürckheim village of Leinenhaussen."

AMERICAN RECORDS

Muddy Creek Reformed KB, Lancaster co.:
Jacob Simon and wife Magdalena had:
   4. Margaret b. 26 June 1753, bp. 15 July 1753
      Sp.: Jacob Wüst [q.v.] and wife Anna Barbara
   5. A daughter (n.n.) bp. 23 Sept. 1755
      Sp.: Christopher Roblet and Maria Dorothea Bruecker

470. SIMON, PHILIP   Liniehausen,
Minerva, 1770   Langensoultzbach=
S-H, I: 730   67360 Woerth
EUROPEAN RECORDS

Langensoultzbach Lutheran KB:
Joh. Philip Simon, carpenter and *Erbeständer* at Liniehausen, son of Jacob
Simon of Birlenbach and his wife Barbara nee Breining, m. Anna Catharina
Eisenhardt, daughter of the late Ulrich Eisenhardt, also *Erbeständer* at
Liniehausen and his wife Maria Barbara nee Hessler. Children:
   1. Joh. Philip b. 22 Oct. 1752, d. 4 May 1754
   2. Philip Carl b. 30 Oct. 1754, d. 22 Apr. 1757
   3. Catharina Salome b. 7 Dec. 1757
   4. Johannes b. 11 Feb. 1761

AMERICAN RECORDS

[Philipp Simon's mark on the shiplist, S-H, II: 844 is the same mark in the KB by the bp. entries.]

1790 Census:
One Philip Simon, Huntington, Manallen, Manheim & Tyrone twps., York co.; 1 male over 16; 1 female.
The next name in the census is John Simmon; 1 male over 16, 2 males under 16; 3 females.

471. SLABACH, JOHANNES   Rott=
Mary, 1733   67160 Wissembourg
S-H, I: 131, 132, 133, 134
  with Maria Elisabeth (woman) and Henry, age 16; Tewald, age 13; Dorothea, age 5.

EUROPEAN RECORDS

Birlenbach Lutheran KB:
Johannes Schlappacher and wife Elisabetha from Rott had:
      Maria Dorothea b. 9 Oct. 1726, bp. 10 Oct. 1726
      Dorothea Margaretha b. 3 Aug. 1728, bp. 5 Aug. 1728

Zweibrücken Manumissions Protocoll, 1733:
Johannes Schlebbach moves to Pennsylvania.

AMERICAN RECORDS

Muddy Creek Reformed KB, Lancaster co.:
Heinrich Schlabbach signed the 1743 Reformed Church doctrine.
Henry Schlappach and wife Elisabeth had children:
      1. Anna Catharina bp. 28 Aug. 1743
         Sp.: Christopher Steinel and Anna Catharina
      2. John George b. 19 June 1753, bp. 5 Aug. 1753
         Sp.: Christopher Schaub; George [Schaub] and Barbara.
      3. Maria Barbara bp. 16 Jan. 1762
         Sp.: George Hefft; Maria Barbara Kieffer.
      4. John b. 19 July 1767, bp. 9 Aug. 1767
         Sp.: George Hefft and wife Dorothy
      5. Christopher b. __ ___ 1771
         Sp.: Christopher Hefft; Anna Eva Fuesser, single.

George Schlaebach, single, Reformed, m. 5 Oct. 1779 Rosina Eschelman, daughter of Christian Eschelman.

Conf. 1769: George Schlebach, age 16 y.
Conf. 1771: Elizabeth Schlabach, age 15 y.
Conf. 1775: Philip Schlabach, age 17 y.
Conf. 1775: Margaret Schlabach, age 17 y.

Lancaster co. Will Book F-I: 478:
Henry Schlabach, Brecknock. 3 Jan. 1793 - 29 Aug. 1793.
Wife: Elizabeth. Children: George, Christopher, Catharine, wife of Henry
Weith; Dorothea, wife of Jacob Zeller; Elisabeth, wife of Peter Blaser;
Barbara; Philip; John. Exrs: John and Christopher Schlabach.

472. SORG, DIEBOLDT   Hattmatt=
Ship Unknown   67330 Bouxwiller
[one Diebolt Sorg arrived on the *Peggy,* 1753,
S-H., I: 546, 547, 549 but his age is given as 27].

EUROPEAN RECORDS

Imbsheim Lutheran KB:
Diebold Sorg, son of Diebold Sorg, *Stabhalter* at Hattmatt, m. 7 Feb. 1719
Margretha, daughter of Hans Denninger, forester here. They had:
    1. Hans Jacob b. 7 June 1719, bp. 9 June 1719
    2. **Hans Dieboldt** b. 19 Nov. 1720, bp. 22 Nov. 1720
    3. Joh. Adam b. 13 June 1722, bp. 16 June 1722
    4. Anna Margretha b. 29 Nov. 1723
    5. Eva Dorothea b. 15 Mar. 1727
    6. Johann Georg b. 28 Jan. 1733
    7. Valentin (see below)
[There may be other children in this family; the Imbsheim KB only contains
Hattmatt records to 1736].

AMERICAN RECORDS

St. Michael's and Zion KB, Philadelphia:
Buried 14 Sept. 1764 - the widow Margretha Sorg, nee Tanninger, from the
Principality Hanau in Alsace, age 63 years.

Valentin Sorg m. 8 Mar. 1767 Anna Maria Does.

Buried 29 Sept. 1797: Valentin Sorg b. 20 Feb. 1744 in Hattmatt in Hanau-
Lichtenberg, son of Sebold and Margaretha Sorg. Married Maria Deff and
had 11 children, 4 living.

473. SPACH, ADAM age 60   67350 Pfaffenhoffen
Charming Betty, 1733
S-H, I: 134, 135, 136 [name on list: Spag]
  with Adam Spag, age 12

EUROPEAN RECORDS

Oberbronn Lutheran KB:
Hans Adam Spach, the weaver here, m. 14 Feb. 1719 Salome, daughter of
Martin Müller, citizen at Oberbronn [=67110 Niederbronn-les-Bains]. [It is
mentioned in this marriage record that this weaver was divorced from his
former wife because of infidelity].

Pfaffenhofen Lutheran KB:
Hans Adam Spach, *bildweber* here, and wife Salome nee Müller had children:
  1. Adam b. 10 Jan. 1720, bp. 16 Jan. 1720
     Sp.: Jonas Brunner, citizen here; Joh. Jacob König, the pastor's
     son from ?Schal____[Schalkendorf?]; Joh. Theobald_____?,
     schoolmaster here; Eva Rosina, daughter of Herr _ Scholl.
  2. Eva Barbara b. 25 Mar. 1723

AMERICAN RECORDS

Reichel, *Moravians of North Carolina,* p. 188:
Adam Spach b. 1720 in Alsace, Germany. Came to North Carolina in 1756;
died in 1801 in Friedberg.
See also Grace L. Tracey and John P. Dern, *Pioneers of Old Monocacy,*
Baltimore, 1987: p. 210 for MD land transactions of Adam Spuch or Spough.

For more information on Adam Spach, see:
Henry Wesley Foltz, *Descendants of Adam Spach.* Published by Wachovia
Historical Society, Winston-Salem, NC; Raleigh NC (1924).
Meynen's Bibliography #7518.

Adam Spaught nat. Frederick co, MD, April 1749

474. SPECHT, JACOB   67580 Mertzwiller
King of Prussia, 1764
S-H, I: 695
EUROPEAN RECORDS

Mertzweiler Lutheran KB:
Jacob Specht, single, linenweaver and son of the late citizen and linenweaver

at Gumprechtshoffen, m. 17 Jan. 1764 Anna Margaretha Bowe, daughter of the late Jacob Bowe, former citizen here.

[The signature of Jacob Specht by this marriage entry matches the signature of the immigrant in S-H, II: 790. His brother, Johan Georg Specht, witnessed the marriage and also signed the KB. He arrived on the ship *Sarah*, 1764 [q.v.].

AMERICAN RECORDS

PA Genealogical Magazine Vo. XXVII, No. 1, 1971, p. 54-61:
Jacob Specht and wife were indentured to Mahlon Kirkbride, two years each, as redemptioners for their passage money.

475. SPECHT, JOHANN GEORG   67110 Niederbronn-les-Bains
Sarah, 1764
S-H, I: 692

EUROPEAN RECORDS

Gumprechtshoffen Lutheran KB:
Hans Georg Specht and wife Anna Barbara had a son:
    Joh. Georg b. 5 Jan. 1734

Niederbronn Lutheran KB:
Joh. Georg Specht, citizen and linenweaver here, and wife Anna Margaretha nee Kleiber [Klauber in another record] had children:
    1. Catharina Salome b. 26 June 1761, bp. 28 June 1761
    2. Anna Margaretha b. 8 Oct. 1763, bp. 9 Oct. 1763

Oberbronn Lutheran KB:
Joh. Peter Klaiber, citizen and *Rothgerber*, son of the late Burckhard Klaiber from Ulm [W-7900 Ulm], m. 6 Aug. 1720 Maria Elisabetha, daughter of Joh. Peter Lips, citizen and *Rothgerber* here. Children:
    1. **Anna Margaretha** b. 16 June 1721, bp. 19 June 1721
    2. Maria Magdalena b. 7 July 1723
    3. Anna Maria b. - July 1724
    4. Anna Magdalena b. 2 Nov. 1726

AMERICAN RECORDS

St. Michael's and Zion KB, Philadelphia:
Buried 10 Oct. 1771: Anna Margaretha Specht, b. in Oberbrunn 19 Jan. 1721; m. the surviving widower Georg Specht on 10 Jan. 1758 in Niederbrun. They came to this land 26 Oct. 1764. Aged 51 y. 9 mo.

Georg Specht, widower in Passyunk, m. (2) 21 Jan. 1772 Anna Margretha Metzler, single, in Philadelphia.

Buried 10 Aug. 1799- Joh. Georg Specht, born in Alsace 6 Jan. 1734; married (1) Margaretha; married (2) M. Metzler. One son living.

476. SPILL, HANS GEORG   Oberkutzenhausen=
Minerva, 1770   67250 Soultz-sous-Forêts
S-H, I: 729
  [Surname translated as *Sch*ill in S-H].

EUROPEAN RECORDS

Kutzenhausen Lutheran KB:
Johann Theobald Spill, citizen at Oberkutzenhausen, and wife Eva had:
   Johann Georg b. 2 June 1724, bp. 4 June 1724

Joh. Georg Spill, single son of Diebold Spill, citizen at Oberkutzenhausen, m. 12 Aug. 1760 Maria Elisabetha Heinrich, daughter of Joh. Jacob Heinrich, citizen and schoolmaster at Oberkutzenhausen.
[She was a sister of the wife of Joh. Georg Müller, also a passenger on the *Minerva*, 1770.] Children:
   1. Georg Heinrich b. 6 June 1762
   2. Hans Michel b. 27 July 1764
   3. Jacob b. 4 Aug. 1766
   4. Johannes b. 7 Feb. 1769

AMERICAN RECORDS

PA, Third Series, Vol. 14:
George Speel, Passyunk, Philadelphia co. tax list, 1780.

1790 Census:
Henry Speil, baker, Philadelphia city, middle district:
1 male over 16; 2 males under 16; 5 females.

John Speile, baker, Philadelphia city, southern district:
1 male over 16; 1 male under 16; no females.

St. Michael's and Zion KB, Philadelphia:
Buried 11 Nov. 1795- Georg Spiel, b. 4 June 1726 in Alsace, son of Theobald Spiel; married 1761 to Elisabetha and had four children; two sons are living; came to Pennsylvania in 1770.

477. SPRECHER, HANS GEORG   67510 Lembach
John & William, 1732
S-H, I: 102, 104, 105
    Catharina Spreakering on 103

EUROPEAN RECORDS

Lembach Lutheran KB:
Hans Sprecher had children (bp. not located in this KB:)
        1. Jacob, conf. 1728, son of Hans Sprecher.
            Died 20 Mar. 1730: Jacob, son of Hans Sprecher,
            citizen here and his late wife Anna nee Friederich.
            Aged 17 years, 8 mo. less 6 days. Buried 21 Mar. 1730.
        2. Hans Görg, conf. 1729, son of Hans Sprecher
        3. Maria m. 21 Jan. 1731 Johannes Nagel [q.v.]

Hans Sprecher, widower, m. 24 Nov. 1720 at Lembach **Catharina nee Hügelin**, widow of the late Johann Nagel, former *Dragoner unter Churpfaltzischen Truppen.* [Her son Johannes Nagel m. 1731 his daughter Maria Sprecher. It seems likely that she is the Catharina Spreakering on the ship list, with her step-son Hans Georg Sprecher and son Johannes Nagel].

AMERICAN RECORDS

Rev. John Casper Stoever's Records:
George Sprecher m. 28 May 1755 Eva Margaretha Schwab, Lebanon.
They were sp. in 1755 for a child of Rev. Joh. Caspar Stoever.
A Jacob Sprecher m. 5 Mar. 1759 Dorothea Blecher, Lebanon.
John Martin Bindtnagel m. 25 Apr. 1761 Maria Elisabetha Sprecher, Derry.
George Sprecher m. 2 May 1771 Margaretha Boger, Lebanon and Hanover.

Egle, *History of Lebanon Co.:*
Georg Sprecker of Lebanon twp., died about 1758 leaving a wife Eva Margaret and children:
        1. Georg, in 1758 residing at Carlisle, PA
        2. Frederick
        3. Julianna, m. Christian Laffery of Cumberland co., PA

George Sprecker nat. 10 Apr. 1758 (no location stated).

478. SPRING, NICKEL   Diedendorf=
Edinburgh, 1750   67260 Sarre-Union
S-H, I: 430

EUROPEAN RECORDS

Wolfskirchen Lutheran KB:
Hans Nickel Spring, from Diedendorf, m. 15 Oct. 1737 Anna Margaretha Karcher. They had:
1. Elisabetha b. 9 Dec. 1738
2. Joh. Nickel b. 15 Sept. 1740
3. Margaretha b. 19 Dec. 1742
4. Lorentz b. 20 Oct. 1745
5. Johann Theobald b. 19 Nov. 1749

Diedendorf was a predominately Reformed parish. Lutheran residents of Diedendorf appear in the Wolfskirchen parish records before 1746, when a separate Lutheran record was started for Diedendorf.

AMERICAN RECORDS

Trinity Lutheran KB, Lancaster:
Nicolaus Spring, a married man, d. 4 Oct. 1753, buried the next day.
His widow d. 1 Nov. 1753, buried the following day.

Elisabet Spring(in), single, was a sp. in 1762 for a child of Joh. Philip Schmitt.

Philip Kolb, yeoman of Lancaster Borough, m. 1 Oct. 1763 Margaret Spring, spinster.

Theobald Spring [also Dewald, Spreng] and wife Hanna had children:
  1. Elisabeth b. 13 Apr. 1779, bp. 25 June 1779
  2. Maria b. 20 June 1782, bp. 25 Aug. 1782
  3. Susanna b. 6 Aug. 1784, bp. 1 June 1785
  4. Anna b. 15 Sept. [____], bp. 1 Aug. 1790

First Reformed KB, Lancaster:
Nich. Spring and wife Christina had children:
  1. Elisabetha b. 28 Jan. 1757, bp. 2 Oct. 1757
  2. Jacob b. 6 Dec. 1768, bp. 11 Jan. 1769.

479. SPRINGER, JACOB age 32   Ingelshoff,
Virtuous Grace, 1737   Uttenhoffen=
S-H, I: 176, 177, 178   67110 Niederbronn-les-Bains

EUROPEAN RECORDS

Gundershoffen Lutheran KB:
Jacob Springer, son of the late N.N. Springer from Reutingen in Switzerland, Canton Bern [CH-3647 Reutigen, BE], m. 17 Jan. 1702 at Uttenhoffen, Maria Ottilia, daughter of the late Dorst Völckel former citizen at Uttenhoffen. They had a son:
  Johann Jacob b. 27 June 1704

Jacob Springer, single tailor from Uttenhoffen, son of the late Jacob Springer, m. 5 Feb. 1733 at Guntershoffen, Anna, daughter of Adam Weiss, *Erbestander auf dem Ingelshoff.* [An Adam Weiss, age 60, also arrived on the *Virtuous Grace,* 1737.] Jacob and Anna Springer had children:
  1. Anna Barbara b. 21 Dec. 1733
  2. Magdalena b. 19 Apr. 1735
  3. Jacob b. 1 Apr. 1737

AMERICAN RECORDS

Lancaster co. Wills, Y-2: 576:
Jacob Springer, Rapho twp., 24 Nov. 1781 - 9 Feb. 1782
Wife: Susanna. Children: Jacob, Philip, Conrad, John and Christina, wife of John German. Exrs: Abraham Frederick and David Nicky.

Trinity Lutheran KB, Lancaster:
Jacob Springer and wife Barbara had:
1. Salome b. 15 June 1781
2. Barbara b. 9 Feb. 1783
3. Anna Maria b. 12 Dec. 1785
4. Susanna b. 12 Feb. 1789
5. Catharine b. 3 Oct. 1791 (Reformed KB)
6. Jacob b. 11 July 1794
7. Heinrich b. 19 Dec. 1796

480. SPRINGER, PETER   Uttenhoffen =
SPRINGER, HANS GEORG   67110 Niederbronn-les-Bains
Phoenix, 1749
S-H, I: 405
EUROPEAN RECORDS

Gundershoffen Lutheran KB:
Jacob Springer, son of the late N.N. Springer from Reutingen, Canton Bern, Switzerland [CH-3647 Reutigen, BE], m. 17 Jan. 1702 at Uttenhoffen Maria Ottilia, daughter of the late Dorst Völckel, former citizen at Uttenhoffen. They had son:
Peter b. 29 Jan. 1706

Joh. Peter Springer, son of the late Jacob Springer, former citizen at Uttenhoffen, m. 5 Feb. 1733 at Griesbach, Anna Elisabetha, daughter of Mathias Schmid, former schoolmaster at Rothbach. They had children:
1. **Joh. Georg** b. 14 Dec. 1733
2. Anna Elisabetha b. 11 Mar. 1735
3. Anna Margaretha bp. 22 Mar. 1737
4. Peter bp. 9 Dec. 1740

Peter Springer, citizen and weaver at Uttenhoffen m. 12 Jan. 1745 at Mertzweiler, Anna Barbara, daughter of Abraham Knochel, citizen at Gunbrechtshoffen. Children:
5. Catharina b. __ Jan. 1746
6. Salome b. 9 Jan. 1748, bp. 11 Jan. 1748
   [the father's signature by this baptism matches
   the immigrant's signature on S-H, II: 453.]

AMERICAN RECORDS

Moselem Lutheran KB, Richmond twp., Berks co.:
Joh. Georg Springer, smith, single son of Peter Springer from Donegal, m.

14 Dec. 1756 Catharine Merkel, single daughter of Nicholaus Merkel.
They had children:
> Esther b. 1 Apr. 1768, bp. 8 May 1768
> Sp.: Christian Schuck and Rosina.
> Hanna b. 16 Feb. 1771, bp. 1 Apr. 1771. No sp. given.

481. STAMBACH, HANS GERG   Preuschdorf=
Dragon, 17 Oct. 1749   67250 Soultz-sous-Forêts
S-H, I: 423   Langensoultzbach=
                                                      67360 Woerth

EUROPEAN RECORDS

Preuschdorf Lutheran KB:
Hans Jacob Stammbach, servant of Matthis Eyermann at Lampresloch
[Lampertsloch=67250 Soultz-sous-Forêts], and wife Anna, had a son:
> Joh. Georg b. 28 May 1706, bp. 30 May 1706

Langensoultzbach Lutheran KB:
Hans Georg Stambach, son of Hans Jacob Stambach, citizen at Merckweiler
[Merkwiller=67250 Soultz-sous-Forêts], m. 8 Jan. 1731 Catharina, daughter
of Ulrich Brücker, citizen at Sultzbach. [See Brücker immigrants]. Children:
> 1. Johann Georg bp. 15 Nov. 1731
>   Sp.: Philipps Stambach, citizen at Mertzweiler; Agnes, wife of
>   Philipps Schuh; Hans Georg Brücker, citizen in ?Weinenheim;
>   Anna, wife of Albrecht ?Hiebert.
> 2. Anna Catharina bp. 4 June 1734
> 3. Joh. Philipp b. 14 May 1737
> 4. Joh. Jacob b. 1 Apr. 1740, died 10 Apr. 1740
> 5. Joh. Jacob b. 7 Feb. 1742
> 6. Joh. Heinrich b. 12 Nov. 1745

482. STAMBACH, HANS JACOB   Birlenbach=
St. Mark, 1741   67160 Wissembourg
S-H, I: 296, 298, 299

EUROPEAN RECORDS

Birlenbach Lutheran KB:
Hans Jacob Stambach was a sp. in 1734 for a child of Hans Jacob Haüser
and wife Catharina.

Hans Jacob Stambach was a sp. in 1735 for a child of Hans Adam Stambach in Keffenach [=67250 Soultz-sous-Forêts.]

Zweibrücken Manumissions Protocoll, Cleeburg, 1740:
Joh. Jacob Stambach of Burlenbach moves out of the country.

483. STAMBACH, JACOB   Kutzenhausen=
Robert & Alice, 1739   67250 Soultz-sous-Forêts
S-H, I: 264, 267, 270

EUROPEAN RECORDS

Kutzenhausen Lutheran KB:
Johannes Stambach, son of Felix Stambach and Anna Maria, married in 1717 Maria Catharina Meyer, daughter of Jacob Meyer and wife Anna, all Reformed religion. Johannes Stambach died 17 Jan. 1733, age about 57 years. Felix Stambach, Reformed citizen here, died 3 Nov. 1729, aged 86 years, 3 months, 12 days. Jacob Meyer, Reformed citizen in Merckweyler, died 1 Feb. 1716, age 63 years. Anna, widow of the late Jacob Meyer of Merckweiler, Reformed, died 19 Feb. 1726, age 70 years; buried in Oberkutzenhausen.
Johannes Stambach, citizen at Unterkutzenhausen, and wife Maria Catharina had children:
    1. Johann Jacob b. 9 Jan. 1719, bp. 11 Jan. 1719
    2. Maria Barbara b. 25 July 1721, bp. 27 July 1721
    3. Nicolaus b. 19 Aug. 1723, bp. 22 Aug. 1723
    4. Lorentz b. 8 Dec. 1725, bp. 11 Dec. 1725
    5. Johann Peter b. 11 Feb. 1729, bp. 13 Feb. 1729
    6. Johann Philipp b. 9 June 1731, bp. 10 June 1731

Catharina, widow of Johannes Stambach, m. 17 Nov. 1733 at Niederkutzenhausen, Niclaus Honig [q.v.], also em. on *Robert & Alice*, 1739.

AMERICAN RECORDS

Trinity Lutheran KB, Lancaster:
Joh. Georg Schmeisser m. 22 May 1740 Barbara Stambach.

Rev. John Casper Stoever's Records:
Jacob Stambach (Conewago) had a daughter:
    1. Maria Catharina b. 22 Sept. 1740; Sp.: Joh. Georg Kuntz [q.v.]
       and daughter Maria Catharina and Maria Elisabetha Morgenstern.

Rev. Jacob Lischy's records, York co.:
Jacob Stambach and wife Margreth had children:
2. Anna Barbara bp. 18 Mar. 1745, Codorus
   Sp.: Georg Schmeisser and Anna Barbara
3. Jacob bp. 17 June 1750
4. Maria Elisabetha bp. 17 June 1750
   Sp.: Lorentz Stambach and Barbara
5. Anna Barbara bp. 14 June 1752
   Sp.: Niclaus Stambach and Anna Barbara
6. Philliph bp. 20 Nov. 1754; Sp.: Philliph Stambach

Peter Stambach and wife Catharina had children:
1. Anna Maria bp. 30 Apr. 1749; Sp.: Emerich Bott and Anna Maria
2. Susanna bp. 29 Mar. 1751
3. Maria Elisabetha bp. 10 Aug. 1755
4. Magdalena bp. 2 Apr. 1760
5. Anna Margreth bp. 3 Mar. 1762

Niclaus Stambach and wife Margretha had children:
1. Joh. Jacob bp. 16 Dec. 1749; Sp.: Jacob Stambach and Margreth
2. Anna Margreth bp. 29 Mar. 1751
Niclaus Stambach and wife Barbara had;
3. Johannes bp. 14 Oct. 1753
4. Anna Elisabetha bp. 15 Jan. 1755
Niclaus Stambach died in 1760, and Letters of Adm. on his estate were
granted to Peter Stambach.

Lorentz Stambach and wife Anna had children:
1. Catharina bp. 4 Nov. 1750; Sp.: Peter Stambach and Catharina
2. Jacob bp. 29 Mar. 1752; Sp.: Sebastian Hellman and Margaretha
3. Elisabetha Magdalena bp. 26 May 1754
4. Peter bp. 7 Mar. 1756
5. Margreth bp. 4 June 1758; Sp.: Jacob Stambach and Margreth
6. Joh. Philliph bp. 17 Sept. 1760

Philipp Stambach and wife Barbara had children:
1. Joh. Heinrich bp. 26 Sept. 1762
2. Joh. Michel bp. 3 Oct. 1764
3. Elisabeth bp. 27 July 1766

484. STAMBACH, PHILIP, age 19   Durstel=
Friendship, 1739   67320 Drulingen
S-H, I: 265, 268, 271

EUROPEAN RECORDS

Durstel Lutheran KB:
Ulrich Stambach of Durstel and wife Eva Catharina nee Gangloff had a son:
Johann Philipp b. 21 Apr. 1719, conf. 1733

Buried 14 Mar. 1745: Anna Catharina Stambach, widow of Ulrich Stambach, nee Gangloff, from Lohr [=67290 Wingen-sur-Moder]. Her father was Andreas Gangloff and her mother was Anna Eva. She was b. 21 Jan. 1680, and m. 27 Aug. 1698 Ulrich Stambach. They had ten children, four sons and six daughters, of whom two sons and one daughter went to America. [see Ulrich Stambach and Anna Catharina Stambach, wife of Friedrich Eberhard]. She was widowed on the 4 Oct. 1729. She d. 12 Mar. 1745, aged 65 years. Was a widow for 15 years.

AMERICAN RECORDS

Augustus Lutheran KB, Trappe, Montgomery co:
Johann Philip Stambach m. __ 1745 in the Oley Mountains Maria Christina Kuhnz(in) [see Kuntz].

New Hanover Lutheran KB, Montgomery co.:
Johann Philip Stambach and Anna Christina had:
   1. Maria Magdalena b. 29 June 1747, bp. 6 Sept. 1747
      Sp.: Adam and Catharine Linck and Maria Catharina Kuntz

Jordan Lutheran KB, South Whitehall twp., Lehigh co:
Philip Stambach and Anna Christina had:
   2. Anna Catharina b. 7 Jan. 1746, bp. 31 Mar. 1746
   3. Johann Daniel (twin) bp. 12 Mar.1749
   4. Anna Barbara (twin) bp. 12 Mar. 1749
   From baptismal certificate:
   5. Anna Margaretha b. 5 Jan. 1754 in Albany twp., Berks co.,
      daughter of Philip Stambach and Christina nee Kuntz

Rev. Daniel Schumacher's records:
Philip Stambach and wife Christina had children:
   6. Anna Maria bp. 14 Sept. 1756, 11 weeks old, in Allemangle
      Sp.: Christian Hechler and Anna Maria
   7. Anna Elisabeth bp. 6 Nov. 1758 in Allemangel
      Sp.: Bernhard Kuntz and Catharina
   8. A Child bp. 8 May 1763, 9 weeks old, in Allemangel
      Sp.: Johannes Küstler and Barbara
   9. Maria Susanna (twin) bp. 25 Oct. 1767, in Allemangel

4 weeks old. Sp.: Jacob Gürtner and Maria Elisabeth
10. Anna Christina (twin) bp. 25 Oct. 1767
    Sp.: Jurg Adam Leibelsperger and Catharina Barbara
11. Son Jacob, named in will
12. Son Philip, named in will.

Conf. 1761 in Allemangel, Albany twp.: Maria Magdalena Stammbachen;
    Anna Catharina Stammbachen.
Conf. 1764 in Weisenberg: Daniel Stammbach
Conf. 1767, Easter Sunday, Apr. 19 in Allemangel:
    Maria Barbara Stammbachen
Conf. 1769 in Allemangel, Rogate Sunday:
    Anna Maria Stammbachen; Anna Margaretha Stammbachen

Northampton co. Wills:
Philip Stambach, Lynn twp. 8 Nov. 1776 - 25 Oct. 1777
Wif: Christine. Children: youngest sons Jacob and Philip; daughter Anna
Elisabeth; daughter Catharine wife of George Probst; son-in-law Philip
Kuntz; daughter Anna Maria; daughter Christina; daughter Susanna; son
Daniel. Exrs: Wife Christina and son Daniel.
Wit: George Sausela, Abraham Boli.

Inventory dated 15 Mar. 1777, totaled £498.5.0
Appraisers: Andreas Hagenbuck, William Stumpff.

Philip Stambach, Linn twp., Northampton co., nat. Autumn 1765.

485. STAMBACH, ULRICH   Durstel=
St. Andrew, 1741   67320 Drulingen
S-H, I: 305, 306
    [appears on A list as Ulrich Hanbach, age 34]

EUROPEAN RECORDS

Durstel Lutheran KB:
Johann Ulrich Stambach, son of Ulrich Stambach of Durstel, m. 12 Jan.
1734 at Adamsweiler Susanna Maria Klein, daughter of Jacob Klein of
Struth [=67290 Wingen-sur-Moder].
Eva Catharina nee Gangloff, widow of Johann Ulrich Stambach, d. 12 Mar.
1745. Her obituary mentions that two sons and one daughter went to
America. [See also Philip Stambach and Friedrich Eberhard.]

486. STARK, JACOB   Uhrwiller=
Brotherhood, 1750   67350 Pfaffenhoffen
S-H, I: 447

EUROPEAN RECORDS

Uhrwiller Lutheran KB:
Hans Jacob Storckh, son of the late Joh. Storckh, *gerichtsmann*, m. 18 Sept.
1714 Maria, daughter of Peter Lemmel, citizen at Moltzheim [=67120
Molsheim]. Children:
    1. Johannes bp. 3 Feb. 1715
    2. Barbara bp. 2 Nov. 1717
    3. Maria bp. 4 Sept. 1719
    4. Theobald [q.v., Stork] bp. 18 Nov 1722
    5. **Jacob** bp. 5 Dec. 1725
        Sp: Joh. Peter, son of Joh. Peter Scheer; Joh. Peter, son of Jac.
        Lauffer; Hedwig, daughter of Pastor Erici Strelin.

AMERICAN RECORDS

Anita L. Eyster, *Notices by German and Swiss Settlers in the Pennsylvanische
Berichte and the Pennsylvanische Staatsbote*, in Pennsylvania German
Folklore Society, Vol. III (1938):12: 1752, Feb. 1:
Jacob Storck arrived some time back in the fall from Ritters Hofen, Hattner
District, Alsace. His mother Anna Maria Storck, son Dewald and daughter
Anna Maria arrived also last fall. The mother and daughter are free of
charges and she is very anxious to see her son Jacob. If he is serving and
cannot come, let him write and she will come to him. She is in Phila. at
Johann Kuhn's, not far from the Reformed Church.

Jacob Stork, Chester, nat. 29 Sept. 1768 in Philadelphia

487. STARTZMANN, EVA CATHARINA   Rexingen=
between 1753-1755   67320 Drulingen

EUROPEAN RECORDS

Berg und Thal Lutheran KB:
Hans Martin Startzmann, carpenter at Rexingen, and wife Christina nee
Arneth had:
    1. Johann Henrich b. 28 Feb. 1720 [q.v.]
    2. Eva Catharina b. 3 Dec. 1722

Eva Catharina Startzmann had two children:
  1. Eva Christina b. 26 Dec. 1745, illegitimate
  Records of Saarwerden county office for Rexingen:
  The child's father (not named) denies fatherhood.
  2. Anna Maria b. 7 June 1753, illegitimate
  Records of Saarwerden county office for Rexingen:
  The child's father (not named) has escaped to America.

AMERICAN RECORDS

Moselem Lutheran KB, Richmond twp, Berks co:
Johan Michael Haefel [Haeffele, Haefelin], son of Carl Haefel, m. 5 Aug.
1755 Eva Catharina, single daughter of Martin Stortzmann. Children:
  1. Johan Carl b. 3 Apr. 1756, bp. 16 May 1756
  Sp.: Joh. Carl Haefele and Eva
  2. Johan Carl b. 22 May 1757, bp. 29 May 1757
  Sp.: Carl Haefele and Eva
  3. Eva b. 22 Feb. 1759, bp. 11 Mar. 1759
  Sp.: Carl Haefele and Eva
  4. Michael b. 16 Feb. 1761
  5. Anna Elisabeth b. 23 June 1765
  6. Maria Eva. b. 12 Nov. 1767

Zion Reformed KB, Hagerstown, MD:
Michael Hefele and wife Eva Catharina had:
  7. Johann Henrich b. 28 June 1771, bp. 16 Sept. 1771
  Sp.: Henrich Stirtzman [q.v.-Startzman] and wife Eva.

488. STARTZMANN, HANS MARTIN   Rexingen=
Robert and Alice, 1738   67320 Drulingen
S-H, I: 213, 214, 216

EUROPEAN RECORDS

Berg Lutheran KB:
Hans Martin Startzman, son of Hans Martin Startzman, miller at the
Kuppertsmühl, *Litzelsteinisch Herrschafft,* m. 13 Feb. 1714 Christina,
daughter of Hennrich Arneth, schoolmaster at Rexingen. Children:
  1. **Johann Martin** b. 19 July 1717, bp. 25 July 1717
  Sp.: Joachim Schmidt, Ottweiler; Hans Nickel, son of Caspar
  Reütenauer of Rexingen; Catharina, daughter of Heinrich Arnet,
  schoolmaster at Rexingen.
  2. Johann Heinrich [q.v.] b. 28 Feb. 1720, bp. 3 Mar. 1720

3. Eva Catharina [q.v.] b. 3 Dec. 1722, bp. 6 Dec. 1722
4. Johann Caspar b. 21 Nov. 1725
5. Justina Christina b. 24 Nov. 1728, died

AMERICAN RECORDS

A Martin Stutsman, Cowisseoppen, Berks co., nat. by affirmation, 10 Apr. 1753.

489. STARTZMANN, JOHANN HEINRICH   Rexingen=
Bilander *Vernon*, 1747   67320 Drulingen
S-H, I: 363
EUROPEAN RECORDS

Berg und Thal Lutheran KB:
Hans Martin Startzmann, carpenter in Rexingen, and wife Christina nee Arneth had a son:
Johann Henrich b. 28 Feb. 1720

Johann Henrich Startzmann, tailor in Rexingen, son of the late Martin Startzmann, m. 10 Sept. 1743 Anna Margaretha, daughter of the late Benedict Führer of Rexingen. Children:
1. Johann Martin b. 5 May 1744, bp. 8 May 1744
2. Johann Henrich b. 10 Feb. 1746

Verification of this emigrant provided by Dr. Bernd Gölzer from the compiled records of Dr. Gerhard Hein:
Records of Saarwerden county office for Rexingen:
27 Jan. 1750, heirs of Martin Startzmann: "the son Henrich is in America and has nothing to receive from here."

AMERICAN RECORDS

Frederick Lutheran KB, Frederick, MD:
Henrich Störtzmann had:
3. Catharina b. 3 Mar. 1750, bp. 4 Apr. 1750
Sp.: Henrich Reitenauer [q.v.] and wife Catharina

Salem Reformed KB, Hagerstown, MD:
Henrich Startzman and wife Eva had:
1. Joh. Henrich b. 2 Jan. 1771, bp. 17 Feb. 1771
Sp.: Henrich Müller and wife Catharine

Zion Reformed KB, Hagerstown, MD:
Henrich Stirtzman and wife Eva were sp. in 1771 for a child of Michael
Hefele. They were sp. in 1773 for a child of Jacob Reidenauer.

St. John's Lutheran KB, Hagerstown, MD:
Henry Storzmann [also Stoetzman, Rotzman, Stortzman] and wife Eva had:
    2. Juliana b. 21 Mar. 1774, bp. 10 Apr. 1774
    3. Daniel b. 1 Jan. 1777, bp. 30 Mar. 1777
    4. Eva b. 21 Nov. 1779
    5. Susanna b. 5 Apr. 1782

An Adam Stortzman, and Peter Stortsman appear in these records in the
1780s, plus others later.

490. STEFFAN, ADAM   Goersdorf=
Bennet Gally, 1750   67360 Woerth
S-H, I: 428

EUROPEAN RECORDS

Preuschdorf Lutheran KB:
Joh. Friedrich Steffan and wife Maria Salome nee Greiner, of Görsdorf, had
a son:
    Adam b. 8 Feb. 1726, bp. 9 Feb. 1726

Hans Adam Steffan, single, son of Friederich Steffan citizen at Görschdorff,
m. 28 Jan. 1749 Maria Magdalena, daughter of the late Valentin Eichenlaub,
former citizen in Retschweyler [Retschwiller=67250 Soultz-sous-Forêts].
They had a daughter:
    1. Chatharina Magdalena b. 7 Nov. 1749, died.

AMERICAN RECORDS

Adam Steffan's signature on pg. 61 of the Preuschdorf marriage record is a
perfect match with S-H, II: 490.

491. STEINMANN, MICHAEL age 40   Breitenacker Hof
Barclay, 1754   Ingolsheim=
S-H, I: 595, 597, 599   67250 Soultz-sous-Forêts

EUROPEAN RECORDS

Hunspach Reformed KB:
Michael Steinmann of Ingelsheim, *Hoffmann* at Breidenacker, and wife
Catharina had children:
1. Eva Margaretha b. __ Apr. 1738
2. Maria Catharina b. 18 Dec. 1740
3. Johann Jacob b. 14 Dec. 1743
4. Dorothea b. 23 Mar. 1747
5. Johann Michael b. 23 Oct. 1749
6. Johann Philipp b. 1 May 1752

Zweibrücken Manumissions Protocoll, Clee- and Catharinenburg, 1754:
Michel Steinmann of Breidenacker [Breitenacker] leaves with wife and six
children for America.

492. STEPHAN, ULRICH
after 1741   Hoffen=
[Not in lists]   67250 Soultz-sous-Forêts

EUROPEAN RECORDS

Hoffen Reformed KB:
Ulrich Stephan, son of Johannes Stephann, former schoolteacher here, m.
21 May 1737 Anna Maria, daughter of Johannes Schirmer, geese herdsman
here. They had children:
1. Johann Michel b. 9 Sept. 1737, bp. 15 Sept. 1737
   Sp.: Hans Jacob Schwab, carpenter; Joh. Michel, son of Lorentz
   Weimer; Elisabetha, wife of Jost Stephan, *hindersäss* at
   Betschdorff
2. Maria Elisabetha b. 3 Dec. 1738, bp. 7 Dec. 1738
   Sp.: Hans Michel, son of Lorentz Weimer; Anna Maria wife of
   Jacob Schwob, carpenter; Elisabetha, wife of Jost Stephan,
   hindersäss at Rittershofen
3. Anna Maria b. 23 Jan. 1741, bp. 29 Jan. 1741
   Sp.: Joh. Georg Oleyer son of Joh. Michel Oleyer.
   Elisabetha, wife of Jost Stephan, *schirmer* at Rittershofen
   Elisabetha, wife of Georg Jauchzy

Died 13 Nov. 1749 Veronica nee Blattner, wife of Johannes Schirmer, the
geese herdsman here, age 70 years.
Died 2 May 1730, buried 3 May 1730, Johann Stephan, former schoolteacher
at Hofen, age 54 years, 9 months.
Died 25 Oct. 1737, Johann Michel, son of Ulrich Stephan, mastertailor and
hindersäss, age 1 month, 16 days.

AMERICAN RECORDS

Lebanon Moravian Seelen-Register, 1754:
Ulrich Stephan b. 2 Oct. 1710 at Affolde (Affottern) in Canton Bern, [CH-3416 Affoltern im Emmental, BE] Switzerland, Reformed. Wife: Anna Maria b. 30 Aug. 1716 in Petschdorf [67660 Betschdorf] in Elsass, Reformed. They had children:
1. Elisabetha b. 3 Dec. 1738
2. Michael b. 26 Nov. 1743
3. Johannes b. 21 Dec. 1745
4. Heinrich b. 2 June 1748
5. Anna Maria b. 1 Oct. 1750
6. Dorothea b. 1 Oct. 1753
from Lebanon Moravian KB:
7. Johann Peter b. 3 June 1757, died
8. Johann Peter b. 3 June 1759

Heidelberg Moravian KB, Berks co:
Died 5 Apr. 1771- Anna Maria Rieth, b 30 Aug. 1717 in Alsace, in County Zweibrücken (!). Her father was Johannes Schirmer, a member of the Reformed Church. She m. (1) Ulrich Stäffen in 1737 and they came to this land together. They became members of our congregation in 1750. They had 6 sons and 4 daughters. After the death of her first husband she m. (2) Caspar Rieth at Hebron on 30 June 1761. [in another record in the KB her date of birth is given as 30 Aug. 1716].

493. STEUER, TOBIAS   Griesbach=
Robert and Alice, 1738   67110 Niederbronn-les-Bains
S-H, I: 212, 214, 215

EUROPEAN RECORDS

Gundershoffen Lutheran KB:
Tobias Steurer, single *mühlartz* in the Griesbacher Mill, earlier *"in der Schlesselig zu Bancken in dem Ampt Brigischen"?*, son of the late N.N. Steurer, former miller there, m. 15 Jan. 1726 Anna Magdalena, daughter of the late Meister Isaac Bannwitz, former miller at Griesbach. Children:
1. Johann Georg b. 3 Feb. 1727, bp. 5 Feb. 1727
   Sp.: Jacob Stähli; Hans Georg, son of Georg Teutsch; Anna Barbara, daughter of the late Hans Peter Duchmann.
2. Anna Elisabetha b. 7 Oct. 1728, bp. 9 Oct. 1728; d. 1730.
   Sp.: Joh. Samuel Stumpff, farrier; Anna Elisabetha, wife of Bernhard Müller of Oberbronn; Anna Maria, daughter of Hanns

Georg Teutsch, citizen at Griesbach.
3. Tobias b. 5 Nov. 1730.

494. STIEFEL, JACOB   Mitschdorf=
Thistle of Glasgow, 1730   67360 Woerth
S-H, I: 31, 33, 34

EUROPEAN RECORDS

Preuschdorf Lutheran KB:
Hans Jacob Stieffel, apprentice carpenter, son of the late Hans Georg
Stieffel, from Frickenhausen in the Dukedom Würtenberg [W-7443 Fricken-
hausen], m. 27 Nov. 1725 at Mitschdorff Catharina Stocker, daughter of
Hans Michael Stocker, citizen at Mitschdorff.
Marginal note by marriage record: "went to the New Land". They had:
1. Anna Margaretha b. 4 Aug. 1726, bp. 6 Aug. 1726; died.

Jacob Stieffel's wife was a sister of Christian Schramm's wife and Friedrich
Pfeifer's wife, also passengers on the *Thistle of Glasgow*, 1730. They were
also sisters of Michel Stocker who arrived on the *Britannia* in 1731.

AMERICAN RECORDS

St. Michael's Lutheran KB, Germantown:
Jacob Stiefell and Catharina Stiefelin were sp. in 1746 for a child of
Heinrich Acker [q.v.].

495. STIEGELMAN, JOH. JACOB age 25   67110 Niederbronn-les-Bains
Peggy, 1753
S-H, I: 545, 547, 549 [signed Stigelmann]

EUROPEAN RECORDS

Niederbronn Lutheran KB:
Joh. Georg Stiegelman, butcher, and wife Anna Barbara had children:
1. Maria Catharina b. 14 ?July 1711
2. Johannes b. 26 Sept. 1713
3. Joh. Daniel b. 16 Nov. 1718
4. Eva Margretha b. 23 July 1721
5. Maria Luiysa [Louisa] b. 18 Feb. 1724
6. **Joh. Jacob** b. 28 Dec. 1726, bp. 31 Dec. 1726

488 EIGHTEENTH CENTURY EMIGRANTS

Lancaster Moravian Burial Records:
Died 26 May 1807- Jacob Steigelman, b. 29 Dec. 1726 in Alsace. Came to America in 1753. Married spring 1759 Eva Barbara nee Ranck; had eleven children, three sons and one daughter survive.
Eva Barbara Steigelman, widow, nee Ranck, d. 25 Apr. 1808. She was b. 11 Mar. 1732 in PA.
Buried 15 June 1760- a stillborn daughter of Jacob and Eva Barbara Steigelman.
Buried 11 Mar. 1762- Georg Michael, son of Joh. Jacob and Eva Barbara Steigelman, age 10 months.

Jacob Stigliman, Lancaster, nat. Apr. 1764.

496. STÖCKEL, HEINRICH 67690 Hatten
Jeneffer, 1764
S-H, I: 700

AMERICAN RECORDS

Hatten Lutheran KB:
Heinrich Stöckel, swineherder, Reformed, son of Hans Stöckel, former citizen in Lobsingen, Canton Basel [?CH-3251 Lobsigen, BE] m. 13 Apr. 1728 Anna Christina Denger, Reformed, daughter of Hans Denger, herdsman. They had sons:
    1. **Joh. Heinrich** b. 3 Feb. 1729, bp. 6 Feb. 1729
    2. Philipp Jacob [q.v.] b. 1 May 1732, bp. 4 May 1732

497. STÖCKEL, PHILIP JACOB 67690 Hatten
Betsey, 1765
S-H, I: 707

EUROPEAN RECORDS

Hatten Lutheran KB:
Heinrich Stöckel, swineherder, Reformed, son of Hans Stöckel, former citizen in Lobsingen, Canton Basel [?CH-3251 Lobsigen, BE] m. 13 Apr. 1728 Anna Christina Denger, Reformed, daughter of Hans Denger, herdsman. They had sons:
    1. Joh. Heinrich [q.v.] b. 3 Feb. 1729
    2. **Philipp Jacob** b. 1 May 1732, bp. 4 May 1732

AMERICAN RECORDS

St. Paul's Lutheran KB, Upper Saucon twp., Lehigh co:
Philip Jacob Steckel and wife Anna Maria had:
1. Johann Matthias b. 11 Oct. 1766, bp. 27 Oct. 1766
   Sp.: Matthias Müller and wife Anna Sophia
2. Georg Henrich b. 23 Feb. 1769, bp. 24 Mar. 1769
   Sp.: Matthias Müller and wife Anna Sophia

Philip Jacob Steckel and Anna Maria were sp. in 1768 for a child of Georg Ruck and wife Margaretha.

Tohickon Lutheran KB, Bucks co:
Henry Stoeckel and wife Christina had:
1. Samuel b. 4 June 1790, bp. 8 Aug. 1790
   Sp.: Matthew Stoekel; Barbara Steinbach.

498. STOCKER, MICHAEL age 31   Mitschdorf=
Britannia, 1731   67360 Woerth
S-H, I: 48, 52, 54   Preuschdorf=
   with Margerite age 24   67250 Soultz-sous-Forêts

EUROPEAN RECORDS

Preuschdorf Lutheran KB:
Hans Michel Stocker, son of the late Jacob Stocker of Mitschdorf, m. 25 Nov. 1692 Maria Remp, daughter of Hans Jacob Remp of Mitschdorf. They had children:
1. Anna Maria bp. 21 Mar. 1694; m. 1718 Joh. Christian Schramm [q.v., emigrant in 1730].
2. Catharina b. -- Dec. 1696, d. 1697
3. Maria Elisabetha b. 4 Mar. 1698; m. 1720 Friedrich Pfeifer [q.v., emigrant in 1730].
4. **Hans Michel** b. 24 Nov. 1701, bp. 27 Nov. 1701 [see below]
5. Maria Catharina b. 25 June 1704; m. 1725 Hans Jacob Steifel [q.v., emigrant in 1730].
6. Anna Margretha b. 10 July 1707, d. 1714
7. Maria Barbara b. 3 Apr. 1713

Hans Michael Stocker, son of Hans Michel Stocker, citizen at Mitschdorff, m. 30 Jan. 1725 Anna Margretha Stephan. She was b. 30 ?Mar. or May? 1708, an illegitimate daughter of Catharina Stephan. A marginal note by marriage: "went to the new land." They had children:
1. Anna Margretha b. 10 Nov. 1725, d. 1726
2. Michel b. 31 Aug. 1727, bp. 5 Sept. 1727

3. Anna Maria b. 7 Dec. 1728, bp. 9 Dec. 1728
4. Maria Barbara b. 20 Sept. 1730, bp. 25 Sept. 1730

AMERICAN RECORDS

New Hanover Lutheran KB, Montgomery co:
Conf. 1749: Michael Stocker age 16, Jürg Burchhart's Servant

Zions Lutheran KB, Lower Macungie twp., Lehigh co.:
Michael Stockert and wife Anna Margaretha had:
    Johann Georg b. 5 Nov. 1769.

Northampton co. Will Abstracts:
Michael Stocker, Macungie. Will 4 Jan 1771/24 Jan. 1771
Wife: Margaret; Children: Mary, Elizabeth, Catharina, Susanna, and others.
Exrs: Wife and George Shitz. Wit: Adam Gramus and Sebastian
Truckenmiller.

Frederick Lutheran KB, Frederick MD:
A Mich. Stoker and wife Anna Barbara had a daughter:
    Anna Barbara b. 1 Apr. 1758, bp. Pentecost 1758
    Sp.: Maria Barbara, single daughter of Mich. Römer.

499. STÖHR, JOHANNES   Langensoultzbach=
STÖHR, HENRICH   67360 Woerth
STÖHR, PHILIP
St. Andrew Galley, 1737
S-H, I: 178, 180, 183

EUROPEAN RECORDS

Langensoultzbach Lutheran KB:
Johannes Stöhr, of Sultzbach, and his wife Margaretha, nee Dock, had
children:
    1. Johann Henrich b. 6 Jan. 1715
    2. Philipp Henrich bp. 20 Feb. 1716
    3. Anna Elisabetha bp. 22 Apr. 1717
    4. Maria Dorothea bp. 20 Dec. 1722

AMERICAN RECORDS

Emanuel [Warwick] Lutheran KB, Elisabeth twp., Lancaster co.:
Johannes Stör and wife Margaretha were sp. in 1744 for a child of Joh.
Mattheis Pflantz.

Heidelberg Moravian KB, Berks co.:
Heinrich Stohr, born in Langen Sulzbach in Alsace 11 Jan. 1715; he m.
Maria Barbara Frey who was b. 16 June 1715 [She was widow of Peter
Brücker, q.v.]. They had children [the first four ch. are also recorded in the
Muddy Creek Moravian KB, Lancaster co.]:
1. Anna Margaretha, b. 2 Aug. 1740, bp. by Pastor Rieger.
   Sp.: David Biehler and his wife
2. Philipp, b. 26 Aug. 1742, old style, bp. in Sept.
   by Caspar Stöver. Sp.: Philipp Stöhr
3. Anna Maria, b. 11 July 1744, old style, bp. by Jacob Lyschi;
   Sp.: Philipp Stöhr and wife
4. Heinrich, b. 25 Nov. 1746, old style, bp. by Johannes Brucker.
   Sp.: Michael Rancke, David Bischoff and Heinrich Schmidt
5. Johannes, b. 10 Mar. 1751, old style, bp. 29 Mar. 1751
   by Brother Christian Rauch; Sp.: Heinrich Beck, Johannes Meyer,
   Philipp Stöhr, Friedrich Gerhardt and Peter Frey
6. Elisabeth, b. 3 Mar. 1749, bp. 9 Apr. 1749 by Leonhardt Schnell
   Sp.: Christina Beckel, Maria Catharina Conrad, Hanna Neubert,
   J. A. See___. Elisabeth d. 30 Sept. 1749, new style, buried 2 Oct.
7. Johann Jacob, b. 12 Mar. 1753, bp. 30 Mar. 1753 by Rauch;
   Sp.: Johannes Meyer, Jacob Miller, Heinrich Schmidt, Nicolaus
   Glad and Johann Heinrich Miller
8. Christian, b. 13 May 1755, bp. 15 may by Brother Antony Wagner;
   Sp.: Friedrich Gerhard, Johannes Meyer, Georg Brendel, Jacob
   Miller and Jacob Conrad. Christian d. 19 Jan. 1758
9. Anna Rosina b. 12 Oct. 1757, bp. 13 Oct. 1757 by Wagner;
   Sp.: Elisabeth Wagner, Maria Margaret Meyer, Christina Böckel,
   Barbara Frey, Maria Elisabeth Glat, Anna Barbara Frey, Barbara
   Gerhard, Eva Elisabeth Brendel

Philipp Stor from Langen Sulzbach in Lower Alsace was b. 18 Feb. 1716,
new style, and bp. 20 Feb. 1716 by Herr Cramer, pastor at that place. The
sponsors were Christina Joost and Philipp Schuh. He was m. in May 1742
by Caspar Stöver (Stöver's private record says April 27) in his house to Miss
Anna Maria Holler, daughter of Johan Nicolaus Holler, citizen of Unkstein
and his wife Anna Maria, married at Warwick (Stöver's record gives her
name as Holder). They had children:
1. Barbara, b. in Warwick, Lancaster co., 31 Aug. 1743,
   bp. by Caspar Stöver in Warwick in the Lutheran church.
   Sp.: Heinrich Stör and his wife Barbara
2. Anna Elisabeth, b. 17 Aug. 1745 in Heidelberg in Lancaster co.,
   bp. by Pastor Wagner in Heidelberg in the Lutheran schoolhouse.
   Sp.: Tobias Bechtel and wife Anna Elisabeth
3. Maria, b. 25 Aug. 1747, old style, in Heidelberg in Lancaster

co., bp. in the meeting house of the Brethren at the same place,
on the 2nd Sunday after Trinity, by Brother Leonhard Schnell.
Witnesses: Christina Bökel, Margaretha Meyer and Maria
Margaretha Conrad. Maria d. 11 Nov. 1751.
4. Christina, b. 10 Sept. 1749 in Heidelberg, Lancaster co. and bp.
in the Brethren meetinghouse on 25 Oct. 1749 by Friderich
Cammerhoff. Sp.: Christina Böckel, Margaretha Meyer, Maria
Barbara Stör, Mrs. Rauch, Mrs. Cammerhoff and Hanna Neibert.
Christina d. 29 Oct. 1751
5. Maria Magdalene, b. 11 Sept. 1751 in Heidelberg, bp. in the
meetinghouse on 24 Sept. 1751 by Brother Mattheus Reüz.
Sp.: Barbara Beck, Christina Böckel, mother Stör, Maria
Elisabeth Glad, Barbara Stör and Anna Sibilla Fischer
6. Maria Margaretha, b. 27 Apr. 1754, bp. 5 May 1754 by Brother
Anton Wagner. Sp.: Maria Catharina Conrad, Maria Margaretha
Meyer, Christina Böckel, Maria Elisabeth Müller, Anna
Catharina Schuchar and Elisabeth Wagner.

Quitopehille Moravian KB, Lebanon co.:
7. Anna Maria b. 26 June 1756
8. Catharina Barbara b. 3 Sept. 1758
9. Johannes b. 19 Mar. 1761
10. Maria Elisabetha b. 4 Apr. 1763, died
11. Regina b. 7 Sept. 1764
12. Joh. Philip b. 27 Feb. 1767
13. Joh. Henrich b. 23 Aug. 176_?

500. STÖHR, SUSANNA MARIA   Langensoultzbach=
ship unknown, 1763   67360 Woerth
                            EUROPEAN RECORDS

Langensoultzbach Lutheran KB:
Nicolaus Stöhr, weaver, and wife Johanna Elisabetha nee Müller, had a
daughter:
        Susanna Maria bp. 21 Jan. 1732 at Sultzbach [Langensoultzbach]
        Marginal note by bp. record: "went to Pennsylvania in 1763".

501. STORK, THEOBALD   Uhrwiller=
Janet, 1751   67350 Pfaffenhoffen
S-H, I: 475
(with mother Maria and sister Anna Maria, not in lists)

                            EUROPEAN RECORDS

Uhrweiler Lutheran KB:
Hans Jacob Storckh, son of the late Joh. Storckh, *gerichtsmann*, m. 18 Sept.
1714 Maria, daughter of Peter Lemmel, citizen at Moltzheim [=67120
Molsheim]. Children:
1. Johannes bp. 3 Feb. 1715
2. Barbara bp. 2 Nov. 1717
3. Maria bp. 4 Sept. 1719
4. **Theobald** bp. 18 Nov. 1722; conf. 1736
    Sp: Joh. Georg son of Jac. Lauffer; Joh. Peter, son of Joh. Peter
    Scheer; Ottilia, daughter of Peter Strigel?.
5. Jacob [q.v., Stark] bp. 5 Dec. 1725

AMERICAN RECORDS

Anita L. Eyster, *Notices by German and Swiss Settlers in the Pennsylvanische
Berichte and the Pennsylvanische Staatsbote*, in Pennsylvania German
Folklore Society, Vol. III (1938): 12:   1752, Feb. 1:
Jacob Storck arrived some time back in the fall from Ritters Hofen, Hattner
District, Alsace. His mother Anna Maria Storck, son Dewald and daughter
Anna Maria arrived also last fall. The mother and daughter are free of
charges and she is very anxious to see her son Jacob. If he is serving and
cannot come, let him write and she will come to him. She is in Phila. at
Johann Kuhn's, not far from the Reformed Church.

St. Michael's and Zion Lutheran KB, Philadelphia:
Buried 15 Sept. 1763: the widow of Jacob Storck born in Moltzheim
[=67120 Molsheim] in Alsace. Age 73 years, 4 months, 3 weeks.
Buried 17 Jan. 1788: Theobald Stork b. 6 Dec. 1725 in Uhrweiler [Uhrwiller
=67350 Pfaffenhoffen]. Married Barbara Haeger(in). Had 2 children.

Theobald Stork, Moyamensing, Philadelphia co., nat. autumn, 1765

502. STRAUSS, JOHANN LUDWIG   67430 Diemeringen
Phoenix, 1749
S-H, I: 404

EUROPEAN RECORDS

Diemeringen Lutheran KB:
Conf. 1720 - Johann Ludwig Strauss, son of Jacob Strauss, joiner here.
Johann Ludwig Strauss, son of Jacob Strauss, joiner here, m. 27 Sept. 1735
Catharina Dorothea, widow of the late Daniel Greiner.

[her 1st m. 3 Feb. 1729 - Daniel Greiner, widower and Catharina Dorothea,

daughter of the late Henrich Schöneberger, tile maker at Dehlingen.]
[See also immigrant Andreas Greiner.]

503. STROH, FRIEDERICH   Bischtroff-sur-Sarre=
Priscilla, 1749   67260 Sarre-Union
S-H, I: 398

EUROPEAN RECORDS

Pistorf (Bischtroff) Lutheran KB:
Johannes Stroh of Pistorff and wife Dorothea had a son:
     Georg Friederich b. 9 Feb. 1712; conf. 1724

Georg Friedrich Stroh, cooper, m. 7 May 1737 Anna Elisabetha, daughter
of Jacob Quirin, beer brewer from Wolffskirchen [=67260 Sarre-Union].
They had children:
     1. Joh. Daniel b. 30 May 1738, bp. 1 June 1738
     2. Joh. Nickel b. 9 Jan. 1740, bp. 11 Jan. 1740
     3. Georg Friedrich b. 9 Nov. 1741, bp. 11 Nov. 1741
     4. Johann Michael b. 2 Dec. 1743, bp. 4 Dec. 1743
     5. Maria Margretha b. 3 Jan. 1746, bp. 6 Jan. 1746
     6. Anna Margretha b. 6 Sept. 1748, bp. 8 Sept. 1748

Verification of this emigrant provided by Dr. Bernd Gölzer from the
compiled records of Dr. Gerhard Hein:
Records of Saarwerden county office for Pisdorf:
Dated 9 Apr. 1748, Friedrich Stroh has debts, will sell house.
Dated 14 Aug. 1749, Georg Friedrich Stroh has moved away to the New
Land without manumission with his wife and children. They (officials)
confiscated his movables at Saarbrücken and brought them back to Pisdorf
for auctioning.

AMERICAN RECORDS

Quitopahilla Reformed KB, Lebanon co.:
Friedrich Stroh and wife Anna Elisabetha had:
     7. Anna Maria b. 8 Mar. 1751

Emanuel [Warwick] Lutheran KB, Elisabeth twp., Lancaster co.:
Friederich Stroh had a son:
     8. Joh. Nicolaus b. 1 Mar. 1753, bp. 4 Mar. 1753
          Sp.: Joh. Nicolaus Ensminger and wife Margaretha
Hill Lutheran KB, Annville, Lebanon co.:
Friederich Stroh had:
     9. Maria Barbara b. 17 Oct. 1757, bp. 19 Oct. 1757

Sp.: Adam Bach and wife

Georg Stroh and wife Anna Engel (belong in Lebanon) had a son:
    1. Joh. Philip b. 22 Dec. 1768, bp. 1769

Salem Lutheran KB, Lebanon:
Buried 22 Apr. 1806- Georg Friedrich Stroh, son of Joh. George Stroh and
wife Elisabeth. Born 9 Nov. 1741 in Pöstorf, Europe. He came to this
county in his tenth year. Confirmed. He was married to Mar. Engel Groh.
They had two children, one is living. His wife died one year ago. Sickness
was consumption.

Died May 1805- Maria Engel Stroh, daughter of Leonhard Groh and
Susanna. Born Oct. 1744 in Mühlbach, Lancaster co. Baptized and
confirmed. On 5 July 1764 she m. George Stroh. They had two children;
one daughter survives. Sickness: pleurisy and chills. Age 50 y. 7 mo.

Died 7 Feb. 1818: Anna Maria Elisabeth Stroh, wife of Michael Uhler. [He
was a son of Anastasius Uhler and Dorothea]. They had ten children (his
obituary) or sixteen children (her obituary). She was b. Mar. 1751, age 66 y.,
10 mo.

Rev. John Casper Stoever's Records:
Joh. Daniel Stroh m. 16 June 1761 Catarina Barbara Uhler, Lebanon.
[Six children bp. at Hill Church].
Michael Stroh m. 15 Sept. 1767 Eva Barbara Goettel, Heidelberg and
Hanover.
Joh. Martin Uhler m. 15 Mar. 1768 Anna Elisabetha Stroh, Lebanon town.
Joh. Michael Uhler m. 20 Apr. 1773 Anna Maria Elisabetha Stroh, Lebanon.
Leonhardt Stroh m. 14 Apr. 1779 Anna Maria Goettel, Hanover.
[For European records on this Uhler family, see Burgert, *The Northern
Kraichgau*, p. 370.]

504. STROH, JACOB   Wolfskirchen=
Halifax, 1754   67260 Sarre-Union
S-H, I: 652, 654
                        EUROPEAN RECORDS

Pisdorf Lutheran KB:
Joh. Theobald Stroh, of Wolfskirchen, and wife Christina nee Juncker had
a son:
        Jacob b. __ Dec. 1727

Wolfskirchen Lutheran KB:
Died 30 Oct. 1764: Christina, wife of Joh. Theobald Stroh.
Died 8 Nov. 1765: Joh. Theobald Stroh.

Verification of this emigration supplied by Dr. Bernd Gölzer, from the county records of Nassau-Saarwerden, compiled by Dr. Gerhard Hein:
Records of the notary public for Wolfskirchen:
16 Nov. 1764, cession of Christina Juncker Stroh: the son Jacob Stroh has moved to America 9 years ago.

AMERICAN RECORDS

Rev. Daniel Schumacher's records:
Jacob Stroh and Maria Catharina had:

> Johann Peter b. 14 June 1760, bp. 27 Feb. 1761 across the Lehigh Sp.: Peter Anthony; Anna Eva Küstern; Joh. Caspar Altmann; Christina Altmann, single

----

Jacob Stroh, Lehi, Northampton co. nat. Fall 1765.

505. STROH, JOST   Rimsdorf=
Anderson, 1751   67260 Sarre-Union
S-H, I: 451

EUROPEAN RECORDS

Bischtroff [Pisdorf] Lutheran KB:
Jost Stroh, son of Johannes Stroh of Pistorff, m. 22 Feb. 1735 Anna Margaretha Müller, daughter of Joh. Nicolaus Müller, citizen and shepherd at Harskirchen [=67260 Sarre-Union].

Neusaarwerden Lutheran KB:
Jost Stroh, farmer at Rimsdorf, and wife Anna Margaretha nee Müller had children:

> 1. Johannes b. 6 Feb. 1736
> 2. Johann Nicolaus b. 19 Feb. 1739
> 3. Probably Joh. Georg b. ca 1741, bp. not located
> 4. Johann Daniel b. 11 Jan. 1746
> 5. Johann Peter b. 23 Sept. 1747, d. 23 Feb.1748

Verification of this emigrant provided by Dr. Bernd Gölzer from the compiled records of Dr. Gerhard Hein:
Records of Saarwerden county office for Pisdorf:
Inventory of Johannes Stroh, dated 14 Feb. 1753: the eldest son Jost lived

in Rimsdorf and afterwards has moved to the New Land, where he stays now. [See also Friedrich Stroh, his brother.]

AMERICAN RECORDS

Emanuel [Warwick] Lutheran KB, Elisabeth twp., Lancaster co.:
Jost Stroh had a son:
>   Johann Friederich b. 3 June 1755, bp. 21 June 1755
>   Sp.: Daniel Stroh; Maria Ellisa Schmidt(in). He d. 6 Aug. 1758.

A Nickel Stroh and wife Eva appear in this KB from 1771-1789.

Trinity Lutheran KB, Lancaster:
Joh. Georg Stroh from Reinssdorf in Nassau-Saarbrücken m. __ Apr. 1763 Anna Magdalena Ruscher, single.   [According to the Neusaarwerden Lutheran KB, there was only one Stroh family in Rimsdorf, that of Jost Stroh. He is listed in the 1742 census as 33 years old, with 4 children. Therefore, it is likely that this Joh. Georg Stroh is his son, although the bp. record has not been located.]

506. STUTZMAN, PETER age 16   Hinsingen=
Lydia, 1741   67260 Sarre-Union
S-H, I: 300, 301, 302

EUROPEAN RECORDS

Keskastel Lutheran KB:
Hans Peter Stutzman from *Sigritzweil?, Landvogtey Dhun Berner Geb.* [CH-Sigriswil, BE], son of the late Hans Peter Stutzman, m. 14 Jan. 1716 at Altweiler Anna Magdalena, daughter of Hans Jacob Lung from Altweiler [Altwiller=67260 Sarre-Union.] Children:
>   1. Hans Nickel bp. 8 Nov. 1716 at Altweiler
>   2. Anna Barbara bp. 27 Feb. 1722
>   3. **Hans Peter** bp. 6 Feb. 1724 at Hinsingen
>   Sp.: Hans Peter Kercher, woolweaver at Neusaarwerden;
>   Clad Rouche from Hinsingen; Eva Margretha, daughter of
>   Hans Nickel Guth of Neusaarwerden.
>   [Note in KB: record extracted 3 May 1741].

AMERICAN RECORDS

Rev. John Casper Stoever's Records:
One Christian Stutzmann m. 19 Mar. 1778 Catarina Ecket, Berks county,

across the Blue Mountain.

Trinity Tulpehocken Reformed KB, Jackson twp., Lebanon co:
One Peter Stutzmann m. 1 June 1807 Elizabeth Artzt.

Schuylkill co. Will Book 1: 262:
Michael Artz of Mahantongo twp. Dated 16 Sept. 1822, prob. 7 Oct. 1822,
Wife: Catharine. Children: Michael; Jacob; **Elisabeth, wife of Peter
Stutzman;** Catharine, wife of Jacob Dinger; Margaret; Barbara, wife of
Frederich Rebuck. Exrs: Jacob Dinger (son-in-law), and Michael Artz
(son).

507. SUMI, HANS PETER age 59	Rexingen=
SUMI, HANS JACOB age 22	67320 Drulingen
SUMI, HANS PETER age 20	67510 Lembach
SUMI, OTTO FREDERICK age 15	

Richard and Elizabeth, 1733
S-H, I: 127, 129, 130 [appears on list as Somey]
   [with Maria Magdalena, age 58; Hans Michael, age 10; Johannes, age 5;
   Maria Magdalena, age 24. Also an Anna Barbara Haltin, age 50 with
   family.]
                          EUROPEAN RECORDS

Diedendorf Reformed KB:
Peter Sumy, son of Caspar Sumy from Sanen, Canton Bern [CH-3792
Saanen, BE] m. 30 Oct. 1705 Magdalena, daughter of Abraham Haldy at
Berg in Lothringen [Berg-sur-Moselle=57570 Cattenom]

Drulingen Lutheran KB:
Peter Sumi, herdsman at Rexingen, and his wife had a daughter:
            1. Maria Magdalena b. 19 Dec. 1706, bp. 23 Dec. 1706
               Sp.: Melcher Kundt, inhabitant at Berg; Andreas Klein,
               son of the dairyman at Rexingen; M. Susanna, daughter
               of Hans Michel Renner, *Hoffmann* at ?Waderhoff; Maria
               Margretha, daughter of Hans Michael Reitenauer, Rexingen.

Lembach Lutheran KB:
Joh. Peter Sumi, herdsman, and wife Maria Magdalena nee Halden had:
            Johannes b. 25 May 1723, bp. 18 May 1723

Langensoultzbach Lutheran KB:
Hans Peter Sommi, from Switzerland, and wife Magdalena nee Halti had:
            Johann Rudolph bp. 15 July 1725; d. 20 June 1727

Görg Andreas b. 11 Dec. 1728, bp. 14 Dec. at Lembach;
d. 19 Dec. 1728

[The herdsmen lived a nomadic life, and the birth records of several of their children have not yet been located.]

AMERICAN RECORDS

Rev. John Casper Stoever's Records:
Peter Sumi (Swatara) had a daughter:
   1. Anna Margaretha b. 9 Apr. 1751, bp. 23 June 1751
      Sp.: John Adam Stein and wife
Michael Sumi (Swatara) had a daughter:
   1. Anna Margaretha b. 29 Mar. 1751, bp. 23 June 1751
      Sp.: Anna Margaretha Guschwa
John Peter Wissenant m. 7 Feb. 1737 Maria Magdalena Suni, Cocalico

Trinity (Tulpehocken) Ref. KB, Jackson twp., Lebanon co.:
Peter Summi and wife had a son:
   John Frederick bp. 28 May 1749. Sp.: Mr. Stein
Peter Summois had:
   John George bp. 26 Mar. 1753. Sp.: George Dollinger and wife
Michael Summi and wife had a daughter
   Magdalena bp. 11 June 1749. Sp.: Mrs. Summi, grandmother
Frederick Summois and wife Anna Mar. had:
   1. Barbara Elizabeth b. ca. 1748, bp. 14 June 1753,
      5 years old. Sp.: William Leitner and wife
   2. John Michael b. ca. 1750, bp. 14 June 1753
      3 years old. Sp.: Michael Summois and wife
[Peter Summy appears in NC land records in 1768; Frederick Summy appears in NC land records in 1778.]

508. SÜSS, GEORG   67360 Woerth
Minerva, 1771
S-H, I: 734

EUROPEAN RECORDS

Pfaffenhoffen Lutheran KB:
Philipp Gottfried Süss, single, from Wörth, son of Nicolai Süss, farmer, m. 11 Feb. 1744 at Niedermodern [=67350 Pfaffenhoffen], Maria Catharina, daughter of Joh. Georg Erb, citizen and farmer at Niedermodern.

Woerth Lutheran KB:
Philipp Gotfried Süss and wife Maria Catherina nee Erb had a son:

Joh. Georg b. 13 Aug. 1753, bp. 15 Aug. 1753
Sp.: Herr Joh. Martin Dörschler, schoolteacher;
Dorothea, daughter of Johannes Bürg, citizen at Gerstorff
[Goersdorf = 67360 Woerth]; Peter Erb, citizen at Niedermodern.

AMERICAN RECORDS

St. Michael's and Zion Lutheran KB:
George Suess m. 3 Feb. 1778 Maria Margaretha Muhlefeld, widow.
Buried 12 July 1783- Georg Süss, son of Gottfried and Anna Catharina Süss,
b. 13 Aug. 1753 in Alsace. Died 11 July 1783, age 29 y., 11 mo., 25 days.

509. SÜSS, JOH. GEORG   67360 Woerth
Bennet Gally, 1750
S-H, I: 429

EUROPEAN RECORDS

Woerth Lutheran KB:
Nicolaus Süss and wife Maria Elisabetha nee Deckert had children:
  Joh. Georg b. 17 Apr. 1718
  Johanna Salome b. 20 Feb. 1721

AMERICAN RECORDS

Heidelberg Moravian KB, Berks co. Family register:
Johann Georg Suess from Alsace, b. 17 Apr. 1718, and his wife Maria
Catharina nee Dock, b. 11 Jan. 1726. Children:
  1. Johann Georg b. 23 Mar. 1754
  2. Julianna b. 15 Feb. 1756, d. 17 Aug. 1762
  3. Johann Paul b. 11 Nov. 1757
  4. Elisabeth b. 26 June 1759, bp. 1 July 1759
  5. Catharina Barbara b. 28 Dec. 1760
  6. Johann Jacob b. 13 Feb. 1763
  7. Gottfried b. 9 Feb. 1765
The Süss family moved to Monocacy 1 Oct. 1765

Graceham Moravian KB, Frederick co., MD:
John George Süss, son of peasants, Lutheran, born 1718 at Wertheim an der
Saur, Lower Alsace, and with 2 sisters came to America in 1750. Married
1752 to Maria Catharina Dock, Lutheran, who came to America with
brothers and sisters in 1751. She was born 1726 in Bischweiler in Alsace.

George Suss of Frederick co., Md., German, Moravian, nat. 7 May 1767.

510. TRAUTMAN, CATHARINA age 62   Mattstall=
Samuel, 1733   67510 Lembach
S-H, I: 108 [Catharina Trootmen on list]

EUROPEAN RECORDS

Langensoultzbach Lutheran KB:
Christoph Trautman and wife Anna Catharina nee Emerich [Emerig in one record] had children:
1. Johann Philipp bp. 13 July 1698 (Langensoultzbach)
2. Maria Catharina b. __ Jan. 1700 at Mattstall (Lembach KB)
   Sp.: Hans Henrich Schleber, citizen and weaver at Mattstall; Catharina, wife of Meister Peter Knobel, carpenter; Christina, wife of Henrich Trautmann.
   She m. Peter Entzminger [q.v.-also on *Samuel*]
3. Maria Barbara b. 19 Apr. 1703

Christoph Trautman d. 21 June 1726
The widow Anna Catharina (nee Emerich) Trautman emigrated with her daughter and son-in-law.

511. TRITTE (TRITT), CHRISTIAN   Diedendorf=
Robert and Alice, 1739   67260 Sarre-Union
S-H, I: 264, 267, 271   Niederstinzel=
                                                       57930 Fénétrange

EUROPEAN RECORDS

Diedendorf Reformed KB:
Hans Peter Tritt, citizen and tailor at Diedendorff, son of Fridrich Tritt from St. Stephan, Canton Bern [CH-3771] m. 6 Jan. 1711 Veronica, daughter of Jacob Kärn, potter at Buchberg, Schaffhauser Gebiet [CH-8451 Buchberg, SH]. Children:
1. Otto bp. 21 Oct 1711
2. Ursula Maria bp. 8 Nov. 1713
3. Johann Peter [q.v.] bp. 13 Aug. 1715, father residing in Vinstingen
4. Christian bp. 1 Jan. 1719, father residing in Stensel; conf. 1733.
   Sp.: Christian Allemand, *Hoffman* at the castle; Joh. Nicolaus Bolinger, master joiner at Stensell; Christina, daughter of Johann Allemand.

Veronica Kern, widow of Peter Tritte from Niederstinsell m. (2) 26 May 1724 David Bühler [q.v.] born in [CH-3657] Schwanden, Canton Bern.

AMERICAN RECORDS

Muddy Creek Reformed KB, Lancaster co.:
Christian Trit and wife Catharine had:
1. Maria Margaret bp. 25 May [1746].
    Sp.: Nicholas Zoeller and Margaret
2. John Werner (Triet) [bp. 26 May ?1751]
    Sp.: John Werner Boeller

A David Boller signed the Reformed Church doctrine in 1743.

512. TRITTE (TRITT), HANS PETER   Diedendorf=
Robert and Alice, 1739   67260 Sarre-Union
S-H, I: 264, 267, 271

EUROPEAN RECORDS

Diedendorf Reformed KB:
Johann Peter Tritt, citizen and tailor in Vinstingen [Fénétrange], and wife
Veronica Kärn from Schaffhausen had a son:
    Johann Peter b. 13 Aug. 1715
    Sp,: Johann Georg Uri, citizen in Vinstingen; Benedict Koch,
    herdsman in Vinstingen; and Maria Votrin, daughter of Abraham
    Votrin, miller in Vinstingen.
    [See 1739 immigrant Christian Tritte for further detail on family].

AMERICAN RECORDS

Muddy Creek Reformed KB, Lancaster co.:
Peter Trit and wife Catharine had:
    1. John Jacob bp. 30 Mar. [1746]. Sp.: Jacob Bechtel and Barbara
    2. Catharine Barbara bp. 29 Aug. 1747. Sp.: Anna Barbara Dieterich
    3. Anna Elizabeth bp.7 Dec. 1748. Sp.: George Haege and Anna Eva

Peter Tritt and wife sp. a child of Abraham Kern [q.v.] in 1747, Muddy
Creek Lutheran KB.

Christ Lutheran KB, York:
John Peter Triett and wife Anna Barbara had:
    John Paul b. 7 Dec. 1752, bp. 13 Dec. 1752
    Sp.: John Paul Michael and wife Christina

Peter Trett, Windsor, York co., nat. 11 Apr. 1763.

513. TSCHANTZ, JOH. ABRAHAM   Asswiller=
Hero, 1764   67320 Drulingen
S-H, I: 698
   [appears on list: Abraham (X) Schantz; did not sign]

EUROPEAN RECORDS

Assweiler Lutheran KB:
Kilian Tschantz, Reformed, of Assweiler, and wife Maria Dorothea nee
Hildebrand had a son:
      Johann Abraham b. 10 Mar. 1745, Conf. 1760
      Notation in KB: "he has moved to Pennsylvania."

Verification of this emigration supplied by Dr. Bernd Gölzer, from the
county records of Nassau-Saarwerden, compiled by Dr. Gerhard Hein:
Emigration notation from the Assweiler Lutheran KB, according to Dr.
Hein.

514. TUCHMANN, CHRISTMAN   Gundershoffen=
Dragon, 17 Oct. 1749   67110 Niederbronn-les-Bains
S-H, I: 423
EUROPEAN RECORDS

Gundershoffen Lutheran KB:
Christmann Tuchmann, son of Hans Adam Tuchmann, citizen at
Niedermodern [=67350 Pfaffenhoffen], m. 15 Jan. 1743 Anna Maria
daughter of Jacob Husser, citizen at Gundershoffen. They had:
     1. Catarina bp. 5 Oct. 1743
       Sp.: Christman Diemer; Maria Catharina, wife of Abraham Huser;
       Catarina, daughter of Jacob Voltz.

AMERICAN RECORDS

St. Paul's Lutheran KB, Upper Hanover twp., Montgomery co.:
Christian Tuchmann and wife had:
     2. Eva Maria b. 3 June 1753, bp. 17 June 1753.
       Sp.: Lehnert Eichly; Anna Maria Baumann.

Old Goshenhoppen Lutheran KB, Montgomery co:
Christmann Tuchmann and wife Anna Maria had:
     3. Maria Elisabetha b. 23 Feb. 1757, bp. 25 Apr. 1757
      She d. 14 May 1757 of whooping cough
      Sp.: Henrich Keppel and wife Greta Elisabeth

Trinity Lutheran KB, New Holland, Lancaster co;
Christian [elsewhere in record: Christman] Tuchman and wife Anna Maria
had children:
4. Johann Michael b. 11 Jan. 1760, bp. 10 Feb. 1760
   Sp.: Michael Schmidt and Christina
5. Christina b. 17 Aug. 1761, bp. 20 Sept. 1761
   Sp.: Michael Schmidt and Christina
6. Christian b. 25 May 1764, bp. 5 Aug. 1764
   Sp.: Georg Martz and wife
7. Maria Elisabeth b. 9 Apr. 1767, bp. 8 June 1767
   Sp.: Hans Adam Tuchmann and Christine

Joh. Philip Hardung of Caenarvon twp. m. 13 Dec. 1763 Catharina
Tuchmann of Earl twp. Their first two children were sp. by Christman
Tuchmann and Anna Maria.

1764 Communicants list: Christman Tuchman, Anna Maria Tuchman,
Margrita Tuchman. 1766 Communicants list: Catharina Tuchmann.

515. TUCHMANN, PETER   Gundershoffen=
Dragon, 17 Oct. 1749   67110 Niederbronn-les-Bains
S-H, I: 423
                    EUROPEAN RECORDS

Gundershoffen Lutheran KB:
Hans Jacob Duchmann, son of Hanns Peter Duchmann, citizen, innkeeper
and *Gerichtsschöffen* at Niedermottern [Niedermodern=67350 Pfaffenhoffen]
m. 8 Jan. 1697 Eva Magdalena, daughter of Hanns Stephan Damron.

Hanns Peter Duchmann, son of Hanns Jacob Duchmann of Nidermottern,
m. 14 Jan. 1727 Anna Barbara, daughter of Christian Gortner, citizen at
Guntershoffen. Children:
1. Johann Wilhelm b. 1 Sept. 1727
2. Catharina Dorothea bp. 30 June 1731
3. Barbara bp. 27 Dec. 1733
4. Anna Margretha bp. 7 Aug. 1735
5. Peter bp. 2 Jan. 1738
6. Maria Salome bp.30 Nov. 1739
7. Hans Peter bp. 8 Oct. 1741

Peter Tuchmann, widower and citizen here, m. 17 Sept. 1743 Magdalena,
daughter of Jacob Huser, citizen here. They had:
8. Dorothea bp. 5 Feb. 1745

Sp.: Hans Georg Mallo; Anna, wife of Ulrich Biehlmann; Anna Barbara, wife of Jacob Wenner.

AMERICAN RECORDS

St. Michael's and Zion KB, Philadelphia:
Henrich Datz m. 2 Oct. 1760 Barbara Tuchmann.

Colonial Maryland Naturalizations:
Nat. 15 Sept. 1758 - Peter Tuchmannus, 8 years away from Alsace, a Lutheran at Fredericktown.

516. TUCHMANN, STEPHAN   Gundershoffen=
Sally, 5 Oct. 1767   67110 Niederbronn-les-Bains
S-H, I: 714

EUROPEAN RECORDS

Gundershoffen Lutheran KB:
Hans Jacob Duchmann, son of the late Hanns Peter Duchman, m. 30 Nov. 1728 Anna Maria, daughter of Hanns Georg Teutsch, citizen at Griesbach. Joh. Jac. Thuchman, citizen here, and wife Anna Maria had a son:
   Johann Stephan bp. 23 Aug. 1740

Stephan Tuchmann, single son of Jacob Tuchmann, was a sp. in 1760 for a child of Jacob Jung. He signed the entry in the KB, and his signature matches the ship list, S-H, II: 820.

AMERICAN RECORDS

Reading Lutheran KB:
Stephann Tuchmann, son of Jacob Tuchmann, Lower Alsace, m. 19 Nov. 1769 Anna Barbara Medler, daughter of George Medler, Bern twp.

Berks co. Wills:
George Metler, Bern, June 5, 1785 - codicil May 30, 1793, probate Feb. 23, 1796 (trans.) To son Daniel all my land and personal estate. To son George £150. To my daughter Anna Barbara Duckman £100; to my daughter Catharine Hinckel £100. To daughter Maria £150. To my daughter Maria Christina Albrecht £100. Son David to provide for wife Maria who is executor. Codicil names David executor instead of wife. Wit.: John Eckert and George Rick.

517. TUSSING, PAULLUS   Eywiller=
(DUSIN), NICHOLAS   67320 Drulingen
Halifax, 1754
S-H, I: 652, 654

EUROPEAN RECORDS

Berg Lutheran KB:
Paulus Doussing, single smith, son of Joseph Doussing, farmer at ?Eyseyser
m. 15 Jan. 1737 Anna Margretha, daughter of Nickel Heckel, farmer at
Eyweiler. They had:
> 1. **Johann Niclaus** b. 29 Jan. 1738
> 2. Johann Jacob b. 20 Nov. 1739
> 3. Johann Georg b. 1 Apr. 1742
> 4. Maria Catharina [surname Tousaint] b. 31 Dec. 1743

AMERICAN RECORDS

Jordan Lutheran KB, Lehigh co.:
Paulus Tussing and wife Margaretha had:
> Margaretha Barbara b. 23 Sept. 1756
> Johannes b. 17 July 1758

Keller's Lutheran KB, Bucks co.:
Married 26 July 1759: Nicholas Dossing and Maria Margaret Huzel,
daughter of _____? of Nockamixon twp.; married in the schoolhouse here,
by William Kurtz, after banns had been read three times.

Hocker, *German Settlers of Pennsylvania:*
Wochentlicher Pennsylvanischer Staatsbote, dated 1 June 1773:
Hans Nickel Duszing, master mason, Frederick (MD?).

518. TUSSING, PETER, age 35   Hirschland=
Lydia, 1741   67320 Drulingen
S-H, I: 300, 301, 303 [signed Thussing]

EUROPEAN RECORDS

Hirschland Lutheran KB:
Joseph Tussing [the surname also appears as Toussaint] from Hirschland
m. 21 Oct. 1704 Maria nee Garardin [Girardin] from Rauweiler. They had:
> Petrus bp. 23 Jan. 1707, conf. 1720

Sp.: Petrus Biber from Hirschland; Petrus Duran from Luxin; Anna Christina Dussinger from Hambach; Anna Elisabetha Cheredin [Girardin] from Rauweiler.

Joh. Petrus Tussing m. 18 May 1734 Catharina Grosmann. She was b. 14 Oct. 1706, conf. 1720, daughter of Joh. Paulus Grossman and Anna Maria nee Bieber.

Peter Tussing and wife Catharina had children:
1. Agnes b. 3 Apr. 1735, d. 1735
2. Maria Elisabetha b. 2 Sept. 1736
3. Johann Paulus b. 7 July 1739

Verification of this emigrant provided by Dr. Bernd Gölzer from the compiled records of Dr. Gerhard Hein:
Records of Saarwerden county office for Hirschland: Dated 5 July 1752: Peter Tussing, the son of Joseph Tussing, moved to America 12 to 14 years ago with wife and children. He had manumission and at that time he received his share (of inheritance).

AMERICAN RECORDS

Emanuel [Warwick] Lutheran KB, Elisabeth twp., Lancaster co.:
Peter Tussing had children:
4. Philipp b. 16 Mar. 1745, bp. 7 Sept. 1745
   Sp.: Joh. Philipp Schäffer and wife Christina
5. Anna Elisabetha b. 20 Jan. 1747, bp. 8 Feb. 1747
   Sp.: Philipp Beyer and wife Anna Elisabetha
6. Johann Philipp b. 9 June 1748, bp. 19 June 1748
   Sp.: Philipp Beyer and wife
7. Maria Catarina b. 8 Sept. 1750, bp. 23 Sept. 1750
   Sp.: Jacob Schmidt [q.v.] and wife
8. Johann Friedrich b. 23 Mar. 1754, bp. 14 Apr. 1754
   Sp.: Friedrich Stroh [q.v.] and wife
9. Johann Jacob b. 9 Mar. 1759, bp. 1759
   Sp.: Michael Lauery and wife.

Peter Tussing was a sp. in 1742 for a child of Michael Grossmann [q.v.].

Lancaster Will Book C-I: 151:
Peter Dussing, Warwick twp. 16 Nov. 1770-9 Dec. 1770.
Wife: Catharine. Children: Philip, plus others who are not named.
Exrs: Jacob Vierling and John Krach.

Lancaster Will Book D-I: 454:
Paul Dussing, Lebanon twp. 29 Apr. 1782-12 Apr. 1784.
Wife: Anna. Children: John, Elizabeth, Susanna, Magdalena, Paul and Philip.
Exrs: Christopher Uhler and Nicholas Weis.

Salem Lutheran KB, Lebanon:
Buried 30 Oct. 1801: Susanna Embich, daughter of Paul Dusing and
Margreta, b. 17 Oct. 1762. She m. 18 May 1784 Bernhardt Embich and had
nine children.

519. URSENBACHER, ABRAHAM   67430 Diemeringen
Edinburgh, 1751
S-H, I: 461

                              EUROPEAN RECORDS

Diemeringen Lutheran KB:
Johann Jacob Ursenbacher, linenweaver from [67240] Bischweiler, and wife
Christina nee Werein, had children:
1. Joh. Jacob b. 25 Mar. 1716
2. **Abraham** b. 7 Feb, 1718, bp. 10 Feb. 1718. He was conf. 1734 at
   Diedendorf [=67260 Sarre-Union]. Sp.: Abraham Messerle, a
   Swiss servant of *Herr Amptmann* Haffeiner; Caspar Urban, son of
   Barthel Urban, butcher and *Amtschreiber* here; and Christina,
   daughter of H. Adam Biber, master miller here; Anna Maria,
   daughter of Jacob Stutzmann, *Herrsch. Hoffmann.*
3. Isaac b. 23 Nov. 1719
4. Anna Christina b. 2 Aug. 1724 (surname spelled Orsenbacher)
5. Anna Maria b. 15 June 1731

On 17 Aug. 1751, Maria Sophia, daughter of Joh. Peter Bieber, *des
Fuhrmann,* had an illegitimate daughter named Maria Sophia, bp. 19 Aug.
1751. The father was Abraham Ursenbacher, son of the late Jacob
Ursenbacher, former linenweaver here, Reformed religion. Sponsors were:
Joh. Friedrich, son of Johannes Kress [q.v.], the hatmaker and Maria
Salome, daughter of Matthias Schneider, *Kohlenbrenner in der Ratzweiler
Waldungen* and Maria Sophia, daughter of Michael Roller, baker at [57910]
Hambach, Reformed religion.

Swiss in Hanau-Lichtenberg:
One Andreas Ursenbach from [CH-3361] Heimenhausen, BE is listed in
Reitweiler [Reitwiller= 67370 Truchtersheim] in 1666.

                              AMERICAN RECORDS

Rev. Daniel Schumacher's records:
Abraham Ursenbacher and his wife Apollonia had a daughter:
    Anna Barbara born in Heidelberg 21 Sept. 1764; bp. 7 Oct. 1764.
    Sp.: Hans Nicolaus Bürger and Otilia.
Schumacher mentioned in this record that Abraham Ursenbacher was once imprisoned by the Indians, but set free.

Hocker, *German Settlers of Pennsylvania:*
Newspaper dated 20 Aug. 1757: Abraham Orszenbacher is listed as residing in Indianfield (Franconia twp., Montgomery co.).

520. UTZ, HANS GEORG age 50
    UTZ, HANS JACOB age 27
Richard and Elizabeth, 1733
S-H, I: 127, 129, 130
with Maria Catherina Uts age 24,
and Barbara Holler age 77.

Mietesheim=
67580 Mertzwiller
Mattstall=
67510 Lembach

EUROPEAN RECORDS

Mertzweiler Lutheran KB;
Hans Georg Utz, citizen at Mietesheim, and wife Eva had a son:
    1. Hans Jacob bp. 26 Feb. 1705
        Sp.: Hans Georg Seyffert; Philips Leininger; Elisabetha,
        daughter of Hans Mohl, all citizens at Mietesheim

Matstall Lutheran KB:
Hans Jacob Utz, son of Hans Görg Utz, herdsman at Mattstall, m. 24 Feb. 1727 at Mattstall, Maria Catharina, daughter of the late Jacob Haller, former citizen at Bobenhausen, Switzerland [elsewhere: Wobenhausen]. They had:
    1. Hennrich b. 4 July 1730, bp. 9 July 1730, d. 1733
        Sp.: Hennrich Holler, tiler here [q.v.]; Joh. Hennrich
        Trauttmann, citizen and forester; Anna Elisabetha Villhard,
        wife of Joh. Daniel Müller, citizen and *Gerichtsschöffen* here.

AMERICAN RECORDS

St. Michael's and Zion KB, Philadelphia:
Communicants list, 1734: Jacob Uts and Joh. Georg Utz

Germantown Lutheran Church, 1738 list of donors: Jacob Uts.

521. VEITH, JOHAN JÖRG   Langensoultzbach=
Francis & Elizabeth, 1742   67360 Woerth
S-H, I: 328

EUROPEAN RECORDS

Langensoultzbach Lutheran KB:
Hans Georg Feit (Veit), daylaborer at Sägmühl, and wife Eva nee Keller,
had:
1. Anna Maria bp. 10 Mar. 1727
2. Hans Georg bp. 8 Sept. 1729
   Sp.: Melchior Rautenbach, Windstein; Anna Magdalena _____?;
   Daniel, son of Jacob Weiss of Imsweiler; Anna Maria Wirth.

AMERICAN RECORDS

Trinity Lutheran KB, Lancaster:
Georg Veit, from Langen Sulzbach in Alsace, m. 10 Dec. 1764 Elisabet
Bäsch, single.

Another Johann Georg Veith d. 28 Feb. 1752, aged 31 y., 5 mo., 1 week and
6 days. His widow Christina m. (2) 23 Oct. 1752 Christian Geiger, widower.

522. VELTEN, JOH. HEINRICH   67690 Hatten
Hamilton, 1767
S-H, I: 715 [Name on list: Henry Felton]

EUROPEAN RECORDS

Hatten Lutheran KB:
Joh. Heinrich Velten, shoemaker, son of Christian Velten, and wife Eva
Gallmann, daughter of Jacob Gallmann, joiner, had children:
1. Eva b. 29 Oct. 1750
2. Jacob Heinrich b. 30 Jan. 1753
3. Catharina Margaretha b. 23 Sept. 1755
4. Joh. Philip b. 25 Mar. 1758
5. Gottfried b. 4 June 1760
6. Christian b. 25 Sept. 1762

AMERICAN RECORDS

St. Michael's and Zion KB, Philadelphia:
Buried 4 Nov. 1771- Maria Elisabeth Veltin, born in *?Hohennz-leben* by
Berlin, 20 Mar. 1717. She m. (1) Johann Vog. She m. (2) the now widower

Henr. Velten. Her age 54 y. 7 mo.

Heinrich Felden, widower, m. 21 Jan. 1772 Maria Weller.

St. Michael's Lutheran Cemetery, Germantown:
Johann Henrich Velten, b. 6 Mar. 1725 in Buchweiler [probably Bischwiller],
d. 30 Nov. 1793.

523. VOGLER, NICKLAS   Ingolsheim=
St. Mark, 1741   67250 Soultz-sous-Forêts
S-H, I: 296, 298, 299
                         EUROPEAN RECORDS

Hunspach Reformed KB:
Nicklaus Vogler, son of Jacob Vogler, former citizen at Ingolsheim, m. 18
Jan. 1735 Susanna Maria, daughter of Hans Georg Niess, citizen here.
Children:
    1. Hans Michel b. 4 Nov. 1735, bp. 6 Nov. 1735
    2. Susanna Maria b. 15 Jan. 1739

                         AMERICAN RECORDS

Rev. Jacob Lischy's records, York co.:
Niclaus Vogler and wife Susanna had:
    3. Hans Görg bp. 27 Oct. 1745
        Sp.: Görg Meyer and Barbara
    4. Maria Magdalena [surname Vogel] bp. 22 Mar. 1752
        Sp.: Michael Haug [q.v.] and Maria Magdalena
    5. Jacob bp. 1 Sept. 1754 [surname Vogel]
        Sp.: Jacob Schäffer and Barbara

Susanna Voglerin sp. a child of Michael Hauck [q.v.] in 1751.
Michel Vogel and Elisabetha Haug were sp. for a child of Bernhardt Haug
[q.v.] in 1762.

524. VÖLLKLE, HEINRICH   Roppenheim=
Minerva, 1770   67480 Roeschwoog
S-H, I: 730
                         EUROPEAN RECORDS

Roppenheim Lutheran KB:
Joh. Michael Völckel, son of Joh. Michael Völckel, m. 22 Apr. 1732 Maria

Catharina, daughter of the late Johannes Geysert [Geissert], former innkeeper and butcher here. They had son:
    Georg Heinrich b. 5 Aug. 1746

Georg Henrich Voelckel, son of Joh. Michael Voelckel, m. 15 Nov. 1768 Maria Magdalena, daughter of Joh. Peter Gerst of Oberhoffen. They had:
        1. Maria Magdalena b. 29 Aug. 1769
        [father signed the entry Johann Heinrich Völkel]

AMERICAN RECORDS

Hocker, *German Settlers of Pennsylvania:*
Philadelphische Correspondenz, **dated 26 May 1789:**
Inquiry for Michael Gerst, who arrived at Philadelphia seventeen years ago from Oberhoffen, five hours from Strasburg, in Lower Alsace, and worked at his trade with Jacob Ritter, blacksmith, Third Street, Philadelphia. His sister, Magdalena, who married _____ Volckel, is also sought.

St. Michael's and Zion KB, Philadelphia:
Henrich Fällkle, newly buried, and wife Maria had:
        2. Christina bp. 18 Oct. 1772, 2 months old.
            Sp.: Joh. Georg Hafner and wife Christina

Buried 14 Sept. 1772: Heinrich Felckly; came two years ago to this land with wife and two children, from Ropnem in Nieder Elsass, seven hours from Cron Weisenburg. Born in 1747, son of Michael Felckly and Margaretha. Conf. at age 15. In his 21st year, m. the widow Maria Magdalena.

525. VOLTZ, JERG   Griesbach=
Phoenix, 1750   67110 Niederbronn-les-Bains
S-H, I: 441   Gundershoffen=
[with father-in-law   67110 Niederbronn-les-Bains
   Killian Jack, q.v.]
                        EUROPEAN RECORDS

Gundershoffen Lutheran KB:
Johann Georg Voltz, son of the late Johann Georg Voltz, former citizen at Griesbach, m. 27 Apr. 1750 Catharina Barbara daughter of Kilian Jacke [q.v.] citizen at Guntershoffen. [His signature by this marriage record, pg. 262 of the KB, matches signature on ship list, S-H, II: 511.]

AMERICAN RECORDS

Christ (Tulpehocken) Lutheran KB, Stouchsburg, Berks co:
Joh. Georg and An. Barb. Fols had:
  1. An. Barbara b. 7 Mar. 1752, bp. 8 Mar. 1752
     Sp.: Joh. Georg Mallo [q.v.] and wife
  2. Georg b. 17 Dec. 1753, bp. 25 Dec. 1753
     Sp.: Georg Mallo and wife

Chalkley, III: 127: Augusta co. Wills:
George Fults (Foltz) will; 10 Feb. 1772-16 Mar. 1773.
To wife Catharina Barbara, all est. until youngest child Susanna comes to age of 12 years. Oldest son George; youngest son John Phillips, infant; daughters Hanna, Eve, Susanna. Wit: Adam Loff or Lock, Adam Harpole, Nicholas Oswedy. Widow Catharine Barbara qualified with Nicholas Harpole, Adam Lock.

Chalkley, III: 414: Augusta co. Deed Book 11: 689
17 Aug. 1764. Frederick Kister and Hannah to George Fults for £20, 35 A at a place called the Little Walnut Bottom on the mountain between the South Fork and the South Branch of Potowmack.

526. VOLTZ [FOLTZ], PETER   Gundershoffen=
Dragon, 17 Oct. 1749   67110 Niederbronn-les-Bains
S-H, I: 423
[error in translation of name: Hans Peder *Goltz* in S-H.]

EUROPEAN RECORDS

Gundershoffen Lutheran KB:
Hans Jacob Voltz, son of the late [n.n.] Voltz, citizen at Wörth [67360] m. 2 Feb. 1712 Eva Elisabetha, daughter of the late Michael Gass[?er], former miller here.
Hans Jacob Voltz, citizen and cooper here, and wife Eva had a son:
       Johann Peter b. 21 July 1726, bp. 25 July 1726

Peter Voltz, single son of Jacob Voltz, m. 18 Jan. 1745 Eva Elisabetha, daughter of Kilian Jack [q.v.]. They had:
  1. A son [n.n.] b. __ Mar. 1747, bp. 25 Mar. 1747
     Sp.: Stephan Duchmann; Joh. Georg Remer;
     Anna Dorothea, wife of Andreas Mallo.
  2. Johann Peter b. 31 Mar. 1749, bp. 1 Apr. 1749
     Sp.: Johann Georg Römer, schoolmaster; Johann Stephan
     Duchmann; Anna, wife of Andreas Mallo.
[The father's signature by this baptism matches his signature in S-H, II: 481.]

AMERICAN RECORDS

Heidelberg Moravian KB, Berks co:
Family register:
Peter Foltz, also written Volz, was born in Guntershofen in Lower Alsace, 25 July 1726 and was bp. at the same place. He married Miss Eva Elisabeth Jack from the same place. Children:
1. Johann Stephan b. 29 Mar. 1747 [elsewhere 25 Mar.]
2. Johann Peter b. 1 Apr. 1749
3. Andreas b. 6 Mar. 1751, bp. 29 Mar. 1751
4. Johann Jacob b. 25 May 1754, bp. 29 May 1754
5. Johannes b. 18 Oct. 1755, bp. 19 Oct. 1755
6. Elisabetha b. 14 Sept. 1757, bp. 15 Sept. 1757
7. Friedrich b. 10 Dec. 1759, bp. 11 Dec. 1759
8. Eva Catharina b. 16 Jan. 1762, bp. 17 Jan. 1762
9. Rosina b. 22 May 1764, bp. 24 May 1764
10. Johann Heinrich b. 14 Aug. 1766

Peter Folz's family, with seven children, left on 7 May 1767 for North Carolina.

VOTRIN, VAUTRIN, see also WOTRING.

527. VOTRIN, JOHANNES   Kirrberg=
Robert and Alice, 1739   67320 Drulingen
S-H, I: 264, 267, 270

EUROPEAN RECORDS

Rauwiller Reformed KB:
Johannes Wotring [Jean Votrin] and wife Eva nee Kuntz [also appears in records as Cuntz] had children:
1. Maria b. 5 Sept. 1734
2. Maria Elisabetha b. 6 Jan. 1737
3. Susanna b. 6 Aug. 1738

AMERICAN RECORDS

Christ Lutheran KB, York:
John Wodring and wife Anna Maria had:
4. Anna Maria Salome b. 6 Apr. 1743, bp. 28 May 1743
Sp.: Peter Pengele and wife Maria

Rev. Jacob Lischy's records, York co.:
Johannes Wodering and Anna Maria had:
5. Catharina bp. 30 July 1745

Sp.: Daniel Heckendorn and Catharina
6. Salome, bp. 16 Apr. 1749
   Sp.: Johannes Kontz and Catharina
7. Maria Elisabeth bp. 19 May 1752
   Sp.: Johannes Binckely and Catharina
8. Maria Elisabeth bp. 26 May 1754

York Moravian KB, York:
Joh. *Daniel* Votrin b. 1711 in Helleringen, Lorraine, Reformed. Came to America 1739; m. (1) 1733 Eva Kohnz; m. (2) 1740 Anna Maria Rebmann of Utenhoffen, Alsace. [Graceham Moravian KB says m. (2) *1744* Anna Maria Rebmann from *Gehrsdorf,* Alsace.] Their children:
1. Johannes b. 21 Dec. 1741
2. A. Catharina b. 16 May 1745
3. Juliana, b. 13 Aug. 1746
4. Mar. Salome b. 18 Mar. 1749
5. A. Elisabeth b. 20 Feb. 1751
6. Mar. Elisab. b. 16 Mar. 1754
7. Barbara b. 27 Feb. 1757

Heidelberg Moravian KB, Berks co.:
Johannes Votring, son of Johann Daniel Votring of Manacosie, m. 13 Sept. 1763 Elisabeth Glad, daughter of Nicolaus and Anna Maria Glad of this place.

528. VOTRING, SAMUEL
Phoenix, 1749
S-H, I: 404

Bischtroff-sur-Sarre=
67260 Sarre-Union

EUROPEAN RECORDS

Pistorf (Bischtroff) Lutheran KB:
Abraham Votrin, (son of Hans Peter Wautrin) from Vinstingen [=57930 Fénétrange] and wife Catharina Broth (elsewhere Brodt) had:
Hans Samuel bp. 3 Feb. 1707
Sp.: Samuel Broth; Hans Adam, son of Jacob Hauer; Maria Elisabetha Bricard.
See Abraham Wotring for additional data.

Diedendorf Reformed KB:
Samuel Voitrin, son of the deceased miller at Vinstingen, m. 18 July 1736 Maria Elisabetha, daughter of Georg Philipp Becker, miller at Pistorff.

Pistorf (Bischtroff) Lutheran KB:
Samuel Wodring, the young miller, and his wife Maria Elisabetha nee Becker had children:
>   1. Eva Magdalena b. 14 Nov. 1738, bp. 16 Nov. 1738
>   Sp.: Gustavus Müller, innkeeper here; Carl Klein, the schoolteacher's son; Eva, wife of the *Herr Meyer* here; Maria Magdalena, daughter of Philip Henrich Becker, the old miller.
>   2. Philipp b. 18 Feb. 1741, bp. 20 Feb. 1741
>   Sp.: Moritz Pforius, the hunter here; Peter Textor, son of Peter Textoris from Burbach; Anna Margretha, wife of Isaac Textoris, Burbach; Margretha, daughter of Joh. Michel Klein, schoolteacher
>   3. Samuel, Jr., b. ca. 1743, bp. not located in European records but appears in PA records.
>   4. Johann Nickel, b. 23 Dec. 1745, bp. 25 Dec. 1745
>   Sp.: Herr Henrich Karcher, citizen and *handelsmann*; Mstr. Hans Nickel Schuster, shoemaker; Anna Margretha, widow of the late Hans Nickel Bader; Anna Maria, wife of Mstr. Sebastian Klein, cooper at Burbach.

AMERICAN RECORDS

Charles Roberts et al, *History of Lehigh County, Pennsylvania*, Vol. III:
Samuel Wotring took out a warrant for 66A of land in Whitehall twp., [now Lehigh co.] on 4 July 1754. On 25 Aug. 1766 he deeded his land to his son, Samuel Wotring, Jr.

Egypt Reformed KB, Lehigh co.; PA, Sixth Series, Vol. 6:
Samuel Wotring and wife were sp. in 1756 for a child of Peter Frantz [q.v.] and wife Eva Elisabeth.

Footnote to Egypt records, pg. 140:
Nicholas Wotring was born in Pistorf, Lorraine, in April, 1745, and died 15 July 1818.

Raymond Bell and Mabel Granquist, *The Vautrin - Wotring - Woodring family; Lorraine - Alsace - Pennsylvania*. Washington, PA (1953, revised 1958).
Samuel Wotring, Jr. and wife Mary Barbara nee Hoffman had 11 children; their baptisms recorded at Schlosser's Reformed Church, Unionville. His wife was a daughter of Michael Hoffman [q.v.].

See also Charles Roberts et al, *History of Lehigh County, Pennsylvania*, Vol. III, p. 1420-1425, for additional detail on the Woodring families.

529. WAGEMANN, TOBIAS
Bilander *Vernon*, 1747
S-H, I: 363 (Wagheman on list)

Herbitzheim=
67260 Sarre-Union

EUROPEAN RECORDS

Herbitzheim Lutheran KB:
Joh. Tobias Wagemann, son of the late Joh. Wilhelm Wageman, formerly
citizen in Firfeldt [W-6927 Fürfeld] in Würtemberg m. 10 Apr. 1738 Anna
Eva Eisemann, daughter of the late Christian Eisemann, citizen here. They
had children:

1. Johann Conrad b. 9 Feb. 1739, bp. 16 Feb. 1739
   Sp.: Joh. Conrad Böse, master weaver and citizen here;
   Catharine, wife of Johannes Weibel, stockingweaver;
   Christian Ochy; Eva Margaretha, wife of Peter Wannemacher,
   tiler here.
2. Johann Michael b. 26 Jan. 1741, bp. 28 Jan. 1741
   Sp.: Joh. Michael Keppel, citizen and church censor here;
   Anna Maria, wife of Jacob Altmann; Johannes Ochy.
3. Johann Gustav b. 12 Dec. 1742, bp. 13 Dec. 1742, died
4. Johann Jacob b. 26 Sept. 1744, bp. 28 Sept. 1744.
   He died 6 Dec. 1746.
5. Eva Elisabetha b. 24 Jan. 1747, bp. in house
   Sp.: Nickel Schneider, church censor here; Joh. Jost, son
   of Johann Ochy; Anna Eva, wife of Friederich ?_____;
   Anna Elisabetha, daughter of Samuel Witmer.

AMERICAN RECORDS

St. Michael's Lutheran KB, Germantown:
Tobias Wageman and wife Anna Eva had children:

6. Maria Dorothea bp. 9 Nov. 1749, aged 7 weeks
   Sp.: Andreas Honeder and Dorothea

Tobias Wageman and wife Margaretha had:

7. Margaretha b. 15 Mar. 1755, bp. 13 July 1755
   Sp.: Michael Mayer and wife.

530. WALD, OSWALD age 41
Britannia, 1731
S-H, I: 48, 52, 54
    with Anna Barbara age 34, Hans Heinrich age 4, and Roselva (? Saloma)
age 6

67360 Woerth

EUROPEAN RECORDS

Woerth Lutheran KB:
Oswald Wald, single son of the late Oswald Wald, citizen here, m. 16 Feb.
1723 Barbara, daughter of Isaac Friedrich, former citizen at Niedermodern
[=67350 Pfaffenhoffen]. Children:
   1. Maria Salome b. 17 Mar. 1725
   2. Joh. Heinrich b. 17 Aug. 1727, bp. 18 Aug. 1727
   3. Oswald b. 14 Oct. 1729, bp. 19 Oct. 1729

AMERICAN RECORDS

Indianfield Lutheran KB, Montgomery co.:
Henry Waldt and Catharina had children:
   1. Magdalena b. 3 Apr. 1753, bp. 21 Apr. 1753
      Sp.: John Ludwig Pilger, widower, & Magdalena Barnhard, single
   2. Maria Salome b. 3 June 1761, bp. 28 June 1761
      Sp.: Solomon Ruckestoll
   3. Andrew b. 30 Oct. 1768, bp. 29 Nov. 1768
   4. Anna Elisabetha b. 6 Feb. 1774, bp. 13 Mar. 1774 at Old
      Goshenhoppen Lutheran Church.
   5. Solomon b. 4 Feb. 1777, bp. 16 Feb. 1777 at Old Goshenhoppen

A Caspar Wald was sp. here in 1757 for a child of Andrew Säger. Casper
Wald and wife Barbara had ten children from 1764 to 1782.

Indianfield Cemetery, tombstone inscription:
   Oswald Wald 1772

Old Goshenhoppen Cemetery, Montgomery co.:
   Heinrich Wald, b. in 1728; died 29 Mar. 1808.

   Anna Catharina Walt, wife of Heinrich Walt, b. 24 Nov. 1732;
   d. 25 Mar 1812.

Oswald Walt, Philadelphia co., nat. 1740
Henry Wald, Upper Salford twp., Philadelphia co., nat. Autumn 1765

531. WALKER, GEORG   Oberbronn=
Edinburgh, 1751   67111 Niederbronn-les-Bains
S-H, I: 462
with stepfather Blasius Beckh [q.v.]

EUROPEAN RECORDS

Oberbronn Lutheran KB:
Anna nee Schmid m. (1) Matthis Walcker, citizen and nailsmith at Mühlhausen [=67350 Pfaffenhoffen]. She m. (2) 2 Jan. 1741 Blasius Beck, a single butcher's apprentice from [W-7470] Ebingen in Wurtemberg. Children of her first marriage who appear in the Oberbronn records:
   1. Georg Walcker, conf. 1747, son of the late Matthis Walcker.
   2. Joh. Jacob Walcker, conf. 1750, son of the late Matthis Walcker.

AMERICAN RECORDS

St. Michael's and Zion Lutheran KB, Philadelphia:
Georg Walcker was a witness at a marriage in 1760.
Jacob Walker m. 27 Dec. 1757 Sophia Margretha Gumelin, in the parents' house, in presence of parents of both parties.
Buried 12 Mar. 1781: Jacob Walker, born in Buschweiler 20 Aug. 1734; d. 11 Mar. 1781, age 46 years, 6 months, and 6 days.

Muhlenberg's Journals, II:296:
Georg Walker was elected deacon at St. Michael's and Zion Lutheran congregation on 6 Jan. 1766.

George Walker, Philadelphia, nat. April 1764

532. WAMBACH, GEORG   67580 Mertzwiller
Dragon, 17 Oct. 1749
S-H, I: 423
   [with step-father Martin Schröter, q.v.]

EUROPEAN RECORDS

Mertzweiler Lutheran KB:
Georg Wambach, single son of Georg Wambach, Lutheran schoolmaster here, m. 22 Jan. 1731 Anna Barbara, daughter of Christian Dürrenberger. They had children:
   1. **Johann Georg** b. 13 Dec. 1731, bp. 16 Dec. 1731
   2. Catharina Barbara b. 25 Nov. 1733
   3. Maria Elisabetha b. __ Dec. 1735, bp. 23 Dec. 1735
   4. Joh. Peter b. __ Sept. 1738
   5. Anna Barbara b. 3 Oct. 1741
   6. Christian b. __ June 1744, bp. 19 June 1744
[See Hans Jerg Dierenberger for additional Dürrenberger data].

Martin Schröter [q.v.], widower and linenweaver here, m. 16 May 1747 Anna Barbara, widow of Georg Wambach, the younger.

AMERICAN RECORDS

Hocker, *German Settlers of Pennsylvania:*
Pennsylvanische Geschichts-Schreiber, newspaper dated 1 June 1750:
Martin Schroeter, with Johannes Schneider, Lancaster, indentured his four children last autumn, and wants to know what became of them. They are: daughters, Christina and Elisabeth; stepsons, Hansz Georg Wambach and Peter Wambach. He also seeks his brother-in-law, Johannes Anstert.

newspaper dated 1 Feb. 1754:
Martin Schroeder's stepson, Peter Wannebach, is in service with Michael Drachel, on the Great Lehigh. He seeks information about his parents.

533. WAMPFLER, HANS PETER age 40	Keskastel=
WAMPFLER, HANS PETER age 18	67260 Sarre-Union
WAMPFLER, MICHAEL age 16	Altwiller=
Lydia, 1741	67260 Sarre-Union
S-H, I: 300, 301, 302	

EUROPEAN RECORDS

Keskastel Lutheran KB:
Peter Wampffler, linenweaver at Hinsingen, and wife Veronica had:
1. Anna Magdalena bp. 7 June 1720
   Sp.: Samuel Mettauer, linenweaver at Kastel; A. Magdalena, wife of Peter S___tz of Newhausel; Anna Magdalena ?___.
   (Record extracted 3 May 1741)
2. Hans Peter bp. 4 Aug. 1722
   Sp.: Hans Peter Klein, Harskirchen; Johannes Wampffler; Anna Elisa, wife of Jacob Lang of ?Zollingen; Maria Barbara, ?daughter of Michel Buttner (Ext. 3 May 1741).
3. Michael b. ca. 1724

Harskirchen Lutheran KB:
4. Anna Fronica b. 5 Nov. 1726, bp. 7 Nov. 1726 at Altweyler
5. Anna Barbara bp. 24 July 1729 at Altweyler [Altwiller]
6. Anna Elisabetha bp. 3 Dec. 1732 at Altweyler
7. Anna Catharina bp. __ ___ 1734
8. possible Georg, bp. not located

An old half-timbered barn at the lordship's mill in Altwiller
dates to the beginning of the eighteenth century.

AMERICAN RECORDS

Hill Lutheran KB, near Annville, Lebanon co:
Mattheis Boger m. 7 Jan. 1746 Anna Magdalena Wampflerin.
Jacob Brenneyssen m. 13 Jan. 1747 Anna Veronica Wampflerin.
[See Burgert, *The Northern Kraichgau* for Boger and Brenneisen].

Rev. John Casper Stoever's Records:
John Peter Wampler m. 26 Sept. 1743 Anna Barbara Brenneiss(en), Swatara.
They had children:
>   1. Joh. Michael b. 6 Oct. 1747, bp. 8 Nov. 1747
>   Sp.: Joh. Michael Wampfler and wife
>   2. Joh. Jacob b. 28 Sept. 1749, bp. 1 Nov. 1749
>   Sp.: Johan Peter Wampfler and wife Maria Barbara
>   3. Anna Elisabetha bp. 28 Oct. 1750
>   Sp.: Michael Wampfler and wife

Georg Wampfler and wife were sp. in 1762 for a child of Mattheis Boger.

Quittopahilla Reformed KB, Lebanon co.:
Hans Adam Wampler and wife had a daughter:
  Maria Barbara bp. 21 May 1749
  Sp.: Valentin Kueffer and wife

Michael Wampler and wife Anna Elisabetha had a daughter:
  Elisabetha bp. 12 Aug. 1752
  Sp.: Mathias Boger and wife Magdalena; Jacob Brenneisen and wife.

Quittopahilla Moravian KB:
Georg Wambler and wife Elisabetha nee Stephan had:
  1. Maria Elisabetha bp. 18 July 1759

534. WAMPFFLER, JOH. CHRISTIAN   Herbitzheim=
WAMPFFLER, CHRISTIAN   67260 Sarre-Union
WAMPFFLER, JOH. LUDWIG
WAMPFFLER, JÖRG
Bilander *Vernon,* 1747
S-H, I: 364
                    EUROPEAN RECORDS

Diedendorf Reformed KB:
Joh. Christian Wampffler, linenweaver at (?Spach)-bach, [?Spechbach =
68720 Illprerth] son of the late Christian Wampffler, m. 14 May 1715 Anna,
daughter of Jacob Tritt(er) of Herbisheim.

Keskastel Lutheran KB:
Hans Christian Wampffler, linenweaver and *bildweber,* and wife Anna had:
  1. Hans Georg bp. 9 Aug. 1716 at Herbisheim
    Sp.: Hans Georg Isenmann; Hans Peter Wampffler; Anna,
    daughter of the schoolmaster Johannes Bentz.
  2. Christian bp. 6 Feb. 1718
    Sp.: Lazarus Bitsch; Christian ?Pont; Barbara, daughter of
    Jacob Dritt [Tritt].
  3. Maria Catharina bp. 21 Oct. 1719
Herbitzheim Lutheran KB:
Joh. Christian Wamffler, weaver in Herbitzheim and wife Anna had:
  4. Anna Magdalena bp. 7 Mar. 1721, d. 10 Jan. 1742,
    age 20 years, 10 months, 1 day.
    Sp.: Johannes Wamffler; Anna Elisabetha Bentz, single;
    Magdalena Heller, single.

5. Margaretha bp. 12 Oct. 1722; sp. in 1740
6. Maria Barbara b. 26 Aug. 1724, bp. 27 Aug. 1724
   Sp. Justus Erb, Maria Barbara Gelbach; Elisabetha Bentz.
7. Hans Adam b. 15 June 1726, bp. 18 June 1726; d. 31 July 1733
8. Joh. Ludwig b. 13 Oct. 1730, bp. 17 Oct. 1730

Christian Wampffler, the younger, inhabitant at Herbitzheim and wife
Justina Magdalena had:
1. Anna Margaretha b. 17 Mar. 1746, bp. 20 Mar. 1746
   Sp.: Johannes Wampffler, citizen and linenweaver here;
   Joh. Nickel, son of Christian Hochstädter, the *Herrschaffl.*
   Hoffbestander here [q.v.]; Anna Maria, wife of Ulrich
   Hochstädter, *"des Melcker auf dem Witterwald"*; Anna
   Margaretha, daughter of Joh. Nickel Schneider, citizen and
   church censor at Herbitzheim.

Verification of this emigrant provided by Dr. Bernd Gölzer from the
compiled records of Dr. Gerhard Hein:
Records of Saarwerden county office for Herbitzheim:
Justina Margretha, wife of Christian Wampfler, Jr., was a daughter of
Philipp Christillus, smith at Herbitzheim, and his wife Louisa Pistorius.
Dated 13 Dec. 1765, inventory of Louisa Pistorius Christillus: the daughter
Justina has moved to America with her husband Christian Wampfler.

AMERICAN RECORDS

Christ Lutheran KB, York co.:
Died 30 Mar. 1758 - Anna Wampler, b. 26 Jan. 1686, buried in the
Reformed churchyard in York. Her father was Jacob Tritten, her mother
Ann nee Feusser, from Berrothau [?Baerenthal] in Alsace. Came to
America in 1747 with her husband, Christian Wampler, whom she had
married in 1715. They had eight children, five survive.

Died Easter, 1758 - Georg Hoffeins, b. 10 Nov. 1726 in Blanckenloch, Baden
Durlach [Blankenloch = W-7513 Stutensee], son of John Hoffeins and
Catharina nee Hensch. Came to America in 1751; m. 1753 Margaret nee
Wampfler. They had three children, two survive. Buried in the Lutheran
churchyard 28 Mar. 1758.

Trinity Lutheran KB, Lancaster:
Communicants list, 1747- Justina Magdalena Wamblerin, husband Reformed.
Communicants list, 1748- Justina Magdalena Wampfler.

Rev. Jacob Lischy's records, York co.:
Christian Wampffler and wife Justina had:
  Anna Rosina bp. 26 June 1757
  Sp.: Christoph Michel and Anna Rosina

Joh. Görg Wamffler and wife Eva had:
  Joh. Görg bp. 23 Apr. 1758
  Sp.: Görg Ernst Meyer and Eva

First Reformed KB, York:
Two Christian Wampflers signed the church doctrine in 1754.
Christian Wampfler was the *Baumeister* for the new church in 1763.
George Wampfler and wife Eva nee Hannspach had:
  1. Maria Catharina b. 17 Aug. 1760, bp. 24 Aug. 1760
    Sp.: Geo. and Cath. Amspacher (Christ Luth. York)
  2. Elisabeth b. 19 June 1762, bp. 27 June 1762
    Sp.: Nicklaus Schaeffer and wife
  3. Margaretha bp. 10 Apr. 1744. Sp.: Ludwig Fridlein
  4. A child b. 27 July 1777, bp. 24 Aug. 1777
    Sp.: Gottfried Gruber and wife

York co. unrecorded Wills:
Christian Wampffler, probated 12 Oct. 1764.
Exrs: Abraham Weldie, Johannes Hunsicker [original in German; neither the
original will or a contemporary translation which is noted in the related
memorandum are known to exist.]

535. WANNEMACHER, SAMUEL   Herbitzheim=
WANNEMACHER, JOH. GEORG   67260 Sarre-Union
Phoenix, 1749
S-H, I: 404
EUROPEAN RECORDS

Herbitzheim Lutheran KB:
Joh. Peter Wannemacher, master tiler at Herbitzheim, and wife Eva
Margaretha had children:
  1. **Joh. Georg** bp. 10 Jan. 1720 (Keskastel Luth. KB); conf. 1734
    at Herbitzheim. Sp.: Tillman Bawr, Meyer; Hans Georg
    Eisenmann; Jannette, wife of Herr Ludwig Haldy.
  2. Joh. Peter bp. 26 May 1722
  3. Catharina Regina b. 31 Dec. 1724, bp. 2 Jan. 1725
  4. Susanna Catharina b. 28 June 1727
  5. Joh. Conrad b. 23 Nov. 1729

6. Samuel b. 17 Dec. 1731, bp. 20 Dec. 1731
Sp.: Samuel Haldy, son of Herr Joh. Ludwig Haldy;
Conrad Würtz, son of Joh. Würtz, *hoffmann* here;
Anna Johanna Pistor wife of the *Rathwirth* here.

Johann Georg Wannemacher, tiler, son of Mstr. Joh. Peter Wannemacher, *Herrschaffl. Ziegler* here, m. 19 Jan. 1740 Elisabetha Catharina, daughter of Nickel Keppel, citizen and inhabitant at Dehlingen, [Dehlingen = 67430 Diemeringen], *Rheingraffl. jurisdiction.* They had:
1. Johann Peter b. 3 Jan. 1741, bp. 5 Jan. 1741
Sp.: Johannes Würtz, son of Johannes Würtz; Joh. Peter Eisemann, son of Georg Eisemann; Catharina Regina Wannemacher, daughter of Mstr. Joh. Peter Wannemacher, *Ziegler* here.

Diemeringen Lutheran KB:
Georg Wannenmacher and wife Elisabetha Catharina had:
2. Maria Christina b. 26 July 1742, d. 21 Feb. 1743
One of the sp. was Peter Wannemacher of Herbitzheim, the child's grandfather.
3. Catharina Regina b. 4 Feb. 1744, bp. 7 Mar. 1744
4. Christina Margaretha b. 2 Mar. 1746, bp. 10 Mar. 1746
5. Eva Elisabetha b. 13 Aug. 1747, bp. 15 Aug. 1747
One of the sp. was Eva Margaretha, wife of Peter Wannemacher, of Herbitzheim, the child's grandmother.

Verification of this emigrant provided by Dr. Bernd Gölzer from the compiled records of Dr. Gerhard Hein:
Records of Saarwerden county office for Herbitzheim:
Dated 11 Jan. 1759, inventory of Joh. Peter Wannenmacher: sons Georg and Samuel Wannenmacher moved to the New Land ten years ago.
Records of the notary public for Dehlingen:
Record dated 1763 mentions Georg Wannenmacher and wife Catharina Elisabetha Köppel of Dehlingen are in America.

AMERICAN RECORDS

St. Michael's and Zion KB, Philadelphia:
Samuel Wannemacher was a sp. in 1752 for a child of Johan Jacob Gilger.

One of the signers on a petition for protection from the Indians, dated 5 Oct. 1757, Forks of the Delaware:
George Wannemacher

Rev. Daniel Schumacher's records:
Regina Wannemacher was a sp. in 1760 for a child of Andreas Schitterly in Lehigh twp.

Jürg Wannemacher and wife Elisabetha had:
Maria Elisabetha bp. 8 Apr. 1760, Lehigh twp.
Sp.: Wilhelm Best; Anna Maria Altmans; Conrad Schneider and wife Elisabetha.

Peter Wannemacher and wife Christina had:
Elisabetha Catharina bp. 6 July 1760, Lehigh
Sp.: Conrad Schneider and wife Elisabetha

Georg Wannemacher, Lechaw [Lehigh] twp., Northampton co. nat. Autumn 1765.

536. WEBER, JACOB   67510 Lembach
John and William, 1732
S-H, I: 102, 103, 105
with Christina (Bever), Jacob (Bever), and Dorothy (Bever)

EUROPEAN RECORDS

Lembach Lutheran KB:
Felix Weber and Magdalena nee Pfeiffer had:
Hans Jacob b. 11 ?June 1696

Johann Jacob Weber, citizen here, and wife Eva Christina nee Stahl had children:
1. Maria Dorothea b. 28 Sept. 1726, bp. 2 Oct. 1726
Sp.: Joh. Carl, son of the late Peter Hördt; Anna Dorothea nee Stock, wife of Hans Adam Metz; Maria Dorothea nee Rummel, wife of Hennrich Frey.
2. Catharina Magdalena b. 20 May 1729, died 26 May 1729
3. Johannes b. 17 Aug. 1730, bp. 20 Aug. 1730
Sp.: Johann Eberth; Johann Leonhard Weiss; Sophia Magdalena, daughter of Herr Joh. Jacob Benckler, *Schultheissen* here.

AMERICAN RECORDS

St. Paul's (Blue) Lutheran KB, Upper Saucon, Lehigh co:
Died 25 Nov. 1752 - Eva Christina, wife of Jacob Weber, aged 52 years. Buried 27 Nov. 1752.

Andreas Erdman and wife Dorothea had a son:
>Johann Jacob b. 14 Mar. 1750, bp. 25 Mar. 1750
>Sp.: Jacob Weber and Christina

Died 6 Jan. 1753 - Anna Dorothea, wife of Andreas Erdmann aged 26 years
and 3 months. Buried 8 Jan. 1753.

John Weber and wife Sara had:
>1. Jacob b. 5 Mar. 1750
>2. Andreas bp. 15 Oct. 1752
>>Sp.: Andreas Erdman and Dorothea
>3. Johann Georg b. 5 Oct. 1760.

537. WEIMER, JACOB   Hunspach=
Janet, 1751   67250 Soultz-sous-Forêts
S-H, I: 474
EUROPEAN RECORDS

Hunspach Reformed KB:
Georg Weimer of Hunspach, and wife Maria Barbara, had a son:
>Hans Jacob b. 19 Jan. 1727, bp. 26 Jan. 1727
>Sp.: Hans Jacob Weimer of Leiterschweiler [Leiterswiller =
>67250 Soultz-sous-Forêts]; Hans Martin Lorentz; Agnes,
>daughter of Hans Ruedehofer.

**F. Krebs "18th-Century Emigrants from the Palatinate, Lower Alsace, and
Rheinhessen", in D. Yoder, Ed. *Rhineland Emigrants:* (1981) 67:**
By decree of the Zweibrücken Government dated July 12, 1764, the property
of Jacob Weimer of Hundsbach, Lower Alsace "who is at this time in
America", was declared fallen to the treasury on account of illicit emigration.
He had requested the delivery of his property left behind in his home village
to the sum of 254 florins, 11 batzen, and 3 shillings.

AMERICAN RECORDS

It is mentioned in the minutes of the Coetus of Pennsylvania in 1768 that
Jacob Weymer was forty years of age.

This is possibly the Jacob Weymer who became a Reformed minister, and
served a parish in PA until 1770, when he moved to MD and served a parish
in the Hagerstown area. The Hagerstown record indicated that he died 12
May 1790, aged 66 years. He left a widow, Mary Salome, and no children.

Hagerstown Reformed KB:
Jacob Weimar and wife Salome were sp. in 1780.

See William J. Hinke, *Ministers of the German Reformed Congregations in Pennsylvania and Other Colonies in the 18th Century* (1951): 152-155, and Charles Glatfelter, *Pastors and People,* Vol. I: 163 for further information.

Jacob Wymer, Longswamp twp., Berks co., nat. Autumn, 1765.

538. WEIMER, JACOB   Hoffen=
Janet, 1751   67250 Soultz-sous-Forêts
S-H, I: 475 Jacob (O) Weimmer

EUROPEAN RECORDS

Hunspach Reformed KB:
Lorentz Weymer, weaver, *gemeinsmann* at Hofen, and wife Maria Barbara nee Weymer had:
> 1. **Johann Jacob** b. 13 June 1727, bp. 15 June 1727; conf. 1740
>   Sp.: Jacob Weymer of Leiterschweiler [Leiterswiller = 67250 Soultz-sous-Forêts]; Hans Michel, son of Hans Michel Rott; Maria Barbara, daughter of Hans Jörg Niess.

Hoffen Reformed KB:
> 2. **Andreas** b. 21 Mar. 1730, conf. 1744
>   Sp.: Andreas Niess of Hunspach; Joh. Michael Claus of Hofen; Maria Salome, wife of Hans Jacob Weimer of Leitersweiler.
> 3. Joh. Bernhard b. 11 July 1734, conf. 1749

AMERICAN RECORDS

Hocker, *German Settlers of Pennsylvania:*
Newspaper dated 23 Oct. 1761:
Andreas Weimar, Albany county, seeks his brother Jacob, born in Hoffen, in Alsace, near Weissenburg, who came to America nine years ago. Notify Peter Paris, Philadelphia, at the corner house at Moravian alley on Second Street.

F. Krebs "18th-Century Emigrants from the Palatinate, Lower Alsace, and Rheinhessen", in Don Yoder, Ed., *Rhineland Emigrants* **(1981): 67:**
By decree of Feb. 1, 1759, it was ordered by the Zweibrucken Government that the property of Jacob Weimer of Hofen, Lower Alsace, who had "gone to America", be collected for the treasury.

St. Paul's (Wolfs) KB, West Manheim twp., York co.:
Joh. Jacob Weymar and wife Catharina had children:
1. John Jacob bp. 5 Apr. 1767
2. Andrew bp.6 June 1768. Sp.: John Jacob Ob and Maria Catharina
3. Catharine bp. 4 Feb. 1770
    Sp.: William Stromeyer and Anna Maria

Westmoreland co. Wills:
One Jacob Weimer of Mt. Pleasant twp., Westmoreland co. left a will dated 13 Apr. 1813, proved 11 May 1813. Names wife Martha; daughter Johanna; Jacob Lindensmith, son of Daniel, to have the rifle as his share; children not designated by name; Exr: friend Christian Erret. Wit: Jacob Painter and Jacob Farver.

539. WEINBERGER, MARTIN   Langensoultzbach=
Sandwich, 1750   67360 Woerth
S-H, I: 449
                              EUROPEAN RECORDS

Langensoultzbach Lutheran KB:
Adam Weinberger and his wife Anna Elisabetha nee Spielmann of Sultzbach had a son:
    Johann Martin b. 27 Feb. 1707
    Sp.: Martin, son of Hans Georg Süss; Otthilia, wife of Burchard Spielman; Emanuel, son of Joachim Weinberger; Susanna Catharina daughter of Hans Georg Weymer.

Martin Weinberger, son of Adam Weinberger, citizen here, m. 11 Sept. 1735 Catharina Barbara, daughter of Philips Bastian, citizen at Wört [67360 Woerth]. They had children:
1. Johann Jacob b. 12 July 1739, bp. 15 July 1739; d. 8 Feb. 1741
2. Catharina Margaretha b. 28 Nov. 1741
3. Georg Henrich b. 9 June 1744
4. Maria Barbara b. 31 Jan. 1748

                              AMERICAN RECORDS

Signature in KB by the 1748 baptism, matches his signature in S-H, II: 524.

540. WEISHAAR, JOHANN GEORG   Keskastel=
Edinburg, 14 Sept. 1753   67260 Sarre-Union
S-H, I: 522, 525

EUROPEAN RECORDS

Keskastel Lutheran KB:
Johannes Weishaar, *Tabackspinner,* and wife Euphrosina had children:
1. Hans Nickel bp. 13 Jan. 1717 at Schopperten [=67260 Sarre-Union]
2. Anna Magdalena bp. 10 Apr. 1718, Keskastel
3. **Hans Georg** bp. 30 Apr. 1721
   Sp. Hans Georg Fischer; Diebold ?Klein;
   Catharina, wife of Christoph Schuher?
4. Susanna Margaretha bp. 29 Apr. 1725
5. Hans Christian bp. 4 July 1728.

AMERICAN RECORDS

Frederick Lutheran KB, Frederick, MD:
Joh. Georg Weisshaar sp. a child of Johann Adam Behm in 1765.

Georg Weisshaar and wife Appolonia had children:
1. Anna Maria b. 16 Feb. 1765
2. Maria Catharina b. 25 Dec. 1766

Buried 10 Feb. 1784, the dyer Joh. Georg Weishaar, b. 29 Apr. 1721 in Castel in Elsass [in France]. Married Feb. 1746 Rufinus Behm's daughter Maria Appellonia with whom he had 3 sons and 7 daughters, of whom 1 son and 6 daughters live. Died of an obstruction the 8th, aged 62 years, 9 months, 10 days. Married 38 years.

[See Burgert, *Western Palatinate,* p. 55 for immigrant Joh. Rauff Böhm.]

George Wisshaar of Frederick co., German, nat. 11 Sept. 1765.

541. WEISS, BENEDICT age 36   67110 Niederbronn-les-Bains
Hope, 1733   Ingelshoffen=
S-H, I: 116, 120, 121   67110 Niederbronn-les-Bains
   with Barbra Weesen age 36, Maria Greta Wees age 5½

EUROPEAN RECORDS

Niederbronn Lutheran KB:
Benedict Weiss, Reformed, and wife Barbara had a daughter:
   1. Maria Margaretha b. 7 Aug. 1727

Gundershoffen Lutheran KB:
Benedict Weiss of Ingelshoffen and wife Barbara had:
  2. Joh. Jacob b. 2 Jan. 1729, bp. 5 Jan. 1729
  3. Anna Magdalena b. 8 June 1730, bp. 11 June 1730
  4. Eva Barbara b. 29 Aug. 1731, bp. 21 (sic) Aug. 1731
  5. Johann Peter bp. 10 Dec. 1732

AMERICAN RECORDS

Northampton co. Wills:
Benedict Weiss, Weisenberg twp. dated 8 Mar. 1757 prob. 14 June 1757.
Son Peter to have the plantation. Two daughters are mentioned, but not
named. Wit: Andreas Reiss, Christian Miller, Silvester Holbe.
Adm. to Peter Weiss, Andreas Reis and Silvester Holbe, 15 June 1757; the
widow Barbara renounced her right to administer in favor of son Peter, 16
June 1757. Inventory 16 June 1757.

Peter Weiss is mentioned in the will of Silvester Holbe of Lynn twp. in 1779
as a son-in-law.

Weisenberg Union KB:
Undated burials before 1764, by Rev. Daniel Schumacher: died, the wife of
the deceased Benedick Weiss.

Weisenberg Union KB and Lowhill Union KB, Lehigh co.:
Peter Weiss and wife Elisabetha had children:
  1. Anna Maria b. 5 Apr. 1765 [Weissenberg]
  2. Elisabeth b. 10 Apr. 1776 [Lowhill]
  3. Susanna b. 7 Aug. 1780 [Lowhill]

542. WEISS, JOHANN PHILIPP   Durstel=
Robert & Alice, 1738   67320 Drulingen
S-H, I: 212, 214, 216   Bettwiller=
                                                67320 Drulingen

EUROPEAN RECORDS

Durstel Lutheran KB:
Johannes Weiss, son of Joh. Philipp Weiss of Bettweiler [=67320 Drulingen]
m. 1 May 1714 at Durstel Maria Catharina Bohn, daughter of Joh. Martin
Bohn of Adamsweiler [=67320 Drulingen]. Children:
  1. Johann Philipp b. 9 Dec. 1714 at Bettweiler
  2. Johann Jacob b. 19 Sept. 1717
  3. Maria Elisabetha b. 16 Sept. 1720, d. 23 Aug. 1738

4. Johann Nicolaus b. 29 Nov. 1723, conf. 1737
5. Anna Margaretha b. 9 Mar. 1727

Buried 22 Mar. 1747: Maria Cathrina Weiss, nee Bohn, daughter of the late J. Martin Bohn, farmer. She was b. 1689; she m. 1 May 1714 Johannes Weiss, son of Philipps Weiss, and had __ sons and two daughters. One son married and went to America. She died aged 58 years.

Joh. Philipps Weiss, son of Joh. Weiss, wagoner, m. 12 June 1735 at Bettweiler, Anna Margreth Marty, daughter of Christian Marty, weaver there.

AMERICAN RECORDS

St. Michael's and Zion KB, Philadelphia:
One Philip Weiss, widower, m. 1 Jan. 1776 Maria Catharina Wolf.

543. WEISS, JOH. LEONHARD age 29   67510 Lembach
Samuel, 1733
S-H, I: 106, 111, 112
  with Maria Greta, age 38

EUROPEAN RECORDS

Lembach Lutheran KB:
Married 9 Oct. 1731 Joh. Leonhart Weiss, single *hausknecht*, son of the late Hans Georg Weiss, citizen and smith at Schweirningen, Hochfurst. Anspach [?W-8881 Schwenningen] and Maria Margaretha daughter of Hans Georg Hermann, Hirschthall, Zweibrücken.
Joh. Leonhard Weiss at Lembach and Maria Margaretha had:
    1. Rosina Barbara b. 7 July 1732 bp. 8 July 1732
      Sp.: Joh. Daniel Rümmel, son of Joh. Rümmel, baker at Lembach; Anna Rosina Moseder, daughter of Pastor Moseder, Lembach; M. Barb. wife of Gabriel Bastian, innkeeper.

544. WEISS, MICHEL age 29   Hunspach=
Richard & Elizabeth, 1733   67250 Soultz-sous-Forêts
S-H, I: 127, 129, 130
  A Magdalena Wisen age 25 on ship

EUROPEAN RECORDS

Hunspach Reformed KB:
Andreas Weiss, *Gemeinsman* and linenweaver at Hunspach, and Margreth nee Niess had:
> 1. Hans Michel b. 23 Mar. 1704, bp. 24 Mar. 1704
> Sp.: Hans Michel, son of Matthes Niess of Hunspach; Hans Martin, son of Martin Hauck; Anna Catharina, daughter of Michel Niess of Hofen.

Zweibrücken Manumissions Protocoll, Cleeburg, 1733:
Michel Weiss of Hundtsbach moves to Pennsylvania.

545. WEISS, SAMUEL   Langensoultzbach=
Duke of Bedford, 1751   67360 Woerth
S-H, I: 458

EUROPEAN RECORDS

Langensoultzbach Lutheran KB:
Samuel Weiss, nightwatchman in Sultzbach, and wife Maria Magdalena nee Sch___tzin had:
> Louisa Carolina Friderica b. 7 Dec. 1748

He made his (W) mark in KB, the same mark used on the ship list.

AMERICAN RECORDS

Moselem Lutheran KB:
One Samuel Weis and wife Elisabeth had:
> Anna Maria b. 15 July 1790, bp. 15 Aug. 1790

Samuel Weiss, Longswamp twp., Berks co., nat. Autumn 1765.

546. WELSCHANS, ABRAHAM   Kirrberg=
Robert and Alice, 1739   67320 Drulingen
S-H, I: 264, 267, 270

EUROPEAN RECORDS

Diedendorf Reformed KB:
Abraham Welschhans, son of Jacob Welschhans of Kirberg, m. 18 July 1700
Anna Haschard, daughter of Isaac Haschard [q.v.-Haschar]. They had:
> 1. Margaretha b. 10 July 1701
> 2. Maria Johanna b. 20 June 1702

3. Anna Judith b. 10 Mar. 1705
4. Maria Magdalena b. 30 Oct. 1707
5. Johann Henrich b. 24 June 1710
6. Abraham bp. 26 Feb. 1713
   Sp.: Abraham Brion; Georg Hachar; Isaac Hachar;
   Susanna Georg, wife of Jacob Pilla
7. Joh. David bp. 5 Apr. 1716
8. Johann Jacob bp. 19 Feb. 1719 [q.v. S-H 300, 301, 302]
9. Johanneta bp. 3 June 1721
   Sp.: Thomas Fichter, Hellering; Jacob Frölich, Kirberg;
   Anna Grojean, Kirberg; Johanneta Nägelin, Schönburg
10. Maria Elisabetha bp. 27 June 1723

EUROPEAN RECORDS

First Reformed KB, Lancaster:
Abraham Welschhans and wife Margaret nee Bryon [q.v.-Brion] had:
   1. Anna Catharina b. 9 Oct. 1742, bp. 7 Nov. 1742
   Sp.: Jacob Welschhans and wife Elisabetha nee Schlepp
   [See Schleppi]

Abraham Welschans signed Lischy's Constitution at York on 17 Mar. 1745.
He also signed the Trinity (First) Reformed Church doctrine in 1754.

Rev. Jacob Lischy's records, York co.:
Abraham Welschhans and wife Margretha had:
   2. Magdalena Elisabetha bp. 23 May 1745 [also recorded in
      Tinity Reformed KB, York]. Sp.: Mathias Burckhardt;
      Friedrich Burckhardt; Magdalena Schlebi; Elisabetha
      Cerper [Cörper].
   3. Maria Magdalena bp. 30 Apr. 1749
      Sp.: Joseph Welschhans and Magdalena
   4. Anna Maria bp. 28 Apr. 1751
   5. Daniel bp. 24 June 1753
   6. Joh. Wilhelm bp. 25 May 1755
   7. Elisabeth bp. 31 July 1757
   8. Johann Heinrich bp. 9 Dec. 1759
   9. Johannes bp. 3 June 1764

547. WELSCHANS, JACOB age 25   Kirrberg=
Lydia, 1741   67320 Drulingen
S-H, I: 300, 301, 302

EUROPEAN RECORDS

Diedendorf Reformed KB:
Abraham Welschans, citizen at Kirberg, and wife Anna Haschar had a son:
>   Johann Jacob bp. 19 Feb. 1719
[See 1739 immigrant Abraham Welschans for additional family data.]

Rauwiller Reformed KB:
Joh. Jacob Welschans, son of Abraham Welschans from Kirburg, m. 27 Oct.
1740 Elisabeta, daughter of Joh. Adam Schlepi [q.v.].

AMERICAN RECORDS

First Reformed KB, Lancaster:
Jacob Welschhans and wife Elisabetha nee Schleppi had:
>   1. Jacob b. 22 Sept. 1742, bp. 10 Oct. 1742
>   Sp.: Jacob Schober; Abraham Hascher

Rev. Jacob Lischy's records, York co.:
Jacob Welschhans signed Lischy's Constitution at York on 17 Mar. 1745.

Jacob Welschhans and Elisabeth had:
>   2. Balthazar bp. 6 July 1746
>   Sp.: Baltzer Spengler and Magdalena
>   3. Abraham bp. 13 May 1750? also recorded in KB as 8 July 1750.

Christ Lutheran KB, York:
Jacob Welshans and wife Elisabeth had:
>   4. Elizabeth b. 9 Mar. 1752, bp. 29 Mar. 1752
>   Sp.: Balthaser and Maria Magdalena Spengler
>   5. Elizabeth b. 26 Oct. 1753, bp. 25 Dec. 1753

Rev. Jacob Lischy's records, York co.:
Jacob Welschans and Eva Elisabeth had:
>   6. Joh. Conrad bp. 19 Apr. 1761

Christ Lutheran KB, York:
Abraham Welshans, b. 18 Apr. 1750, son of ____ ? and Elizabeth Welshans,
d. 18 Oct. 1758 aged 8 years and 6 mo; buried in the Reformed churchyard.

548. WELSCHANS, JOSEPH   Kirrberg=
Robert and Alice, 1739   67320 Drulingen
S-H, I: 264, 267, 270

EUROPEAN RECORDS

Diedendorf Reformed KB:

Hans Peter Welschhans, son of Jacob Welschhans of Kirberg, m. 6 Dec. 1705 Susanna Fuhrmann, daughter of Abraham Fuhrmann of Berg. They had a son:

>   **Joseph** bp. 9 Dec. 1714
>   Sp: Peter Zeller, schoolmaster in Kirberg; Joseph Schneider, citizen and weaver in Kirberg; Anna, daughter of Isaac George.

AMERICAN RECORDS

Rev. Jacob Lischy's records, York co.:

Joseph Welschhans signed Lischy's Constitution at York on 7 Mar. 1745. Joseph Welschhans and wife Magdalena had:

>   1. Joh. Jacob bp. 28? Apr. 1746
>   Sp.: Jacob Ob and Maria Elisabeth Reiff
>   2. Anna Catharina bp. 8 Oct. 1752
>   Sp.: Görg Meyer and Anna Barbara
>   3. Joseph bp. 2 Mar. 1755
>   Sp.: Görg Schramm and Elisabetha
>   4. Elisabeth bp. 9 Oct. 1757
>   Sp.: Ludwig Kraft and Catharina

Trinity (First) Reformed KB, York:

Joseph Welschhans signed the church doctrine in 1754. He was a church elder in 1762.

Christ Lutheran KB, York:

Joseph and Magdalena Welshans had:

>   5. Joseph b. 2 Feb. 1760, bp. 24 Feb. 1760
>   6. John Peter b. 16 Oct. 1761, bp. 22 Nov. 1761

Trinity (First) Reformed KB, York:

Jacob Welschhans and wife Anna Maria had:

>   1. Magdalena b. 14 Nov. 1767, bp. 24 Jan. 1768
>   Sp.: Joseph Welschhans and wife
>   2. Heinrich b. 31 Dec. 1769, bp. 8 Apr. 1770
>   3. Maria Elisabetha b. 29 Mar. 1773, bp. 13 June 1773

Joseph Welschance nat. 10 Apr. 1760. (No residence given.)

549. WENGER, NICHOLAUS   Kirrberg=
[unnamed ship], 20 Oct. 1747   67320 Drulingen
S-H, I: 370

EUROPEAN RECORDS

Diedendorf Reformed KB:
Samuel Wenger, son of Peter Wenger from Bolcher, BE [CH-3611 Pohlern, BE], citizen and inhabitant in Kirberg m. 16 July 1709 Anna nee Matti from Allmetten, Berner Geb. [elsewhere in KB: Erlenbach, Bern = CH-3762 Erlenbach im Simmental, BE]. They had:

1. **Johannes Nicolaus** bp. 1 Jan. 1711
   He was a baptismal sp. there in 1739.
2. Johann Peter bp. 14 Nov. 1713
3. Maria Catharina bp. 9 Aug. 1716
   [surname Wingert], father listed as *Ackerman* in Kirberg.
4. Catharina Elisabeth bp. 1 Jan. 1723
5. Anna Barbara bp. 10 Mar. 1726

Johann Nicolaus Wenger, single, from Kirberg had an illegitimate child with Anna Margaretha Batscheli, daughter of Wilhelm Batscheli of Kirberg:
1. Susanna Margaretha b. 7 Jan.1740, d. 14 Jan. 1740

There is a Christian Wenger and a Johannes Wenger also on the ship. These names also appear in the Diedendorf records as well as Hirschland KB.

Verification of this emigrant provided by Dr. Bernd Gölzer from the compiled records of Dr. Gerhard Hein:
Records of Saarwerden county office for Kirberg:
Dated 8 Dec. 1747, inventory of Anna Matti Wenger: the eldest son Nickel, 35 years old, single, left for America.

AMERICAN RECORDS

Zion's (Ziegel) Union KB, Windsor twp., Berks co.:
Nicklos Wengert and wife Catharina had children:
1. Leonhart b. 1 Jan. 1755
2. Georg b. 9 July 1758
3. Adam b. 12 Nov. 1762
4. Peter b. 12 Aug. 1764

Berks Co. Adm:
Nicholas Wenger, Windsor twp., adm. granted to the widow Catharina Wenger, 21 Mar. 1769.

550. WERNER, PHILIPP   Niederkutzenhausen,
Richmond, 1763   Kutzenhausen=
S-H, I: 684, 685   67250 Soultz-sous-Forêts

EUROPEAN RECORDS

Kutzenhausen Lutheran KB:
Joh. Philip Werner, carpenter and *schirmer* at Niederkutzenhausen, m. 9
June 1739 Anna Dorothea, daughter of Lorentz Eyer and his wife Anna
Magdalena nee Senn. They had a son:
        Joh. Philip b. 14 May 1742

Anna Dorothea Eyer, the mother, was a sister of the mother of Martin
Forsch [q.v.] also a passenger on this ship.

AMERICAN RECORDS

1790 Census:
One Philip Werner, Heidelberg twp., Berks co.:
        1 male over 16; 2 males under 16; 2 females

Another Philip Werner, Northern Liberties, Philadelphia co.:
        1 male over 16; 3 males under 16; 2 females

551. WESTERMEYER, JOHANNES   67510 Lembach
Hamilton, 1767
S-H, I: 716
EUROPEAN RECORDS

Lembach Catholic KB:
Johannes Westermeyer, son of the late Nicolai Westermeyer and his wife
Magdalena nee Waliser of Killendorff, m. ?14 Nov. 1763 Odillia Kiemel,
daughter of the late Andreas Kiemel and wife Susanna nee Vital in
Lembach. Witnesses at the marriage were Vitus Waltz, Johannes Herdt,
Jacob Klein, and Martin Westermeyer, brother of the bridegroom.

AMERICAN RECORDS

Michael Tepper, ed., *Emigrants to Pennsylvania*, Baltimore, 1975, p. 261:
[Excerpted from *Pennsylvania Magazine of History and Biography*, Vol.
XXXIII, no. 4, p. 501, 1909]
The following list of German families arrived at Philadelphia, appears in an
advertisement in Henry Miller's *Staats Bote* of Feb. 9, 1758. [Note by

compiler: this date of the newspaper is obviously in error, and should be 1768. See corrected list in Appendix B of this volume].
"The following German families, and a couple of unmarried persons, are now in the city; all held for their passage from Holland, and desiring to bind themselves out for same ......" Among those named in this list are:
Johannes Westermeyer, maker of wooden shoes, from the Alsace region, village of Köllendorf and his wife Aldiga from Fischbach in Alsace. [Note: there is no Fischbach in Alsace; evidently Lembach is intended.]

Johannes Westermeyer made his mark, a **W**, in the marriage record, pg. 225 of the KB; it is the same mark on the ship list, S-H, II: 824.

552. WETZEL, HANS MARTIN age 31   Goersdorf=
Britannia, 1731   67360 Woerth
S-H, I: 48, 51, 52, 54
    with Maria Barbara age 33, Hans Martin age 6, Nicholaus age 4, Katharina age 3
                     EUROPEAN RECORDS

Preuschdorf Lutheran KB:
Hans Nicol Wetzel and his wife Maria Barbara, nee Motz (daughter of Hans Motz of Lampertsloch [=67250 Soultz-sous-Forêts]), had a son:
        Hans Martin b. 6 Sept. 1700, bp. 8 Sept. 1700.

Johann Martin Wetzel, son of Nicklaus Wetzel, master miller, m. 6 Jan. 1720 at Gerstorff, Maria Barbara, daughter of the late Hans Nicklaus Geist of Gerstorff. A notation in the KB, beside this record: "went to the new land." They had children:
        1. Joh. Martin b. 28 Feb. 1721, d. 1723
        2. Joh. Martin b. 15 Oct. 1723, bp. 17 Oct. 1723
        3. Joh. Nicol b. __ Feb. 1726
        4. Chatharina b. 1 Dec. 1728, bp. 2 Dec. 1728

                     AMERICAN RECORDS

Rev. John Caspar Stoever's records:
Martin Wetzel and wife Maria Barbara were sp. in 1739 for a child of Bernhardt Weinmar [q.v. Weimer] at Monocacy.

Frederick Lutheran KB, Frederick MD:
Martin Wetzel, Sr. and wife were sp. in 1750 for a child of Michel Reissner; also sp. in 1750 and 1751 for children of Zacharias Barth; sp. in 1749 a child of Georg Kuntz. Martin Wetzel had a son:

Johann Jacob b. ?22 Dec. 1744? bp. 2 Feb. 1744
Sp.: Jacob Brunner and wife

Signers of Pastor Muhlenberg's Constitution, 24 June 1747:
Martin Wetzel (his mark); Martin Wetzel, Jr.; Nicolaus Wetzel

For land transactions and additional family records see:
Grace L. Tracey & John P. Dern, *Pioneers of Old Monocacy,* Baltimore,
1987. Pg. 207-210.

Colonial Maryland Naturalizations:
Martain Wezler nat. 19 Oct. 1743.

553. WEYLL, JOHANN JACOB   Oberbronn-Zinswiller=
Patience, 1751   67110 Niederbronn-les-Bains
S-H, I: 456
EUROPEAN RECORDS

Oberbronn Lutheran KB:
Johann Jacob Weyll and wife Anna Maria nee Dick had children:
1. Johann Fridrich b. 16 May 1724, bp. 19 May 1724
2. Maria Barbara b. 10 Aug. 1726, bp. 11 Aug. 1726
3. Johann Jacob b. 18 May 1728
4. Catharina Christina b. 7 June 1731, bp. 10 June 1731
5. Johann Peter b. 12 May 1734, bp. 14 May 1734
6. Joh. Phillip b. - Dec. 1737, bp. 4 Dec. 1737
7. Anna Maria b. - May 1742, bp. 13 May 1742

Signature from KB: Signature from S-H, II: 534:

AMERICAN RECORDS

Trinity Lutheran KB, Lancaster:
Communicant's list, 1751: Catharina Christina Weilin.

Died 19 July 1752- Jacob Weil, a widower who came from Germany last
year, buried 20th; aged 56 years.

Peter Weyl and wife Elisabet had children:
1. Anna Eva b. 5 Sept. 1762, bp. 10 Oct. 1762
Sp.: Jacob Stähle and wife Anna Eva

2. Christian b. 8 Apr. 1767, bp. 19 Apr. 1767

Philipp Weyl from Oberbrunn in Alsace, m. 31 May 1763 Magdalena Graff, single. They had children:
1. Jacob b. 7 June 1764, bp. 17 June 1764
    Sp.: Jacob Martin and wife Eva
2. Johannes, d. 18 May 1766, age 1 year, 7 weeks.

554. WEYMER, BERNHARDT   Hoffen=
John and William, 1732   67250 Soultz-sous-Forêts
S-H, I: 102, 104, 105
    with wife Barbara, son Johannes

EUROPEAN RECORDS

Hunspach Reformed KB:
Johannes Weymart and wife Anna Catharina nee Anthony, had a son:
    Johann Bernhard b. 30 Aug. 1702, bp. 3 Sept. 1702

Hans Bernhardt Weymar, son of Hans Weymar, citizen at Hofen, m. 29 June 1723 in the church at Hofen, Barbara, daughter of the late Willhelm Dörrmann, former citizen and *Bütels* at Hunspach. They had:
1. Maria Eva b. 27 Apr. 1724, bp. 30 Apr. 1724
2. Johannes b. 12 Nov. 1726, bp. 17 Nov. 1726

AMERICAN RECORDS

Maryland Commission Book, 82, in *Maryland Historical Magazine,* XXVI: 1931 and XXVIII: 1932:
Bernard Weimer, Planter of Baltimore Co., native of Germany, nat. 20 May 1736.

Rev. John Casper Stoever's Records:
Bernardt Weinmar (Monocacy) had a son:
    John Bernhardt b. 15 Apr. 1739, bp. 17 June 1739
    Sp.: Martin Wetzel [q.v.] and wife Maria Barbara

Monocacy Lutheran KB, Frederick, MD:
Anna Maria Weymar, daughter of Bernhardt Weymer, was a sp. in 1745.
Johannes Weymar had:
1. Johann Friedrich b. 11 Aug. 1750, bp. 4 Sept. 1750
    Sp.: Friedrich Willhäut and wife

Anna Barbara, daughter of Bernhard Weimar, sp. a Willheit child in 1756.

Frederick, MD, Lutheran KB:
Friederich Willheit, son of the late Friederich Willheit, m. 25 June 1747
Anna Maria Weimar, daughter of Bernhard Weimar.
[for Willheit, see Burgert, *The Northern Kraichgau*, p. 398-399.]

See Grace L. Tracey and John P. Dern, *Pioneers of Old Monocacy*, Baltimore
(1987): p. 191-192 for additional data and land transactions in MD.

555. WIEDERHOLT, CARLE   Eschwiller=
Billander *[Elizabeth]*, 1751   67320 Drulingen
S-H, I: 452
                          EUROPEAN RECORDS

Hirschland Lutheran KB:
Hans Nickel Wetterhold from Eschweiler, *Hochgräff*. Ottweiler jurisdiction,
shepherd, and wife Anna Maria had:
>   Hans Carl bp. 24 Feb. 1718
>   Sp.: Carl Ensminger from [67430] Diemeringen; Hans Nickel
>   Martzloff; Anna Utilia __?; Anna Eva ?Fritz from Dommfessel
>   [Domfessel= 67430 Diemeringen]

Two other Wetterhold immigrants, Johan Nickel Wetterhold and J. Jacob
Wetterhold, who arrived on the ship *Halifax*, 1754 [S-H, I: 652, 654] are also
likely from this area, and may even be members of this same family. The
Wetterholds were shepherds and moved freely throughout the region.
Several entries for Nicolaus Wetterhold appear in the records studied, but
there is not sufficient data for clear identification. The following records
were located:

Pisdorf Lutheran KB:
Caspar Wetterholdt and wife Anna Christina nee Urban had six children,
including a son:
>   Johann Nickel b. 1 Aug. 1726, bp. 4 Aug. 1726.

Herbitzheim Lutheran KB:
Johann Nicolaus Wetterhold, shepherd at Altweiler, had sons confirmed at
Herbitzheim:
>   Conrad, conf. 1734
>   Johann Nicolaus, conf. 1737
>   Johann Jacob, conf. 1741

Bütten Lutheran KB:
Joh. Nickel Wetterhold, son of the late Nickel Wetterhold, m. 11 Jan. 1752
Catharina Elisabetha, daughter of Peter Dormeyer.

AMERICAN RECORDS

St. Michael's and Zion KB, Philadelphia:
Carl Wiederholt m. 31 Mar. 1752 Susanna Widmann.

German Reformed KB, Germantown, Philadelphia co.:
Charles Widerhold and Susanna had:
1. Elizabeth b. 19 Feb. 1753, bp. 18 Mar. 1753
   Sp.: The father and Barbara Widman
2. Jacob [surname spelled Wiethold]
   bp. 14 Dec. 1755
   Sp.: Jacob Hegi and wife Anna Maria
3. Georg b. 11 July 1758, bp. 13 Aug. 1758
   Sp.: Georg Alsentz, Pastor
4. Joh. Godfried bp. 18 Jan. 1761
   Sp.: Joh. Godfried Thiel and wife
5. Margaret b. 25 Oct. 1763, bp. 4 Dec. 1763
   Sp.: Parents
6. Susanna [father deceased] b. 7 Sept. 1766, bp. 12 Oct. 1766
   by Rev. Bucher, at Frederickstown, on the Swatara.
   Sp.: the mother.

Rev. Daniel Schumacher's records:
Jacob Wedderhold and wife Susanna Catharina had children:
1. Johann Jacob bp. 31 Aug. 1760, five weeks old, in Linn.
2. Susanna Christina bp. 3 Oct. 1762, five weeks old.

Jacob Wedderhold, already dead, murdered by the Indians, and his widow
Susanna Catharina had:
3. Catharina Barbara b. 23 Nov. 1763, bp. 15 Dec. 1763.

Johann Nickolaus Wedderhold and wife Catharina had:
1. Elisabeth bp. 16 May 1762 in Linn.
   Sp.: Samuel Schneider; Elisabeth Widerstein.

Additional data on the Lehigh county Wetterholds may be found in:
Charles Roberts et al, *History of Lehigh County, Pennsylvania,* **Vol. III.**

Charles Witterhold, Germantown, Philadelphia co., nat. 11 Apr. 1763.

556. WIRT, ULRICH   57119 Lixheim
Two Brothers, 1748
S-H, I: 378, 379, 381

EUROPEAN RECORDS

Diedendorf Reformed KB:
Ulrich Wirth and wife Catharina nee Scheürer, daughter of Johannes
Scheürer from Weyer [=67320 Drulingen], had a son:
> Joh. Ulrich bp. 29 Nov. 1714
> Sp.: Johannes Scheürer from Weyer; Johannes Teusch, shoemaker;
> Anna Elisabetha daughter of Jacob Hegle, both of Wolffskirchen

Rauwiller Reformed KB:
Ullerich Wirth, linenweaver, m. 10 Feb. 1740 Maria, daughter of Henrich
Schmit. They had:
> 1. Johann Jacob b. 22 Jan. 1741 in Lixheim
> 2. Balthasar b. 24 Feb. 1743
> 3. Daniel, twin, b. 17 Jan. 1745
> 4. Samuel, twin, b. 17 Jan. 1745
> 5. Maria Eva b. 5 Mar. 1747

Verification of this emigrant provided by Dr. Bernd Gölzer from the
compiled records of Dr. Gerhard Hein:
Records of Saarwerden county office for Rauweiler:
Ulrich Wirth had a sister Barbara Wirth who married Daniel Stutzmann.
Stutzmann died before 14 June 1782, and his inventory mentions his wife's
siblings: Christina Wirth, who moved to America, single, 36 years ago; and
Ulrich Wirth who moved to America, married, 32 years ago.

AMERICAN RECORDS

Tax List Whitehall twp., Northampton [now Lehigh] co., 1762:
> Ulrich Werth
Whitehall tax list, 1772: Jacob Wert
Whitehall tax list, 1772: Balthaser Wert
Weisenberg tax list 1771: Daniel Wert
Weisenberg tax list 1772: Samuel Werth

Unionville Reformed KB, Neffs, Lehigh co.:
Jacob Werth and wife Anna Catharina had:
> 1. Jacob b. 10 Dec. 1765
Jacob Werth and Anna Christina had:
> 2. Burckhard b. 15 July 1771

3. Joh. Georg b. 9 Feb. 1773
4. Maria Barbara b. 1 May 1775
5. Catharina Margaret b. 4 June 1777
6. Michael b. 7 Oct. 1779
7. Susanna Margareth b. 16 Mar. 1783
8. John b. 30 Mar. 1785

Several families migrated from Heidelberg, Whitehall and Lowhill twp., in Lehigh co. to Menallen twp., York co. in 1785. This Wirth (Wert) family was included in that migration. Jacob Wirth d. 3 Oct. 1805 and is buried at Bender's Church, Butler twp., Adams co. His wife Anna Christina Wirth d. in Sept. 1812 aged 67 y. 4 mo.

Adams Co. Will Book A: 312:
Jacob Werts, Straban twp., yeoman. 30 Sept. 1805 - 18 Oct. 1805.
Wife: Christena. Children: Jacob; Burk; Michael; George; John; Cristena, wife of John Slusser; Catharine, wife of Peter Ruffelsbarger; Barbara, wife of Peter Berger; Margaret, wife of George Rudisell; Susana, wife of Nicholas Detrick. Exrs: Sons Jacob and Burk. Wit: George Eyster, William Gilliland.

Unionville, Heidelberg, and Rev. Abraham Blumer's records, Lehigh co.:
Balthaser (Balser) Wert and wife Anna had children:
    1. Maria Gertrude b. 31 Dec. 1772 (Unionville)
    2. Catharina b. 3 May 1775 (Unionville)
    3. Catharina bp. 28 May 1779 (Unionville)
       [Rev. Helffrich's burial records give her date of birth as
       6 Jan. 1776.] She m. J. George Rex.
    4. Christian bp. 13 Oct. 1776
       [His tombstone at Heidelberg Union Church, Lehigh co., gives
       his birth date 17 Dec. 1776.] He m. Margaretha Rex.
    5. William b. ca. 1781, died 4 Apr. 1785, age 4 y.
       [Rev. Abraham Blumer's records].
    6. Joh. Conrad b. 9 Nov. 1785, d. 5 Feb. 1845
    7. Martin b. ca. 1790
    8. Nicholas b. ca. 1795
       [These last 3 children appear in the Heidelberg records.]

Daniel Wert lived in Weisenberg twp. He and his wife Anna Margaret had children:
    1. Maria Elisabeth bp. 28 Mar. 1773 at
       Weisenberg Lutheran Church, Lehigh co.
    2. Christina Barbara bp. 26 Mar. 1775 (Weisenberg)

Samuel Werth and wife Juliana had children:
1. Anna Maria b. __ June 1771, (Unionville KB)
   Sp.: Ulrich Werth and wife Anna Maria
2. Anna Catharina b. 31 May 1773 (Lowhill KB)
3. Susanna b. 16 June 1775 (Weisenberg KB)

It is possible that Samuel Werth died in service in the Revolutionary War. He was enrolled as a private in Capt. Hagenbuch's Co. of the "Flying Camp", Perth Amboy muster roll dated 6 Aug. 1776. Adm. on his estate in 1777, Northampton co., Est. # 721.

Ulrich and Catharina Werth had other children after their arrival in PA, but baptismal records have not been located. The following appear in records of the Unionville, Heidelberg, and Lowhill churches:

Christina Barbara Werth m. 18 Oct. 1774 Joseph Nelig (Rev. Abraham Blumer's records).

Christian Werth b. ca. 1750, m. 9 Apr. 1776 Barbara Nelig (Blumer's records).

Jost Werth and wife Maria had children:
1. Johan Nicholas b. 5 Oct. 1784, (Lowhill KB)
2. Salome b. 11 Feb. 1787 (Unionville KB)

Johan Nicholas Wert m. 5 Nov. 1782 Margaret Leydel (Rev. Abraham Blumer's records).

All sons in this family appear on the rosters of Northampton co. militia companies; several were on active duty during the Revolutionary War.

557. WITTMER, SAMUEL   Herbitzheim=
Bilander *Vernon*, 1747   67260 Sarre-Union
S-H, I: 363
                         EUROPEAN RECORDS

Diedendorf Reformed KB:
Hans Jacob Widmer from Zollingen and wife Elisabeth Hirtzeler had a son:
    Samuel bp. 17 Apr. 1701

Herbitzheim Lutheran KB:
Samuel Wittmer and his wife Barbara, both Reformed had children:
    1. Anna Elisabetha, appears in the record as a sponsor in 1747

for a child of Tobias Wagemann [q.v.]
2. Anna Barbara b. 13 Dec. 1728, bp. 16 Dec. 1728; d. 1730.
Sp.: Joh. Martin Holtzbacher, apprentice butcher from Kirn;
Philip Samuel Page, servant; Maria Barbara Hochstätter and
Anna Huntzinger
3. Anna Barbara b. 29 Feb. 1731
4. Johann Conrad b. 23 Sept. 1733, bp. 27 Sept. 1733
Sp.: Joh. Conrad Böse, linenweaver here; Stephan Bentz;
Anna Eva Eisemann, daughter of the late Christian Eisemann;
Catharina Baur, daughter of Peter Baur of Dehlingen [=67430
Diemeringen]
5. Johann Peter b. 19 Sept. 1736, bp. 21 Sept. 1736
Sp.: Johannes Wampfler, master weaver here; Peter Würtz;
Elisabetha Heck nee Schädlin at Neusaarwerden [=67260 Sarre-
Union]; Christina Margaretha, daughter of the late Philip
Jacob Nieser of [6660] Saarbrucken
6. A daughter (n.n.), b. 5 Feb. 1739, bp. 8 Feb. 1739
7. Johan Michael b. 25 Nov. 1741, bp. 27 Nov. 1741; d. 1742.
8. Christina Margaretha b. 13 Mar. 1743, bp. 15 Mar. 1743.
She died 29 Oct. 1744
9. Maria Catharina b. 24 Sept. 1745, bp. 26 Sept. 1745.
She died 22 Aug. 1746.

Died 20 Nov. 1723 - Anna Maria Wittmar, a Swiss from Canton Bern.

Died 19 Jan 1729 - Jacob Witmar, Reformed Swisser and weaver from
Ermingen [67960 Oermingen], age 58 y.

AMERICAN RECORDS

St. Michael's and Zion KB, Philadelphia:
Peter Witmar m. 7 Oct. 1757 by license Sarah Maria Salome Schüttin. Wit:
Christian Schneider and Jacob Christler.

Peter Witmar and wife Salome had:
1. Joh. Georg b. 23 Apr. 1758; Sp.: Parents
2. Joh. Peter b. 11 Jan. 1760, bp. 13 Sept. 1760
Sp.: Jacob Schutt and wife Catharina
2. Anna Catharina b. 11 July 1762, bp. 1 Oct. 1762
Sp.: Samuel Witmar and Barbara, grandparents.

Egle, *Notes and Queries,* 1899 Annual Vol.: 165:
"Peter Witmer, founder of the Witmer family seated in the region contiguous
to Sunbury, was born in 1737 in Hertzheim, Nassau-Dillenberg, Kingdom of

Prussia. He was connected with the older Witmer family of Lancaster county, PA. Coming to Pennsylvania when young, he married, in 1757, a Miss Marie Solomana, who was born in Upper Alsace, France (now Germany), October 24th 1740. Rev. Handschue, a noted Lutheran divine, consummated the marriage. The early years of his married life were spent in Lancaster county.

In 1766 he located on a very large tract of land on the west side of the Susquehanna, one mile above the present village of Port Trevorton, in Snyder county. He effected his removal from Columbia to this place by means of a flat-boat. He was one of the first settlers of this region, and a prominent citizen. He died in July, 1793, leaving a wife and family of whom presently. Will filed at Sunbury, probated July 31, 1793. Over 300 acres of the estate is still in the hands of his descendants. The place was an important point in the early days. Witmer carried on a ferry, saw mill and distillery.

The children of Peter and Marie Witmer were the following:
    i.   Georg, b. 23 Apr. 1758
    ii.   Peter, b. 11 Jan. 1760
    iii. Maria Catharine, b. __? July 1761
    iv.   Maria Solomana, b. 3 Sept. 1762
    v.   John Jacob, b. __ Feb.1764
    vi.   Maria Magdalena, b. __ June 1766
    vii. Anna Maria b. __ Oct. 1767
    viii. Maria Barbara, b. __ Jan. 1769
    iv.   Samuel. b. 4 Apr. 1771
    x.   Margaretha, b. 28 Dec. 1772
Of the above, George died in 1769 and John in 1778. Anna Maria became the wife of John Motz and removed to Centre county. Maria Magdalena married John Thornton. He died 1816 (?) and the family with the widow, removed to Greensburg, Ohio. Some of the other daughters were also married to men whose names are unknown to the writer."

558. WOLFERSBERGER, JOHANNES   Mattstall=
Thistle of Glasgow, 1730   67510 Lembach
S-H, I: 31, 33, 34
[only the surname appears on the list]

EUROPEAN RECORDS

Mattstall Lutheran KB:
Joh. Wolffisberger, son of Joh. Erhard Wolffisberger, citizen at Wolschheim, Hochgraff. Hanau-Liechtenb. Herrschaff [=67700 Saverne], m. 27 Jan. 1721 Anna Margaretha, daughter of Phillips Entzminger, smith and inhabitant at

Mattstall. Children:
1. Johan Peter b. 16 Oct. 1721, bp. 19 Oct. 1721

Niederbronn Lutheran KB:
Hans Wolffensperger and wife Maria Margretha had:
2. Maria Ursula bp. 24 Oct. 1723
She died 8 Sept. 1727 (Langensoultzbach KB)

Langensoultzbach Lutheran KB:
3. Jacob Friedrich bp. 1 June 1727

AMERICAN RECORDS

Muddy Creek Lutheran KB, Lancaster co.:
Anna Maria Wolfferssperger sp. in 1737 a child of Peter Schmidt [q.v.].
Joh. Peter Wolfferssperger sp. in 1759 a child of Peter Schmidt.
Margaretha Wolffersperger sp. in 1747 a child of Nicolaus Enssminger, Cocalico.

Johannes Wolffssperger had:
Catharina b. 3 Aug. 1733, bp. 17 Sept. 1733
Sp.: Catharina Göringen

Hans Görg Wolfersberger signed the 1743 Muddy Creek Reformed Church doctrine.

PA Patent Book AA-l: 540:
Under warrant issued 11 Apr. 1744 there was surveyed to John Wolfsberger, Lancaster co. a tract in Lebanon twp. of 671 acres adjoining Pentz Knoll, Theobald Poff, David Fisher, and Oswald Knave. Wolfsberger died intestate leaving Peter, Frederick, John, and Philip, sons, and Catherine, wife of Jacob Frey, and Anna Maria, wife of Martin Hefflefinger, daughters. Patent was issued to all his children 6 May 1761. Recorded 2 Oct. 1761.

Dauphin co. Wills:
Peter Wolfbarger, Sr., Heidelberg, 2 Mar. 1793 - 14 Oct. 1802; signed a marriage contract with wife Elizabeth on 6 Mar. 1784. Wife Elizabeth to have £7 yearly. Mentions plantation sold to sons Peter Jr. and George for £1000. To eldest son Frederick £5 more than others. Son Frederick, son George Michael, son John, daughter Margaret wife of Daniel Henning, daughter Ann wife of John Thoma, son Peter, son George are to share est. Friends Henry Weiss, Sr. and Joseph Bambarger Sr. exrs. Wit. by Henry Herkleroth, Samuel Rex.

Articles of Agreement - dated 2 Mar. 1793 - between Peter Wolfesbarger Sr. Heidelberg twp., and Peter Wolfesbarger Jr. and George Wolfersbarger, sons of Peter Wolfersbarger Sr. Peter Wolfersbarger Sr. by deed dated 28 May 1791, conveyed his plantation to 2 sons, Peter Jr. and George. They are in turn to provide him with his maintenance and at his (Peter Sr.'s) death, they are to provide for widow Elisabeth and pay £1000. Wit. by Henry Herkleroth, Samuel Rex.

Egle, *History of Lebanon County,* **p. 356:**
Frederick Wolfersberger of Heidelberg; d. prior to 1767, leaving a wife, Elizabeth, who afterwards married Michael Mayer, and among others, children:
> 1. John; 2. Catharine m. Jacob Gemberling [q.v.]; 3. Anna Maria.

Peter Wolfersberger, Sr., of Heidelberg; d. Sept. 1802, leaving a wife, Elizabeth, and children:
> 1. Frederick; 2. George Michael; 3. John; 4. Margaret; m. (1)
> George Storn; (2) Daniel Henning; 5. Anna; m. John Thomas;
> 6. Peter; d. Dec. 1812, leaving a wife, Catharine.

George Michael Wolfersberger, late of Culpeper co., VA; d. prior to 1791 leaving children:
> 1. Sarah; 2. George; 3. Hannah; 4. John; 5. Margaret;
> 6. Elizabeth; 7. Catharine.

559. WOLF, JOH. CHRIST. FRIED.   67340 Ingwiller
Two Brothers, 1751
S-H, I: 465
                    EUROPEAN RECORDS

Ingweiler Lutheran KB:
Johann Christ Fried Wolff, inhabitant and goldsmith, and wife Anna Christina nee Kühn had had children:
> 1. Johann Friederich b. 1 Oct. 1736, bp. 5 Oct. 1736
>   Sp.: Mstr. Valentin Jonas; Johannes Jund & Maria Magdalena
>   Zibig, daughter of Dr. Jeremias Zibig.
> 2. Anna Christina b. 20 Nov. 1737, died.
> 3. David Hermann b. 2 June 1740, bp. 3 June 1740
> 4. Christina Sophia b. 9 Dec. 1741
> 5. Catharina Salome b. 2 Oct. 1744
> 6. Catharina Margaretha b. __ Dec. 1746
> 7. Catharina Rosina b. 27 Apr. 1749, bp. 29 Apr. 1749
> 8. Christian Friederich b. 29 Dec. 1750, bp. 31 Dec. 1750

Signature from KB:

Signature from S-H, II: 457:

AMERICAN RECORDS

Muhlenberg's Journals, Vol. II: 34:
Conf. 21 Feb. 1764: Catharina Margretha, daughter of Christian Friderich Wolf, in her eighteenth year.

St. Michael's and Zion Lutheran KB:
Johann Christ Friederich Wolf and wife Anna Christina had children:
　　9. Johann Christian b. 21 Dec. 1751, bp. 26 Dec. 1751
　　　Sp.: Johann Georg Horn and wife Catharina
　　10. Hans Friedrich b. 13 Oct. 1754, bp. 27 Oct. 1754
　　　Sp.: Hans Georg Hafner and Catharina.
In 1760, Christ Friedr. Wolff, wife Anna Christina, and their daughters Christina Sophia and Cathar. Salome were witnesses at a marriage.
Georg Philip Weissmann m. 12 Jan. 1762 Catharina Salome Wolff. Witnesses were Johannes Weissmann and wife Margar. Barbara; Christ Fred. Wolff and wife Christina; Joh. David Nauty.
Jacob Riel m. 9 Dec. 1762 Christina Sophia Wolff. Witnesses were Christ. Fred. Wolff, Adolf Riel, Johannes Kuhn, Ludwig Wirth, Johannes Weismann, Georg Thürmer.

Buried __ Oct. 1768: Christina Sophia Riel, wife of Jacob Riel; daughter of Christian Friedrich Wolff & Christina, b. 9 Dec. 1741 at Ingweiler in Alsace; came to America with her parents eighteen years ago. Conf. 1759 and m. 1762. Had three children.

Buried 15 Nov. 1773: Johann Christian Friedrich Wolf, son of the late Dr. Joh. Christian Wolf in Eisleben in the Pfaltz, b. 17 Dec. 1701, bp. and conf. He married in 1743 (?1734) the surviving widow Christina and had fifteen children: eight sons and seven daughters. Three sons and 2 daughters are living. In 1747 he came here with his family. Aged 72 years less 1 month and 3 days.

Buried 15 Nov. 1773: Catharina Salome, wife of Georg Philip Weisman, daughter of the late Joh. Christian Friederich Wolf and his still living wife Christina. (see his burial above, same day). She was b. 4 Oct. 1744 in Ingweiler, a town in Nieder Elsass, under the Count of Hanau; came 1747 with her parents to this land; conf. at age 17 by Pastor Handschue. She m.

12 Jan. 1763 Georg Philip Weismann and had six children, two sons and two daughters are living. Aged 29 years 1 month and 2 weeks.

560. WOTRING, ABRAHAM age 33   Vinstingen=
Richard and Elizabeth, 1733   57930 Fénétrange
S-H, I: 127, 129, 130
  with Anna Margaretha Wootring, age 32; Hans Peter, age 9; Anna Margaretha, age 7; Maria Magdalena, age 4½; Anna Louisa, age 2 [probably should read Anna Lisa = Anna Elisabetha]

EUROPEAN RECORDS

Diedendorf Reformed KB:
Abraham Wautrin, son of Hans Peter Wautrin, and wife Catharina Brot [Brodt] of Lixin [57119 Lixheim] had a son:
      Abraham bp. 11 July 1700
[His brother, Samuel Wotring [q.v.] bp. 3 Feb. 1707 also emigrated].
Abraham Vautrin, son of Abraham Vautrin, miller at Vinstingen [today 57930 Fénétrange], m. 19 Mar. 1723 Anna Margaretha, daughter of Peter Mertz, citizen at Hangenweiller, Lützelsteiner Herrschafft. [Hangviller= 57370 Phalsbourg]. Children:
      1. Joh. Peter bp. 5 Mar. 1724
      2. Anna Margaretha bp. 20 Oct. 1725 at Hirschland [= 67320 Drulingen].
      3. Maria Magdalena bp. 16 Mar. 1728
      4. Anna Elisabetha bp. 29 June 1730
      5. Joh. Jacob bp. 3 Aug. 1732

AMERICAN RECORDS

Egypt Reformed KB, Lehigh co.:
Abraham Wudring and wife Anna Margreth had:
      6. Johann Wilhelm, bp. not located, conf. 1753 at Egypt.
      7. Anna Barbara bp. 22 Mar. 1739; conf. 1754
          Sp.: Ulrich Burghalter and Anna Barbara
          [She m. Adam Ochs b. 1733; d. 1789].

Charles Roberts et al, *History of Lehigh County, Pennsylvania,* **Vol. III:**
Two more children are listed:
      8. Abraham b. ca. 1745, bp. not located, but he had 3 children bp. at Egypt.
      9. Eva b. ca. 1747 m. David Hahn [q.v.]

Egypt Reformed KB, Lehigh co.: Deaths recorded in PA 6: 6: 132
Abraham Wutring died 28 Nov. 1752. He was born 11 July 1700; lived in
marriage 27½ years and had 16 children, of whom 8 still live as long as God
wills. His age was somewhat over 52 years.

Northampton co. Adm:
Letters of Adm. on his estate were granted to Peter Wotring and Paul
Polliet [Balliet - q.v.].

Charles Roberts et al, *History of Lehigh County, Pennsylvania*, Vol. III:
The eldest daughter Anna Margaretha m. Johannes Schneider [q.v.] and
their family was involved in the Indian massacre on 8 Oct. 1763.
The next daughter Maria Magdalena m. Paul Balliet [q.v.].
The third daughter Anna Elisabetha m. Martin Andreas.

See Raymond M. Bell and Mabel Granquist, *The Vautrin-Wotring-Woodring
family; Lorraine-Alsace-Pennsylvania*, Washington, PA (1953, revised 1958)
for additional family data.

Peter Woodring, Egypt, Bucks co., nat. 11 Apr. 1752.
Abraham Wotring, Bucks co., nat. Apr. 1742.

WOTRING see also VOTRIN, VOTRING.

561. WÜRTZ, JOHANN FRIEDERICH   Herbitzheim=
Bilander *Vernon,* 1747   67260 Sarre-Union
S-H, I: 364
                         EUROPEAN RECORDS

Herbitzheim Lutheran KB:
Johann Friederich Würtz, inhabitant at Herbitzheim, and wife Anna Eva had
children:
> 1. Johannes b. ca Jan. 1740, d. 27 May 1740 age 5 mo. 2 days
> 2. Maria Margaretha b. 6 May. 1742, bp. 8 May 1742
>   Sp.: Joh. Nickel, son of Georg Eisemann; Christina Hänel,
>   single daughter of Henrich Hänel of [67430] Diemeringen;
>   Johannetta Bentz, single daughter of Joh. Nickel Bentz.
> 3. Johann Henrich b. 3 Feb. 1745, bp. 5 Feb. 1745

Other Würtz in KB, including Daniel Würtz, Ref. who came from Weinau
in der Schweitz [CH-4858 Wynau, BE] and lived at the Luderbacher Hoff.
He d. 2 Jan. 1730, age 58 y.

Verification of this emigrant provided by Dr. Bernd Gölzer from the compiled records of Dr. Gerhard Hein:
Records of Saarwerden county office for Berg und Thal:
Anna Eva, wife of Friedrich Würtz, was a daughter of Jonas Schickner of Mackweiler and his wife Anna Elisabetha nee Freund. On 10 Apr. 1769, inventory of her aunt Anna Barbara Freund: Eva Schickner, married to Friedrich Würtz is in America.
Records of Saarwerden county office for Mackweiler:
Record dated 1748, children of Jonas Schickner: Anna Eva and husband Friedrich Würtz have emigrated to America and have renounced their share of the inheritance of Jonas Schickner.

AMERICAN RECORDS

Fred. Wertz, Upper Milford twp., Northampton co., nat. Autumn, 1765.

562. WÜST, JACOB age 28   Liniehausen,
St. Andrew, 1743   Langensoultzbach=
S-H, I: 348   67360 Woerth
EUROPEAN RECORDS

Langensoultzbach Lutheran KB:
Jacob Wüst of Sultzbach and wife Anna Catharina nee Jung had children:
1. Johann Georg b. 15 Aug.1706
2. Susanna b. 9 May 1709
3. **Joh. Jacob** b. 18 Feb. 1712
4. Maria Christina b. 9 Apr. 1715
5. Johannes b. 19 Jan. 1718, d. 18 Aug. 1732
6. Johann Henrich b. 16 Oct. 1720

Jacob Wüst, *Erbeständer* at Liniehausen, and wife Margretha nee Hausel (?also appears as Hässler, Sichler) had children:
7. Johann Christoph bp. 18 Nov. 1725
8. Catharina bp. 3 Jan 1727
9. **Maria Esther** bp. 3 Nov. 1728
10. Maria Catharina bp. 25 Nov. 1731

AMERICAN RECORDS

Muddy Creek Lutheran KB, Lancaster co.:
Joh. Jacob Wüster and wife sp. a child of Christian Krebs [q.v.] in 1744.
Joh. Jacob Wüste and Christina Krebs sp. a child of Joh. Peter Franckhaussen [q.v.] in 1744.

Jacob Wüst m. 24 Mar. 1745, at Muddy Creek, Catarina Barbara Riegel. They had:

1. Barbara b. 19 Jan. 1746, bp. 29 Mar. 1746
   Sp.: Christian Krebs[q.v.] and Eva Franckhausserin
2. Susanna Catarina b. 29 Feb. 1748, bp. 27 Mar. 1748
   Sp.: Martin Frey and wife [q.v.]
3. Eva Margaretha b. 20 Aug. 1749, bp 10 Sept. 1749
   Sp.: Peter Franckhausser and wife, Eva [q.v.]
4. Jacob b. 20 Apr. 1751, bp. 19 May 1751
   Sp.: Peter Franckhausser and Maria Esther Wüstin
5. Christian b. 30 Aug. 1755, bp. 14 Sept. 1755
   Sp.: Jacob Simon and his wife [q.v.]
6. Abraham b. 27 Aug. 1758, bp. 10 Sept. 1758
   Sp.: Abraham Schneider and Margaretha Beckin, both single

Jacob Wuest and wife Barbara sp. a child of Jacob Simon [q.v.] in 1753, Muddy Creek Reformed KB.

563. WÜTERICH, MARTIN   Hunspach=
_____, 1752   67250 Soultz-sous-Forêts

EUROPEAN RECORDS

Hunspach Reformed KB:
Peter Wüterich, *Schirmsverwanther* at Hunspach and wife Margreth, had a son:
Hans Martin b. 11 Nov. 1718, bp. 13 Nov. 1718; conf. 1734

Martin Wütterich, son of the late Peter Wütterich, former *Schirms Verwanther* here, m. 8 May 1752 Dorothea, daughter of Jacob Kauff from Seebach [= 67160 Wissembourg].

Dorothea, daughter of Jacob Kauff from Seebach, conf. 1733

Zweibrücken Manumissions Protocoll, Clee- and Catharinenburg, 1752:
Martin Witterich of Hunspach leaves for America.

AMERICAN RECORDS

Frederick Reformed KB, Frederick, MD:
Martin Widerich and wife Maria Dorothea first appear in this record as sponsors in 1759.
A Georg Witerich and wife Catharina had 9 children bp. from 1775 to 1792.

Died 7 Nov. 1801: Dorothy Witterich, wife of Martin Witterich, aged 83 years, 2 mo.

Colonial Maryland Naturalizations:
Martin Witterich of Frederick co., German, a member of Reformed, Fredericktown, nat. 28 Sept. 1762.

Half-timbered houses line the streets of Hunspach,
one of the most charming villages in the region.

564. ZEHNER, JACOB
    ZEHNER, MICHAEL
Betsey, 1765
S-H, I: 706, 707

Kutzenhausen =
67250 Soultz-sous-Forêts

EUROPEAN RECORDS

Kutzenhausen Lutheran KB:
Joh. Michel Zehner, b. ca 1709, and wife Anna Catharina nee Krätel, had children:
1. Susanna Catharina b. 15 Nov. 1737, d. 1746
2. Maria Elisabetha b. 21 Dec. 1739, d. 1741
3. Maria Barbara b. 21 Oct. 1742, d. 1747
4. **Joh. Michel** b. 5 June 1745
5. **Joh. Jacob** b. 18 Dec. 1747
6. Joh. Georg b. 22 June 1750
7. Magdalena b. 24 Mar. 1753

Although too young to appear on the ship list, it would appear that the two youngest children in this family also emigrated; both Georg Zehner and Magdalena Zehner appear in the Westmoreland co. records in 1775.

AMERICAN RECORDS

Greensburg Lutheran and Reformed KB, Westmoreland co.:
Michael Zehner and wife Barbara had children:
1. Juliana b. 18 Feb. 1781, bp. 16 Sept. 1781
   Sp.: Johannes Ruff and Juliana Schrother
2. Maria Barbara b. 9 May 1785, bp. 29 June 1785
3. Jacob b. 10 Jan. 1787, bp. 15 Apr. 1787
   Sp.: Jacob Zehner and Catharina.

Jacob Zehner and wife Catharina had children:
1. Jacob b. 19 Apr. 1775, bp. 28 May 1775
   Sp.: Jacob Schrötter and Anna Maria
2. Magdalena b. 5 Aug. 1776, bp. 12 Oct. 1777
   Sp.: Georg Matheis and Magdalena
3. Michael b. 12 Mar. 1779, bp. 27 June 1779; sp.: parents.
4. Joh. Georg b. 28 Feb. 1781, bp. 25 Mar. 1781
   Sp.: Georg Zehner and Anna Maria
5. Philip b. 1 Jan. 1783, bp. 20 Apr. 1783
   Sp.: Daniel Mathes and Catharina
6. Catharina b. 8 Feb. 1784, bp. 1 Jan. 1785 (Lutheran KB)
7. Wilhelm b. 12 Mar. 1786, bp. 28 Mar. 1786
   Sp.: Michael Zehner and Barbara
8. Anna Maria b. 12 Oct. 1789, bp. 30 Jan. 1790
   Sp.: Georg Zehner and Anna Maria

Georg Zehner and Anna Maria had children:
  1. Georg b. 5 Jan. 1775, bp. 16 Jan. 1775
     Sp.: Christian Ehret and Magdalena Zehner
  2. Maria Elisabetha b. 31 July 1778, bp. 12 Aug. 1778
     Sp.: Adam Fritschmann and Catharina
  3. Christian b. 30 Apr. 1780, bp. 21 May 1780
     Sp.: Christian Ehret and Maria Elisabetha
  4. Joh. Heinrich b. 10 Feb. 1782, bp. 10 Mar. 1782
  5. Joh. Philip b. 11 Mar. 1784, bp. 11 Apr. 1784 (Reformed KB)
  6. Jacob b. 10 May 1787, bp. 28 Oct. 1787 (Lutheran KB)
     Sp.: Jacob Zehner and Catharina.

The church records in Kutzenhausen start in 1714.

APPENDIX A

The families presented here were contributed by Dr. Bernd Gölzer. They were compiled by Dr. Gölzer from the records of the Saarwerden county office and the various church book compilations of Dr. Gerhard Hein. Dr. Hein has compiled a series of privately mimeographed publications about the inhabitants of northwestern Alsace. These volumes include numerous church book transcriptions, the 1742 census of Saarwerden county, and are supplemented with data from the county office records and notary public records. There are currently eighty volumes in Dr. Hein's series; since they are not regularly published, copies are available in just a few selected libraries and historical societies in Germany and France.

Most of the emigrants presented in this appendix do not appear in the Pennsylvania passenger lists, but that does not rule out their arrival, perhaps through a port other than Philadelphia; these county office records, with their emigration notations on certain individuals, provide the needed reference to prove the emigration, especially valuable in the case of the women who do not appear in the passenger lists.

Dr. Gölzer also provided similar data from the county records on several other families who had been located in the passenger lists or European church book notations, and had previously identified villages of origin known from American sources. These data provided welcome verification of the emigration from the European county office records. These notations will be found scattered throughout the main text with the pertinent family, and are not repeated in this appendix.

565. BAUER, GERTRUD   Bütten=
                                                            67430 Diemeringen
Bütten Lutheran KB:
Conrad Bauer of Bütten and wife Anna Maria nee Köppel had a daughter:
     Gertrud who appears in the Bütten records as a sp. in 1752 and
     1754.

The obituary of Conrad Bauer, 6 Mar. 1758, mentions that he left two sons
and three daughters; one of the daughters moved, single, to the New Land.

566. BORNER, JOHANNES   Siltzheim=
Leslie, 1749   67260 Sarre-Union
S-H, I: 420
     [appears on list as Barner]

Siltzheim Catholic KB:
Nickel Borner of Siltzheim and wife Elisabetha nee Riss had a son:
     Johannes b. 19 Oct. 1716

1742 Census of Siltzheim: Niclaus Borner, daylaborer, 55 years old, 6
children, 1 house, 1 garden, Catholic, meadows, acreage, debts: 210 Gulden,
fortune -- bad.
Records of Saarwerden County office for Siltzheim: Dated 16 Feb. 1764,
inventory of Nickel Borner: the son Johannes, 48 years old, has moved to
the New Land in Spring, 1748.

567. CONRADI, GOTTFRIED   Dehlingen=
Favourite, 1785   67430 Diemeringen
S-H, III: 10
     with Cath. Conrad, Jno Conrad, Carlina Conrad

Dehlingen Lutheran KB:
Gottfried Conradi, miller at the Klappacher Mühle, son of Georg Elias
Conradi, m. 29 Aug. 1782 at Dehlingen Catharina Tamerich, daughter of
Daniel Tamerich, joiner of Grehweiler. They had:
     Johann Elias b. 28 June 1783.

This emigrant provided by Dr. Bernd Gölzer from the compiled records of
Dr. Gerhard Hein:
"He moved with his wife and a little son to America on 25 Apr. 1785."
[See Joh. Henrich Gödel and Georg Henrich Hornung who also arrived on
the *Favourite, 1785.]*

568. DEUTSCH/TEUTSCH, ELISABETHA JOHANNA   Asswiller=
67320 Drulingen

Asswiller Lutheran KB:
Johann Marcellus Teutsch of Assweiler and wife Anna Margaretha
Hischmann had a daughter:
Elisabetha Johanna b. 5 Aug. 1720

In the 1776 obituary of Joh. Marcellus Teutsch: "one daughter moved to
America with her husband." Judging from the family records and from the
details on other children in the obituary, this refers to the daughter
Elisabetha Johanna.

569. ENSMINGER, CHRISTIAN   67430 Diemeringen

Diemeringen Reformed KB:
Hans Peter Ensminger of Diemeringen and wife Catharina Dorothea, nee
Schönenberger, had a son
Christian b. 1 Nov. 1709, conf. 1724

Records of Saarwerden county office for Berg und Thal:
Dated 10 Apr. 1769, inventory of Nickel Schönenberg of Berg: Christian
Ensminger, the son of Hans Peter Ensminger and Catharina Dorothea nee
Schönenberg, is in America.

570. FAUL, CHILDREN OF JOHANNES   Keskastel=
ca. 1764   67260 Sarre-Union
W-6781 Nünschweiler

Georg Faul of Keskastel had a son Johannes who lived in Nünschweiler in
Zweibrücken. Johannes Faul died before 3 May 1763.

Records of Saarwerden county office for Keskastel:
Dated 3 May 1765, inventory of Georg Faul of Keskastel: the son Johannes
is dead. His children have removed to the New Land.

Werner Hacker, *Auswanderungen aus Rheinpfalz und Saarland* (Stuttgart,
1987): 316, #3469: 14 May 1764, the children of Johannes Faul have moved
away without permission, one son into French service, two daughters
perhaps to America in 1764.

571. FEDER, JOHANN PETER   Neusaarwerden=
before 1785   67260 Sarre-Union

Neusaarwerden Lutheran KB:
Johann Andreas Feder, butcher in Neusaarwerden, son of Johannes Feder, butcher in "Marx-Muggendorf" in Grafschaft Bayreuth [Muggendorf=W-8551 Wiesenttal], m. 25 Apr. 1747 Louisa Catharina Pfirsch, daughter of Johann Peter Pfirsch. They had a son:
        Johann Peter b. 15 Apr. 1752, conf. 1766

Records of Saarwerden county office for Neusaarwerden:
Dated 16 Sept. 1785, inventory of Johann Andreas Feder: the son Johann Peter, 32 years old, in America.

572. FEUERSTEIN, LORENZ   Thal=
ca. 1741   67320 Drulingen

Berg und Thal Lutheran KB:
Lorenz Feuerstein, son of Hans Feuerstein of Thal, appears in the KB as a bp. sponsor in 1730 and 1731.

12 Dec. 1744: according to a letter dated 26 Oct. 1742 written by Michel Marck [q.v.], "on the River Lehigh (Leesau) in the Island of Pennsylvania" to Burbach, Saarwerden Co., the son of Johannes Feuerstein of Thal died on the journey to the Island Pennsylvania, at sea. Lorenz' siblings in Thal become heirs.

573. FINCK, PAULUS   Weyer=
_ _ _ _, 1751   67320 Drulingen

Hirschland Lutheran KB:
Valentin Finck, son of Benedict Finck of Weyer, m. (1) 17 Apr. 1708 Anna Elisabetha Klein. He m. (2) 14 June 1718 Anna Elisabetha Giess (or ?Gross), of Eyweiler. A son of the second marriage was:
        Johann Paulus b. 25 July 1720 at Weyer

Records of Saarwerden county office for Weyer:
Dated 20 Mar. 1760: Valentin Finck granted part of his property to his children. The record lists two sons from his second marriage: Joh. Friedrich Finck of Weyer, and Paulus Finck who nine years ago emigrated to America.

574. GIRARDIN, JACOB   Weyer=
ca. 1763   67320 Drulingen

Hirschland Lutheran KB:
Jacob Toussaint [also Thoussing, Tussing] m. 13 Jan. 1699 Anna Jannet
Balliet [also Baliad]. They had twelve children; Jacob Toussaint died 6 Aug.
1714. His widow m. (2) 16 Nov. 1717 Paulus Männlein. One of the children
of the first marriage was:
    Anna Margaretha b. 20 Apr. 1712 at Weyer

Records of Saarwerden county office for Weyer:
Inventory of Paulus Männlein who died in 1762: the inventory lists his
children and the step-children, among them Margretha Toussaint who, with
her husband Jacob Girardin of Rauweiler, has moved to America in 1763.

575. GÖDEL (GOETTEL), JOH. HENRICH   Dehlingen=
Favourite, 1785   67430 Diemeringen
S-H, III: 10
    appears on list as Henry Gottel, with Philipina; Charlotta; Philipina, Jr.;
    Christian; Frederica; Elizabeth; Henry; Louis.

Dehlingen Lutheran KB:
Joh. Henrich Gödel [also Goettel], schoolteacher of Dehlingen, and wife
Philippina nee Graeckmann of Offenbach had children:
    1. Maria Charlotta, conf. 1783, 14 years old
    2. Christian Wilhelm b. 29 Sept. 1773
    3. Philippina b. 23 Jan. 1775
    4. Maria Friederica Elisabetha b. 19 Oct. 1776
    5. Maria Elisabetha b. 18 Mar. 1778
    6. Johann Henrich, twin, b. 11 Sept. 1780
    7. Johann Carl, twin, b. 11 Sept. 1780, d. 3 June 1783
    8. Georg Philipp b. 12 Nov. 1782, d. 14 Nov. 1782
    9. Daniel Ludwig b. 24 Nov. 1783

This emigrant provided by Dr. Bernd Gölzer from the compiled records of
Dr. Gerhard Hein:
"He moved with wife and seven children to America on 25 Apr. 1785."
[See also Horning and Conradi].

576. GREINER, CHRISTIAN   Zittersheim=
between 1737-1739   67290 Wingen-sur-Moder

Zittersheim Lutheran KB:
Christian Greiner, carpenter of Zittersheim m. (1) 15 Oct. 1711 Anna Maria
Munsch. They had ten children.
At the marriage record of the daughter Anna Margaretha (recorded in the
Lützelstein Lutheran KB) dated 29 Jan. 1739 it is recorded that her father,
Christian Greiner of Zittersheim "has moved to the New Land."
The first wife Anna Maria nee Munsch d. 12 May 1735. Christian Greiner
m. (2) 16 Feb. 1736 Anna Maria Burghardt. No children from the second
marriage are recorded there.

577. GUTH, ISAAC   Burbach=
                                                       67260 Sarre-Union
Records of Saarwerden county office for Burbach:
Hans Heck of Burbach and wife Anna Maria nee Marq (Marc) had a
daughter Anna Catharina who m. Isaac Guth.

Dated 5 Nov. 1745, inventory of Anna Maria Heck nee Marq: the daughter
Anna Catharina was married to Isaac Guth. According to a letter from
America dated 21 Oct. 1742 they lived in "Manactany an der Schuhkielt"
[?Maxatawny on the Schuylkill] and both are now dead leaving four children
there.

[See Daniel Heck, 1753 immigrant, in main text for additional Heck data.]

578. HERTZOG, children   Mackwiller=
                                                       67430 Diemeringen
Bütten Lutheran KB:
Jacob Hertzog, Reformed cowherd of Mackweiler, and wife Johanneta nee
Geyer had children:
    1. Salome, conf. 1748, m. 28 Nov. 1758 Nickel or Henrich Müller.
    2. Diebold, conf. 1745, m. 10 June 1766 at Mackweiler
       Christina Stutzmann.
    3. Maria Margaretha b. 29 Jan. 1743, d. 10 Feb. 1744
    4. Anna Catharina b. 1 Dec. 1744, conf. 1759
    5. Maria Elisabetha b. 31 Aug. 1747, d. 28 Dec. 1747
    6. Johann Jacob b. 5 Mar. 1749, conf. 1763
    7. Eva Elisabetha b. 12 Aug. 1756, d. 7 Oct. 1757

Records of Saarwerden County office for Mackweiler:
Jacob Hertzog died before 31 May 1777. The daughter Salome inherits
everything although there are living siblings who moved to the New Land,
and deceased siblings of Salome who left issue.

579. HILDENBRAND, JOHANN CARL   Asswiller=
                                                        67320 Drulingen

Assweiler Lutheran KB:
Joh. Georg Hildenbrand, farmer at Assweiler, and wife Anna Christina nee
Wettstein had a son:
>   Johann Carl b. 27 Jan. 1741

Annotation in Assweiler Lutheran KB: "he moved to PA." 1775 obituary of
father Joh. Georg Hildenbrand: this couple had 9 children; the eldest son
died, the second son moved to America, the third and fourth sons are
married here; three single sons and two single daughters are still alive."

580. HORNUNG, GEORG HENRICH   Dehlingen=
Favourite, 1785   67430 Diemeringen
S-H, III: 10
> appears on list as Geo. Horn, in cabin #34 with the Conradi family [q.v.].
> Others on ship: Ottilia Horn; Geo. Horn, Jr.; Casper; Jacob; Christian.

Dehlingen Lutheran KB:
Georg Henrich Hornung, Reformed, shepherd, and wife Ottilia nee
Hülsenkopp, Reformed from Schalbach, had a son:
>   Johann Christian b. 9 Feb. 1785

This emigrant provided by Dr. Bernd Gölzer from the compiled records of
Dr. Gerhard Hein:
"He moved with wife and four children to America on 25 Apr. 1785".
[See also Gödel and Conradi].

581. JUNKER, JOST   Wolfskirchen=
                                                        67260 Sarre-Union

Wolfskirchen Lutheran KB:
Johannes Junker, daylaborer at Wolfskirchen, and wife Maria Elisabetha nee
Klein had a son:
>   Jost b. 2 Nov. 1761

Records of the Notary Public for Wolfkirchen:
Dated 4 Apr. 1783 and 9 Mar. 1792, inventory of Johannes Junker, or
cession of his widow: the son Jost is a soldier under the Regiment La
Marque; has been transferred from the Nassau Infantry in order to be
transported to America.

582. KARCHER, JOHANN GEORG
ca. 1767

Wolfskirchen=
67260 Sarre-Union

Wolfskirchen Lutheran KB:
Joh. Theobald Karcher, tanner of Wolfskirchen, and wife Anna Magdalena nee Ludmann had children:

Anna Barbara b. 13 Apr. 1731
Johann Georg b. 31 May 1744

Records of the Notary Public for Wolfskirchen:
Dated 10 Dec. 1768: the son Johann Georg has moved to America in 1767; the daughter Anna Barbara, married, moved to America 16 years ago.

583. KÖNIG, DAVID

Diedendorf=
67260 Sarre-Union

Diedendorf Reformed KB:
David König, schoolteacher at Diedendorf, and wife Anna Maria nee Weiss had a son:

David, conf. 1746 at Diedendorf

Records of Saarwerden county office for Diedendorf:
Dated 3 Mar. 1757, inventory of Anna Maria Weiss König: the son David is a weaver in Switzerland. Dated 1764: David König appears as a sponsor in the Diemeringen Lutheran KB, where it is mentioned that he had been in America, but returned. He remained there, never married, and his will dated 4 July 1791 leaves everything to his sister's daughter Sophia Weber of Neusaarwerden.

584. KUCHEN or KUOHREN, ABRAHAM
ca. 1741

Berg=
67320 Drulingen

Berg und Thal Lutheran KB:
Andreas Fäss of Berg, Reformed, and wife Anna nee Eichenberger had a daughter:

Maria Eva b. 12 Oct. 1713 at Berg; conf. 1728 at Diedendorf.

Records of Saarwerden County office for Berg und Thal:
Dated 26 June 1766, inventory of Anna Eichenberger Fäss: the eldest daughter Maria Eva Fäss and her husband Abraham Kuchen or Kuohren have moved to the New Land 25 years ago with manumission.

585. KUNTZ, JOH. NICKEL   Diedendorf=
one on *Francis and Elizabeth,* 1742 S-H, I: 328   67260 Sarre-Union
another on *Samuel,* 1740 S-H, I: 289, 291
another Nicholas Koontz on *Two Brothers,* 1748 S-H, I: 378, 380, 381 with
others from Diedendorf.

Diedendorf Reformed KB:
Felix Kuntz and wife Esther nee Huber had a son:
    Joh. Nickel bp. 11 Apr. 1720, conf. 1733

Records of Saarwerden county office for Notary Public of Sarre-Union:
Dated 20 Feb. 1766, inventory of Jacob Huber, Jr., brother of Esther Huber:
Joh. Nickel Kuntz of Diedendorf, son of Felix Kuntz and wife Esther nee
Huber, has left for America "more than 25 years ago." The mother of Joh.
Nickel Kuntz was deceased, and her brother died leaving no children. The
inventory lists his nieces and nephews who were the heirs to his estate.

586. LAMBERT, JACOB   Siltzheim=
before 1786   67260 Sarre-Union

Siltzheim Catholic KB:
Joseph Lambert, farmer of Siltzheim, and wife Christina nee Orditz had a
son:
    Jacob b. 30 July 1750

Records of Saarwerden County office for Siltzheim:
Dated 9 Mar. 1758, inventory of Joseph Lambert: the son Jacob, 8 years
old. Dated 20 Apr. 1786: the son Jacob resides in Pennsylvania.

587. LARUETTE, JOH. JACOB   Harskirchen=
after 1791   67260 Sarre-Union

Harskirchen Lutheran KB:
Joh. Jacob Laruette, schoolteacher of Harskirchen, son of Nickel Laruette,
innkeeper at Harskirchen, m. (1) 26 Nov. 1767 Eva Margaretha Klein,
daughter of Anstet Klein, innkeeper at Harskirchen. They had 7 children.
Eva Margaretha Klein d. 14 Apr. 1782. At the marriage of their son Johann
Jacob Laruette to Catharina Margaretha Müller on 26 June 1798 it is
recorded that both parents (i.e. Jacob Laruett and Johann Georg Müller,
q.v.) have emigrated to America.

588. MÄNNLEIN, ISAAC
ca. 1741

Thal=
67320 Drulingen

Berg und Thal Lutheran KB:
Isaac Männlein, smith of Thal, m. 25 Dec. 1712 Anna Maria Dintinger.
Children:
1. Maria Magdalena b. 20 July 1713; she m. 1741 Ludwig Urban and remained in Berg.
2. Anna Margaretha b. 1 Feb. 1715, d. 4 Mar. 1715
3. Maria Catharina b. 9 Feb. 1716
4. Anna Margaretha b. 1 Mar. 1718; she m. 1738 Joh. Weidmann.
5. Anna Maria b. 15 Oct. 1719, d. 1719
6. Johannes b. 17 Nov. 1721
7. Anna Dorothea b. 6 Nov. 1723
8. Johann Andreas b. 26 Nov. 1725
9. Johann Joseph b. 3 May 1728
10. Johann Peter b. 21 Jan. 1731
11. Kunigunda b. 31 Oct. 1734

Records of Saarwerden County office for Berg und Thal:
Dated 1 May 1741: Isaac Männlein has moved to the New Land. Family is not on 1742 Census of Thal.

589. MÜGLER, JOHANN DANIEL

Burbach=
67260 Sarre-Union

Pisdorf [Bischtroff] Lutheran KB:
Peter Mügler, smith at Burbach, and wife Anna Eva nee Bader had a son:
Johann Daniel b. 24 Jan. 1722

Peter Mügler d. 27 Mar. 1743 in Strassburg.

Records of Saarwerden county office for Burbach:
Dated 20 Apr. 1748, inventory listing the children of Peter Mügler: the son Johann Daniel, 28 years old, smith, is in the New Land.

590. MÜLLER, JOHANN GEORG
after 1791

Harskirchen=
67260 Sarre-Union

Harskirchen Lutheran KB:
Johann Georg Müller, son of Thiebold Müller of Harskirchen, m. 4 May 1779 Anna Maria Müller, daughter of Jacob Müller, innkeeper at

Harskirchen. At the marriage of their daughter to Joh. Jacob Laruett [q.v.] on 26 June 1798 it is annotated that both parents (i.e. Johann Georg Müller and Jacob Laruett) have emigrated to America.

591. MÜLLER, JOSEPH

Rauwiller=
67320 Drulingen

Rauwiller Reformed KB:
Joseph Müller on the Schneckenbusch [=57400 Sarrebourg] farm, m. 23 June 1743 at Rauweiler Maria Elisabetha "who went to America together with Michael Marx of Burbach." [This entry is confusing; Michael Marck arrived in 1741; possibly he returned to the area, or this may refer to his son Michael Marck. However, no later Marck appears in the ship lists, nor does Joseph Müller appear.]

592. NEHLICH, BALTHASAR
____, 1765

Voellerdingen=
67430 Diemeringen

Voellerdingen Marriage Contract:
Balthasar Nehlich, son of Georg Nehlich of Diedingen, m. 31 Aug. 1752 at Voellerdingen Catharina Kiefer, daughter of Henrich Kiefer and Margaretha nee Rauscher of Voellerdingen.

Records of Saarwerden County office for Voellerdingen:
Dated 1 Apr. 1769: Catharina nee Kiefer, and husband Balthasar Nehlich have moved to America four years ago.

593. ORDITZ, JACOB
ca. 1768-69

Siltzheim=
67260 Sarre-Union

Siltzheim Catholic KB:
Jacob Orditz, Catholic, m. 9 Jan. 1764 Anna Maria Zimmer, daughter of Nickel Zimmer.
Nickel Zimmer of Siltzheim and wife Margaretha Lambert had a daughter:
Anna Maria b. 6 Jan. 1739

Jacob Orditz and Anna Maria had children:
1. Appolonia b. 20 Mar. 1765
2. Barbara b. 25 May 1766
3. Eva Elisabetha b. 10 July 1768

Records of Saarwerden County office for Siltzheim:
Dated 14 Dec. 1774, inventory of Nickel Zimmer: the daughter Anna Maria
and her husband Jacob Orditz removed seven years ago to the New Land.

594. PATRIARCH, CATHARINA   Siltzheim=
before 1757   67260 Sarre-Union

Siltzheim Catholic KB:
Matthias Patriarch and wife Anna Maria had a daughter:
        Catharina b. 1 Feb. 1722

Records of Saarwerden county office for Siltzheim:
Dated 5 Nov. 1757, inventory of Catharina's brother Michael Patriarch, who
died without issue: the sister Catharina is in the New Land.

595. PAULI, JOH. NICOLAUS   Siltzheim=
possibly on *Chance,* 1756   67260 Sarre-Union
S-H, I: 683

Siltzheim Catholic KB:
Paulus Pauli of Siltzheim and wife Christina nee Müller had a son:
        Joh. Nicolaus b. 30 Oct. 1729

Records of Saarwerden county office for Siltzheim:
No date given: the fourth child of Paulus Pauli has moved to America with
permission in 1754.

596. PFORRIUS, FRIEDERICH SAMUEL   Herbitzheim=
before 1788   67260 Sarre-Union

Herbitzheim Lutheran KB:
Herr Moritz Pforrius, Forester at Herbitzheim, and wife Maria Margaretha
nee Reeb had a son:
        Friederich Samuel b. 11 Sept. 1750, bp. 15 Sept.1750
        Sp.: Johann Bernhard Horstmann, Lutheran Pastor here;
        Samuel Haldy; Friedericka Elisabetha, daughter of Herr Clemens
        Textor, Pastor at ?Pildorf [?Pisdorf]

Died 26 Jan. 1766: Johannes Moritzius Pforrius, age 51 y. less 13 days.
Died 15 Oct. 1787: Anna Margaretha, widow of Herr Moritz Pforius, *Fürstl
Nassau Weilburgischen Oberförster* in Herbitzheim, age 68 y. 6 mo., 19 days.

Records of Saarwerden county office for Herbitzheim:
Dated 12 Feb. 1766, inventory of Moritz Pforrius: son Friedrich is 15 y. old.
Dated 22 May 1788, inventory of Margaretha Reeb Pforrius: Son Friedrich,
37 ½ years old, has been in America, his whereabouts unknown.
Records of Saarwerden county office for Neusaarwerden:
Dated 17 Nov. 1790, inventory of Joh. Nicolaus Pforrius: his (Nephew)
Friedrich Pforrius, 39 years old, allegedly in America.

597. PREUSS, PHILIPP   Weyer=
                                                     67320 Drulingen

Weyer Lutheran KB:
Philipp Preuss (also Preiss), son of Friedrich Preuss of Weyer, m. 19 ___
1763 Maria Dorothea, daughter of David Euler of Hirschland. They had:
> 1. Stillborn daughter b. 11 Jun 1766
> 2. Jacob b. 20 Oct. 1768

Hirschland Lutheran KB:
Master carpenter David Euler m. (1) Anna Margaretha nee Wehrung; he m.
(2) Catharina Elisabetha nee Werthmüller. A daughter of the first marriage
was:
> Maria Dorothea bp. 27 Dec. 1730

David Euler(t)'s obituary in the Hirschland KB, dated 25 Mar. 1759
mentions that he died in Zweibrücken. He was with the French army in
Frankfurth am Mayn, when he was stricken with *hitzigen fieber*, and died
soon after his return to Zweibrücken. His second wife Catharina Elisabetha
nee Werthmüller d. 2 Oct. 1771, aged 55 years.

Records of Saarwerden county office for Hirschland:
Dated 18 Apr. 1772: Anna Elisabetha Werthmüller Euler died. The heirs
are listed among them Dorothea Euler, wife of Philipp Preuss. They moved
to America three years ago.

598. RODHUT, NICKEL   Dehlingen=
before 1770   67430 Diemeringen

Dehlingen Lutheran KB:
Hans Ulrich Köppel, wagoner of Dehlingen, and wife Maria Elisabetha nee
Weinland had a daughter:
> Anna Elisabetha b. 6 Aug. 1741, conf. 1754.

Records of Saarwerden county office for Dehlingen:
The daughter Anna Elisabetha is mentioned in a record dated 1769 as the wife of Nickel Rodhut. Another record, dated 21 Nov. 1770: the daughter Anna Elisabetha and her husband Rodhuth are in America.

599. RUDIO, ANDREAS   Hinsingen=
ca. 1743   67260 Sarre-Union

Keskastel Lutheran KB:
Hans Nickel *Cherudio* and wife Margaretha had:
> 1. Andreas bp. 11 Nov. 1710 at Keskastel
> 2. Anna Maria bp. 6 Jan. 1713

Altweiler Lutheran KB:
Andreas Rudio, son of Hans Nickel Rudio of Hinsingen, m. 8 Feb. 1735 Anna Margaretha Quirin, daughter of Jost Quirin of Pisdorf [Bischtroff =67260 Sarre-Union]. Children:
> 1. Friedrich Carl b. 2 Jan. 1736, Pisdorf
> 2. Johann Henrich b. 15 Feb. 1738, d. Feb. 1738, Pisdorf
> 3. Johann Matthias b. 15 Apr. 1739, Hinsingen

On 4 Sept. 1743, Hans Nickel Rudio had a comforting sermon held for his son and son's wife, also his daughter, and two grandchildren who died on their voyage to Pennsylvania aboard the ship. The daughter was possibly Anna Maria Rudio who appears in the KB as sponsor in 1736 and 1739.

600. SCHÄFER, MARIA ELISABETHA   Weyer=
SCHÄFER, HANS THEOBALD   67320 Drulingen

Hirschland Lutheran KB:
David Schäfer, herdsman, d. 9 Jan. 1745 at Weyer, aged 47 y. His widow Ottilia nee Rauscher d. on Michael's Day, 1757.

Records of Saarwerden county office for Weyer:
Dated 28 Jan. 1758, inventory lists their five children, and mentions that daughter Maria Elisabetha and son Hans Theobald went to the New Land four years ago.

601. SCHMIDT, PAULUS   Kirrberg=
                                                    67320 Drulingen

Records of Saarwerden county office for Kirberg:
Dated 13 Mar. 1777, inventory of Jacob Schmidt: his son Paulus is 21 years
old. Dated 16 Apr. 1785: the son Paulus died according to a certificate of
death as a soldier under the Regiment Nassau Infantry in America in the
year 1781.

602. SCHMIDT, PHILIPP   Siltzheim=
ca. 1763   67260 Sarre-Union

Siltzheim Catholic KB:
Andreas Schmidt of Siltzheim and wife Anna Maria nee Geisskopf had a
son:
        Philipp b. 16 Dec. 1720

Philipp Schmidt and wife Anna Maria nee Orditz had:
        1. Ludwig b. 31 Jan. 1747
        2. Appolonia b. 7 Feb. 1748
        3. Johann Georg b. 11 Apr. 1750
        4. Michael b. 23 Oct. 1752
        5. Franz b. 24 Feb. 1755
        6. Barbara b. 30 June 1757
        7. Eva b. 10 Aug. 1758
        8. Philipp b. 11 Mar. 1761

Records of Saarwerden county office for Siltzheim:
Dated 9 May 1765, Philipp Schmidt of Sültzen [Siltzheim] has a couple of
years ago moved to the French Islands. [The French Islands usually stand for
Cayenne].

603. SCHMIDTGALL, possibly CATHARINA MARGARETHALützelstein=
after 1779   La Petite Pierre=
                                                67290 Wingen-sur-Moder

Lützelstein Lutheran KB:
Jacob Schmidtgall m. __ Jan. 1742 Catharina Margaretha Beck, daughter of
Hans Michael Beck, cordwainer at Lützelstein. She d. 12 Jan. 1787 and her
obituary mentions that "they had ten children, five of them died, one
daughter is in America, one married son and three married daughters reside
here." Their daughter:
        Catharina Margaretha b. __ Mar. 1748, conf. 1762
        She last appears in the record as a sp. in 1779.

604. SCHNEIDER, CHILDREN OF JOHANNES   Keskastel=
before 1780   67260 Sarre-Union

Keskastel Lutheran KB:
Johannes Schneider of Keskastel and wife Margaretha had a son:
        Johannes b. 20 Oct. 1728

Johannes Schneider, Catholic of Willerwald [=57430 Sarralbe] and wife
(n.n.) had children:
        Johannes; Elisabetha Margaretha; Catharina; Margaretha.
Johannes Schneider died ca. 1761.

Records of Saarwerden county office for Keskastel:
Dated 1 Apr. 1766: the widow has moved to Hungary with the four children.
Dated 19 Aug. 1780: the children are in the New Land.

605. SCHORPP, ANNA EVA   Siltzheim=
ca. 1754   67260 Sarre-Union

Siltzheim Catholic KB:
Joh. Thomas Schorpp of Siltzheim and wife Margaretha nee Rundio had a
daughter:
        Anna Eva b. 12 Aug. 1724

Records of Saarwerden county office for Siltzheim:
Dated 18 Nov. 1735, inventory of Margaretha Rundio: the daughter Anna
Eva is 12 years old. Dated 21 Feb. 1755, inventory of Thomas Schorpp: the
daughter Anna Eva has moved to the New Land in 1754.

606. SCHWING, SOPHIA   Diedendorf=
                                                                   67260 Sarre-Union
Diedendorf Reformed KB:
Jean Schwing [surname also appears in KB as Join, Lajoin, Longjoin] of
Diedendorf, m. 11 Jan. 1708 Maria Jacobea Müller, daughter of Henrich
Müller, innkeeper at Diedendorf. They had nine children, the youngest was:
        Sophia, conf. 1742

Records of Saarwerden county office for Diedendorf:
Dated 2 Mar.1757, inventory of Peter Schwing, son of Jean Schwing. He
died single and the inventory names six siblings: Hans Michael, Ottilia,
Susanna, Christina, Eva Elisabetha, and Sophia who six years ago (ca. 1751)
emigrated to America.

607. SCHUBDREIN, DANIEL   Weyer=
                                                        67320 Drulingen

Hirschland Lutheran KB:
Daniel Schubdrein (also Schubder), carpenter at Weyer, and wife Anna
Margaretha had children:
1. Johann Jacob bp. 21 Dec. 1714; m. 14 Nov. 1741 at
   Hirschland Anna Eva Schäfer. He d. 18 Mar. 1775
2. Anna Maria bp. 13 Sept. 1716, m. 13 Jan. 1747 at
   Weyer Joh. Georg Klein.
3. Anna Margaretha bp. 10 Aug. 1718, m. Peter Freyermuth
4. Joseph bp. 16 Feb. 1721
5. Daniel bp. 3 Aug. 1723
6. Johann Peter bp. 17 Feb. 1726
7. Catharina bp. 29 Mar. 1729
8. Hans Nickel bp. 21 Oct. 1732

Records of Saarwerden county office for Weyer:
Dated 24 Aug. 1775, inventory of Johann Jacob Schubdrein, mentions that
the father Daniel Schubdrein left for the New Land (obviously with some of
the other family members; last entries in KB for the younger children are in
1747, 1748.)   The inventory also mentions that Catharina Elisabetha,
daughter of the deceased Johann Jacob Schubdrein, went to the New Land
about seven years ago without manumission, and is married there.

608. SONNSTÄDT, ANNA DOROTHEA   Berg=
ca. 1755   67320 Drulingen

Berg und Thal Lutheran KB:
Johann Jacob Sonnstädt appears in the KB from 1749 to 1761 as
schoolteacher of Berg. He d. 12 Apr. 1761. His first wife was Veronica
Kirchhofer.

Records of Saarwerden county office for Berg und Thal:
Dated 20 Aug. 1761 and 16 Mar. 1780: Anna Dorothea Sonnstädt, the only
child from the first marriage of Johann Jacob Sonnstädt, has moved ca. 1755
to the New Land. When she left she obtained her maternal inheritance.
One has no news of her.

609. TUSSING (TOUSSAINT), JOH. JACOB   Weyer=
ca. 1751   67320 Drulingen

Hirschland Lutheran KB:
Johann Jacob Tussing [in some records Toussaint], stonemason of Weyer, son of Joh. Jacob Thoussing, m. 24 Nov. 1721 Anna Maria Männlein of Weyer. Their son:
> Johann Jacob b. 23 Feb. 1727, conf. 1739

Records of Saarwerden county office for Weyer:
An inventory in 1763, after the death of Johann Jacob Tussing, reports that the son Johann Jacob has moved twelve years ago to the New Land and one has no news on his whereabouts.

The church in Zollingen was erected in 1853. Before that date, residents of Zollingen appear in nearby parish registers.

610. WEIDMANN, MARCEL   Zollingen=
                                                     67260 Sarre-Union

Pisdorf [Bischtroff] Lutheran KB:
Marcellus Weydmann, son of the late Johann Peter Weydmann, m. 31 Aug.

1706 in Zollingen Gerdrut, daughter of Johannes Altmann of Öhrmingen [67970 Oehrmingen]. They had:
   1. Anna Margretha bp. Pfingstag (June) 1707
? 2. Anna Ottilia b. 10 Feb. 1709

This emigrant provided by Dr. Bernd Gölzer from the compiled records of Dr. Gerhard Hein:
There are no records on this family in the area after 1709. Dr. Hein has two editions of the Pisdorf Lutheran KB: The first one dated 1977 and a new edition of 1981. The 1977 edition mentions an annotation in the Pisdorf KB in 1707: "Moved to India, to the Island Pennsylvania". The 1981 edition does not mention this and does not mention the daughter #2.

611. WEIDMANN, JOHANN CARL   Dehlingen=
                                                         67430 Diemeringen

Dehlingen Lutheran KB:
Johann Carl Weidmann, son of Hans Leonhard Weidmann of Dehlingen, m. 10 Feb. 1763 Anna Eva, widow of Nicolaus Rauscher. She was a daughter of Peter Hafner of Mackweiler [Mackwiller=67430 Diemeringen] and his wife Anna Barbara nee Hertzog; conf. 1748 at Bütten Lutheran KB. They had one child b. and died in 1763.

Records of Saarwerden county office for Mackweiler:
Dated 13 Oct. 1768, inventory of Peter Hafner: the daughter Anna Eva is married to Carl Weidmann of Dehlingen. They emigrated in Spring, 1764, to the New Land.

612. WEIDMANN, JOH. LUDWIG   Dehlingen=
   before 1758   67430 Diemeringen

Dehlingen Lutheran KB:
Hans Matthias Weidmann of Dehlingen and wife Anna Margaretha nee Angst had a son:
         Joh. Ludwig bp. 21 Mar. 1726, conf. 1739

Records of Saarwerden county office for Dehlingen:
Dated 6 Feb. 1758, inventory of Hans Matthias Weidmann: the eldest son Ludwig, 31 years old, is in America. Deed book, Dehlingen: 20 records from 1770-1788 concern Ludwig Weidmann, who is in America, but who is having items bought for him. On 25 Feb. 1786, he sends a letter of authorization from Savannah, GA to have his property in Dehlingen sold and the money to be forwarded to him.

613. WEISS, MARX (MARC)   Altsaarwerden
  before 1742   Sarrewerden=
not in lists; died on voyage   67260 Sarre-Union

Diedendorf Reformed KB:
Daniel Weiss, carpenter at Altsaarwerden, son of Benedict Weiss, citizen at Reutli, Grafschaft Büren, [CH-3295 Rüri b. Büren, BE] Canton Bern, m. 14 Nov. 1716 Anna Magdalena Stüber, daughter of Nickel Stuber of Saarwerden. They had a son:
  Markus bp. 30 Oct. 1717, conf. 1733

Marx Weiss, citizen and carpenter at Altsaarwerden, son of Daniel Weiss, m. 12 Feb. 1738 Margaretha Lantz, daughter of Durst Lantz, citizen at Altsaarwerden. Children:
  1. Jacob b. 24 Sept. 1739

Records of Saarwerden county office for Burbach:
1742 church census of Burbach mentions that a daughter of Durst Lantz is in America. Durst Lantz d. before 15 Nov. 1745; estate records mention the daughter Anna Margaretha is married to Marc Weiss, citizen of Altsaarwerden; he died on the voyage to or in America.

Diedendorf Reformed KB:
Durst Lantz of Burbach, son of Melchior Lantz of Kilchberg [CH-3422 Kirchberg, BE] m. 8 May 1708 in Burbach Anna Maria Marc, daughter of Jean Marc of Burbach. Their daughter:
  Margaretha b. 26 Dec. 1718, conf. 1733

614. WILMSTÄTTER, JOHANN THEOBALD   Rexingen=
                                                  67320 Drulingen
Berg und Thal Lutheran KB:
Michael Wilmstätter, daylaborer at Rexingen, and wife Catharina Magdalena nee Ulrich had a son:
  Johann Theobald b. 16 Mar. 1751

Records of Saarwerden county office for Rexingen:
"Theobold Wilmstätter, son of Michael Wilmstätter of Rexingen, was transferred in the recent American War from Nassau Infantry Regiment to the Regiment Lamarck and died there, according to a certificate of death" (before 29 Oct. 1785). His heirs are a half-sister, and his uncle.

APPENDIX B

A Correction to a Published List of Immigrants

The following list was originally published in the *Pennsylvania Magazine of History and Biography* (1909) Vol 33, No. 4, pg. 501, contributed by R. G. Swift; it was reprinted in Michael Tepper, ed; *Emigrants to Pennsylvania* Baltimore: Genealogical Publishing Co., Inc. (1975), p. 261 complete with all of the errors.

The first major error appears in the date. The 1909 translation states that the following list of German families appears in an advertisement in Henry Miller's *Staats Bote* of 9 February <u>1758</u>. However, all of the names that could be identified in the ship's lists arrived on ships in <u>1767</u>. It appeared that there might be a 10 year error in the published date 1758. A visit to the Library Company of Philadelphia to search the available original issues of Henry Miller's *Staats Bote* located the list in the issue dated 9 Feb. <u>1768</u>. A comparison of the original newspaper item with the published translation revealed that, in addition to the date error, there were numerous other discrepancies, especially in place names. Since several families on this list also appear in this volume of emigrants, a correction to this earlier published list seems advisable. It will be noted that some of the place names, even with a corrected transcript, differ from the spelling used today, and also the jurisdictions have changed since 1768. Almost all of the male passengers listed here can be identified as arriving on either the ship *Hamilton*, 6 Oct. 1767 or on the ship *Minerva*, 29 Oct. 1767, S-H, I: 716, 717, 718, 719. The Alsatians arrived on the *Hamilton*, and information on their families will be found in the main text.

"Philadelphia, the 9 February [Hornung] 1768
The following German families and a couple of unmarried persons, are now in this city; all held for their passage from Holland, and desiring to bind themselves out for the same; they are in present need; they hope to find their friends and kinfolk to insure their indebtedness to *Willing and Morris* as they themselves are unable to pay, since they (Willing & Morris) are willing to give credit either to their friends or themselves if they bind themselves out."

Johannes Hobert, joiner, born in the Chur-Mannz territories, village of Lembach; his wife **Maria Elisabetha Kettel(in)** from the village Langenkandel, in the Zweybrücken territory.

Johann Jacob Müller, a farmer, is born in the Grafschaft Dierdorf, village of Dirnbach; his wife **Margaretha Elisabetha Thomasz(in).**

Johann Wilhelm Kaper, a farmer, is born in the Grafschaft Dierdorf, village of Poterbach; his wife **Annagir Hoffmann(in)** from the village of Werlebach.

Johannes Müller, a farmer, born in the Chur-Pfalz jurisdiction , village of Bretzen; his wife **Anna Elisabetha Sandhöffer(in),** from the Margraffschaft Anspach, village of Bürgenhausen.

Johann Müller, a farmer, born in the Hessen-Darmstadt jurisdiction, from the Herrschaft Itter; his wife **Anna Maria Müller(in).**

Eva Schleichhart(in), a seamstress, born in Alsace, village of Lembach. [See Schweickert in main text].

Joseph Bläs, tailor from the Chur-Mannz jurisdiction, village of Burtzele; his wife **Dorothea Kartz(in),** born in Alsace, Dorfschaft Lembach. [See Joseph Blesch in main text].

Bastian Dauber, a farmer, born in the Hessen-Cassel jurisdiction, Amt Marpurg, village of Leidehoffen; his wife **Anna Elisabetha Litt(in)** from the Braunfels jurisdiction, village of Oberhofen.

Johann Derbald Hauck, a farmer, born in the Zweybrücken jurisdiction, village of Hunbach [Hunspach]; his wife **Barbara Schunckel(in),** from the village of Haffen [Hoffen]. [See Joh. Diebold Hauck in main text].

Johann Jacob Albrech, a farmer, born in the Zweybrücken jurisdiction, village of Langenkandel; his wife **Anna Maria Nirlind,** born in Landau.

Johann Philip Bott, a farmer, born in Alsace, village of Fachbach; his wife **Anna Maria Malone** from the village of Krüszbach.

Johann Kobbeloch, linenweaver, born in the Zweybrücken jurisdiction, village of Langenkandel; his wife (nee) **Seyler(in)** from the village Börlebach. [See Jörg Friedrich Knobelloch in main text].

Anna Catharina Notz(in), born in the Zweybrücken jurisdiction, village of Langenkandel.

Johann Georg Hoch, a farmer, born in the Zweybrücken jurisdiction, village of Bürlebach; his wife **Maria Dorothea Baur(in),** born in Alsace, village of Lembach. [See Georg Hoch in main text].

Jeremias Algeyer, farmer and wine-grower, born in Kirchheim am Neckar; his wife **Elisabetha Margaretha Schäf(in),** born in Güglingen.

Johann Nicolas Albrecht, farmer and wine-grower, born in Kirchheim am Neckar; his wife **Christina Krausz(in),** born in Leham.

Johannes Westermeyer, from the Alsace region, village of Köllendorf, a wooden-shoe maker; his wife **Adilga,** born in Fischbach in Alsace. [See Johannes Westermeyer in main text].

Johann Georg Schäfer, musician, born in Chur-Pfalz territory, Ober-Amt Lindenfels; his wife **Elsa,** born in Clembach, in Chur-Pfalz.

APPENDIX C

Possible Immigrants

The following families are presented in this appendix as possibly being the immigrants on the stated ships, but sufficient data has not been located to actually verify their emigration. The families listed here disappear from the European records, and an immigrant with the name appears in the Pennsylvania lists, but the available data does not provide unquestionable identification. In several cases, they arrived on ships that carried other passengers from the Alsatian villages. Rather than delete the data, this group is presented here with the hope that eventually sufficient information will be located to prove or disprove the assumption that they might be the immigrant family in question.

615. BECK, GEORG   Wolfskirchen=
?Anderson, 1751   67260 Sarre-Union
S-H, I: 451 [Yerick (x) Beck]
Others in S-H

EUROPEAN RECORDS

Wolfskirchen Lutheran KB:
Georg Beck, carpenter, m. 4 Nov. 1732 Anna Barbara Karcher. They had children:

    1. Joh. Nicolaus b. 18 Aug. 1733
    2. Catharina Margaretha b. 24 June 1735
    3. Anna Barbara b. 21 Sept. 1737
    4. Joh. Nicolaus b. 23 Apr. 1740
    5. David b. 23 June 1746
    6. Child (n.n.) b. 7 Feb. 1749

AMERICAN RECORDS

One George Beck, Bethlehem, Northampton co., nat. Autumn, 1765
Another John George Beck, Philadelphia, nat. 10/12 Apr. 1762.

616. BERNHART, PETER   Niederstinzel=
St. Mark, 1741   57930 Fénétrange
S-H, I: 296, 298, 299

EUROPEAN RECORDS

Diedendorf Reformed KB:
Peter Bernhard, shepherd at Altweiler, [Altwiller=67260 Sarre-Union] then at Niederstinsel, son of Matthias Bernhard of Kleinmünchweiler, Blieskasteler Amt, m. 24 Aug. 1721 Anna Elisabetha Wittmer, daughter of Ulrich Wittmer of Altweiler. They had children:
1. Anna Elisabetha bp. 13 Oct. 1723, conf. 1739
2. Anna Barbara bp. 17 June 1726, d. 27 Mar. 1728
3. Anna Barbara bp. 3 Sept. 1732
4. Johann Daniel bp. 7 July 1735

AMERICAN RECORDS

One Peter Bernhard, Philadelphia co., nat. Apr. 1744.

617. BRAUN, RUDOLPH age 30   67350 Pfaffenhoffen
Loyal Judith, 1732
S-H, I: 87, 90, 91
[did not sign; appears on A list as Roland Brown; on B and C lists as Rudolph (x) Brown.]

EUROPEAN RECORDS

Pfaffenhoffen Lutheran KB:
Rudolph Braun, single, from Cappeln, [CH-3273 Kappelen, BE] Canton Bern, Switzerland, m. 23 Jan. 1731 Catharina, widow of the late Rudolph Pflughaupt, former *Schirmer* at Niedermothern, [Niedermodern = 67350 Pfaffenhoffen]. [her first m. not recorded there].

618. BÜTTNER, HENNRICH   Hinsingen=
     BÜTTNER, HANS MICHEL   67260 Sarre-Union
Bilander *Vernon,* 1747
S-H, I: 363

[The Michael Buttner on the *Vernon,* 1747, was previously identified in Burgert, *Northern Kraichgau* as an immigrant from Schwaigern. There was a Michael Buttner from Schwaigern who later appeared in Lancaster, PA, but the currently available evidence would indicate that he was not the immigrant who arrived on this ship. His exact date of arrival is unknown. The 1747 immigrant Michael Büttner arrived with Hennrich Büttner (see below). There were several other passengers on this ship who appear in the Keskastel parish records; based on this evidence, it is possible that the following family is the 1747 immigrant group:]

EUROPEAN RECORDS

Harskirchen Lutheran KB:
Hans Michel Büttner, carpenter at Hinsingen, and wife Anna Margaretha had a son:
Hans Henrich bp. 6 Nov. 1701

Keskastel Lutheran KB:
Johann Hennrich Büttner, son of Hans Michael Büttner, master carpenter at Hinsingen, m. 13 Oct. 1722 at Altweiler Barbara Schneider, daughter of Adam Schneider, the shepherd at Altweiler. They had:
1. Hans Michel bp. 14 Nov. 1723
2. Hans Georg bp. 7 Feb. 1726

AMERICAN RECORDS

Old Goshenhoppen Lutheran KB, Montgomery co.:
Henrich Bittner and wife Christina had a daughter:
Anna Margaretha b. 24 July 1751
Sp.: Jacob Grotz and wife Elisabeth.

619. DIEDRICH, HANS ADAM   Wolfskirchen=
Patience, 1751   67260 Sarre-Union
S-H, I: 456

EUROPEAN RECORDS

Wolfskirchen Lutheran KB:
Joh. Adam Diederich m. 12 Feb. 1737 Christina Bieber from Hirschland [her surname also given as Biber in records]. They had:
1. Maria Christina b. 9 Nov. 1737
2. Jacob b. 10 Jan. 1739
3. Joh. Adam b. 8 Nov. 1740
4. Catharina b. 21 Oct. 1742
5. Maria Elisabetha b. 14 Sept. 1744

6. Joh. Jacob b. 10 June 1746
7. Johann Nickel b. 16 Mar. 1748, d. 1750
8. Anna Magdalena b. 20 July 1750
   [Last entry for family in KB]

AMERICAN RECORDS

Rev. Daniel Schumacher's records:
One Johann Adam Diederich and wife Maria Barbara nee Steenbrucker had:
1. Anna Catharina bp. 23 May 1763, 3 days old, in Heidelberg.
   Sp.: Jurg Schneider; Anna Barbara Steinbruchen
2. Johann Adam bp. 25 Dec. 1764 in Heidelberg, 14 days old
   Sp.: Abraham Steinbruch; Barbara Köckin
3. Johann Simon bp. 19 May 1766 in Weisenberg; died.
   Sp.: Simon Moser and Christina
4. Johann Georg bp. 24 May 1767 in Heidelberg
   Sp.: Simon Moser and Christina
5. Johann Jacob bp. 13 Aug. 1773, 3 weeks old, in Weisenberg
   Sp.: Sebastian Werner and Maria Margaretha.

Adam Diederick, Lowhill twp., Northampton co., nat. Autumn, 1765.

620. DIEDRICH, JOH. JACOB   Wolfskirchen=
Halifax, 1752   67260 Sarre-Union
? S-H, I: 483
[with Mathias Müller, and Nickel Quirin, q.v.]

EUROPEAN RECORDS

Wolfskirchen Lutheran KB:
Joh. Jacob Diedrich, weaver, m. 7 Feb. 1736 Catharina Mertz [her surname
also given in records as Märtz, Murtz]. They had:
1. Joh. Nicolaus b. 31 Aug. 1737
2. Anna Margaretha b. 15 June 1739
3. Jacob b. 1 June 1741
4. Jacob b. 30 June 1744
5. Anna Catharina b. 25 Feb. 1747
6. Joh. Jost b. 10 Feb. 1750, d. 1751
7. Anna Eva b. 27 Feb. 1752, d. 1 Apr. 1752
   [Last entry for family in KB]

AMERICAN RECORDS

St. Michael's and Zion KB, Philadelphia:
Jacob Diedrich, newcomer, sp. in Jan. 1753 a child of John Mich. Christian
(from Bischwiler) [67240 Bischwiller].

Jacob Dietrich and wife Magdalena, Reformed, had a son:
   Johan Jacob b. 14 Jan. 1753, bp. 21 Jan. 1753
   Sp.: Abraham Wild; Eva Seipold; Joh. Michael Christian.

Jacob Diedrich m. 27 Feb. 1755 Dorothea Johanna Margr. Sternbekin.
Wit: David Schaefer [q.v.] and wife; Johannes Kaufman.

One Jacob Dietrick, Greenwich twp., Berks co., nat. Sept. 1761.

621. FISCHER, CHRISTOPH   Oberbronn-Zinswiller=
Phoenix, 1750   67110 Niederbronn-les-Bains
S-H, I: 440

EUROPEAN RECORDS

Oberbronn Lutheran KB:
Christoph Fischer, single mason, son of the late Leonhard Fischer, citizen
and stonecutter at Heylbronn [=W-7100 Heilbronn] m. 26 Nov. 1737 Maria
Catharina, daughter of the late David Schild. They had children:
   1. Johann Caspar b. 29 Aug. 1738, bp. 31 Aug. 1738
   2. Maria Catharina b. 23 Jan. 1741, bp. 25 Jan. 1741
   3. Joh. Jacob b. 25 Feb. 1744, bp. 27 Feb. 1744
      Sp.: Joh. Jacob Weyll [q.v.]; Hans Adam Kober [q.v.];
      Anna Ursula wife of Dietrich Metsch, stocking weaver here.
   4. Maria Barbara b. 13 May 1745, bp. 15 May 1745
   5. Christoph b. 17 Jan. 1749, bp. 18 Jan. 1749.

622. FUCHS, ULRICH   Oberbronn-Zinswiller=
Phoenix, 1750   67110 Niederbronn-les-Bains
S-H, I: 440
EUROPEAN RECORDS

Oberbronn Lutheran KB:
Ulrich Fuchs, born in Canton Bern, Switzerland, widower, m. 19 Feb. 1737
Maria Elisabeth daughter of the late Herr Joh. Martin Weber, fromer school
praeceptoris here. She died in childbirth, Nov. 1737.
Meister Ulrich Fuchs, son of the late Hans Fuchs, former citizen at

Hinterlach [possibly CH-3800 Interlaken, BE], Canton Bern, m. 20 May 1738 Salome, daughter of the late Joh. Georg Bauer, citizen and *des Gerichts* here. Ulrich Fuchs and wife Salome nee Bauer had:
1. Wilhelm Friderich b. 14 Dec. 1739, bp. 16 Dec. 1739
2. Johann Bernhard b. 29 Dec. 1742, bp. 1 Jan. 1743
3. Maria Barbara b. __ Feb. 1745
4. Maria Elisabeth b. 24 Oct. 1749 bp. 26 Oct. 1749
Sp.: Johann Georg Walcker [q.v.] son of the late Matthis Walcker, former nailsmith; Anna Maria, daughter of Joh. Jacob Helm; Maria Elisabeth, wife of Andreas Diemer.

[A Dewalt Fooks on ship list, possibly a son of the first marriage.]

623. GROSJEAN, JACOB
Queen of Denmark, 1751
S-H, I: 472

Hellering-lès-Fénétrange=
57930 Fénétrange

EUROPEAN RECORDS

Diedendorf Reformed KB:
Johannes Grosjean, son of Abraham Grosjean, m. 24 Apr. 1713 Judith Vautrin, daughter of Hans Peter Vautrin of Helleringen.

Jean Grosjean and wife Judith nee *Wotreng* had a son:
Johann Jacob bp. 18 Dec. 1725
Sp.: Jacob Gassert, citizen and inhabitant at Helleringen; Lorentz Leyenberger, Helleringen; Catharina Brodt, wife of Abraham Wotring, citizen and miller at Vinstingen; Anna Maria Nunemacher, wife of Georg Adam, citizen at Helleringen.

624. HEINTZ, JACOB
Minerva, 1770
S-H, I: 730

Retschwiller=
67250 Soultz-sous-Forêts

EUROPEAN RECORDS

Kutzenhausen Lutheran KB:
Married 18 July 1769 after proclamation here and in Sultz:
Johann Jacob Heintz, citizen and master cooper at ?Rötschweiler (Retschweiler), son of the late Philipp Heintz, farmer there, and Maria Catharina Rieth, daughter of Stephan Rieth, citizen and farmer at Feldbach. (No children there.)

625. HOLTZINGER, RUDOLPH age 44
Britannia, 1731
S-H, I: 48, 52, 53
  with Magdalena age 26

Rountzenheim=
67480 Roeschwoog
Merkwiller-Pechelbronn=
67250 Soultz-sous-Forêts

EUROPEAN RECORDS

Kutzenhausen Lutheran KB:
Rudolph Holtzinger, born in Switzerland, now citizen and woolspinner at
Runtzenheim, Fleckenstein Jurisdiction, m. 19 Mar. 1726 at Merckweiler,
Magdalena, daughter of Jacob Meyer, citizen and shoemaker at Merckweiler,
both Reformed religion. (No children there.)

626. MUTSCHLER, JOHANN DANIEL
Snow *Ketty,* 1752
S-H, I: 496

Langensoultzbach=
67360 Woerth

EUROPEAN RECORDS

Langensoultzbach Lutheran KB:
Andreas Mutschler and wife Margaretha had:
  Johann Daniel bp. 6 Oct. 1701
Barbara, wife of Daniel Mutschler from Wörth, was a sp. in 1723 for a child
of Hans Georg Mercker.

AMERICAN RECORDS

St. Michael's and Zion KB, Philadelphia:
Johann Daniel Mutschler m. 2 Oct. 1758 Susanna Dorothea Schroetlin.
Wit: Johann Philip Burghardt and wife; Michael Frick; Andreas Burghardt.
Children:
  1. Johann Michael b. 30 July 1759, bp. 5 Aug. 1759.
    Sp.: Johann Michael Frick & Susanna Margaretha Wartin.
  2. Johannes b. 31 July 1761, bp. 16 Aug. 1761.

627. STETTLER, CHRISTIAN
Thistle, 1738
S-H, I: 221, 222, 224

Rauwiller=
67320 Drulingen

EUROPEAN RECORDS

Rauwiller Reformed KB:
Christian Stettler from Guthingen, Switzerland [possibly CH-8594 Güttingen, TG], m. 17 Feb. 1733 Anna, daughter of the late Görg Huntsinger, also from Switzerland.

[No children there - they probably moved on, as did so many of the Swiss who were transient through this region.]

AMERICAN RECORDS

Rev. Jacob Lischy's records, York co.:
A Christian Stettler and wife Elisabeth had a daughter:
> Sussanna Marg. bp. 8 Sept. 1751
> Sp.: Wentel Metzler and Maria Marg. Lentz

Jordan Lutheran KB, Lehigh co.:
A Christoph Stettler and wife Catharina were sp. in 1744 for a child of Abraham Knerr [q.v.].

628. SULTZBERGER, JACOB age 20   Hunspach=
St. Andrew, 1741   67250 Soultz-sous-Forêts
S-H, I: 303, 306, 307

EUROPEAN RECORDS

Hunspach Reformed KB:
Henrich Sultzberger, son of Conrad Sultzberger from Switzerland, m. 24 Jan. 1713 Maria Magdalena Schertenlaub from Neuhoff. Henrich Sultzberger, residing at the Neuhof by Hunspach, and wife Magdalena nee Schertenlaub had a son:
> Hans Jacob b. 3 Dec. 1718, bp. 8 Dec. 1718; conf. 1734

Note on the Indexes

The first index, Index of Ships, contains the name of the ships and the year of arrival. When a more specific date of arrival is given, it is because there were two ships with the same name in the same year; for example, there were two *Dragons* arriving in 1749, and two *Sallys* arrived in 1767. The reader is referred to Volume III of Strassburger and Hinke, *Pennsylvania German Pioneers*, pp. 251-221, for a complete alphabetical listing of the known ship arrivals.

The second index, Index to Names, is a full name index of all names appearing in the text. The searcher should keep in mind, when using this index, that there are several spellings used for each given name and surname. In all cases, the spellings used in the text are those given in the original records; names are frequently misspelled, phonetically spelled or given with both a German and French spelling. Therefore, the index should be used with care (and with some imagination). There are a few suggestions included in the text and index to lead the searcher to other possible spellings, when there is a change in the initial letter. For example, Votrin, Vautrin see also Wotring. Variant spellings also occur in the given names, and Hans Jerg, Johann Georg, Johann Görg, Hans Georg, and John George might be five spellings for the given names of the same person; furthermore, it is likely that this same person might appear in the records as simply Georg or George. The umlaut has been ignored in the alphabetical arrangement, out of consideration for American readers not familiar with European alphabetical arrangements.

John, 158
Louisa, 158
Liebs,
  Wendel, 454
Lieser,
  Maria Elisabetha,
   336
  Michael, 336
Linck,
  Adam, 372, 479
  Anna Magdalena, 372
  Catharine, 479
  Joh. Jacob, 372
  Maria Elisabeth,
   372
  Maria Magdalena,
   372
Lindemann,
  Anna Barbara, 47,
   344
  Catharina, 344
  Elisabetha, 345
  Eva Barbara, 323
  Georg, 343
  Joh. Georg, 47
  Joh. Nicolaus, 344
  Johann Georg, 343,
   344
  Nicholas, 344
  Niclaus, 323
  Nicolaus, 343, 344
  Veronica, 343, 344
Lindenmann,
  Anna ?, 344
  Anna Barbara, 344
  Anna Catharina, 344
  Anna Dorothea, 344
  Barbara, 344
  Georg, 344
  Jacob, 344
  Joh. Georg, 344
  Joh. Michael, 344
  Johann Georg, 344
  Maria Catharina,
   344
  Maria Salome, 344
  Nicolai, 344
  Nicolaus, 344
Linderman,
  Nicholas, 345
  Nichs., 345
Lindermann,
  Barbara, 344
  Elisabetha, 345
  Georg, 344
  Mar. Magdalena, 345
  Nicholas, 345
  Nicolaus, 345
Linner,
  Catharina Louise,
   345
Lipp,
  Samuel, 434
Lippert,
  Barbara, 420
  Jacob, 420

Johann, 420
Maria Barbara, 420
Lips,
  Joh. Jacob, 48
  Joh. Peter, 470
  Johann Martin, 454
  Maria Elisabetha,
   470
  Wendel, 454
Lischer,
  Catharina Louise,
   345
  Johann Philipp, 345
  Maria Salome, 345
  Philip Jacob, 345,
   362
  Salome, 345
Lischy,
  Jacob, 109, 215
Lithweiler,
  John, 200
  Magdalena, 200
Litt(in),
  Anna Elisabetha,
   580
Liwig,
  Peter, 192
  Susanna, 192
Lober,
  Barbara, 21
Lochner,
  Anna, 383
  Henry, 383
Lock,
  Adam, 513
Loeffler,
  Reinhard, 465
Loesch,
  Hermanus, 252
Loescher,
  Catharina, 347
  Jacob, 347
Loff,
  Adam, 513
Logel,
  Anna, 111
Long,
  Barbara, 200
  Catharine, 153
  David, 200
  Peter, 449
Longacre,
  Barbara, 328
  Jacob, 328
  Peter, 328
Longjoin,
  family, 5
  see Schwing, 574
Loreht,
  Dorothea, 198
Lorentz,
  Eva, 371
  Hans Martin, 527
  Margaretha, 435
  Maria Eva, 205
Lorenz,

Anna Maria, 435
Eva, 107
Geo. N., 107
Joseph, 435
Loreth,
  Dorothea, 198
  Johannes, 198
Löscher,
  Anna Margaretha,
   346
  Barbara, 346
  Catharina, 346
  Catharina Barbara,
   346
  Catharina
   Elisabetha, 346
  Eva, 346
  Eva Margaretha, 346
  Hans Georg, 346
  Jacob, 346
  Joh. Georg, 346
  Margaretha, 346
  Nicholas, 126
  Peter, 346
Loscherin,
  Cathrina, 346
  Cathrina, Jr., 346
Losser,
  Maria, 181
  Nicolaus, 181
Löster,
  Elisabetha, 345
  Jacob, 345
Lotz,
  Johannes, 307
  Maria, 307
Löw,
  Anna Barbara, 349
  Anna Cleophe, 174,
   347, 348
  Anna Maria, 349
  Catharina Juliana,
   348
  Christman, 174
  Christman(n), 347,
   349
  Conrad, 175, 260,
   349
  Hans Jacob, 348
  Hans Peter, 349
  Hans Theobald, 349
  Joh. Christmann,
   348
  Joh. Peter, 348
  Joh. Philipp, 348
  Johann Peter, 349
  Maria Barbara, 175,
   349
  Maria Catharina,
   349
  see Lau, 329
Lowein,
  Anna Gluf, 347, 349
  Barbara, 347, 349
  Christian, 347, 349
  Margaret, 347, 349